Conflicts of Interest

Corporate Governance and Financial Markets

Conflicts of Interest

Corporate Governance and Financial Markets

Edited by

Luc Thévenoz and Rashid Bahar

CENTRE DE DROIT
BANCAIRE ET FINANCIER

Published by:
Kluwer Law International
P.O. Box 316
2400 AH Alphen aan den Rijn
The Netherlands
E-mail: sales@kluwerlaw.com
Website: http://www.kluwerlaw.com

Sold and distributed in North, Central and South America by:
Aspen Publishers, Inc.
7201 Mc Kinney Circle
Frederick, MD 21704
United States of America

Sold and distributed in all other countries except in Switzerland by:
Turpin Distribution Services Ltd.
Stratton Business Park
Pegasus Drive, Biggleswade
Bedfordshire SG18 8TQ
United Kingdom

Sold and distributed in Switzerland by:
Schulthess Médias Juridiques SA
Zwingliplatz 2, Postfach
CH-8022 Zurich
and
21, rue du Mont-Blanc
CH-1201 Geneva

This book is part of the 'Publications du Centre de droit bancaire et financier' series.

ISBN 90-411-2578-7

Printed and bound in Great Britain by
CPI Antony Rowe, Chippenham and Eastbourne

ISBN 978 3 7255 5332 7

www.schulthess.com

Summary of Contents

Table of Contents

Chapter 11
Conflicts of Interest in the Distribution of Investment Funds 337

Luc Thévenoz

Chapter 12
United States Mutual Fund Investors, Their Managers and Distributors 363

Tamar Frankel

List of Contributors

Dr Sandro Abegglen
Attorney-at-Law, Partner, Niederer Kraft & Frey, Zurich; Privat Docent, University of Berne; LL.M., University of Texas at Austin School of Law.

Dr Rashid Bahar
University of Geneva, Attorney-at-Law, Bär & Karrer, Zurich.

Dr Guido Bolliger
Head of Risk Management, Olympia, Capital Management, Paris, Formerly International Center for Asset Management and Engineering (FAME).

Dr Michel Dubois
Professor, University of Neuchâtel.

Dr Pascal Dumontier
Professor, University of Geneva.

Dr Tamar Frankel
LL.M., S.J.D., Harvard Law School, Professor, Boston University.

Dr Alain Hirsch
Professor Emeritus, University of Geneva; Counsel, Schellenberg Wittmer, Geneva.

Dr Manuel Kast
Formerly University of Lausanne and International Center for Asset Management and Engineering (FAME).

Marc Kruithof
LL.M., Yale Law School, Law Lecturer, University College Ghent, Assistant, Ghent University.

Karim Maizar
Attorney-at-Law, Bär & Karrer, Zurich.

Dr Leo Schrutt
Member of the Extended Executive Board, Julius Baer.

Dr Luc Thévenoz
Professor, University of Geneva, Director, Centre for Banking and Financial Law, Commissioner, Swiss Federal Banking Commission.

Dr Rolf Watter
LL.M., Georgetown, Professor, University of Zurich, Attorney-at-Law, Bär & Karrer, Zurich.

Stefan Wieler
Investment Research and Portfolio Construction Private Banking, Julius Baer.

Dr Eddy Wymeersch
Professor, Ghent University, Chairman, Belgian Banking, Finance and Insurance Commission.

Dr Jean-Baptiste Zufferey
LL.M., Michigan School of Law, Professor, University of Fribourg, Vice-Chairman, Swiss Federal Banking Commission.

Preface

This book presents the results of a two-year research project, bringing together academics and practitioners in both law and finance from Europe and the US under the auspices of the Centre for Banking and Financial Law of the University of Geneva (www.unige.ch/cdbf). It analyzes conflicts of interest focusing on three areas where the problems are particularly acute: executive compensation, financial analysts and asset management. Formulating an appropriate response has become a central concern for academics, policy makers and practitioners interested in financial regulation and corporate governance. Rather than a minute analysis of black-letter law, this book analyses the guiding principles and policies, thus nourishing the current debate at national, European and international levels. The outcome of this interdisciplinary and transnational dialogue is, we hope, a series of fresh and innovative contributions and a systematic introduction, placing conflicts of interest in their broader context.

To achieve this result, in addition to the research of each author, we organized two meetings, during which each author discussed their respective papers. First, in September 2005, we held a closed workshop over three days at the Study Centre Gerzensee, a foundation of the Swiss National Bank, during which the contributors presented their work-in-progress and engaged in an intense and fruitful discussion. This workshop also benefited from the presentation and comments of Hubert de la Bruslerie, Philipp Hildebrand, Alain Hirsch, Karl Hofstetter, Samantha Meregalli Do Duc, Henry Peter, Laurent Probst, Peter Spinnler and Christian Soguel.

Six months later, the authors met again at a public conference held at the University of Geneva, during which key conclusions were debated among a panel of academics and practitioners from law and finance, including Christian Bovet, Peter Böckli, Rajna Gibson, Alain Hirsch, Gérard Hertig, Patrick Odier, Henry Peter and Peter Spinnler, as well as all of the authors whose work is included in this book. We are indebted to all the participants in both seminars for their invaluable comments and would like to thank each of them once again for their contributions.

We would particularly like to thank Christian Bovet for his participation at the earliest stages of the project and Alain Hirsch for his guidance both on the general parameters of the project and on the specifics of the book. Our thanks go also to Rosemary Williams, who, through her careful editing, improved the quality of this book, and to Gervais Muja, who assisted the two of us with the administration of the project and in particular organizing the conference. Finally, we would like to acknowledge gratefully financial support from the *Ecoscientia Stiftung zur Förderung besonderer Anliegen in Ausbildung und Wissenschaft*, who generously funded this project.

Luc Thévenoz and Rashid Bahar
Geneva, July 2006

Foreword

This book examines some important conflicts of interest arising in the field of corporate governance and financial services. It was appropriate to concentrate on specific and actual issues, allowing a precise and thorough analysis. We should nonetheless remember that conflicts of interest are a general phenomenon, arising in many aspects of life: in particular in public life (for members of government, parliament, administrations, tribunals, even universities), in economic life (for persons engaged in providing services of any kind, such as legal, management, financial, fiscal, information technology), and even in many other fields (for instance in family relations, non-profit organisations, etc.).

Conflicts of interest are not easy to define. They imply the existence of a duty of loyalty of an 'agent' towards another person or organization (the 'principal') conflicting with an interest (or with another duty) of the agent. Such interest is often of a financial nature, but can also be non-financial. The conflict may not affect the agent personally, but only a related person, such as a relative, business partner, friend or acquaintance. Conflicts of interest are as difficult to define as the notion of 'independence', which is ultimately related to the personal situation (at the time) and character of each person.

Conflicts of interest are often perceived as an evil to be avoided at any cost, especially in the context of clear and shocking abuses. However, we must not forget that conflicts of interest arise constantly and inevitably due to the fact that we have multiple social and economic relations. Such relations are the essence of our life and of our experience. A person without conflicts of interest would often be quite incompetent to understand and handle the task assigned to him. Who would like to receive an advice from such a person?

As this book will show, conflicts of interest should generally not be prohibited, but should be properly managed. All duties of loyalty are not identical. On the contrary, the importance of most duties of loyalty depends on the object of the service rendered, the relations of the agent with the principal, the legitimate expectations of the principal, the nature and importance of the conflicting interest of the agent, etc. It follows that the duties of loyalty are not absolute, but depend on all circumstances, including the extent to which the duties can be modified based on mutual agreement between the agent and the principal.

Conflicts of interest may not only matter to the principal (in a particular relationship with his agent), but can affect the reputation of the agent and indeed of his entire profession. If conflicts of interest arise in public life, they may even affect the authority of the state.

Most importantly, even in cases in which conflicts of interest do not have material adverse consequences, they can give rise to negative public perceptions. Such perceptions may unfortunately often be more significant than the conflict of interest itself.

Nonetheless, the authors have wisely focused on the material effects of actual conflicts of interest. One may hope that their balanced views will inform not only academics and practitioners, but also legislators, regulators and eventually even the media and the general public.

Alain Hirsch

Chapter 1

Conflicts of Interest: Disclosure, Incentives, and the Market

*Rashid Bahar and Luc Thévenoz**

Conflicts of interest captured the attention of media and policy makers at the turn of the twenty-first century. Everywhere from corporations to investment banks, conflicts of interest were decried as the source of countless problems. The public called for action and governments and regulators replied with often-draconian laws and regulations, starting with the ominous Sarbanes-Oxley Act of 2002.[1] In this book, we decided to take a step back and analyze the issue more rationally. From the outset, we were aware that it would be pointless to write a monumental treatise on the issue. The law has become far too scattered and specialized to be grasped even-handedly or analyzed adequately from a purely economic perspective. We chose instead to focus on a small sample of specific situations, and examine them from various perspectives in order to reflect the extent and diversity of relationships and markets in which conflicts of interest have become a significant concern.

This book discusses three areas where conflicts of interest were, and remain, a central concern of policy makers world-wide: executive compensation, financial

* Rashid Bahar works with the Centre for Banking and Financial Law, University of Geneva, and as an Attorney-at-law, with Bär & Karrer. Luc Thévenoz is professor at the University of Geneva, Director of its Centre for Banking and Financial Law, and Commissioner of the Swiss Federal Banking Commission. We would like to thank the participants of the August 2005 Gerzensee Seminar for their comments, which have inspired this article, and Alain Hirsch for the fruitful discussions of earlier drafts of this chapter.

1. Sarbanes Oxley Act of 2002, P.L. 107, 204,<www.sec.gov/about/laws/soa2002.pdf>.

L. Thévenoz and R. Bahar (eds.), *Conflicts of Interest: Corporate Governance and Financial Market*, pp. 1–29.

analysis, asset management and the distribution of financial products.[2] It considers various aspects of conflicts of interest in each of these areas from a legal as well as an economic point of view, combining the insights of scholars, regulators, and practitioners.

This fragmented view of the problem notwithstanding, a number of strong patterns can be discerned through this kaleidoscope.[3] These patterns revolve around the definition of conflicts of interests and the types of relationships that trigger a duty of loyalty. They include the mechanisms available to handle conflicts of interest, from prohibition to disclosure and managerial processes, as well as the extent to which the duty of loyalty may be waived or contracted around. Two further issues emerge in all areas: compensation and enforcement. Compensation is inherent in any commercial transaction; it is simultaneously a source of conflicts of interests and a possible means of reducing these conflicts by creating the proper incentives. Similarly, current law will remain a dead issue unless it is effectively enforced. How the law can be effectively enforced, and by whom, are significant issues discussed in various chapters in this book.

In this introduction we shall review each of these issues in order to highlight the salient themes. We hope that this introduction will serve as a springboard to "plunge" into the rest of the book. We shall attempt a summary definition of conflicts of interest and review the remedies used by the legal system to counter them,[4] with a closer look at compensation and market mechanisms.

I. WHAT ARE CONFLICTS OF INTEREST?

A. THE TRADITIONAL APPROACH: FIDUCIARIES AND THE DUTY OF LOYALTY

Interests conflict in any business relationship. Every bargain, even an outright sale, causes at least two different interests to clash with each other,[5] yet they do not fall under the ambit of rules on conflicts of interest. Traditionally, the law only

---

2. Other areas of interest for research are accountancy firms, rating agencies and universal banking. See A. Crockett, T. Harris, F.S. Mishkin and E.N. White, *Conflicts of Interest in the Financial Services Industry: What Should We Do About Them?* (Geneva and London, International Centre for Monetary and Banking Studies and Centre for Economic Policy Research, 2003), pp. 27 *et seq.*, 39 *et seq.* and 55 *et seq.*
3. See also K.J. Hopt, 'Trusteeship and Conflicts of Interest in the Corporate, Banking, and Agency Law: Toward Common Legal Principles for Intermediaries in the Modern Service-Oriented Society' in *Reforming Company and Takeover Law in Europe*, G. A. Ferrarini *et al.* (eds) (Oxford, New York, Oxford University Press, 2005), p. 86.
4. See also for a cross-jurisdictional survey, K. Clark et al., *Conflicts of Interest – Jurisdictional Comparisons in the Law and Regulation for the Financial Services, Auditing and Legal Professions 2005/2006* (London, The European Lawyer, 2005).
5. M. Ekelmans, 'Conflits d'intérêts: contrats d'intermédiaires' in *Les Conflits d'intérêts* (Brussels, Bruylant, 1997), p. 7.

intervenes in situations in which one party owes the other party a specific duty of loyalty; something more than the ordinary duty to act in good faith in business. In such circumstances, the first party must protect and promote the interests of the other party.[6] In other words, the first party is in a delicate situation, being in charge of two conflicting interests. Both common law and civil law jurisdictions have tackled this issue and the outcomes are fundamentally similar. Moreover, there is a clear trend towards convergence of both legal systems.[7] Nevertheless, the differences in sensibility and in remedies are deep rooted and a brief examination of the genealogy of these rules yields precious insights.

In common-law jurisdictions, as Tamar Frankel reminds us in her chapter, this duty is one of the fiduciary duties originating from the law of trusts. The duty of loyalty is a legal consequence of entrusting the trustee with the interests of the beneficiary. Originally the trustee received property. As the scope of the fiduciary relationship expanded, the link between a transfer of property and the duty of loyalty faded away. But this connection remains and explains the deeply property law-like characteristic of the duties of a common law fiduciary.[8]

By contrast, civil-law jurisdictions connect the duty of loyalty to the obligations under a mandate contract,[9] i.e. a contract whereby one party, the agent or mandatee, undertakes to perform a service for or manage the interests of the other party, the principal. The archetypical mandate is a mandate of representation, which empowers the agent to act on behalf of the principal.[10] Such a duty of loyalty may arise from the performance of other services by anyone from a company director to a mere employee. The institution is fundamentally a contractual one, divorced from property-based claims.

Because the execution of the mandate, rather than its result, is at the core of the contract, the duty of care and diligence has traditionally assumed a central position. As Mark Kruithof points out in his chapter, continental jurisdictions do not consider conflicts of interest as such to be a problem. Decision making in a conflicted situation is not a breach of duty. Private law usually calls for at least prima facie evidence of damage or undue profits before condemning the conflicted actions.[11]

Despite this historical difference, the gap between these two legal traditions is less significant than it appears, and there are certain convergences between Continental and Anglo-American legal systems. Indeed, it is indisputable that directors

---

6. V. Simonart, 'Conclusions générales' in *Les Conflits d'intérêts* (Brussels, Bruylant, 1997), pp. 303–304.
7. For an overview of this issue in corporate governance, see the volume of essays edited by M.J. Roe and J.N. Gordon, *Convergence and Persistence in Corporate Governance* (Cambridge: Cambridge University Press, 2004).
8. See T. Frankel, Chapter 12, p. 364–367, below.
9. Under Swiss law, Art. 394 *et seq.* Code of obligations (CO) RS 220.0.
10. See V. Simonart, 'Conclusions générales', p. 308, identifying the power to act in the interest of someone else as a defining moment on the way to a correct understanding of conflicts of interest.
11. See M. Kruithof, Chapter 10, p. 303–304 and 309–310, esp. no. 139, below.

and officers everywhere owe a duty of loyalty to their companies, and that asset managers owe a similar debt to their clients.

B. The Ever-Broadening Scope of Conflicts of Interest

Conflicts of interest are not limited to individual relationships. If they are widespread, the adverse effects of these conflicts can plague entire markets. If investors believe the agency costs of equity are too high, they will avoid buying shares in favour of bonds, thus limiting the access of business to capital. Similarly, lacking trust in asset managers or collective investment schemes, investors will forego the advantages of this form of investment: the expertise of the agent and the economies of scale offered by asset pooling. Instead, investors will make and implement their investment decisions alone and risk the potentially adverse consequences. From a macroeconomic viewpoint, those consequences can be dire in terms of misallocation of resources: capital markets may dry up and savings may vanish or be inefficiently invested. Conflicts of interest thus are a source of concern not only for individual principals, but also for society at large, and indeed the state.[12] Public regulation is necessary insofar as individuals may not be able to fend for themselves and cannot enforce their rights alone.

The regulation of financial markets has, however, introduced a new paradigm; a new approach with new tools. In addition to contract or fiduciary law claims, regulators took this issue into their own hands, using the instruments of administrative law. This new approach is obvious with regard to asset management and investment funds. EU rules such as the UCITS Directive,[13] the Investment Services Directive of 1993,[14] and its successor, the Directive on Markets in Financial Instruments,[15] all provide for an administrative duty of loyalty, or at least on conflicts of interest, which is supplementary to the requirements of private law.[16] Swiss law has followed

12. A. Crockett, T. Harris, F. S. Mishkin and E.N. White, *Conflicts of Interest in the Financial Services Industry: What Should We Do About Them?*, pp. 76–77. For to the duty of loyalty of worker representatives on German co-determined boards see K.J. Hopt, 'Trusteeship and Conflicts of Interest in the Corporate, Banking, and Agency Law: Toward Common Legal Principles for Intermediaries in the Modern Service-Oriented Society', p. 76.
13. Council Directive of 20 December 1985 on the coordination of laws, regulations and administrative provisions relating to undertakings for collective investment in transferable securities (UCITS) (85/611/EEC) OJ L 375/3, 1985 (hereafter 'UCITS Directive'). This directive has been modified by several subsequent directives. A current, consolidated text is available at <www.eur-lex.europa.eu/LexUriServ/LexUriServ.do?uri=CELEX:01985L0611-20050413:EN:NOT>.
14. Council Directive 93/22/EEC of 10 May 1993 on investment services in the securities field, OJ L 141/27, 1993 (hereafter 'ISD').
15. Directive 2004/39/EC of the European Parliament and of the Council of 21 April 2004 on markets in financial instruments, amending Council Directives 85/611/EEC and 93/6/EEC and Directive 2000/12/EC of the European Parliament and of the Council and repealing Council Directive 93/22/EEC, OJ L 145/1, 2004 (hereafter 'MiFID').
16. Art. 18 MiFID; art. 10 (2) and 17 UCITS Directive; art. 10 and 11 ISD.

the same trend with the Investment Funds Act[17] and the Stock Exchange Act:[18] both impose a duty to act in the client's best interests and an implied rule on conflicts of interest that is expanded by regulatory and self-regulatory instruments.[19]

The increasing role of regulators is also obvious in the realm of corporations. Until recently, the border between corporate and securities law was clear-cut: the latter tackled only issues of disclosure, leaving the internal affairs of the company, and the entire governance system, to corporate law.[20] The emergence of corporate governance codes, and their integration in various listing rules, has eroded this difference. These codes opened the way for securities regulators to intervene at the core of corporate governance and gave it a new dimension. In particular, as one of us points out in his chapter, whereas traditional corporate law was not strongly concerned with issues of executive compensation,[21] securities law, broadly speaking, required the disclosure of compensation packages and called for increased scrutiny over the governance practices of boards and remuneration committees in particular.[22]

The regulatory action improved enforcement and, optimally, compliance with these rules. Regulators are not subject to the usual problems that plague the dispersed mass of small investors. They have better tools to tackle the issue directly. Moreover, regulators can take enforcement action even if no damage has been suffered or can be proved. Non-compliance alone can trigger measures by authorities.[23]

In addition to stronger enforcement, the regulatory approach to conflicts of interest also led to an expansion of the scope of fiduciary duties. Formerly, regulation was primarily concerned with the prudential supervision of institutions, including

---

17. Loi fédérale du 18 mars 1994 sur les fonds de placement (Loi sur les fonds de placement, LFP) RS 951.31, abbreviated in English as 'IFA' Trend confirmed by the loi fédérale du 23 juin 2006 sur les placements collectifs de carpitaux (loi sur les placements collectifs, LPCC), FF 2006 5533, which is set to enter in force in 2007.
18. Loi fédérale du 24 mars 1995 sur les bourses et le commerce des valeurs mobilières (Loi sur les bourses, LBVM) RS 954, abbreviated in English as 'SESTA'.
19. See art. 11 (1)(a) SESTA; art. 12 and 20 IFA.
20. See *Santa Fe Industries Inc. v. Green* 430 U.S. 462, 478–480 (1977).
21. Until the recent revision of the Swiss Code of Obligations, Swiss law included only one provision on compensation. The provision governed *tantièmes*, an instrument that is rarely used in practice. However, general principles of corporate law and, in particular, the general duty of diligence and loyalty ensured that the issue did come within the ambit of the law. See [R. Bahar Chapter 3, p. 91–92, below and refs. Since 7 October 2005, Parliament has enacted a new provision on the disclosure of executive compensation: Code des obligations (CO) (Transparence des indemnités versées aux membres du conseil d'administration et de la direction), Modification du 7 octobre 2005, FF 2005 5593. Subsequently the government moved forward and published a consultation paper on the revision of corporate law that would allow companies to put remuneration packages to the ballot. Art. 627 (4) draft CO. *Begleitbericht zum Vorentwurf zur Revision des Aktien- und Rechnungslegungsrechts im Obligationenrecht vom 2. Dezember 2005*, <www.bj.admin.ch>, p. 40. See R. Bahar, Chapter 3, p. 92, below.
22. See, e.g., the SWX Corporate Governance Directive.
23. See generally S. Shavell, 'The Optimal Structure of Law Enforcement' (1993) *Journal of Law and Economics* 36, 255, 263–271 on various forms of enforcement and their advantages.

the adequacy of their organization and their capital base. More recently, regulators have been more inclined to probe the very content of the agreement between intermediaries and their customers by enforcing rules of conduct and trying to prevent market abuse, thus delving into the particulars of the relationship.[24]

This heightened scrutiny went hand in hand with an expansion of the circle of beneficiaries of the duty of loyalty. Regulators often take the view that financial intermediaries owe loyalty to the investing public at large. The first wave of investor-protection regulation was limited to a series of reinforced pre-contractual duties, requiring issuers to disclose all material and relevant facts and barring them from defrauding investors.[25] This regulation has changed recently: allotment rules for new issues,[26] and more specifically rules of conduct for analysts,[27] require financial intermediaries to take action to prevent conflicts of interests from tainting their interactions with the public at large. In both cases, the regulator considered that the duty of loyalty of securities dealers requires them to treat all clients fairly when a conflict arises between those clients' individual interests.[28]

The case of analysts is exemplary in this respect. As Sandro Abegglen points out in his chapter, sell-side analysts, who are hired and paid by underwriters and M&A advisors, do not enter into a direct contractual relationship with investors. Unlike buy-side analysts, who are paid to advise clients on how to invest their assets, there is no doubt where the interests of sell-side analysts lie: with their securities house and possibly with the firm whose securities the securities house underwrites, and not with the investor.[29] Empirical studies reviewed by Michel Dubois and Pascal Dumontier show that the market is not deceived, and discounts the enthusiastic language of sell-side analysts.[30] Although the Global Research Analyst Settlement of 2003[31] and various regulatory and self-regulatory initiatives[32] have enabled greater integrity in the marketplace, the overall efficiency of the new arrangements has yet to be tested. Has the problem been solved or merely shifted? The UK

24. Although this trend is new in banking and investment services, insurance regulators have traditionally exercised this scrutiny. See Art. 46 (1)(f) of the Loi fédérale sur la surveillance des entreprises d'assurance (Loi sur la surveillance des assurances, LSA) RS 961.01.
25. The U.S. Rule 10b-5 is most likely emblematic of this trend.
26. See the Directive of the Swiss Bankers Association on the Issuance Market, <www.ebk.ch/f/regulier/rundsch/pdf/04-02_Anhang/Zirkular7332.pdf> (in French).
27. Swiss Bankers Association's Directives on the Independence of Financial Research <www.swissbanking.org/en/3566_e.pdf>.
28. See e.g. Decision of the Federal Banking Commission of 19 March 2003, in regard to the *Bank Vontobel*, Bulletin CFB 45 (2003) 165. Art. 11 SESTA.
29. Art. 8 of the Swiss Bankers Association Code of Conduct for Securities Dealers, <www.swissbanking.org/en/8019_e.pdf>. See S. Abbegglen, Chapter 5, p. 171, below.
30. M. Dubois and P. Dumontier, Chapter 6, p. 187 et seq., below.
31. Global Research Analyst Settlement of 2003, <www.sec.gov/spotlight/globalsettlement.htm>.
32. See in Switzerland, the Swiss Bankers Association's Directives on the Independence of Financial Research, <www.swissbanking.org/en/3566_e.pdf>. The Federal Banking Commission required all supervised banks and securities dealers to comply with the terms of this instrument as a self-regulation norm recognized as a minimum standard. See the Circulaire CFB 04/2 du 21 avril 2004, Normes d'autorégulation reconnues comme standards minimaux par la CFB.

Financial Services Authority recently expressed a suspicion that issuers are trying to pressure investment banks into breaching the rules governing the independence of financial analysts by delaying the selection of the lead underwriter.[33]

C. Erosion and Waivers of the Duty of Loyalty

This expansion of the duty of loyalty beyond its original scope is creating stress in business relationships. Whereas in the words of Cardozo, for a trustee not 'honesty alone, but the punctilio of honour the most sensitive, is . . . the standard of behaviour',[34] this rule was relaxed early in the development of corporate law by the business judgment rule.[35] And few would argue that an investment banker is bound by the same rules as a trustee. This gradual erosion was not the product of contractual innovations or conscious judicial decisions, but rather was simply the evolution of the marketplace.

Loyalty comes at a cost. For the agent, this fact is obvious. Paraphrasing Cardozo's famous dictum once again, agents cannot simply act in accordance with common market practice; they must take additional steps to meet the high standards of behaviour expected of them.[36] Principals, however, also have to bear the costs of loyalty: conflicts of interests may prevent them from hiring the most experienced and specialized agents to defend their interests.[37] The principals may have to settle for a lower standard of quality in exchange for higher integrity, and the trade-off is not easy to quantify.

---

33. See FSA, 'Competitive Initial Public Offerings' List! No. 11, Supplementary Edition November 2005, 1 <www.fsa.gov.uk/pubs/ukla/list11_suped.pdf>.
34. *Meinhard v. Salomon*, 164 N.E. 545 (N.Y.1928) at 546.
35. See on this topic, §4.01(c) American Law Institute Principles of Corporate Governance; *Aronson v. Lewis*, 473 A.2d 805 (Del. 1984) 812; *Smith v. Van Gorkom*, 488 A. 2d 858 (Del. 1985). See also under Swiss law, e.g. SJ 1982 221, c. 3a, 225; ATF 113 II 52, c. 3a, 57; R. Bahar, *Le rôle du conseil d'administration lors des fusions et acquisitions: une approche systématique* (Zurich, Schulthess, 2004) pp. 90–98; L. Glanzmann, 'Die Verantwortlichkeitsklage unter Corporate Governance-Aspekten', *Revue de droit suisse* 119 (2000) II 135, 165–166; A.R. Grass, 'Management-Entscheidungen vor dem Richter: Schranken der richterlichen Überprüfbarkeit von Geschäftsentscheiden in aktienrechtlichen Verantwortlichkeitsprozessen', *Revue suisse de droit des affaires* 72 (2000) 1–10; A.R. Grass, *Business Judgment Rule: Schranken der richterlichen Überprüfbarkeit von Management-Entscheidungen in aktienrechtlichen Verantwortlichkeitsprozessen* (Zurich, Schulthess, 1998); Trigo Trindade and Bahar, 'Droits des actionnaires minoritaires en Suisse', p. 396; H.C. von der Crone, 'Auf den Weg zu einem Recht der Publikumsgesellschaften', *Revue de la société des juristes bernois* 133 (1997) 73, 107; P. Widmer and O. Banz, in *Basler Kommentar zum Schweizerisches Privatrecht*, N.P. Vogt, R. Watter, and H. Honsell (eds) (Basle, Geneva, Munich, Helbing & Ichtenhahn, 2002) ad art. 754 CO, no. 31.
36. *Meinhard v. Salomon*, 164 N.E. 545 (N.Y.1928) at 546.
37. This point is made cogently by M.C. Jensen and W.H. Meckling, 'Theory of the Firm: Managerial Behavior, Agency Costs and Ownership Structure' *Journal of Financial Economics* 3 (1976) 328.

Considering how difficult it is to measure loyalty, the law usually enshrines loyalty as a mandatory duty. This policy does not seek merely to protect the weaker party. A principal, however sophisticated and commercially alert, cannot waive her fiduciary's duty of loyalty. As Tamar Frankel points out, this problem stems from common-law jurisdictions with the proprietary nature of the duty. At most, a principal may consent to a conflict of interest once she is aware of it, and can presumably measure the adverse consequences of the conflict.[38]

Although this principle may appear far reaching, and might be expected to prove a considerable handicap to the financial industry, ways around the roadblock are built by the absolute nature of the duty of loyalty. First, the parties can narrow the scope of the service or the interests entrusted. Execution-only brokers, for instance, promise nothing more than a diligent, careful and loyal execution of exchange orders. These brokers do not provide any form of financial advice to their customers. They do not even promise to ensure that the trades match the risk profile of their clients. Perhaps the future lies with an explicit definition of the services an intermediary promises to provide: execution-only; trade-related advice; general assessment of the financial situation of the client; and investment management.

Nevertheless, views to the contrary notwithstanding, we do not believe that this evolution is redefining the duty of loyalty. It remains a discrete variable: a fiduciary is either loyal or she is not; she cannot be more or less loyal. She can only contract in the domain of her loyalty. Once she enters into this area, she is bound to an unlimited loyalty to her principal. The face of this duty may change, depending on the circumstances and the nature of the relationship. But the duty itself remains fundamentally the same: the agent must act in the interest of the principal.

II. COMPENSATION

A. Compensation as a Source of Conflicts of Interest

Compensation schemes are arguably one of the main sources of conflicts of interest. This fact is somewhat surprising, because the compensation an agent or fiduciary receives is part of the bargain between the fiduciary and the principal and falls outside the scope of the former's duty of loyalty. In addition, the fiduciary and the principal both agreed to the compensation scheme, at least implicitly. Thus, even if a given type of remuneration creates perverse incentives, it will not automatically fall under conflict of interest rules. However, in many instances, it does. The remuneration can fall under conflict of interest rules, for example, if an agent fails to carry out his duties to the best interest of his principal, due to misguided incentives. In such cases, the incentive scheme does not, as such, constitute a breach of the

38. See T. Frankel, Chapter 12, p. 365 et seq., below.

duty of loyalty, but instead encourages the fiduciary to take action that contravenes his duty of loyalty.

From asset managers to financial analysts, payment schemes have created perverse incentives. Corporate history is rife with stories of bonus schemes that have run amok, encouraging pushing managers to dump products on clients in order to meet quarterly sales targets, at the expense of the firm's long-term interest in maintaining proper relations with customers.[39] Stock option plans can also engender an entire series of conflicts of interest and perverse incentives, ranging from short-term bias to excessive payouts at the expense of shareholders as the result of a failure to understand the value of the options granted under the plan.[40]

Not only existing shareholders stand to lose from perverse effects of stock option plans: managers themselves may feel tempted to 'cook the books' and engage in other fraudulent activities to boost their profits. Managers may also use milder schemes and engineer false expectations to create an appearance of over-performance.[41] As a result, the entire market may lose confidence in the accuracy of financial reports. Guido Bolliger and Manuel Kast confirm empirical findings that corporate managers with high incentive schemes influence the stock price by analyst guidance and other forms of expectation management.[42] Using informal channels they persuade the market to reduce earnings forecasts, which will be beaten by the results subsequently reported. As Guido Bolliger and Manuel Kast show, equity-based plans, management shareholdings, and bonus plans foster this behaviour. Financial analysts are willing victims in this scheme. They depend on good relations with management in order to access information. It is therefore quite logical for them to issue biased forecasts so as to secure future information from management.[43]

This conflict is not the only one to which analysts are exposed. More generally, sell-side analysts working for investment banks who act as underwriters for the companies they cover have implicit incentives to issue favourable reports. They do not directly generate revenues: institutions offer their reports for free, hoping that they will yield new investment banking or trading business. Sell-side analysts thus have a limited interest in objective and independent research if it comes at the expense of trading or underwriting business.[44]

This conflict of interest is more or less explicit, ranging from a direct link between analyst compensation and the performance of the investment banking division or the trading desk, to more subtle and less controllable career considerations. Nevertheless, as Michel Dubois and Pascal Dumontier show, only the

---

39. See, for numerous examples, M.C. Jensen, 'Paying People to Lie: The Truth about the Budgeting Process' (2003) *European Financial Management* 9, 379.
40. See L.A. Bebchuk and C.M. Fried, *Pay without Performance*, pp. 137–185.
41. See R. Bahar, Chapter 3, p. 113–116, below.
42. See G. Bolliger and M. Kast, Chapter 4, p. 137 et seq., table 2, below.
43. See R. Bahar, Chapter 3.
44. See FSA, 'Competitive Initial Public Offerings' List! No. 11, Supplementary Edition November 2005, 1 <www.fsa.gov.uk/pubs/ukla/list11_suped.pdf>.

investment recommendations, and not the earnings forecasts, reveal actual bias. More significantly, these authors also point out that the market is not gullible and is quite capable of taking such bias into account.[45] This leaves us wondering whether the regulatory tsunami of the last five years, which is vividly described by Sandro Abegglen[46] and Jean-Baptiste Zufferey,[47] will actually yield any benefit in this area. This attempt to restore public confidence may have succeeded in terms of media spin, but at what cost remains to be seen.

Although the regulatory pressure was less felt in this area, asset managers are also exposed to conflicts of interest because of the structure of their compensation. 'Churning portfolios' – generating excessive trading to increase revenue – is a well-known risk that most investors are aware of and can monitor. They may be less aware of other quirks. Independent asset managers typically enjoy some form of revenue sharing with the brokers who execute their orders on behalf of investors. In this book, we make frequent use of the word 'retrocessions' to designate commissions paid by banks and securities brokers to asset managers out of their own fees. Typically, institutional investors bargain with their asset managers for a net fee, and the asset managers guarantee that their clients will benefit from any connected income received from third parties. This is often explicitly regulated with regard to companies that manage investment funds. The same problem nonetheless exists with regard to individual investors, who lack the commercial power to achieve the same bargain. It has not yet drawn the attention of Swiss or EU regulators, except for the UK Financial Services Authority's 'new menu' approach for independent financial advisors.[48]

However, this may be changing. In the related area of distribution of investment funds to retail investors, the Swiss Fund Association, with the backing of the Swiss Federal Banking Commission, has called for the disclosure of various types of commissions that fund managers pay to distributors and other intermediaries. Yet, as one of us (Luc Thévenoz) points out in his paper, the problem extends beyond the question of conflicts of interest to encompass competition law and perhaps the controversial issue of corruptive practices.[49] Indeed, the competition for shelf-space in the fund industry and the fostering of open architecture raise fundamental questions for the industrial organization of the financial sector. Moreover, whereas a retrocession can be viewed as the purchase of precious shelf-space, a relatively innocuous transaction similar to what goes on every day in supermarkets, we could also see it as a form of corruption. Whenever a fund manager offers retrocessions, she is implicitly inducing the distributors to disregard the interest of their clients. In this respect, her behaviour does not differ fundamentally from that of a firm that pays a public servant a kickback for contracting with it.

45. M. Dubois and P. Dumontier, Chapter 6.
46. S. Abegglen, Chapter 5, p. 171 et seq., below.
47. J.-B. Zufferey, Chapter 7, p. 211 et seq., below.
48. Financial Services Authority, *Reforming Depolarisation: Implementation*, Policy Statement 04/27, November 2004, available at www.fsa.gov.uk, discussed by L. Thévenoz, Chapter 11, p. 351, below.
49. L. Thévenoz, Chapter 11, p. 337, below.

B. Compensation as a Solution to Conflicts of Interest

In the realm of conflicts of interest, compensation assumes the appearance of the two-faced Roman god Janus: On one side, compensation is a source of conflicts, while on the other, it is a remedy. This ambivalence is obvious with respect to executive compensation. Corporate governance commentators, particularly Jensen and Murphy, called for incentive plans as a solution to the agency conflict between shareholders and managers, and advocated the use of numerous performance-based schemes, ranging from bonuses to stock-option plans.[50] In hindsight, however, many of these proposals seem to have failed to attain their objective. Rather than aligning the interests of managers with those of shareholders, they created perverse incentives, in the worst case inducing executives to commit fraud and other crimes.

Does this mean that incentive plans are useless and that managers should again be paid like bureaucrats? Probably not. The floodgate is open and the challenge now is to design an appropriate compensation package. Which is precisely what Rolf Watter and Karim Maizar set out to do in their chapter. From a corporate governance perspective, they explain the legal principles that must be respected by boards of directors and compensation committees. They also describe the constraints imposed by the legal system on the structure itself.[51] Performance-based fees, however, are used beyond the corporate arena. It is not uncommon for these fees to be paid to asset managers and fund managers.[52] Looking beyond the scope of the financial industry, U.S. law and economics commentators have praised attorneys' contingency fees as mechanisms helping plaintiffs, who are often unsophisticated and do not know the law, to ensure that their lawyers only advise them to litigate if they have a good chance of success.[53]

C. Intrinsic Motivation and Non-Monetary Incentives

Half-way between the ideal answer to conflicts of interest and their very source, compensation schemes are obvious targets for regulation. Although there have been no widespread attempts in the financial industry to regulate the amount of compensation payable to a financial intermediary or corporate officer, certain forms of compensation have been banned. For instance, lawyers in many continental European jurisdictions are barred from receiving contingency fees;[54] they are, however,

50. See the twin papers published in 1990 by M.C. Jensen and K.J. Murphy, 'CEO Incentives – It's Not How Much You Pay, But How' (1990) *Harvard Business Review* 68, 138, and 'Performance Pay and Top-Management Incentives' (1990) *Journal of Political Economy* 98, 225–264.
51. R. Watter and K. Maizar, Chapter 2, p. 31 et seq., esp. at 49 et seq., below.
52. See in the US, U.S. General Accounting Office, *Mutual Funds: Information on Trends in Fees and Their Related Disclosure*, GAO-03-551T (Washington, D.C.: 12 March 2003), finding an increase in management fees due to the use of performance-based fee schedules.
53. R. Cooter and T. Ulen, *Law and Economics* (3rd edn, Reading, MA, *et al*, Addison-Wesley, 2000), p. 390.
54. See Art. 3.3 of the Code of Conduct for lawyers in the European Union, <www.ccbe.org/doc/En/code2002_en.pdf>.

often allowed to receive a success fee in addition to their non-performance-based pay.[55] The policy reason is that contingent remuneration jeopardizes the independence and integrity of lawyers. From this perspective the lawyer is part of the judicial system, and if he were too committed to the interests of his clients, he might be induced into forgetting his duties as an officer of the court. Does this suggest that the legal system expressly seeks to decouple the interests of the agent from those of the principal? Or is it an implicit and early recognition that remuneration too strongly dependent on the success of the agent creates overreaching effects detrimental to the interests of the principal?

Regulators also followed this approach with respect to financial analysts: under the rules adopted by the Swiss Bankers' Association, sell-side analysts are barred from investing in firms they cover.[56] This is obviously quite paradoxical from an incentive theory perspective. It implies that analysts will be more conscientious if they are disinterested than when their vested interests are involved. This policy is even more disturbing because buy-side analysts who also act as asset managers are obviously free to apply their own recommendations to the portfolio they manage.

In the corporate arena, several commentators have been critical of the practice of offering stock options to directors on the grounds that they could lose their independence. Peter Böckli, for example, in his treatise on Swiss corporate law, strongly advises against giving directors any form of stock-option-based compensation. He suggests only that directors should be invested in the companies they serve.[57]

However, a fundamental assumption underlies these policies: that financial incentives have a corrupting effect. Either they attract the wrong type of people to the job or they crowd out other values such as integrity and intrinsic motivation.[58] This second danger is a major source of concern, because it undermines reputation-based incentive schemes, which may be more effective in disciplining fiduciaries.[59] Indeed, unless an individual agent is at the very end of his career, he will inevitably seek to preserve his reputation to secure promotion within the firm or on the general labour market. Similarly, firms may want to preserve their reputation for integrity in order to secure future business.

III. REMEDIES: DISCLOSURE AND ORGANIZATIONAL MEASURES

A. Can the Market Solve the Problem?

Early on, Eugene Fama suggested that the market would constrain agents and thus solve the agency problem. In a competitive market, any agent who does not pull her

55. See in particular Art. 19(3) of the Code de Déontologie of the Swiss Lawyers' Association, <www.bgfa.ch/fr/01_gesetze/03_standesregeln.htm?eintrag_id=549>.
56. Para. 33 Swiss Bankers Association Directives on the Independence of Financial Research, <www.swissbanking.org/en/3566_e.pdf>.
57. See P. Böckli, *Schweizer Aktienrecht* (3rd edn, Zurich, Schulthess, 2004) 13, no. 244–246.
58. See R. Bahar, Chapter 3, p. 88, below.
59. See *ibid.*

weight will be outdone by more loyal agents who promise better performance at a lower cost. In the corporate environment, individuals are disciplined by the market for managers and directors. Firms are active in product and capital markets and, if they are unable to control their agency costs, their competitors will offer better products at cheaper prices and will be able to finance themselves at a lower cost. Ultimately, the market for corporate control may save the investors: a competing management team may take over control and will then curtail agency costs. If in spite of these constraints the management does not improve, failure and bankruptcy are inevitable and the firm will be eliminated from the market economy. However, all these constraints are relatively loose and will operate only if the disloyalty is egregious.[60]

This argument also works for other conflicts of interest. Underwriters, for example, are at the heart of a conflict of interest between the firms whose securities they underwrite and the investors to whom they seek to offer them; and yet this does not seem to create excessive problems. Reputation and competition in this market sector seem to keep a check on disloyalty.[61] And this is not solely an effect of primary market regulation; as George Stigler and later Carol Simon pointed out, the market already encouraged substantial disclosure before the enactment of the Securities Act of 1933. The new regulation did not affect the mean returns of securities traded on the NYSE, or even of seasoned issues of securities traded on smaller exchanges.[62] At the time the 'money trust' of J. P. Morgan and other financiers ruled Wall Street, disclosure was already substantially developed. As this example hints, market participants often intentionally look for conflicted partners, hoping that their fiduciary is 'in the know.'

The market could also work with respect to the distribution of financial products or asset management. If a fund distributor allows retrocessions to influence her decisions, her competitors will outrace her by offering investors better products. If an asset manager churns the portfolio of her clients, thus increasing the overall costs of her services, in a competitive market, her customers may decide to change to a cheaper service provider.

There is a catch, however. If the markets are not competitive, they will not be a sufficient constraint to discipline the agent, in which case rules may prove necessary. Moreover, most agency services suffer from a fundamental problem: the quality of the service is not directly observable[63] and a third party can only infer them from the outcome and other proxies. The agent can invest to build a reputation. She can hire an auditor to certify that she is complying with applicable

---

60. E.F. Fama, 'Agency Problems and the Theory of the Firm' (1980) 88 *Journal of Political Economy* 207. See also A. Crockett, T. Harris, F.S. Mishkin and E.N. White, *Conflicts of Interest in the Financial Services Industry: What Should We Do About Them?* p. 7.
61. Ibid. pp. 15 and 73.
62. C.J. Simon, 'The Effect of the 1933 Securities Act on Investor Information and the Performance of New Issues' (1989) *The American Economic Review*, 79 S2:295–318; G.J. Stigler, 'Public Regulation of the Securities Markets' (1967) *Journal of Business* 37, 117–142.
63. A. Crockett, T. Harris, F.S. Mishkin and E.N. White, *Conflicts of Interest in the Financial Services Industry: What Should We Do About Them?* p. 7.

rules. An agent can join a professional association and commit herself to a 'code of conduct' or other 'ethical principles.'[64] Investment banks followed a similar strategy after the analyst scandals that followed the bursting of the Internet bubble; and they responded by voluntarily reforming their internal organization[65] and promoted directives and codes of conduct.[66] Often, these actions will suffice to overcome the information asymmetry. However, in other cases it may be more difficult to separate 'good' types from 'bad' types; worse still, opportunistic individuals will be able to capture a firm's reputational rents, eventually destroying the firm's accumulated goodwill and possibly damaging the credibility of the entire industry.[67] Regulation and supervision may prove necessary to solve this 'lemons' problem[68] and, ultimately, to ensure an efficient outcome.[69]

Competition policy can thus be an answer to conflicts of interest.[70] Alternatively, as Davis points out, conflict of interest rules can be read as a part of broader set of rules intended to solve the problem of lack of competition in certain markets.[71] For instance, if disclosure is required, and in particular if its accuracy is implicitly certified through enforcement, this may help make the market more transparent and hence more competitive.

However, regulation comes at a cost: if rules on conflicts are excessively tough, they prevent specialized actors from sharing their knowledge. This can present a problem when the benefits of specialization exceed the agency costs. Put bluntly, a qualified but conflicted agent is often preferable to an honest but incompetent one.[72] Rules can also be anti-competitive and lead to the fragmentation of markets. To a certain extent, this is the case in the financial industry, where regulatory pressure encourages greater protection of the retail investor, thus reinforcing the segmentation of the market between institutional and retail investors.

B. PROHIBITION

Traditionally, most legal systems called for the fiduciary to abstain from acting in a conflicted situation. This rule is still operative and applies regularly to certain

64. See e.g. this proposal in connection with rating agencies, ibid. p. 52.
65. Ibid. p. 24.
66. See e.g. the Swiss Bankers Association's Directives on the Independence of Financial Research <www.swissbanking.org/en/3566_e.pdf>.
67. A. Crockett, T. Harris, F.S. Mishkin and E.N. White, *Conflicts of Interest in the Financial Services Industry: What Should We Do About Them?* p. 77.
68. See G. Ackerlof, 'The Market for "Lemons": Quality Uncertainty and the Market Mechanism' (1970) *Quarterly Journal of Economics* 84, 488–500.
69. A. Crockett, T. Harris, F.S. Mishkin and E.N. White, *Conflicts of Interest in the Financial Services Industry: What Should We Do About Them?*, p. 74.
70. See ibid. p. 81, suggesting this solution for the rating agency industry, but excluding it for analysts, auditors and most financial institutions.
71. K.B. Davis, Jr., 'Judicial Review of Fiduciary Decisionmaking – Some Theoretical Perspectives' (1985) *Northwestern University Law Review* 80, 1, 6.
72. M.C. Jensen and W.H. Meckling, 'Theory of the firm: Managerial behaviour, agency costs and ownership structure', p. 328.

intermediaries. Lawyers in particular are traditionally barred from representing two clients with conflicting interests. In the financial and corporate world, some global firms learned the hard way that this rule is still alive and kicking.[73] Although bound by a duty of independence rather than a duty of loyalty, auditors are increasingly called upon to turn down any business that may compromise their integrity.[74]

However, due to its rigidity,[75] this approach is waning in the financial industry: From asset managers to financial analysts, none of the commentators recommends such a radical approach, at least as a mandatory rule. In the United States, the Gramm-Leach-Bliley Act of 1999[76] undid the Glass-Steagall Act of 1933,[77] indicating that even the archetypical conflict between investment banking and commercial banking is no longer a source of concern for lawmakers.[78] In Europe, as Marc Kruithof rightly notes, neither the UCITS Directive nor the Directive on Markets in Financial Instruments requires financial institutions to take measures to avoid conflicts of interest. Instead, financial institutions are merely required to mitigate these conflicts and treat their clients fairly.[79]

Nevertheless, one of us (Luc Thévenoz) suggests in his paper that a rule calling for a prohibition of conflicts of interests could be used as a default rule which parties could contract out of subject to mutual consent based on appropriate disclosure. Even in these circumstances, however, the prohibition is not absolute, nor is the rule seriously intended to apply. Rather, it serves as a backdrop against which the parties can negotiate and achieve an efficient outcome.[80]

At the same time, the costs of managing conflicts of interest, and the reputation risks they create, seem to prompt some financial firms to spontaneously disaggregate into smaller, more specialized and less conflicted business units. Marc Kruithof and Eddy Wymeersch both note that some financial conglomerates have spun off their

---

73. *Marks & Spencer PLC v Freshfields Bruckhaus Deringer* [2004] EWHC 1337 (Ch), upheld Court of Appeal [2004] EWCA Civ 741; *Prince Jefri Bolkiah v KPMG* [1999] 1 All E.R. 517 [House of Lords].
74. See e.g. Commission Recommendation of 16 May 2002 – Statutory Auditors' Independence in the EU: A Set of Fundamental Principles (Text with EEA relevance) (notified under document number C(2002) 1873), OJ L 191/22, 2002. In Switzerland, see Art. 727c CO and in the banking area, Circ. CFB 05/03 Sociétés d'audit, items 15ff. In the US, see 17 CFR § 210.2-01(b) and (c) defining independence requirements for auditors.
75. K.J. Hopt, 'Trusteeship and Conflicts of Interest in the Corporate, Banking, and Agency Law: Toward Common Legal Principles for Intermediaries in the Modern Service-Oriented Society' p. 71–72; v. Simonart, 'Conclusions générales', p. 313.
76. Act of 12 November 1999, Pub. L. 106–102
77. Act of 16 June 1933, ch. 89, 48 Stat. 162.
78. See R.S. Kroszner, 'Is the Glass-Steagall Act Justified? A Study of the U.S. Experience with Universal Banking Before 1933' (1994) *The American Economic Review* 84, 810–832, showing that the benefits of the separation by no means exceeded the costs they imposed. For a history of the Glass-Steagall Act of 1933 and good review of the literature overturning the underlying conventional wisdom about universal banking see A. Crockett, T. Harris, F.S. Mishkin and E.N. White, *Conflicts of Interest in the Financial Services Industry: What Should We Do About Them?*, pp. 56 *et seq.*
79. M. Kruithof, Chapter 10, p. 303 et seq., below.
80. L. Thévenoz, Chapter 11, p. 349 et seq., above.

asset management business from their banking activities into a separate division accounting to the holding company and on an equal footing with bank and insurance activities in the organizational design.[81] This outcome comes surprisingly close to a reinstatement of the Glass-Steagall Act of 1933; the difference being that the command-and-control approach of the New Deal era is replaced by the more contemporary repertoire of incentive-based mechanisms; instead of outright bans, it is now organizational constraints and the costs of compliance that are leading to disaggregated firms.

C. Organizational Measures

Rather than barring conflicted firms from acting, regulators have increasingly required these firms to manage the problem through organizational measures.[82] Chinese walls, originally designed as a defence against allegations of insider trading, have become a widespread conflict management tool in most financial conglomerates: The separation between the back and front office, between the client trading desk and the firm's proprietary trading desk, are well known and accepted.[83] In the aftermath of recent analyst-related scandals, organizational rules forced institutions to separate analysts from the corrupting influence of investment bankers.[84] There is nothing very new here: effectively this is an extension of Chinese walls to new business lines in integrated firms. However, how best to achieve efficient and reliable Chinese walls is a problem that still needs further research.[85]

In the realm of corporate governance, remuneration committees and independent directors have now become part of the standard palette of institutional measures devised to limit managerial influence on the pay setting policy.[86] But the road to a truly independent executive compensation procedure is still long and arduous. Personal and professional relations cast doubt on apparent independence. In addition, a problem of cognitive dissonance may make directors unduly lenient, thus worsening the problem; in other words, psychological factors induce directors, most of whom are or have been executives themselves, to adjust their perception of reality in favour of the interests of executives.[87]

---

81. Marc Kruithof, Chapter 10, p. 270 et seq., below; Eddy Wymeersch, Chapter 9, p. 333 et seq., below.
82. See K.J. Hopt, 'Trusteeship and Conflicts of Interest in the Corporate, Banking, and Agency Law: Toward Common Legal Principles for Intermediaries in the Modern Service-Oriented Society', pp. 80–81.
83. Art. 19 (1) and (2) SESTA.
84. See e.g. Global Research Analyst Settlement of 2003, <www.sec.gov/spotlight/globalsettlement.htm>; Swiss Bankers Association's Directives on the Independence of Financial Research, <www.swissbanking.org/en/3566_e.pdf>.
85. See e.g. the five-fold test set out by the House of Lords in *Bolkiah v. KPMG* (no. 72 above).
86. See L.A. Bebchuk and C.M. Fried, *Pay without Performance* (Cambridge, MA; London, England, Harvard University Press, 2004), p. 33.
87. See R. Bahar, Chapter 3, p. 96–97, below; L.A. Bebchuk and C.M. Fried, *Pay without Performance* (Cambridge, MA; London, England, Harvard University Press, 2004), p. 33.

The European and Swiss law both require financial groups to carry out their investment fund management activities via a separate entity, which must be clearly segregated from the depository bank.[88] This segregation is far from being complete: most management companies are part of a financial group,[89] and directors of management companies are not independent. Moreover, directors of investment companies are not found at the top levels of group management. Thus, hierarchy and career concerns may temper the autonomy of the company vis à vis the interests of other divisions.

The same criticism can be levelled at the position of the compliance function more generally. We conclude that any conflict management policy must enhance the status of compliance officers and turn them into a core part of the business. During the semester that led to his book, Tamar Frankel sketched the SEC's attempted solution, which is to raise the status of compliance officers by granting them rapid and direct access to SEC staff, a privilege envied by lawyers and management alike.[90] Pushing the organizational strategy to its extreme, the suggestion might be made that all financial companies be required to create a new 'C-Officer': a Chief Conflict Management Officer. She would rank on an equal standing with the chief financial officer or the chief risk officer, which would offer her and her function increased weight within the organization. While this is probably impractical, solutions must be found to put compliance at the top of the value chain.

The problem with rules on management of conflicts of interest is that they smack of a command-and-control approach to regulation, with all the problems that entails, in particular the one-size-fits-all assumption. It would be better to experiment with alternative solutions, which might lead to identifying better institutional arrangements. In addition, if small financial firms were subject to the same rules as larger institutions, they would have to bear comparable compliance costs in absolute terms, which would be disproportionate to the benefits. Thus, in extreme cases, regulation will actually create a barrier to entry for smaller organizations which are arguably less exposed to conflicts of interest.[91]

The classic answer to this criticism lies with self-regulation. By allowing the industry to regulate itself, the legal system avoids some of its traditional pitfalls, including remoteness from market reality and undifferentiated solutions. Self-regulation is based on industry-wide consensus and can produce a higher degree of compliance. However, self-regulation is not without its drawbacks. It lacks the legitimacy based on democratic decision-making, and is prone to regulatory capture and anticompetitive practices. Left to its on devices the industry may be tempted to cater to its own interests rather than those of the investor, particularly the dispersed retail

88. Art. 9 IFA, confirmed and reinforced by Art. 28(5) of the Federal Act on Collective Investments of Capital of 23 June 2006. Art 5(2) UCITS Directive.
89. Commission Staff Working Paper Annex to the Green Paper on the Enhancement of the EU Framework for Investment Funds, COM (2005) 314 final, p. 21.
90. T. Frankel, Chapter 12.
91. G. Hertig, 'On-Going Board Reforms: One-Size-Fits-All and Regulatory Capture' (2005) *Oxford Review of Economic Policy* 21, 273–275.

investor. Similarly, it can also use the rhetoric of high ethical standards to curtail competitors. As Jean-Baptiste Zufferey hints in his discussion of self-regulation, this may well have been the case with analysts in Switzerland.[92] Lacking any differentiation based on size and specialization, the Swiss Bankers' Association directive was perhaps more a media spin to protect the reputation of global players than the outcome of a sound policy reflection on the problem.

Regulators could, and arguably should, experiment with other forms of regulation. They could, for instance, limit themselves to formulating broad objectives and allow each regulated institution to implement them as it sees fit. Rather than control the specifics of the design, the regulator would then only ensure that the approach was reasonably tailored to its objective, unless major dysfunctions were detected.[93] If a given firm appears to have adopted an inappropriate policy, the regulator would be required to step in and, in extreme cases, impose a standardized set of solutions. This approach, to an extent, underlies several recent regulatory efforts, notably the Basel II Capital Standards, which allows sophisticated institutions to use internal models to measure their credit, market, and operational risks as long as these instruments meet high standards of reliability. Otherwise, standard rules apply.[94]

D. Disclosure

As the outright prohibition of conflicts of interest has waned, disclosure has increasingly become the favoured instrument of policy makers. Rather than force a given organizational arrangement on principal and fiduciary alike, as required by most rules on management of conflicts, disclosure seeks to overcome the information asymmetry between the parties. It brings hidden profits and interests out into the light.[95]

This approach is particularly inviting in the area of compensation. No one is arguing any longer for a government-imposed compensation schemes in the financial industry.[96] Competition authorities in Europe and Switzerland have strongly deprecated industry-wide fee setting arrangements.[97] Thus regulation of

92. J. B. Zufferey, Chapter 7, p. 220, below.
93. G. Hertig, 'On-Going Board Reforms: One-Size-Fits-All and Regulatory Capture', pp. 8–10 (2005) *Oxford Review of Economic Policy* 21, 273–275.
94. Basel Committee on Banking Supervision, 'International Convergence of Capital Measurement and Capital Standards a Revised Framework' (Bank for International Settlements, Basel: 2004), nos. 756–760.
95. See L. D. Brandeis, *Other People's Money and How Bankers Use It* (New York, 1914; reprint, St. Martin's Press: New York, 1995), p. 89.
96. See K.J. Hopt, 'Trusteeship and Conflicts of Interest in the Corporate, Banking, and Agency Law: Toward Common Legal Principles for Intermediaries in the Modern Service-Oriented Society', p. 70.
97. See e.g. *Kartellkommission*, 'Untersuchung der Kartellkomission: Die gesamt schweizerisch wirkenden Vereinbarungen in Bankgewerbe' [1989] Publications de la Commission suisse des cartels et du Préposé à la surveillance des prix [VKKP], 7 *et seq.*, which set out a far-reaching set of recommendations that to a large extent opened the Swiss banking industry to competition.

the compensation scheme itself is not a viable option, and rightly so. Instead, the focus has been turned on transparency.

At an individual level, disclosure empowers the principal to decide whether or not to do business with a conflicted fiduciary. In the realm of bilateral relations, customers can simply decide not to contract, or to terminate an existing agreement. If they have sufficient bargaining power, customers can try to persuade the fiduciary to take steps to manage the conflict of interest in a more effective way. In the corporate realm, investors can sell their shares and disassociate from a company that does not handle conflicts appropriately. This approach also improves the monitoring of the fiduciary's actions and enables the principal to more easily prove any wrongdoing.[98]

Disclosure also enables the market mechanism to work towards an efficient, albeit less than optimal, solution.[99] The decisions of individual market participants will aggregate into a collective reaction to the conflict of interest, which will factor in the costs and benefits of relying on a conflicted, but competent, service provider. In certain cases, the trade-off will work and customers and investors will opt for this solution. In other situations, customers will simply reject the solution and seek to find an alternative.

In financial markets, most service providers are repeat players who expect to be involved for the long term. Disclosure of past performance thus helps the market to appraise how a fiduciary acted. It also allows the institution to build a reputation for integrity, even in highly conflicted situations. Historically, underwriters, such as J.P. Morgan, were able to instil confidence in investors that they would cater to their interests, even if they themselves were involved in a nexus of opposing interests.[100] Prescribing all-encompassing moral standards and integrity would be impossible. However, disclosure helps to reinforce such social practices by sorting the good types, the 'sugar puffs', from the bad, the 'lemons'.[101]

As one of us (Rashid Bahar) points out, the solution is far from perfect. To be effective, disclosure must be full and complete. However, in a world of increasing commoditization of services, it is not possible to rely entirely on bilateral negotiations to achieve efficient disclosure. The same problem plagues any regulatory approach that does not focus sufficiently on the policy and the pay-performance sensitivity of incentive plans.[102]

98. R. Kraakman, P. Davies, H. Hansmann, G. Hertig, K.J. Hopt. H. Kanda and E.B. Rock, *The Anatomy of Corporate Law: A Comparative and Functional Approach* (Oxford, Oxford University Press, 2004), pp. 195–196. See also K.J. Hopt, 'Trusteeship and Conflicts of Interest in the Corporate, Banking, and Agency Law: Toward Common Legal Principles for Intermediaries in the Modern Service-Oriented Society', p. 70.
99. See R. J. Gilson and R. Kraakman, 'The Mechanisms of Market Efficiency' (1984) *Virginia Law Review* 70, 552. See also the follow-up article focusing on behavioural finance: R.J. Gilson and R. Kraakman, 'The Mechanisms of Market Efficiency Twenty Years Later: The Hindsight Bias' (2003) *Journal of Corporate Law* 28, 715.
100. D. Skeel, *Icarus in the Boardroon* (Oxford, New York, Oxford University Press, 2005), pp. 57–58.
101. See G. Ackerlof, 'The Market for "Lemons": Quality Uncertainty and the Market Mechanism'.
102. See, focussing on the disclosure of executive compensation in Switzerland, R. Bahar, Chapter 3, p. 107, below.

Moreover, the lack of homogeneous requirements hinders any form of inter-firm comparison and thus impedes market discipline. Standardization of disclosure schedules is necessary to minimize transaction costs and to avoid counterproductive information. Through standardization, various actors – investors, creditors, regulators, and academics – can access the information they need directly, rather than be potentially misguided by spin. More importantly, they can compare the performance and policies of firms. But standardization also facilitates the ranking of executive remuneration, which may inflate compensation packages due to a ratcheting effect; the so-called 'Lake Wobegon' effect. In other words, any executive can compare her pay-check with those of her peers and demand a raise if hers is below average, i.e. below the market standard.[103]

Like any regulation, disclosure rules may induce certain actors to comply, but they also create opportunities for arbitrage. Less scrupulous actors will seek to hide the most embarrassing information in their disclosure schedules. This is obvious in the context of executive compensation, where management uses equity-based plans and pension schemes as instruments to channel compensation to executives. These payments are troublesome not only because they are not disclosed to investors, but also because they may give false incentives to managers.[104] Although the picture is less bleak with respect to the disclosure of retrocessions, the same risk exists and to a certain extent has taken the form of soft commissions.[105] Thus, although transparency can potentially help, there is no guarantee that it will deliver on all its promises.

Finally, in order for disclosure to achieve its goals, an enforcement mechanism is also required.[106] Several potential solutions are available: a regulatory scheme is but one example. Auditors have long performed this function in the area of financial reporting and underwriters have staked their reputation and liability on the accuracy of offering prospectuses.[107]

Management of conflicts of interest, therefore, may be inevitable: this is the conclusion of most enquiries into executive compensation. Compensation committees and shareholder votes are increasingly being hailed as recommended practices. Even in the fund industry, the formalistic separation between distributors and managers has acquired a new importance in the context of the new interest in 'fund governance'.[108] Thus, the use of independent managers may perhaps push fund

---

103. R. Bahar, Chapter 3, p. 118–119, below.
104. *Ibid.*, p. 113–115, below.
105. See T. Frankel, Chapter 12, p. 380–381, below.
106. A. Crockett, T. Harris, F.S. Mishkin and E.N. White, *Conflicts of Interest in the Financial Services Industry: What Should We Do About Them?*, p. 8.
107. See R.H. Kraakman, 'Gatekeepers: The Anatomy of a Third-Party Enforcement Strategy' (1986) *Journal of Law, Economics, and Organization* 2, 53, 63–66. See more recently in the post-Enron environment, J.C.J. Coffee, 'Gatekeeper Failure and Reform: The Challenge of Fashioning Relevant Reforms' (2004) *B.U. Law Review* 84, 301, 308–315, A. Hamdani, 'Gatekeeper Liability' (2003) *Southern California Law Review* 77, 53.
108. Commission Staff Working Paper Annex to the Green Paper on the Enhancement of the EU Framework for Investment Funds, COM (2005) 314 final, p. 38–44.

management companies to deal with conflicts of interest more adequately. From this perspective, disclosure is one of the numerous tools for managing conflicts of interest. It depends, however, on an external management system: the market or the individual actors should be able to use the information provided to them. They should, thus, be able to appraise whether it is worth putting their trust in the conflicted agent and whether the internal controls set up to avert any adverse consequences exist and are effective.

IV. ENFORCEMENT

Thanks to the American legal realists,[109] the dichotomy between 'law in action' and 'law in the books' is well known. Conflicts of interests in the financial industry provide a striking example of this problem. In theory, the legal doctrines are relatively well established, however, there is something of a chasm between the legal nirvana of conflict of interest rules and the harsh reality of everyday practice. This dichotomy is mainly attributable to enforcement. It does not imply that law must yield to reality. However, legal policies must be realistic and policy makers need to think how they will implement their advice to ensure it is effective in practice.

A. PRIVATE LAW REMEDIES OF THE PRINCIPAL

The main problem with the enforcement of conflict of interest rules stems from the very nature of the duty of loyalty. Compliance with this duty cannot be directly observed; at best it can be guessed at through proxies. Thus, a first set of rules attempts to facilitate the enforcement efforts of principals by introducing a number of presumptions. Early on fiduciary law set out a presumption of breach of loyalty and a heightened standard of review whenever an agent was acting in a conflicted situation: the agent had to prove the intrinsic fairness of her actions so as not to be held in breach. Although common law jurisdictions have formulated this doctrine in its strictest form,[110] milder versions also exist in civil law jurisdictions. Thus, for instance, Swiss corporate law recognizes that the business judgment rule no longer applies in situations in which a conflict of interest creates the suspicion that directors or officers did not act in the best interest of the corporation.[111]

---

109. See e.g. Roscoe Pound, 'Law in Books and Law in Action' (1910) *American Law Review* 44, 12, 18.

110. See § 4.01 (c) American Law Institute Principles of Corporate Governance; *Aronson v. Lewis*, 473 A.2d 805 (Del. 1984) 812; *Smith v. Van Gorkom*, 488 A. 2d 858 (Del. 1985).

111. See e.g. SJ 1982 221, c. 3a, 225 ; ATF 113 II 52, c. 3a, 57. L. Glanzmann, 'Die Verantwortlichkeitsklage unter Corporate Governance-Aspekten' *Revue de droit suisse* 119 (2000) II 135, 165–166, A.R. Grass, 'Management-Entscheidungen vor dem Richter: Schranken der richterlichen Überprüfbarkeit von Geschäftsentscheiden in aktienrechtlichen Verantwortlichkeitsprozessen' *Revue suisse de droit des affaires* 72 (2000) 1–10, A. R. Grass,

Beyond the level of scrutiny exercised by courts, remedies play a decisive role in the effective enforcement of conflict of interest rules. In this respect, common law jurisdictions have a decisive advantage over civil law. Grounded in the language of property law, Anglo-American fiduciary law allows the wronged principal not only to sue for damages, but also to force the fiduciary to disgorge any undue profits. As law and economics scholars have pointed out, this remedy debars the fiduciary from making any profit at the expense of the principal and thus creates appropriate incentives for the principal to fulfil his obligations.[112] Although, in certain continental jurisdictions, a disgorgement-type remedy is in theory available under the title of unjust enrichment[113] or the Swiss *gestion d'affaires sans mandat*,[114] continental legal systems seem to lack a doctrinal foundation for recognizing a generalized right to disgorgement.[115] In any case, this right lacks any bite in practice, probably because lack of information and procedural hurdles make the right difficult to enforce.

B. Class Actions and Derivative Suits

The classical remedies of private law fail to deliver either in the corporate world or in the financial industry. The costs of litigation are too high for most private investors. Civil actions are confined to the more affluent institutional investors and high net worth individuals and are beyond the reach of most retail investors, because the costs of litigation would exceed the possible benefits.[116] Collective action problems and rational apathy accentuate this problem in the corporate environment. An individual

---

Business Judgment Rule: Schranken der richterlichen Überprüfbarkeit von Management-Entscheidungen in aktienrechtlichen Verantwortlichkeitsprozessen (Zurich, Schulthess, 1998); Trigo Trindade and Bahar, 'Droits des actionnaires minoritaires en Suisse', p. 396, H.C. von der Crone, 'Auf den Weg zu einem Recht der Publikumsgesellschaften' *Revue de la société des juristes bernois* 133 (1997) 73, 107; P. Widmer and O. Banz, in *Basler Kommentar zum Schweizerisches Privatrecht*, N. P. Vogt, R. Watter, and H. Honsell (eds) (Basle, Geneva, Munich, Helbing & Lichtenhahn, 2002) ad art. 754 CO, no. 31.

112. R. Cooter and B.J. Freedman, 'The Fiduciary Relationship: Its Economic Character and Legal Consequences' (1991) *New York University Law Review* 66, 1053–1056.
113. Art. 62 CO.
114. Art. 423 CO.
115. See K.J. Hopt, 'Trusteeship and Conflicts of Interest in the Corporate, Banking, and Agency Law: Toward Common Legal Principles for Intermediaries in the Modern Service-Oriented Society', p. 85. For an attempt to identify a general disgorgement theory within a continental legal system, see C. Chappuis, *La restitution des profits illégitimes: le rôle privilégié de la gestion d'affaires sans mandat en droit privé suisse* (Basle, Frankfurt, Geneva, Helbing & Lichtenhahn, 1991); C. Chappuis, 'La remise du gain: les temps sont mûrs' in *Quelques questions fondamentales du droit de la responsabilité civile*, F. Werro (ed.) (Bern, Staempfli, 2002) p. 51; C. Chappuis, 'La restitution des profits illégitimes, le retour' in *De lege ferenda: réflexions sur le droit désirable en l'honneur du professeur Alain Hirsch*, A. Héritier-Lachat and L. Hirsch (eds) (Geneva, Slatkine, 2004), p. 341.
116. See, in relation to consumers in competition law, the Green Paper Damages Actions for Breach of the EC Antitrust Rules (2005), p. 9.

shareholder will not invest in monitoring and litigation if she can free-ride on the efforts of other players.[117]

Thus the level of enforcement obtained through traditional routes is bound to be suboptimal. To overcome this hurdle, legal systems have experimented with a number of procedural strategies. Derivative suits and class actions create the preconditions for litigation entrepreneurs to take the enforcement of rules into their own hands: such procedural institutions enable a lawyer to act in the interests of a diffuse mass of affected persons. This system has been grafted on to private law and does not modify the core set of substantive rules on conflicts of interest. Interestingly, it also assumes that the legal system will enable lawyers to play a more entrepreneurial role by permitting payment schemes based on contingent fees.[118]

From a policy perspective, the chief effect is to improve the effectiveness of sanctions. Moreover, it diminishes the administrative costs of numerous lawsuits by consolidating them all into a single venue. This strategy has a major downside: civil procedure remains a costly means of enforcement and the 'one case at a time' approach may arguably lead to inconsistency.[119] Moreover, litigation entrepreneurs usually lack the more specialized information required to pursue a broader policy of enforcement.[120] Finally, the entire system may be taken hostage by opportunistic suits, where one shareholder or shareholder's attorney tries to hold out unless a company it is willing to settle.[121]

C. CRIMINAL LAW

Traditionally, if private action is lacking but a public interest is involved, there is a call for deterrence through the criminal justice system. A public prosecutor can call to account and punish misfeasors[122] using a wide array of legal mechanisms. In addition to the monetary sanctions, such as damages and disgorgement, and to injunctions, criminal law enables the legal system to act upon persons who would otherwise evade its grasp.[123]

---

117. See e.g. R. Kraakman, P. Davies, H. Hansmann, G. Hertig, K.J. Hopt, H. Kanda and E.B. Rock, *The Anatomy of Corporate Law: A Comparative and Functional Approach*, p. 116–119.
118. E.g. ibid. See also J.C. Coffee, Jr., 'The Unfaithful Champion: The Plaintiff as Monitor in Shareholder Litigation' (1985) *Law & Contemporary Problems* 48,5; R. Romano, 'The Shareholder Suit: Litigation without Foundation' (1991) *Journal of Law, Economics, and Organization* 7, 55.
119. See in relation to product liability law R. Epstein, *Simple Rules for a Complex World* (Cambridge, MA, London, Harvard University Press, 1995) pp. 240–243. See in relation to competition law the Green Paper Damages Actions for Breach of the EC Antitrust Rules, p. 9.
120. R. Epstein, *Simple Rules for a Complex World*, p. 243.
121. See D.R. Fischel and M. Bradley, 'Role of Liability Rules and the Derivative Suit in Corporate Law: A Theoretical and Empirical Analysis' (1985) *Cornell Law Review* 71, 271–274.
122. See K.J. Hopt, 'Trusteeship and Conflicts of Interest in the Corporate, Banking, and Agency Law: Toward Common Legal Principles for Intermediaries in the Modern Service-Oriented Society', p. 85.
123. S. Shavell, *Foundations of Economic Analysis of Law* (Cambridge, MA, and London, Harvard University Press, 2004) p. 510. See also more generally S. Shavell, 'Criminal Law and the Optimal Use of Nonmonetary Sanctions as a Deterrent' *Columbia Law Review* 85 (1985) 1232.

Due to the gravity of these sanctions, criminal law calls for a heightened burden of proof and is only suitable for the most severe and egregious breaches of loyalty. However, as the Global Research Analyst Settlement of 2003[124] has shown, this approach can strongly impact the financial world. Nevertheless, although it may deter fiduciaries from committing the worst violations, this approach is unsuitable to tackle minor breaches.

D. Regulatory Enforcement

The last, although probably the most popular alternative strategy to private enforcement by the principal is regulation – including supervised self-regulation. This approach avoids the pitfalls of civil procedure and criminal law. The centralized enforcement authority can monitor the market as a whole. Obviously, the authority will lack information on specific violations, but at the very least it can focus on the big picture with the assistance of a specialized staff with dedicated resources. In this way, the authority can monitor compliance with broad policy purposes and tackle systemic dysfunctions.[125]

We noted this advantage previously in the rule-making arena, but the advantage is even more significant in the area of enforcement. Thanks to the inexpensive enforcement mechanisms provided by administrative law, it can ensure a certain degree of standardization. As one of us points out in his paper, the SEC had to provide tabular forms in order to ensure that investors could compare the disclosure of executive compensation packages. Such a rule is not significantly more costly to apply than a general duty to disclose compensation packages, but it nonetheless enables the enforcement authority to ensure from a superficial inquiry that issuers comply with the rule. Investors ultimately benefit from standardized information which they could not have obtained otherwise.[126] In Switzerland, individual investors could arguably have obtained the information disclosed in the corporate governance schedules prior to the enactment of the rules. Investors, however, were noticeably silent. It was left to the Federal Banking Commission to pressure the Stock Exchange into adopting a mandatory scheme for the disclosure of executive compensation.[127]

Moreover, administrative law can enforce precautionary rules before any harm is done, thus playing a key role in preventing violations and maintaining trust in the markets – as well as restoring trust in the aftermath of a scandal.[128] This advantage is

---

124. Global Research Analyst Settlement of 2003, <www.sec.gov/spotlight/globalsettlement.htm>.
125. See Shavell, 'The Optimal Structure of Law Enforcement', pp. 590–598; R. Kraakman, P. Davies, H. Hansmann, G. Hertig, K.J. Hopt. H. Kanda and E.B. Rock, *The Anatomy of Corporate Law:A Comparative and Functional Approach*, p. 211. See also, in the context of product liability, R. Epstein, *Simple Rules for a Complex World*, pp. 236–237.
126. R. Bahar, Chapter 3, p. 110–112, below.
127. Rapport de gestion CFB 2000, 213; Rapport de gestion CFB 2001, 221. This eventually led to the implementation of the Corporate Governance Directive.
128. S. Shavell, 'The Optimal Structure of Law Enforcement', pp. 590–598.

particularly interesting in the area of conflicts of interests, as the breach of loyalty itself is hard to detect. For instance, formal rules on Chinese walls are easy to monitor, whereas the information flow itself is difficult for even a regulator to supervise, let alone a customer.

However, as with rule-making, micro-management by the regulator remains a notable drawback of public enforcement.[129] Conversely, with an increasing volume of regulations, regulators are bound to prioritize their enforcement efforts. As a result, certain rules are likely to remain on the books without ever being acted upon. Although all rules ideally have an equal standing, in a world of limited resources, the phenomenon is inevitable. This development sets a new challenge for policy makers and regulators: Rather than refuse to acknowledge reality, they ought to acknowledge this prioritization and explain it following a rational process, such as cost-benefit analysis or another methodology.

V. CONCLUSION

Conflicts of interest lie at the heart of modern financial architecture; an architecture which is based on increasing intermediation. Conflicts of interest can potentially arise every time an intermediary acts for the benefit of a third party to whom she owes a duty of loyalty, if the agent has a personal interest in the transaction or acts also on behalf of persons who themselves have a vested interest. As the network of relations becomes increasingly dense, the likelihood of such conflicting interests increases. This development challenges the classical legal framework in both common law and civil law jurisdictions, which seeks to avoid conflicts of interest.

Traditionally, this issue was tackled by private law, and more specifically by property and contract law. After the Great Depression, most Western democracies looked to regulation and administrative law to deal with instances of conflicts of interests. Regulation and supervision have become increasingly significant in financial industries. The pace of reform has increased in the European Union in order to foster the creation of an integrated financial market. Switzerland, while not participating in this grand effort, has mirrored these developments. Throughout the world, the scandals that accompanied the end of the stock exchange bubble of the 1990s merely served to accelerate the trend.

This thickening of the legal framework is not devoid of ambiguity. In parallel with this phenomenon, market participants have sought to relax the core duty of loyalty. The commoditization of financial services and the increased horizontal integration of market-players has made this phenomenon unavoidable. Is it realistic to require the same degree of independence from an investment banker in a global marketplace dominated by ten players as from a trustee in a pre-industrial society,

129. G. Hertig, 'On-Going Board Reforms: One-Size-Fits-All and Regulatory Capture', (2005) *Oxford Review of Economic Policy* 21, 273–274.

especially if we expect the banker to be experienced and aware of the latest developments in the industry? Innovations such as execution-only brokers and other efforts to narrow down the service provided are just one manifestation of this effort.

The complexity of the problem is also obvious with regard to remedies to conflicts of interest. A pure *laissez-faire* policy is not appropriate. Market pressure is not a panacea that can solve all problems related to conflicts of interest. Weak or imperfect competition caused by market structures, transaction costs and information asymmetry prevents this mechanism from disciplining agents. However, prohibiting them to act in conflicted situations is far too radical. It bars principals from using a conflicted but qualified agent in circumstances in which expertise is more important than loyalty. Regulators have therefore increasingly relied on organizational measures to solve the problem, which had the result of creating a new problem: namely how to reconcile this command-and-control approach with the organizational autonomy that market-players need if they are to adapt to their rapidly changing environment, without considering the subtle interaction between regulation and competition? This is why disclosure was hailed as an ideal remedy. However, disclosure also has its dark side. Its effectiveness, for example, relies on standardization. Moreover, disclosure, like any type of intervention, opens the gate to regulatory arbitrage that may have perverse effects. In fact no system is perfect, although an approach based on light organizational rules and clear disclosure schedules is arguably the best option.

But the formulation of an adequate remedy for conflicts of interest is only a partial solution to this problem. The real issue is enforcement. To postulate a duty of loyalty is simple; to ensure compliance is a far more strenuous task. Starting from private law remedies available to the principal, we observed various attempts to overcome the high costs of private litigation, ranging from class actions and derivative suits to criminal law and regulatory enforcement. Each attempt creates new challenges: how to coordinate private actions into a consistent policy; how to overcome the risk that regulators focus on minor issues and micro-manage an industry while missing the bigger picture; and so on. This calls for the formulation of new policies and methodologies to assess the effectiveness of enforcement techniques and further research.

Conflicts of interests are here to stay and the challenges they pose are increasingly complex. Despite the numerous developments of the past ten years, as this book demonstrates, there is still a long way to go. We hope that this book will help guide policymakers, scholars and practitioners as they attempt to formulate answers to problems old and new.

REFERENCES

Ackerlof, G., 'The Market for "Lemons": Quality Uncertainty and the Market Mechanism' *Quarterly Journal of Economics* 84 (1970) 488.

Bahar, R., *Le rôle du conseil d'administration lors des fusions et acquisitions: une approche systématique* (Zurich, Schulthess, 2004).

Basel Committee on Banking Supervision, 'International Convergence of Capital Measurement and Capital Standards a Revised Framework' (Bank for International Settlements, Basel, 2004).

Bebchuk, L.A., and C.M. Fried, *Pay without Performance* (Cambridge, MA, London, Harvard University Press, 2004).

Böckli, P., *Schweizer Aktienrecht* (3rd edn, Zurich, Schulthess, 2004).

Brandeis, L. D., *Other People's Money and How Bankers Use It* (New York, 1914; reprint, St. Martin's Press: New York 1995).

Chappuis, C., *La restitution des profits illégitimes: le rôle privilégié de la gestion d'affaires sans mandat en droit privé suisse* (Basle; Frankfort; Geneva, Helbing & Lichtenhahn, 1991).

Chappuis, C., 'La remise du gain: les temps sont mûrs' in *Quelques questions fondamentales du droit de la responsabilité civile*, F. Werro (ed.) (Bern, Staempfli, 2002), 51.

Chappuis, C., 'La restitution des profits illégitimes, le retour' in *De lege ferenda: réflexions sur le droit désirable en l'honneur du professeur Alain Hirsch*, A. Héritier-Lachat and L. Hirsch (eds) (Geneva, Slatkine, 2004), 341.

Coffee, J.C., Jr, 'Gatekeeper Failure and Reform: The Challenge of Fashioning Relevant Reforms' *B.U. Law Review* 84 (2004), 301.

Coffee, J.C., Jr, 'The Unfaithful Champion: The Plaintiff as Monitor in Shareholder Litigation' *Law & Contemporary Problems* 48 (1985), 5.

Cooter, R., and B.J. Freedman, 'The Fiduciary Relationship: Its Economic Character and Legal Consequences' (1991) *New York University Law Review* 66, 1,045.

Cooter, R., and T. Ulen, *Law and Economics*, Addison-Wesley series in economics (3rd edn, Reading, MA, et al, Addison-Wesley, 2000).

Crockett, A., T. Harris, F.S. Mishkin and E.N. White, *Conflicts of Interest in the Financial Services Industry: What Should We Do About Them?* (Geneva and London, International Centre for Monetary and Banking Studies and Centre for Economic Policy Research, 2003).

Davis, K.B., Jr., 'Judicial Review of Fiduciary Decisionmaking – Some Theoretical Perspectives' (1985) *Northwestern University Law Review* 80, 1.

Ekelmans, M., 'Conflits d'intérêts: contrats d'intermédiaires', *Les Conflits d'intérêts*, (Brussels, Bruylant, 1997), p. 7.

Epstein, R., *Simple Rules for a Complex World* (Cambridge, MA, London, Harvard University Press, 1995).

Fama, E.F., 'Agency Problems and the Theory of the Firm' (1980) *Journal of Political Economy* 88, 207.

Fischel, D.R. and M. Bradley, 'Role of Liability Rules and the Derivative Suit in Corporate Law: A Theoretical and Empirical Analysis' (1985) *Cornell Law Review* 71, 261.

Gilson, R.J., and R. Kraakman, 'The Mechanisms of Market Efficiency' (1984) *Virginia Law Review* 70, 552.

Gilson, R.J., 'The Mechanisms of Market Efficiency Twenty Years Later: The Hindsight Bias' (2003) *Journal of Corporate Law* 28, 715.

Glanzmann, L., 'Die Verantwortlichkeitsklage unter Corporate Governance-Aspekten' (2000) *Revue de droit suisse* 119 II, 135.

Grass, A.R., 'Management-Entscheidungen vor dem Richter: Schranken der richterlichen Überprüfbarkeit von Geschäftsentscheiden in aktienrechtlichen Verantwortlichkeitsprozessen' (2000) *Revue suisse de droit des affaires* 72, 1.

Grass, A.R., *Business Judgment Rule: Schranken der richterlichen Überprüfbarkeit von Management-Entscheidungen in aktienrechtlichen Verantwortlichkeitsprozessen* (Zurich, Schulthess, 1998).

Green Paper: Damages actions for breach of the EC antitrust rules, COM(2005) 672 final, 2005.

Hamdani, A., 'Gatekeeper Liability' (2003) *Southern California Law. Review* 77, 53.

Hertig, G., 'On-Going Board Reforms: One-Size-Fits-All and Regulatory Capture' (2005) *Oxford Review of Economic Policy* 21, 269.

Hopt, K.J., 'Trusteeship and Conflicts of Interest in the Corporate, Banking, and Agency Law: Toward Common Legal Principles for Intermediaries in the Modern Service-Oriented Society' in G.A. Ferrarini, K.J. Hopt, J. Winter and E. Wymeersch (eds), *Reforming Company and Takeover Law in Europe* (Oxford, New York, Oxford University Press, 2005), p. 51.

Jensen, M.C., 'Paying People to Lie: the Truth about the Budgeting Process' (2003) *European Financial Management* 9, 379.

Jensen, M.C., and W.H. Meckling, 'Theory of the Firm: Managerial Behaviour, Agency Costs and Ownership Structure' (1976) *Journal of Financial Economics* 3, 305.

Jensen, M.C., and K.J. Murphy, 'CEO Incentives – It's Not How Much You Pay, But How' (1990) *Harvard Business Review* 68, 138.

Jensen, M.C., 'Performance Pay and Top-Management Incentives' (1990) *Journal of Political Economy* 98, 225.

Kraakman, R., P. Davies, H. Hansmann, G. Hertig, K. Hopt, H. Kanda, and E.B. Rock, *The Anatomy of Corporate Law: A Comparative and Functional Approach* (Oxford, Oxford University Press, 2004).

Kraakman, R.H., 'Gatekeepers: The Anatomy of a Third-Party Enforcement Strategy' (1986) *Journal of Law, Economics, and Organization* 2, 53.

Kroszner, R.S., 'Is the Glass-Steagall Act Justified? A Study of the U.S. Experience with Universal Banking Before 1933' (1994) *The American Economic Review 84*, 810.

Roe, M.J., and J.N. Gordon (eds) *Convergence and Persistence in Corporate Governance* (Cambridge: Cambridge University Press, 2004).

Romano, R., 'The Shareholder Suit: Litigation without Foundation' (1991) *Journal of Law, Economics, and Organization* 7, 55.

Shavell, S., 'Criminal Law and the Optimal Use of Nonmonetary Sanctions as a Deterrent' (1985) *Columbia Law Review* 85, 1,232.

Shavell, S., 'The Optimal Structure of Law Enforcement' (1993) *Journal of Law and Economics* 36, 255.

Shavell, S., *Foundations of Economic Analysis of Law* (Cambridge, MA and London, Harvard University Press, 2004).

Simon, C. J., 'The Effect of the 1933 Securities Act on Investor Information and the Performance of New Issues' (1989) *The American Economic Review* 79, S2: 295.

Simonart, v., 'Conclusions générales' in *Les Conflits d'intérêts*, (Brussels, Bruylant, 1997), p. 299.

Skeel, D., *Icarus in the Boardroon* (Oxford, New York, Oxford University Press, 2005).

Stigler, G.J., 'Public Regulation of the Securities Markets' (1964) *Journal of Business* 37, 117.

Trigo Trindade, R., and R. Bahar, 'Droits des actionnaires minoritaires en Suisse' in *Rapports suisses présentés au XVIème Congrès international de droit comparé*, (Zurich, Schulthess, 2002), p. 381.

von der Crone, H.C., 'Auf den Weg zu einem Recht der Publikumsgesellschaften' (1997) *Revue des juristes bernois* 133, 73.

Widmer, P., and O. Banz, in N. P. Vogt, R. Watter and H. Honsell (eds), *Basler Kommentar zum Schweizerisches Privatrecht: OR II*, (Basel, Geneva, Munich, Helbing & Lichtenhahn, 2002).

Chapter 2

Structure of Executive Compensation and Conflicts of Interests – Legal Constraints and Practical Recommendations under Swiss Law

*Rolf Watter and Karim Maizar**

I. INTRODUCTION

The design of executive compensation packages has been extensively analyzed in a number of areas, such as (corporate) law, accounting, economic sciences, sociology (organizational behaviour), and psychology.[1] The subject is highly politicized, as mass media in particular pay a great deal of attention to the level (and, less frequently, the structure) of such packages, often calling for regulation, including compensation ceilings. This paper will first analyze the (economic) context of executive compensation, from which potential conflicts of interests[2] may arise

---

* Prof. Dr. Rolf Watter, LL.M. (Georgetown), Attorney-at-law, Bär & Karrer, Zurich, professor at the University of Zurich. lic.iur Karim Maizar, Attorney-at-law, Bär & Karrer, Zurich. Our text is based on the laws and regulations as in force per 1 May 2006; it considers the literature and court decisions published up to that date.

1. For references see e.g. K.J. Murphy, 'Executive compensation' April 1998,<papers.ssrn.com/abstract_id=163914>, and M.C. Jensen and K.J. Murphy, 'Remuneration: Where we've been, how we got to here, what are the problems, and how to fix them' *European Corporate Governance Institute Working Paper* 44/2004 (July 2004), 2 <papers.ssrn.com/abstract_id=561305>.
2. A conflict of interest arises when a person who has undertaken to safeguard the interests of another person has to resolve an issue which may result in a conflict with his/her own interests and/or

L. Thévenoz and R. Bahar (eds.), *Conflicts of Interest: Corporate Governance and Financial Market*, pp. 31–85.

(section II). We shall then examine how Swiss law addresses conflicts of interests in connection with (i) the design and structure of executive compensation packages (section III) and (ii) the pay-setting process (i.e. competences, organizational issues) (section IV). Thus we hope not only to explain the parameters set *de lege lata,* but also to suggest guidelines and recommendations on defining a compensation system which is in the best interests of the company and its shareholders, and show how the corporate bodies (shareholders, board members and executives) should interact in order to mitigate conflicts of interests.

In this article we shall use the term 'executive' in a broad sense that encompasses not only top management, but also directors who hold an executive position – which in Switzerland is often (but by no means always) the case with the CEO (who is then called a *'Delegierter'*); other top managers such as CFOs, COOs and key division heads are not usually board members of Swiss companies, although this is not excluded by law. We shall use the terms 'managers' and 'directors' in a more specific sense, i.e. members of the management and members of the board respectively.

II. THE ROLE OF EXECUTIVE COMPENSATION FROM AN ECONOMIC POINT OF VIEW

A. The Agency Problem

If an executive owns 100 per cent of a company, his personal and business interests are naturally aligned: his strategic and operational decisions will normally serve his personal interests as well.[3] If ownership of a company's shares is dispersed and decision-making is vested with persons other than the owners, conflicts of interests will arise, because ownership is separated from control, as A.A. Berle and G.C. Means[4] were the first to demonstrate with regard to (public) companies. They observed, *inter alia*, that shareholders cannot always monitor or direct executives' actions, so the executives who exert day-to-day control in such companies have considerable discretion in their decision-making, which they may use to further their personal interests at the expense of those of the shareholders.[5]

---

the interests of third parties. See e.g. H.C. von der Crone, 'Interessenkonflikte im Aktienrecht' (1994) *Revue suisse de droit des affaires 66, 2.*

3. M.C. Jensen and W.H. Meckling, 'Theory of the firm: Managerial behaviour, agency costs and ownership structure' (1976) *Journal of Financial Economics* 3, 305; M.C. Jensen and K.J. Murphy, no. 1, 23 *et seq.*; H.C. von der Crone, 'Verantwortlichkeit, Anreize und Reputation in der Corporate Governance der Publikumsgesellschaft' (2000) *Revue de droit suisse* 119, II 241; Gion Giger, *Corporate Governance als neues Element im schweizerischen Aktienrecht* (Zurich, Schulthess, 2003), p. 31.
4. A.A. Berle and G.C. Means, *The Modern Corporation and Private Property* (New York/Chicago/Washington, Harcourt, Brace & World, 1932).
5. A.A. Berle and G.C. Means, no. 4, 119 *et seq.* In contrast to later authors, Berle and Means did not suggest that managers should be bound to shareholders' interests, but rather that managers

Since M.C. Jensen and W.H. Meckling,[6] the problem of managerial discretion (and thus power) has been analyzed as the 'agency problem'. The separation of ownership and control can be understood to be an agency relationship in which executives act as agents of shareholders.[7] Based on the premise of the resourceful, evaluating, maximizing man ('REMM'),[8] agency theory suggests that executives will always try to maximize their own welfare, which may diverge from the interests of shareholders.[9]

The interests of managers and shareholders can diverge in a number of ways.[10] Managers, for example, may be tempted to substitute leisure for effort[11] or seek

---

should use their discretionary power to assume a social responsibility of the company by taking into account interests other than those of the shareholders alone: 'It is conceivable – indeed it seems almost essential if the corporate system is to survive – that the "control" of the great corporations should develop into a purely neutral technocracy, balancing a variety of claims by various groups in the community and assigning to each a portion of the income stream on the basis of public policy rather than private cupidity' (A.A. Berle and G.C. Means, no. 4 above, 352 *et seq.*, especially 356).

6. M.C. Jensen and W.H. Meckling, no. 3 above.
7. The separation of ownership and control formulated by A.A. Berle and G.C. Means is focused on public companies. However, it is indisputable that the same applies to non-public companies. M.C. Jensen and W.H. Meckling, no. 3 above, 308 *et seq.*, define the agency relationship as 'a contract under which one ore more persons (the principal[s]) engage another person (the agent) to perform some service on their behalf which involves delegating some decision making authority to the agent'. Consequently, the agency theory also applies to non-listed companies. In practice, however, most privately held companies will be owned and, at least in part, controlled by the same individuals. Although this may also be true of many public companies in Switzerland, the management of a company (*Geschäftsführung*) is often fully or partially delegated from the board of directors to the managers. As a result, an agency relationship also exists between the board of directors and the management even (though to a lesser extent) in companies without dispersed ownership. The implications of the agency theory, therefore, also apply to such companies.
8. The premise of the REMM is somewhat disputed in economic literature. However, REMM is not intended to describe the behaviour of any particular individual but rather that of an aggregate of individuals. As such, it is still considered the best model for analyzing human behaviour. See e.g. M.C. Jensen and W.H. Meckling 'The nature of man' (1994) *Journal of Applied Corporate Finance* 7(2), 4 *et seq.*; M. Ruffner, *Die ökonomischen Grundlagen eines Rechts der Publikumsgesellschaften* (Zurich, Schulthess, 2000), p. 60 with further references; K. Mathis, *Effizienz statt Gerechtigkeit?*, (Berlin, Duncker & Humblot, 2004), p. 27.
9. See M.C. Jensen and W.H. Meckling, no. 3 above, 308; L.A. Bebchuk and J.M. Fried, *Pay without performance – The unfulfilled promise of executive compensation* (Cambridge, Massachusetts/London, Harvard University Press, 2004) p. 16; A. Picot, H. Dietl and E. Franck, *Organisation – Eine ökonomische Perspektive*, (3rd edn, Stuttgart, Schaeffer-Poeschel, 2002) p. 88 *et seq.*; M. Ruffner, no. 8 above, p. 58 *et seq.*; R. Suter, *Corporate Governance & Management Compensation* (Zurich, Versus, 2000) p. 56 *et seq.*
10. See e.g. R.A. Brealey and S.C. Myers, *Principles of corporate finance* (7th edn, New York, McGraw-Hill, 2003) p. 316 *et seq.*; R. Suter, no. 9 above, p. 65 *et seq.*
11. L.A. Bebchuk and J.M. Fried, no. 9 above, p. 16 *et seq.*; L. Glanzmann, 'Die Verantwortlichkeitsklage unter Corporate-Governance-Aspekten' (2000) *Revue de droit suisse* 119, II 141; D.M. Weiss, *Aktienoptionspläne für Führungskräfte* (Cologne, Schmidt, 1999), p. 41 *et seq.*; S.M. Bainbridge, 'Executive compensation: Who decides?' (2005) *Texas Law Review* 83, 7 *et seq.*

to minimize firm-specific risks.[12, 13] Further, they may engage in empire building, entrench themselves in their positions,[14] in particular by trying to block takeover attempts, or favour the retention of earnings within the company rather than distribution to shareholders.[15] Generally speaking, managers will be tempted to maximize their welfare by maximizing their compensation and discretion while minimizing their personal risk.[16]

Agency costs are a consequence of these diverging interests.[17] They comprise e.g. the costs of monitoring and the costs of establishing incentives, in the form of (*inter alia*) performance-based compensation.[18] Generally, shareholders will be happy to bear these costs as long as the marginal profit from the separation of ownership and control is higher than the marginal agency costs.

B. Overview of Remedies Against the Agency Problem

In theory, several mechanisms are in place which might overcome, or at least mitigate, the conflicting interests of shareholders and managers,[19] in particular the following:

- Market Forces:[20] such as the market for corporate control, the market for debt and equity capital, the market for managers,[21] and the market for

12. Executives tend to be risk averse: they invest their monetary and human capital in the company and are therefore (unlike shareholders) not diversified.
13. S.M. Bainbridge, no. 11 above.
14. L.A. Bebchuk and J.M. Fried, 'Executive compensation as an agency problem' (2003) *Journal of Economic Perspectives* 17, 71 *et seq.*
15. St.M. Bainbridge, no. 11 above, 8 *et seq.* with further references.
16. R. Suter, no. 9 above, p. 62 *et seq.*; R. Weilenmann, *Value based compensation plans* (Bern/Stuttgart/Vienna, Haupt, 1999) p. 170 *et seq.*; D.M. Weiss, no. 11 above, p. 45.
17. Agency costs were first analyzed by M.C. Jensen and W.H. Meckling, no. 9 above. They distinguish (i) monitoring expenditures by the principal, which include costs in connection with the establishment of incentives designed to limit the aberrant activities of the agent; (ii) bonding expenditures, in which the principal pays the agent to expend resources to guarantee that the agent will not take certain actions which would harm the principal or to ensure that the principal will be compensated if the agent does take such actions; and (iii) the residual loss, which is the cost that cannot be avoided despite the use of monitoring/incentives and bonding expenditures.
18. See e.g. R. Suter, no. 9 above, p. 49.
19. See e.g. M.C. Jensen, 'The modern industrial revolution, exit and the failure of internal control systems' (1993) *Journal of Finance* 48, 850; A. Picot, H. Dietl and E. Franck, no. 9 above, p. 268 *et seq.*; T. Spillmann, *Institutionelle Investoren im Recht der (echten) Publikumsgesellschaften* (Zurich, Schulthess, 2004), p. 206 *et seq.*; G. Giger, no. 3 above, p. 37 *et seq.*; R. Suter, no. 9 above, p. 49 *et seq.*; D.M. Weiss, no. 11 above, p. 57 *et seq.*
20. E.F. Fama, 'Agency problems and the theory of the firm' (1980) *Journal of Political Economy* 80, 288 *et seq.*; see also e.g. A. Picot, H. Dietl and E. Franck, no. 9 above, p. 276 *et seq.*; T. Spillmann, no. 19 above, p. 207 *et seq.*; G. Giger, no. 3 above, p. 38 *et seq.*; L.A. Bebchuk, J.M. Fried and D.I. Walker, 'Managerial power and rent extraction in the design of executive compensation' (2002) *The University of Chicago Law Review* 69, 774 *et seq.*; L.A. Bebchuk and J.M. Fried, no. 9 above, p. 53 *et seq.*; Reto Suter, no. 9 above, p. 123 *et seq.*; D.M. Weiss, no. 11 above, p. 57 *et seq.*

products and services, and which are generally said to be reinforced by reputation mechanisms;[22]

- Legal/regulatory/internal sanctions: which lead e.g. to personal liability;[23]
- Institutional control mechanisms: in particular monitoring/supervision of the board by the shareholders and of the management by the board,[24] but also appropriate internal organizational structures, e.g. committees at board level;[25]
- Incentives: in particular performance-based compensation.[26]

Although market forces, sanction regimes, and institutional control mechanisms may help to *prevent* decisions that are not in line with shareholders' interests, they do not substantially *induce* managers to make *a priori* decisions that are in the shareholders' best interests. In addition, each of these mechanisms has various shortcomings.[27] This is where incentives come into play, in particular performance-based compensation, which will be described in more detail below.

Although scholars admit that market forces can do something to correct agency problems, they are considered far too weak to ensure a substantial alignment of interests between shareholders and managers: see L.A. Bebchuk and J.M. Fried, no. 9 above, p. 53; T. Spillmann, no. 19 above, p. 217; G. Giger, no. 3 above, p. 42. For more on the role of the market for managers, see no. 21 below.

21. The market for managers is often criticized as being incomplete on the grounds that it is manipulated by the managers themselves: see e.g. A. Picot, H. Dietl and E. Franck, no. 9 above, p. 281 *et seq.* The incompleteness of the market is seen e.g. in the steady and inexorable rise in manager compensation, which, according to the critics, does not correlate with any shortage of managers or increase in their (marginal) productivity. For a good overview see e.g. M. Benz and A. Stutzer, 'Was erklärt die steigenden Managerlöhne? – Ein Disskussionsbeitrag' (2003) *Die Unternehmung* 57 (1), 5 *et seq.* (also <www.iew.unizh.ch/wp/iewwp081.pdf>).
22. Due to the information asymmetry between principals and agents, principals have to rely on the reputation of agents whether they want to or not. Conversely, it is argued that agents should have an incentive not to act opportunistically in order to maintain or even increase the number of principals interested in hiring them. See H.C. von der Crone, no. 3 above, 259 *et seq.,* and H.C. von der Crone, 'Freiheit und Verantwortung in der Corporate Governance' in *Corporate Governance, Symposium zum 80. Geburtstag von Arthur Meier-Hayoz*, P. Forstmoser, H.C. von der Crone, R.H. Weber and D. Zobl (eds.) (Zurich/Basle/Geneva, Schulthess, 2002) p. 78 *et seq.*; for further references G. Giger, no. 3 above, p. 412.
23. See e.g. H.C. von der Crone, no. 3 above, 242 *et seq.* and L. Glanzmann, no. 11 above, 139 *et seq.*
24. See e.g. A. Picot, H. Dietl and E. Franck, no. 9 above, p. 268 *et seq.* In theory, the board of directors of a company is presumed to be the most crucial body to supervise the management: '*They are the link between the people who provide capital and the people who use that capital to create value*' (R. A. Monks and N. Minow, cited in: R. Suter, no. 9 above, p. 129).
25. Such as independence requirements, rules to be observed in situations of conflicts of interests (e.g. abstention from voting) or the formation of committees: see below sections IV.A.3 and IV.B.3. Also G. Giger, no. 3 above, p. 42; T. Spillmann, no. 19 above, p. 214.
26. For a recent overview, see D. Leu, *Variable Vergütungen für Manager und Verwaltungsräte* (Zurich, Schulthess, 2005) p. 34 *et seq.*
27. See the references in no. 20 *et seq* above.

C. Incentives and Performance-based Compensation in Particular

Compensation that depends on a particular performance measure (performance-based compensation) is viewed as the key method to align the interests of the managers with those of shareholders.[28] The idea behind such compensation schemes is that the business risk is (partly) shifted on to the executive:[29] good performance is rewarded while poor performance is punished.[30] Or, in the words of Bebchuk/Jolls, 'performance-based pay tie[s] managers' fates to shareholders' return'.[31] Although the efficiency of monetary incentives, and performance-based compensation in particular, is not unquestioned,[32] many companies have implemented such compensation arrangements.[33]

---

28. The impetus for the shift towards performance-based compensation during the 1990s was predominantly provided by M.C. Jensen and K.J. Murphy (see e.g. M.C. Jensen and K.J. Murphy, 'Performance pay and top-management incentives' *Journal of Political Economy* 98 (1990) 225; M.C. Jensen and K.J. Murphy, 'CEO incentives – It's not how much you pay, but how' *Harvard Business Review* May/June (1990) 138 *et seq.*; further references can be found in L.A. Bebchuk and J.M. Fried, no. 9 above, p. 19 and there particularly no. 11; A. Brandenberg, *Anreizsysteme zur Unternehmenssteuerung* (Wiesbaden, Deutscher Universitäts-Verlag, 2001) p. 5; M. Ruffner, no. 8 above, p. 132; H.C. von der Crone, no. 3 above, 252.
29. Optimal compensation contracts must reflect the trade-off between the goals of providing efficient risk-sharing and providing the managers with incentives to perform appropriate actions; see M.C. Jensen and K.J. Murphy, no. 1 above, 17.
30. A. Brandenberg, no. 28 above, p. 5; Gion Giger, no. 3 above, p. 390.
31. L.A. Bebchuk and C. Jolls, 'Managerial value diversion and shareholder wealth' (1999) *Journal of Law, Economics and Organization* 15, 489.
32. Critics often complain that the agency theory assumes that managers' motives are *solely* extrinsic (and chiefly monetary) rather than acknowledge that individuals' motives are more broadly based, e.g. that they derive utility from the activity itself or wish to comply with given normative standards for their own sake (intrinsic motivation). The critics argue that extrinsic motivation may impair intrinsic motivation and thus may turn out to be counterproductive: see e.g. B.S. Frey and M. Osterloh, 'Yes, managers should be paid like bureaucrats' *CESIFO Working Paper No.* 1379 (January 2005) <papers.ssrn.com/abstract_id=555697>; further B.S. Frey, 'Die Grenzen ökonomischer Anreize' *Neue Zürcher Zeitung*, 18 May 2005 (no. 114) 25; D. Leu, no. 26 above, p. 35 *et seq.*; R. Suter, no. 9 above, p. 27 *et seq.*; G. Giger, no. 3 above, p. 397 *et seq.*; D. Portmann, *Mitarbeiterbeteiligung* (Bern, Staempfli, 2005) n. 74; T. Spillmann, no. 19 above, p 215 with references.

    According to a recent study of 342 Swiss companies conducted by the *Lehrstuhl für Human Resource Management* at the University of Zurich, performance-based compensation is a greater incentive for low-status employees than for top management. See U. Bernard and M. Becker, 'Worte zählen mehr als Geld – Die indirekte Anreizwirkung leistungsabhängiger Löhne' *Neue Zürcher Zeitung,* 14 April 2005 (no. 86), 29.
33. In Switzerland, variable compensation represents approximately 33 per cent, and long-term incentive compensation (e.g. shares) 13 per cent of the total compensation. See e.g. *Handelszeitung*, 18 May 2005 (no. 20), 9. For surveys in the USA, see e.g. M.C. Jensen and K.J. Murphy, no. 1 above, 23 *et seq.* Recently, share option programs have lost some of their attractiveness. The Microsoft Corporation, for instance, has stopped granting share options to employees and now grants shares instead. Whether this is a shift in philosophy or rather a consequence of changing accounting rules and tax laws, combined with much less favourable equity markets remains to be seen.

To measure or reward performance in performance-based compensation systems, the company has to decide on appropriate performance criteria.[34] Usually, such criteria are based on market, accounting, firm-value and/or strategic measures:

- Market measures, e.g. the share price or total shareholders' return (the latter adjusts the share price to take account of dividend pay-outs), are commonly used for performance because the share price is (still) considered the best proxy to reflect the firm value, i.e. the present value of the entire future stream of expected cash-flows.[35] Market-based compensation is, in essence, quite simple: the higher the (future) market value of the company, the higher the executive's compensation. Thus executives have an incentive to increase shareholder value[36] in order to earn higher pay. Pure market-based compensation schemes usually consist in granting a certain number[37] of shares and/or share options.[38] In case of shares, the compensation will increase or decrease in proportion to the increase or decrease in the share price; in case of options, the compensation will increase or decrease disproportionately,[39] dropping to zero if the share price falls below the strike price. Often, rather than use share price as a direct yardstick to reward performance, companies use other criteria (such as the ones mentioned below) and then pay the variable part of the salary in the form of blocked shares or (restricted) options. If the executive cannot immediately monetize these types of shares or options, this provides the company with an additional market-related long-term incentive to induce the executive which – if structured

---

34. See e.g. D. Leu, no. 26 above, p. 176 *et seq.*; D.M. Weiss, no. 11 above, p. 66 *et seq.*; R. Weilenmann, no. 16 above, p. 38 *et seq.*; S. Reichelstein, 'Die Ungeduld der Manager bändigen – Geeignete Kennzahlen für die Leistungsbewertung' *Neue Zürcher Zeitung,* 10 June 2003 (no. 131), B3; further M.C. Jensen and K.J. Murphy, no. 1 above, 19; H.J. Stern, 'Wertmaximierende Bonussysteme dank interessenausgleichenden Führungsstrukturen – Nicht-monetäre Zielgrössen im leistungsorientierten Lohnsystem?' [2002] *L'Expert comptable suisse,* p. 1,141 *et seq.*
35. M.C. Jensen and C.W. Smith Jr., 'Stockholder, manager, and creditor interests: applications of agency theory' (December 2000) *Harvard Research Paper,* 12, <papers.ssrn.com/abtstract_id=173461>. This view is based on the assumption that the efficient capital market hypothesis is applicable, at least in its semi-strong form.
36. Market-based compensation systems assume that the individual concerned has some influence on the market value, because otherwise there would be no incentive. See e.g. A. Risi, *Mitarbeiteroptionen und –aktien – Bewertung, Rechnungslegung, Besteuerung* (Zurich, Treuhand-Kammer, 1999), p. 76 *et seq.*
37. Rather than issue a given number of shares for the period under review, the company can also grant a higher number of shares if the share price increases over this period. The company can also choose to reward the increase in the share price by granting a cash payment, which is effectively a stock appreciation right.
38. The company can also use a cash-settled market-based compensation system (phantom stock and/or stock appreciation rights).
39. This is why options offer a manager with incentives to invest in projects which increase the risk (and thus the volatility) of the company's cash-flows.

property – also provide an incentive for the executive to stay with the company.[40]

- Accounting criteria, e.g. sales, EBIT, EBITDA, profit, cash-flow or certain key performance indicators such as ROE (return on equity) or ROIC (return on invested capital) are widely used, *inter alia,* because they enable easy determination of the variable pay and are, by and large, not dependent on general market movements (as pure market-based models are). By defining the objectives, which are often also communicated to analysts, the board hopes to offer managers a guideline to increase shareholder value based on the board's strategy and thus align their interests with those of the shareholders. The variable pay is calculated on the basis of these criteria, and is paid either in cash or in (blocked) shares or (restricted) options; the latter add a long-term incentive for the executives to increase the share price.
- Firm value-based criteria (e.g. Economic Value Added [EVA][41] and discounted free cash-flow [DCF]) have recently become more widely used.[42] These criteria provide a measure of performance that goes beyond the market- and accounting-based systems, but is rooted in them: EVA, for instance, compares the company's earnings with the weighted average cost of capital, including the cost of equity, i.e. the weighted average cost of capital multiplied by the invested capital minus the company's income earned before interest, but after tax.[43]
- Strategic criteria, e.g. market share, image, employee or customer satisfaction, productivity and technical innovation, play a less significant role in top executive compensation packages, but a feature in the compensation of

40. We prefer this last method *inter alia* because using criteria different from the pure share price performance enables companies to set targets based on the company's strategy, as well as to set different targets for different functions (i.e. for the CEO, the CFO and each division head). The (future) share price performance will of course still loom large in the executive's mind (and thus continue to be an motivating factor) if he/she is paid in (blocked) shares or options. In any case, when considering the use of options, directors should be particularly mindful of the fact that the share price is (also) influenced by externalities, which enables executives to benefit from positive windfalls, unless precautionary measures are taken. For more on this, see sections III.C.1.a. and III.C.1.c below.
41. EVA is a registered trademark of Stern Stewart & Co.
42. See e.g. D. Leu, no. 26 above, p. 192 *et seq.*
43. See e.g. R. Volkart, *Corporate Finance – Grundlagen von Finanzierung und Investition* (Zurich, Versus, 2003), p. 259 *et seq.*; R.A Brealey and S.C. Myers, no. 10 above, p. 322 *et seq.*; R. Weilenmann, no. 16 above, p. 67 *et seq.* and p. 130 *et seq.*; S. Hostettler, 'Economic Value Added – Lektionen aus der Praxis – Das EVA Konzept richtig eingesetzt als Grundlage einer effektiven finanziellen Corporate Governance' [2003] *L'Expert comptable Suisse,* 117 *et seq.* For a critical analysis of EVA as performance standard, see e.g. P. Gampenrieder, 'Variable Vergütung auf Basis des Economic Value Added – Ein kritischer Beitrag zur Diskussion um die richtige Bemessungsgrundlage' [2002] *L'Expert comptable suisse,* 123 *et seq.*; J. Evans and R. Evans, 'An examination of Economic Value Added and executive compensation' 2002, <papers.ssrn.com/abstract_id=313974>; R. Suter, no. 9 above, p. 153 *et seq.*

some line managers and the heads of certain key staff functions, e.g. heads of sales, supply chain and R&D.[44]

D. Conflicts of Interests in Executive Compensation

Executive compensation is a classic example of a field in which the interests of executives and shareholders collide.[45] The board of directors most often sets the compensation of its executive and non-executive members and is therefore confronted with a clear conflict of interest, because these directors naturally will want to maximize their own compensation, to the detriment of shareholders.[46]

There is less of a conflict if the executives are not board members, but their interests will still diverge from those of the shareholders, depending on the structure of their compensation. For instance, compensation that depends on long-term corporate solvency, i.e. any type of deferred payment, may induce executives to reduce the volatility of cash flows, because their expected payoff increases as cash-flow risk and the probability of default decline.[47] Executives will also have incentives to retain funds within the company and reduce debt, even where such actions have a negative impact on the value of the company.

Equity-based compensation (whether paid in shares or options)[48] tempts executives to adopt a restrictive dividend policy, but favours share buy-back as a substitute.[49] Moreover, it creates an incentive to increase the share price through short-term actions,[50] although it is unclear whether the share price in fact mirrors such actions.[51, 52] In addition, as executives' possession of share options or shares constitutes a risk concentration, they may be tempted to mitigate this risk by either selling or, if restrictions apply, entering into (personal) hedging and/or derivatives contracts. Alternatively, executives may try to diversify firm-specific risk, for example, by creating a conglomerate. In addition, if share options are granted, decreases

44. D.M. Weiss, no. 11 above, pp. 72.
45. For an overview see e.g. D. Leu, no. 26 above, pp. 114 *et seq*.
46. Directors – if different from the owners – are just as subject to the agency problem as managers are, and because managers are not assumed to prioritize shareholders' interests-automatically, directors cannot be expected to do so either. See e.g. L.A. Bebchuk and J.M. Fried, no. 14 above, 73; M.C. Jensen and K.J. Murphy, no. 1 above, 22.
47. M.C. Jensen and C.W. Smith Jr., no. 35 above, 11 *et seq*.
48. The strike price of options is generally not adjusted for dividends or nominal capital reductions.
49. Of course, the shareholders have the last word under Swiss law on dividends, but executives can influence this decision to an important degree, e.g. by restricting pay-outs from subsidiaries, which then limits the amount of distributable reserves in the top company.
50. Such as the disclosure of positive price sensitive information prior to exercising options, e.g. innovations and share buy-back programs
51. D.M. Weiss, no. 11 above, pp. 98 *et seq*.
52. See H.C. von der Crone, no. 3 above, p. 253 *et seq*.; T. Bühner and M. Wallmeier, 'Aktienkurs-basierte Mitarbeiterentlohnung in der Schweiz – Zielkonflikt zwischen Anreizsystem und Steuersparmodell?' [2004] *L'Expert comptable Suisse,* 556; D.M. Weiss, no. 11 above, p. 74 *et seq.* with various references; R. Suter, no. 9 above, p. 151 *et seq.*; A. Risi, no. 36 above, p. 70 *et seq.*

in share price may create a temptation to try to amend the terms of the options, particularly the exercise price ('re-pricing').[53] Finally, there is a danger that managers may try to adopt (or persuade the board to adopt) a share option or share participation plan before the disclosure of (positive) share-price-sensitive information in order to profit from the ensuing share price increase, or may delay such information until after a plan is implemented. A similar conflict arises in existing plans, where executives may delay publication of positive news until after the grant date.

Using accounting criteria as a measure of performance to determine the variable component of the pay package can create a number of conflicts.[54] For instance, certain accounting parameters give executives a direct interest in the choice of options (or early adoption of new standards)[55] within the accounting standard.[56] Furthermore, accounting measures are past-oriented; a fact that may lead executives to focus on the relevant (short-term) accounting period rather than on long-term objectives.[57] For example, if an executive's compensation is geared to sales, he may be tempted to boost sales late in the year by granting rebates, which in turn set a lower price level for the future, and thus in the long term lead to lower shareholder returns. Likewise, executives who believe that they cannot achieve a performance target in a given year will try to shift sales or profits into the next year by delaying revenues or accelerating expenses.[58] Another problem is created when – as often occurs – performance targets are set in such a way that they are always expected to exceed those of the preceding year:

> [D]oing badly in any given year negatively affects that year's bonus but positively affects the next year's bonus. The same scheme also lessens the reward for performing well: improving performance in any given year raises the bar and makes it hard to get a bonus the next year.[59]

53. See e.g. R. Suter no. 9 above, pp. 71 and 80 *et seq.*; H.C. von der Crone, 'Risiko und Corporate Governance' in *Aktuelle Fragen des Bank- und Finanzmarktrechts – Festschrift für Dieter Zobl zum 60. Geburtstag*, H.C. van der Crone, P. Forstmoser, R.H. Weber, R. Zāch (eds) (Zurich, Schulthess, 2004) p. 559; Ibid., no. 3 above, 253.
54. For an overview, see e.g. A. Risi, no. 36 above, p. 70 *et seq.*; D.M. Weiss, no. 11 above, p. 69; R.A Brealey and S.C. Myers, no. 10 above, pp. 321 and 326 *et seq.*
55. A recent example relates to the abandonment of linear good-will amortization in favour of impairment testing. Early adoption is an attractive prospect for executives whose rewards are based on EBIT or profit.
56. In Switzerland, executives cannot themselves change the accounting standard, as appears to be the case in the US. See also e.g. M.C. Jensen and C.W. Smith Jr., no. 35 above, 12; H. Hax, 'Manipulierbare Massstäbe als Knacknuss – Noch kein Patentrezept für erfolgsabhängige Saläre' *Neue Zürcher Zeitung,* 10 June 2003 (no. 131), B3; A. Risi, no. 36 above, p. 70 *et seq.*; D.M. Weiss, no. 11 above, p. 69; R.A Brealey and S.C. Myers, no. 10 above, pp. 321 and 326 *et seq.*
57. D.M. Weiss, no. 11 above, p. 67.
58. M.C. Jensen and K.J. Murphy, no. 1 above, 70 *et seq.*: 'And if we see that we are not going to make it we are then better off to take a bigger hit this period so we can do better next period'.
59. L.A. Bebchuk and J.M. Fried, no. 9 above, p. 124 *et seq.*

Reliance on particular accounting figures is also problematic because it never accurately reflects the full economic reality. If pay is geared to profits, this may prevent executives from making investments that have no short-term benefit, e.g. spending money on research and development, market expansion or employee training. In addition, this type of performance measure may constitute an incentive to postpone restructurings that entail short-term costs, such as the closing of an unproductive facility.[60]

By contrast, if compensation is based on EBITDA, an executive might, for example, prefer the construction of a new factory over an outsourcing solution, even if the latter would be a more favourable option overall for the company and its shareholders. If we assume, for example, that the price of a new factory is 1,000 and will cost 70 per annum in interest payments and 100 per annum in depreciation, and that production costs and raw materials amount to 250 while sales amount to 500, then the 'build' alternative will generate a bottom line profit of 80. If the company could purchase the same goods from an outsourcing partner at 400, it would generate a bottom-line profit of 100, i.e. an increase of 25 per cent, but the EBITDA associated with the 'build' solution would be 250, as compared to 100 for the outsourcing solution. In other words, while sourcing the products from the third party would be more efficient for the company and its shareholders, it would produce a much lower EBITDA. As a result, management might be tempted to build the factory rather than purchase the products, because, if the managers' pay is geared towards EBITDA, interest costs and amortization will be of less concern to them.

Economic-value-based compensation is subject to much the same shortcomings as accounting-based measures. When applying EVA, for instance, the respective value is derived from accounting figures by means of conversions[61] or estimates.[62] Consequently, the downside of these systems is that they are difficult to measure[63] and are open to manipulation. Furthermore, EVA favours projects with immediate payback.[64]

Finally, strategy-based compensation is often based on soft factors, which makes it, to some degree, discretionary. In addition, this type of compensation can create misplaced incentives. A manager who is rewarded for an increase in the market share, for example, may lower prices in order to achieve this increase, which could be detrimental to the long-term strategy and interests of the company.

---

60. D.M. Weiss, no. 11 above, p. 68.
61. 'Conversions' refers to operating conversions, funding conversions, tax conversions and shareholder conversions. In theory, more than 160 conversions and adjustments exist. However, in practice, usually only five to ten conversions are made, and sometimes even fewer. For more details, see e.g. R. Volkart, no. 43 above, p. 260.
62. See also P. Gampenrieder, no. 43 above, 126; D.M. Weiss, no. 11 above, p. 72; and A. Risi, no. 36 above, p. 73. S. Hostettler, no. 43 above, 118, stresses that it is not the absolute level of EVA that counts, but the measure of its development. Thus, S. Hostettler argues, the weak resistance to manipulation can be relativized.
63. See A. Risi, no. 36 above, p. 73.
64. R.A Brealey and S.C. Myers, no. 10 above, p. 324.

Against this background, it becomes clear that the structure of an executive compensation package, in particular the performance-based part, is crucial to achieving an alignment of interests between shareholders and executives. Therefore, if structuring does not exclude conflicts, special control mechanisms will have to be put into place.

III. CONFLICTS OF INTERESTS AND THE DESIGN OF EXECUTIVE COMPENSATION ARRANGEMENTS UNDER SWISS LAW

Given the vast potential for conflicts of interests in executive compensation, it is scarcely necessary to point out that the very structure of compensation arrangements plays a crucial role in mitigating such conflicts. In the following section we will analyze the objectives (A) and key factors (B) of executive compensation from a Swiss legal perspective. We shall then address the legal restrictions that apply to the various elements of compensation arrangements, and make some recommendations on how they should be designed in order to mitigate conflicts of interests (C). We conclude the section with an overview of our own recommended package (D).

A. Objectives of Executive Compensation Arrangements

Swiss corporate law remains silent on the question of how to structure compensation arrangements for executives or which specific principles need to be observed.[65] The same is true of Swiss employment law,[66] which – while dealing with various forms of compensation[67] – does not prescribe any form for, or lay down any specific principles applicable to, executive compensation. It is therefore the statutory general duty of care and the general duty to act in the best interest of the company

65. Swiss corporate law addresses (executive) compensation only indirectly. Art. 653 (1) CO allows the use of conditional share capital for the purposes of employee participation programs (see also art. 652b (2) CO, which permits the exclusion of shareholder's pre-emptive rights if additional share capital is used for employee participation programs). The law also allows the granting of *Tantiemen* to directors. For more on the *Tantiemen,* see section IV.A.1 below.
66. The relationship between a manager (who is not a member of the board of directors) and a company is legally described as an employment agreement pursuant to art. 319 *et seq.* CO (see e.g. D. Portmann, no. 32 above, no. 13 with further references). Employment law also applies to executive members of the board of directors, as the relationship between the company and such executive is considered to be governed by corporate law (*organschaftliches Verhältnis*) and employment law (*arbeitsrechtliches Verhältnis)* (see e.g. ATF 130 III, 213 *et seq.* with further references; and R. Müller, 'Die arbeitsrechtliche Situation der VR-Delegierten in der Schweiz' [2001] *Pratique juridique actuelle,* 1,367 *et seq.*
67. See art. 322–322d CO for the forms of compensation stipulated in the law. Forms other than the ones specified there are, however, admissible (see e.g. T. Geiser, 'Arbeitsrechtliche Aspekte im Zusammenhang mit Leistungslohn' [2001] *Pratique juridique actuelle,* 382 *et seq.*, or D. Portmann, no. 32 above, no. 34 *et seq.*

(duty of care and loyalty)[68] that the board must observe when designing executive compensation packages.

The implication of these duties must be derived from the company's overall objective. In other words, the first task is to determine how the phrase 'interest of the company'[69] should be interpreted. While this is not the place to go through the entire shareholder/stakeholder debate,[70] it does seem clear that a company under Swiss law is principally designed as a for-profit organization,[71] and therefore that its executives must aim to maximize the value of the company and thus of the shareholders' participations.[72] In the words of Jensen and Murphy:

> [I]if our objective is to maximize the efficiency with which society utilizes its resources (that is to avoid waste and to maximize the size of the pie), then the proper and unique objective for each company in the society is to maximize the long-run total value of the firm.[73]

Thus the main objective of compensation must be to achieve this value-enhancement (by finding and retaining top talent at rates which are reasonable for the company), while at the same time aligning the interests of the executives with those of the shareholders in order to overcome the negative impact of the separation of ownership and control.[74]

B. Key Factors

When designing a compensation arrangement that will accomplish the compensation objectives described above, the board of directors (or the compensation committee)[75] must make decisions on the following interrelated questions:[76]

- What will be the overall target level of compensation for a defined period (assuming average performance, but taking into consideration the effects of a possible over-achievement) and the key contract terms, particularly minimum contract and notice periods?[77]

68. Art. 717 (1) CO.
69. Interestingly, Swiss law defines these duties with respect to the company, and not directly with respect to the shareholders.
70. For references, see e.g. T. Spillmann, no. 19 above, p. 96, especially no. 535.
71. See arts 620 (3) and 660 (1) CO.
72. See R. Watter, in H. Honsell, N.P. Vogt and R. Watter (eds), *Basler Kommentar zum Schweizerischen Privatrecht, Obligationenrecht II* (2nd edn, Basle/Geneva/Munich, Helbing & Lichtenhahn, 2002), no. 37 ad art. 717 CO.
73. M.C. Jensen and K.J. Murphy, no. 1 above, 15.
74. See also M.C. Jensen and K.J. Murphy, no. 1 above, 19; L.A. Bebchuk and J.M. Fried/David I. Walker, no. 20 above, 762 *et seq.*; D. Leu, no. 26 above, pp. 53 *et seq.*
75. For simplicity's sake, we shall refer in what follows only to the board of directors. For more on compensation committees, refer to sections IV.A.3.c and IV.B.3.a below.
76. M.C. Jensen and K.J. Murphy, no. 1 above, 19 *et seq.*
77. In general, the larger the variable part of the compensation, and the more the payment is deferred, the higher the target level. Deferred payment can take the form of e.g. (blocked) shares or options, which may be partly forfeited if the executive quits his/her job.

- What will be the ratio between fixed and (variable) performance-based compensation and the way performance is measured?[78]
- In what form will the compensation be paid (cash, shares, options etc.) and when will compensation be paid (i.e. immediate payment versus e.g. payment into a bonus bank[79] in case of cash payments, or transfer and exercise restrictions in case of shares and options?

Swiss law does not provide any explicit guidelines with regard to these key factors. Here again it is the general duty of care and loyalty that sets the broad parameters. In the following sections, we will try to illustrate the implications.

1. Overall Target Level of Compensation and Key Contract Terms

First, the board of directors will have to decide the overall target level of executive compensation, assuming average performance, as well as what downside the executive must carry in case of underperformance and vice versa. This target level, together with the down- and upsides, will be set at a level likely to induce the desired executive to take on the position and stay for a reasonable time. In order to attract and retain an executive, a company must offer an overall package of benefits that meets or exceeds his opportunity costs.[80] When determining the overall target level of compensation, it is important for the board to take into account all elements of a compensation package; i.e. not only cash and equity-based compensation, but also all benefits and allowances. When determining the length of the contract or the notice period, the board must bear in mind that the company has to retain flexibility should the executive not perform as desired.[81]

It follows from the board's duty of care and loyalty that it will have to set the level so as to minimize the total cost to the company while still attracting the desired talent.[82] Clearly, this guideline (quite rightly) gives the board considerable discretion. In our view the following factors should be taken into consideration, though the overall level will also be influenced by the answers to the two other questions, i.e. the ratio of fixed to variable compensation and the compensation is paid:[83]

---

78. The relationship between pay and performance defines which actions and results are rewarded and which are penalized.
79. For more on the use of bonus banks, see section III.C.2 below.
80. See e.g. L.A. Bebchuk, J.M. Fried and D.I. Walker, no. 20 above, 762.
81. Swiss employment law requires companies and employees to adhere to equal periods of notice; see art. 335a (1) CO.
82. See e.g. M.C. Jensen and K.J. Murphy, no. 1 above, 19.
83. See e.g. P. Forstmoser, A. Meier-Hayoz and P. Nobel, *Schweizerisches Aktienrecht* (Bern, Staempli, 1997), para. 28 no. 130; P. Böckli, *Schweizer Aktienrecht* (3rd edn, Zurich, Schulthess 2004), para. 13 no. 240 *et seq.*; Ivo W. Hungerbühler, *Der Verwaltungsratspräsident* (Zurich, Schulthess, 2003), p. 177 *et seq.*; R. Ruedin, 'Rémunération de l'administrateur de société anonyme' in *Wirtschaftsrecht zu Beginn des 21. Jahrhunderts – Festschrift für Peter Nobel*

- The company's financial situation, its position within the industry and payment levels in peer companies;[84, 85]
- The required skills, position and responsibility of the job offered and the financial risk associated with it (e.g. unlimited personal liability or[86] difficulty of finding another job if the executive gets fired[87]);[88]
- The compensation that the desired executive might receive (after tax) elsewhere, perhaps in another industry.[89]

It is often argued that the market value of an executive is decisive for the overall level of compensation. While this argument is certainly not entirely misguided,[90] we think that the company should start from an analysis of its own needs and financial resources, and then seek executives who fit this definition and are willing to work within the defined parameters. If the company cannot find executives on its preferred terms, it will have to re-think them.[91]

2. The Relationship between Fixed and Variable Compensation

a. In General

Executives tend to be risk averse.[92] They invest their monetary and human capital in the company, and are therefore not diversified (unlike shareholders). Consequently,

---

zum 60. Geburtstag, R. Waldburger, Ch. Baer, U. Nobel and B. Bernet (eds) (Bern, Staempfli, 2005), p. 317 *et seq.* Each of these authors analyze these principles with regard to directors' compensation. We, however, take the view that these principles apply also to management compensation.

84. However, a number of problems are involved with peer group comparisons; see section III.B.3 below.
85. ATF 86 II, 162 *et seq.* and ATF 105 II, 122. An exception to this rule may be when a financially distressed company attempts to attract an executive.
86. This fact, however, is offset by the fact that companies regularly pay the D&O insurance premiums.
87. Within the compensation package, we believe that this aspect should be addressed by a severance payment, and not by higher compensation.
88. ATF 111 II, 480 *et seq.*
89. P. Böckli, no. 83 above, para. 13 no. 240 *et seq.* with further references; P. Forstmoser, A. Meier-Hayoz and P. Nobel, no. 83 above, para 28 no. 130.
90. The key question relative to this argument is whether executives can, in fact, be said to have a market value, when the 'market' is so lacking in transparency, as well as somewhat distorted; see also no. 21 above. According to L.A. Bebchuk and J.M. Fried, no. 9 above, p. 22, the validity of the arguments depends on whether the outcomes of the market value are largely generated by arm's-length bargaining between the executive and the board: 'If the market as a whole is distorted by the absence of at arm's length bargaining, general conformity to market terms cannot allay concerns about the amount and the structure of compensation'. A crucial problem with the accuracy of arm's-length bargaining is the role of compensation surveys; see section IV.B.3.a below.
91. More in favour of a clear market-value-approach is the view of D. Leu, no. 26 above, p. 284 *et seq.*
92. D. Leu, no. 26 above, p. 51 *et seq.*

executives are exposed to firm-specific risks, and therefore generally favour a compensation package that includes higher fixed and immediately payable[93] compensation over a package with an element of high variability.[94] However, the key objective of variable compensation is precisely to (partly) shift the business risk to the executive in order to achieve the desired alignment of interests. Fixed compensation may provide an incentive to work, but this does not necessarily mean that it provides incentives to work 'right', i.e. in the interests of the company and its shareholders. For this reason, variable compensation should always play an important role in executive compensation packages. Of course, a company that requires an executive to accept variable, i.e. risky, elements of compensation will have to provide higher total compensation to offset risk-bearing costs, and a higher target level, but the company should be amply rewarded for this, thanks to the incentive mechanism.[95]

In considering the ratio between fixed and variable compensation,[96] it will not come as a surprise that – once again – Swiss law is silent on the issue and, clearly, offering a specific recommendation is impossible. However, the following considerations may provide a guideline:

The incentive effect of fixed salary compensation is marginal.[97] In fact, a very high fixed salary, together with deferred but guaranteed and/or secured[98] payments, such as pensions,[99] high severance payments in case of early termination, or golden parachutes in case of a change in control are likely to dilute the incentive effect of the performance-based compensation element. Conversely, if an executive is (hypothetically)[100] to receive variable compensation only, failure to reach a minimum

---

93. Theoretically, fixed compensation can also be paid in shares or options, so long as they cannot be monetized immediately. This form of compensation has the characteristics of variable payment. See also section III.B.3 below.
94. M.C. Jensen and K.J. Murphy, no. 1 above, 21.
95. See M.C. Jensen and K.J. Murphy, no. 1 above, 21; H.C. von der Crone, no. 54 above, 559.
96. For more on the criteria to be observed when determining the ratio between fix and variable pay, see D. Leu, no. 26 above, p. 167 *et seq.*
97. One incentive may be that good performance is likely to lead to future increases in salary; see M.C. Jensen and C.W. Smith Jr., no. 35 above, 11. But cf. no. 32 above, where reference is made to authors who argue that excessive performance-based compensation may impair the intrinsic motivation of an executive.
98. Interesting to note in this context is that the Swiss pension fund system, which requires contributions to be paid into a separate fund structure, provides almost total protection against future company bankruptcy.
99. For an empirical study, see particularly L.A. Bebchuk and R.J. Jackson Jr., 'Putting executive pensions on the radar screen' (April 2005) *Harvard Law School Discussion Paper No. 507,* <papers.ssrn.com/abstract_id=694766>.
100. Clearly, a certain element of fixed compensation will always have to remain, not only for the executive to cover his/her basic needs, but also for legal reasons (see D. Leu, no. 26 above, p. 167 with further references); a significant variable compensation may come into play if the fixed compensation exceeds the cost of meeting the executive's basic needs (see A. Risi, no. 36 above, p. 60).

salary level may either induce him or her to take serious risks to achieve the desired level, or simply frustrate him or her from the start. In addition, if fixed pay is in cash and variable pay in shares or options, the company should consider the cash needs of the executive, including the amount of tax he or she must pay on non-cash compensation.[101]

b. Choice of Performance Measure

Variable compensation is dependent upon parameters that must somehow be measured. We have already discussed the main performance measures and some of their shortcomings.[102] Irrespective of which performance parameters are used, performance measures must accomplish three main objectives:[103]

- Alignment of interests between executives and shareholders;
- Measurability;
- Resistance to manipulation.

Accounting-based parameters are easy to measure. However, as mentioned earlier,[104] they cannot always optimally align interests, and can, to a certain extent, be manipulated.[105] The problem of the alignment of interests is mitigated if the variable compensation based on these measures takes the form of (blocked) shares or share options instead of cash (or, if made in cash, then paid into a bonus bank). This also does something to address the manipulation problem, if one assumes that control mechanisms will detect the problem sooner or later, and before the expiry of the blocking period.[106] Value-based measures (such as EVA) are quite likely to achieve an alignment of interests with those of the shareholders, because they are a direct attempt to measure shareholder wealth. As a result, the application of EVA in particular by companies has increased recently. We have seen that the disadvantage of these parameters is that they are rather difficult to measure and prone to manipulation. Strategy-based parameters involve similar problems.[107]

---

101. Swiss tax law generally taxes shares when they are granted (or vested), taking account vesting periods, but with a discount factor. This approach has long applied to options; see below no. 193.
102. See above section II.D.
103. D.M. Weiss, no. 11 above, p. 69. Further objectives can be found in A. Risi, no. 36 above, p. 66 *et seq.*
104. See above section II.D.
105. For examples, see e.g. R.A. Brealey and S.C. Myers, no. 10 above, p. 326 *et seq.* and D.M. Weiss, no. 11 above, p. 69. See also A. Risi, no. 36 above, p. 71.
106. See below sections III.B.3 and III.C.1.
107. See above section II.D.

Stock-market-based parameters achieve an alignment of interests because measuring a reward against a share price encourages executives to focus on increasing the share price. The problem once again is one of manipulation[108] and also, more importantly, sensitivity to general market movements, which enable executives to receive windfall profits in a bullish market and punishes them during downturns.

Clearly, there is no ideal choice for a performance parameter. This is because economic reality differs too widely from one company to another: one board might decide that its company's strategic positioning makes increased market share the key factor, and so decide to reward increased sales rather than profits (at least for a time); another board might conclude that operational excellence, best measured in terms of EBITDA, is more important; and yet another board might decide that EVA is the right measure for its business. What matters most is that the board be aware of the shortcomings of the various performance measures and select, to as great a degree possible, the control mechanisms best suited to its particular circumstances.[109]

3. Form of Compensation

Compensation, whether fixed or variable, may be paid in various forms: cash, shares, share options, retirement benefits, perks or allowances, such as a fancy company car with driver, house and travel, or even education for executives' children.[110] While a minimum amount will have to be paid in cash in order for the executive to cover his/her basic needs, including tax payment on non-cash compensation, the remainder (often but not necessarily tied to variable payments) can take various forms, such as additional cash payments, whether immediate or deferred (the latter referring to e.g. payments into a bonus bank, phantom stock or stock appreciation rights) or restricted or unrestricted shares or options.

When considering these various forms, the board of directors must give careful consideration to the interactions between forms and the incentives associated with each. For example, blocked shares and options are not designed solely to align the interests of the holder with those of shareholders; they also include an important retention element if the shares/options do not vest unless the executive stays for a specified minimum period of time. In the following section, we will elaborate on the pros and cons of the various forms of compensation, including legal restraints applicable to each.

Finally, the board will also have to consider other effects, such as taxation (or social security contributions) for each form of payment, as it affects both the company and the executive.

108. See above section II.D.
109. See also sections IV.A.3 and IV.B.3 below.
110. See also D. Leu, no. 26 above, p. 218.

C. Legal Restrictions and Practical Recommendations Regarding Executive Compensation Elements

1. The Use of Shares and Share Options

a. General

Equity-based compensation enables the executive to participate financially in the company's success by profiting from dividends,[111] voting rights[112] and price appreciation. In addition, owning equities encourages the executive to take more firm-specific risks.[113] Finally, equity-based compensation can help retain an executive, because it facilitates restrictions on vesting and/or selling respectively exercise. Though shares and share options are conceptually comparable elements, the latter are a greater incentive to managers than the former, owing to their leverage effect.[114] Consequently, a larger number of shares is required to provide the same financial incentive as share options.[115] Options also help to control the issue of under-leverage:[116] higher leverage becomes more attractive to the manager, since it increases the volatility of the equity and thus the value of options.[117]

The degree to which options encourage executives to accept additional risk depends mainly on their exercise price.[118] In theory the exercise price can be set above, below or at the share price at the grant date, or can vary over time, e.g. with movements in broad stock indices or with the company's capital costs.[119] Overall, there is no such thing as an optimal exercise price. The choice depends on a number of factors, some of which are firm-specific (growth opportunities and debt load) and others that depend on the manager's risk preferences.[120] In reality, most options in Switzerland are granted with an exercise price equal to the market price of the shares at the grant date ('at-the-money'). The theory being that the executive should only profit if the share price increases as a result of his/her efforts.

111. Option holders, however, generally do not profit from dividends, unless the strike price is adjusted for them.
112. The exercise of voting rights is also considered to have (indirect) financial value; see T. Spillmann, no. 19 above, p. 83, especially no. 468 with further references. Again, option holders do not *directly* benefit from these rights until they exercise the option.
113. L.A. Bebchuk and J.M. Fried, no. 9 above, p. 159.
114. See e.g. R. Suter, no. 9 above, p. 89 *et seq.*; T. Bühner and M. Wallmeier, no. 52 above, 556; H.C. von der Crone, no. 53 above, p. 559 and no. 36.
115. H.C. von der Crone, no. 53 above, p. 560.
116. Executives compensated with fixed but deferred compensation have incentives to reduce the firm's debts even if such reductions adversely affect the company value.
117. See M.C. Jensen and C.W. Smith Jr., no. 35 above, 12.
118. L.A. Bebchuk and J.M. Fried, no. 9 above, p. 159.
119. M.C. Jensen and K.J. Murphy, no. 1 above, 57.
120. L.A. Bebchuk and J.M. Fried, no. 9 above, p. 160.

b. Legal Restrictions

A number of legal issues affect shares and options. For the purposes of this article, we will limit ourselves to the most crucial ones.[121]

When considering restrictions on the exercise of options and the selling of granted shares,[122] two recent decisions of the *Obergericht* of the Canton of Lucerne are of particular significance. In both cases the *Obergericht* held that restricted share options that constitute a 'wage element' ('*Lohnbestandteil*') must be considered void and that the employer is obliged to pay the full value of the options as of the grant date at the time the employee's wage becomes due.[123] This finding was based on article 323b (3) of the Code of Obligations (CO), pursuant to which an employer is required to pay wages that are at the free disposal of the employee (the so-called '*Truckverbot*'). The Swiss Federal Supreme Court, to which appeal was made, did not explicitly address the question of whether the *Truckverbot* applies to restricted shares or options that constitute a wage element, but held that the *Truckverbot* applies to all employees, including managers.[124] The Supreme Court, therefore, implicitly upheld the reasoning of the Lucerne *Obergericht*.[125] This implies that restricted shares and share options that are a wage element must be considered void, unless they are transferable or may be returned to the employer.[126] While the implications of this result for executive compensation packages are rather baffling,[127] we believe that proper drafting of the employment agreement could avoid this problem.[128]

---

121. For an in-depth legal analysis, see e.g. B. Walti, *Mitarbeiterbeteiligung – Aktien- und Optionspläne* (Zurich, Schulthess, 1998); C. Helbling, *Mitarbeiteraktien und Mitarbeiteroptionen in der Schweiz* (2nd edn, Zurich, Schulthess, 2003); D. Portmann, no. 32 above; further, see R. Knecht, *Mitarbeiterbeteiligung in der Praxis* (Bern, Staempfli, 2001); and R. Lyk, *Die Mitarbeiteraktie in der Schweiz* (Zurich, Organisator, 1989)
122. See also M. Staehelin, 'Gesperrte Optionen – als Lohn unzulässig?' (2005) *Revue suisse de jurisprudence* 101, 181 *et seq.*; D. Portmann, no. 32 above, no. 253 *et seq.*
123. Decisions of the *Obergericht des Kantons Luzern,* both dated 3 March 2004. See *Luzerner Gerichts- und Verwaltungsentscheide* (LGVE) [2004] I N 20.
124. See ATF 4C.239/2004 and ATF 4C.237/2004.
125. The same conclusion is drawn by M. Staehelin, no. 122 above, 181.
126. See ATF 4C.239/2004 and ATF 4C.237/2004; further, see M. Staehelin, no. 122 above, 181. D. Portmann, no. 32 above, no. 192 *et seq.* also concludes that restricted shares and options that are a wage element (*Lohnbestandteil)* are void. However, some authors reject this view: see the references in D. Portmann, no. 32 above, no. 192 and particularly no. 755.
127. A thorough analysis of these decisions is outside the scope of this paper. However, we would encourage courts to reconsider the general applicability of art. 323b (3) CO (*Truckverbot*) vis-à-vis managers, because the social motivation behind the provision may no longer be operative in the case of high-ranking employees. See also F. Vischer, *Der Arbeitsvertrag* (Basle/Geneva/Munich, Helbing & Lichtenhahn, 2005), p. 111 with further references and M. Staehelin, no. 122 above, 185 *et seq.* Even if the *Truckverbot* does apply, in our view, the courts should bear in mind that the granting of shares/options is not *solely* in the interests of the employer. This means that the courts must weigh the respective interests of the employer and the manager before coming to a decision. (See also M. Staehelin, no. 122 above, 185.) In so doing, the court should give due consideration to the advantages of shares and share options

In contrast, the Federal Supreme Court recently also held that restricted shares that do not have to be considered a wage element and that are of secondary importance relative to the overall value of the wage do not, as a rule, fall within the scope of the *Truckverbot*, if the employee's relationship is terminated prior to the lapse of the vesting period.[129]

Some authors have argued that blocked shares or options may violate the statutory provisions regarding due dates of employees' claims ('*Fälligkeitsregelung*'[130]).[131] They hold that selling or exercise restrictions are only allowed in so far as the shares or options concerned do not constitute a wage element (*Lohnbestandteil*).[132] Again, we do not believe that these theories – which we consider irrelevant to executive compensation – are a serious problem when designing compensation packages, but they should be taken into account when drafting employment agreements.[133]

Another critical issue is the vesting of options and shares (and the exerciseability of options) if vesting/exercise is impossible after the employment agreement is terminated. Two problems in particular must be considered.[134] First, pursuant to article 152 (1) CO, the parties are obliged to refrain from any conduct that may impair the position of the other party before the fulfilment of a condition. If the fulfilment is prevented by the bad faith of one party, the law assumes that the condition is nonetheless fulfilled (article 156 CO). Therefore, the question arises whether a manager whose employment agreement has been terminated by the company prior to vesting can claim that the vesting has nevertheless occurred, particularly absent any legitimate reasons for the termination.[135] Secondly, pursuant to article 335a (1) CO, any disparity between the periods of notice applicable to the employer and the employee is invalid. With respect to vesting provisions, it could be argued that the employee's freedom to terminate the employment is restricted by the prospective loss of the shares or options, even if the periods of notice are formally equal.[136]

---

for the executive: his share participation, tax privileges, etc. (See also D. Leu, no. 26 above, p. 88 *et seq.*)

128. E.g. by defining the fixed amount as a 'wage element' (*Lohnbestandteil*) while defining the variable part as a bonus (in the sense of a *Gratifikation*), or by giving the executive a choice between shares/share options and a cash option. However, a mere definition in the contract will not suffice – what counts is that the definition expresses the true will of the parties (art. 18 (1) CO). See also sections III.C.1 and III.C.2 below.
129. See ATF 131 III 615.
130. Art. 323 (1) CO and art. 339 (1) CO.
131. D. Portmann, no. 32 above, no. 261 *et seq.*
132. D. Portmann, no. 32 above, no. 253 *et seq.*; see also F. Vischer, no. 127 above, p. 111.
133. See no. 128 above.
134. For more information, see D. Portmann, no. 32 above, no. 274 *et seq.* and F. Vischer, no. 127 above, p. 110 *et seq.*
135. See ZR 102 (2003) N. 5, 21 *et seq.* and D. Portmann, no. 32 above, no. 274 *et seq.*
136. M. Staehelin, no. 122 above, 181. In its decision dated 18 November 2002, the *Obergericht* of the Canton of Zurich came to the conclusion that the principle of equal notice periods is formal in nature, which eliminates the issue of vesting provisions: see ZR 102 (2003) N. 5, 21 *et seq.*, in particular 26. See also D. Portmann, no. 32 above, no. 291 *et seq.*

Again, we believe that proper contract drafting can largely resolve these two issues, but unfortunately some uncertainty remains.

Further restrictions have to be observed when considering the re-pricing of share options (which is, for economic reasons, in any case inadvisable).[137] Since the reduction of the exercise price, as well as the exchange of out-of-the-money options for new options results in a dilution of existing shareholders,[138] it has been argued that the right of re-pricing would have to be included in the shareholders' resolution in regard to the creation of conditional capital, if such capital is used for the options.[139]

As far as disclosure is concerned, shares allotted during a given year, as well as ownership at year's end and the number of share options held by board members and managers including the grant year, must be disclosed in the annual reports of listed companies.[140] In addition, on 7 October 2005 the Swiss Parliament added a new provision to the Code of Obligations, requiring listed companies to disclose the compensation of their directors and managers.[141] Pursuant to this new provision, individual directors of listed companies will be required to disclose their compensation, plus shares and share options held, though management compensation may be disclosed collectively. The provision will enter into force at the beginning of 2007.

Finally, depending on the circumstances, the grant of shares and share options to executives, as well as the sale of such shares or share options by executives, may be subject to the new SWX Directive on the Disclosure of Management Transactions.[142]

c. *Recommendations*

Equity-based compensation, if well designed, provides not only a retention incentive for executives, but also helps to align their interests with those of shareholders. However, the design of the plan is crucial in order to avoid distortions.

When determining the exercise price of options, it is important to remember that the performance sensitivity of out-of-the-money options (i.e. options with an

137. See section III.C.1 above.
138. A. von Planta, 'Les plans d'intéressement – Aspects du droit commercial' in: *Les plans d'intéressement/Stock option plans*, G. Bovet (ed.) (CEDIDAC, Lausanne 2001), p. 54 *et seq.*
139. See D. Leu, no. 26 above, p. 306 *et seq.*; D. Portmann, no. 32 above, no. 230; A. von Planta, no. 138 above, p. 54 *et seq.*
140. See the SWX Swiss Exchange Directive on Information Relating to Corporate Governance: <www.swx.com/download/admission/regulation/guidelines/swx_guideline_20020701-1_en.pdf>.
141. Art. 663bbis CO; the text with the final wording is published in BBl 2005 5963, also <www.admin.ch/ch/d/ff/2005/5963.pdf>.
142. <www.swx.com/download/admission/regulation/guidelines/swx_guide-line_20050701-2_en.pdf>. See also N.J. Frei and L. Giovanoli, 'Management muss Transaktionen offenlegen – Keine Namensnennung – Sanktionen durch die SWX' (28 July 2005) *Neue Zürcher Zeitung* (no. 174), 29.

exercise price above the share price at the date of grant) is much greater than that of at-the-money (or in-the-money for that matter) options.[143] The incentives may diminish, however, if the option is too far out of the money.

The company should also bear in mind that the share price is influenced by external factors which lie beyond the influence of executives.[144] This means that executive compensation in the form of shares or options (or tied to the share price) is independent of performance if the share price increases or decreases coincidentally, e.g. as a result of general market or sector trends.[145] From an executive's point of view, windfall effects are generally positive, because they increase the value of options due to volatility.[146] From a shareholder's viewpoint, however, options should be designed to achieve incentives at the lowest possible cost. When executives are rewarded for windfalls that have nothing to do with their performance, the costs incurred by the company could be better spent in such a way either to create the same incentives for lower costs or use the same amount of money to create even more powerful incentives.[147] According to a study conducted in 2002, the estimated cost of providing conventional options to executives in the 100 largest NYSE-listed companies was 41 per cent higher than the cost of providing options that screened out general market trends.[148] It is therefore crucial to eliminate or reduce windfalls in order to reduce costs. There are several ways of doing this,[149] e.g. by tying the share option's exercise price to a market or sector index, to a group of competitors (peer group), or to the company's capital costs.[150] Another way to filter out general market trends is to link the vesting of options to the achievement of performance targets.[151] For example, it could be agreed that (all or part of the) options will vest only if the company's share price beats the market or a basket of similar shares over a specified period.[152]

A further aspect of option design concerns dividends. Because paying dividends lowers the value of the options, non-dividend-adjusted options deter executives from recommending the distribution of dividends to directors and shareholders.[153] Unless executives use the excess cash to buy back shares, the result will be that they keep the shares in the company rather than distributing them to the shareholders.

143. See the various references in L.A. Bebchuk and J.M. Fried, no. 9 above, p. 161.
144. See e.g. R. Suter, no. 9 above, p. 153; A. Risi, no. 36 above, p. 77 *et seq.*
145. See e.g. D.M. Weiss, no. 11 above, p. 93 *et seq.*
146. L.A. Bebchuk, J.M. Fried, and D.I. Walker, no. 20 above, 797.
147. L.A. Bebchuk and J.M. Fried, no. 9 above, p. 139.
148. J.J. Angel and D.M. McCabe, 'Market-adjusted options for executive compensation' (2002) *Global Business and Economics Review* 4, 14.
149. See e.g. L.A. Bebchuk and J.M. Fried, no. 9 above, p. 140 *et seq.*
150. T. Bühner and M. Wallmeier, no. 52 above, 556; L.A. Bebchuk and J.M. Fried, no. 9 above, p. 140 *et seq.*; M.C. Jensen and K.J. Murphy, no. 1 above, 58; D. Leu, no. 26 above, p. 249.
151. L.A. Bebchuk and J.M. Fried, no. 9 above, p. 142; M.C. Jensen and K.J. Murphy, no. 1 above, 57.
152. Scholars have also suggested linking the exercise of options with profitability, which should be set at a certain percentage above the interest rate of state bonds: see e.g. *Neue Zürcher Zeitung*, 4 January 2005, no. 2 above, 21.
153. See the references in: M.C. Jensen and K.J. Murphy, no. 1 above, 61, no. 51.

For this reason, we recommend adjusting the strike price of share options to take into account any dividends or return on capital paid to shareholders.[154]

In regard to the exercise (or selling) of options or disposing of shares, it must be borne in mind that equity-based compensation should ensure that executives cannot benefit from short-term increases in share prices that are achieved at the expense of long-term value destruction. The shares and options should, therefore, be subject to a vesting period[155] (which also achieves a retention incentive) and options should become exercisable (or shares sellable) only after a specified minimum period, e.g. vesting after two years, exercise and selling after four years. In order to increase the incentive effect, the vesting of shares and/or share options could be tied to performance targets.

There is another reason for introducing such restricted periods: if executives are granted unrestricted shares or share options, they can immediately sell the shares or exercise the options and sell the underlying shares upon vesting. The company would then have to give the executive new shares or options in order to maintain the same level of incentives, otherwise the company will have to deal with the consequences of executives' having weaker performance incentives than with restricted shares or options.[156]

For this reason, executives' freedom to sell vested shares or options should be limited. In order to avoid the danger under Swiss law which we described earlier (i.e. that restrictions are invalid if the shares or share options are considered to be a wage element), we recommend granting shares and options as a bonus (*Gratifikation*)[157] and not as part of the contractual compensation (i.e. a wage element).[158] Alternatively, the company could offer executives a choice between a cash payment and a (more valuable) equity-based compensation.[159] The company can then argue that the mandatory employment law provisions do not apply, because if the executive chooses the shares or options over the cash, he or she is assumed to be acting not as an employee, but as an investor.[160] The disadvantage of the first approach, from the executive's viewpoint, is that he has no contractual right to enforce the granting of the shares. The only disadvantage of the second approach is that if the executive (unexpectedly) takes the money, the incentive is lost.

---

154. M.C. Jensen and K.J. Murphy, no. 1 above, 61; A. Risi, no. 36 above, p. 85.
155. See also D. Leu, no. 26 above, p. 220.
156. L.A. Bebchuk and J.M. Fried, no. 9 above, p. 175.
157. For more details on how to design gratifications to prevent them from being considered a *Lohnbestandteil*, see M. Staehelin, no. 122 above, 182 *et seq.* A gratification is always, to some extent, at the employer's discretion.
158. Note, however, that the higher the variable part is in relation to the fixed part, the more likely it is that a court will identify the variable part as a wage element. On the other hand, courts are also likely to consider the absolute level of the fixed part, e.g. as compared to the compensation of a middle-ranking manager. If this absolute level still permits a decent standard of living, courts are more likely to consider the variable part as 'icing on the cake' and thus not a wage element.
159. M. Staehelin, no. 122 above, 182.
160. See ATF 130 III 495 *et seq.* and M. Staehelin, no. 122 above, 182.

Another critical issue is re-pricing practices. If the exercise price falls below the share price (out-of-the-money options), executives may argue that, in order to reinstate the incentives associated with options, the exercise price must be revised.[161] In our view this should not be considered.[162] Options are designed to create incentives to align the interests of executives and shareholders; this incentive is diluted if an executive can expect the company to engage in re-pricing to offset the consequences of adverse share price movements.[163] In the end, a re-pricing would mean nothing more nor less than rewarding a poor share price performance. Furthermore, the risk of negative share price movements as a result of general market or sector trends can be eliminated *a priori* through the use of indexed options as demonstrated above. Finally, it is questionable whether re-pricing is legally valid, at least when the underlying shares come out of conditional capital.[164]

From an incentive point of view, it is worth considering forcing managers to have additional 'skin in the game' (i.e. a greater vested interest in the company's performance) by purchasing – on top of what they receive as compensation – shares (or even options) with their own money (possibly using executive loans[165]).[166] Executives who purchase shares or options will be more likely to recognize the opportunity cost of these shares or options and will strive to earn a fair return on their investment. Another consequence is that executives will actually lose money if the share price drops. Further, executives must not be allowed to use financial engineering to hedge the risk that their shares or options decline in value.[167] We think it possible to argue that hedging shares or options which are intended as incentives constitutes a breach of the general contractual fiduciary duty of an executive to his company.[168] For safety's sake, a suitable provision should be explicitly agreed between the company and the executive.

Finally, it is important to note that equity-based compensation for executives requires more stringent monitoring by the board of directors (i.e. the compensation committee and also perhaps the audit committee), because it may encourage executives to manipulate financial reports and/or operating decisions so as to increase the share price and generate larger short-term payoffs.[169]

---

161. Alternatively, a company could grant new share options with a lower exercise price.
162. See also the Swiss Code of Best Practice (section 26) <www.economiesuisse.ch/d/content.cfm?upid=DD23731B-DCDF-4F99-960C0AE389A96E3C&type=pdf&filetype=pdf>.
163. L.A. Bebchuk and J.M. Fried, no. 9 above, p. 166; T. Bühner and M. Wallmeier, no. 52 above, 556.
164. See section III.C.1 above.
165. See section III.C.4 below.
166. M.C. Jensen and K.J. Murphy, no. 1 above, 58. A combination is also possible, i.e. linking the grant of options to the prior purchase of shares; see no. 152 above.
167. The position could be hedged by acquiring put options on the shares underlying the manager's call option.
168. See also D. Leu, no. 26 above, p. 150 and *Bericht der Regierungskommission Corporate Governance* (Baums ed.) (Cologne, Schmidt, 2001), p. 90 *et seq.*
169. See sections IV.A.3 and IV.B.3 below.

2. The Use of Bonus Plans

a. General

The economic issues related to designing bonus plans are largely identical to the issues of (variable) pay in general: within a target amount, performance criteria must be defined as well as the payment method (cash or shares/options, immediately or deferred). As we explained in the preceding section, we consider that under Swiss law, it is a good idea to refer to certain aspects of compensation (restricted shares or options) as bonus plans rather than pure variable pay.[170]

b. Legal Restrictions

Swiss employment law contains provisions related to performance-related pay.[171] It is widely acknowledged that, apart from the performance-related pay as defined by law, additional forms of performance-related pay may be agreed upon between the parties.[172] The difficulty with bonus plans, however, is that legal authors as well as Swiss courts disagree on what, by law, constitutes a bonus.[173] This will be important if the agreement is not explicit in all respects, and even more so if the employee later claims that certain clauses in the bonus plan are contrary to Swiss mandatory law.

Many authorities consider any bonus as constituting a wage element (*Lohnbestandteil*) and therefore an enforceable contractual claim of the executive vis-à-vis the company, meaning that the board cannot refuse to pay the bonus if the specified conditions are fulfilled. Hence it is imperative that the contract specify the intention of the parties as to whether the bonus is to constitute an enforceable contractual claim or to remain at the company's discretion.[174] If the parties decide on the former, they may encounter the problems described above if the bonus is paid in restricted options or shares. We therefore recommend that if the bonus is paid in restricted shares, the grant of the shares should be declared to be a bonus at the discretion of the employer. Alternatively, if this is not acceptable to the employee,

170. See above at no. 157.
171. E.g. a 'gratification' pursuant to art. 322d CO (*Gratifikation*), or a share in the company's profits pursuant to art. 322a CO (*Anteil am Geschäftsergebnis*). On performance-related pay from an employment law point of view; see e.g. T. Geiser, no. 67 above, 382 *et seq.*
172. See T. Geiser, no. 67 above, 391.
173. Some qualify a bonus as gratification in the sense of art. 322d CO (*Gratifikation*) which is, absent an agreement of the parties to the contrary, in the sole discretion of the employer and thus no enforceable claim of the employee. Others, in contrast, take the view that a bonus should be considered a share in the company's profit in the sense of art. 322a CO (*Anteil am Geschäftsergebnis*) with the consequence that a bonus is automatically considered as an enforceable claim of the employee. Finally, some authors argue that a bonus is a *contractus mixtus* or *sui generis*. For an overview, see D. Portmann, no. 32 above, note 34 *et seq.*; further T. Geiser, no. 67 above, 382 *et seq.*
174. Art. 18 (1) CO. See also T. Geiser, no. 67 above, 391; D. Portmann, no. 32 above, no. 39 and 43.

he should be allowed to choose between a (lower) cash payment and restricted shares as described above.[175]

Finally, it must be noted that bonus payments to directors and managers of listed companies must be disclosed in the corporate governance section of the annual report as part of the total compensation (executives and non-executives combined).[176]

c. *Recommendations*

Once target compensation and the proportion of variable pay have been determined (and ideas on the form of payment exist), the board needs to address the selection of the performance measure for the bonus pay, as discussed previously with regard to variable compensation in general.[177] Although there is no one-size-fits all solution, it is important that the measure chosen sets the appropriate incentives for the executives and that these incentives be consistent with the corporate strategy. Furthermore, the incentives may have to be targeted to various functions within a company. If the company's focus is on gaining market share, it should reward sales (or market share gains); if the focus is on operational efficiency, EBITDA might be the right measure, at least for the CEO (while financing costs and control of working capital might be an appropriate target for the CFO in this scenario). In other companies, bottom-line profits or return on equity or on assets might be appropriate yardsticks.

Because it is possible to align such performance measures (which as shown above can also relate to EVA, or to factors such as customer satisfaction) to the strategy and to individual functions, we think that these measures are preferable to a bonus plan tied directly to the share price. Conversely, we think it is more effective if payments under bonus plans are made in (restricted) shares or options. If payments are made in cash, we recommend using a phantom stock plan or bonus bank concept.

As mentioned above, the board of directors must also assess the advantages and disadvantages of each performance measure, including the dangers of manipulation.[178] Since the main disadvantage of annual or other periodic bonus pay systems is that they may encourage executives to think in the short term, deferred payment systems (either restricted shares or options or deferred cash payments based on a phantom stock concept or payments into a virtual bonus bank[179] which releases payments only if targets are also met in subsequent years) should generally be chosen.

---

175. See above section III.C.1.
176. See the SWX Swiss Exchange Directive on Information Relating to Corporate Governance, no. 140 above, section 5.2. See also no. 141 above for the recent amendment of the CO.
177. See above section III.B.2.
178. See above section II.D.
179. M.C. Jensen and K.J. Murphy, no. 1 above, 75; D. Leu, no. 26 above, pp. 213 *et seq.*; R. Weilenmann, no. 16 above, pp. 324 *et seq.*; further D. Portmann, no. 32 above, no. 52 with further references.

Plans should not merely define a threshold, because in that case the motivation to continue performing is likely to decrease once the target is attained. Rather, they should, at linear or non-linear intervals, define further levels at which the bonus earned will be increased.[180] While a cap may make sense with regard to the company's compensation policy or liquidity needs, it is important to note that executives capable of producing above the 'cap' will tend to stop producing once they have reached the cap and will transfer performance results that could have been realized during the current period into the next.[181] We therefore advise, as a rule, against the introduction of caps.

Finally, the board should – as noted above[182] – decide whether the bonus is to constitute an enforceable contractual claim of the executive (*Lohnbestandteil*) or is to remain at the company's discretion. To avoid breaching mandatory employment laws, the board ought to choose for the latter.

3. The Use of Severance Payments

a. General

As discussed briefly previously, executives invest all of their human capital in the company and are thus more risk averse than (diversified) shareholders. This risk aversion may lead to excessively cautious, inefficient investments, or to the executives entrenching themselves in their positions, e.g. by blocking beneficial takeovers that could result in their dismissal. This is where golden parachutes (i.e. severance payments if an executive is dismissed following a change of control)[183] and general severance payments (made in case of termination, sometimes only early termination) come into play. Either of these inducements may compensate for, or even overcome, managers' general risk aversion, i.e. remove managerial resistance to takeovers and other actions that might lead to job losses. They therefore serve to align the executives' interests with those of shareholders.[184] Rather than a risk

---

180. See also D. Leu, no. 26 above, p. 285 *et seq.*
181. M.C. Jensen and K.J. Murphy, no. 1 above, 71.
182. See section III.C.2 above.
183. An alternative to golden parachutes has been suggested by B. Brechbühl, 'Goldene Fallschirme oder silberne Brücken? Ein Beitrag zu den Kontrollwechselklauseln' (2004) *Revue suisse de jurisprudence* 100 32 *et seq.* B. Brechbühl considers that a (limited) extension of the notice period is preferable to a golden parachute, because it enables the new controlling shareholder either to benefit from the manager's know-how during the extended notice period or to let the manager go, in which case the extended notice period could lead to the same result as a golden parachute.
184. M.P. Narayanan and A.K. Sundaram, 'A safe landing? Golden parachutes and corporate behavior' *University of Michigan Business School Working Paper No. 98015,* August 1998, <papers.ssrn.com/abstract_id=131869>; D.M. Weiss, no. 11 above, p. 44 *et seq.* with further references; H.C. von der Crone, no. 54 above, p. 558 with further references.

premium incorporated into the annual salary, the executive may be satisfied with a severance payment, should he/she lose his/her job.[185]

b. Legal Restrictions

If agreed upon prior to the commencement of the employment relationship, the promise of severance payments is generally not problematic from a legal perspective. Severance payments reduce the annual salary[186] and compensate only a specific risk (i.e. that the employment may be terminated at a time earlier than either party anticipated when making the employment contract),[187] which is in the best interests of the shareholders.

On the other hand, the board's statutory duty to safeguard the interests of the company[188] often restricts its ability to enter into such arrangements during an existing employment relationship. The board is only likely to do so in order to avoid costly litigation[189] or to encourage managers to favour a takeover bid.[190, 191] Even more problematic are *ex gratia* payments made at the end of an employment agreement, as they can scarcely be said to be in the legitimate interests of the company.

Big golden parachutes for executives of a listed company that are agreed upon only after the publication of a public tender offer, with the intention of blocking that offer, are void unless the shareholders meeting has agreed to the arrangement.[192]

---

185. H.C. von der Crone, no. 53 above, p. 560. See also M. Dreher, 'Change of control-Klauseln bei Aktiengesellschaften' [2002] *Die Aktiengesellschaft (AG),* 214 *et seq.*
186. If this is not the case (and if the board is aware of it), the promise is problematic: see B. Brechbühl, no. 183 above, 34; P. Böckli, no. 83 above, para. 13 no. 257.
187. Entering into a short-term contract with a severance payment is better for the company than entering into a long-term arrangement, because the company requires flexibility in the event that the executive does not perform as desired. Put another way: a contract that can be terminated within three months and that carries a two-year's salary severance payment will have much the same effect as a three-year agreement.
188. Art. 717 (1) CO.
189. P. Böckli, no. 83 above, para. 13 n. 257.
190. However, a transaction bonus might actually be better suited to achieve this goal.
191. The duty to safeguard the interests of the company pursuant to art. 717 (1) CO is relevant not only with regard to Swiss corporate law, but also from a Swiss takeover-law perspective. In the context of the recent takeover struggle over Saia-Burgess Electronics Holding AG, the Swiss Federal Banking Commission confirmed the Swiss Takeover Board's earlier decision, pursuant to which severe violations of art. 717 (1) CO even *prior* to the publication of a public tender offer may be deemed an illicit takeover defence measure once a public tender offer is launched. See Recommendation V of the Swiss Takeover Board (23 August 2005) and the decision of the Swiss Federal Banking Commission of 19 September 2005, both of which are available at <www.takeover.ch>. See also the critical analysis of these decisions by R. Bahar at <www.unige.ch/cdbf>, no. 346, 25 September 2005.
192. See art. 29 (2) of the Federal Stock Exchange Act in connection with art. 35 (2) lit. c of the Takeover Ordinance of the Swiss Takeover Board. Pursuant to a recent decision of the Swiss Federal Banking Commission, golden parachutes may be problematic with regard to not just corporate law, but also to takeover law: see no. 191 above.

The main idea behind this rule is that big golden parachutes impair the efficiency of the market for corporate control and remove or at least attenuate the discipline imposed on the executives by that market.[193]

Finally, golden parachutes and severance payments have to be disclosed in the annual report of listed companies if and when granted.[194]

c. Recommendations

The board of directors will have to bear in mind that a severance payment that is extraordinarily large – like any high (guaranteed) deferred payment – is apt to dilute performance-based incentives *a priori*.[195] Furthermore, oversized golden parachutes may tempt an executive to engineer a change of control, particularly if the company is facing difficult times, even though a takeover might not at this point in time or at this price level be in the best interests of shareholders.[196] On the other hand, the board of directors should also consider the positive effects of golden parachutes and severance payments described above.

In principle we are in favour of negotiating golden parachutes and severance payments. However, the board should ensure that the amount does not distort incentives and is in line with the company's interests. More specifically, the board must be mindful of the fact that severance payments that are triggered by an early termination or a change of control are quite often related to underperformance by both the executive and the firm, which is most likely attributable to the executive's management.

Severance payments in case of early termination should be geared to length of service, i.e. they should decrease over time. Their size should only compensate for the manager's loss (including reputational loss) from the early termination, including the loss if the parties agree to a waiting period during which the executive must not accept a job offer from a competitor.

Furthermore, payments under golden parachutes should only be made if the takeover attempt is successful (i.e. if the transaction is closed) and – in our opinion – only if the executive loses his job following the change in control. While one can argue that this restriction limits the executives' interest in a transaction, we believe that a specific transaction bonus can better address that point.

Severance promises should contain a proviso that the payment only becomes due if the employment has not been terminated by the employer for cause in the sense of article 337 CO. No payment should be due in case of termination by the

---

193. For more on market forces, see section II.B above.
194. See the SWX Swiss Exchange Directive on Information Relating to Corporate Governance, and no. 141 for the recent amendment of the CO.
195. See above section III.B.2.
196. See e.g. M. Dreher, no. 185 above, 216. This view has been disproved by the study conducted by M.P. Narayanan and A.K. Sundaram, no. 184 above, on 245 companies listed on NYSE between 1980 and 1994. The study concluded that golden parachutes offer managers not just a feeling of security, but also the confidence to restructure their companies without having to worry about losing their jobs if the company is then put in play.

executive, except possibly if the executive has reason for resigning pursuant to article 337 CO.

Finally, it should be stipulated that severance payments may be made in instalments, so that payments can stop if the executive finds a new position shortly after losing his previous one, or breaches any waiting periods to which the parties may have agreed.

4. The Use of Executive Loans

a. General

An alternative (or supplement) to granting shares is to extend loans to executives to enable them to buy company shares or exercise granted share options (with the aim of keeping the shares).

The benefits of such executive loans are that they increase the executives' stake in the company and thus reduce agency conflicts.[197] Because shares and options are presently often taxed in Switzerland upon grant or vesting,[198] loans to executives can frequently help them to pay tax on an income which they cannot convert into cash for quite a long period of time.

b. Legal Restrictions[199]

Whenever a loan is granted to an executive (irrespective of whether the recipient is a director or manager), the board of directors must ensure that the loan is granted at arm's length;[200] in particular, the loan should not carry favourable interest rates. If it does, the parties must realize that this is a further compensation element: tax and social security issues should also be taken into account.[201]

Shares purchased with such loans should be pledged to the company and not be transferable by the executive unless he/she repays the loan, e.g. on termination of the employment relationship. We believe that the company, considering the compensation element, may accept the shares as valid security, even though the

---

197. See K.Shastri and K.M. Kahle, 'Executive loans' *EFA 2003 Annual Conference Paper No. 184,* February 2003,<papers.ssrn.com/abstract_id=423447>.
198. See the Circular of the Swiss Federal Tax Administration (EStV) No. 5/1997: <www.estv.admin.ch/data/dvs/druck/kreis/d/w97-005d.pdf>. The Swiss Parliament is currently amending the applicable tax regime (see <www.parlament.ch/afs/data/ d/gesch/2004/d_gesch_20040074.htm>); pursuant to this amendment, restricted share options will no longer be taxed upon vesting but on exercise. For an overview of the legislation process and further material see <www.efd.admin.ch/d/dok/faktenblaetter/efd-schwerpunkte/3_best_mitarbbet.htm>.
199. For an overview see P. Böckli, no. 86 above, para. 12 no. 544 *et seq.* For a detailed analysis see e.g. L. Glanzmann, *Der Darlehensvertrag mit einer Aktiengesellschaft aus gesellschaftsrechtlicher Sicht* (Bern/Stuttgart/Vienna, Hopt, 1996) and L. Bochud, *Darlehen an Aktionäre aus wirtschaftlicher, zivil- und steuerrechtlicher Sicht* (Bern, Staempfli 1991).
200. Art. 717 (1) CO.
201. See above section III.B.1.

liquidity of these shares may be questionable, especially if the financial situation of the company deteriorates.[202] The provisions in the CO regarding the acquisition of own shares are in our opinion not applicable.[203]

In exceptional circumstances, the grant of loans could be considered a hidden profit distribution in the sense of article 678 (2) CO, or an unlawful repayment of capital.[204] However, here again our opinion is that this is generally not the case in view of the compensation element of the loan. The problems just described can thus only arise if the company (a) knows that the executive has no other funds to repay the loan and (b) has reason to believe that the share price is overvalued and will go down.

Finally, executive loans have to be disclosed in the annual report of listed companies.[205]

c. Recommendations

Executive loans offer the advantage of providing the executive with 'skin in the game'. An executive who is required to use his own money (albeit borrowed) to buy shares or options is likely to have stronger incentives than if the shares or options were merely given to them. We therefore consider an executive loan to be worth considering when designing compensation packages. As we have said, the board must ensure that the loan is actually used for acquiring equity and is repaid once the shares or options are sold, which is best achieved if the shares or options purchased are directly pledged to the company.

The above considerations apply *mutatis mutandis* if the company guarantees a bank loan taken out by an executive in order to buy shares.

5. The Use of other Forms of Compensation

a. General

Executive compensation arrangements usually contain a number of other benefits, such as a company car (or car allowance), club memberships, housing and travel allowances (also for family members), pension promises, allowances for financial or other advice, education for children etc.

Scholars are divided in their judgment of the legitimacy of such benefits in executive compensation arrangements.[206] Some authors point out that these benefits

202. P. Böckli, no. 86 above, para. 4 no. 346.
203. See also P. Böckli, no. 83 above, para. 4 no. 347 *et seq.*
204. For more details see the authors listed in no. 199 above.
205. See the SWX Swiss Exchange Directive on Information Relating to Corporate Governance; see no. 141 above, with regard to the recent amendment of the CO.
206. For an overview see D. Yermack, 'Flights of fancy: corporate jets, CEO perquisites, and inferior shareholder returns' March 2005, <papers.ssrn.com/ abstract_id=529822> and R.G. Rajan and J.Wulf, 'Are perks purely managerial excess?' May 2004, <papers.ssrn.com/ abstract_id=546291>.

may tend to increase the recipient's social status, which in turn might motivate lower-ranking executives to try harder to earn a promotion. Others argue that such benefits simply reduce the company's value without providing executives with any incentives to increase it. An interesting study showed that firms that disclosed such benefits underperformed in average shareholder returns as compared to market benchmarks by more than four per cent annually.[207] Another study found evidence that perks are offered most often in situations in which they are likely to enhance managerial productivity.[208]

Considering the objectives of compensation,[209] such benefits may help to induce and retain an executive due to their attractiveness (which sometimes includes the fact that such benefits are not taxed as income),[210] but it is doubtful whether they do anything to align the interests of the executive with those of shareholders.

b. Legal Restrictions

The disclosure duties imposed on companies listed on SWX Swiss Exchange by the SWX Directive on Corporate Governance[211] require the disclosure of fringe benefits.[212]

Apart from the disclosure duty, Swiss law does not place any specific restraints on the payment of benefits, except of course the director's general duty of care and loyalty. The implications of this are addressed below.

c. Recommendations

If a board of directors decides to use fringe benefits in order to induce and retain executives, we strongly recommend that these benefits be treated as a wage element. The various benefits must be valued and suitably offset by adjustments to salary or other forms of pay,[213] and it is worth considering whether an incentive element can be brought into the benefits, e.g. by tying them to performance targets.

---

207. See the study by D. Yermack, no. 206 above.
208. The study by R.G. Rajan and J. Wulf, no. 206 above, indicates that perks are often linked to the location of the company headquarters, e.g. executive jets are less common in firms that are headquartered in countries with large populations and less common in firms that are in close proximity to a major airports.
209. See above section III.A.
210. The failure to declare fringe benefits in the wage statement (*Lohnausweis*) has led to an overhaul of the form on which this is done. The new form (mandatory from 2006) is intended to capture fringe benefits more specifically than its predecessor. For further information, see e.g. <www.steuerkonferenz.ch/pdf/2004-2_medienmitteilung_internet.pdf>.
211. See no. 140 above.
212. See the relevant section in the SWX Swiss Exchange commentary: <www.swx.com/download/admission/regulation/guidelines/swx_guideline_20020701-1_comm_en.pdf>. Unfortunately, the term 'fringe benefits' is not defined. However, it can be assumed that the benefits described here would be included. The same applies in our opinion with regard to the new article 663bbis CO, see no. 141.
213. See e.g. E.F. Fama, no. 20 above, 288 *et seq.*

D. Our own Recommended Package

Considering all the legal restrictions and our own recommendations, and taking into account that systems should not be overly complicated, if we controlled the board of a listed company, we would consider the following compensation package (at least as a starting point):

- Fixed compensation in cash – such compensation to be sufficient to guarantee the executive (a) a decent standard of living and (b) the means to pay taxes on all compensation elements;
- Variable compensation based on two or three criteria (which would differ depending on the executive, i.e. be different for the CEO, the CFO and the divisional heads); such criteria to be in line with the corporate strategy, with linear compensation for over-fulfilment of each criterion;
- All variable compensation (for legal reasons we would always offer the executive a cash option, making sure to keep the option less attractive than variable compensation) to be paid in options[214] (knowing that shares are more popular these days), such options having the following characteristics:
  - Exercise price equal to the share price at the grant date; the exercise price to be adjusted based on a basket of peer companies, further adjusted for dividend payments, and with no re-pricing;
  - Immediate vesting of one-third, a further one-third vesting if the same performance criteria are also achieved the following year, and one-third vesting the year after. No vesting if executive terminates without a valid reason;
  - Exercise period starting in year 3 and lasting until year 10.
- Decreasing severance payments, starting with five years' fixed compensation, dropping to zero after ten years of employment. Golden parachute equal to the total compensation received in the two years preceding the change of control.
- Limited allowances and benefits;
- Executive loan possibly to purchase shares in an amount equal to one year's target compensation.

IV. COMPETENCES AND CONFLICTS OF INTERESTS IN EXECUTIVE COMPENSATION

Conflicts of interests arising in connection with executive compensation may be addressed not only with regard to the design and structure of the compensation, but also with regard to the pay-setting process, which involves not only the question 'who decides?' but also 'how?'

Bearing in mind the specifics of Swiss law, we will analyze these questions by examining separately (executive) directors' compensation (A) and then management compensation (B). We conclude the section with an analysis of the pros and

214. Options would be valued using recognized methods.

cons of the highly debated question of whether the principal, i.e. the shareholders, should be involved in the pay-setting process (C).

A. (EXECUTIVE) DIRECTORS' COMPENSATION

1. Overlapping Competences of the Board of Directors and the Shareholders Meeting

The shareholders meeting, under Swiss law the 'supreme' corporate body,[215] has its competences set forth in article 698 (2) CO.[216] Among these competences is the entitlement of the shareholders meeting to include so-called *Tantiemen*,[217] a form of profit sharing offered to directors,[218] in the company's articles of incorporation. The distribution of *Tantiemen* must be resolved by the shareholders meeting and may only come out of profits after deduction of the necessary allocation to the reserves and a dividend of five per cent (on nominal value) to the shareholders.[219] The amount of *Tantiemen* may either be fixed in the articles of incorporation[220] or resolved on a case-by-case basis at the shareholders meeting.[221] Although allowing directors a profit share by way of *Tantiemen* was intended to align their interests with those of the shareholders,[222] *Tantiemen* are, in fact, highly rare in Swiss companies. The main reason for this – apart from directors' lack of enthusiasm for such risky compensation[223] – is the adverse tax consequences.[224] Because *Tantiemen* are so rare, the shareholders' decision-making powers in this area are of little use to them and hence are not an appropriate method to control the board of directors.

---

215. Art. 698 (1) CO.
216. Further competences are set forth in other legal acts, such as the Federal Stock Exchange Act and the Federal Merger Act.
217. Art. 698 (2)(4) CO and art. 627 (2) CO.
218. *Tantiemen* are payable to board members only. See the wording of art. 677 CO. Further e.g. P. Kurer, in *Basler Kommentar zum Schweizerischen Privatrecht, Obligationenrecht II*, H. Honsell, N.P. Vogt and R. Watter (eds) (2nd edn, Basle/Geneva/Munich, Helbing & Lichtenhahn, 2002), no. 11 ad art. 677 and D. Leu, no. 26 above, p. 108 *et seq.*
219. See art. 677 CO.
220. In such a case, the shareholders' resolution pursuant to art. 698 (4) CO has no constitutive effect and the *Tantiemen* can be considered a (variable) wage element (*Lohnbestandteil*). See A. Nussbaumer and H.C. von der Crone, 'Ausschüttung von Tantiemen' (2005) *Revue suisse de droit des affaires* 75, 94.
221. See e.g. P. Kurer, no. 218 above, no. 7 ad art. 677; A. Nussbaumer and H.C. von der Crone, no. 229 above, 94 with further references.
222. However, the connection between the individual performance of a board member and the company's balance sheet profit is considered weak and thus not very incentive-based. See e.g. G. Giger, no. 3 above, p. 401.
223. When a company is in crisis and the board is under particular pressure, the board members have no or little prospect of compensation if paid with *Tantiemen*.
224. As part of the company's profits, *Tantiemen* are taxable at the company level and may not be deducted as expenses from the taxable net profits (in contrast to fees). In addition, *Tantiemen* are subject to personal income tax. For further tax consequences, see e.g. P. Kurer, no. 218 above, no. 18 ad art. 677.

Furthermore, the issuing of shares and/or share options which are to be funded out of conditional share capital requires a shareholders' resolution.[225] However, the decision to set up a specific share participation or share option plan remains in the power of the board of directors[226] and does not have to be put to the shareholders, although the latter can, in theory, refuse to accept the capital increase until and unless they learn more about the specific plan. If treasury shares (including repurchased shares) rather than conditional capital are used as a source for equity plans, shareholders are not involved at all.

In addition to *Tantiemen* and the creation of conditional share capital, the board of directors is competent to set the compensation of its members.[227] Needless to say, this is an abundant source of potential conflicts of interests.

2. Is Directors' Compensation a Non-transferable Duty of the Board of Directors?

Article 716a (1) CO lays down the fundamental decision-making powers of the board of directors, which cannot be delegated to either management or shareholders but are considered non-transferable.[228] Directors' compensation is not explicitly listed in this catalogue. Is it included implicitly? The answer to this question matters due to its implications for the possibility of delegating the (final) decisions over directors' compensation arrangements to a compensation committee (along with the potential liability associated with such decisions). In addition, the answer also determines whether the board can submit *de lege lata*, such compensation issues to the shareholders meeting.

Under Swiss law, the power to run a company is generally vested with the board of directors, but may be duly delegated to particular members of the board or to managers.[229] Article 716a (1)(1) CO gives the board of directors non-transferable

225. The shareholders' resolution 'only' concerns the creation of conditional share capital for the purposes of employee participation plans (see art. 653 (1) CO). Despite the wording of art. 653 (1) CO, share options and share participation plans based on conditional share capital are not limited to employees, but can also be extended to members of the board or other individuals who hold executive functions and who are not necessarily in an employment relationship with the company. See e.g. P.R. Isler and G.G. Zindel, in *Basler Kommentar zum Schweizerischen Privatrecht, Obligationenrecht II*, H. Honsell, N.P. Vogt and R. Watter (eds), (2nd edn, Basle/Geneva/Munich, Helbing & Lichtenhahn, 2002), no. 16a ad art. 653; see further C. Helbing, no. 121 above, p. 35 *et seq.*

226. B. Walti, no. 121 above, p. 166, even argues that the decision on the plan is a non-transferable decision of the board of directors. See also D. Portmann, no. 32 above, no. 84.

227. See e.g. P. Forstmoser, A. Meier-Hayoz and P. Nobel, no. 83 above, para. 28 no. 129; P. Kurer, no. 218 above, no. 22 ad art. 677. But cf. v. Aepli, 'Zur Entschädigung des Verwaltungsrates' (2002) *Revue suisse de droit des affaires* 72, 272 *et seq.* and R. Ruedin, no. 83 above, p. 329 *et seq.*, who argue that directors' fees should be resolved by the shareholders meeting in analogy with the *Tantiemen*.

228. For further duties that are not considered transferable, see e.g. P. Böckli, no. 83 above, para. 13 no. 287; C. Chapuis, in *OR Handkommentar*, J.K. Kostkiewicz, U. Bertschinger, P. Breitschmid and I. Schwander (eds) (Zurich, Schulthess, 2002), no. 1 ad art. 716a.

229. See arts 716 (2) and 716b (1) CO.

responsibility for the ultimate direction of the company (*Oberleitung*). This includes deciding the company's strategy in accordance with its corporate purpose and selecting the instruments for achieving that purpose.[230] The board is also responsible for determining the organization of the company (article 716a (1) (2) CO), in particular that of top management,[231] and for appointing and supervising the latter (article 716a (1) (4) and (5) CO). Two conclusions can be drawn from this list: either (a) based on these rules, it would be inconsistent not to include at least the *basic principles* of directors' compensation in this list, especially as the creation of incentives plays such a considerable role in the life of a company;[232] or (b) all decisions (on the policy and on specific arrangements) can validly be delegated to the compensation committee[233] and thus, by implication, also to shareholders.[234]

On balance, we believe that while there should be a clear link between compensation and strategy (inasmuch as performance parameters should fit the strategy) and overall direction of the company (since compensation should align the interests of executives and shareholders), both elements would favour a non-transferable board duty. However, it would be inconsistent to exclude shareholders altogether from the decision process, since it is they who elect the board and can remove its members at any time (articles 698 [2][2] and 705 CO) and therefore have considerable influence on who decides the strategy and direction of the company. In our view, shareholders can therefore decide not only the principles of directors'

---

230. R. Watter, no. 72 above, no. 4 ad art. 716a.
231. R. Watter, no. 72 above, no. 8 ad art. 716a.
232. P. Böckli, no. 83 above, para. 13 no. 426; P. Böckli, C. Huguenin and F. Dessemontet, *Expertenbericht der Arbeitsgruppe 'Corporate Governance' zur Teilrevision des Aktienrechts* (Zurich, Schulthess, 2004) pp. 133 *et seq.*; D. Leu, no. 26 above, p. 112; D. Daeniker, 'Vergütung von Verwaltungsrat und Geschäftsleitung schweizerischer Publikumsgesellschaften' *Revue suisse de jurisprudence,* 101 (2005) 386 *et seq.*; on employee participation programs as a non-transferable duty of the board of directors see B. Walti, no. 121 above, p. 167 *et seq.*; D. Portmann, no. 32 above, no. 84.
233. This is in fact common practice in many companies; however, the committee will generally inform the board of its decisions, permitting the board to revisit a decision, in the event that it is dissatisfied with the results of the decision.
234. R. Watter, 'Verwaltungsratsausschüsse und Delegierbarkeit von Aufgaben' in *Neuere Tendenzen im Gesellschaftsrecht – Festschrift für Peter Forstmoser*, H.C. Von der Crone, R.H. Weber, R. Zäch and D. Zobl (eds) (Zurich, Schulthess 2003), 196 (dealing only with delegation to a committee); H.C. von der Crone, A. Carbonara and L. Marolda Martínez, 'Corporate Governance und Führungsorganisation in der Aktiengesellschaft' (2004) *Revue suisse de jurisprudence,* 100, 409, who take the view that not only the principles, but also the specific determination of a compensation package may be delegated; U. Bertschinger, 'Zuständigkeit der Generalversammlung der Aktiengesellschaft' in *Festschrift für Jean Nicholas Druey*, R.J. Schweizer, H. Burkert and U. Gasser (eds) (Zurich, Schulthess, 2002), p. 324; R. Müller, no. 66 above, 1,375; I.W. Hungerbühler, no. 83 above, 177; P. Forstmoser, A. Meier-Hayoz and P. Nobel, no. 83 above, para. 28 no. 128; P. Kurer, no. 218 above, no. 22 ad art. 677; in addition, H.C. von der Crone, no. 2 above, 254 *et seq.*

    Furthermore, in 1960 a case was brought before the Swiss Federal Supreme Court in which the articles of a company provided for the directors' compensation to be fixed by the shareholders meeting (see ATF 86 II 162). In its decision, the Swiss Federal Supreme Court implicitly upheld this provision.

compensation, but in our opinion they are – theoretically[235] – entitled to vote on even more specific aspects, such as individual arrangements.[236] We therefore come to the conclusion that not only the principles of directors' compensation, but all aspects of directors' compensation are *not* a non-transferable duty of the board of directors and may therefore be delegated to a committee or – through the articles of incorporation – even to the shareholders meeting.

3. Dealing with Conflicts of Interests

a. Duty to Abstain from Voting

As we have seen, the board of directors has considerable discretion with regard to the compensation of its members. However, a board member who decides his/her own compensation is clearly conflicted, since he/she will naturally try to maximize it despite his/her obligation to safeguard the interests of the company.[237]

Swiss corporate law does not explicitly address this conflict of interest,[238] but legal authors agree that a conflicted board member must abstain from voting on matters which affect him/her directly, based on the board member's statutory duty of loyalty[239] which requires him/her to always put the company's interests before his/her own.[240]

A violation of the duty to abstain from voting constitutes a breach of the duty of loyalty, which may result in personal liability if damage can be proven.[241] This threat of personal liability is a mechanism for overcoming the agency problem on

---

235. A shareholders' vote on directors' compensation, however, requires by law a basis in the company's articles of incorporation (see art. 716 (1) CO). Also see e.g. R. Watter, no. 72 above, n. 1 ad art. 716. We do not, however, believe that it is favourable to empower the shareholders meeting with such extensive competences for reasons set out in more detail in section IV.C.2 below.
236. Of course, the possibility for shareholders to indirectly influence the compensation arrangements remains insofar as they are able to refuse to elect a director who receives a package with which shareholders are dissatisfied (although, as a matter of fact, they are unlikely to be given the relevant information unless they specifically request it).
237. Art. 717 (1) CO.
238. Pursuant to the recently published draft on a partial reform of Swiss corporate law as proposed by the Swiss Federal Council (see the *Begleitbericht zum Vorentwurf zur Revision des Aktien- und Rechnungslegungsrechts im Obligationenrecht vom 2. Dezember 2005*, <www.bj.admin.ch>), a provision is proposed to be included in the CO dealing with conflicts of interests on the board and management level.
239. Art. 717 (1) CO.
240. See e.g. P. Böckli, no. 83 above, para. 13 no. 643; H.C. von der Crone, no. 2 above, 5; L. Handschin, 'Treuepflicht des Verwaltungsrates bei der gesellschaftsinternen Entscheidfindung' in *Neuere Tendenzen im Gesellschaftsrecht – Festschrift für Peter Forstmoser*, H.C. Von der Crone, R.H. Weber, R. Zäch and D. Zobl (eds) (Zurich, Schulthess, 2003) pp. 169 *et seq.*; D. Leu, no. 26 above, 118 *et seq.*
241. Art. 754 CO.

the assumption that the threat of sanctions will deter board members from breaching their duties.[242]

It should be noted, however, that abstention is ineffective in instances such as when the board is to decide the compensation of all non-executive directors, because this will mean that the executive directors decide the compensation of the very people who are subsequently going to decide their (the executives') salaries and supervise their activities.

b. No Self-Dealing

If a conflicted director has a voice in deciding his/her own compensation, this constitutes self-dealing. The Swiss Federal Supreme Court has consistently held that, as a matter of general contract law, an agreement concluded by way of self-dealing is invalid unless (i) no disadvantage can ensue to the party represented (which can be proven e.g. by a fairness opinion confirming that the agreement is at arm's length) or (ii) the agreement was previously authorized, or has subsequently been approved, by the represented party.[243] If the represented party is a legal entity, the Swiss Federal Supreme Court held that another board member who has signatory power (*recte*: the necessary competence – *Geschäftsführungsbefugnis*)[244] may authorize or subsequently approve an agreement concluded by a conflicted board member which has not been authorized or approved by a superior corporate body.[245]

If a board member wants a personal compensation agreement this will have to be done on behalf of the company by other members with the necessary competence. Board members must adhere to the statutory duty of care and loyalty,[246] i.e. they must ensure that the compensation agreement with the board member in question is at arm's length.[247] If there are no other board members, it is theoretically up to the shareholders meeting to authorize or subsequently approve the agreement. However, we are not aware of such practices in Switzerland.[248]

---

242. L. Glanzmann, no. 11 above, 140; see also no. 23 above.
243. See e.g. ATF 126 II 361, 363 with further references to earlier cases.
244. B. Stutz and H.C. von der Crone, 'Kontrolle von Interessenkonflikten im Aktienrecht – Urteil des Bundesgerichts 127 III 332 vom 2. Mai 2001 i.S. Erbengemeinschaft J.M. (Berufungsklägerin) gegen K. AG (Berufungsbeklagte) sowie Urteil des Bundesgerichts 4C.397/1998 vom 15. Juni 1999 i.S. W, C und T (Berufungskläger) gegen H Immobilien Holding AG (Berufungsbeklagte)' (2003) *Revue suisse de droit des affaires* 74, 102 *et seq.* If the other board member does not have the necessary competence, a third party could invoke a 'good-faith defence' with respect to the representation authority of that board member. However, if the third party is a member of the same board, this defence is not available because he/she knew, or ought to have known, that the other board member lacked the necessary competence.
245. See ATF 127 III 332.
246. Art. 717 (1) CO.
247. See e.g. P. Böckli, no. 83 above, para. 13 no. 646.
248. See also D. Daeniker, no. 232 above, 385; R. Ruedin, no. 83 above, 329 *et seq.*, who even takes the view that all directors' compensation must be ratified during the shareholders meeting.

c. *The Role of Compensation Committees and Independent/Non-Executive Directors*

An institutional solution to the abstention and self-dealing problems is the formation of a committee.[249] Under Swiss law, the formation of committees is not explicitly prescribed.[250] However, the (non-binding) Swiss Code of Best Practice recommends setting up at least an audit, a nomination, and a compensation committee.[251] Many Swiss public companies have set up such committees.[252]

One of the main postulates of the corporate governance movement is that the board and its committees should include non-executive and/or even independent[253] members.[254] Such directors are believed to decide more objectively on the appropriateness of particular issues than executive directors,[255] and the arrangement makes it possible to separate operational responsibilities (executive directors) from supervision (non-executive and/or independent directors). Furthermore, non-executive and independent directors are considered to inspire confidence in the shareholders.[256] It is very common for Swiss companies to have a majority of non-executive and even independent board members.[257]

Against this background, a compensation committee mainly (or uniquely) composed of such non-executive or even independent directors,[258] which is set up to deal with the compensation of all board members (and management), can be considered as an institutionalized measure that reduces conflicts of interests, particularly for executive directors, because it automatically excludes them from voting, while at the same time resolves the self-dealing problem.

---

249. D. Leu, no. 26 above, 118 *et seq.*
250. The formation of committees is, however, undoubtedly admissible. See art. 716a (2) CO.
251. See Swiss Code of Best Practice, sections 23, 25, and 27, no. 162 above.
252. From a legal perspective, the formation of committees offers the advantage that directors who are not on them are freed from liability for their decisions so long as the delegation of tasks to be fulfilled by the committee complies with legal requirements. See art. 716b (1) CO. For more details see R. Watter, no. 234 above, 183 *et seq.*
253. The term 'independent' is broader than 'non-executive.' For an overview of the definitions of independence in the USA, UK and the EU, see G. Hertig, 'On-going board reforms: One-size-fits-all and regulatory capture' (March 2005) *European Corporate Governance Institute Working Paper N. 25/2005*, <papers.ssrn.com/abstract_id=676417>. For the definition used in the Swiss Code of Best Practice (section 22, no. 162 above), see K. Hofstetter, 'Corporate Governance in der Schweiz' (2002) *Bericht der Expertengruppe Corporate Governance 34*, <www.economiesuisse.ch/d/ content.cfm?upid=625F94F2-A025-4414-83C5FED2AC82701F& type=pdf&filetype=pdf>.
254. For a detailed analysis of the independent director see C.J. Meier-Schatz, 'Der unabhängige Verwaltungsrat' in *Festschrift für Jean Nicholas Druey,* R.J. Schweizer, H. Burkert and U. Gasser (eds) (Zurich, Schulthess, 2002), p. 479 *et seq.* with various references.
255. Executive directors have invested all of their human capital with one company whereas non-executive and independent directors are diversified. See Ibid. p. 494.
256. K. Hofstetter, no. 253 above, p. 39.
257. See the references in C.J. Meier-Schatz, no. 254 above, p. 484 and there particularly no. 34 and 35.
258. See Swiss Code of Best Practice, section 25, no. 162 above.

However, despite their advantages, compensation committees (and non-executive and/or independent directors) have not been spared from criticism. In the first place, non-executive directors – if different from the owners – are also subject to an agency problem. Just as it has to be assumed that managers do not automatically seek to safeguard shareholders' interests, it cannot always be expected that directors will do so either.[259] This in turn may negatively impact managers' ability to appropriately set their own compensation and that of their fellow board members. Directors in particular have economic incentives to support compensation arrangements that are favourable to other board members, if only to legitimize their own (high) compensation.[260] In addition, although a compensation committee ought to be composed of compensation experts, frequent criticisms are levelled that the members of such committees (especially independent board members) lack both time and firm- or sector-specific know-how. It is also argued that social and psychological factors (collegiality, team spirit, loyalty, a natural desire to avoid conflict within the board team) negatively impact independent and/or non-executive directors' ability to appropriately exercise their role.[261]

Despite these potential shortcomings, we are inclined to encourage the establishment of compensation committees. If the committee has deficiencies, it is, in the end, the shareholders' responsibility to make changes to the board. We will elaborate on the role of shareholders in the next section.

d. The Role of Shareholders

The shareholders meeting is, under Swiss law, the supreme corporate body[262] in a company. It elects, and can at any time dismiss, the directors, who in turn appoint the managers.[263]

Interestingly, apart from the *Tantiemen*, the CO grants shareholders only indirect powers to influence director remuneration. They can vote against the creation of conditional share capital which would serve as basis for a share option or share participation plan for board members[264] (but cannot in principle vote on specific equity-based plans enacted using that capital). Conversely, they can put pressure on the board (and the management) by withholding the discharge of liability

259. L.A. Bebchuk and J.M. Fried, no. 14 above, 73; M.C. Jensen and K.J. Murphy, no. 1 above, 22.
260. L.A. Bebchuk and J.M. Fried, no. 9 above, p. 30.
261. See also L.A. Bebchuk and J.M. Fried, no. 9 above, p. 30 *et seq.*; C.J. Meier-Schatz, no. 254 above, p. 487 *et seq.*; G. Hertig, no. 253 above, 13 *et seq.*
262. Art. 698 (1) CO.
263. Unless they perform the management themselves, or delegate it to members of the board (the delegation requires a basis in the company's articles of incorporation and thus a shareholders' resolution, art. 716b [1] CO).
264. See art. 653 (1) CO. Pursuant to art. 704 (1)(4) CO, a qualified majority of two-thirds of the votes cast and the absolute majority of the nominal capital represented at the shareholders meeting is required to create conditional share capital.

(*Décharge*)[265] or dismissing existing directors and electing new ones.[266, 267] Clearly, information is crucial for exercising these indirect powers. Swiss rules at present stipulate (or will stipulate in the near future) the following:

Based on article 697 (1) CO, any shareholder has a right to request information concerning business matters from the board of directors at the shareholders meeting. Information must be provided in so far as it is necessary for the exercise of the shareholder's voting rights.[268] The compensation of directors (and managers) clearly fulfils this requirement because it affects the company's financial situation and may prove useful when considering potential legal action for the restitution of excessive compensation.[269] It is for this reason that we disagree with those authors who admit only information on the overall sum of compensation paid to members of the board (and to managers).[270, 271] In practice, however, shareholders are always reluctant to exercise this right.

Since 1 January 2002, companies whose shares are listed on the SWX Swiss Exchange have had to comply with the SWX Directive on Information Relating to Corporate Governance.[272] This directive requires[273] issuers to publish in a separate section of the annual report, *inter alia*, information on the issuer's compensation policy, meaning the total compensation (fees, salaries, credits, bonuses, benefits in kind) of executives (executive board members and managers) as well as non-executive board members, along with share ownership and share/option

265. Art. 698 (2) (5) CO only specifies the discharge of liability of the members of the board of directors. It is clear, however, from art. 754 (1) CO in conjunction with art. 758 (1) CO that the shareholders may also vote on the discharge of the management (depending on the motions of the board of directors to be published in the invitation to the shareholders meeting).
266. Art. 705 CO. The right to elect and dismiss directors can in fact be considered the most powerful right of the shareholders meeting; it can also have an indirect influence on the composition of the management. See also T. Spillmann, no. 19 above, 156 and there note 823.
267. See also K. Hofstetter, 'Schlüsselrolle institutioneller Investoren in der Corporate Governance' in *Aktuelle Fragen des Bank- und Finanzmarktrechts, Festschrift für Dieter Zobl*, H.C. von der Crone, P. Forstmoser, R.H. Weber, R. Zäch (eds) (Zurich, Schulthess, 2004), p. 520.
268. Art. 697 (2) CO.
269. Art. 678 (2) CO. See also P.V. Kunz, 'Das Informationsrecht des Aktionärs in der Generalversammlung' [2001] *Pratique juridique actuelle*, 889 *et seq.*; G. Giger, no. 3 above, p. 400 *et seq.* Pursuant to the recently published draft on a partial reform of Swiss corporate law as proposed by the Swiss Federal Council (see the *Begleitbericht zum Vorentwurf zur Revision des Aktien- und Rechnungslegungsrechts im Obligationenrecht vom 2. Dezember 2005*, <www.bj.admin.ch>), the CO is proposed to be amended in order to include an explicit provision entitling shareholders of non-listed companies to obtain information on executive compensation.
270. See P. Forstmoser, 'Informations- und Meinungsäusserungsrechte des Aktionärs' in *Rechtsfragen um die Generalversammlung*, J.N. Druey and P. Forstmoser (eds) (Zurich, Schulthess, 1997), p. 105 and no. 103.
271. See also G. Giger, no. 3 above, p. 400 *et seq.*
272. See no. 140 above. See also the SWX Swiss Exchange commentary <www.swx.com/download/admission/regulation/guidelines/swx_guideline_20020701-1_comm_en.pdf>.
273. The information on compensation, shareholdings and loans must imperatively be disclosed, i.e. no comply-or-explain principle applies. See note 7 to the directive.

allotments for executives and non-executives, loans granted, and the highest total compensation (though without naming individuals).

Finally, the Swiss Code of Obligations has recently been amended to the effect that (*inter alia*), the total compensation of board members (and managers) of companies whose shares are listed on a stock exchange must be disclosed in the notes to the balance sheet.[274] The future provisions of the CO will go beyond the requirements of the above-mentioned SWX Swiss Exchange Directive inasmuch as the compensation of board members (but not of managers) will not have to be disclosed as a total but individually.

In addition to these (formal) shareholders' rights, (institutional) shareholders may of course try to exert influence on the board and the management informally.[275]

Apart from these rather indirect powers, the shareholders meeting has, in our view, the (albeit not uncontested) capacity to intervene directly in the company's compensation policy by e.g. demanding the opportunity to approve the compensation principles established by the board or even by including it (or parts of it) in the company's articles of incorporation. This type of policy could theoretically cap the remuneration (although we would not consider this to be a good idea), define the relationship between fixed and variable compensation, or direct in which form variable compensation should be paid. While the shareholders can also block the election of a board member (e.g. a board member who is promised a compensation package considered too high), we do not believe they can not block the hiring of a manager.[276]

In reality, shareholders rarely ever try to exercise these rights, and the question arises whether, *de lege ferenda*, shareholders' rights should be enhanced. We will return to this point in section IV.C.

B. Management Compensation

1. Competence of the Board of Directors

Swiss law does not explicitly define who is competent to set the management compensation. It is clear, however, that apart from the creation of conditional share capital for the purposes of a share participation or share option plan, which requires a shareholders' resolution, it is the board of directors which, as part of its overall management competence (*Geschäftsführung*),[277] is competent to set the management compensation.

---

274. For more details, see section III.C.1 above and particularly no. 141.
275. Such as personal discussions on the occasion of road shows or analyst conferences. See further T. Spillmann, no. 19 above, p. 250 *et seq.*
276. Again, shareholders have of course the possibility recall board members who have chosen a manager – but this will have only an *ex post* effect.
277. Art. 716 (2) CO.

2. Is Management Compensation a Non-Transferable Duty of the Board of Directors?

We have analyzed this question with regard to directors' compensation, and we take the same view with regard to management compensation, i.e. that the principles of management compensation are not a non-transferable duty of the board of directors, and that either the compensation committee (if the power is delegated to it) or shareholders (although this does not happen in practice) can define a binding compensation policy[278] which covers not only directors' compensation but also that of the management.[279] Shareholders, however, cannot oppose the election of a manager and we see no way that they can vote on specific arrangements for managers.

3. Dealing with Conflicts of Interests

a. The Role of the Board of Directors, Compensation Committees, and Non-Executive and Independent Directors

Pursuant to article 716a (1)(4) and (5) CO, the board of directors is ultimately responsible not only for the appointment and dismissal of managers (*cura in eligendo*), but also for supervising them (*cura in custodiendo*).[280] The law, however, is silent on how this supervision should be exercised. Legal authors agree that it is not limited to legal and regulatory compliance, but extends to economic aspects of decisions made and processes instituted.[281] This duty necessitates an appropriate reporting and internal control system in order to determine and evaluate performance and avoid or mitigate potential risks.[282]

The implication of this supervision duty in the area of management compensation is that the board should take particular care to ensure that the measurement of performance criteria is not manipulated by executives. It will most likely never be possible to completely eliminate shortcomings in compensation packages. But the board must introduce (minimal) performance-evaluation and monitoring systems

---

278. We also feel this is necessary so that a company can have parallel policies for both board and management.
279. See section IV.A.2 above. For a contrary view, see H.C. von der Crone, A. Carbonara and L. Marolda Martínez, no. 234 above, 409; P. Böckli, no. 83 above, para. 13 no. 426; D. Leu, no. 26 above, p. 112 *et seq.* Slightly unclear is the view expressed by D. Daeniker, no. 232 above, 387, who argues that the determination of management compensation may be delegated to a compensation committee, but not the shareholders meeting.
280. See art. 716a (1)(4) and (5) CO.
281. See e.g. P. Böckli, no. 83 above, para. 13 no. 374 *et seq.*; B.U. Glaus, *Unternehmensüberwachung durch schweizerische Verwaltungsräte* (Zurich, Treuhand-Kammer, 1990); E. Homburger, *Zürcher Kommentar zum Schweizerischen Zivilgesetzbuch, Obligationenrecht, V 5b, Der Verwaltungsrat* (Zurich, Schulthess, 1997), no. 589 ad art. 716a; C.J. Meier-Schatz, no. 254 above, p. 485 *et seq.* with various references.
282. P. Böckli, no. 83 above, § 13 note 374 *et seq.*; R. Watter, no. 72 above, n. 20 ad art. 716a.

in order to ensure that the managers have not abused weaknesses in compensation packages (e.g. by taking advantage of options in an accounting system, shifting sales to another period or pursuing strategies which produce short-term share price increases).[283] The duty is wider, however, in the sense that the board will need to check continually whether the performance criteria used are still the best to achieve the designated strategy.

We believe, in this context, that close co-operation between the compensation committee and the audit committee (which, with the help of the internal and external auditors, ought to be able to judge whether the accounts are drawn up in order to favour executives) is crucial. It is also important for the entire board to understand that there are certain inherent shortcomings of compensation committees consisting of independent/non-executive board members with regard to directors' compensation.

In addition to the issues described previously,[284] the following applies specifically to management compensation: As mentioned earlier, just as it can be assumed that managers do not automatically seek to safeguard shareholders' interests, it cannot be expected that directors will do so either.[285] This may undermine their supervision of the management,[286] in particular if the compensation scheme of the directors is identical to that of the managers.[287] Apart from the lack of time and inside know-how and the social and psychological factors,[288] the fact that managers exercise a great deal of influence over appointments to the board may also negatively impact the directors' ability to properly supervise the management.[289]

Finally, the determination of management compensation by relying on peer group comparisons (benchmarking) is being increasingly criticized[290] for two main reasons. First, compensation surveys of compensation consultants[291] (which often

283. R. Watter, no. 234 above, 196; M.C. Jensen and K.J. Murphy, no. 1 above, 48. B. Walti, no. 121 above, p. 171 *et seq.* Johnson, Ryan and Tian, who found a link between high equity-based compensation and the incentive for executives to commit corporate fraud, suggest that anti-fraud measures should be tighter the more executives are compensated with equity. See no. 56 above.
284. See section IV.A.3 above.
285. L.A. Bebchuk and J.M. Fried, no. 14 above, 73; M.C. Jensen and K.J. Murphy, no. 1 above, 22.
286. Pursuant to art. 716a (1)(5) CO, the supervision of the management is vested with the board of directors as a non-transferable duty.
287. A sad example of such lacking supervision due to the identical compensation scheme between directors and managers was discovered at Royal Dutch/Shell, see H.-J. Luhmann, 'Der Shell-Skandal als Indiz für die kommende Erdölverknappung – Fatale Verquickung von Karriere, Bonus und Reserven-Buchhaltung' *Neue Zürcher Zeitung,* 23 February 2006 (no. 45), 27.
288. See above section IV.A.3.
289. L.A. Bebchuk and J.M. Fried, no. 9 above, p. 30 *et seq.*; C.J. Meier-Schatz, no. 254 above, p. 487 *et seq.*
290. See M.C. Jensen and K.J. Murphy, no. 1 above, 55 *et seq.*; L.A. Bebchuk and J.M. Fried, no. 9 above, p. 37 *et seq.* and p. 70 *et seq.*; M. Benz and A. Stutzer, no. 21 above, 9 *et seq.* with further references.
291. These consultants are often conflicted themselves inasmuch as they also offer other services (e.g. search services) for which they hope to be hired after serving as consultants for

label compensation as 'below market', 'at market' or 'above market') may severely constrain the compensation committee's negotiating power, as it encourages managers to demand compensation packages that are not 'below market'.[292, 293] In this context it is important to remember that independent board members who lack firm- and sector-specific know-how are more likely to be tempted to turn to compensation consultants in order to get a feeling for the fair compensation level. Second, setting management compensation by relying on peer group comparisons creates an incentive for managers to influence the composition of the peer group to include businesses in related sectors (or in the same sector but another geographical location) which they know pay well.

b. The Role of Shareholders

With the exception that they cannot dismiss them,[294] shareholders have the same (indirect) powers vis-à-vis the managers as vis-à-vis the directors.[295]

C. Shareholders' Approval for Directors' and/or Management Compensation?

1. Recent Developments

In the wake of recent excesses in executive compensation around the world, the question is now often asked of whether directors' and/or management compensation matters should be brought before the shareholders meeting. This idea is supported by recent studies in the USA, which aim to demonstrate that most boards are unable to conclude arm's-length compensation agreements with executives. The directors bow to the power of management, or follow the advice of biased compensation consultants.[296] In other words, there is a widespread feeling that the control

---

executive pay. Since it is management who will hire them, they have no incentive to displease management.

292. According to M.C. Jensen and K.J. Murphy, survey information provided by compensation consultants has led to systematic increases in executive pay levels, because no executive wants to be paid 'below market.' The authors also think that compensation consultants are rarely retained by the compensation committee, but rather by the company's management or human resources department, which obviously creates potential conflicts of interests. We therefore recommend that if compensation consultants are used at all, it should be in conjunction with other instruments for determining the compensation package. See M.C. Jensen and K.J. Murphy, no. 1 above, 55 *et seq.* and M. Benz and A. Stutzer, no. 21 above, 9 *et seq.* with further references.
293. It is interesting to note that transparency of compensation packages may be counterproductive because it greatly increases the disadvantage of peer group comparisons. The board should remember that peer group comparisons in themselves will never suffice to appropriately set the compensation level.
294. In addition, shareholders also have the power to decide whether the delegation of management competences is admissible at all (art. 716b [1] CO).
295. See section IV.A.3 above.
296. See in particular the recent study by L.A. Bebchuk and J.M. Fried, no. 9 above.

mechanisms available to the board of directors (i.e. the agent) to avoid or mitigate conflicts of interests in the area of executive compensation have failed and that the time has come to enhance the powers of the shareholders (i.e. the principal).

In 2002, the UK adopted a new act pursuant to which the directors' remuneration report[297] must be put on the agenda of the shareholders meeting.[298] A negative vote does not void any agreements, i.e. is 'merely' advisory. In other words, the shareholders' vote is tantamount to a vote of confidence in the work of the compensation committee, focusing in particular on the appropriateness of compensation levels.[299] On 14 December 2004, the Commission of the European Union followed suit and adopted a recommendation,[300] pursuant to which member states are invited to amend their legislation in order to ensure, *inter alia,* that the remuneration policy,[301] including a summary and explanation of the terms of executive directors' contracts,[302] as well as equity-based compensation plans (share participation or share option plans but also compensation that is calculated based on the share price movement),[303] are an explicit item on the agenda of the annual general meetings of listed companies.[304] The shareholder vote may be either binding or advisory.

The debate recently extended to Switzerland.[305] The Swiss expert group on 'Corporate Governance' suggests amending the current article 698 CO to the effect that the articles of a company may provide that resolutions of the board of directors with regard to the compensation policy of board members and management have to

297. The report must include information about compensation committees, performance-related remuneration and liabilities in respect to director contracts, as well as detailed information about director remuneration.
298. The Directors' Remuneration Report Regulations 2002, statutory instrument 2002 no. 1986, <www.opsi.gov.uk>.
299. J.N. Gordon, Executive compensation: If there's a problem, what's the remedy? The case for 'Compensation Disclosure and Analysis' *European Corporate Governance Institute Law Working Paper no.* 35/2005 and *Columbia Law and Economics Research Paper no.* 273 (25 February 2005), 25 *et seq.* <papers.ssrn.com/abstract_id=686464>.
300. Commission Recommendation of 14 December 2004 fostering an appropriate regime for the remuneration of directors of listed companies (2004/913/EC) OJ L 385/55, 2004. The member states are only 'invited' to adopt the provisions of the recommendation in their member state law until 30 June 2006. They are not obliged to do so.
301. Such as the importance of variable and non-variable components, performance criteria for variable components, the link between remuneration and performance, the main parameters and rationale of annual bonus schemes and the main characteristics of supplementary pension or early retirement schemes. See art. 3.3 of the recommendation.
302. Such as information on the duration of contracts with executive directors, notice periods, details of provision for severance payments and other payments linked to early termination. See art. 3.4 of the recommendation.
303. I.e. phantom stock or stock appreciation rights.
304. Art. 4.1 of the recommendation. In addition, share-based remuneration for directors should always be subject to the prior approval of the shareholders.
305. See e.g. D. Leu, no. 26 above, p. 133 *et seq.*; G. Giger, no. 3 above, p. 410 *et seq.*; K. Hofstetter, no. 267 above, p. 520; see P. Böckli, C. Huguenin and F. Dessemontet, no. 232 above, p. 131 *et seq.*; U. Bertschinger, no. 234 above, p. 324.

be submitted to the shareholders meeting for approval.[306] As we have said, we do not entirely believe that such an amendment is necessary, because the present law already allows this type of submission, which could go even further and directly contain elements of the policy. On the other hand, we recognize that there is at present no sign of shareholders wanting to take advantage of this possibility, so that it might make sense for the law to include at least an 'invitation' to submit such resolutions to shareholders.

In addition, when the Swiss Federal Parliament was in the process of amending the Code of Obligations to enforce transparency of directors' and management compensation in listed companies,[307] some members submitted motions which would have required listed companies to include in the articles of incorporation the competence of the shareholders meeting to approve directors' compensation.[308] However, these motions were finally rejected by Parliament.[309]

2. Pros and Cons of Shareholders' Approval

Generally, the question of whether shareholders should receive (additional)[310] rights in compensation matters *de lege ferenda* boils down to the following main issues:

- Whether certain aspects of directors' and/or management compensation should be an explicit and mandatory item on the agenda of the shareholders meeting, or whether they should only be tabled upon request by a certain number of shareholders;
- Which aspects of compensation should be submitted to shareholders;
- Whether the shareholders' vote should be binding or advisory.

We do not consider it necessary that a vote on remuneration at every shareholders meeting be mandatory, but we would encourage the legislator to rethink the necessary thresholds for tabling any item by tying the shareholding level not to nominal capital, but to market value of shares held, or a percentage of the shares.[311] For this

306. See P. Böckli, C. Huguenin and F. Dessemontet, no. 232 above, pp. 14 and 225. In the opinion of these authors, the shareholders meeting can decide 'yes' or 'no', but can not submit another compensation policy. Nevertheless, in the recently published draft of the Swiss Federal Council in regard to a partial reform of Swiss corporate law (<www.bj.admin.ch>), the idea of the Swiss expert group on 'corporate governance' was not picked up.
307. See above section III.C.1 and particularly no. 141.
308. See <www.parlament.ch/ab/frameset/d/s/4708/126184/d_s_4708_126184_126275.htm>.
309. See <www.parlament.ch/ab/frameset/d/n/4709/206748/d_n_4709_206748_206808.htm>.
310. As we mentioned previously, we believe shareholders can introduce a policy into the articles or ask for their approval for a policy to be mandatory, and they can of course dismiss directors.
311. Art. 699 (3) CO sets a threshold of 10 per cent of the share capital for calling a meeting; to table an agenda item for a meeting already called requires holding shares with a total nominal value of CHF 1,000,000.

    Pursuant to the recently published draft on a partial reform of Swiss corporate law as proposed by the Swiss Federal Council (see the *Begleitbericht zum Vorentwurf zur Revision des Aktien- und Rechnungslegungsrechts im Obligationenrecht vom 2. Dezember*

reason, we believe that shareholders should take the initiative, if they are dissatisfied with the compensation system in 'their' company, and resolve an amendment in the articles requiring the board to submit the company's compensation policy to a shareholders' vote (or even include elements of such policy directly in the articles).[312] However, even if the articles of association included a cap, we do not believe that this would necessarily invalidate a future agreement between the company and a new manager in excess of this cap, since the latter would not be disclosed in the Commercial Register although accepting an agreement that exceeded the cap might make the board liable.[313] Furthermore, we do not think that the introduction into the articles of a policy, or the requirement for shareholder approval of a policy, would influence agreements already concluded.[314]

With respect to the possible scope of the shareholders' vote, we do not believe that it should relate to specific compensation agreements of directors and/or managers. While such a vote would certainly help to overcome the problem of conflicts of interests (the principal decides), the downside of such intervention is obvious: The board of directors would be unable to offer a definitive contract, which would significantly impair recruitment because of the uncertainty and the possible embarrassment of a negative shareholder vote.[315] In addition, if existing executives' compensation packages are rejected, the executives in turn are likely to leave the company. We would further argue that the shareholders meeting is not the appropriate corporate body to decide specific management issues, because it lacks case-specific knowledge[316] and the ability to negotiate. Finally, in case of a negative shareholder vote, it would be necessary to convene another shareholders meeting (to approve a new arrangement), which, at least for public companies, would incur unreasonable costs.[317]

2005,<www.bj.admin.ch>), the CO is intended to be amended by setting a threshold of five per cent of the share capital or votes, a holding of shares with a total nominal value of CHF 1,000,000 or a total market value of CHF 5,000,000 for calling a meeting; to table an agenda item for a meeting already called, the draft proposes a threshold of five per cent of the share capital or votes, a holding of shares with a total nominal value of CHF 1,000,000 or a total market value of CHF 2,000,000.

312. A similar view is taken by D. Leu, no. 26 above, p. 137. As mentioned previously in no. 235, a provision in the company's articles of incorporation would be mandatory to duly empower the shareholders meeting to decide on compensation matters.
313. This only applies if the newly hired manager can claim that he did not know about the cap, i.e. acted *bona fide*.
314. Does this mean that the board would then have to terminate existing agreements and offer new ones? This question could be clarified by shareholders' introducing a policy, or by the board introducing one if the policy must be submitted to shareholders.
315. J.N. Gordon, no. 299 above, 25.
316. L.A. Bebchuk and J.M. Fried, no. 9 above, p. 201.
317. Alternatively, it could be provided that if the shareholders vote 'no' then it is up to the board of directors to conclude the compensation agreement. See G. Giger, no. 3 above, pp. 410 with further references. However, this would be very close to making the shareholders' vote advisory.

Furthermore, we believe that advisory shareholders' votes are already possible under the present system[318] (if properly tabled on the agenda – we do not believe in spontaneous votes such as recently took place in one large Swiss company).[319] They might even have certain advantages over binding votes on the policy. The advantage of such votes (which, in our opinion, could apply to specific compensation agreements and also to policies, specific equity plans or the overall compensation level) is that they create a reputational control mechanism: Directors and managers will try to avoid negative exposure in order to keep their attractiveness in the directors and managers market and therefore have an incentive to structure compensation agreements/plans/policies/overall levels in a way that is likely to get past a shareholders' vote.[320] The hope is that '*although a negative vote does not void any contracts or other compensation arrangements, the public force of such a negative expression may lead to a 'voluntary' re-negotiation and a shake-up in the firm's compensation-setting process.*'[321] In the UK, where the shareholders meeting has an advisory vote on the remuneration report, this vote has already had considerable success.[322] Further, we would argue that greater involvement of shareholders in executive compensation may induce companies to discuss executive compensation issues in advance with large shareholders,[323] which in turn would enhance the importance of shareholder supervision as control mechanism within the agency context of a company. This shareholder control, of course, also works in case of binding shareholders' votes, but the advisory vote has the further advantage that existing agreements are not voided and there is even some future flexibility, e.g. if an extraordinarily talented CEO is on the market but demands corresponding compensation.

In considering the pros and cons of shareholders' approval in compensation matters, it is important to bear in mind that *de lege lata* shareholders in Swiss-listed companies already have not just the right to ask questions in regard to compensation, but also the information they require to determine whether compensation is properly handled in their company. If they are dissatisfied, they can, *de lege lata*, do the following:

- Refuse to elect a board member who is promised excessive compensation;
- Dismiss the board and substitute one that promises to change the compensation policy;

---

318. See e.g. P. Böckli, no. 83 above, § 12 n. 42.
319. Shareholders meeting of UBS AG, held on 21 April 2005. See the press release <www.ubs.com/1/e/investors/agm/2005/media_release.html> and the voting results at: <www.ubs.com/1/e/investors/agm/2005/votingresults.html>.
320. For more references on the role of reputation as a control mechanism, see above section II.B.
321. J.N. Gordon, no. 299 above, 26.
322. Shareholders of GlaxoSmithKline roundly rejected a large golden parachute for the CEO. This decision resulted in an overhaul of the company's remuneration committee, a two-thirds reduction in the CEO's golden parachute and stricter terms for vesting options. Other pay packages have been renegotiated. See Jeffrey N. Gordon, no. 299 above, 26 with further references.
323. According to J.N. Gordon, no. 299 above, 26, UK institutional shareholders appear to be mobilized by the vote on the remuneration report rather, as US ones were by the 'just vote no' campaigns against re-electing directors of underperforming firms.

- Express their dissatisfaction with the compensation as a whole, or with individual agreements, by way of a non-binding advisory vote;
- Resolve a change in the articles of association to require approval of the compensation policy prepared by the board or even define certain elements of such policy in the articles (e.g. that compensation should be partly variable – a cap is theoretically also possible but probably not a good idea).

However, with regard to the approval of a compensation policy, if it is to be of real use to the shareholders, the policy should, in our view, contain at least the following elements:

- General principles in regard to the overall level of compensation for directors (executive as well as non-executive) and management. Merely to say that the compensation should be 'competitive' is, in our view, insufficient. On the other hand, we see no need to set an absolute level. A company could, however, state (e.g.) that it intends to remunerate its board and top management with a fixed salary not exceeding 0.3 per cent of its sales, and that variable compensation should not in general exceed 0.8 per cent of sales.
- General principles governing the relationship between fixed and variable compensation for directors (executive as well as non-executive) and management;
- Information on (or definition of) the performance measures applied;
- General principles governing the form of compensation for directors (executive as well as non-executive), i.e. whether the compensation is in the form of cash, (restricted) shares or options (in which case the policy should also specify whether such options are normally issued with strike prices at or above market level, whether such strike prices are adjusted e.g. based on indices, after which period, if any, they vest and when and for how long they become exercisable);
- Specific rules for the granting of shares and share options, e.g. the possibility (or exclusion) of re-pricing and hedging;
- Monitoring and reporting duties;
- General principles governing severance payments;
- General principles governing the use of executive loans and other perquisites;

Against this backdrop, it becomes clear that the only shortcoming is that the shareholders have only limited power to change existing packages. However, as we have stated, this is in any case undesirable.

V. CONCLUSION

For these reasons, we arrive at the following conclusion with respect to executive compensation and dealing with the conflicts of interest associated with defining and negotiating that compensation.

A. THE DESIGN OF EXECUTIVE COMPENSATION ARRANGEMENTS

If the executive function in a company is exerted by persons other than the owners, conflicts of interest arise between the two groups. In order to align the potentially diverging interests, a company must strive to create, *inter alia*, monetary incentives for the executive that provide for a (partial) shift of the business risk to the executive. This leads to the conclusion that performance-based elements should be the cornerstone of every executive compensation package.[324] When designing executive compensation packages that include performance-based elements, the board of directors has a number of performance criteria to choose from (such as accounting-, market-, value- or strategic-based measures). Their choice should be based on the company's strategy, as defined by the board. Because each of these criteria have shortcomings, it is crucial for the board to realize that poorly designed performance measures may be counterproductive (see our examples in section II.D above). Therefore, apart from carefully designing the performance criteria to be applied, the board must institutionalize appropriate control mechanisms in order to monitor executives' actions and prevent them from attempting to profit from the shortcomings inherent in the respective performance criteria.

When designing executive compensation packages, a board of directors should be mindful of the overall objective, namely finding and retaining top talent at rates that are reasonable for the company, while simultaneously aligning the interests of the executives with those of the shareholders. This means that the board must pay particular attention to the three determining factors of compensation:

- The overall target level of compensation;
- The relationship between fixed and variable components;
- The form of compensation.

These factors are strongly interrelated.[325] With regard to setting the overall target level of compensation, the board must take particular care to take into consideration all elements of compensation (particularly fringe benefits) and to start from an analysis of the company's needs and financial resources and then seek executives who fit this definition and who are willing to work within the defined parameters.

If the company cannot find executives on its preferred terms, it will have to adjust its offer. Generally speaking, we would like to stress that, in our view, it is the structure of executive compensation that matters, rather than its level.

While it is difficult to make general suggestions on how compensation should be structured, we have set out a system which is relatively simple and incorporates the elements we deem most significant (see section III.D). This system centres upon our conviction that variable pay should be in (restricted) shares or (preferably) options, which provide greater flexibility in as much as their strike prices can

324. Performance-based compensation should not be limited to managers, but should also be applied to executive directors. In Switzerland, the remuneration of directors is only weakly linked to performance. See *Handelszeitung*, 5 October 2005, B8.
325. For more details see section III.B above.

be adjusted. This also enables companies to include built-in retention elements. In addition, if such compensation has a long-term character (which we would encourage), this will counteract the shortcomings of certain accounting criteria, assuming that manipulations will sooner or later be discovered. However, certain specific legal constraints will have to be observed when designing such compensation structures.

We favour severance payments (but not for non-executive directors), but promised payments must decrease over time. Moreover, we believe that golden parachutes can serve to align the interests of shareholders and executives with respect to takeovers. However, the board must be mindful of the fact that severance payments triggered by early termination or change of control quite often correlate with underperformance by both the executive and the firm, most often as the direct result of the executive's management.

Finally, we believe that granting loans to executives can be a useful tool, but only if such loans are used to purchase shares or options, or to pay taxes associated with the granting of shares and options.

B. Competences in Executive Compensation

The easiest way to eliminate conflicts between shareholders and executives is to include the principal in the decision-making process. Shareholders are already *de lege lata* granted rather broad powers, but only rarely use them. These powers include an entitlement to include in the articles of association a requirement for the board to submit the compensation policy to the shareholders meeting. Shareholders can also make advisory votes, which are not binding, but which are often followed in other countries due to their reputational implications. Such votes can even be taken on individual compensation packages. In short, we do not entirely see the necessity of interference by legislators in this field, with the exception that the law should lower the thresholds for placing items on the agenda of a shareholders meeting.

Legally, the board's duty of loyalty and care plays a key role in executive compensation, which ultimately does not define simply the content of a company's compensation policy, but also the way in which individual agreements are negotiated. This duty of care and loyalty also defines the amount of supervision that will be necessary to prevent the beneficiaries from twisting the rules. Other rules of Swiss company or employment law play only a minor role. Certain issues that arise out of a few (unfortunate) court cases can be avoided if contracts are properly drafted.

The role of the board should, in our view, be strengthened by (largely) staffing it with independent and/or non-executive directors who exert monitoring functions on the compensation committee. In addition, we believe that close co-operation between the compensation committee and the audit committee is important where accounting parameters are used to measure variable pay.

To conclude, we urge shareholders to take a more active role in assessing the compensation systems of the firms they choose to invest in. The quality of management, and the way its efforts are rewarded constitute one of the key drivers of shareholder value, and successful firms are a benefit not only to their owners, but also to the economy and to society at large.

Chapter 3

Executive Compensation: Is Disclosure Enough?

*Rashid Bahar**

Executive compensation is at the heart of heated debates on corporate governance. The issue has drawn perhaps more media attention than any other company-law-related subject, most likely due to the more stringent disclosure rules introduced in the last decade. Pundits, however, are calling for even more regulatory intervention. Recently, the Swiss Parliament decided to reinforce the current self-regulatory regime with a statutory provision.[1] The *Expertenbericht der Arbeitsgruppe 'Corporate Governance' zur Teilrevision des Aktienrechts*, a report on Corporate Governance published by a government-appointed group of experts, suggests a number of additional routes.[2] At the European level, the Commission Recommendation of 14 December 2004, fostering an appropriate regime for the remuneration of

---

* Centre for Banking and Financial Law, University of Geneva. Attorney-at-Law, Bär & Karrer. I would like to thank Dr Thomas Schultz, Dr Valerie Meyer and the participants at the University of Geneva and Université catholique de Louvain in March 2005 and the Gerzensee Seminar in August 2005 for their valuable comments.

1. See *Message relatif à la modification du code des obligations (Transparence des indemnités versées aux membres du conseil d'administration et de la direction) du 23 juin 2004*, FF 2004 4223; Code des obligations (CO) (Transparence des indemnités versées aux membres du conseil d'administration et de la direction), Modification du 7 octobre 2005, FF 2005 5593.
2. See P. Böckli, C. Huguenin-Jacobs and F. Dessemontet (2003); P. Böckli, C. Huguenin-Jacobs and F. Dessemontet (2004).

L. Thévenoz and R. Bahar (eds.), *Conflicts of Interest: Corporate Governance and Financial Market*, pp. 85–136.

directors of listed companies,[3] also calls for broad reforms in this area. The purpose of this paper is to assess the success of disclosure in controlling executive compensation.

The article consists of four sections. Section I sets out the goals of executive compensation. This section distinguishes three main goals in particular, including the use of pay as an incentive mechanism and a remedy to agency conflicts. It also considers the practical difficulties involved in setting up an effective performance-based compensation system.

Section II considers the governance of executive compensation, highlighting the inherent conflict of interest and the agency problem generally and examining why neither improved corporate governance at board level nor shareholder action can effectively solve these problems.

Section III examines the interaction between disclosure and executive compensation. This section discusses the current regulatory framework and assesses its efficacy, but also stresses the new problems resulting from this remedy.

Section IV takes a step back and considers the underlying problem with the governance of executive compensation: the lack of emphasis on shareholders. The author suggests how shareholders can be put back at the centre of the corporate system.

I. PURPOSE OF EXECUTIVE COMPENSATION

A. THREE PERSPECTIVES ON EXECUTIVE COMPENSATION

1. Fairness

In the last decade, executive compensation has been the subject of debate among numerous circles in Europe and the United States. Corporate governance specialists, compensation experts and institutional investors have long discussed how to pay executives and board members, but they are not alone: unions, political parties and the media at large have also taken strong stances on the issue.

These different actors take different views on what executive compensation ought to be and what principles and policies should guide the applicable laws and regulations. Putting it briefly, two approaches collide.

First, the media and politicians echo a concern that absolute levels of executive compensation are too high, if not indecent. Behind this concern lies a general call for more distributive justice in society at large.

This paper does not inquire further into this 'moral' or 'fairness-based' critique.[4] However, the main weakness of this approach lies in its focus on a single group of individuals, executives and directors, while letting others, such as show-business and sporting celebrities and wealthy heirs, enjoy their wealth immune to

---

3. Recommendation of 14 December 2004, fostering an appropriate regime for the remuneration of directors of listed companies (2004/913/EC), OJ L 385/55, 2004.
4. L.A. Bebchuk and J.M. Fried (2004), p. 8.

such attacks.[5] In spite of its theoretical shortcomings, this theory enjoys a measure of popularity with the public at large and is very often voiced by politicians and other leading opinion makers, including trade unionists and journalists.[6] As such, the theory sets an additional, although undesirable, constraint on executive compensation,[7] and therefore cannot be entirely ignored when examining the issue of executive compensation.[8]

2. Agency

A second approach focuses on the agency conflict between managers and shareholders: in most companies, investors do not manage the company's affairs, trusting that the managers will carry out this task for them. This constitutes what economists term an agency relationship, which in turn creates an agency conflict: the incentives of the agents (the managers) are not aligned with those of the principals (the shareholders).[9]

This problem is particularly acute in publicly traded companies without a controlling shareholder, where, as A.A. Berle and G. Means (1932) noted in their classic study, ownership is separated from control. Although this paper focuses on such entities, it is important to stress that the problem permeates all types of business organizations, including small and medium-sized enterprises where shareholders are more active. For instance, in a typical Continental European Mid-Cap, a strong blockholder may effectively monitor management, but at the same time he may also be colluding with executives to the detriment of the other shareholders.

To limit the agency conflict, the principals may monitor their agents in an attempt to ensure that the latter are actually acting in their interests. On the other side of the bargaining table, the agents may also take measures to prove to the principals that they have the investors' interests at heart; they may, for example, hire accountants, set up a compliance system or comply with corporate governance codes. Nevertheless, these steps entail costs for the principals or the agents, which add to the residual agency cost.[10] All these efforts drain resources away from more productive uses.

Instead of focusing only on agency costs and trying to find more efficient means to monitor or bond managers, economists have argued that compensation could be used to mitigate the agency conflict. Assuming that executives are influenced by financial incentives, a generous payment scheme can be beneficial for shareholders

5. Ibid; S.M. Bainbridge (2005), 1,621.
6. See e.g. the book by D. Schütz (2005).
7. See K. Murphy (1999), 2, 251–2,254.
8. M.C. Jensen and K. Murphy (1990b), 254; P.L. Joskow, N.L. Rose and C.D. Wolfram (1996), 165.
9. See S. Ross (1973), 165; M.C. Jensen and W.H. Meckling (1976), 308. See also the theoretical work pioneered by B. Holmstrom (1979), 74; B. Holmstrom (1982), 324; S.J. Grossman and O.D. Hart (1983), 7.
10. M.C. Jensen and W.H. Meckling (1976), 308.

and the firm more generally.[11] From this perspective, as M.C. Jensen and K. Murphy (1990a, 1990b) have suggested, it is not how much managers are paid, but how they are paid that matters: High pay is not a problem if it yields better performance. Conversely, there is no point in paying managers a low wage if they then act like bureaucrats.[12]

3. Intrinsic Motivation

Even in academic circles, the agency approach to executive compensation is subject to criticism. A third approach to remuneration, one promoted by L.A. Stout (2003) and B.S. Frey and M. Osterloh (2005), casts doubt on the idea that financial incentives motivate top executives appropriately. These authors claim that large, performance-driven packages are not necessary and can even have perverse effects. Rather than suggest focusing on other sources of extrinsic motivation, such as the need for esteem, self-actualization, prestige and intrinsic motivation, where the activity of the agent increases the utility.[13]

From this perspective, high-powered incentive plans are dangerous, because they can crowd out other sources of motivation[14] or crowd in managers who conform to the type of the self-centred, profit-seeking individual that underlies the agency theory.[15] Once executive compensation corresponds to the quality of management, the need for intrinsic motivation decreases and gradually fades away. At the same time, incentive packages legitimize the self-serving behavioural assumption that is at the heart of agency theory: as a result of incentive packages, greed becomes good (to paraphrase the character Gordon Gecko in the 1987 film *Wall Street*).

The crowding out of ethical values using money as an incentive is well documented by behavioural scientists. U. Gneezy and A. Rustichini (2000), for instance, observed that fining parents for picking up their children late from a day-care centre led to a significantly *lower* level of punctuality. Instead of feeling guilty for being late, parents felt they could simply buy themselves out.[16] This may constitute an argument against high-powered incentive packages, and might explain the low pay-performance sensitivity of executive compensation packages.

However, once the dyke is breached it is hard to prevent the flood. The crowding-out effect of monetarizing performance is not reversible: In the day-care study, when the fine was discontinued, punctuality remained at the lower level. The use of financial penalties had already undermined norms of good conduct and the

11. See, from the theoretical perspective, the seminal papers by S. Ross (1973), 134; B. Holmstrom (1979), 74; S.J. Grossman and O.D. Hart (1983), 7.
12. M.C. Jensen and K. Murphy (1990a), 138; M.C. Jensen and K. Murphy (1990b), 225. See also L.A. Bebchuk and R. Jackson (2005), 8. However, see also B.S. Frey and M. Osterloh (2005).
13. See L.A. Stout (2003), 1; B.S. Frey and M. Osterloh (2005), 11–14.
14. B.S. Frey and M. Osterloh (2005), 16–21.
15. Ibid. 23–25. See also E. Fehr and S. Gächter (2002); E. Fehr and B. Rockenbach (2003).
16. B.S. Frey, F. Oberholzer-Gee and R. Eichenberger (1996); B.S. Frey and F. Oberholzer-Gee (1997); U. Gneezy and A. Rustichini (2000).

parents no longer felt compelled to pick up their children on time.[17] Thus, although high-powered performance packages may be les than optimal, it may already be too late to rely solely on intrinsic motivation to provide adequate incentives to managers. Performance-based pay may thus be unavoidable.

B. Executive Compensation as a Source of Agency Conflicts

The disadvantage of using remuneration to solve the agency conflict is that, if agents, executives or the board, are in charge of setting the compensation policy, they may fall prey to agency conflicts and thus fail to provide managers with desirable incentives.[18] The managers may receive numerous perks and other fringe benefits quite regardless of their performance. This may translate into excessively luxurious facilities at corporate headquarters, a corporate art collection or the executive jet.[19]

Moreover, incentives are not always beneficial. They may induce managers to focus myopically on the short term. They may also lead managers to strive to meet an earnings target for the current quarter at the expense of future earnings or long-term relationships. In the most extreme cases, managers may even engage in dubious practices, such as earnings management, expectations management or even outright fraud.[20]

C. Risk Aversion and Non-Diversification of Managers

A more intractable difficulty relates to diversification and risk aversion. From the perspective of the economy at large, firms ought to take risks if the weighted probability of profit is sufficiently high. Some may lose money, some may even go bankrupt, but others will create considerable profits, outweighing the losses of the others. Investors, particularly shareholders, also share this interest in risk taking. Through a diversified portfolio, shareholders can buy into most firms and thus set off their losses against their profits.[21]

17. U. Gneezy and A. Rustichini (2000), 1–18.
18. This is the fundamental critique underlying the managerial power theory of L.A. Bebchuk, J.M. Fried and D.I. Walker (2002); L.A. Bebchuk and J.M. Fried (2004).
19. See M.C. Jensen and W.H. Meckling (1976), 312. However, this outlay may be useful to the company and its shareholders: a firm that had its headquarters in a run-down shack would undoubtedly experience difficulties in hiring and retaining qualified employees and acquiring the trust of its clients. In a word, such expenditure may serve to enhance productivity or signal the status of the beneficiary. R.G. Rajan and J. Wulf (2004) question whether most perks are actually a sign of managerial excess, pointing out, for instance, that CEOs who have a corporate jet tend to be based in relatively remote locations.
20. See generally F. Degeorge, J. Patel and R. Zeckhauser (1999); M.C. Jensen (2003); and M.C. Jensen, K. Murphy and E.J. Wruck (2004), 45–48. See also B.S. Frey and M. Osterloh (2005).
21. M. Ruffner (2000), p. 218. See the groundbreaking paper by H. Markowitz (1952) and, for a general introduction, R.A. Brealy and S.C. Myers (2003), p. 187.

By contrast, managers and employees cannot diversify their exposure.[22] They can work for only one firm at a time and they rely exclusively on their job for their salary. If their employer goes bankrupt, they risk losing all their future salary and the firm-specific human capital they invested in learning how the organization operated. If the firm performs badly or even goes out of business, the CEO is likely to have a hard time finding a comparable job. The CEO's track record will be stained, and in any case most CEOs are hired internally, rarely jumping from the highest position in one company to a comparable position in another.[23] Overall, this fact makes managers more inclined to be risk averse. They will nearly always tend to stick with a safe bet, even if taking a risk might reap higher profits.[24]

D. The Difficulty of Designing an Appropriate Compensation Scheme

As we have seen, a well-designed executive compensation scheme can mitigate, but not avert, all three types of agency conflict-related problems by tying the fate of managers to that of their shareholders. If pay and performance are linked, the manager will feel the consequences of his actions, and will thus feel the need to maximize the corporation's performance in order to receive the highest pay-off.

However, the ideal compensation scheme is highly difficult to design. Indeed, no such scheme can ever be perfect; no compensation scheme short of transferring all of the profits and risks of the company to the manager will avoid the agency conflict.[25] Short of giving away the firm, even less-radical versions of highly sensitive pay-performance contracts are hard to implement: shareholders are not likely to let managers take away a huge slice of the firm. Conversely, few executives are willing, e.g. by personally assuming liability, to compensate firms and their shareholders for negative performance caused by their poor management.[26]

Second, a compensation scheme must take account of the risk-aversion of undiversified managers. To coin a phrase: a dollar of fixed compensation in the hand is worth more to a manger than a dollar of variable compensation in the bush. Assuming that the company and its shareholders are risk-neutral, or at least less risk-averse, than the manager, it will cost the company more to use an incentive scheme than to pay the manager a flat salary.[27]

22. F.H. Easterbrook and D.R. Fischel (1991), pp. 29–30; M. Ruffner (2000), p. 218. See, in the specific context of options, B.J. Hall and K.J. Murphy (2002), 8–21.
23. See the empirical data in C.E. Fee and C.J. Hadlock (2003).
24. F.H. Easterbrook and D.R. Fischel (1991), pp. 29–30; M. Ruffner (2000), p. 219; S.M. Bainbridge (2005), 1,621. This point was also made by M.C. Jensen and W.H. Meckling (1976), 314.
25. See, from a theoretical point of view, the seminal papers of B. Holmstrom (1979); S.J. Grossman and O.D. Hart (1983).
26. M.C. Jensen and K. Murphy (1990b), 244.
27. Ibid. See also, in the specific context of options, B.J. Hall and K.J. Murphy (2002).

Finally, factors other than the sheer efforts of the executives influence the performance of a company.[28] Many factors are beyond the control of executives and, if incorporated in the incentive scheme, enable executives to profit from random events; in other words: pure 'luck': M. Bertrand and S. Mullainathan (2001), for example, show how oil price fluctuations impact the performance of companies in the oil industry, and how exchange-rate variations and sector-wide fluctuations affect a broader set of firms. In both cases, these fluctuations are directly reflected in the value of executives' equity compensation, although executives could not influence them in any way.[29]

In view of the uncertainties and difficulties of designing an appropriate incentive scheme, the issue of who gets to decide the compensation comes to the fore. As there is no real consensus on the purpose or content of incentive schemes, it is not advisable to regulate the structure of executive compensation. Failing a substantive standard, decision-making power is of prime importance. The person, or group of persons, who set up the executive compensation package has more or less unfettered discretion.

II. GOVERNANCE OF EXECUTIVE COMPENSATION

A. The Bargaining Paradigm and its Shortcomings

1. Limited Decision-Making Power of Shareholders

Under Swiss law, executive compensation is generally deemed to fall within the residual competence of the board of directors,[30] if not its exclusive domain.[31] In other words, the board can determine its own compensation without consulting the shareholders. Swiss corporate law does not specify any specific rules on executive compensation granting shareholders a right of governance, except for *tantièmes*.

Using *tantièmes*, the general meeting of shareholders can allot a share of the earnings to the company's directors.[32] Under Swiss law, this type of compensation requires an express provision in the articles of incorporation and cannot take place unless the mandatory payments have been made into the statutory reserve funds and the company has paid out a dividend of at least five per cent of the nominal value of the shares.[33]

The percentage of *tantièmes* payable to directors can either be definitively specified in the articles of incorporation,[34] or can be left to the discretion of the

---

28. This point is clearly made from a theoretical point of view by B. Holmstrom (1979).
29. M. Bertrand and S. Mullainathan (2001), 907–910.
30. Art. 716 (2) CO. See D. Daeniker (2005), 384; R. Ruedin (2005), p. 329.
31. Art. 716*a* (1)(4) CO. See P. Böckli (2004), §13, no. 426.
32. R. Ruedin (2005), p. 321.
33. Art. 677 CO and Art. 698 (1)(4) CO.
34. A. Nussbaumer and H.C. von der Crone (2005), 94. See ATF 75 II 149. In such a case, exceptionally, each director is entitled to sue for the payment of his share of the *tantièmes*, even if the general meeting did not vote for the payment.

general meeting,[35] which in either case will have to vote for the payment. In practice, however, Swiss public companies seldom use this instrument, because, unlike other forms of compensation, they cannot be expensed.[36] Instead, these companies usually prefer to pay their directors and executives performance fees or bonuses, which are deductible from the taxable profit.

The other exception to directors' power over executive compensation is the issuance of new shares and, in particular, the creation of conditional capital to hedge the company's obligation to deliver shares under a stock option or a stock ownership plan.[37] But even then shareholders have little say: they do not vote on the specifics of the plan, or even on the plan's underlying policy. Shareholders are simply asked to allow the company to issue a given number of new shares. The board is not required to submit the terms and conditions of the employee stock option plan to shareholders prior to the general meeting. And if the board does not want to put the issue to the vote, it can have recourse to share buybacks[38] or a hedging agreement with a financial institution.[39]

In summary, Swiss shareholders have only a limited say on executive compensation; the board of directors is the key decision-maker. It sets its own compensation, as well as that of managers, regardless of how it decides to pay them: through board membership fees, service agreements, employment contract or a stock option plan.

The *Expertenbericht der Arbeitsgruppe 'Corporate Governance' zur Teilrevision des Aktienrechts*, a report on corporate governance published by a government-appointed group of experts, does not suggest any radical reforms to the governance of executive compensation. It reluctantly suggests allowing companies to pass an amendment to their articles of incorporation, requiring the general meeting to vote on equity incentive plans,[40] without considering other aspects of compensation policy. This proposal was taken up by the government as a part of its plan to revise company law,[41] without examining other options.

---

35. P. Kurer (2002) ad art. 677 CO, no. 7; R. Ruedin (2005), p. 324.
36. P. Kurer (2002) ad art. 677 CO, no. 18. As *tantièmes* are paid out of the company's profits, they are not expensed and thus cannot be deducted, unlike fees or salary payments. At the same time, *tantièmes* provide the director with an additional source of taxable income. See e.g. P. Kurer (2002) ad art. 677 CO, no. 18; P. Böckli (2004), §12, no. 5; D. Daeniker (2005), 385.
37. Art. 653 (1) CO. Although the wording of this provision refers only to employees, there is no doubt that directors too may benefit from such a stock option plan. See e.g. P. Isler and G. Zindel (2002) ad art. 653 CO, no. 16a.
38. Art. 659 CO. Under Swiss law, the board of directors, and not the general meeting, is competent to decide to buy back shares on the basis of the general applicability of art. 716 (1) CO. See H. Peter and R. Bahar (2000), p. 25; A. von Planta and C. Lenz (2002) ad art. 659 CO, no. 2a; P. Böckli (2004), §4, no. 235. Compare with Art. 19 of the Second Company Law Directive 77/91/EEC of 13 December 1976, OJ L 26, 31.1.1977, p. 1 (requiring the approval of the general meeting).
39. See *Association CANES c. Nestlé S.A.*, ATF 117 II 290.
40. P. Böckli, C. Huguenin-Jacobs and F. Dessemontet (2004), pp. 131–134.
41. Art. 627 (4) draft CO. *Begleitbericht zum Vorentwurf zur Revision des Aktien- und Rechnungslegungsrechts im Obligationenrecht vom 2. Dezember 2005*, available at: <www.bj.admin.ch>, p. 40.

2. Decision-Making Power of the Board of Directors

The board's power to set executive compensation fits with the general governance framework at the heart of most corporate law systems. Management of company affairs is not a matter for shareholders to ponder; it is the job of directors and managers. Shareholders have neither the time nor the qualifications to carry out this activity. Even if they did, they would be faced with substantial collective action problems. Therefore, they appoint directors to act for them. These specialized agents are empowered to select and supervise management and take all important corporate decisions.[42] Thus directors should also be able to set the remuneration of managers. This applies in particular to performance-based pay, which must go hand in hand with strategic orientations and objectives. The variable elements in the compensation package should depend on the strategic choices, and it would be hard to require the board to set the direction if it could not also set the incentives.[43]

Under the dominant approach to corporate law, executive compensation can safely rest with the board, which will bargain with management.[44] This system promises an arm's-length process and results in a presumably fair outcome. It also puts a small group of specialized agents in charge of the negotiation. Directors can contribute their knowledge and expertise and thus achieve a better result than the shareholders could be expected to reach if left to their own devices.[45] Directors are also bound by a statutory duty of care and loyalty, and thus can be expected to act in the best interests of the company.[46]

Several market mechanisms reinforce the bargaining-by-the-board paradigm and constrain the board's discretion to set executive compensation: The board must take account of the labour market in which it operates. It must consider the general conditions under which CEOs in the same sector and geographic location are hired. If the board is not sufficiently generous with regard to compensation, it will simply not be able to hire qualified executives. However, if it is too generous, the directors themselves will suffer. Directors must sell themselves on the directorship market and risk losing their reputation as good directors.[47] The firm will also suffer in the product market, due to the competitive disadvantage that results from unqualified

---

42. See art. 716 (1) CO defining the core attributes of the board of directors under Swiss law. See also under US law, Del. Code Ann. tit. 8, §141(a) (2001); Model Bus. Corp. Act Ann. §8.01 cmt. (1995).
43. P. Böckli, C. Huguenin-Jacobs and F. Dessemontet (2004), pp. 133–134.
44. D. Daeniker (2005), 386. See. L.A. Bebchuk and J.M. Fried (2004), p. 17–18, who are extremely critical of this view.
45. See in defence of this view P. Böckli, C. Huguenin-Jacobs and F. Dessemontet (2003), p. 8; D. Daeniker (2005), 386.
46. Art. 717 (1) CO.
47. E.F. Fama (1980), 297–298.

CEOs or over-generous compensation packages. In time, this will affect the bottom line and in extreme cases could lead to the downfall of the firm.[48]

3. Shortcomings of the Bargaining Paradigm

a. Conflicts of Interest at Board Level

In the last few years, several authors, in particular L.A. Bebchuk, J.M. Fried and D.I. Walker (2002) and L.A. Bebchuk and J.M. Fried (2004), have challenged this contractual paradigm[49] due to one key shortcoming: directors are agents. Although directors owe a duty of loyalty to the company, their very status carries the risk that they will not do their absolute best to negotiate the best deal for the company. But this issue is not peculiar to executive compensation; it permeates the entire corporate system. What makes remuneration unusual is that, unlike other corporate decisions, it directly impacts the status of directors and managers. In the worst case, the board of directors sets the compensation of its members, thus creating an egregious conflict of interest.[50]

From a formalistic standpoint, the board can easily avoid this conflict. A director is in a conflict only when his own compensation package is under review. In such a situation, he is under a duty to abstain from voting.[51] When the other directors decide on his package, they will seem to have avoided the conflict,[52] but in reality the problem will persist because most non-executive directors receive comparable packages, which means that all board members will have a personal interest in favouring their peers.[53] In other words, directors indirectly set their own compensation packages and the conflict of interest remains. Oddly enough, this

48. F.H. Easterbrook (1984), 554–564. See also F.H. Easterbrook and D.R. Fischel (1991), pp. 19–20. But see L.A. Bebchuk and J.M. Fried (2004), p. 57–58.
49. L.A. Bebchuk, J.M. Fried and D.I. Walker (2002); L.A. Bebchuk and J.M. Fried (2003); and L.A. Bebchuk and J.M. Fried (2004). See also M.C. Jensen (2003); M.C. Jensen (2004); and M.C. Jensen, K. Murphy and E.J. Wruck (2004).
50. P. Böckli, C. Huguenin-Jacobs and F. Dessemontet (2003), pp. 7–8; *Message relatif à la modification du code des obligations (Transparence des indemnités versées aux membres du conseil d'administration et de la direction) du 23 juin 2004*, FF 2004 4223, 4227. See also R. Ruedin (2005), pp. 329–330.
51. There are, however, no express requirements for dealing with conflicts of interest under Swiss corporate law. This duty stems from the duty of loyalty (Art. 717 [1] CO) and Art. 15 Swiss Code of Best Practice for Corporate Governance. The duty to abstain is widely recognized by Swiss legal scholars. See e.g. R. Watter (2002) ad art. 717 CO, no. 15; P. Böckli (2004), §13, no. 643–644, but see H.C. von der Crone (1994), 5. Case law also recognizes such a duty for contractual actions (though it has not been discussed with regard to internal decisions: see ATF 127 III 332, c. 2a/bb; ATF 126 III 361, c. 5a.
52. But cf. B. Brechbühl (2004), 34 (considering that if a director in untenable conflict, he must submit the compensation decision either to the entire board or to the general meeting of shareholders under the principles developed in ATF 127 III 332).
53. R. Ruedin (2005), pp. 329–330. See also D. Daeniker (2005), 386–387 (rejecting delegation to the board).

problem, unlike executive compensation, has attracted little attention from either the general public or the experts,[54] perhaps simply because the amounts at stake are substantially lower.[55]

Although the problem is less acute with respect to executive directors and managers, because they can remain aloof of the board meeting and negotiate with non-executive directors, the issue is not negligible. They may have connections with non-executive members, through interlocking directorships; they may be in a position to impact the position of the non-executives, for instance if the latter have other links with the company. This can lead to further conflicts of interest, which must again be tackled through abstention.[56]

Non-managing directors are often themselves executives or former executives of other companies.[57] Although legally this is not a sufficient reason to question their loyalty (except in cases of interlocking directorships, where the conflict of interest is clear), they are likely to feel more sympathetic to the interests of executives. This may be a conscious decision or, as suggested by L.A. Bebchuk and J.M. Fried (2004), a cognitive dissonance. Behavioural scientists have noted that individuals develop beliefs to support positions consistent with their own self-interest. This allows them to avoid the discomfort of enjoying benefits that they believe to be undeserved.[58] Therefore, a director who holds an executive position with another company will not scrutinize the compensation scheme of managers too harshly if she herself profits from a similar package.

b. *Influence of Management at Board Level*

In addition to these conflicted situations, executives can also exert substantial influence on the decision-making process at board level, even if they do not take part in the discussions of the compensation committee or the board itself. Boards and committees rarely have sufficient time or information to make informed decisions. Very often, compensation packages are assembled by the Human Resources department and reviewed by management before being submitted to the board or the remuneration committee for approval.[59] Management may also hire compensation consultants to ensure they have a solid case before proceeding.[60] The compensation

54. But see P. Böckli, C. Huguenin-Jacobs and F. Dessemontet (2003), pp. 7–8; *Message relatif à la modification du code des obligations (Transparence des indemnités versées aux membres du conseil d'administration et de la direction) du 23 juin 2004*, FF 2004 4223, 4227; B. Brechbühl (2004), 34; R. Ruedin (2005), pp. 329–330.
55. In Switzerland, the highest-paid non-executive directors earn an average CHF 300,000 annually, whereas the best-paid executives average more than CHF 20 million.
56. L.A. Bebchuk and J.M. Fried (2004), pp. 29–30.
57. Ibid., p. 31.
58. Ibid., p. 33.
59. Ibid., pp. 37–39; M.C. Jensen, K. Murphy and E.J. Wruck (2004), 50–51.
60. K. Murphy (2002), 853–854; L.A. Bebchuk and J.M. Fried (2004), pp. 37–39; M.C. Jensen (2004), 50, 55–56.

committee and the board of directors will be more or less compelled to rubber-stamp the proposal of management.[61]

This problem is obviously acute if the executive whose compensation is under review is already working for the company or is even on the board. Under the Swiss Code of Best Practice for Corporate Governance, the CEO is entitled to take part in the deliberations of the compensation committee, except where his own remuneration is under discussion.[62] The pre-existing relationships of directors and managers strengthen this distortion of the negotiation process: the former are often ex-managers of the same company, or executives in other companies. In either case they may be lenient, either because they want to favour their former protégés who have made it to the executive suite or because they personally stand to profit if the overall level of executive compensation is high; they will be in a stronger position when negotiating their own remuneration with their own boards.[63]

The development of corporate governance over the last decade has certainly contributed to reducing the influence of management on how a board determines executive compensation, but has not yet slowed the steady escalation of that compensation.[64] One reason for this is the composition and psychology of boards.

c. *Lack of Emotional Independence*

The entire environment of directors tends to discourage the development of the sort of emotional independence that would enable them to negotiate at arm's length with executives. As L.A. Bebchuk and J.M. Fried (2004) note, even 'independent' directors are likely to have some social connection with the CEO and other senior executives; and may in fact even be close friends.[65] This comment, originally applied to the businesses in the US, applies even more directly to Switzerland; a small country in which the pool of potential directors is relatively small. Moreover, even if a director does not know the CEO prior to her appointment, she will become acquainted with him in the course of her work and feel indebted to him, particularly if the CEO was involved in bringing her on board; a situation that creates a reciprocity requirement.[66]

Even the most independent director knows that her job is not limited to setting the executives' compensation packages. She also must collaborate with them to run the company. She has to be a team player if she wants to contribute constructively to business and financial decisions, which are a key part of her job as director. Therefore, even when hiring a new CEO who cannot exert any direct influence

61. Cf. K. Murphy (1999), pp. 2,517–2,518, suggesting that while compensation committees are not simply rubber stamps, they do systematically favour CEOs.
62. See Section 25 Swiss Code of Best Practice for Corporate Governance.
63. K. Murphy (1999), pp. 2,517–2,518.
64. K. Murphy (2002), 852. This does not mean that corporate governance is useless in terms of improving pay–performance sensitivity. See L.A. Bebchuk and J.M. Fried (2004), pp. 81–83.
65. L.A. Bebchuk and J.M. Fried (2004), p. 31.
66. Ibid; M.C. Jensen, K. Murphy and E.J. Wruck (2004), 54–55.

on the board, she cannot take an overly aggressive stance against executives when discussing their pay without the running the risk of jeopardizing the functioning of the board as a whole.[67] Professional negotiators working on behalf of executives are aware of this fact and obviously are not afraid to exploit it:

> 'Joe [Bachelder, perhaps the most famous of such negotiators] took me aside after one contract,' says Michael Valentino, an executive who has worked at several drug companies, 'and told me: "I knew on Day One that we were going to get everything you wanted." When Mr. Valentino asked why, Mr. Bachelder told him that the hiring company had mistakenly put its general counsel in charge of the talks. 'When this is over, you're going to be that guy's boss,' Mr. Bachelder explained. 'He knows that. He can't fight you too hard on anything.'[68]

This problem is worsened by the fact that directors are the agents of distant and diffuse principals. The average director hardly ever sees the shareholders. At best, she will see and hear a small, unrepresentative group of them at the annual general meeting. This problem is even more acute for non-executive directors, because they, unlike the executives, do not often participate in discussions with institutional investors or analysts who may echo the concerns of the shareholders. By contrast, directors come into contact and interact with executives on a regular basis. They see each other at board meetings, take decisions together or are briefed by the executives. They are a team and seek a common goal. Independent directors, therefore, are likely to feel emotionally closer to the executives than to their shareholders. In spite of their duty to achieve the best deal possible for shareholders, they will be soft on the executives, if not ostentatiously generous.[69]

B. Corporate Governance Solutions

1. Improvements at Board Level

To mitigate these shortcomings, corporate governance analysts have championed several measures to improve control over executive compensation, for example smaller boards.[70] J.E. Core, R.W. Holthausen and D.F. Larcker (1999) find that CEO compensation increases when the board is larger.[71] D. Yermack (1996) also observes that pay/performance sensitivity decreases as the size of the board increases.[72]

67. L.A. Bebchuk and J.M. Fried (2004), pp. 39–41; M.C. Jensen, K. Murphy and E.J. Wruck (2004), 54–55.
68. G. Anders, 'Upping the Ante: As Some Decry Lavish CEO Pay, Joe Bachelder Makes It Happen', *Wall Street Journal*, 25 June 2003.
69. L.A. Bebchuk and J.M. Fried (2004), pp. 33–37.
70. Ibid., p. 81.
71. J.E. Core, R.W. Holthausen and D.F. Larcker (1999), 371.
72. D. Yermack (1996), 185.

In Switzerland, apart from initiatives at company level, these measures are essentially a matter of self-regulation by the Swiss Code of Best Practice for Corporate Governance, a non-binding corporate governance code drawn up by *economiesuisse*, a lobby of Swiss companies, together with SWX Swiss Exchange, and endorsed by major firms and institutional investors. Unlike comparable codes, it is not subject to the 'comply or explain' rule. Companies are free to disregard its principles without even having to explain why. With respect to executive compensation, the Swiss Code of Best Practice recommends that companies set up a compensation committee, which ought to consist of a majority of independent[73] and non-executive directors.[74] This corporate governance code is far from perfect: it advises committees to consult the chair of the board and the leading executive (i.e. the CEO), except when reviewing the remuneration of these persons. In other words, the chair and the CEO can influence compensation policy directly at committee level.[75] Moreover, although the committee is in charge of preparing compensation packages and policies for both board members and executives, the final say rests with the board, which retains the exclusive competence to decide upon such matters.[76]

Though the rules are not binding, most Swiss listed companies do follow them: in 2004, 44 per cent of the 100 largest companies included in the SPI index included a remuneration committee and an additional 40 per cent have set up a joint remuneration and appointments committee, leaving only 16 per cent with no similar institutional mechanism.[77] And compliance with these rules is still on the rise. In 2003, 22 per cent of companies had neither a remuneration committee nor a joint appointments/remuneration committee. On a more qualitative level, 40 per cent had a sufficiently independent committee, while 35 per cent had a committee that was insufficiently independent, or included an executive as a member[78]

At the international level, as suggested by Commission's Recommendation of 15 February 2005 on the role of non-executive or supervisory directors of listed companies and on the committees of the (supervisory) board, these committees

73. Under Section 25 Swiss Code of Best Practice for Corporate Governance. 'Independent members shall mean non-executive members of the Board of Directors who never were or have not been for three years members of the executive management and who have no or comparatively minor business relations with the company.' Cf. on independence Annex 2 to Commission Recommendation of 15 February 2005 on the role of non-executive or supervisory directors of listed companies and on the committees of the (supervisory) board (Text with EEA relevance) (2005/162/EC), OJ L 52/51, 2005.
74. See Section 25 Swiss Code of Best Practice for Corporate Governance.
75. Ibid., Section 25. The same principle is applicable under Section 2.3 (2) of Annex 1 to Commission Recommendation of 15 February 2005 on the role of non-executive or supervisory directors of listed companies and on the committees of the (supervisory) board (Text with EEA relevance) (2005/162/EC), OJ L 52/51, 2005.
76. Section 25 Swiss Code of Best Practice for Corporate Governance.
77. See Ethos (2004), p. 28.
78. Ethos (2003), p. 17.

should be entitled to choose their own compensation consultants rather than rely on an adviser selected and briefed by management.[79]

The development of corporate governance practices during the last decade has certainly contributed to reducing management's influence on executive compensation. However, it seems that these process-based approaches have done little to prevent the inflation of remuneration packages,[80] although some of the blame may be laid on other factors such as the stock market boom or misperception of the real cost of options.[81]

2. Control by Shareholders

Ideally, shareholders should be able to remedy an imperfect decision-making process at board level. If given appropriate powers to monitor the compensation scheme effectively, the principals can, in theory, correct the shortcomings of their agents.[82] This approach seems to work at least when large shareholders can counteract the power of management. M. Bertrand and S. Mullainathan (2001) point out that companies with large blockholders are less likely to reward their CEOs for events beyond their control; in other words, for simply getting lucky.[83] J.C. Hartzell and L.T. Starks (2003) also point out that firms with institutional investors tend to have lower levels of executive compensation and higher pay–performance sensitivity.[84]

This monitoring assumes the existence of institutional arrangements enabling shareholders to take an active part in the governance of the company. Traditionally, corporate law analysts have distinguished three kinds of monitoring mechanism: control by voice, control by exit and control in court by legal remedies. All three are at best imperfect tools for tackling executive compensation.

a. Lack of Control by Vote

Currently, control by vote has only a limited impact on executive compensation. As we have seen, under Swiss law, shareholders are not entitled to vote on executive compensation; the issue is left to the board of directors and its committees. In exception cases, shareholders can be called upon to pay *tantièmes* to directors or vote on a capital increase to fund a stock option plan. However, in both instances, this right has no real practical effect and is easily circumvented.[85]

---

79. See Section 3.3 (2) of Annex 1 to Commission Recommendation of 15 February 2005 on the role of non-executive or supervisory directors of listed companies and on the committees of the (supervisory) board (Text with EEA relevance) (2005/162/EC), OJ L 52/51, 2005.
80. K. Murphy (2002), 852.
81. L.A. Bebchuk and J.M. Fried (2004), pp. 73–74; M.C. Jensen, K. Murphy and E.J. Wruck (2004), 35–44.
82. L.A. Bebchuk and J.M. Fried (2004), p. 83.
83. M. Bertrand and S. Mullainathan (2001), 301.
84. See also J.C. Hartzell and L.T. Starks (2003), 2,351.
85. See Section II.A.1 above.

In default of a right to vote on a compensation scheme, shareholders can in theory refuse to grant a discharge of liability to the members of the board and managers[86] or, even more radically, remove them from the board.[87] But these instruments are quite ineffective: the discharge has mainly a symbolic effect.[88] The removal of a director is the proverbial use of a sledgehammer to crack a nut: it can only be directed at board members and not at executives. Indeed, an executive director suffers little from such a removal, because the shareholders can only strip her of her directorship; they are not entitled to terminate the employment contract.[89] The only objective this type of strategy achieves is to remove individuals whose track record is otherwise irreproachable; a dilemma that is likely to make the shareholders hesitate before implementing it.[90]

At a purely expressive level, shareholders can pass a non-binding resolution on any issue, including executive compensation. The shareholders of UBS AG, a large Swiss bank, tried this at their annual general meeting on 21 April 2005.[91] However, such decisions pose two problems. First, by definition, they cannot constrain the actions of the board of directors.[92] Second, to ensure a transparent and orderly decision-making process, they have to be properly tabled.[93]

Finally, active shareholders can also try to influence the board through informal channels. However, for such bargaining in the shadow of the law to be effective, institutional investors need to either have legally enforceable shareholder rights or be able to influence corporate policy through their exit.

86. Art. 698 (2)(5) CO and Art. 758 (1) CO. Although Art. 698 (2)(5) CO is only directed at directors, it is generally admitted that the discharge vote can be extended to all members of the corporate executive. P. Böckli (2004), §12, no. 23.
87. Art. 705 (1) CO.
88. Formally, the discharge is the recognition by the general meeting and shareholders that they do not have any grounds for legal action against members of the board of directors. However, the scope of this discharge is limited to disclosed facts and this resolution is only enforceable on shareholders who voted in favour of the discharge (Art. 758 (1) CO). In the absence of a US-style 'demand' procedure, any shareholder, despite the discharge resolution, can sue a director if she simply did not vote at the general meeting. See on the situation in the US L.A. Bebchuk and J.M. Fried (2004), pp. 47–48; J.N. Gordon (2005), 691–693. The only limitation to her right of action is the requirement that she sue within six months of the decision (Art. 758 (2) CO). This requirement replaces the ordinary limitation period pursuant to Art. 760 CO. Thus, the discharge is legally quite ineffectual, but it does have a very strong symbolic function and is comparable to a vote of no confidence by shareholders.
89. Pursuant to art. 716(1)(4) CO, the appointment of persons to manage and represent the company is an inalienable and non-transferable attribute of the board of directors.
90. J.N. Gordon (2005), 700–701.
91. See the press release available at <www.ubs.com/1/e/investors/agm/2005/media_release.html>, and the voting results at <www.ubs.com/1/e/ investors/agm/2005/votingresults.html>.
92. See, on non-binding decisions, R. Trigo Trindade and R. Bahar (2002), p. 395 (with references).
93. See also R. Watter and K. Maizar, Chapter 2, p. 80 above.

b. Control by Exit

In many other areas of corporate law, shareholders may express their discontent in a forum other than the general meeting. They can, for example, sell their shares and vote with their feet.[94] As shareholders take this road, the share price of the company will fall. This sends a clear signal to the management that if they do not act, another company may take control or, at best, their own company will suffer should it need to raise money from external sources.

This mechanism also has limited effectiveness. Executive compensation is unlikely to cause a significant exit; if remuneration is the only source of discontent, it is unlikely to trigger massive share dumping. Executive compensation is only one of a host of performance drivers. Other factors, such as competitive position or the talent of the management team, are arguably more important.

Certain institutional investors are captive consumers of shares in publicly listed companies. Regulatory requirements, the size of their portfolios and the imperatives of diversification prevent them from selling their biggest capitalizations, which incidentally pay the highest salaries to their managers and/or board members.

Moreover, control by exit is an extremely costly and clumsy mechanism. A takeover is a costly transaction. A bidder will be interested only if the discount is substantial, without taking account of the costs of overcoming defence mechanisms. As far as executive compensation is concerned, the amounts at stake are not sufficient to justify the costs.[95] Thus, R.K. Aggarwal and A.A. Samwick (1999) find that firms whose executives are relatively overpaid are no more likely to be taken over.[96] Similarly, if the company has sound finances, it will not need to refinance itself externally. The company's own means will suffice and, even if it has to go outside, the company will borrow before increasing its equity.[97] All in all, the market constraint that results from shareholder exits is on the whole quite weak for most public companies.

c. Control by Courts

If voice and exit are not effective remedies, the last recourse of shareholders against an inappropriate compensation scheme is in the courts. The statute grants shareholders two legal instruments to address this issue.[98] First, if they can prove that the compensation received by a director or, arguably, an executive is grossly disproportionate to the services rendered and the economic situation of the company,

94. This mechanism of control by exit was originally developed by A.O. Hirschmann (1970).
95. L.A. Bebchuk and J.M. Fried (2004), p. 56.
96. R.K. Aggarwal and A.A. Samwick (1999), 2,012–2,030.
97. Under the 'pecking order' theory of financing, this preference for internal financing and debt finance over new equity issues stems from the informational asymmetry between insiders, such as management, and outsiders. See S.C. Myers (1977), 147; S.C. Myers and N.S. Majluf (1984), 187. For a general presentation of empirical evidence, see M. Harris and A. Raviv (1991), 306–307.
98. P. Böckli, C. Huguenin-Jacobs and F. Dessemontet (2003), p. 18.

shareholders can force her to repay any such undue benefit to the company.[99] Second, if they can prove that the board breached its duty of diligence and loyalty by offering a manager an inappropriate compensation scheme, they are entitled to sue for any damages incurred by themselves or the company as a direct result of the breach.[100]

Without entering into the legal preconditions for such claims,[101] I would stress their practical difficulties. Short of a discovery-like procedure, the claimant usually lacks the appropriate information to be able to substantiate his claim, making it extremely difficult to win such a suit.[102] The claimant in this case bears the burden of proof, and the Swiss business judgment rule further darkens these already grim prospects. Under this rule, management enjoys very broad discretion in a non-conflicted situation, provided he acts on an informed basis in what he believes to be the best interests of the company.[103] Finally, the costs of such proceedings are relatively high for a shareholder of a public company. The case will be brought on behalf of the company, which means that costs will be calculated on the basis of the entire damage incurred by the corporate body, not just the shareholders who brought the action. Moreover, because under Swiss law the loser bears both parties' costs on top of the court costs, the system strongly encourages claimants to think twice before bringing suit.[104] In fact, the entire system is skewed against the plaintiff.

In a recent case, the Swiss Federal Banking Commission, following the Takeover Board, limited the protection offered by the business judgment rule in the context of takeover.[105] These regulators held that, under Swiss private law, to grant a golden parachute in the wake of a hostile takeover bid would grossly breach the duty of loyalty owed to the company. Without discussing the merits of this case – which are questionable –[106] this decision is unlikely to achieve a broad effect, for two reasons. First, the enhanced scrutiny exists only in the context of takeover bids. Second, the deciding factor in this case was exactly when the golden parachute was granted. The decision of the Federal Banking Commission implies that, had the golden parachute been provided for in the original employment contracts, it would most likely have been valid. Moreover, had the golden parachute been independent of a change of control, the regulator would have probably have been more reluctant

99. Art. 678 (2) CO.
100. Art. 754 (1) CO.
101. On the application of Art. 678 (2) CO to executive compensation, see e.g. V. Aepli (2002), 276; D. Daeniker (2005), 388.
102. R. Trigo Trindade and R. Bahar (2002), p. 446 (with references).
103. SJ 1982 221, c. 3a, 225; ATF 113 II 52, c. 3a, 57; H.C. von der Crone (1997), 107; A.R. Grass (1998); L. Glanzmann (2000), 165–166; A.R. Grass (2000); R. Trigo Trindade and R. Bahar (2002), p. 396; P. Widmer and O. Banz (2002) ad art. 754 CO, no. 31.
104. R. Trigo Trindade and R. Bahar (2002), p. 437–438 and p. 446 (with references).
105. Decision of the Federal Banking Commission of 19 September 2005, in re Saia Burgess; Recommendation V of the Takeover Board of 23 August 2005, in regard to Saia Burgess.
106. See R. Bahar (2005).

to criticize it.[107] In short, a well-advised board might arguably be able to simply jump the hurdle set by this enhanced scrutiny.

C. Conclusion

Under Swiss corporate law, as in other jurisdictions, executive compensation is first and foremost a matter for the board: it is up to the directors to negotiate the compensation package with other directors and executives. This approach is consistent with the general corporate governance system, but fails to deal with the conflicts of interest and agency problems that plague directors. Moreover, the entire system is biased in favour of over-compensation, due to the influence that managers can exert on the process and the psychological factors that push directors to be generous with executives, rather than take a critical view of the compensation policy.

Recent corporate governance initiatives have strived to overcome these shortcomings through increased reliance on compensation committees and independent directors, but despite some successes they have failed to prevent the inflation of executive compensation. This weakness is worsened by the lack, or at least the limitations, of control mechanisms at shareholder level using voice, exit or courts. We therefore must look for another means to improve the current institutional arrangement.

III. DISCLOSURE AND EXECUTIVE COMPENSATION

A. Is Disclosure a Solution to the Conflict of Interest?

Over the last decade, regulators and promoters of corporate governance codes have increasingly relied on transparency to resolve the conflict of interest over executive compensation. This increased disclosure is fostered by statute, agency regulation and corporate governance codes. The approach is based on the assumption that if investors are aware of the compensation scheme, they will be in a position to check and react against managerial excesses.[108] In other words, by forcing companies to disclose information, the proponents of this approach hope to lower the costs of monitoring by shareholders and thus reduce the agency costs linked to executive compensation.

Switzerland has followed this route. In this section, I will present the Swiss regulatory framework with regard to the disclosure of executive compensation. Then I will point out its substantive and formal shortcomings, showing that hopes of a solution to the conflict of interest through increased disclosure are likely to prove illusory, at least under the current disclosure scheme.

---

107. See ibid.
108. See e.g. R. Ruedin (2005), p. 332.

1. The Swiss Regulatory Framework

In Switzerland, the traditional route to obtaining information on executive compensation is through the shareholders' right to request information at the general meeting.[109] The scope of this right is limited to the information shareholders require to exercise their other rights. Most scholars argue that the company is only required to disclose the global compensation paid to directors or executives,[110] however a minority of scholars seem to take a more generous stance and call for disclosure of individual amounts.[111] As a result this uncertainty, companies are able to withhold detailed information: shareholders seeking to obtain the information are left to seek a ruling in the courts, which would be too costly for most investors. Moreover, the right to request information is not an effective information mechanism, as it does not require issuers to disclose any information unless expressly requested to do so by a shareholder; a situation that enables issuers to play a game of cat and mouse with active shareholders.

SWX Swiss Exchange, the main stock exchange, as one of its listing conditions under the Corporate Governance Directive requires issuers to disclose their executive compensation policies, in addition to data on corporate governance. Unlike the rest of the Corporate Governance Directive, the rules on the disclosure of compensation, shareholdings and loans are mandatory and an issuer cannot avoid compliance by giving specific reasons for non-disclosure.[112]

As a matter of principle, the directive calls for the disclosure of the:

> 'basic principles and elements of compensation and shareholding programs of acting and former members of the issuer's board and senior management as well as the applicable authority and procedure'.[113]

More specifically, the directive calls for the disclosure of five types of compensation:

- The total compensation, including all salary, bonuses, fees and benefits in kind,[114] but notably excluding the value of options and shares;[115]
- The allotment of shares;[116]

109. Art. 697 CO.
110. P. Forstmoser (1997), p. 105; E. Homburger (1997) ad art. 717 CO, no. 957; G. Krneta (2001), no. 1,789. See also *Message relatif à la modification du code des obligations (Transparence des indemnités versées aux membres du conseil d'administration et de la direction) du 23 juin 2004*, FF 2004 4223, 4225.
111. V. Aepli (2002), 275; R. Ruedin (2005), p. 333. On the acceptance of individual disclosures in specific circumstances see P. Böckli (2004), §13, no. 260.
112. Section 7 of the Annex to the Corporate Governance Directive.
113. Ibid., section 5.1.
114. Ibid., section 5.2.1.
115. Authentic Decision of the Admission Board of SWX Swiss Exchange of 11 November 2002; See also Commentary on the Corporate Governance Directive, p. 27.
116. Section 5.4. of the Annex to the Corporate Governance Directive.

- Options, including warrants and synthetic shareholding programs;[117]
- Additional fees, e.g. consultancy fees or legal fees paid to a board member, an executive or party closely linked to either of these groups of individuals, such as the law firm of a lawyer that sits on the board of a company (if they exceed half the ordinary remuneration of such a person);[118]
- Loans and other forms of credit extended to board members.[119]

The directive also obliges issuers to disclose separately the amount of any severance payment offered to an executive who resigns[120] and all forms of compensation to former directors and senior managers.[121] This enables investors to detect any golden parachutes offered to outgoing managers and other deferred compensation and benefits to former directors.

The Corporate Governance Directive also requires the disclosure of all shares hold by directors and top managers and options.[122] This disclosure schedule enables investors to assess to what extent executives and directors are invested in the company. However, whereas all shareholdings must be disclosed, the Commentary on the Corporate Governance Directive calls only for the disclosure of convertible bonds and warrant bonds, i.e. bonds with an option attached, and only if the bond was part of a compensation scheme.[123]

The treatment of stock options under the Corporate Governance Directive is quite surprising. The value of allotted, granted and vested options does not have to be disclosed in the annual report, even implicitly as a part of the total compensation package. The Corporate Governance Directive requires only the disclosure of the allotment year, the duration, the subscription ratio and the exercise price of these options.[124] Using this information, analysts and most sophisticated investors can value the options, but the general public does not have access to this information, although it is necessary to calculate this value in order to identify the best-paid director.[125] This issue is all the more puzzling because even the value of cash-settled derivatives, such as ‘naked options,’ ‘stock appreciation rights,’ and ‘phantom stocks’ does not have to be disclosed.[126]

The Corporate Governance Directive does not require disclosure of the compensation packages of individual directors and managers. Other than consulting fees and other remuneration to directors, senior managers and related parties,[127]

117. Ibid., section 5.6.
118. Ibid., section 5.7.
119. Ibid., section 5.8.
120. Ibid., section 5.2.3.
121. Ibid., section 5.3.
122. Ibid., sections 5.4 and 5.6.
123. Commentary on the Corporate Governance Directive, p. 30.
124. Section 5.6 of the Annex to the Corporate Governance Directive, p. 31.
125. Commentary on the Corporate Governance Directive, p. 30.
126. See Section 5.6 of the Annex to the Corporate Governance Directive and Commentary Corporate Governance Directive, p. 31.
127. Section 5.7 of the Annex to the Corporate Governance Directive.

listed companies are only required to spell out the total compensation paid to senior management, including executive directors, and the aggregate amounts paid to non-executive directors.[128] As a matter of principle, issuers are not obliged to detail the remuneration of each member of the board or of every manager; they need only disclose the payment package of the best-paid director.[129]

The fact that issuers need only disclose the total payment creates a particularly acute problem of comparison. Only the global compensation of the board is disclosed, although directors rarely carry out the same tasks.[130] On mixed boards, executives will earn much more than non-executive directors. Even among non-executive directors, some tasks, such as acting as an independent chairman or membership of an audit committee, are much more time-consuming than others. This system also makes cross-firm comparisons extremely difficult; it complicates comparison within the same firm from one year to another. The boards of some companies have a large number of directors, while others have fewer directors, while at management level the disparities are even greater: some firms have a very lean top management, others a much broader one.

This feature is a positive invitation to dilute the most outrageous payment packages among an array of more reasonable ones. Construing this notion very broadly, the Zehnder Group tried to make the argument that its top management team included 58 members;[131] a bold view that was eventually condemned by the Admission Board, the regulating body of the Stock Exchange, who ruled that 'top management' refers only to the CEO, the CFO, heads of key divisions and other individuals who are directly accountable to the board of directors.[132] This case illustrates quite well the problem of definition posed by the assumptions underlying the Corporate Governance Directive. From this perspective, the American approach seems more sensible: disclosing the compensation package paid to the five best-paid executives offers a clearer picture of a firm's remuneration policy.[133]

A similar problem of comparison arises with respect to the disclosure of the package given to the best-paid director. Although the justification – directors, unlike managers, are always subject to a conflict of interest with respect to their own compensation[134] – is convincing in theory, it is more questionable in practice.[135] First, the debate over corporate compensation centres on executives, and the CEO in particular. Because the Swiss corporate governance system allows companies to put their executives on the board of directors,[136] they can choose whether or

128. Ibid., sections 5.2.2, 5.3.2, 5.4, 5.5, 5.6 and 5.8.
129. Ibid., section 5.9.
130. See R. Ruedin (2005), p. 332.
131. See Decision of 30 September 2004, DK/CG/I/04, available at <www.swx.com/download/admission/being_public/sanctions/publications/decision_cg300904_de.pdf>.
132. See Decision of 30 September 2004, DK/CG/I/04, c. 5–9 available at <www.swx.com/download/admission/being_public/sanctions/publications/decision_cg300904_de.pdf>.
133. See item 402, Regulation S-K.
134. See e.g. P. Böckli, C. Huguenin-Jacobs and F. Dessemontet (2003), p. 8.
135. P. Böckli (2004), §14, no. 244.
136. See art. 716b (1) CO.

not to disclose their executive compensation package: if an issuer does not want to disclose its CEO's salary, it can simply refrain from appointing her to the board.[137] Second, inter-firm comparisons are also hindered: in some firms, the CEO is a director, whereas in others she is not and the best-paid director will generally be the chairman of the board; a non-executive director.[138]

The Swiss legislator considered that this directive offered insufficient disclosure. Therefore, the Swiss parliament recently passed an act to amend the Code of Obligations to require listed companies to disclose additional information.[139] Under this act, which is likely to come into force 1 January 2007, listed companies will, in addition to their current obligations, be required to disclose the compensation, shareholdings and options of individual directors and provide details for the best-paid executive (*membre de la direction*), regardless of whether or not she sits on the board of directors.[140] The rest of the bill broadly reflects the content of the current SWX Corporate Governance Directive and thus stops short of requiring effective transparency and comparability.

2. The Substantive Shortcomings of the Swiss Regulatory Framework

a. Insufficient Disclosure of Deferred Compensation

In addition to the problem of defining precisely who is subject to disclosure, the current regulatory framework fails to appropriately capture all forms of compensation. No duty applies, for example, to disclose deferred compensation schemes, pension schemes or other long-term incentive plans that are not due or payable by the company during the current accounting year, [141] though these amounts will be disclosed once they are paid out to the manager or any related person, such as a designated beneficiary.[142] Until then, the amounts can remain hidden from the investing public. In addition, payments from a standard pension fund, as opposed to an employer-controlled pension fund, arguably do not need to be disclosed at any time, even if the funds were funded by the company.[143]

From an accounting perspective, this approach may be justifiable: the company has incurred a conditional liability towards the directors or the executives, which will not accrue until later.[144] But, by focusing on the books and applying

137. Commentary on the Corporate Governance Directive, p. 27.
138. See M. Boemle (2003), 499–500.
139. See Code des obligations (CO) (Transparence des indemnités versées aux membres du conseil d'administration et de la direction) Modification du 7 octobre 2005, FF 2005 5593.
140. See Art. 663b^{bis} (4)(1) and (2) CO (as amended).
141. Section 5.2. of the Annex to the Corporate Governance Directive *a contrario*. See also Commentary Corporate Governance Directive, p. 26.
142. Section 5.2.3 of the Annex to the Corporate Governance Directive.
143. See R. Watter (2003), pp. 60–61.
144. See IAS 1, pp. 25–26.

the accrual principle, this system misses the whole point of disclosing executive compensation: the purpose of transparency in this field is not to monitor what was paid, but to figure out whether the payment scheme provides directors and managers with appropriate incentives.[145] This deficiency is surprising, because most of the scandals that rocked Swiss companies in 2001 and 2002, and that eventually led to the Corporate Governance Directive and the bill on the revision of the Code of Obligations regarding transparency of executive compensation, were related to pension schemes and golden parachutes.[146] However, this is not the only problem with the Swiss regulatory framework.

b. Insufficient Disclosure of Stock Option Plans

Focusing on the critical question of stock options, the current solution is even worse. The Corporate Governance Directive does not require companies to provide detailed information on the type of option granted. The financial statements have to disclose the year in which they were granted, the strike price and the duration of the option,[147] but are not obliged to publish the value of the options granted, the prevailing market conditions at grant or whether they are subject to a waiting period.[148] Thus, literally millions of Swiss francs can be secretly paid out.[149] If the underlying stock is volatile, the public has no way of finding out whether the options were in-the-money or out-of-the-money and thus will be unable to judge the incentive effect of the compensation scheme.

Moreover, option re-pricing by lowering the strike price of previously granted options is not subject to any specific disclosure requirement. Such transactions will go unobserved by investors unless they carefully compare the disclosures from one year to another. It is relatively easy, therefore, to conceal the re-pricing of stock options, although such transactions may entail substantial transfers to managers and greatly dilute the incentive effect of these instruments. Although Swiss companies have hitherto been spared any major scandal relating to stock option plans, the current regulatory framework is simply asking for trouble.[150]

c. No Disclosure of the Unwinding of Incentive Schemes

Finally, the disclosure framework focuses exclusively on compensation granted by the company and on managers' shareholdings. The framework does not capture dealings by managers and third parties which may counteract or 'unwind' the

145. L.A. Bebchuk and J.M. Fried (2004), p. 192.
146. P. Böckli, C. Huguenin-Jacobs and F. Dessemontet (2004), p. 133.
147. Section 5.6 of the Annex to the Corporate Governance Directive.
148. R. Watter (2003), p. 61.
149. P. Böckli (2004) §14, no. 245.
150. See P. Böckli, C. Huguenin-Jacobs and F. Dessemontet (2004), p. 133.

incentive effect of the compensation scheme.[151] For instance, there is no requirement for the executive compensation schedule of the annual report to disclose any options managers may purchase from a financial institution in order to protect themselves against the risks from a stock option plan or a blocked shareholding scheme.[152]

In certain circumstances, this information may have to be disclosed under the heading of management transactions.[153] Relying on this data, it seems that managers are willing to divest. In the first experiences with this regulation, between 1 July 2005, when the regulation came into force, and 17 August 2005, 68 per cent of the notifications filed with the SWX pertained to the sale of securities. In terms of value, these notifications involved an amount of CHF 59 million (exceeding by a ratio of 1:4.5 the CHF 13 million involved in purchases) and one per cent of the notifications related to put options (as opposed to 10 per cent related to call options).[154] These sales may be related to imperatives of liquidity or diversification, but in any case they weaken the effect of equity-based plans.

However, the management transaction scheme is not designed to inform investors about corporate governance but to deter insider dealing, which may in turn mean that the information provided is not sufficient to provide an estimate of the incentive effect of the compensation scheme. Moreover, as this information is not disclosed in the corporate governance section of the annual report, the general investing public (but not analysts or markets) may believe that the compensation package is more performance-driven than it in fact is.

d. No Discussion or Analysis of Compensation Policy

A more fundamental flaw in the framework adopted by the Corporate Governance Directive, as well as the proposed revision of the Code of Obligations, is the lack of information on the pay–performance sensitivity of compensation packages or even the general policy followed by the board of directors. The current requirements focus on hard data: total amount of compensation received and number of shares and options held by directors and managers. No explicit information is available on performance-based compensation other than options.[155]

Moreover, although the Swiss Code of Best Practice for Corporate Governance requires compensation committees to link pay and performance and states that ‘The

---

151. E. Ofek and D. Yermack (2000), 1,374–1,381; L.A. Bebchuk and J.M. Fried (2004), pp. 174–185; M.C. Jensen, K. Murphy and E.J. Wruck (2004), 67.
152. Sections 5.5 and 5.6 of the Annex to the Corporate Governance Directive only require the disclosure of current shareholdings and option positions resulting from stock option plans; it does not impose any duty to disclose sales of options or hedging transactions.
153. See generally Art. 74a SWX Listing Rules and the Directive on the Disclosure of Management Transactions.
154. See SWX, ‘Favourable experience with disclosure of management transactions,’ Media release 18.8.2005, available at <www.swx.com/media_release20050818_en.pdf>.
155. Section 5.2.1 of the Annex to the Corporate Governance Directive requires that such variable compensation be simply included in the calculation of the total compensation package.

remuneration should be demonstrably contingent upon sustainable company success and the individual contribution by the person in question. False incentives should be avoided,'[156] the disclosure schedule set forth by the Corporate Governance Directive does not enable shareholders to check that the board of directors and its compensation committee actually pursued this goal. At most, it would be possible to construe the general disclosure of the principles and elements of compensation as a requirement to state the compensation policy openly.[157] But, even this bullish approach does not call for the disclosure of the pay–performance sensitivity of the compensation package.

By contrast, following the English example,[158] the Commission's Recommendation of 14 December 2004, fostering an appropriate regime for the remuneration of directors of listed companies (Text with EEA relevance) (2004/913/EC), calls on companies to disclose their compensation policy in a 'remuneration statement'[159] which should clearly explain the relationship between fixed and variable compensation, setting forth the criteria used to measure performance for bonus schemes and determining the entitlement to shares or options.[160] It also requires that sufficient information be provided on the link between pay and performance.[161] Finally, to prevent the use of pension schemes to conceal executive compensation, the remuneration statement must describe the main characteristics of directors' retirement plans.[162] This approach focuses on the real issue of executive compensation; namely the link between pay and performance.

3. Formal Shortcomings of the Regulatory Framework

In addition to its substantive shortcomings, the Corporate Governance Directive also fails to convey the information in a user-friendly manner. The directive prescribes what the company must disclose, but does not state, or even suggest, how to disclose it.[163] This approach follows the general philosophy of the SWX Listing

156. Section 26 Swiss Code of Best Practice for Corporate Governance.
157. See R. Watter (2003), p. 60.
158. See The Directors' Remuneration Report Regulations 2002, SI 2002 no. 1986.
159. Art. 3.1 Commission recommendation of 14 December 2004 fostering an appropriate regime for the remuneration of directors of listed companies (Text with EEA relevance) (2004/913/EC), OJ L 385/55, 2004.
160. Ibid., art. 3.3 (a) and (b).
161. Ibid., art. 3.3 (c).
162. Ibid., art. 3.3 (d).
163. The only requirements relate to the location of the corporate governance disclosure in the annual report. Under Section 6 of the Corporate Governance Directive, it must be published in the annual report, as opposed to the financial statements, and be included in a separate chapter. Issuers are entirely free to communicate the information in whichever form they believe is more suitable for their needs. They can disclose compensation in either textual or tabular form as long as all the required information is provided.

Rules, which, unlike US and UK regulations,[164] allow issuers to structure their prospectus as they wish, provided they discloses all information required by the applicable Schedule and complies with a few general principles.[165]

This discretion enables issuers to leave their executive compensation packages more or less opaque, leaving them free to engage in all manner of public relations spin to limit outside criticism. Issuers can package the figures among factual information or can dress up certain perks. Or, they can indulge in various strategies to conceal the exact amount and structure of executive compensation packages. This creates two related problems. At firm level, it prevents outsiders from analyzing whether the executive compensation policy is sensible and whether it appropriately links pay with performance. At market level, it complicates comparisons by analysts and other interested parties, because no two firms follow the same disclosure format.[166]

The US experience is instructive. As L.A. Bebchuk and J.M. Fried (2004) recall, before 1992 the SEC required firms to publish executive compensation, but allowed them to choose the format of the disclosure. Firms seized on this discretion to obscure the form and amount of their compensation. The SEC reacted in 1992, tightening its rules to require the disclosure of executive compensation using standardized tables.[167]

Standardized tables have their pros and cons. On the one hand, they facilitate market-wide comparisons and make it easy to check whether all the required information has actually been disclosed. But, they can also lead to oversimplification and create an incentive to use forms of compensation that do not have to be disclosed in the standardized table.

This topic is similar to another discussion in the field of financial reporting. Financial statements present a summary overview of a firm, allowing easy comparisons with other companies, but they do not provide an accurate picture of the company's 'real' financial situation. Moreover, as revealed by recent accounting scandals and the debate over the expensing of stock options that has raged over the last decade, even if a company discloses information in the notes to the financial statements, it makes a big difference whether or not it is actually on or off the balance sheet.[168] Nevertheless, in spite of these shortcomings, no one seriously contests the necessity and the usefulness of financial statements in the form of a balance sheet, a profit and loss account and a cash-flow statement. In the realm

---

164. See for the US Regulation S-K, item 402 and for the UK Schedule 7A of the Companies Act 1985, as amended by the Directors' Remuneration Report Regulations 2002, SI 2002 no. 1986.
165. Art. 36 Listing Rules.
166. L.A. Bebchuk and J.M. Fried (2004), pp. 67–68.
167. The particulars of disclosure are set out in Regulation S-K (17 CFR 229), specifically, item 402 (executive compensation), item 403 (security ownership) and item 404 (related party transactions). See also L.A. Bebchuk and J.M. Fried (2004), pp. 67–68.
168. In some cases, not even the notes to the accounts constitute adequate disclosure of complex financial transactions. According to some commentators, in certain circumstances, it may even be more efficient – from an investor-protection perspective – simply to ban the transaction rather than approve disclosure. See S. Schwarcz (2004), 21–24.

of stock options, however, it seems that the form of the disclosure actually does matter. If the use of these instruments is merely mentioned in the notes, rather than expensed, managers (but not economists or analysts) will tend to regard the instruments as being free of charge.[169]

If the analogy holds, this conclusion can be extended to the disclosure of executive compensation. A standardized compensation package has the advantage of requiring companies to disclose forms and amounts in a simple and direct manner. It may lack subtlety, but this could be compensated for through a separate qualitative discussion, explaining the process and policy underlying executive compensation in general and the disclosed figures in particular.

B. Efficacy of Disclosure: The 'Spot the Compensation' Game

1. Transparency as a Source of Shareholder Empowerment

Even if the disclosure system were perfect, it is far from certain that it would be sufficient to align managers' compensation packages with their performance. Indeed, for transparency to operate as a control over executive compensation, shareholders must be able to voice their objections in one way or another. As we have seen, the three mechanisms used to control managers – voice, exit and the courts – are largely ineffective in controlling executive compensation:[170] the operative threshold is too high. These instruments limit the discretion of the board of directors and executives while preventing only the most egregious abuses.

J. N. Gordon (2005) views disclosure as a tool to make directors more accountable.[171] From this perspective, transparency can help improve the governance of executive compensation. It increases the shareholder awareness, and it diminishes the costs borne by active shareholders by reducing the cost of analyzing executive compensation packages. This, in turn, enables shareholders to more easily react to inappropriate schemes.

Moreover, forcing disclosure enables a broader audience of investors to be aware of the scandalous compensation packages awarded to particular managers. L.A. Bebchuk, J.M. Fried and D.I. Walker (2002) and L.A. Bebchuk and J.M. Fried (2004) view disclosure as a cost – a so-called 'outrage cost' – imposed on managers and directors, which does something, though not much, to limit overall management power.[172] From this perspective, transparency increases outrage costs, which makes it a stronger constraint on managerial power.

169. See B.J. Hall and K.J. Murphy (2003), 65–67.
170. See Section II.B.2 above.
171. J.N. Gordon (2005), 693–698.
172. L.A. Bebchuk, J.M. Fried and D.I. Walker (2002), 786–788; L.A. Bebchuk and J.M. Fried (2004), pp. 64–65.

2. Transparency as a Cause of Inefficient Remuneration

a. In General

The constraint on managerial discretion resulting from transparency, however, has perverse effects. Managers and directors may seek to diminish the outrage costs through means other than a more efficient compensation package: they may simply have recourse to less-transparent structures. This entails two costs, in addition to the lack of pay–performance sensitivity. First, such schemes are costly to set up: management may spend a great deal of time on designing them. They may also require the services of expensive consultants, bankers, lawyers and accountants to ensure the validity of the structure. Second, disguised forms of compensation are likely to cost the firm more than the cost of the benefits conferred on the managers. In other words, were it not for the outrage costs, it would be cheaper to pay the manager the perceived value of the benefit in cash rather than in kind.[173]

b. Perks

Perks and other benefits in kind are quite typical in this respect: they can be camouflaged as professional expenses. For instance, if the board provides its top manager with an executive jet, the cost of the flight will not be disclosed as a part of the executives' compensation package, so long as the jet was used in a business capacity rather than a purely private one. This luxury first and foremost benefits managers. Thus the corporate jet has become synonymous with agency costs. Yet, as R.G. Rajan and J. Wulf (2004) suggest, such perks are not always inefficient. A corporate jet, for instance, enables executives to manage their schedules more effectively, and spend more time on the job by eliminating time wasted at check-in or at the boarding gate, and more generally by eliminating the dependency on the time-schedules and connections of commercial carriers. This benefit may be particularly important for executives of companies that are not located close to major hubs; these executives make up the majority of users of corporate jets, according to a study by R.G. Rajan and J. Wulf (2004). All things considered, the use of a jet can often prove to be in a company's best interests.[174]

The main problem is determining whether, and to what extent, the use of the jet is merely a professional expense and not merely a disguised form of compensation. This difficulty is precisely what makes the benefit a convenient way to channel compensation to executives without running the risk of outrage. This, in addition to tax considerations, may explain why numerous benefits, such as a company car, apartment or club membership, are part of the standard package offered to executives. Moreover, as J. N. Gordon (2005) has pointed out, perks are difficult

173. This concept is a familiar one to economists. See e.g. L.A. Bebchuk and J.M. Fried (2004), p. 108.
174. R.G. Rajan and J. Wulf (2004).

to value accurately, which makes them all the more attractive, even if they have to be disclosed as part of the total compensation package.[175]

c. Options

This same observation can be extended to other forms of compensation. Obviously, options, more than any other payment in kind, can be used to make high remuneration more palatable to shareholders. Undoubtedly, an option plan can be used as an incentive mechanism, as suggested by M.C. Jensen and K. Murphy (1990b) in their seminal paper.[176] But they can also be used as a discreet way of conveying money into executives' pockets, as suggested by L.A. Bebchuk and J.M. Fried (2004), who devote a considerable part of their book to this instrument.[177] Interestingly, M. Bertrand and S. Mullainathan (2001) note that a substantial number of executives are compensated for developments beyond their control; in other, words for luck rather than performance.[178]

The difficulty of valuing such instruments makes it more difficult for shareholders and investors at large to determine the precise amount the board of directors agreed to pay its managers. In particular, as B.J. Hall and K. Murphy (2003) point out, bearing in mind the risk aversion of managers, and the fact that options granted under a typical stock option plan are not tradable, options actually cost the company more than the value they bring to their beneficiary.[179] Unlike traditional options, which can be traded at any time on an exchange, stock option plans granted to executives are not assignable and often represent a sizeable portion of an individual executive's assets and income. From the executive's perspective, an option is not worth its Black and Scholes valuation and she will want to be indemnified for the additional risk she bears and hence will demand more options.[180]

However, the company will be willing to bear this cost, because it offers tax benefits to the company and its managers and will not provoke outrage. Corporate governance considerations actually strengthened this motive for using stock options. The very fact that options to a certain extent link executive pay with corporate performance served to make them more palatable to most activists.

The American tax reform of 1992 is emblematic. After a wave of outrage over executive compensation, the United States Congress passed a bill that barred the expensing of non-performance-based compensation in excess of USD one million.[181] Far from scaling down executive pay, the enactment of this new rule had two consequences. First, it led to an increase of non-performance-based compensation

175. J.N. Gordon (2005), 694.
176. M.C. Jensen and K. Murphy (1990b), 232–238.
177. See L.A. Bebchuk and J.M. Fried (2004), pp. 137–171.
178. M. Bertrand and S. Mullainathan (2001), 901.
179. See B.J. Hall and K.J. Murphy (2002); B.J. Hall and K.J. Murphy (2003), 55–56.
180. F. Black and M. Scholes (1973). For an introduction to option pricing generally see R.A. Brealy and S.C. Myers (2003), pp. 565–662.
181. IRC §162 (m), 26 USC, §162 (m).

up to the threshold. Second, it accelerated an existing trend to grant more options to executives, because this type of instrument did not fall under the scope of the rule. These two perverse effects can be seen as a consequence of implicit government approval of such levels of compensation.[182]

The fact that stock options did not have to be expensed as an accounting cost only made matters worse. Until recently, under US GAAP, option grants were not expensed, despite the fact that they entail an opportunity cost. Rather than handing out options to executives, the company can sell them to investors to raise cash. The loss of this consideration is a cost, which ought to be expensed. Efficient capital markets were neutral to such accounting quirks and appropriately discounted the share price. Nevertheless, as Hall and Murphy (2002) and Murphy (2002) point out, managers chose to ignore this cost because it did not impact their bottom line or their profitability.[183]

d. Pension Funds

Over the past few years, pension schemes appear to have been used as a 'camouflage technique'. This form of compensation has certain features that make it a particularly attractive way of paying executives covertly. In the US, for example, payments into a pension fund are not required to be disclosed as part of the executive compensation package. In addition, payments to former executives do not have to be disclosed either. Therefore, in the words of Bebchuk and Jackson (2005), executive pension funds are a technique to increase executive compensation 'off the radar screen.'[184] And this development is not specific to the US legal system. Swiss companies have also been censured for attempting to use pension funds to camouflage payments to executives.[185]

This problem is aggravated by the fact that pension scheme payments are rarely contingent on the performance of the executive. Defined contributions into these

---

182. See B.J. Hall and K.J. Murphy (2003), 62 (reporting mixed evidence). See also T. Perry and M. Zenner (2001), 460–483; N.L. Rose and C. Wolfram (2002), S143–S166.
183. K. Murphy (2002), 860. This irrational focus on accounting figures is not specific to options. He cites two anecdotal cases in which accounting changes impacted the use of certain instruments without affecting the stock price. In 1993, when the US Financial Accounting Standards Board (FASB) imposed a current accounting charge for anticipated post-retirement health benefits (Statement 106 of the Financial Accounting Standards Board), managers anticipated a drop in stock prices. This did not happen, which shows that with or without accounting information, markets are efficient. Nevertheless companies dramatically cut down their benefits. A similar phenomenon was observed five years later, when the FASB imposed an accounting charge on re-priced options. It might have been expected that companies with declining stock prices would stop re-pricing options. Instead, these companies cancelled their existing options, waited six months, and then granted new options at a lower exercise price. The outcome was the same, with the exception that a substantial risk was borne by employees, who were not aware of the exercise price for that period and there was a perverse incentive to keep the price down for the next six months. See B.J. Hall and K.J. Murphy (2002), 66–67; K. Murphy (2002), 860–861.
184. L.A. Bebchuk and R. Jackson (2005), 827–831.
185. P. Böckli, C. Huguenin-Jacobs and F. Dessemontet (2004), p. 133.

types of schemes are based on fixed compensation or target bonus levels. Thus, not only do these instruments enable companies to understate the compensation paid to executives, they also lead to an overestimation of the pay–performance correlation.[186]

C. Transparency as a Problem

Considering this bleak depiction of the legal landscape, it is tempting to conclude that insufficient disclosure is better than no disclosure at all. But, this would be too hasty. Transparency causes an entire range of problems for corporate governance.

The first argument that is generally raised against increased disclosure – the protection of the private sphere of corporate executives[187] – should not, in my opinion, be considered a major hurdle. When a manager accepts a job as an executive of a public listed company, the manager ought to accept that he is accountable to the shareholders, and therefore his pay will be scrutinized by the investing public and financial intermediaries in the broadest sense, including analysts and journalists who are expected to independently verify and process information. This imperative constitutes an overwhelming private and public interest, counteracting the manager's right to privacy and data protection.[188] If managers are unwilling to undergo disclosure, they must renounce the right to raise equity from the public and rely on other sources of finance, such as debt or private equity, which carry other mechanisms to ensure that managers will perform and the company will meet its obligations.

1. Political Costs of Transparency

Beyond the camouflage issue and managers' attempts to avoid disclosure, transparency has a more perverse effect from the perspective of shareholders and managers alike. 'The public' does not consist solely of the investors and their agents. It also includes workers, and the unions and political parties that represent their interests. Even if shareholders are undisturbed by the payments made to executives and are, for reasons good or ill, unwilling to take any action on this issue, other constituencies may take a different view.

Increased disclosure may enable these other constituencies to benefit from published information about executive compensation. This fact is cause for concern if one assumes, as most corporate analysts do, that the corporate governance system is mainly a way of protecting shareholders from abuses by management, rather than other constituencies who have access to contractual or legal mechanisms to cater

186. L.A. Bebchuk and J.M. Fried (2004), p. 26.
187. Art. 28 of the Swiss Civil Code protects the personality of all individuals. This right is deemed to include the right of every person to protect his private sphere from undue intrusions.
188. See art. 13 (1) Data Protection Act and art. 28 (2) CC. See also P. Böckli, C. Huguenin-Jacobs and F. Dessemontet (2003), p. 8.

to their concerns. Thus, even if shareholders are not outraged by the levels and forms of executive compensations, workers may call on politicians to intervene and attempt to limit the payout to managers.[189]

A second problem arises if the general public is outraged by high absolute levels of executive compensation without considering pay–performance sensitivity, which mainly interests shareholders. As D. Daeniker (2005) notes, in Switzerland, the increased disclosure did not lead to greater shareholder activism, but rather to the tabloids' printing a who's-who of the best-paid managers without bothering to discuss the relation between pay and performance.[190] In response, boards may try to avoid the outrage costs by relying on an inefficient compensation package that will not shock the general public.[191] In summary, although disclosure may constrain managerial discretion, it can also prevent shareholders from forcing management to maximize the firm's value.

Taking a step back, this problem is likely the reason why continental European jurisdictions have traditionally been more reluctant to disclose executive compensation. Indeed, the risk of political intervention is more acute in a left-leaning political environment, in which unions are strong and social democrats are more willing to take a stance in favour of workers and cap executive compensation (against the interests of shareholders). Therefore, as M.J. Roe (2002) suggests, in these types of environments, corporate governance is more likely to evolve towards a concentration of power in the hands of large block-holders, who can effectively monitor directors and management without relying on public disclosure.[192] In such a setting, shareholders are actually likely to side with management and oppose increased disclosure, for fear that it may lead to increased political interference.[193] This may explain why strong union and political pressure was needed to induce German listed companies to disclose individual executive compensation figures – a standard practice in the UK.[194]

From a policy perspective, this problem is not entirely unavoidable. As G.A. Ferrarini and N. Moloney (2005) point out, if instead of focusing on absolute levels of compensation, the disclosure schedule stresses pay–performance sensitivity and the effectiveness of governance, it is less likely to invite popular hostility and thus avoids this problem.[195]

189. See *Message relatif à la modification du code des obligations (Transparence des indemnités versées aux membres du conseil d'administration et de la direction) du 23 juin 2004*, FF 2004 4223, 4226 (expressly mentioning that transparency of executive compensation should serve to balance the interests of, inter alia, other stakeholders).
190. D. Daeniker (2005), 389.
191. M.C. Jensen and K. Murphy (1990b), 254; P.L. Joskow, N.L. Rose and C.D. Wolfram (1996), 168–179.
192. M.J. Roe (2002), pp. 30–33 and 47.
193. Ibid., pp. 41–43; J.N. Gordon (2005), 693, no. 57.
194. G. Hertig (2005), 271.
195. G.A. Ferrarini and N. Moloney (2005), 311–312.

2. The Lake Wobegon Effect: All Managers are above Average

A more serious problem was dubbed the 'Lake Wobegon'[196] effect or, more prosaically, 'benchmarking'. This effect revolves around a perverse dynamic. One of the most important duties of any board of directors is to choose the CEO and the rest of the executive team. In principle, the board will be convinced that it hired the best (or one of the best) managers in its industry. At the very least, it will believe that it has an above-average CEO, particularly if it has searched high and low for what R. Khurana (2002) calls the 'star CEO'. When the time comes to compensate the executives, this behavioural trait will lead the board to offer above-average packages to management. As this approach is repeated by all companies, the overall level of compensation will climb.[197]

The irony of this escalation is that nobody wins. It is obvious that companies and shareholders pay more. But executives themselves are probably no happier. As moral philosophers and economists since Adam Smith have pointed out,[198] to a certain extent humans do not seek wealth for its own sake, but rather for the status it confers.[199] If all executives earn more, no one executive can expect to acquire a better status from his increased compensation package. Thus even managers are caught in this infernal spiral.

Transparency is not directly to blame for this problem. Long before the disclosure of executive compensation was required, boards of directors could rely on compensation consultants to provide them with information on how competitors and other firms in the peer group generally paid their managers.[200] But transparency does aggravate the problem in two respects. First, transparency makes it much easier to discern levels of pay across the board, thus encouraging inflation. Whereas compensation consultants limit their comparison to a handful of peer companies, and can use their specialized skills to question the validity of certain comparisons, disclosure leads to complete transparency without these safeguards – producing yet more inflation. However, this problem is a minor one in comparison with another: the legitimizing effect of transparency.

Disclosure rules have a legitimizing effect. Without even accounting for the healing effect of disclosing conflicts of interest under the rules governing the duty of loyalty, laboratory experiments have shown that agents will act more opportunistically if they disclose their conflicts of interest.[201] Most likely, these agents

196. Lake Wobegon is the fictional Minnesota setting for radio entertainer Garrison Keillor's tales and yarns. He concludes each weekly show with, 'That's the news from Lake Wobegon, Minnesota, where all the women are strong, all the men are good-looking, and all the children are above average.' See <www.prairiehome.org>.
197. M.C. Jensen, K. Murphy and E.J. Wruck (2004), 56.
198. See the citation by H.L. Cole, G.J. Mailath and A. Postlewaite (1992), 1,092.
199. G. Akerlof (1976); R. Layard (1980). See also R.M. Landers, James B. Rebitzer and Lowell J. Taylor (1996), examining a similar phenomenon involving partners in a law firm.
200. K. Murphy (1999), pp. 2,517–2,518.
201. See D. M. Cain, G. Loewenstein and D. A. Moore (2005), 8–18.

assume that their principal can discount the biased nature of their activity, and are convinced that transparency absolves them from any moral issue arising out of their opportunistic actions[202]. Applied to executive compensation, this line of argument would lead managers to feel that they need not be shy when negotiating their package, as even the most shocking arrangement can be disinfected by disclosure. Directors will also be comforted by publicizing arrangements. As more firms fall into this trap, the effect will be accentuated in practice by the norm-setting effect of transparency.

3. Transparency as a Norm-Setting Mechanism

a. Economic Function of Social Norms

Over the past decade, legal scholars have become increasingly interested in the existence and effect of social norms in the commercial context.[203] The term 'social norm' is usually employed to refer to widely occurring patterns of behaviour. Compliance with social norms does not stem from a hierarchical power relation as with legal rules, but rather from peer pressure and, taking an economic approach to this issue, the 'signalling' benefits of belonging to a group.[204]

E.A. Posner (1998, 1999), borrowing from M. Spence's signalling theory, offers a model for understanding social norms as signals that can be summarized as follows:[205] If we assume there are two types of persons, a 'good' type and a 'bad' type, third parties will always prefer to do business with good types and shun bad types. However, 'good' types often cannot be distinguished from 'bad', and parties cannot simply ask the potential partner to which type he belongs, because the 'bad' types will be inclined to lie and pass themselves off as good ones. As a result, 'good' types are required to try to find a way to communicate, or signal, their type to other parties. One way to do this is to offer some kind of legally enforceable promise, e.g. a warranty that would be too costly for a bad type. Another way is to behave in a way that would not be in keeping with a bad type. The signalling effect makes it possible to distinguish between good types and bad types. As a result, this behavioural pattern will become a socially accepted norm and will be complied with by most 'good types'.[206]

In this model, the rule itself is unimportant; it may be as trivial as wearing a tie; it may be efficient or inefficient; it may even be unfair. What matters most is that only the good types find that the benefits of being seen as such by potential

202. See D. M. Cain, G. Loewenstein and D. A. Moore (2005).
203. See e.g. L. Bernstein (1996); R. Cooter (1996); E.A. Posner (1999), 22. See also the very influential studies by S. Macaulay (1970); R.M. Axelrod (1983); R. Ellickson (1991).
204. See generally R. Cooter (1998), 587; E.A. Posner (1999), p. 14.
205. E.A. Posner (1998), 767–771; E.A. Posner (1999), pp. 22–36. See also M. Spence (1973).
206. E.A. Posner (1998), 776–778; E.A. Posner (1999), pp. 22–36.

business partners outweigh the costs of complying with the rule. In other words, the existence of a norm does not guarantee its efficiency, or its fairness.[207]

b. Transparency as a Norm-Creating Device

Transparency can act as catalyst for other norm-setting devices: a good executive compensation package is often seen as a sign of good corporate governance. To a large extent, the jury is still out on what constitutes good or bad compensation structures. From the perspective of adaptive efficiency,[208] it may be better to leave it up to each individual corporation to determine the best option and to find out through a process of trial and error what system ensures the best outcome. In this context, transparency as such in theory does not matter greatly; in fact it could act as a control mechanism. The truth is that good practice is difficult to observe and measure.

The problem is that executive compensation is an appealing proxy for measuring the quality of corporate governance at board level, although certainly not the only one.[209] With the exception of a few extremely formal procedures – which are far from being empirically proven – such as separation of the functions of chairman and CEO, the use of committees of independent directors, and the frequency of board meetings, the corporate governance practices of individual firms are difficult for an outsider to observe. How can one examine, much less measure, whether or not a director prepares her meetings appropriately? Whether she is 'independent in mind' and critical of management? Whether she handles investor relations with an appropriate degree of candour? For this reason, easily quantifiable criteria are often used to measure corporate governance in academic and non-academic studies alike.[210] Even then, interestingly, the evidence for the efficiency of particular acknowledged 'best practices,' such as board independence, is at best mixed.[211]

Transparency enables outsider to more easily observe and measure just how these procedures impact the structure and level of executive compensation. If most firms adopt a more or less standard practice, any outlier will, by comparison, be suspected of poor management. Therefore, unless a given firm has strong beliefs in regard to what constitutes a good compensation package and can explain its view to the markets – a difficult task, needless to say – it will tend to blend in and follow whatever standard behaviour other companies have adopted in order to avoid being branded as a bad type.

---

207. E.A. Posner (1998), 798–799; E.A. Posner (1999), pp. 22–36.
208. D.C. North (1990), p. 81.
209. Other proxies are formal elements, such as the existence of committees, frequency of board meetings, number of outside or independent directors, and separation of chairman and CEO positions.
210. See e.g. La Porta/Lopez-de-Silanes/Shleifer (1999); Ethos (2003); Ethos (2004).
211. Compare S. Bhagat and B. Black (1999) and S. Bhagat and B. Black (2002) with A. Klein (1998).

From an efficiency standpoint: this normalization of compensation practices has two important consequences. First, the social norm may crystallize an inefficient compensation package. This, in fact, may have been what happened with stock options. They were initially praised as an appropriate instrument to provide incentives to managers and overcome the agency conflict.[212] No company could afford not to offer them to its managers, without running the risk of being viewed as *passé*. The result was an explosion in that particular means of executive compensation.[213] The enthusiasm was so widespread that it took the corporate scandals that followed the bursting of the corporate bubble to make the same analysts more critical of this instrument.[214] Although enthusiasm was tempered after the collapse of the bull market, it is not unlikely that other inefficient patterns of compensation will take off and generate new social norms.[215]

The second problem is linked to the diversity of corporate ventures. No single type of executive compensation will suit all firms. There are many different types of companies, and the type of remuneration package needed to encourage owners to act in the best interests of their shareholders varies from one company to the next.[216] Perhaps stock options work well in a rapidly evolving new economy, but not in industries with a longer product development pipeline. Similarly, a package that is suited to the executives of a multinational blue-chip company is perhaps not suited to a mid-cap. Yet, in each of these cases, if a social norm arises around executive compensation, firms will feel a strong pressure to comply with it or run the risk of being shunned by the capital markets.

c. The Expressive Function of Codes of Best Practice

This pressure is increased by the development of corporate governance principles and codes of best practice. Although these self-regulatory instruments aim to create a flexible alternative to government regulation and to insulate the corporate environment from political interference, they also have an expressive function: they express a moral – or at least normative judgment – on what is presumed to be the best practice in the field, even if they are not mandatory. Other market participants will view the dissident's practices as suboptimal and informally make sure he suffers for them.[217]

---

212. See the influential papers by M.C. Jensen and K. Murphy (1990a); M.C. Jensen and K. Murphy (1990b)
213. See the data in Hall/K. Murphy (2003), 51. See also K. Murphy (2004), 5 (showing that the explosion in stock options is not limited to the US, but has crossed over to Europe).
214. See e.g. M.C. Jensen (2004); M.C. Jensen, K. Murphy and E.J. Wruck (2004).
215. According to data from K. Murphy (2004), the percentage of options as a part of total pay decreased in 2002–2003 in the US, but continued to grow in Europe, albeit at a slower rate. However, in both cases, the influence of bearish stock markets remains uncertain.
216. G. Hertig (2005), 274–275.
217. See C. Sunstein (1996), 2,031–2,033; R. Cooter (1998), 592–593 on the expressive function of law.

A similar phenomenon occurred several years ago in the US, when the tax code was modified to limit the deductibility of non-performance pay in excess of a million dollars.[218] Rather than cap base compensation, this amendment led to an overall increase in compensation packages: they increased performance-based remuneration, which remained fully deductible. In addition, and rather perversely, a significant number of companies raised their base pay up to the one million dollar threshold.[219] Thus the statute actually increased the amount of non-performance-based compensation

The same trend is likely to manifest itself even if a corporate governance code expressly allows dissidents to defend their position through a 'comply-or-explain' system. Indeed, the expressive function of a norm is not contingent on its enforcement by a court or regulator. A specific rule, even a non-binding or default rule, offers a strong lead that most actors are likely to follow.[220] This is precisely what happens with a corporate governance code: it implicitly – or even explicitly (e.g. 'best practice') – enshrines its proposed approach as the right one. The dissident must bear the burden of proving that his approach is justified.[221] In Switzerland, Ethos, an institutional investor based in Geneva and noted for its activism, called for the Swiss Code of Best Practice for Corporate Governance to adopt the 'comply or explain' approach to ensure better compliance with its principles.[222] Similarly, G. Hertig (2005) notes how analysts and even loan officers feel increasingly compelled not to recommend companies that do not follow corporate governance standards.[223]

The expressive function of codes of best practice has an adverse effect on corporate governance. As I said previously, the debate on the purpose of executive compensation remains open and we are far from a consensus. The existence of corporate governance code and its normative power may discourage companies from testing new incentive schemes, thus preventing the emergence of perhaps more efficient solutions. In the long run, this may lock most firms in a standardized, but mediocre, executive compensation scheme.[224]

Similarly, the one-size-fits-all approach that underlies most codes of best practice is also likely to prevent atypical firms from implementing an incentive scheme that would be more appropriate for their size or type of business. They may also burden such firms with organizational costs that exceed the benefits.[225]

---

218. Section 162(m) Internal Revenue Code.
219. See N.L. Rose and C. Wolfram (2002), S143–S166.
220. R. Cooter (1998), 593–595. See also C. Sunstein (2002), 132–133; R. Korobkin (2003), 1,282.
221. G. Hertig (2005), 274.
222. Ethos (2003), p. 24.
223. G. Hertig (2005), 274.
224. D. C. North's concept of adaptive efficiency postulates that a society that locks itself into a given social configuration will lose its capacity to change. By contrast, a society that encourages experimentation will be more likely to find efficient solutions through a process of trial and error. D.C. North (1990), p. 81.
225. G. Hertig (2005), 273–274.

D. Conclusion

Faced with such a bleak picture, what is the usefulness of increased transparency? By making more information readily available to investors, it facilitates shareholder action. Nonetheless, the data disclosed to the public is incomplete. Some forms of compensation will go unnoticed, giving the impression that the overall level is lower and, perhaps, that pay is more sensitive to performance than it really is. This may lead managers to use inefficient forms of compensation so as to avoid public scrutiny.

In the previous section, we examined the current Swiss disclosure framework set out in the Corporate Governance Directive and proposed amendments to the Code of Obligations. These rules are far from perfect. Their numerous formal and substantive shortcomings make it more difficult to assess the level and pay–performance sensitivity of compensation at firm level and virtually prevent any sensible cross-company analysis. These gaps in the disclosure system could be easily remedied through more comprehensive regulation. However, if this breach is closed, another will soon appear somewhere else. The game is endless and, at some point, the legislator or regulator will have to consider whether the costs of disclosure are compensated by additional benefits. However, the fundamental problem will remain; shareholders will react only to the most egregious abuses.

Moreover, the disclosure of compensation data worsens three problems of executive compensation. First, transparency may increase popular hostility to executive compensation and drive legislators to tackle the problem using inappropriate means or by setting remuneration at an inadequate level. At the same time, the 'Lake Wobegon effect' pushes up levels of executive compensation, because firms always aspire to pay their CEOs above the benchmark. Finally, disclosure, together with corporate governance codes, has a norm-creative function which encourages most firms to go with the pack to avoid being the outlieroutsider. Therefore, although disclosure of executive compensation may have a laudable purpose, the current governance structure needs to be revised if disclosure is to effectively achieve its purpose.

IV. REVISING THE GOVERNANCE OF EXECUTIVE COMPENSATION

A. Current Governance of Executive Compensation: Managers and Politicians

If we take a step back and look at who determines executive compensation, the answer is quite surprising. At the level of individual firms, directors, who are themselves often executives of other companies, sit on compensation committees and discuss how much to pay the managers. However, directors are subject to conflicts of interest or, more broadly, to agency problems. On a higher level, politicians, members of parliament and (to a lesser extent) of government, also influence the design of executive compensation. Obviously they can use the tax system to favour certain forms of compensation and disadvantage others. They can also tackle executive compensation more explicitly by setting caps, or changing the disclosure system. However, most politicians do not legislate in the sole interests of investors. They also cater to the interests of other constituencies, such as labour, consumers and creditors.

This picture, however, omits one key interested party: shareholders. Although the very purpose of most corporations is to yield profit for shareholders,[226] the residual owners are not well equipped at company level to tackle the problem of inadequate compensation. They do not vote directly on executive compensation except in the context of the issuance of new share. Nor are they even called upon to approve the decisions of the board of directors *ex post facto*. The one recourse a shareholder possesses to penalize a company with an inappropriate compensation policy is by selling their shares. But this will have a limited impact on managers of financially sound companies, who do not need to raise capital from the markets and can, to an extent, insulate themselves from the market for corporate control. Due to these constraints on shareholder action, investors scrutinize only the worst abuses of executive compensation. Most inappropriate forms of compensation remain unaffected.

Shareholders cannot hope to take the issue to a political forum, where other interest groups with greater clout might only exacerbate the situation.[227] They may try to avoid this risk by relying on self-regulatory bodies, such as stock exchanges, or other privately sponsored soft-law makers.[228] Alternatively, they may use informal mechanisms while using the formal options as threats. However, these techniques are only available to larger institutional investors who are willing to spend the time and money involved in an active exercise of shareholder rights, thus creating the risk of regulatory capture to the detriment of smaller shareholders.[229]

226. See, under Swiss law, art. 620 (3) CO. The broad purpose is implemented in specific cases either by the board or by the general meeting and this implementation is the source of ongoing controversies. See R. Bahar (2004), pp. 98–108 (and references); C. Lambert (1992).
227. Obviously the validity of this statement depends on the overall political climate. In a social democratic environment, shareholders will be extremely reluctant to use lobbying to solve corporate law problems. In a more right-leaning environment, shareholders, drawing on populist influences, may acquire some influence in the aftermath of financial scandals. See M.J. Roe (1994), pp. 26–49 (with respect to financial institutions in the US); M.J. Roe (2002), pp. 29–37.
228. This matches M.J. Roe's 'Delaware model': Because most companies incorporated in Delaware do not have any other substantial tie with that state, the politics of Delaware corporate law are schematically the product of a bargaining game between managers and shareholders. By contrast, other constituencies are present at the federal level. M.J. Roe (2004), 2500–2504.
229. G. Hertig (2005), 278–279.

B. The Solution: Empower Shareholders

1. Put Shareholders at the Centre of the Debate

The best way to improve executive compensation is to put the principals at the centre of the debate. Disclosure helps. It lowers the threshold for shareholder action: greater transparency decreases the cost of obtaining information on executive compensation. It facilitates intervention by active investors and provides passive investors with information they would not bother to find otherwise,[230] but it also has its costs. As I hinted above, perhaps the best way to improve accountability would be to focus disclosure on process and policy.[231]

Among other oft mentioned options, increased shareholder activism is clearly an avenue worthy of further exploration. However, it is not necessarily the road to salvation. Although institutional shareholders can and do contribute to increased pay–performance sensitivity,[232] it is worth noting that shareholder passivity is not necessarily a bad thing. There is no way that shareholders can manage companies and set executive compensation. In fact, the possibility of investing money in a firm *without* having to manage it is arguably (together with limited liability, a precondition to this characteristic) the most significant feature of any system of company law. It is at the very heart of the company as an organizational form. For this reason, it is scarcely surprising if most small investors take little interest in how the company is managed, even before we consider the collective action problems plaguing any publicly held company. This separation between ownership and control also enables specialized managers to tap into the capital of numerous investors who would be entirely unable to manage the company themselves.

Recently, institutional investors have increasingly worked to change the picture through various forms of activism. They have promoted corporate governance codes and lobbied for change at government level.[233] However, the fact that it is always the bigger institutional investors who are willing to spend time and money on the active exercise of shareholder rights creates the risk of regulatory capture, to the detriment of smaller shareholders.[234]

---

230. See e.g. L.A. Bebchuk and J.M. Fried (2004); J.N. Gordon (2005), 693–698. This idea is also at the heart of a number of reform processes both in Switzerland and in Europe more generally. See Commission Recommendation of 14 December 2004, fostering an appropriate regime for the remuneration of directors of listed companies (Text with EEA relevance) (2004/913/EC), OJ L 385/55, 2004; *Message relatif à la modification du code des obligations (Transparence des indemnités versées aux membres du conseil d'administration et de la direction) du 23 juin 2004*, FF 2004 4223.
231. J.N. Gordon (2005), 693–698.
232. J.C. Hartzell and L.T. Starks (2003), 2,351.
233. See e.g. <www.icgn.org> at European level. In Switzerland, ethos promotes shareholder activism.
234. G. Hertig (2005), 278–279.

Interestingly, as it occurs, the most active institutional investors are the pension funds of public institutions.[235] Politically active constituencies, particularly trade unions, are far better represented on these bodies than on other institutional investors. These actors are more likely to feel they are accountable to the polity at large rather than to their beneficiaries, namely present and future retired employees. It must be remembered, however, that most institutional investors are also agents. As such, they are likely to fall prey to their own conflicts.[236]

2. Shareholder Votes on Executive Compensation

Rather than rely on shareholders themselves, it may be more efficient to remind the agents for whom they are acting. Disclosure contributes to this focus on investors and improves the accountability of directors.[237] However, it will not produce any effect unless it is followed by action.

Under the current system, the stock-exchange penalizes issuers who do not comply with disclosure requirements,[238] but the only disclosure rules it can effectively enforce are the quantitative ones. It is much more difficult to take action against an issuer whose disclosure is qualitatively unsatisfactory.

A milder form of sanction could come from the shareholders. For shareholders to decide executive compensation[239] is, in my opinion, out of place. As described previously, under the current corporate governance system, shareholders can pass binding resolutions on structural issues, such as the capital of the company or the appointment of directors and auditors.[240] Strategic decisions are the prerogative of the board of directors.[241] If compensation policy were transferred to the shareholders, the board would be deprived of one of its tools for controlling management by setting what it believes to be appropriate incentives.[242]

A similar objection applies to votes on specific forms of remuneration, such as equity-based incentive plans. Nevertheless, a trend in that direction is observable. In 2003, US Stock Exchanges moved to subject all incentive plans to shareholder approval.[243] In the EU, the Commission Recommendation of 14 December 2004 on an appropriate regime for the remuneration of directors of listed companies took

235. For instance, CALPers, the California State pension fund, is one of the largest shareholders in the world.
236. This issue had already been raised in the US by R.J. Gilson and R. Kraakman (1991), 871–876. See also B. Black (1992), 850–853.
237. See J.N. Gordon (2005), 693–698.
238. Art. 82 SWX Listing Rules provides various penalties for breaches of the Rules and thus, indirectly, of the Corporate Governance Directive.
239. The argument against voting on directors' compensation is less strong. But, as noted above, in spite of the heightened conflicts of interest, most complaints are focused on executive compensation rather than the remuneration of managers.
240. See art. 698 CO.
241. See art. 716a (1) CO.
242. P. Böckli, C. Huguenin-Jacobs and F. Dessemontet (2004), p. 134.
243. NASD Rule 4350; NYSE Listed Company Manual Rule 303A.

a similar stance and urged EU Member States to require shareholder approval for any equity-based compensation scheme.[244] In Switzerland, the *Expertenbericht der Arbeitsgruppe 'Corporate Governance' zur Teilrevision des Aktienrechts*, a report on Corporate Governance published by a government appointed group of experts on corporate governance, timidly suggested allowing companies to modify their articles of incorporation to provide for such shareholder approval of equity-based plans.[245] This proposal was taken up by the government as a part of its plan to revise company law.[246]

Although such an amendment would not be a complete novelty – *tantièmes* are already subject to a general meeting resolution[247] – it would have a real impact. The amendment would put a popular instrument of executive compensation to the ballot. Thus, the effect of the change would be felt more broadly than with the distribution of *tantièmes*, an obsolete form of compensation.

However, to submit only one institution to shareholder vote is an invitation to regulatory arbitrage, or more bluntly, avoidance; boards may be tempted to channel compensation through other means. For instance, they may pay executives a bonus to match stock performance, possibly subject to adjustments. They may also give up any incentive-based compensation package and increase executives' fixed salaries, forgoing any pay–performance sensitivity. Even L.A. Bebchuk and J.M. Fried (2004), who are more than dubious of current pay policies, stress this risk and recognize that putting desirable pay packages to the ballot may impose unnecessary costs.[248]

Instead of deciding executive compensation, shareholders could be asked to approve the executive compensation policy and ratify its implementation through a non-binding vote, as is current practice in England. [249] This would force the remuneration committee and the board at large to spell out its executive compensation package and its policy with shareholders in mind. Instead of distant and impersonal investors or a few vocal institutional investors, the vote of an annual general meeting has the key advantage of putting all shareholders at the heart of the debate.[250] From a legal perspective, such a vote should not have much more effect than the approval of the annual report or the discharge of liability:[251]At most, one

---

244. Art. 6 Commission Recommendation of 14 December 2004, fostering an appropriate regime for the remuneration of directors of listed companies (text with EEA relevance) (2004/913/EC), OJ L 385/55, 2004.
245. P. Böckli, C. Huguenin-Jacobs and F. Dessemontet (2004), p. 134.
246. Art. 627 (4) draft CO. *Begleitbericht zum Vorentwurf zur Revision des Aktien- und Rechnungslegungsrechts im Obligationenrecht vom 2. Dezember 2005*, available at <www.bj.admin.ch>, p. 40.
247. Art. 698 (2)(4) CO.
248. L.A. Bebchuk and J.M. Fried (2004), pp. 197–198.
249. Section 241A Companies Act 1985 as amended by Section 7, The Directors' Remuneration Report Regulations 2002, SI 2002, no. 1986.
250. J.N. Gordon (2005), 698–699.
251. Art. 698 (2)(4) CO. The effects of the discharge of liability are set out in Art. 758 CO. In practice, however, this resolution has a mainly symbolic value.

could add as a sweetener a protection from claims for the restitution of undue profits.[252] This would actually encourage the board to disclose information on executive compensation.

I do not think, or even hope, that this change would dramatically alter shareholders' attitudes to corporate governance in general, or executive compensation in particular. Shareholders are essentially passive, owing to the deep structure of corporations; they have problems with collective action and are not well equipped to carry out management decisions on their own. As a result, shareholders will more often than not rubber stamp the board's proposals. However, I do believe that forcing directors, and in particular the compensation committee, to come out and face their principals would make them take shareholders' interests more to heart. The prospect of an unpleasant annual general meeting would counterbalance the disagreeableness of having to be hard on executives, thus making directors more accountable to shareholders.

This solution has its limitations. It will not lead to shareholder action, but, I repeat, this is not the purpose. Nor will it prevent the compensation inflation caused by the Lake Wobegon effect and by norm creation. It does not even promise to improve disclosure and avoid camouflage. It simply seeks to draw the board's attention back to the shareholders. From there, it might lead to better performance through better governance.

As mentioned earlier, shareholders can pass a non-binding resolution on any subject, including executive compensation; such votes are uncommon, but not unheard of, in the Swiss corporate environment.[253] Companies could voluntarily submit to this type of system without any changes to the legal framework. However, for such a system to yield tangible results, disclosure has to focus on the right things: it must give more weight to compensation policy and pay–performance sensitivity than to raw quantitative data.

V. CONCLUSION

For at least the last thirty years, corporate analysts have been discussing how to improve governance and overcome, or at least mitigate, the agency conflict without prejudicing the benefits of specialized management by competent individuals. Since the formalization of agency theory, executive compensation has always been designated as one of the best tools for setting correct incentives and aligning interests. In parallel to this endeavour, large increases in the remuneration of CEOs and directors have become the target of popular hostility and have drawn increased media and political attention, adding a new constraint to the overall issue.

After negative experiences, analysts, lawyers and economists have come to realize that executive compensation could also be a source of false incentives

252. See Art. 678(2) CO.
253. Just such a vote took place at the UBS Annual General Meeting 2005 at the request of one shareholder. See press the release at <www.ubs.com/1/e/investors/agm/2005/media_release.html> and the voting results at <www.ubs.com/1/e/investors/agm/2005/votingresults.html>.

and was fraught with its own agency problems and conflicts of interest. Despite improvements in corporate governance at board level, the lack of shareholder control (through the three classic modes of exit, voice and the courts) meant there was no way to prevent abuses once the dikes were breached.

Against this backdrop, disclosure was hailed as the new savior, protector of good-governance practices, able to shed light on dubious practices. In Switzerland, the Corporate Governance Directive has indeed substantially improved the available information about the compensation practices of Swiss listed companies. But it has proven to have several formal and substantial shortcomings. First and foremost, it fails to show how pay is related to performance and to explain what policies the board and the compensation committee are seeking to pursue. Second, it fails to fully account for particular forms of remuneration, such as perks, options and certain payments to pension funds, opening a breach for abusive practices. Finally, on a more formal level, it fails to compel issuers to communicate information in a clear and standardized manner. This in turn makes it more difficult to compare practices across companies.

Despite these shortcomings, disclosure does contribute to improving shareholder control and director accountability. It lowers monitoring costs and enables shareholders to use their rights more effectively. By informing a wider public, it strengthens what L.A. Bebchuk and J.M. Fried (2004) dub the 'outrage constraint'. Perversely, however, disclosure may also induce directors to use less transparent, and possibly less efficient, forms of compensation to avoid this control.

More fundamentally, the outrage constraint is linked not only to the efficiency of the compensation package from the shareholders' perspective, but also to a broader social attitude towards executive remuneration. Thus it may cause executive compensation to fall prey to misguided political restrictions. Far from improving pay–performance sensitivity, it may actually worsen it.

Furthermore, increased transparency facilitates benchmarking and is at the source of the so-called 'Lake Wobegon' effect: salary inflation caused by the desire to grant above-average compensation packages to what are believed to be above-average CEOs.

Finally, disclosure, together with best practice codes, leads to homogeneity in an area in which no one size fits all companies and there is still plenty of room for experimentation. The case for transparency is a complicated one and the regulatory framework must be carefully designed to avoid these risks. This, I suggest, means acting on the governance structure underlying most listed companies.

From this perspective, it is striking to observe how the determinants of executive compensation are essentially set by two groups of actors; broadly speaking, legislators and regulators on the one hand and directors on the other. Shareholders are left out of the picture, although they should be right in the centre. Several avenues have been suggested to address this problem, among them increased activism through institutional investors and shareholder resolutions on executive compensation. These options are risky. They would disrupt the balance of power at the foundation of modern corporations; institutional investors sometimes pursue their own agendas and their interests may diverge from those of most shareholders.

Thus empowering them is to open the gates to a new array of abuses. Moreover, binding resolutions by shareholders would constitute a substantial change to the current institutional arrangement, whereby the affairs of the company are managed by, or at least under the supervision of, the board of directors.

Rather than empowering shareholders directly, it would be preferable to make directors more accountable to shareholders. In this connection, disclosure is clearly an interesting tool. However, it is difficult to enforce and thus has little bite. One way of overcoming these limitations would be to submit the disclosed compensation package to a non-binding shareholder vote. Such a resolution would be comparable to those on the annual report or the discharge of liability; its effects would be mainly symbolic. Thus it would be soft enough not to disrupt the balance of power within the company, yet strong enough to improve the accountability of boards and committees. This hopefully would be sufficient to resolve the agency problems of executive compensation and effectively lead companies to pay directors based on performance.

REFERENCES

Aepli, V., 'Zur Entschädigung des Verwaltungrates' (2002) *Revue suisse de droit des affaires* 72, 269.

Aggarwal, R.K. and A.A. Samwick, 'Executive Compensation, Strategic Competition, and Relative Performance Evaluation: Theory and Evidence' (1999) *Journal of Finance* 54, 1999.

Akerlof, G., 'The Economics of Caste and of the Rat Race and Other Woeful Tales' (1976) *The Quarterly Journal of Economics* 90, 599.

Anders, G., 'Upping the Ante: As Some Decry Lavish CEO Pay, Joe Bachelder Makes It Happen' *Wall Street Journal*, 25 June 2003, A1.

Axelrod, R.M., *The Evolution of Cooperation* (New York, NY: Basic Books, 1983).

Bahar, R., *Le rôle du conseil d'administration lors des fusions et acquisitions: une approche systématique* (Zurich, Schulthess, 2004).

Bahar, R., 'Indemnité de départ dans le contexte d'OPA hostile : mesure de défense inadmissible ? *<www.unige.ch/cdbf>, actualité n° 346 du 25 septembre 2005.*

Bainbrdige, S.M., 'Executive Compensation: Who Decides?' (2005) *Texas Law Review* 83, 1,615.

Bebchuk, L.A. and J.M. Fried, *Pay without Performance* (Cambridge, MA; London, Harvard University Press, 2004).

Bebchuk, L.A. and J.M. Fried, 'Executive Compensation as an Agency Problem' (2003) *Journal of Economic Perspectives* 17, 71.

Bebchuk, L.A., J.M. Fried and David I Walker, 'Managerial Power and Rent Extraction in the Design of Executive Compensation' (2002) *University of Chicago Law Review* 69, 751.

Bebchuk, L.A. and R.J. Jackson, Jr., 'Executive Pensions' (2005) *Journal of Corporation Law* 30, 823.

Berle, A.A. and G. Means, *The Modern Corporation and Private Property* (New Brunswick, NJ, Transaction Publishers, 1932).

Bernstein, L., 'Merchant Law in a Merchant Court: Rethinking the Code's Search for Immanent Business Norms' (1996) *University of Pennsylvania Law Review* 144, 1,765.

Bertrand, M. and S. Mullainathan, 'Are CEOs Rewarded for Luck? The Ones without Principals Are' (2001) *Quarterly Journal of Economics* 116, 901.

Bhagat, S. and Bernard B., 'The Uncertain Relationship between Board Composition and Firm Performance' (1999) *Business Lawyer* 54, 21.

Bhagat, S. and Bernard B., 'The Non-Correlation between Board Independence and Long-Term Firm Performance' (2002) *Journal of Corporation Law* 27, 231.

Black, B.S., 'Agents Watching Agents: The Promise of Institutional Investor Voice' (1992) *UCLA Law Review* 39, 811.

Black, F. and M. Scholes, 'The Pricing of Options and Corporate Liabilities' (1973) *Journal of Political Economy* S2 : 81, 637.

Böckli, P., *Schweizer Aktienrecht* (3rd edn, Zurich, Schulthess, 2004).

Böckli, P., C. Huguenin-Jacobs and F. Dessemontet, *Rapport intermédiaire du groupe de travail 'Gouvernement d'entreprise': Transparence des rémunérations et crédits octroyés aux membres des organes dirigeants des sociétés anonymes du 25 mars 2003*.

Böckli, P., C. Huguenin-Jacobs and F. Dessemontet, *Expertenbericht der Arbeitsgruppe 'Corporate Governance' zur Teilrevision des Aktienrechts* (Zurich, Schulthess, 2004).

Boemle, M., 'Die aktuelle Frage: 'Wie verlässlich und vergleichbar sind die Angaben über die Organentschädigungen im Rahmen der Corporate-Governance-Berichterstattung in den Geschäftsberichten 2002?" [2003] *L' Expert comptable suisse*, 499.

Brealy, R.A. and S.C. Myers, *Principles of Corporate Finance* (7th edn, Boston, etc., McGraw-Hill Irwin, 2003).

Brechbühl, B., 'Goldene Fallschirme oder silberne Brücken' (2004) *Revue suisse de jurisprudence* 100, 32.

Cole, H.L., G.J. Mailath and A. Postlewaite, 'Social Norms, Savings Behavior, and Growth' (1992) *Journal of Political Economy* 100, 1,092.

Cooter, R., 'Decentralized Law for a Complex Economy: The Structural Approach to Adjudicating the New Law Merchant' (1996) *University of Pennsylvania Law Review* 144, 1,643.

Cooter, R., 'Social Norms, Social Meaning, and the Economic Analysis of Law' (1998) *Journal of Legal Studies* 27, 585.

Core, J.E., R.W. Holthausen and D.F. Larcker, 'Corporate governance, chief executive officer compensation, and firm performance' (1999) *Journal of Financial Economics* 51, 371.

Daeniker, D., 'Vergütung von Verwaltungsrat und Geschäftsleitung' (2005) *Revue suisse de jurisprudence* 101, 381.

Degeorge, F., J. Patel and R. Zeckhauser, 'Earnings Management to Exceed Thresholds' (1999) *Journal of Business* 72, 1.

Easterbrook, F.H., 'Managers' Discretion and Investors' Welfare: Theories and Evidence Symposium' (1984) *Delaware Journal of Corporate Law* 9, 540.

Easterbrook, F.H. and D.R. Fischel, *The Economic Structure of Corporate Law* (Cambridge, MA, London, Harvard University Press, 1991).

Ellickson, R., *Order without Law: How Neighbours Settle Disputes* (Cambridge, MA, Harvard University Press, 1991).

Ethos, *Gouvernement d'entreprise des sociétés suisses* (Geneva: Ethos, 2003).

Ethos, *Gouvernement d'entreprise des sociétés suisses* (Geneva: Ethos, 2004).

Fama, E.F., 'Agency Problems and the Theory of the Firm' (1980) *Journal of Political Economy* 88, 207.

Fee, C.E. and C.J. Hadlock, 'Raids, Rewards, and Reputations in the Market for Managerial Talent' (2003) *Review of Financial Studies* 16, 1,315–1,357.

Fehr, E. and S. Gächter, 'Do Incentive Contracts Undermine Voluntary Cooperation?' Institute for Empirical Research in Economics, University of Zurich, 2002.

Fehr, E. and B. Rockenbach, 'Detrimental effects of sanctions on human altruism' (2003) *Nature* 422, 137–140.

Ferrarini, G.A. and N. Moloney, 'Executive Remuneration in the EU: The Context for Reform', (2005) *Oxford Review of Economic Policy* 21, 304.

Forstmoser, P., 'Informations- und Meinungsäusserungsrechte des Aktionärs' *Rechtsfragen um die Generalversammlung* (Zurich: Schulthess, 1997), p. 85.

Frey, B.S. and F. Oberholzer-Gee, 'The Cost of Price Incentives: An Empirical Analysis of Motivation Crowding-Out' (1997) *American Economic Review* 87, 746.

Frey, B.S., F. Oberholzer-Gee and Reiner Eichenberger, 'The Old Lady Visits Your Backyard: A Tale of Morals and Markets' (1996) *Journal of Political Economy* 104, 1,297.

Frey, B.S. and M. Osterloh, *Yes, Managers Should Be Paid Like Bureaucrats*, CESIFO Working Paper No. 1,379, 2005.

Gilson, R.J. and R. Kraakman, 'Reinventing the Outside Director: An Agenda for Institutional Investors' (1991) *Stanford Law Review* 43, 863.

Glanzmann, L., 'Die Verantwortlichkeitsklage unter Corporate Governance-Aspekten' *Revue de droit suisse* 119 (2000) II 135.

Gneezy, U. and A. Rustichini, 'A Fine Is a Price' (2000) *The Journal of Legal Studies* 29, 17.

Gordon, J.N., 'Executive Compensation: If There's a Problem, What's the Remedy? The Case for "Compensation Disclosure and Analysis" 2005 *Journal of Corporate Law* 30, 675.

Grass, A.R., *Business Judgment Rule: Schranken der richterlichen Überprüfbarkeit von Management-Entscheidungen in aktienrechtlichen Verantwortlichkeitsprozessen* (Zurich, Schulthess, 1998).

Grass, A.R., 'Management-Entscheidungen vor dem Richter: Schranken der richterlichen Überprüfbarkeit von Geschäftsentscheiden in aktienrechtlichen Verantwortlichkeitsprozessen' (2000) *Revue suisse de droit des affaires* 72, 1.

Grossman, S.J. and O.D. Hart, 'An Analysis of the Principal-Agent Problem' (1983) *Econometrica* 51, 7.

Hall, B.J. and K.J. Murphy, 'Stock Options for Undiversified Executives' *Journal of* (2002) *Accounting and Economics* 33, 3.

Hall, B.J. and K.J. Murphy, 'The Trouble with Stock Options' (2003) *Journal of Economic Perspectives* 17, 49.

Harris, M. and A. Raviv, 'The Theory of Capital Structure' (1991) *Journal of Finance* 46, 297.

Hartzell, J.C. and L.T. Starks, 'Institutional Investors and Executive Compensation' (2003) *Journal of Finance* 58, 2,351.

Hertig, G., 'On-Going Board Reforms: One-Size-Fits-All and Regulatory Capture' (2005) *Oxford Review of Economic Policy* 21, 269.

Hirschmann, A.O., *Exit, Voice and Loyalty: Responses to Decline in Firms, Organisations and States* (Cambridge, MA, London, Harvard University Press, 1970).

Holmstrom, B., 'Moral Hazard and Observability' (1979) *Bell Journal of Economics* 10, 74.

Holmstrom, B., 'Moral Hazard in Teams' *Bell Journal of Economics* 13 (1982) 324.

Homburger, E., *Der Verwaltungsrat*, in *Zürcher Kommentar zum schweizerischen Zivilgesetzbuch* (Zurich, Schulthess, 1997).

Isler, P. and G. Zindel in *Basler Kommentar zum Schweizerisches Privatrecht: OR II* (2nd edn, Basle, Geneva, Munich: Helbing & Lichtenhahn, 2002) ad art. 652a CO.

Jensen, M.C., 'Paying People to Lie: the Truth about the Budgeting Process' (2003) *European Financial Management* 9, 379.

Jensen, M.C., 'The Agency Costs of Overvalued Equity and the Current State of Corporate Finance' (2004) *European Financial Management* 10, 549.

Jensen, M.C. and W.H. Meckling, 'Theory of the Firm: Managerial Behavior, Agency Costs and Ownership Structure' (1976) *Journal of Financial Economics* 3, 305.

Jensen, M.C. and K.J. Murphy, 'CEO Incentives – It's Not How Much You Pay, But How' (1990a) *Harvard Business Review* 68, 138.

Jensen, M.C. and K.J. Murphy, 'Performance Pay and Top-Management Incentives' (1990b) *Journal of Political Economy* 98, 225.

Jensen, M.C., K.J. Murphy and E.J. Wruck, *Remuneration: Where We've Been, How We Got to Here, What Are the Problems, and How to Fix Them*, ECGI Working Paper, 2004.

Joskow, P.L., N.L. Rose and C.D. Wolfram, 'Political Constraints on Executive Compensation: Evidence from the Electric Utility Industry' (1996) *RAND Journal of Economics* 27, 165.

Khurana, R., *Searching for a Corporate Savior: The Irrational Quest for Charismatic CEOs* (Princeton, N.J.: Princeton University Press, 2002).

Klein, A., 'Firm Performance and Board Committee Structure' (1998) *Journal of Law and Economics* 41, 137.

Korobkin, R., 'The Endowment Effect and Legal Analysis' (2003) *Northwestern Law Review* 97, 1,227.

Krneta, G., *Praxiskommentar Verwaltungsrat* (Bern, Staempfli, 2001).

Kurer, P., in *Basler Kommentar zum Schweizerisches Privatrecht: OR II* (2nd edn, Basle, Geneva, Munich: Helbing & Lichtenhahn, 2002) ad art. 677 CO.

La Porta, R., F. Lopez-de-Silanes and A. Shleifer, 'Corporate Ownership around the World' (1999) *Journal of Finance* 54, 471.

Lambert, C., *Das Gesellschaftsinteresse als Verhaltensmaxime des Verwaltungsrates der Aktiengesellschaft* (Bern, Staempfli, 1992).

Landers, R.M., J.B. Rebitzer and L.J. Taylor, 'Rat Race Redux: Adverse Selection in the Determination of Work Hours in Law Firms' (1996) *American Economic Review* 86, 329.

Layard, R., 'Human Satisfactions and Public Policy' (1980) *The Economic Journal* 90, 737.

Macaulay, S., 'Non-Contractual Relations in Business: A Preliminary Study' (1970) *American Sociological Review*, 56.

Markowitz, H., 'Portfolio Selection' (1952) *Journal of Finance* 7, 77.

Murphy, K.J., 'Executive Compensation' in *Handbook of Labor Economics. Volume 3B. Handbooks in Economics, vol. 5*, (O. Ashenfelter and D. Card eds) (Amsterdam; New York and Oxford: Elsevier Science, North-Holland, 1999), p. 2,485.

Murphy, K.J., 'Explaining Executive Compensation: Managerial Power versus the Perceived Cost of Stock Options' (2002) *University of Chicago Law Review* 69, 847.

Murphy, K.J., *Executive Pay: How Can We Explain Current Levels of Executive Compensation?* 2004, <www.nccr-finrisk.unizh.ch/media/pdf/murphyslides.pdf> (12 December 2005).

Myers, S.C., 'Determinants of Corporate Borrowing' (1977) *Journal of Financial Economics* 5, 147.

Myers, S.C. and N.S. Majluf, 'Corporate Financing and Investment Decisions when Firms Have Information that Investors Do Not Have' (1984) *Journal of Financial Economics* 13, 187.

North, D.C., *Institutions, Institutional Change, and Economic Performance* (Cambridge, New York, NY: Cambridge University Press, 1990).

Nussbaumer, A. and H.C. von der Crone, 'Ausschüttung von Tantiemen (Enstscheid BGer 4C.386/2002 vom 12 Oktober 2004' (2005) *Revue suisse de droit des affaires* 75, 94.

Ofek, E. and D. Yermack, 'Taking Stock: Equity-Based Compensation and the Evolution of Managerial Ownership' (2000) *Journal of Finance* 55, 1,367.

Perry, T. and M. Zenner, 'Pay for Performance? Government Regulation and the Structure of Compensation Contracts' (2001) *Journal of Financial Economics* 62, 453.

Peter, H. and R. Bahar, 'Rachat et options de rachat par une société de ses propres actions (en droit des sociétés)' in *Journée 1999 de droit bancaire et financier* (L. Thévenoz and C. Bovet eds) (Bern, Staempfli, 2000), p. 15.

Posner, E.A., 'Social Norms, Social Meaning, and the Economic Analysis of Law' (1998) *Journal of Legal Studies* 27, 765.

Posner, E.A., *Law, Cooperation and Rational Choice* (Cambridge, MA: Harvard University Press, 1999).

Rajan, R.G. and J. Wulf, 'Are Perks Purely Managerial Excess?' NBER, 2004.

Roe, M.J., *Strong Managers, Weak Owners: The Political Roots of American Corporate Finance* (Princeton, N.J., Princeton University Press, 1994).

Roe, M.J., *Political Determinants of Corporate Governance* (New York, Oxford University Press, 2002).

Roe, M.J., 'Delaware's Politics' (2004) *Harvard Law Review* 118, 2,493.

Rose, N.L. and C. Wolfram, 'Regulating Executive Pay: Using the Tax Code to Influence Chief Executive Officer Compensation' (2002) *Journal of Labor Economics* 20, S138.

Ross, S.A., 'The Economic Theory of Agency: The Principal's Problem' (1973) *American Economic Review* 63, 134.

Ruedin, R., 'Rémunération de l'administrateur de société anonyme', in *Wirtschaftsrecht zu Beginn des 21. Jahrhunderts: Festschrift für Peter Nobel zum 60. Geburtstag* (R. Waldburger, C.M. Baer, U. Nobel and B. Bernet eds) (Bern, Staempfli, 2005) p. 313.

Ruffner, M., *Die ökonomischen Grundlagen eines Rechts der Publikumsgesellschaft* (Zurich, Schulthess, 2000).

Schütz, D., *Gierige Chefs: Warum kein Manager zwanzig Millionen Wert ist* (Zurich, Orell Füssli Verlag, 2005).

Schwarcz, S., 'Rethinking the Disclosure Paradigm in a World of Complexity', (2004) *University of Illinois Law Review*, 1.

Spence, M., *Market Signaling: Informational Transfer in Hiring and Related Processes* (Cambridge: Harvard University Press, 1973).

Stout, L.A., 'On the Proper Motives of Corporate Directors (Or, Why You Don't Want to Invite Homo Oeconomicus to Join Your Board)' (2003) *Delaware Journal of Corporate Law* 29, 1.

Sunstein, C., 'On the Expressive Function of Law' (1996) *University of Pennsylvania Law Review* 144, 2,021.

Sunstein, C., 'Switching the Default Rule' (2002) *New York University Law Review* 77, 106.

Trigo Trindade, R. and R. Bahar, 'Droits des actionnaires minoritaires en Suisse' *Rapports suisses présentés au XVIème Congrès international de droit comparé* (Zurich, Schulthess, 2002) p. 381.

von der Crone, H.C., 'Interessenkonflikte im Aktienrecht' (1994) *Revue suisse de droit des affaires* 66, 1.

von der Crone, 'Auf den Weg zu einem Recht der Publikumsgesellschaften' (1997) *Revue des juristes bernois* 133, 73.

von Planta, A. and C. Lenz, in *Basler Kommentar zum Schweizerisches Privatrecht: OR II* (2nd edn, Basle, Geneva, Munich: Helbing & Lichtenhahn, 2002) ad art. 659–659b, 807 CO.

Watter, R., in *Basler Kommentar zum Schweizerisches Privatrecht: OR II* (2nd edn, Basle, Geneva, Munich, Helbing & Lichtenhahn, 2002) ad art. 716–724, 726–731a, 752–753, 811–816, 819, 897–902, 905–910 et 1156 CO.

Watter, R., 'Die Informationsversorgung des Aktionärs insbesondere die SWX-Richtlinie betr. Information zur Corporate Governance' in *Informationspflichten des Unternehmens im Gesellschafts- und Börsenrecht* (C.B. Bühler ed.) (Bern, Stuttgart, Wien: Paul Haupt, 2003) p. 33.

Widmer, P. and O. Banz in *Basler Kommentar zum Schweizerisches Privatrecht* (2nd edn, Basle, Geneva, Munich, Helbing & Lichtenhahn, 2002).

Yermack, D., 'Higher Market Valuation of Companies with a Small Board of Directors' (1996) *Journal of Financial Economics* 40, 185.

Chapter 4

Executive Compensation and Analyst Guidance: The Link between CEO Pay and Expectations Management

Guido Bolliger and Manuel Kast*** [1]

I. INTRODUCTION

Over the past decade, companies have tried particularly hard to meet analyst expectations.[2] There has been a marked decrease in the tendency of managers to report

* Head of risk management, Olympia Capital Management, Paris, Formerly International Center for Asset Management and Engineering, FAME.

** Formerly University of Lausanne and International Center for Asset Management and Engineering, FAME.

1. This paper was written while both authors were Ph.D. candidates affiliated with the International Centre for Asset Management and Engineering (FAME). The views expressed in this paper are those of the authors and do not represent positions of any current or previous employer.
We should like to thank the following for their helpful comments: Michel Dubois, Pascal Dumontier, Rajna Gibson, William Rees, Michael Rockinger, Nathan Shulman, René Stulz, Ernst-Ludwig von Thadden, and seminar participants at the FAME Doctoral Workshop, University of Geneva; the Second Swiss Doctoral Workshop on Finance; the London Business School Accounting Symposium 2003; and the European Finance Association Annual Meeting 2003. We gratefully acknowledge financial support from the Banque Cantonale Vaudoise (BCV), the International Center for Asset Management and Engineering (FAME) and the National Centre of Competence in Research 'Financial Valuation and Risk Management' (NCCR FINRISK). Any errors are our own.
2. Analyst expectations are commonly equated with the analyst consensus estimate of one year earning per share forecast.

L. Thévenoz and R. Bahar (eds.), *Conflicts of Interest: Corporate Governance and Financial Market*, pp. 137–169.

earnings falling short of analyst estimates.[3] Two principal mechanisms can be used to ensure that reported earnings do not fall short of analyst expectations. First, by manipulating discretionary accruals executives can manage earnings in order to meet or beat analyst expectations. The second method is to inject pessimism into analysts' forecasts by providing them with negative clues leading to downward revisions of the consensus estimates. As a result, firms can more easily meet or beat analyst expectations. The business press is replete with articles referring to this practice. In an article entitled 'The Guidance Game', published in *Fortune* in December 1998, E. Schonfeld wrote:

> '[A] company is allowed to provide the analysts with clues, or so-called guidance, about what it thinks earnings will be. The guidance number usually shows up as the consensus estimate among analysts. If the company meets or just beats the consensus, both that company and the analyst win: The stock goes up and everyone looks smart.'

Fuller and Jensen (2002) attribute the increasing tendency of managers to engage in analyst manipulation strategies to a shift in the nature of executive compensation structure. As stock options have become an increasingly important component of executive compensation, the preservation or enhancement of short-term stock value around the earnings announcement has become a priority for managers. M. Vickers, writing in the 24 May 1998 issue of *Business Week*, corroborated this explanation, saying, 'Companies need to generate positive surprises to keep not only stockholders but also stock-option holders happy – and that group is growing. . . .'

In this paper, we investigate whether the tendency of executives to manage analyst forecasts downward is related to the incentives provided by their compensation packages. Although past research and the financial media have claimed that management of expectations by executives relates to the increasing dependence of their remuneration on short-term trends in stock prices, to date, no direct empirical tests of this relationship have been carried out that take explicitly into account how, and to what degree, management compensation and ownership depend on the firm's stock performance.

In this paper, we will analyze these components of CEO compensation contracts, which, together with stock and option ownership, most influence the extent of analyst guidance, taking into account other firm-specific factors. We approach the problem by considering the characteristic components of the CEO compensation package according to their differing risk and incentive profiles. We have found that CEO compensation components strongly influence the propensity of managers to engage in expectations management strategies. Consistent with common wisdom, we have identified strong positive relationships between the practice of analyst guidance and the value of the CEO's in-the-money exercisable options, and between the sensitivity of the option portfolios to stock price movements and analyst guidance. Moreover, we have found a positive relationship between the value of shares held by CEOs and analyst guidance. Furthermore, we have identified a strong positive

3. See, for example, Brown (2001a).

relationship between analyst guidance and the annual bonuses paid to CEOs, suggesting that meeting or beating analyst expectations is an important determinant of CEO performance assessment. Finally, we will highlight the negative link between CEO base salary and analyst guidance.

In addition, in this paper, we examine the stock market's ability to discern pessimistic biases in analyst consensus forecasts induced by expectations management strategies. We also conducted an event study focusing on the earnings announcement dates to measure the valuation effects triggered by expectations management strategies and find that firms that meet or beat analyst consensus forecasts display strong positive cumulative abnormal returns during the period before and after the announcement date. However, the market is, to an extent, able to discern analyst guidance strategies: companies that are suspected of managing analyst expectations in order to report a positive earnings surprise display a lower abnormal return at the earnings announcement than those that are not suspected of guiding analysts downward.

Our research makes several contributions to the existing literature. As far as we know, we are the first to demonstrate the crucial role of executive compensation in explaining analyst guidance. Our findings that equity-based compensation induces managers to manipulate analysts complement previous research underlining the adverse consequences of such compensation.[4] Secondly, we extend Matsumoto's (2002) analysis, in which she shows that specific characteristics of firms can explain managerial incentives to avoid negative earnings surprises, although without including the incentives created by executive compensation components. Thirdly, our research complements the study of Richardson et al. (2003), who show that the tendency of managers and firms to sell shares after the earnings announcement creates incentives to guide analyst forecasts downward. Our paper considers the CEO's full pay package with several additional compensation and ownership items. We identify which equity and accounting performance-based compensation components lead managers to manipulate analyst expectations downward. We find that CEOs not only time the grant dates of their option awards to coincide with news announcements (Yermack 1997) and corporate voluntary disclosures around fixed award dates (Aboody and Kasznik 2000), but also manipulate analysts in order to maximize CEO compensation. Finally, our study contributes to the earnings surprise literature by demonstrating that positive cumulative abnormal returns for firms that meet or beat analyst forecasts are smaller if the firms are suspected of achieving these returns through expectations management. This result confirms the findings of Bartov et al. (2002), who use a different method to measure expectations management.

The remainder of this paper is organized as follows. In Section 2, we review the literature on expectations management. In Section 3, we suggest hypotheses to explain the cross-sectional relationship between expectations management and CEO compensation components, as well as CEO stock and option ownership.

4. See, for example, Dechow at al. (1996). Bergstresser and Philippon (2003) study the effects of executive incentive compensation on *earnings* management. Our focus is on the management of analysts.

Section 4 presents the sample and the empirical design and Section 5 presents the results of our research. In Section 6, we present the conclusions of our research.

II. REVIEW OF THE LITERATURE

Three important conclusions for expectations management stand out from past research. First, reported earnings affect stock prices. Bartov et al. (2002) show that stocks of firms that meet or beat analyst forecasts command a significantly higher return at the announcement date than those with unfavourable surprises. Furthermore, they find that the cost of managing analyst expectations downward before the announcement date is more than compensated by the stock price reaction to positive earnings surprises at the announcement date. More specifically, in their sample, which is controlled for the magnitude of the revision and the surprise, the stock price response to surprises at the earnings announcement is 1.5 times stronger than the response to analysts' downward revisions before the announcement date. Lopez and Rees (2001) report that firms that meet or beat analyst estimates over a series of consecutive quarters experience positive cumulative abnormal returns on the announcement date. Similarly, Kasznik and McNichols (2002) show that subsequent earnings and subsequent market values are higher for firms reporting positive earnings surprises over a number of quarters. Again, Skinner and Sloan (2002) show that firms that report negative surprises suffer large asymmetric market reactions as compared to those that report positive surprises. This applies particularly to growth firms.

Second, management is concerned about the evolution of short-term stock prices for several reasons. As noted by Richardson et al. (2003), managers of companies that intend to issue new equity are preoccupied with the current price level of their company because it directly impacts the amount of capital raised in the issue. Because many equity issues occur in the period immediately following the public earnings announcement, a sharp price increase at the earnings release is particularly important for the success of such issues. Richardson et al. find that pessimistic forecasting prior to an earnings announcement is more common in firms that are about to issue new equity.

The structure of management compensation packages is another reason why executives care about their firms' near-term stock prices. Murphy (1999) demonstrates a strong increase in the option compensation of US CEOs between 1991 and 1996 across all industrial sectors. He also reports a strong increase in the value of stocks held by S&P 500 CEOs throughout the 1990s. Yermack (1997) examines how CEOs influence the timing of stock option awards with respect to corporate news announcements and finds that they often receive these types of awards in advance of good earnings news that boosts stock prices. By the same token, earnings announcements *before* CEO stock option awards tend to be less favourable. Yermack concludes that CEOs exert influence on the compensation committee and are therefore able to manage the timing of their awards. Aboody and Kasznik (2000) found that CEOs make opportunistic voluntary disclosure decisions that increase the value of their stock option compensation. In particular, the authors investigate the timing of voluntary disclosures with respect to the granting of option awards to the CEOs of firms with fixed award schedules, and find that managers of such firms manage investor expectations downward prior to the award date, by delaying good news and rushing forward bad news. Richardson et al. (2003) showed that analyst forecasts are more pessimistic for firms whose insiders are net sellers of the firm's stock in the aftermath of earnings announcements.

Managers may also fear that a negative earnings surprise will affect their performance evaluation. Matsunaga and Park (2001) showed significant negative effect on the CEO's bonus payment when reported earnings fall short of analyst expectations. Puffer and Weintrop (1991) found an increased probability of CEO turnover when earnings fall short of analyst expectations. In the same vein, Matsumoto (2002) found that managers of firms with high institutional ownership are more likely to take action to avoid negative earnings surprises. She attributes her finding to the pressure for near-term performance that characterizes institutional investors. She also finds that firms that rely on implicit claims with stakeholders, and companies in industries with high litigation risk, are more likely to take action to avoid negative earnings surprises.

The third main conclusion of previous research is that managers have the ability to manage analyst forecasts. This is achieved by means of various mechanisms, including public disclosures (Cotter et al. 2002), informal communications and pressuring analysts to adjust their forecasts away from their actual expectations. A crucial input to the analyst is timely access to new information about the companies concerned, usually provided by companies themselves. Consequently, analysts are forced to cooperate with firms to improve their access to company management (Boni and Womack 2002). Lim (2001) argues that analysts, logically enough, issue biased forecasts in order to obtain valuable future information from management, which is one of their key sources of information. To the extent that the analyst's employer holds important positions or maintains an investment banking relationship with the company covered, the analyst is likely to be subject to additional pressures. Michaely and Womack (1999) and Lin and McNichols (1998) detect a systematic bias in recommendations for companies underwritten by the analyst's institution.

Overall, past research has indicated a strong relationship between the sign of the earnings surprise and the stock price reaction at the earnings announcement; that managers have strong incentives to avoid negative surprises; and that they have devised ways of influencing analysts by using various information channels or by exerting pressure on them to issue forecasts that are compatible with managers' own objectives.

III. HYPOTHESES ON EXPECTATIONS MANAGEMENT AND EXECUTIVE COMPENSATION

In this section we describe the components found in most executive compensation packages (Murphy 1999): stocks, stock options, bonus payments, long-term incentive plans and base salary. For each compensation component, we discuss the incentives that are created for managers to manipulate analysts prior to the earnings announcement. We form hypotheses about the relationship between expectations management and these compensation components as an integral part of the CEO's total firm-related financial exposure.

We define expectations management as the tendency of a company's management to avoid negative earnings surprises by maintaining low analyst expectations. Expectations management is measured by comparing the analyst consensus forecast and the expected earnings forecast according to the model described in section 4.2.[5]

To examine the influence of the CEO's stock compensation and share ownership on expectations management, we utilize two measures: (1) restricted stocks granted to the CEO during the current fiscal year and (2) the CEO's total stock position.

Restricted stocks are 'restricted' because shares are forfeited under certain conditions, typically related to employment retention. Their sale is usually prohibited during a three to five year vesting period. The CEO's total stock position also includes any stocks acquired privately by the CEO and restricted stocks granted in previous years.

Risk-averse and liquidity-constrained managers tend to sell a large portion of their shares as quickly as possible for purposes of liquidity or diversification, possibly aiming for personal target levels of share ownership (Ofek and Yermack 2000). However, due to insider trading restrictions, these sales typically do not occur before the earnings announcement: the bulk of insider trading is concentrated within the week immediately following the earning announcement (Sivakumar and Waymire 1994). Consequently, equity-based compensation components provide executives with strong incentives to take action that leads to a share price increase immediately before and after the earnings announcement date. Moreover, executives benefit from a relatively pessimistic outlook during a fiscal year in which stocks are awarded or purchased. By maintaining low analyst forecasts and saving good news for the earnings announcement, managers will receive a larger number of shares at times when share price is low.

Hence we expect a positive relationship between the total values of CEO share positions and expectations management. We also expect a positive relationship between awards of restricted stocks to managers and manipulation of analysts. However, this relation may prove to be weaker than that of analyst manipulation to the total position in unrestricted stocks, as our data is in regard to the restricted stocks granted in the current fiscal year only, which are probably not yet at the CEO's free disposal.[6] This leads to the first hypothesis.

Hypothesis 1: There is a positive relationship between the value of the shares held by CEOs and expectations management.

Stock options provide a direct, albeit non-linear, link between share price appreciation and managerial rewards. Options-based incentives to manipulate analysts' expectations may stem from two distinct sources: (1) newly awarded stock options, and (2) unexercised stock options granted in previous years.

Newly awarded stock options are usually non-tradable and are typically forfeited if the executive leaves the firm before vesting. Murphy (1999) shows that

5. We use the terms 'expectations management' and 'analyst guidance' synonymously in this paper.
6. For a detailed description of the compensation variables, see section 4.3.

most options expire after ten years, are generally vested over approximately four years, and are granted with strike prices equal to the 'fair market value' on the date of the grant. There are three reasons why newly awarded stock options can encourage executives to manage analyst expectations downward in spite of trading restrictions. First, a low stock price in the year of the option grant will translate into a relatively low strike, thus increasing the future value of the CEO's grant after the positive surprise at the earnings announcement (Aboody and Kasznik 2000). Second, newly awarded options increase executives' risk exposures to their companies. CEOs may thus have an interest in selling non-restricted shares or exercising other options to hedge the additional risk created by the newly awarded options (Ofek and Yermack 2000). Finally, as compared to out-of-the-money options, the value of newly awarded at-the-money options is more sensitive to stock price changes. As a consequence, top-level executives aiming to maximize their yearly stock option compensation may pursue stock price enhancing strategies for behavioural reasons.

In contrast to newly awarded options, exercisable and in-the-money options granted to CEOs in previous years can be cashed in directly after the earnings announcement. The amount of cash that can be raised by exercising the option and reselling the shares immediately is linearly related to the share price. Therefore, CEOs who own considerable amounts of exercisable and in-the-money options will have strong incentives to push strategies that lead to increases in share price. Overall, we would expect executives with large positions in newly awarded and exercisable in-the-money options to have strong incentives to guide analysts. For this reason, the second hypothesis states the following:

Hypothesis 2: There is a positive relationship between expectations management and the value of the options held by the CEO.

Bonus plans awarded to top executives are generally based on a single-year performance measure. Murphy (1999) reports that most companies use two or more performance measures when paying annual bonuses to top executives, and almost all companies rely on some measure of accounting profits to assess performance. Previous research suggests two reasons why bonuses may be related to expectations management. First, the size of the annual bonus is positively related to success in meeting analyst forecasts (Matsunaga and Park 2001). Therefore, managers who receive bonus plan payments directly benefit from meeting or beating analysts' earnings forecasts. Second, analysts' earnings forecasts are reflected in the board of directors' expectations about the future performance of their organizations (Imhoff and Lobo 1984, Fuller and Jensen 2002). Consequently, executives have a strong interest in keeping the directors' expectations at moderate levels (using analyst forecasts) so as to ensure that the performance thresholds set for their bonus plans are relatively low. Accordingly our third hypothesis is as follows:

Hypothesis 3: The relationship between expectations management and the amount paid to CEOs according to annual bonus plans is positive.

The structure of typical long-term incentive plans is similar to the structure of bonus plans, except that long-term incentive plans are typically based on rolling averages of cumulative performance over three to five years. Hence managers can likewise benefit from relatively pessimistic analyst forecasts during the year and a positive surprise at the announcement. Consequently we would expect the relationship between long-term incentive plans and expectations management to be similar to the relationship between bonus plans and expectations management. This leads to our fourth hypothesis.

Hypothesis 4: The relationship between expectations management and the amount paid to CEOs according to long-term incentive plans is positive.

Base salary represents the fixed component in executive compensation contracts. Salaries are typically based on salary surveys over the whole industry supplemented by detailed analysis of selected industry peers. In contrast to the other compensation items described above, the total amount of salary paid to a CEO in a given fiscal year is independent of the company's accounting performance or stock price development in that year. Therefore it is not likely to create any incentive for the CEO to engage in expectations management. On the contrary, CEOs with high salaries may be *less* likely to manage expectations, for two reasons.

First, for any given level of performance-linked compensation items, the higher the CEO's base salary, the less likely are there to be liquidity constraints that might force him/her to cash in any performance-dependent compensation items. Hence, the CEO is less likely to take short-term action in order to increase the value of the positions to be cashed in.

Second, expectations management may prove costly if it increases the risk of shareholder litigation in response to stock price manipulation. Moreover, investors may discount the stock prices of firms that have been caught manipulating analysts. If expectations management jeopardizes the firm's reputation and the credibility of management, it could ultimately result in the loss of the CEO's job, which would be particularly costly for CEOs with high base salaries. These arguments lead to our fifth hypothesis:

Hypothesis 5: The relationship between the salaries paid to CEOs and expectations management is negative.

In the following section, we first describe our sample selection process. We then present the measurement of the variables used in this paper and report their summary statistics. Finally, we describe the methodology used to test our hypotheses.

IV. SAMPLE AND METHODOLOGY

A. Sample Selection

We use data from five sources. CEO compensation information is taken from Standard and Poor's Execucomp database. Execucomp reports components of executive compensation for approximately 1,500 U.S. firms (S&P 500, S&P 400 Mid Cap, S&P 600 Small Cap) between 1992 and 2001. Like Richardson et al. (2003), we use individual analysts' forecasts to calculate a customized consensus estimate. We use this approach to construct a measure of expectations that is more up to date than the I/BE/S monthly consensus mean, which may contain stale forecasts.[7] We

7. Using the I/B/E/S monthly consensus mean instead of our own consensus yields quantitatively very similar results and does not affect any main result.

calculate the monthly consensus forecast for each company using the median of all individual analyst forecasts in that month. The individual analysts' annual earnings forecasts were obtained from Thomson Financial's I/B/E/S Detail History database. Accounting data is taken from Standard and Poor's Compustat. Daily stock returns and market capitalization data are from the Center for Research in Security Prices (CRSP). We use Thomson Financial's CDA Spectrum Historical Tape Files (13F) for institutional investor data.

The initial sample contains 14,873 observations for 3,956 different firms in the Execucomp database. The following categories were excluded from this initial sample: financial institutions (SIC codes 6000–6999), utilities (SIC codes 4800–4999), quasi-regulated industries (SIC codes 8000 and above), and firms with missing data in I/B/E/S, CRSP or Compustat. We also excluded firm–year observations in which the details of options granted to the company's CEO were incomplete or inconsistent (e.g. no maturity date, no exercise price, maturity date earlier than the grant date). In addition, we excluded firm–year observations for any company belonging to an industry that contained fewer than eight companies in that year. Industries are grouped as in Yermack (1995). Finally, we did not use any observations from the year 1992, for which Execucomp reports compensation data for only 433 CEOs.[8] After thus filtering the data, only 174 observations remained for that year. Another reason for excluding 1992 was due to the fact that it was the first year in which executive compensation information was published in the present format; we were anxious not to introduce any self-selection biases in case the characteristics of the firms (not) reporting correlated with the company characteristics used in the construction of our explanatory variables. The final sample contains 8,714 firm–year observations.

B. Sample Selection

Measuring true analyst expectations is always a difficult task. Whether analysts have been manipulated by management into issuing relatively low forecasts (expectations management) cannot, obviously, be directly observed. Previous research has developed two proxies for detecting expectations management. One method (cf. Richardson et al. 2003, Chan et al. 2003) is to track the error in the analysts' forecast over the relevant period. Expectations management is suspected when analyst forecasts are optimistically biased (EPS forecast>EPS announced) at the beginning of the period but end up with a pessimistic bias just prior to the announcement (EPS forecast<EPS announced). The alternative method (cf. Matsumoto 2002, Brown and Higgins 2002) is to model the expected forecast as a function of public information about the firm's performance (measured by EPS changes and stock price returns) and compare it with the last consensus forecast. Expectations management is suspected when the last consensus forecast is below the expected forecast.

We have used the latter (Matsumoto 2002) method because the former measure is inappropriate for our study, for two main reasons. Our main research question is

8. In 1992 only S&P500 companies were included in the database.

whether expectations management is related to various CEO compensation components. Hence our research focuses on the manipulation of analysts (as opposed to earnings). However, any measure that involves comparing forecasts with announced earnings cannot differentiate between analyst and earnings manipulation, since announced earnings are directly subject to earnings management. The Matsumoto measure, on the other hand, is based on comparing the consensus forecast to the expected forecast, which does not contain the current year's announced earnings.[9]

We adapted Matsumoto's (2002) methodology to annual data. She uses an econometric model to forecast future changes in earnings per share (EPS). Two explanatory variables are used in the model: 1) lagged yearly EPS changes and 2) the cumulative excess daily stock price return over the fiscal year. Returns are intended to capture additional value-relevant information that an analyst might use to estimate earnings. The parameters of the model are estimated cross-sectionally by industry group. Once the expected changes in yearly EPS have been determined, the expected EPS for a particular firm/year pair can be estimated. This expectation is then compared with the last analyst consensus forecast in order to detect analyst guidance. Downward guidance of analyst expectation is suspected whenever the last consensus is lower than the expected EPS for a particular firm. From this comparison we generated a dichotomous variable (DOWN), which equals one when guidance is suspected and zero when it is not. A detailed description of Matsumoto's (2002) model can be found in Appendix 2.

Figure 1 depicts the dynamic pattern of the average forecast error over the annual forecast horizon for the full sample and two sub-samples: firm–year observations for which expectations management can be suspected (DOWN=1) and firm–year observations for which expectations management is not suspected (DOWN=0). For each firm and for each month leading up to the earnings announcement, the scaled forecast error is calculated as the median of individual analysts' EPS forecasts minus the announced EPS, deflated by the stock price at the previous fiscal year end:$(FEPS_{it}-EPS_{it})/P_{it-1}$. The graphs display the average values across firms over time. Forecast errors with earnings forecasts issued less than 30 days prior to the earnings announcement are grouped in month 0 (zero), forecast errors using forecasts released in the window (−60, −31) days are in month −1, etc.

For both sub-samples, analysts are, on average, too optimistic at the beginning of the period and become increasingly pessimistic as the earnings announcement approaches. However, at the beginning of the forecast period, analysts appear to be far more optimistic with regard to firms that are suspected of manipulating analysts than to those that are not. The difference in the average scaled forecast error remains statistically significant until eight months before the earnings release date. At the end of the forecast period, there is a reversal in the sign of this difference: analysts are significantly more pessimistic (t-stat. = 1.98) with regard to firms suspected of managing expectations downward. Furthermore, 73.36 per cent of the firm–year observations for which a positive or zero earnings surprise is reported belong to the

9. Announced earnings only enter indirectly into the calculation of the expected EPS change as the *difference* between earnings in the previous year and the year before that. See below.

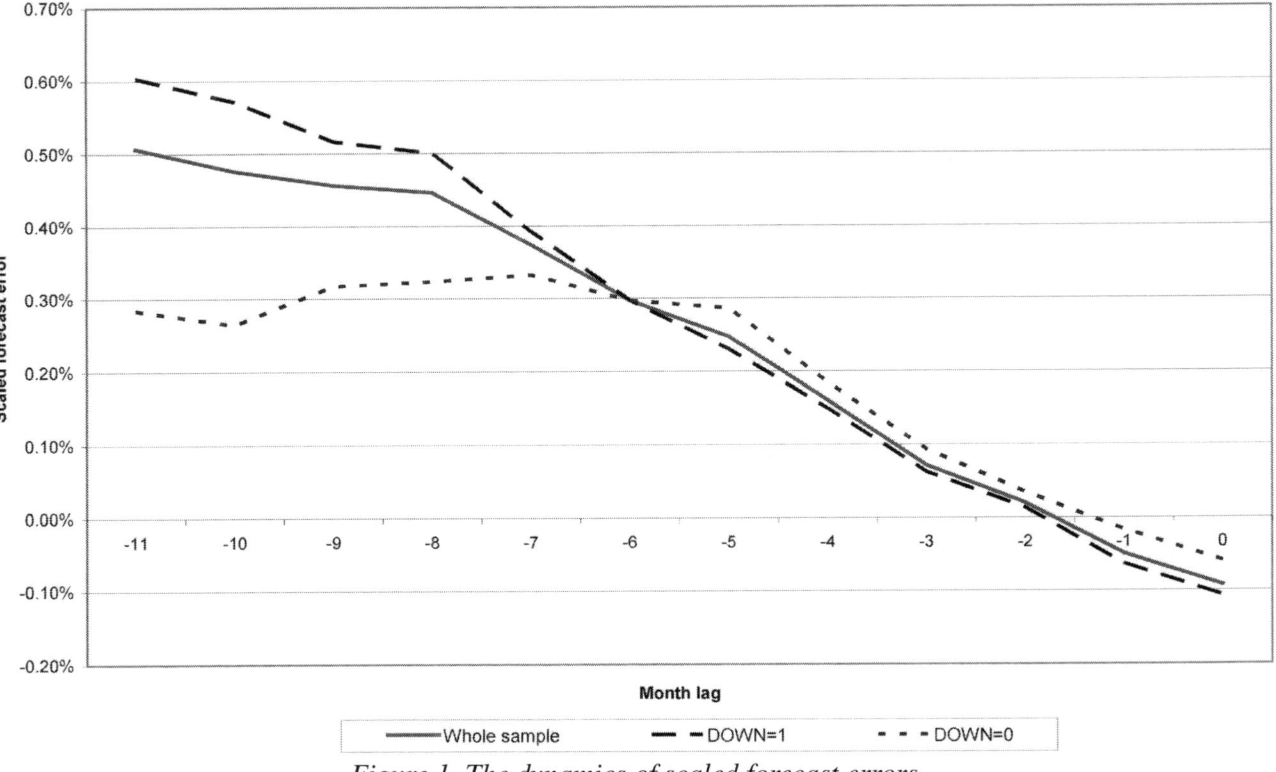

Figure 1. The dynamics of scaled forecast errors

The average forecast error is calculated as the mean of all analyst forecasts of EPS in month t preceding the announcement minus announced EPS. This difference is scaled by stock price at the end of the previous fiscal year. Month -11 is the first and month 0 the last month of the forecasting period. The solid line shows the average scaled forecast error for the entire sample of observations. The broken line displays the average scaled forecast error for firms suspected of managing expectations downward (*DOWN*=1) and the dotted line depicts the average forecast error for firms that are not suspected of managing expectations downward (*DOWN*=0).

sample for which expectations management can be suspected, whereas only 69.11 per cent of the firm–year observations belong to this sample when a negative earnings surprise is reported. A Chi-square test indicates that the dependence between DOWN and firms that report a positive earnings surprise is significant ($\chi^2 = 16.23$, p-value <0.001). Overall, this suggests that our measure for expectations management is capable of distinguishing between firms that manipulate analysts in order to report a positive (zero) earnings surprise and those that do not.

C. Measuring CEO Compensation Components and Ownership Variables

We obtained the following values directly from the Execucomp database: the dollar value of each CEO's annual base salary, the dollar value of the CEO's annual bonus, the amount paid out to the CEO according to the company's long-term incentive plan (*LTIP*), and the value of restricted stock grants (*RSG*) awarded during the year. In addition, we calculated the value of the firm's shares held by the CEO at the end of the fiscal year (*SHARE*) in order to assess the impact on expectations management of the total share position (as opposed to the stock grants awarded in the present year only).[10] We used the value of in-the-money and exercisable options (*INMONEX*) held by the CEO to measure the impact of the entire relevant option position. This item was taken directly from Execucomp and includes all in-the-money exercisable options from grants in the current and also previous years.

Considering the non-linear relationship between share and option price and the ensuing differences in option sensitivity to stock price changes, we constructed a variable to measure the change in the value of the CEO's newly awarded options deriving from a one percent increase in the company's stock price (*OPTSENS*). Following Core and Guay (2001), we estimated the sensitivity of stock option value to stock price as the partial derivative of the option value with respect to stock price ('delta'). The option deltas are based on the Black-Scholes (1973) formula, as modified by Merton (1973) to account for dividend payments.[11] The detailed methodology and the parameters used to calculate the value of the options

10. Execucomp reports the percentage of the firm's shares owned by the CEO as reported in the proxy statement. We multiplied this percentage by the market value (taken from CRSP) at the end of the fiscal year to obtain the value of the firm-share position owned by the CEO. Ownership below one per cent does not have to be reported. Following common practice we set missing values equal to zero. Execucomp also reports the number of the company's shares owned by the CEO. This item makes it possible to calculate positions below the one per cent threshold because it includes voluntary disclosures. Some values above the threshold are inconsistent across the two methods, probably because they were measured at different times. However, our results in this paper do not depend on which data item is used to calculate the value of the CEO's shares.
11. We are aware that the Black-Scholes approach has many limitations when applied to executive stock options: executives are forced by institutional constraints to hedge or arbitrage their option values in the secondary market; their options are subject to forfeiture if they leave the company; and they are not free to trade or sell their options. In addition, company executives are undiversified: their financial as well as human capital is invested disproportionately in their

awarded annually to CEOs are presented in the appendix. In addition, to measure the impact of the options granted over prior years, we used the value of in-the-money and exercisable options (*INMONEX*) held by the CEO. Since Execucomp reports detailed characteristics (e.g. maturity, strike price) only for the options that have been granted during the current fiscal year, we could not calculate a sensitivity measure for the *INMONEX* options to stock price changes as we did for the current year's options. However, the delta of in-the-money options from previous years approaches the value delta relatively quickly once the stock price exceeds the strike. Therefore, if we assume a delta equal to one, the *INMONEX* value could loosely be interpreted as an additional measure of sensitivity.

Table 1, Panel A summarizes the components of CEO compensation. The average amount of restricted stocks (*RSG*) granted to CEOs is relatively small compared to other compensation components, with a mean of USD 308,450. Less than one-third of all CEOs receive any restricted stocks. The mean (median) value of shares held by CEOs is USD 2.61 (USD 0.24) million, with a range from 0 to USD 1.32 billion. The average (median) amount of in-the-money exercisable options held by CEOs (*INMONEX*) is USD 8.88 (1.01) million, with a range from zero to nearly USD 2 billion. A one percent increase in the share price leads to an increase of USD 44,463 in the value of stock options awarded annually to CEOs (*OPTSENS*). This amount varies substantially across sample observations, with a standard deviation of USD 188,150. The mean annual bonus paid to CEOs equals approximately USD 0.53 million, ranging from zero to more than USD 43 million. The average value of payments to CEOs under long-term incentive plans is USD 135,184. Again the amount varies substantially, especially as fewer than 33 per cent of CEOs receive any such payments. Finally, the average annual base salary paid to CEOs equals USD 575,141. As with the other compensation components, the distribution for base salary is highly skewed, some CEOs receiving no annual base salary at all.

Therefore, and for the reasons given below, we measured all compensation and ownership variables as well as some highly skewed control variables with the values assigned by their cumulative distribution functions (hereafter referred to as 'cdf') in the regression analysis. The cdf transformation generates a more uniform distribution of the transformed variables, which enhances the speed of convergence of the parameter estimates to the true population parameters. In addition, the effect of outliers is mitigated without discarding this information completely as was done in censoring the sample. Furthermore, this transformation is consistent with decreased marginal effects as the variables increase. Intuitively, this suggests that the first USD 1,000 of any compensation component have greater importance than a USD 1,000 variation at high income or ownership levels.[12] The

company. As a result, CEOs tend to exercise their options much earlier than outside investors would. However, as pointed out by Core and Guay (2001), the Black-Scholes model can be relied on to produce an instrumental variable to capture cross-sectional variation in option plan deltas.

12. The cdf transformation is similar to the log transformation commonly applied to firm size. However, the log transformation is not appropriate for the compensation and ownership variables, since there are a large number of observations with value zero.

Table 1. Summary Statistics ($ thousands)

	Mean	*Std. dev.*	*Min.*	*T1*	*Median*	*T2*	*Max.*
Panel A: CEO Compensation							
RSG	308.45	7,086.57	0.00	0.00	0.00	0.00	650,812.05
SHARE	2,611.07	25,976.39	0.00	106.03	236.71	539.70	1,318,976.32
INMONEX	8,878.89	44,889.17	0.00	192.48	1014.03	2977.11	1,959,915.45
OPTSENS	44.46	188.15	0.00	3.28	10.52	22.77	9,993.09
BONUS	531.23	938.88	0.00	150.00	300.00	500.00	43511.53
LTIP	135.18	685.66	0.00	0.00	0.00	0.00	16,092.70
SALARY	575.14	309.53	0.00	405.00	518.11	650.00	36,49.13
Panel B: Control variables							
LOSS	0.080	0.271	0.000	0.000	0.000	0.000	1.000
INCEPS	0.669	0.471	0.000	1.000	1.000	1.000	1.000
MEET	0.706	0.456	0.000	1.000	1.000	1.000	1.000
RCOV	0.000	0.454	−1.729	−0.180	0.021	0.212	1.330
IFE	0.023	0.059	0.000	0.004	0.008	0.016	3.012
EARNRET	5.459	2.427	1.000	4.000	5.000	7.000	10.000
LTG	0.175	0.087	−0.250	0.129	0.150	0.186	1.250
LABOR	0.565	0.221	0.024	0.481	0.592	0.689	0.995
DUR	0.417	0.493	0.000	0.000	0.000	1.000	1.000
R&D	0.036	0.068	0.000	0.000	0.006	0.028	1.464
ICLAIM	0.000	1.000	−1.720	−0.560	−0.099	0.521	10.241
LIT	0.355	0.478	0.000	0.000	0.000	1.000	1.000
TRAN	0.049	0.059	0.000	0.017	0.032	0.050	0.538

SHARE is the market value of firm shares held by CEOs at the end of a given fiscal year.
RSG is the value of restricted shares awarded to CEOs in a given fiscal year.
INMONEX is the value of in-the-money exercisable options held by CEOs at the end of the fiscal year.
OPTSENS, or option sensitivity, is the U.S. dollar amount of option value change (options granted during the current fiscal year) if the underlying stock price moves up one per cent.
BONUS denotes the annual bonus paid to CEOs.
LTIP is the sum paid to CEOs in a given fiscal year according to the long-term incentive plan.
SALARY is the annual base salary paid to CEOs. All compensation variables are expressed in thousands of U.S. dollars.
LOSS is an indicator variable which equals one if a loss is reported in the current fiscal year.
INCEPS, or increasing EPS, is an indicator variable that equals one if reported EPS exceed the previous year's EPS.
MEET is an indicator variable which equals one if reported earnings meet or beat the last consensus estimate prior to the announcement.
RCOV, or residual analyst coverage, is the residual from a regression of the log of one plus the number of analysts contributing to the last consensus estimate prior to the announcement on the log market value of the company at the beginning of the fiscal year.
IFE, or initial forecast error, is the absolute value of the difference between the first consensus estimate in the fiscal year and reported EPS, scaled by share price at the beginning of the fiscal year.

EARNRET, or returns on earnings, is the decile rank from industry-specific regressions of cumulative excess returns on yearly changes in earnings.
LTG, long-term growth, is the first consensus long-term earnings growth forecast estimate in the fiscal year.
LABOR, or labour intensity, is defined as one minus the ratio of gross property, plant, and equipment to total gross assets.
DUR is a dummy variable indicating membership of a durable goods industry (SIC codes 150–179, 245, 250–259, 283, 301, 324–399).
R&D is annual research expenses divided by total assets. Missing values for *R&D* are set to zero.
ICLAIM is the score of the factor analysis combining *LABOR*, *DUR*, and *R&D* into a single variable measuring reliance on implicit claims.
LIT is a dummy variable indicating membership of a litigious industry (SIC codes 2833–2836, 3570–3577, 3600–3674, 5200–5961, 7370–7374). Transient institutional investors *TRAN* measures the percentage of a firm's shares held by transient institutional investors. This variable is constructed as in Bushee (1998). The total number of observations is 8,714.

use of the cdf transformation is not problematic for this study, since we are mainly interested in seeing whether distinct components of executive compensation increase or decrease the probability of expectations management (i.e. we are after the sign of the estimated coefficients), rather than in estimating precisely the marginal effect of a USD 1,000 increase in executive remuneration on the probability of analyst manipulation.

D. Control Variables

We included additional explanatory variables to control for earnings thresholds, information environment, growth prospects and further firm-specifics that are potentially related to expectations management. Degeorge et al. (1999) suggest that executives with self-interested motives who are subject to outside monitoring have strong incentives to manipulate earnings around behavioural thresholds. In their analysis of EPS and forecast error distributions, Degeorge et al. find evidence consistent with earnings management in order to exceed zero earnings, past earnings and analyst expectations. We included three control variables to capture these thresholds. The indicator variable *LOSS* equals one if a particular firm reports a loss in the current fiscal year (annual Compustat item A18). *MEET* is a dummy variable that equals one if the firm's reported EPS at the announcement date meets or beats analyst expectations, as measured by the last consensus estimate prior to the announcement date. The indicator variable *INCEPS* equals one if the firm reports a positive earnings variation relative to the previous year.

A priori, the way these threshold variables affect the probability of expectations management is not unambiguous. Degeorge et al. (1999) show that depending on how close latent earnings are below or above a performance threshold, executives will have various incentives to exaggerate reported earnings, rein in, take big baths, or not manipulate at all. Since it is difficult to predict whether analyst guidance will serve as a substitute for, or complement to, earnings management for different levels of latent earnings and for the differing thresholds, we make no prediction regarding the sign of the thresholds included as control variables.

Brown and Higgins (2002) find that guidance increases with the richness of the firm's information environment. They define the information environment as the availability and effectiveness of communication between managers and analysts and show a positive relationship between a firm's analyst coverage and the probability of expectations management. Using the absolute value of the final forecast error as an alternative proxy for information environment, they find a negative relationship between the magnitude of the forecast error and expectations management.

We measured a firm's informational environment by using two related proxies. First, we included residual analyst coverage (*RCOV*) as proposed by Hong et al. (2000). Residual analyst coverage is the residual from the regression of the logarithm of one plus the number of analysts following the firm on the logarithm of the market value of the company taken at the beginning of the fiscal year. The number of analysts for a particular firm–year corresponds to the number of estimates that constitute the last consensus forecast released before the earnings announcement date. Using residual coverage rather than the number of analysts following the firm provides a measure that does not proxy for a firm's market capitalization. As shown by Hong et al. (2000), market value is the most important determinant of analyst coverage. Consistent with Brown and Higgins (2002), we expect a positive relationship between expectations management and residual analyst coverage. Our second proxy for informational environment is the absolute value of the initial forecast error (*IFE*) as in Matsumoto (2002), which we calculate as $|FEPS_{it}{}^{ini} - EPS_{it}|/p_{it}$, where $FEPS_{it}^{ini}$ is the first consensus forecast released by analysts for company i in year t, EPS_{it} is the company's actual earnings per share and P_{it} is the company's share price at the beginning of the fiscal year. Matsumoto shows a strong negative relationship between the initial forecast error and the probability that a firm will meet or beat analyst expectations.[13]

We include the firm's long-term earnings growth forecast (*LTG*) as a proxy for its growth prospects, using the first consensus *LTG* released by I/B/E/S during the fiscal year. Previous research has found that growth firms (high *LTG*) suffer strong and asymmetric reactions to negative earnings surprises (Skinner and Sloan 2002). Brown (2001b) shows that growth firms are more likely to manage analysts than are value firms. He attributes this to the increase in managerial compensation in stocks and options. Due to the asymmetric market reaction to bad news, growth firm managers' portfolios will lose more after a negative earnings surprise than those of value firm managers. Assuming this is correct, if we include stock-based compensation and a proxy for growth jointly as explanatory variables for expectations management, there should not be any difference between the propensities of growth

13. Note that Matsumoto (2002) also uses the logarithm of the firm's market value as a control variable for the firm information environment. Due to potential multi-collinearity problems between market capitalization and most of the compensation variables, we did not include this proxy for the informational environment. Nevertheless, including the logarithm of the market value does not change any main conclusions.

and value firms to engage in expectations management strategies. However, if the motives inducing growth firm managements to avoid negative surprises are not confined to the structure of their management compensation, the growth proxy should remain positive and significant in explaining earnings management. For instance, Liu and Yao (2003) argue that firms use earnings guidance and consensus beating as a mechanism to credibly signal their growth potential. Matsumoto reports that firms with high growth prospects (measured by analysts' consensual long-term EPS growth forecasts) are more likely to take action to avoid negative surprises.[14] Conversely, firms in distress (with very low market-to-book) might depend heavily on short-term earnings surprises in order to obtain additional finance or signal recovery to stakeholders, which would suggest a negative relationship between analyst guidance and growth prospects.

We included three additional variables to control for the value-relevance of earnings, reliance on implicit claims made to stakeholders, and litigation risk. Matsumoto (2002) shows that firms with low earnings value relevance are less likely to avoid negative earnings surprises, since market reactions are expected to be relatively moderate. We use *EARNRET* to control for the value-relevance of earnings. Value-relevance is calculated as the decile rank of the R^2 from yearly industry-specific regressions of cumulative excess returns on yearly changes in earnings.[15] Matsumoto finds that firms depending heavily on implicit claims with stakeholders are more likely to take action to avoid negative earnings surprises. She argues that avoiding negative surprises at the earnings announcement yields more favourable terms of trade with stakeholders, including suppliers, clients and employees. These groups are likely to limit their assessment of a company's financial performance to reported earnings, since the financial press focuses primarily on earnings announcements rather than initial analyst forecasts. To measure reliance on implicit claims, we used the proxies *LABOR*, *DUR* and *R&D*, developed by Bowen et al. (1995). *LABOR* is a measure of labour intensity, defined as one minus the ratio of total gross property, plant, and equipment (Compustat item A7) to firm size, measured by total gross assets (total assets plus accumulated depreciation, depletion, and amortization with Compustat items A6 and A196 respectively). The indicator variable DUR denotes membership of the durable goods industry and equals one for firms with primary (three-digit) SIC codes 150–179, 245, 250–259, 283, 301, and 324–399. *R&D* denotes research intensity, calculated as annual research and development expenditure (Compustat item A46) divided by total assets (Compustat item A6).

14. Instead of *LTG* we performed our estimations using the market-to-book ratio. Our results are not sensitive to this modification.
15. Firms are grouped into industry sets as in Yermack (1995). Every year, for each industry group, we regressed cumulated daily excess returns (cumulated from three days after the fiscal year t–1 earnings announcement date to 20 days before fiscal year *t* earnings announcement) on the change in earnings per share from fiscal year t–1 to fiscal year *t*, scaled by the share price at the end of fiscal year *t-1*. We required each industry group to contain at least eight firms. The firms with R^2s in the highest (lowest) 10 per cent of the distribution are assigned a value of 10 (1).

We then used factor analysis with principal component factors to transform *LABOR*, *DUR* and *R&D* into the single variable *ICLAIM*, representing reliance on implicit claims.[16]

A sharp drop in price at the earnings announcement can give rise to shareholder litigation. Therefore firms that are highly vulnerable to such litigation may take more action to avoid negative earnings surprises. Following Francis et al. (1994), Soffer et al. (2000), Ali and Kallapur (2001), and Matsumoto (2002), to control for litigation risk we included the dummy variable *LIT* to indicate whether a firm belongs to an industry classified as litigious. *LIT* equals one (1) for firms with primary SIC codes 2833–2836, 3570–3577, 3600–3674, 5200–5961, and 7370–7374 (biotechnology, electronics, retailing and calculators).

Finally we controlled for institutional ownership. Matsumoto (2002) finds that firms with a higher percentage of institutional owners are more likely to guide analysts in order to avoid negative earnings surprises. Transient institutional investors with relatively high portfolio turnover, diversified positions and high use of momentum strategies are most likely to create incentives for executives to avoid negative surprises due to their short-term focus. *TRAN* measures the percentage of a firm's shares held by transient institutional investors. In order to classify institutional investors into different types, we applied the cluster analysis approach developed by Bushee (1998), using Thomson Financial's CDA Spectrum Historical Tape Files (13F).

Panel B in Table 1 displays descriptive statistics for the control variables. Only 8.0 per cent of the firm–year observations relate to firms that reported losses. The thresholds for meeting or beating analyst forecasts and reporting increased EPS were reached in 71 per cent and 67 per cent of firm–years respectively. Residual analyst coverage ranges from -1.73 to 1.33, with the median of 0.021 close to zero. *IFE* contains very large outliers. The average long-term growth consensus forecast is relatively high at 17.5 per cent. More than 66 per cent of the firm–year observations have long-term growth forecasts higher than 12.9 per cent. Firms in the durable goods industries account for 41.7 per cent of the firm–year observations; firms in litigious industries account for 35.5 per cent. Due to the replacement of missing values with zeros, *R&D* is highly skewed as well, with about 30 per cent of the values being zero. We used it together with *LABOR* and *DUR* to generate *ICLAIM*, which has zero mean and variance one by construction. Finally, the percentage of firm shares held by transient institutional investors (*TRAN*) is 4.9 per cent on average and ranges from 0.0 per cent to 53.8 per cent.

16. Almost one third of the observations for *R&D* are missing. Following Bowen et al. (1995) and Matsumoto (2002) we replaced missing values by the value zero. The results do not depend on this ad-hoc assumption. We also performed all regressions with *LABOR*, *DUR*, and *R&D* jointly and individually included as additional explanatory variables. The coefficients of *DUR* and *R&D* are never significantly different from zero. Only *LABOR* is (highly) significant and positive, thus behaving in exactly the same way as *ICLAIM*.

E. Measuring the Impact of CEO Compensation on Expectations Management

To test whether executive compensation components are associated with expectations management as postulated in our hypotheses, we performed a logit regression, modelling the probability that analyst expectations have been managed downward. A detailed description of the regression methodology can be found in Appendix 3.

Following previous research on expectations management and forecast guidance, we pooled the observations from 1993 to 2001 and performed the logit regression for the entire sample.[17] In all regressions, we used indicator variables to control for year effects (relative to the base year 1993), as well as for industry effects. In addition, we estimated panel models and performed further sensitivity analyses.

V. RESULTS

A. CEO Compensation and Expectations Management

Table 2 displays the results of the pooled logit regression of the analyst guidance measure *DOWN* on the compensation and ownership variables, controlling for year and industry effects and further firm-specific variables.[18]

Consistent with our first hypothesis, the value of shares owned by the CEO (SHARE) is positively and significantly related to the probability of expectations management. However, the variable RSG (restricted stock grants) is not significantly different from zero and has a negative sign. We attribute this result to the failure of the variable (in the raw form) to measure the value of stock at the disposal of the executive for short-term transactions. RSG measures the value of the restricted stocks awarded in the current year only, when the vesting period has typically not yet ended. SHARE is probably a much better proxy to measure the CEO's incentive from stock ownership than RSG, since it measures the value of the CEO's total position in firm shares.

Supporting our second hypothesis, there is a positive and highly significant relationship between the value of in-the-money exercisable options (INMONEX) and expectations management. Further support for this hypothesis comes from the positive and again highly significant coefficient of OPTSENS, indicating that analyst guidance is positively associated with the stock price sensitivity of option grants.

---

17. See, for example, Matsumoto (2002) and Richardson et al. (2003). This implicitly assumes that observations $i = 1, \ldots, N$ are independent, including consecutive observations of the same firm. In order to correct for firm clustering, we calculated robust standard errors adjusted for clustering. However, the corresponding p-values differ by less than 0.01 for the significant variables, and therefore we do not report these standard errors. (These figures are, however, available upon request.)
18. Coefficients on the year and industry dummies are not reported. Each group of dummy variables is jointly highly significant.

Table 2. The relationship between downward guidance, CEO compensation components and other firm-characteristic control variables. Endogenous variable: DOWN

Variable	*Predicted sign*	*Coefficient*	*p-value*	*Marginal effect*
SHARE	+	0.328	0.0241	0.060
RSG	+	−0.478	0.7800	−0.088
INMONEX	+	0.805	0.0000	0.148
OPTSENS	+	0.415	0.0008	0.076
BONUS	+	0.517	0.0001	0.095
LTIP	+	0.879	0.1789	0.162
SALARY	−	−0.583	0.0000	−0.107
LOSS	+/−	0.294	0.0065	0.051
INCEPS	+/−	−1.052	0.0000	−0.175
MEET	+/−	0.319	0.0000	0.061
RCOV	+	0.018	0.3930	−0.003
IFE	−	−1.023	0.0000	−0.188
EARNRET	+	−0.035	0.9977	−0.006
LTG	+	−0.473	0.9999	−0.087
ICLAIM	+	−0.089	0.9580	−0.016
LIT	+	−0.093	0.7980	−0.017
TRAN	+	0.600	0.0000	0.110
Chi2(46)	1,127.82		N	8,714
Prob > chi2	0.0000		Pseudo R2	0.1394

Pooled logit regression estimates of *DOWN* on compensation variables and other firm characteristics; year and industry effects are included but not reported. All exogenous variables are defined in Table 1. *SALARY, BONUS, LTIP, RSG, SHARE, INMONEX, OPTSENS, IFE, LTG* and *TRAN* are expressed in terms of the values assigned by their cumulative distribution functions. p-values are calculated with robust standard errors and correspond to one-sided hypothesis tests. If no prediction is made (+/−), the p-values are given for two-sided tests. Marginal effects are calculated as $e^{\beta\prime X}/(1+e^{\beta\prime X})^2$, evaluated at the mean of the elements of X. The chi2 statistic and the corresponding p-value are given for the joint test of significance of the model coefficients. *N* is the number of firm–year observations. Pseudo R2 is McFadden's measure of goodness of fit, calculated as $1-(L_u/L_c)$, where L_u denotes the unconstrained Log-Likelihood of the (full) model and L_c denotes the constrained Log-Likelihood of the constrained (intercept only) model.

Consistent with our third hypothesis, the relationship between bonus and analyst guidance is positive and highly significant. Although the large positive coefficient on long-term incentive plans (LTIP) is consistent with our fourth hypothesis, it is not statistically significant.[19]

19. Note that long-term incentive plan payments are zero for 86 per cent of the firm–year observations, which leads to a large standard error. Dropping this variable does not affect the results for the other variables.

Supporting our fifth hypothesis, SALARY has a highly significant negative influence on the probability of expectations management.

The three threshold variables *LOSS*, *INCEPS*, and *MEET* are all strongly significant, with *INCEPS* having a negative coefficient. Consistent with previous research (Matsumoto 2002), the variable proxying for forecasting uncertainty *IFE*, is negative and highly significant. In contrast to Matsumoto, we do not find *EARNRET* significant. Equally insignificant are long-term growth forecast (*LTG*), residual analyst coverage (*RCOV*), implicit claims (*ICLAIM*) and litigation risk (*LIT*).

The rejection of a positive coefficient on *LTG* in particular is in sharp contrast to previous research, which neglects CEO compensation variables. Predictably, as conjectured by Brown (2001b), market-to-book was found positive and significant in explaining analyst management due to the pronounced tendency among growth firms to include stocks and options in the remuneration package.[20] In our sample, we controlled for these effects and found no more positive effect of *LTG* on expectations management. This is consistent with Brown's (2001b) view and contradicts the argument of Liu and Tao (2003) that growth firms use analyst guidance as a device for signalling future earnings growth.

As in Matsumoto (2002), *LIT* is negative and insignificant, whereas *TRAN* is positive (as predicted) and highly significant, which supports the hypothesis that transient institutional investors create pressure on managements to boost short-term performance through analyst guidance.

In summary, the pooled regression with firm-specific control variables, year and industry effects strongly supports our hypotheses about the relationship between expectations management and CEO compensation components (salary and bonus, stock and option positions), as well as option sensitivity.

B. Sensitivity Tests

One potential drawback of the pooled logit specification is unobserved heterogeneity. For instance, the CEO's ability to guide or manipulate analysts is difficult to measure, but may correlate with other explanatory variables, thus causing biased coefficient estimates. The executive's skill at negotiating his/her compensation components with the compensation committee, for example, is likely to correlate with skill at dealing with analysts, and will be reflected in the compensation variables. Differing attitudes toward business ethics or moral standards are just as hard to observe, but undeniably play a role in the CEO's propensity to manage analysts. Therefore we estimated a fixed effects logit model, allowing for unobserved heterogeneity at firm level.

The results of modelling the dependence across units in a panel framework are presented in Table 3. The fixed effects logit regression of *DOWN* on the compensation, ownership, and control variables is displayed in Panel A.

---

20. In order to replicate these results of previous research, we regressed *DOWN* on the market-to-book ratio alone and the year effects: as expected, the coefficient of *MTB* is significantly positive when executive compensation is not controlled for.

Table 3. Fixed and random effects estimates of the relation between downward guidance, CEO compensation components and other firm-characteristic control variables

Dependent variable: *DOWN*		**Panel A: Fixed Effects Logit**			**Panel B: Random effects probit**		
Variable	*Predicted sign*	*Coeff.*	*p-value*	*Marginal effect*	*Coeff.*	*p-value*	*Marginal Effect*
SHARE	+	0.304	0.1873	0.061	0.186	0.0277	0.059
RSG	+	−0.483	0.7182	−0.107	−0.250	0.7422	−0.079
INMONEX	+	1.472	0.0000	0.318	0.466	0.0000	0.148
OPTSENS	+	0.565	0.0003	0.235	0.254	0.0005	0.080
LTIP	+	0.708	0.3269	0.218	0.541	0.1804	0.171
BONUS	+	0.481	0.0056	0.108	0.298	0.0001	0.094
SALARY	−	−0.601	0.0164	−0.140	−0.340	0.0000	−0.108
LOSS	+/−	0.888	0.0000	0.205	0.177	0.0065	0.053
INCEPS	+/−	−1.056	0.0000	−0.254	−0.617	0.0000	−0.180
MEET	+/−	0.295	0.0000	0.075	0.183	0.0000	0.059
RCOV	+	0.217	0.0268	0.047	0.014	0.3630	0.004
IFE	−	−0.290	0.0225	−0.069	−0.608	0.0000	−0.193
EARNRET	+	−0.039	0.9991	−0.010	−0.018	0.9952	−0.006
LTG	+	−1.001	1.0000	−0.251	−0.283	1.0000	−0.090
ICLAIM	+	0.198	0.0758	0.050	−0.052	0.9668	−0.016
LIT	+	−0.189	0.6941	−0.039	−0.054	0.7976	−0.017
TRAN	+	0.737	0.0000	0.176	0.346	0.0000	0.110
Chi2				1,120.14			1,250.07
Prob > chi2				0.0000			0.0000
N				7,548			8,714
Pseudo R2				0.1834			0.1397

Conditional logit (fixed effects) and random effects probit estimates of *DOWN* on all explanatory variables; year effects are included but not reported. Industry effects (not reported) are only jointly significant in the random effects specification and are dropped in the fixed effects estimation. Chi2 is Chi2(25) for fixed effects and Chi2(45) for the random effects specification. All exogenous variables are defined in Table 1. *SALARY, BONUS, LTIP, RSG, SHARE, INMONEX, OPTSENS, IFE, LTG* and *TRAN* are expressed in terms of the values assigned by their cumulative distribution functions. All reported items are defined as in Table 2.

All compensation and ownership components maintain their sign, but compared to the pooled logit estimation, the marginal effect of the in-the-money exercisable options INMONEX is now twice as large. INMONEX and OPTSENS are still highly significant. SALARY and BONUS remain significant at the conventional level. No longer significant, however, is the CEO's position in the firm's stocks SHARE.

In the set of control variables, the thresholds LOSS, INCEPS and MEET remain highly significant. As in the pooled logit estimate, the initial forecast error has the predicted negative influence on expectations management and the percentage of shares held by transient institutional investors has the predicted positive influence at high levels of significance. As before, the signs of EARNRET LTG and LIT are in opposition to the prediction. However, compared to the pooled logit estimation, residual analyst coverage and implicit claims become significant and weakly significant respectively, both with the predicted positive signs.

The strong changes in the magnitudes of LTIP and INMONEX could be a sign of unobserved heterogeneity at the firm or equivalently CEO level, possibly relating to skill or ethical standards. However, the conditional logit approach is flawed owing to the deletion of all firms with the endogenous variable indicating expectations management in all years, as well as firms without expectations management in each year. This means that 1,166 'extreme' observations (13.4 per cent of the sample) are ignored. The results, therefore must be interpreted with some caution. Nevertheless, the fixed effects logit estimation corroborates the pooled logit results: analyst guidance is negatively related to the compensation component of the CEO's salary and positively related to the CEO's bonus, as well as to the CEO's in-the-money exercisable option position and the option sensitivity.

Compared to the fixed effect logit regression, the random effect probit approach has the advantage that it does not discard any firms without time series variation in *DOWN*, but it imposes the restriction that the unit-specific effects must be uncorrelated with the explanatory variables. The results are displayed in Table 3, Panel B. All the variables that were significant in the pooled logit regression remain significant, with the same signs as in the random effects probit regression. Again with the exception of *RSG* and *LTIP*, the coefficients of all compensation and ownership variables support our hypotheses relating expectations management to executive compensation. *SALARY*, *BONUS*, *SHARE*, *INMONEX,* and *OPTSENS* are highly significant.

In a related robustness test, we checked to see whether there is a bias in the standard errors obtained from the pooled logit regressions due to correlated regression residuals across years. We ran separate yearly cross-sectional regressions and calculated the time-series average coefficients and *t*-statistics in the style of Fama and McBeth (1973). Our main results are robust to this estimation methodology as well.[21] The significance levels of *SALARY* and *SHARE* are reduced, but *INMONEX* and *BONUS* remain highly significant, pinpointing the importance of CEO compensation components in motivating analyst guidance. However, *OPTSENS* is no more significant at the conventional level, confirming that the sensitivity of recently granted (and not necessarily exercisable) options has less impact on expectations management.

As additional sensitivity tests, we made the sample conditional on (not) reaching the three behavioral thresholds (profits, increasing earnings, meeting analyst expectations) rather than include each threshold directly in the regressions. The results again support our hypotheses, with the compensation in stock options providing a particularly strong incentive to manage analysts in all the scenarios under test.[22]

21. Results are not tabulated for the sake of brevity but are available on request.
22. Results are not tabulated (available on request). *INMONEX* is always positive and significant, whether or not any of the thresholds are reached. The same holds true for *OPTSENS* except that we have restricted the sample to firms with decreasing EPS. *SALARY*, *BONUS* and *SHARE* are

As another robustness check, we used a dependent variable indicating the occurrence of small earnings surprises, which can be achieved by both analyst and earnings management. The results indicate that the role of in-the-money exercisable options and the CEO's position in the firm's shares is just as important when it comes to explaining small earnings surprises as it is in explaining downward guidance of analyst forecasts.[23]

To summarize, we find that pooling observations, estimating panel models and further sensitivity tests together lend strong support to our hypotheses. Our major conclusions are not sensitive to the method applied.

C. DOES THE MARKET FIGURE IT OUT?

In contrast to earnings management, expectations management does not induce managers to borrow against future earnings in order to reach the target set by analysts. However, investors appear to punish firms that do not reach analysts' expectations (Skinner and Sloan 2003). Yet, to date, it has remained largely unknown whether, and to what extent, the market reacts to predictable expectations management by executives.

We conducted an event study to investigate whether the market takes into account any discernible expectations management strategies. This requires the calculation of the cumulative abnormal returns around the earnings announcement date. The market model was used to adjust returns for risk. Abnormal returns were cumulated from two days before the earning release date until two days after the release date. The methodology used to calculate abnormal returns is described in details in Appendix 4.

The earnings announcement date was taken from I/B/E/S, individual stock returns were obtained from CRSP, and the market index is the CRSP value-weighted stock index. Announcement date returns are missing for 51 observations. Hence we have estimated the model for 8,663 firm–year observations.

In Table 4 we present cumulative abnormal returns conditional on whether a particular company meets or beats analyst expectations and conditional on whether our method points to expectations management.

The cumulative abnormal returns earned by firms that meet or beat analyst forecasts, and are more likely to have achieved this by managing analyst expectations downward, are 0.93 per cent lower than the cumulative abnormal returns of firms reporting a zero or positive surprise without managing expectations downward. Most managers suspected of engaging in analyst manipulation still earn a positive abnormal return, but it amounts to only 1.03 per cent over the period prior to and immediately following the announcement date. This suggests that the market

---

highly significant with the predicted signs in all regressions, so long as the relevant thresholds are reached. When the thresholds have not been reached, these variables generally become insignificant, except *BONUS* conditional on decreasing EPS.

23. Results are not reported but are available on request.

Table 4. Market anticipation of expectations management at announcement date

Earnings surprise	*Expectations management*	*N*	*CAR(p - value)*	*Difference (p - value)*
Zero or Positive	Suspected *(DOWN =1)*	4,489	0.0103	
			(0.0000)	
	Not suspected *(DOWN=0)*	1,630	0.0195	−0.0092
			(0.0000)	*(0.0002)*
Negative	Suspected *(DOWN=1)*	1,758	−0.0163	
			(0.0000)	
	Not suspected *(DOWN=0)*	786	−0.0113	−0.0051
			(0.0019)	(0.2215)

Cumulative abnormal returns (*CAR*) for 8,663 firm–year observations around the earnings announcement date between 1993 and 2001. CARs are estimated with a market model type regression over 252 days ending two days after the earnings announcement with a WLS regression as in Heinkel and Krauss (1998). The event window ranges from two days before the earnings announcement to two days after it. Companies' cumulative abnormal returns are classified into four distinct categories according to whether their earnings surprise is positive or strictly negative and whether expectations management can be suspected. Earnings surprise is calculated as the difference between the announced EPS and the last consensus issued by analysts for a particular firm in a given year. A given company is suspected of managing expectations if $FEPS < E[FEPS]$. $E[FEPS]$ is calculated as described in section 4.

has some ability to anticipate the expectations management strategies implemented by managers. For firms that do not meet analyst expectations, no significant difference is observed in cumulative abnormal returns whether or not expectations management is suspected. This implies that CEOs' gains from managing earnings expectations downward may come at a cost. Thus the findings of Bartov et al. (2002), who analyze quarterly forecast error trajectories, also appear to hold for annual forecasts and the expectations management measure used in this paper.

VI. CONCLUSION

This paper has investigated whether the increasing tendency of executives to manage analyst forecasts downward is, as informally suggested by past academic research and financial media, related to a change in the structure of executive compensation packages. Using the components of CEOs' compensation in conjunction with their share and option ownership, our results are consistent with this explanation. We have shown that CEOs who hold substantial share and option positions are more likely to manage analyst expectations downward. Moreover, other compensation components that are not directly related to share price movements have been shown to have a significant impact on CEOs' motives for guiding analysts. Expectations management is negatively related to salary, indicating that high fixed compensation decreases managers' incentive to manipulate analyst forecasts. We have detected a positive relationship between the annual bonus paid to CEOs and expectations management. This suggests that board of directors' expectations are related to analyst expectations and that meeting analyst expectations may be an important criterion used by boards of directors to measure CEO performance.

In a second test, we found that the cumulative abnormal return for firms that meet or beat analyst forecasts at the announcement date is significantly lower for firms that are suspected of pursuing expectations management strategies. We have shown that this lower return is significantly related to the amount of options held by CEOs. This suggests that the market has some ability to identify which firms are managing analysts in order to meet or beat their forecasts more easily.

Using a large sample, we have documented, for the first time, the importance and impact of CEO compensation components on expectations management. However, our results may not generalize to all market segments, since the substantial amount of data needed to conduct this study requires a sample with relatively large firms. Moreover, since executive compensation components are only available from the main provider on an annual basis, we have used annual EPS forecasts. As a result, our results may not be generalizable to quarterly earnings forecasts.

APPENDIX 1

Measuring the Sensitivity of the CEO's Stock Option Award to a 1 Per Cent Change in the Company's Stock Price

The value of the options awarded yearly to CEOs can be calculated using the following formula:

$$\textit{Award value} = N[Se^{-dT}\Phi(d1) - Xe^{-rT}\Phi(d1 - \sigma\sqrt{T})] \qquad \text{(A1.1)}$$

where

$$d1 = \frac{\ln(S/X) + (r - d + \sigma^2/2)T}{\sigma\sqrt{T}} \qquad \text{(A1.2)}$$

N = Number of shares covered by the award[24]

S = Price of the underlying stock

X = Exercise price

24. We considered all awarded options in our measure, including those awarded to adjust existing options ('reload' options). The results are not sensitive to this inclusion.

r = Risk-free interest rate
d = Expected dividend rate over the life of the option
σ = Expected stock return volatility over the life of the option
T = Time to maturity
Φ = Cumulative probability for the normal distribution

The sensitivity of the CEO's stock option award to a one per cent change in the company's stock price in a given year (*OPTSENS*) is estimated in the following way:

$$OPTSENS = N \cdot \Delta \cdot (S/100) \tag{A1.3}$$

where $\Delta = e^{-dT}\Phi(d1)$

In estimating the parameters of the Black-Scholes formula, we use the following assumptions:

S = Market price of the company's stock on the date of the option grant

r = ln(1+risk-free interest rate), where the risk-free interest rate is the approximate average yield that could have been earned in the year in which the option was granted by investing in a seven-year U.S. Treasury bond. This yield was obtained from Execucomp.

d = ln(1+dividend rate), with dividend rate defined as the company's average dividend rate over the past three years. If, in a particular year, the dividend rate is above the 95th percentile of the distribution of yields for that year, it is reduced to the 95th percentile value. Dividend rate and 95th percentile values were obtained from Execucomp.

σ = Annualized volatility, estimated from past 60 months' returns. If, in a particular year, a company's stock volatility is in the bottom or top five per cent of the cross-sectional volatility distribution, its volatility is increased or decreased to the 5th or 95th percentile values. Annualized volatility and percentile values were taken from Execucomp.

APPENDIX 2

Adaptation of Matsumoto (2002) Model to Yearly Data in Order to Detect Expectations Management

For each firm i in industry j during year t, the yearly change in earnings is modelled as a function of previous year's change in earnings and returns cumulated over the current year:[25]

25. Returns are intended to capture additional value-relevant information that an analyst might use to estimate earnings.

$$\frac{\Delta EPS_{ijt}}{P_{ijt-1}} = \alpha_{jt} + \beta_{1jt} \cdot \frac{\Delta EPS_{ijt-1}}{P_{ijt-2}} + \beta_{2jt} \cdot CUMRET_{ijt} + \varepsilon_{ijt}, \tag{A2.1}$$

where:

$\Delta EPS_{ijt} =$ Earnings per share for firm i in industry group j in year t, less earnings per share for the same firm one year previously, as reported by I/B/E/S.

$P_{ijt} =$ Price per share for firm i in industry group j at the end of year t.

$CUMRET_{ijt} =$ Cumulative daily excess return for firm i in industry group j during year t. Returns are cumulated from three days after year t−1 earnings announcement to 20 days before year t earnings announcement.

The model is estimated for each industry group using all firms in that year that belong to the group. Industry groups are defined as in Yermack (1995). In any year there must be at least eight companies in a particular industry group for the equation to be estimated. The parameter estimates from the previous year are used to determine the expected change in earnings per share ($E[\Delta EPS]$):

$$E[\Delta EPS_{ijt}] = \left[\hat{\alpha}_{jt-1} + \hat{\beta}_{1jt-1} \cdot \frac{\Delta EPS_{ijt-1}}{P_{ijt-2}} + \hat{\beta}_{2jt-2} \cdot CUMRET_{ijt}\right] \cdot P_{ijt-1}. \tag{A2.2}$$

This value is added to the previous year's earnings to obtain an estimate of the expected analyst forecast ($E[FEPS]$) for the current year's earnings:

$$E[FEPS_{ijt}] = EPS_{ijt-1} + E[\Delta EPS_{ijt}]. \tag{A2.3}$$

Like Matsumoto, we define a dichotomous variable *DOWN*, comparing the last analyst consensus forecast prior to the earnings announcement date (*FEPS*) and the expected analyst forecast calculated from the model:

$$DOWN = 1 \; if \; FEPS_{ijt} < E[FEPS_{ijt}]$$

indicating that analyst expectations *may have been* managed downward, and

$$DOWN = 0 \; if \; FEPS_{ijt} \geq E[FEPS_{ijt}]$$

indicating that analyst expectations have *not* been managed downward.

APPENDIX 3

Logistic Regression Model

For the limited-dependent variable model, the existence of a latent variable D^* is assumed such that:

$$\mathrm{DOWN}_i = \begin{cases} 1 & \text{if } D^* > 0 \\ 0 & \text{if } D^* < 0 \end{cases}$$

with, $D^* = x\prime_i \beta + v_i,\, v_i \sim logistic(0, \pi^2/3)$

This corresponds to:

$$\mathrm{Pr}ob(DOWN_i = 1) = \Lambda(x\prime_i \beta) = \frac{e^{x\prime_i \beta}}{1 + e^{x\prime_i \beta}}$$

where Λ is the cdf of the logistic distribution and

$$\begin{aligned} x\prime_i \beta \;=\; & \beta_0 + \beta_1 SALARY_i + \beta_2 BONUS_i + \beta_3 LTIP_i + \beta_4 RSG_i \\ & + \beta_5 SHARE_i + \beta_6 INMONEX_i + \beta_7 OPTSENS_i + \beta_8 LOSS_i \\ & + \beta_9 INCEPS_i + \beta_{10} MEET_i + \beta_{11} IFE_i \\ & + \beta_{12} EARNRET + \beta_{13} LTG_i + \beta_{14} RCOV_i + \beta_{15} ICLAIM_i \\ & + \beta_{16} LIT_i + \beta_{17} TRAN_i + \gamma_1 I_1 + \cdots + \gamma_{N-1} I_{N-1} \\ & + \delta_{94} Y_{94} + \cdots + \delta_{01} Y_{01} \end{aligned} \tag{A3.1}$$

Indicator variables Y_{94} to Y_{01} control for year effects (relative to the base year 1993), which are not captured by the compensation and control variables. The indicator variables I_1 to I_{N-1} represent industry effects.

APPENDIX 4

Abnormal Return Estimation

In order to measure abnormal returns close to the earning announcement date, we estimated the following equation:

$$R_{it} = \alpha_i + \beta_i R_{mt} + \lambda_i D_{it} + \varepsilon_{it} \qquad \text{(A4.1)}$$

$$t \in [A_i - 250; A_i + 2]$$

$$D_{it} = \begin{cases} 1/5 & \text{if } t \in [A_i - 2; A_i + 2] \\ 0 & \text{otherwise} \end{cases}$$

where

A_i = Earnings announcement date for firm i
R_{it} = Log return of stock *i* on day *t* adjusted for capital changes and dividends
R_{mt} = Log return of the market index on day *t*
λ_i = Cumulative abnormal return for stock *i* between $A_i - 2$ and $A_i + 2$.[26]

Equation (A4.1) is estimated with a weighted least square regression as in Heinkel and Kraus (1988) to correct for missing returns.

REFERENCES

Aboody, D. and R. Kasznik, 'CEO Stock Option Awards and the Timing of Corporate Voluntary Disclosures' (2000) *Journal of Accounting and Economics* 29, 73–100.

Ali, A. and S. Kallapur, 'Securities Price Consequences of the Private Securities Litigation Reform Act of 1995 and Related Events' (2001) *Accounting Review* 76, 431–461.

Bartov, E., D. Givoly, and C. Hayn, 'The Rewards to Meeting or Beating Earnings Expectations' (2002) *Journal of Accounting and Economics* 33, 173–204.

Bergstresser, D. and T. Philippon (2003), 'CEO Incentives and Earnings Management, Working Paper', Harvard Business School.

Black, F. and M. Scholes, 'The Pricing of Options and Corporate Liabilities' (1973) *Journal of Political Economy* 81, 637–654.

Boni, L. and K. L. Womack, 'Wall Street's Credibility Problem: Misaligned Incentives and Dubious Fixes? Working Paper', University of Pennsylvania, 2002.

26. As an initial step, we conducted an analysis of abnormal returns around the earnings announcement date. We observed most significant abnormal returns during the five days chosen as the event window.

Bowen, R. M., L. DuCharme, and D. Shores, 'Stakeholders' Implicit Claims and Accounting Method Choice' (1995) *Journal of Accounting and Economics* 20, 255–295.

Brown, L. D., 'A Temporal Analysis of Earnings Surprises: Profit vs. Losses' (2001a) *Journal of Accounting Research* 39, 221–241.

Brown, L. D., 'Small Negative Surprises: Frequency and Consequence, Working Paper', Georgia State University, 2001b.

Brown, L. D. and H. N. Higgins, 'Managers' Guidance of Analysts: International Evidence, Working Paper', Georgia State University, 2002.

Bushee, B. J., 'The Influence of Institutional Investors on Myopic R&D Investment Behavior,' (1998) *Accounting Review* 73, 305–333.

Chan, L. K. C., J. Karceski, and J. Lakonishok, 'Analysts' Conflict of Interest and Biases in Earnings Forecasts, Working Paper', University of Illinois at Urbana-Champaign, 2003.

Core, J. E. and W. R. Guay, 'Stock Option Plans for Non-Executive Employees' (2001) *Journal of Financial Economics* 61, 253–287.

Cotter, J. A., I. Tuna, and P. D. Wysocki, 'The Expectations Management Game: Do Analysts Act Independently of Explicit Management Earnings Guidance? Working Paper', University of Pennsylvania, 2002.

Crichfield T., T. Dyckman, and J. Lakonishok, 'An evaluation of Security Analysts' Forecasts' (1978) *Accounting Review* 53, 651–668.

Dechow, P., R. G. Sloan, and A. P. Sweeney, 'Detecting Earnings Management' (1995) *Accounting Review* 70, 193–225.

Dechow, P., R. G. Sloan, and A. P. Sweeney, 'Causes and Consequences of Earnings Manipulations: An Analysis of Firms Subject to Enforcement Actions by the SEC' (1996) *Contemporary Accounting Research* 13, 1–36.

Degeorge, F., J. Patel, and R. Zeckhauser, 'Earnings Management to Exceed Thresholds,' (1999) *Journal of Business* 72, 1–33.

Fama, E. F., and J. McBeth, 'Risk, Return, and Equilibrium: Empirical Tests' (1973) *Journal of Political Economy* 51, 55–87.

Francis, J., D. Philbrick, and K. Shipper, 'Shareholder Litigation and Corporate Disclosures' (1993) *Journal of Accounting Research* 32, 137–164.

Fuller, J., and M. C. Jensen, 'Just Say No to Wall-Street' (2002) *Journal of Applied Corporate Finance* 14, 41–46.

Gao, P. and R. E. Shrieves, 'Earnings Management and Executive Compensation: A Case of Overdose of Option and Underdose of Salary? Working Paper', University of Tennessee, 2002.

Heinkel, R. and A. Kraus, 'Measuring Event Impacts on Thinly Traded Stocks' (1988) *Journal of Financial and Quantitative Analysis* 23, 71–88.

Hong, H., T. Lim, and J.C. Stein, 'Bad News Travels Slowly: Size, Analyst Coverage, and the Profitability of Momentum Strategies,' (2000) *Journal of Finance* 55, 265–295.

Hotchkiss, E. S. and D. Strickland, 'Does Shareholder Composition Matter? Evidence from the Market Reaction to Corporate Earnings Announcements' (2003) *Journal of Finance* 58, 1,469–1,498.

Imhoff, E. A. and G. J. Lobo, 'Information Content of Analysts' Composite Forecast Revisions' (1984) *Journal of Accounting Research* 22, 541–554.

Jones, J., 'Earnings Management during Import Relief Investigations' (1991) *Journal of Accounting Research* 29, 193–229.

Kasznik, R. and M. F. McNichols, 'Does Meeting Expectations Matter? Evidence from Analyst Forecast Revisions and Share Prices' (2002) *Journal of Accounting Research* 40, 727–759.

Kennedy, P., *A Guide to Econometrics* (4th edn, Oxford, Blackwell, 2000).

Lin, H. and M.F. McNichols, 'Underwriting Relationships, Analysts' Earnings Forecasts and Investment Recommendations' (1998) *Journal of Accounting and Economics* 25, 101–127.

Lim, T., 'Rationality and Analysts' Forecast Bias' (2001) *Journal of Finance* 56, 369–385.

Liu, M.H. and T. Yao, 'The Consensus-Beating Game, Working Paper', Boston College, 2003.

Lopez, T.J. and L. Rees, 'The Effect of Meeting Analyst Forecasts and Systematic Positive Forecast Errors on the Information Content of Unexpected Earnings, Working Paper', Texas A&M University, 2001.

Matsumoto, D. A., 'Management's Incentives to Avoid Negative Earnings Surprises' (2002) *Accounting Review* 77, 483–514.

Matsunaga, S. R. and C. W. Park, 'The Effect of Missing a Quarterly Earnings Benchmark on the CEO's Annual Bonus' (2001) *Accounting Review* 76, 313–332.

Merton, R., 'Theory of Rational Option Pricing' (1973) *Bell Journal of Economics and Management Science* 4, 141–183.

Michaely, R. and K. L Womack, 'Conflict of Interest and the Credibility of Underwriter Analyst Recommendations' (1999) *Review of Financial Studies* 12, 653–686.

Murphy, K. J., 'Executive Compensation,' in *Handbook of Labor Economics*, vol. 3, (O. Ashenfelter and D. Card eds) (Amsterdam, Elsevier, 1999), pp. 2,485–2,563.

Ofek, E. and D. Yermack, 'Taking Stock: Equity-Based Compensation and the Evolution of Managerial Ownership' (2000) *Journal of Finance* 55, 1,367–1,384.

Puffer, S. M. and J. B. Weintrop, 'Corporate Performance and CEO Turnover: The Role of Performance Expectations' (1991) *Administrative Science Quarterly* 36, 1–19.

Richardson, S. A., S. H. Teoh, and P. D. Wysocki, 'The Walk-Down to Beatable Analyst Forecasts: The Role of Equity Issuance and Insider Trading Incentives, Working Paper', University of Pennsylvania, 2003.

Sivakumar, K., and G. Waymire, 'Insider Trading Following Material News Events: Evidence from Earnings' (1994) *Financial Management* 23, 23–32.

Soffer, L., R. Thiagarajan, and B. Walther, 'Earnings Preannouncement Strategies' (2002) *Review of Accounting Studies* 5, 5–26.

Skinner, D.J. and R.G. Sloan, 'Earnings Surprises, Growth Expectations, and Stock Returns or Don't Let an Earnings Torpedo Sink Your Portfolio' (2002) *Review of Accounting Studies* 7, 289–312.

Yermack, D., 'Do Corporations Award CEO Stock Options Effectively?' (1985) *Journal of Financial Economics* 39, 237–269.

Yermack, D., 'Good Timing: CEO Stock Option Awards and Company News Announcements' (1997) *Journal of Finance* 52, 449–476.

White, H., 'A Heteroscedasticity-Consistent Covariance Matrix Estimator and a Direct Test for Heteroscedasticity' (1980) *Econometrica* 48, 817–838.

Chapter 5

Investment Research: How to Solve Conflicts of Interest More Efficiently

*Sandro Abegglen**

As a reaction to the conflicts of interest affecting major Wall Street investment banks in connection with financial research and the issue of securities, which received enormous publicity after the bursting of the dot-com bubble, lawmakers and financial services authorities in many jurisdictions imposed rules to ensure unbiased investment research and recommendations.

While the technical substance of the rules on investment research varies widely by jurisdiction, almost all of them are based on a combination of organizational requirements (for banks), obligations addressed to the financial analysts themselves, and rules for the proper structuring of incentive systems. However, it should not be taken for granted that the new regulations that have been rushed through are in every respect an efficient way of mitigating conflicts of interests in connection with financial analysis, as this paper is intended to show.

I shall first examine some basic facts and define the scope of the problem (section II). I shall then briefly discuss the phenomenon of banks' conflicts of interests in general, and present the main regulatory instruments used to increase the independence of financial analysts' work, using the Swiss rules as an example

* PD Dr. iur. Fürsprecher (attorney-at-law), LL.M. (Austin, Texas); Partner, Niederer Kraft & Frey, Zurich; Privat Docent for Private and Commercial Law and Banking and Financial Markets Law, University of Berne. The author wishes to thank his colleague Thomas M. Brönnimann for helpful review of and comments on this article.

L. Thévenoz and R. Bahar (eds.), *Conflicts of Interest: Corporate Governance and Financial Market*, pp. 171–185.

(section III). Section IV identifies the concepts underlying the relevant conflict of interest regulations. Section V provides policy proposals for achieving a more efficient regulation of conflicts of interest in connection with financial research.

I. HOW SERIOUS ARE CONFLICTS OF INTERESTS – OR: WHY DID NO ONE CRY 'FOUL' UNTIL AS RECENTLY AS 1999?

A. General

In 2002 an SEC director, reacting to press criticisms that made it sound as though the SEC had only just started examining analysts' conflicts of interest, rejected the implication, stating: 'In fact, the SEC began to examine this issue in 1999.'[1] She then went on to state that, in the summer of 1999, SEC staff had begun a review of industry practices regarding the disclosure of research analyst's conflicts of interest. This pronouncement raises the question of just how serious financial analysts' conflicts of interest really are. If they are thought to constitute an important problem, surely that must have been the case for years, if not decades, before the bursting (or, come to that, the inflation) of the dot-com bubble. If so, why was it not considered necessary to address conflicts of interest in the past, and what has changed since to produce the common opinion that financial analysts' conflicts of interest are a serious regulatory concern which needs close attention from policy makers, regulators and the industry – not to mention academics?

As a matter of fact, it is quite astonishing that a regulatory issue as large (when judged by the attention currently being given to the topic) as the conflicts of interest of research analysts should have gone unnoticed by regulators in the recent past. One rather gets the impression that the regulators' feverish activity in this area may be partly due to their desire to avoid questions such as: 'Why did you not address this problem before and avoid all this trouble?' This applies with particular force to the situation in the United States, where the New York State Attorney General, Mr. Elliot Spitzer, made the SEC look as though it had been wrong-footed by the conflicts of interest of financial analysts in investment banks. And even when the SEC did start to address these conflict of interest problems, it looked distinctly sluggish compared to Mr. Spitzer's rapid and effective intervention.

Thus the question I shall address in this paper is: Was sin really so late in coming to financial analysts, and did it come only to Wall Street, or also to other banking centres such as Zurich or London?

---

1. Speech by L. Richards, Director, Office of Compliance Inspections and Examinations, U.S. Securities and Exchange Commission, 'Analysts Conflicts of Interest: Taking Steps to Remove Bias,' available at <www.sec.gov/news/speech/spch559.htm>.

B. DID SIN REALLY COME SO LATE?

Financial analysis and its practitioners may always have been subject to certain temptations: for example, to issue over-positive recommendations, not only to appease the managements of analyzed companies and institutional investors with participations in those companies, but also to help their own employers attract and retain investment-banking business. It is also possible that financial analysts engaged, either on their personal account or on their employer's, in securities transactions taking advantage of as-yet-unpublished investment research reports or buy or sell recommendations, to the detriment of the market.

Moreover, the obvious fact that financial analysis helps to bring in more business for the bank's brokerage/trading department may – but need not (see section V) – lead to conflicts of interest. Sell-side financial analysis always has been and still is heavily subsidized by the brokerage and trading units of banks. In fact, it was long thought that the very purpose of financial analysis was to bring more (institutional) investor business to a bank's brokerage/trading units.

I shall now briefly describe how financial analysis fits into a bank's business setup. It will be helpful to distinguish between three types of financial analysis providers:

- Universal banks/full-service investment banks: These banks offer most, if not the full range of, investment banking, brokerage, and commercial and private banking services. They finance their sell-side research departments out of the profits from their underwriting (investment banking), institutional equity trading and (in some cases) retail brokerage. In addition, profits from the asset management business may be used to fund research (according to industry insiders, up to 50 per cent of an investment firm's research budget may be funded through institutional equity trading). Investment banking revenues are used to fund financial analysis because research may bring in new underwriting business, and institutional equity trading departments fund research because the recipients of the pertinent research reports, large institutional investors, take account of the quality of the research when choosing an investment bank. Moreover, institutional investors may, when making transaction commission payments, specify which piece of research they are paying for.
- Brokerage firms: Most brokerage firms do not engage in investment banking activities but only in brokerage/trading activities for institutional and/or retail clients. They normally depend on transaction commissions to fund sell-side research analysis.
- 'Pure' research providers: These provides are not financial intermediaries in the narrow sense of the term, i.e. they provide neither banking nor brokerage services in any form. Rather, they sell their research work as a product, in consideration of a flat fee or fee per report, to interested customers, normally institutional investors. This last category is not further dealt with in this paper, as independent research providers are less subject to conflicts of interest.

C. Why Attention Now and Not Then?

The funding of investment research, as described above, carries a risk that financial analysts' recommendations may be biased. This applies, first, when research work is funded by trading commissions: a buy recommendation, since it can be acted upon by *any* market participant, will generate more commissions than a sell recommendation, which can be acted upon by investors who already hold the security in question, put aside derivatives and short selling transactions. It also applies when research is subsidized by the underwriting business: negative recommendations are scarcely likely to increase that business. Thus there appears to be potential for conflicts of interest.

However, prior to the dot-com feeding frenzy, the addressees of research reports were mostly institutional investors and other professional market participants. As a result, conflicts of interests, if any, were mitigated or moderated by, in particular, the following circumstances:

- Institutional investors, being aware of the conflicts of financial analysts and their employers, compensated for the potential upward bias by not acting very strongly on buy recommendations, but very strongly on sell recommendations.
- In regard to knowledgeable institutional investors, financial analysts personally, as well as their employers, had a reputation to lose if the recommendations turned out to be incorrect: institutional investors had (and have) the capacity to observe and remember the quality and value of the research work provided to them, and which analyst produced it.[2]
- The very fact that large institutional investors linked their trading orders directly to pieces of research, which they would obviously not do unless they put some value on the research, was a very strong incentive for both financial analysts and their employers to provide real value to such investors. If an investor thought that a bank's financial analysts were so conflicted that they were (e.g.) making buy recommendations when they ought to be making sell recommendations, the investor would promptly transfer its trading business to another bank, or continue to trade with the original bank at a lower fee to factor out the useless 'research'. Over time, the reputation of the bank as a whole would suffer from such behaviour and would be forced to provide brokerage services at lower margins. This in turn would damage the bank's standing, as well as its eligibility for high-profile underwriting mandates, where it is essential that a bank has a good reputation in order to provide the best possible placement results. Accordingly, it is not surprising that studies appears to show that research work carried out by highly reputable banks tends to be less biased than research work by other banks.[3]

---

2. See, e.g., A. Ljungqvist, F. Marston, L.T. Starks, K.D. Wei and H. Yan, Conflicts of Interest in Sell-side Research and The Moderating Role of Institutional Investors, 12 September 2005, available at <www.ssrn.com/abstract=649684>, p. 1 *et seq.*, with an extensive list of references.
3. Ibid.

During the stock exchange bubble of the late 1990s, however, these mitigating effects became far less marked, because suddenly *retail* investors became important purchasers of initial public offerings and therefore also important recipients of sell-side research. It seems that these two elements combined to form a vicious circle, as some financial analysts threw business ethics to the winds, culminating in attitudes such as the one allegedly expressed by a once very famous dot.com analyst in the US: 'I am in the flow of what's going on. What has been a conflict of interest in the past is now regarded as a synergy'.

At the same time, some financial analysts were wallowing in unprecedented levels of remuneration. They apparently saw this as a kind of endgame and ceased to care about their long-term reputation.

However, it appears that this concatenation of events was quite unique and that the scope and gravity of the problems caused to financial research by the dot-com bubble were exceptional (which is not of course to say that no conflicts whatsoever existed at other times).[4]

II. THE APPLICABLE SWISS RULES AS AN EXAMPLE OF HOW FINANCIAL ANALYST CONFLICTS OF INTEREST CAN BE ADDRESSED

A. Preliminary Remark: Conflicts of Interest in Connection with Financial Research are Only One Example of the Numerous Conflicts of Interests Within Banks

Conflicts of interest within banks in connection with financial research are only one example of the numerous actual and potential conflicts of interest with which a bank or securities dealer is confronted when carrying out its business. Accordingly, and typically for the principle-oriented (as opposed to rule-based) Swiss approach to financial services regulation, the same principles and rules that govern banks' conflicts of interest in general are also being used as a basis for solving the conflicts of financial analysts.

Conflicts of interest are deemed to exist if a person (agent) who is *obliged* to safeguard a third party's (principal's) interests has incompatible interests of his own or is *obliged* to safeguard the conflicting interests of another principal. Swiss contract law specifically addresses conflicts of interest in connection with self-contracting and the situation in which an agent is acting for several principals in the same business. According to the relevant rules, an agent can only act in such situations if, in spite of the conflict of interest, there is no risk that a principal will be put at a disadvantage.[5]

---

4. See, in this volume, M. Dubois and P. Dumontier, Chapter 6, as well as L. Schrutt and S. Wieler, Chapter 8.
5. See in detail S. Abegglen, *Wissenszurechnung bei der juristischen Person und im Konzern, bei Banken und Versicherungen – Interessenkonflikte und Chinese Walls bei Banken und Wertpapierhäusern – Privatrecht und Finanzmarktrecht* (Staempfli, Bern, 2004), pp. 344–346.

Financial services providers are subject to a vast number of conflicts of interest. While studies written in continental Europe have linked this to the universal banking principle (as opposed to the regime of separation of commercial and investment banking pursuant to the repealed US Glass Steagall Act), there is no doubt that a regime that segregates the two types of banking business has not eliminated conflict of interests either. In fact, financial analysts' conflicts of interest are a good illustration of the fact that even firms active only in one type of banking business are subject to conflicts.[6]

The importance policy makers and regulators attach to conflicts of interest in financial services is shown by the extensive regulation of such conflicts (including those relating to financial analysis) within the European Union. For example, article 18 of Council Directive 2004/39/EC of 21 April 2004 on Markets in Financial Instruments (the so-called 'Markets in Financial Instruments Directive' or 'MIFID') addresses conflicts of interest in detail. Article 18 (1) MIFID requires investment firms:

> '[T]o take all reasonable steps to identify conflicts of interest between themselves, including their managers, employees and tied agent, or any person directly or indirectly linked to them by control and their clients or between one client and another that arise in the course of providing any investment and ancillary services (providing investment research is considered to be such an ancillary service) or combinations thereof.'

In contrast to MIFID, which also covers conflicts of interest in investment research, MIFID's 'predecessor', namely Council Directive 93/22/EEC of 10 May 1993 on Investment Services in the Securities Field (the so-called 'Investment Services Directive' or 'ISD'), did not apply to investment research (it was not included under either 'investment services' or 'non-core services'). The Council Directive 2003/6/EC of 28 January 2003 on Insider Dealing and Market Manipulation (the 'Market Abuse Directive' or 'MAD') also now provides for consistent EC-wide treatment of the disclosure of conflicts of interest in connection with investment research.

B. Basic Principles for Solving Conflicts of Interest in Swiss Law

1. Statutory Basis: Art. 11 (1) Stock Exchange Act

Art. 11(1) of the Stock Exchange Act imposes on Swiss securities dealers (most Swiss banks have a securities dealer's license that permits them to engage in brokerage business, besides them carrying out the ordinary bank business of taking

6. For a description of the various types of conflicts of interests in the financial services business see S. Abegglen (no. 5 above), p. 346 *et seq.*

deposits and lending to third parties[7]) not only duties of care and duties of information, but also a duty of loyalty (art. 11 [1] lit. c Stock Exchange Act). The securities dealer is required to 'ensure in particular that any conflicts of interest do not adversely impact its customers.' It follows from this provision that the avoidance of conflicts of interest is a top priority; in cases in which this is not possible, the securities dealer must institute organizational measures to ensure that any (potential) conflicts of interest do not adversely affect the client's interests. If this is impossible, the client must be informed; i.e. the conflict of interest situation must be appropriately disclosed. It should be noted that art. 11 (1) lit. c Stock Exchange Act does not stipulate precisely how securities dealers must ensure compliance with this rule. In principle, they are free to choose the appropriate measures in view of the relevant conflicts of interest.[8]

Both the Swiss Federal Banking Commission and the Swiss Federal Court consider compliance with art. 11 (1) lit. c Stock Exchange Act to be highly important. A substantial breach of the duty of loyalty is regarded as a breach of the securities dealer's duty to properly conduct his business (*börsengesetzliche Pflicht zur Gewähr einwandfreier Geschäftstätigkeit*), which he must comply with if he is to obtain and keep his securities dealer's licence, pursuant to art. 10 (2) lit. d Stock Exchange Act. For a securities dealer that is also licensed as a bank, this requirement also derives from art. 3 (2) lit. c of the Banking Act (*bankengesetzliche Gewähr einwandfreier Geschäftstätigkeit*). Compliance with these provisions is of paramount importance for any Swiss bank/securities dealer. Moreover, the duty to ensure the proper conduct of business operations under both the Stock Exchange Act and the Banking Act applies not only to the directors and managers, but also to the bank as an organization.

The duty of loyalty, pursuant to Art. 11 Stock Exchange Act, which comprises an obligation to ensure that clients' interests are not adversely affected by conflicts of interest, is limited to the area of securities trading and its organization and does not apply directly to other financial services.

2. Assurance of Proper Business Conduct (*Gewährspflicht*): An Important Principle in the Management of Conflicts of Interest

The limited applicability of the duty of loyalty pursuant to art. 11 (1) lit. c Stock Exchange Act does not imply that comparable duties do not exist in other areas

7. The dual licensing status (banking and securities dealer's license) is standard for any bank active in the wealth management business, because clients' assets are not only deposited with the bank but also invested in securities, which means the bank must deal in securities; banks without securities dealer status are very rare, but a number of institutions do not have a banking license, because they do not accept cash deposits from customers. In other words, any regulated institution that provides financial research services will normally have at least the status of securities dealer and will therefore be subject to the regulation described in the text.
8. For an extensive discussion of conflicts of interest and the regulatory obligations to be fulfilled in connection therewith, see S. Abegglen (n. 5 above), pp. 320 *et seq.*

of banking. The consistent practice of the Swiss Federal Banking Commission with regard to conflicts of interest makes it quite clear that it considers the same principles as described above under the duty of loyalty to be implied by art. 3 (2) lit. c Banking Act. This important provision of Swiss banking regulations requires the directors and management of a bank, as well as the bank itself, to ensure the proper conduct of business operations (the so-called *Gewährspflicht*).[9] The view that the proper management of conflicts of interest also follows from the *Gewährspflicht* is confirmed by the Swiss Federal Court. The relevant precedent is the well-known Biber case,[10] which is particularly significant in so far as the Swiss Federal Banking Commission applied very strict standards in regard to the handling of conflicts of interest, although the Stock Exchange Act did not apply (for technical reasons that are irrelevant to the present discussion). In the Biber case, the disputed transaction was a proprietary transaction by a bank that had been in possession of advantageous (but not inside) information. Both the Swiss Federal Banking Commission and the Swiss Federal Court considered this to be a breach of the good faith (*Treu und Glauben*) principle, as defined in art. 2 (1) Swiss Federal Civil Code; the bank misused an information advantage by selling shares to clients, alledgedly knowing that their value was substantially less than the current stock market price. In the circumstances of the Biber case, the Federal Court held that such a breach of art. 2 (1) Swiss Federal Civil Code was also a violation of the *Gewährspflicht*[11] laid down in art. 3 (2) lit. c Banking Act.

In a later, equally well-known decision,[12] the Swiss Federal Banking Commission confirmed the requirements as developed in the Biber case. In particular, the Commission held that it is a breach of art. 3 (2) lit. c Banking Act if a bank's conduct is fundamentally opposed to the behaviour to be expected of an honest banker. In addition, the Commission imposed on banks an obligation not to compromise themselves, i.e. damage their reputations and undermine public confidence. Finally, the Commission stated that banks must pay special attention to the principle of art. 2(1) Swiss Federal Civil Code and that conflicts of interest must be resolved in a way that does not put clients or third parties at a disadvantage.

C. Implementation of these Principles

1. Code of Conduct for Securities Dealers

A first general application of art. 11 (1) lit. c Stock Exchange Act is provided in section D (Duty of loyalty) of the Code of Conduct for Securities Dealers dated

9. See e.g. M.L. Aellen, *Die Gewähr für eine einwandfreie Geschäftstätigkeit*, (Berne, Staempfli, 1990); the book is still of fundamental importance.
10. ATF 2A.230/1999/bol of 2 February 2000, Bulletin CFB 40/2000, p. 37 *et seq.*
11. For a detailed discussion of the Biber case, see S. Abegglen (footnote 4), p. 369 *et seq.*
12. Decision of the Federal Banking Commission of 19 March 2003 in regard to the allocation of shares in the initial public offering (IPO) of Think Tools AG, Bulletin CFB 45/2003, 164 *et seq.*

22 January 1997, and issued by the Swiss Bankers Association. The FBC considers the Code of Conduct to be a minimum standard, compliance with which must be monitored by the banking law auditors of all Swiss securities dealers (and any bank holding a securities dealer's license). The Code of Conduct does not contain any specific requirements that are not also covered by the instruments discussed below, and is therefore not further addressed here.

However, it is noteworthy that the principle-based Code of Conduct leaves it in the discretion of the banks which organizational measures be implemented as long as they ensure compliance with the duty of loyalty and appropriate management of conflicts of interest.

2. Directives on the Independence of Financial Research

In contrast to the above-mentioned Code of Conduct, this piece of regulation is rule-based in the sense that banks have less discretion on how to implement the required measures taking into consideration their type of business. The Swiss Bankers Association's Directives on the Independence of Financial Research[13] provide a number of very specific rules for *internal organization* regarding the relationship between financial research on the one hand, and securities trading (including proprietary trading) and sales (N 13–16), the new issues department and investment banking, the loans department and equity participations held by a bank on the other. From an organizational, hierarchical and functional perspective, financial analysis must be separate from all the other specified units. And those units, as well as the financial research department, must be so structured as to ensure that no privileged ('material, non-public') information flows between them that is not simultaneously available to clients of the bank ('Chinese walls'). In the rare cases in which such information is exchanged despite these precautions, the bank's Compliance Unit must be called in to ensure, in particular, that the exchange of information occurs within a regulated framework which will prevent the conflict of interest from having any negative consequences (N 16).

In addition, these directives set forth rules governing *external relationships* (i.e. the relationship of the financial research department and the individual analysts with bank clients and companies being analyzed), and proprietary trading by financial analysts.

Finally, the introduction to the Directives (page 2) states that banks are free to implement the content of the Directives as they see fit; provided, of course, that the minimum requirements are met.

These Directives (dated 24 January 2003) are not part of statutory law but *de facto* have the force of law: this piece of self-regulation has been recognized by the Swiss Federal Banking Commission as a minimum standard with which any Swiss bank or securities dealer engaged in producing and publishing financial

13. Available at <www.swissbanking.org/en/3566_e.pdf>.

research must comply, and as an ongoing requirement for proper business conduct under the relevant Swiss banking and brokerage regulations. Compliance with the Directive is subject to regular audits by external banking and broker/dealer auditors.

III. REGULATORS' TYPICAL APPROACH TO SOLVING CONFLICTS OF INTEREST

A. Overview

The following sections provide a brief overview of the concepts that underlie the general rules intended to prevent or mitigate conflicts of interest.

B. Instruments Most Often Used to Regulate Research Analysts' Conflicts of Interest

Legislation and regulation that addresses conflicts of interest connected to financial research typically use the following instruments:

- Organizational measures: The organizational, functional and hierarchical separation of financial research from all other units and departments within a bank ought to ensure the independence of financial analysts. Banks also must ensure that other departments are not engaged in front running etc., based on knowledge of the contents of as-yet-unpublished recommendations etc. These separations include limitations on relationships and communication between investment banking, trading and asset management on the one hand, and research analysts on the other (Chinese walls). The separations should not only provide information barriers, but also exclude undue influence on analysts from within a bank (e.g. analysts must not be directly supervised by, or report to, a person who is responsible for another business unit in the bank, e.g. proprietary trading). In exceptional circumstances, e.g. in connection with pre-IPO investment research work, financial analysts can be taken 'across' the Chinese Wall, but usually only with the approval of a high-level compliance officer.
- Appropriate compensation structure: Detailed stipulations on the compensation of banks' financial analysts are intended to provide incentives to improve the independence of financial analysts' work, or at least to avoid providing incentives which might bias financial analysts' judgments. In particular, an analyst's compensation must not be tied to a specific investment banking or equity trading transaction, and if it is generally linked to the bank's underwriting and/or equity trading returns, this must be disclosed in the research reports. In addition, it goes without saying that financial analysts may not accept any incentives in whatever form from companies on which they conduct research work.

- Ban on analysts' proprietary trading: Proprietary trading by financial analysts is heavily restricted: In contrast to the popular concept of 'put your money where your mouth is', financial analysts are generally prohibited from investing in securities on which they carry out research work, or even (with certain exemptions) in the sector in which they conduct research work. Front running is strictly prohibited, as are, of course, the execution of transactions that are contrary to analyst recommendations.
- Transparency, disclosure of potential and actual conflict of interests: Banks are usually required to include disclosure statements in their recommendations. An investment bank must disclose if it is engaged in underwriting or other investment banking business with the companies being analyzed. For example, according to the Swiss rules, in every published research report, banks must disclose whether they participated in any issue of securities on behalf of the company being researched within the last three years.
- Relationships with companies being analyzed are governed in detail: A helpful illustration is available in sections 25–32 of the Swiss Bankers Association Directives on the Independence of Financial Research (see the annex to this paper). These rules oblige companies being researched to treat all analysts equally (to prevent them from punishing analysts for unfavourable recommendations),[14] and stipulate quiet periods that a bank that is involved in an initial public offering as a manager or co-manager must observe, during which no new research reports on the company in question, or new recommendations, may be published. Similar rules, usually with shorter quiet periods, apply to secondary public offerings.

C. Conclusion: Three-pillar Approach

A brief analysis of the above commonly applied rules and regulations shows that the underlying regulatory concept has the following three pillars:

- First pillar: Measures, notably Chinese Walls of every type, are taken to ensure that conflicts of interests are not detrimental to clients' interests.
- Second pillar: In situations that generate strong conflicts of interest, these conflicts must be disclosed (e.g. the bank's investment banking mandates; any compensation of financial analysts that is tied to investment banking; the bank's equity holdings in analyzed companies, etc.).
- Third pillar: In situations that constitute a particularly strong incentive for financial analysts to come up with positively biased recommendations, the bank must, under Swiss law, abstain from publishing research reports and

14. For an excellent discussion of the connection between an accounting topic, namely fair value reporting by analyzed companies, and regulation of financial analysts' conflicts of interest see R. Volkart, P. Labhart and E. Schön, 'Fair-Value-Bewertung und Value Reporting' in H. Bieg and R. Heyd (eds), *Fair Value: Bewertung in Rechnungswesen, Controlling und Finanzwirtschaft*, (Munich, Vahlen, 2005), p. 517 *et seq.*

recommendations. Examples include situations in which a bank holds 50 per cent or more of an analyzed company; when a bank performs financial research on the bank's own securities; or when a financial analyst is involved in a commercial relationship with the analyzed company.

The reason for enjoining such restraint on banks is, fundamentally, the belief that the Chinese Walls and other instruments which should be sufficient to ensure the *de facto* independence of financial analysts are viewed with suspicion by the public, who will assume that financial analysts and banks are biased in their judgments whether the financial analysts actually act independently or not. The same anxiety is reflected in the question (whose relevance goes well beyond the conflicts of interest of financial analysts) of whether regulatory Chinese Walls do, in fact, prevent knowledge transfer within a bank, which is a prerequisite e.g. of the due diligence defence in cases in which an underwriting bank argues that the specific knowledge available about a company (in e.g. the loans department) did not have to be taken into consideration when drafting the company's issue prospectus.[15]

An (admittedly extreme and somewhat theoretical) example may serve as an illustration. The Chinese Wall requirements do not (e.g.) allow the loans department to pass material non-public information to the financial analysts. Suppose the loans department is aware that a borrower is about to go bankrupt and the same borrower is being analyzed by the same bank's analysts: in the worst case, this may mean that the bank's analysts are making a buy recommendation on a company the bank knows to have very severe financial problems. In this case – or in a similar situation – the reputation of the bank as a whole is at stake, since it may appear as if the financial analyst has issued a buy recommendation on purpose in order to protect the loan position and to help the bank terminate its exposure to the analyzed company.

IV. POLICY THOUGHTS AND PROPOSALS

A. High Costs of Current Regulation

As the above discussion shows – and as is also plainly obvious from a glance at e.g. the Swiss Bankers Association's Directives on the Independence of Financial Research,[16] or the even more complex art. 18 MIFID, and in particular its implementation measures as advised by the Committee of European Securities Regulators (CESR)[17] – regulations in the area of conflicts of interests place substantial burdens on banks and securities firms that conduct research work and publish research reports and recommendations. The implementation and monitoring of these highly detailed rules are extremely costly and complex. Moreover, because this piece of regulation is rule-based rather than principle-based, it significantly limits the organizational freedom of banks. In addition, it should be noted that internationally

15. See S. Abegglen (n. 5 above), pp. 384–391.
16. Available at <www.swissbanking.org/en/3566_e.pdf>.
17. <www.europa.eu.int/comm/internal_market/securities/isd/index_en.htm>

active financial service providers are not only required to comply with the rules and regulations of their home country. Whenever research reports are 'exported' or 'imported', the various rules of the foreign jurisdictions must be observed. While MIFID and MAD have introduced some consistency to the general rules across the EC, substantial differences exist in non-EC jurisdictions. For example, the rules differ on the thresholds that define when an investment bank must disclose that it holds a participation in a company being analyzed – minimum participation for disclosure in Switzerland, for example, is five percent; and, depending on the jurisdiction, different definitions apply as to what constitutes an investment banking mandate that must be disclosed.

Reactions to the costs that go along with such pieces of legislation vary between equanimity (i.e. full compliance), avoidance of certain research and/or business segments and outsourcing of research work to independent firms and disposal of in-house research units, e.g. to ratings agencies. This shows that the burden of the rules and regulations is substantial. In fact, as Jean-Baptiste Zufferey stated, one can speak of a 'regulatory shower' to which the financial analyst regulation has made its contribution.[18] The question therefore arises of whether it might not be possible to increase the efficiency of the anti-conflicts regulation. In the following section, I will offer an answer to that question in the form of a number of policy proposals.

B. FOUR POLICY PROPOSALS

1. First Proposal: Replace Excessive Rule-based Separation Requirements by Escalating Measures

In general, the extensive, highly technical and detailed requirements regarding organizational, hierarchical and functional *separation* of research units from other departments in banks appear to go too far and may not be necessary to ensure high-quality financial analysis. This is not to question the importance of Chinese Walls, which – independent of the present regulation of financial research – must be in place in banks and security firms to prevent misuse of material non-public (insider) information. However, rather than promulgate highly technical separation requirements that substantially affect a bank's organizational freedom, why not consider less extensive, but still extremely effective, and therefore more efficient, means to ban the management of a bank from exerting pressure on individual analysts to arrive a particular research results? The necessary prohibition could be effectively enforced by placing a range of escalating measures at the disposal of the compliance officer and enabling analysts to lodge formal complaints in response to undue pressure. This means, of course, that the compliance officer must have a position in the hierarchy within the firm, allowing him to effectively fight and sanction abuses, even if committed by higher management.

18. See Chapter 7 by J.B. Zufferey, who is inter alia Vice-Chairman of the Swiss Federal Banking Commission (which is the Swiss financial services authority).

2. Second Proposal: Differentiate Between Institutional (Sophisticated) and Retail Investors

Generally, the rules designed to prevent or limit potential conflicts of interest associated with the preparation of financial research reports do not differentiate between institutional investors (or other professional financial intermediaries) and retail investors as recipients of recommendations. This practice is inefficient, because institutional investors should be in a position to protect themselves, as long as market mechanisms work as required.[19] In particular, it is inefficient to subject banks that provide research work and recommendations only to institutional investors to the very same set of rules that applies to banks that provide recommendations in part or only to retail investors.

3. Third Proposal: Allow Reputation Cost to Work

The effectiveness of reputation as one means of regulation of corporate governance for public companies has been shown in Switzerland most prominently by Hans Caspar von der Crone.[20] Reputation as a regulatory instrument can also be put to work in the context at hand. As described in Sections II.B and II.C, among the most important objectives of investment research are to attract more institutional investor trading business and to increase a bank's reputation, enabling it to charge higher fees for trading and investment banking services. This objective can only be reached because institutional investors do actually observe and remember the quality of research work and investment recommendations, and reward good work by taking trading business to the relevant institution. Hence it is most efficient if a financial analyst's remuneration is geared to the trading commissions generated by institutional investors who appreciated his work (see the fourth proposal below). However, current regulations generally prohibit this type of link, on the assumption that it will encourage the analyst to issue false trading signals. That is incorrect: as long as the analyst's performance and his bank's investment research performance can be monitored (and remembered) by relevant investors (not only institutional but also retail investors), analysts and banks will, in order to keep or increase their reputations (and, accordingly, keep or increase their ability to charge premium fees and command premium salaries), make great efforts to produce high-quality, that is unbiased, investment research. Recently published rankings of banks' and analysts' investment research seem to indicate the usefulness of this reputation concept.[21]

---

19. For the differentiation between institutional investors and retail investors see generally e.g. D.R. Fischel, 'Use of Modern Finance Theory in Securities Fraud Cases Involving Actively Traded Securities' (1982) *Bus. Law* 38, 2 *et seq.*
20. Hans Caspar von der Crone, Verantwortlichkeit, Anreize und Reputation in der Corporate Governance der Publikumsgesellschaft, *Zeitschrift für Schweizerisches Recht* (ZSR) 119 (2000) II 235 *et seq.*
21. A large number of rankings are made available in special-interest publications. Interestingly, even general newspapers such as Neue Zürcher Zeitung (NZZ) have begun to publish rankings

It could be made to work for retail investors, as well, by introducing standardized reporting of a bank research unit's track record with respect to specific securities; all banks could be required to publish such a track record in connection with each piece of research work.[22]

4. Fourth Proposal: Reward Analysts for High Quality Work

This proposal is to be set alongside the third proposal: The general requirement that the remuneration paid to financial analysts may not be dependent upon the performance of one or more specific securities trading or sales transactions and/or commissions generated thereby seems to be contrary to the very purpose of ensuring more high-quality investment research when the recipients of the research are institutional investors. Where there is transparency on the remuneration structure, institutional investors will decide whether to perform their transactions with a specific bank on the basis of the value they put on the research report's conclusions. In the event the research reports of a bank's analysts are biased for the purpose of generating transaction commissions based on unjustified buy or sell recommendations, careful institutional investors will take their business from that bank and give it to a better one.

of the best research units, e.g., 'Die besten Analytiker für Schweizer Aktien', NZZ, 18 October 2003, No. 243, p. 27.

22. Making the provision of this type of information mandatory would be unnecessary; it could be left to investors to decide whether or not to base investment decisions on research recommendations from firms which withhold their ranking.

Chapter 6

Do Conflicts of Interest Affect Analysts' Forecasts and Recommendations? A Survey

*Michel Dubois and Pascal Dumontier**

Because they play a key role in the production and transmission of information among market participants, financial analysts exert considerable influence in capital markets. By collecting and interpreting information related to companies and economic sectors, turning this information into forecasts and recommendations and documenting these forecasts and recommendations in written reports, financial analysts provide investors with highly valuable investment research. Unfortunately, several recent corporate scandals have given rise to a mood of scepticism about analysts' production. These scandals have shaken the confidence of investors, particularly retail investors, in the value of investment research, which ultimately depends upon reliability and objectivity. They have especially questioned the ability of analysts to provide market participants with the assistance they need to evaluate the financial position and performance of listed firms. Following extensive evidence of frequent biases in equity-research disclosures, analysts have increasingly come under suspicion of dishonesty and incompetence. Suspicion of dishonesty is

* Michel Dubois is professor at the University of Neuchâtel. Pascal Dumontier is professor at the University of Geneva. We should like to express our thanks to seminar participants at the 'Conflicts of interest' meeting held in Gerzensee in August 2005 for their valuable comments. Support from the Swiss National Science Foundation (grant no. 105432) is gratefully acknowledged.

L. Thévenoz and R. Bahar (eds.), *Conflicts of Interest: Corporate Governance and Financial Market*, pp. 187–210.

aroused by the multiple conflicts of interest analysts face. Suspicion of incompetence arises from the apparent inability of analysts to guarantee the credibility of the information on which they base their opinions.

Bias in analysts' research is frequently ascribed to various conflicts of interest, which have increased significantly over the last twenty years due to the growing number of integrated banks and the expanding range of their activities. Analysts are suspected of talking up forecasts and recommendations, both to stimulate trading – which brings in commissions – and to satisfy clients whose stock issues are underwritten by their employers. However, as we shall show, empirical findings often refute this common belief. They suggest that analysts employed by firms involved in investment banking do not systematically talk up their findings.

The remainder of this contribution is structured as follows. Section I identifies the factors that may affect analysts' independence and objectivity. Section II and Section III analyse the empirical results so as to appraise the economic consequences of potential conflicts of interest, which may be severe. Section IV provides an overview focusing on the trading activity induced by optimistic forecasts and recommendations, the segmentation of investors who use investment research and the impact of biased research on the market shares of investment banks. Section V analyses the main features of the new regulations intended to re-establish investor confidence in the integrity of financial analysts. Section VI provides our conclusion.

I. THE NATURE AND MAGNITUDE OF CONFLICTS OF INTEREST IN THE SECURITIES ANALYSIS INDUSTRY

A. Who are Financial Analysts and What Do They Do?

Financial analysts are employed by investment banks, brokerage firms, fund management companies, institutional investors, independent research firms and integrated banks, and can be sell-side, buy-side and independent analysts. Sell-side analysts work in the research departments of investment banks, brokerage houses or integrated firms. Institutional investors, such as mutual funds, hedge funds, pension funds and insurance companies, employ buy-side analysts to advise portfolio managers. Independent analysts are not associated with any investment bank, brokerage firm or institutional investor. These analysts conduct research and sell the results to subscribers.

The main task of financial analysts, regardless of their employer, is to forecast profits and losses and determine if securities are over- or under-valued. To this end, analysts collect and process strategic, accounting and financial data from various sources. Using a valuation model in conjunction with their estimates, analysts derive a target price for each stock they cover, and recommend buying when the difference between the target price and the actual quoted price is positive, or selling when it is negative. Their recommendations usually fall into five categories: strong buy, buy, hold, sell and strong sell. In addition, they often publish a detailed research report, which provides quantitative and qualitative analyses to explain and justify the disclosed summary figures (earnings forecasts, growth forecasts, investment recommendations). Previts *et al.* (1994), Bouwman *et al.* (1995) and Block (1999) examine such reports in depth to discern what information is used to produce forecasts and recommendations. They conclude that analysts rely heavily on both accounting figures and narrative information available in corporate reports. They also found that analysts make extensive use of industry reports, reports describing macro-economic conditions and various management communications. Although sell-side, buy-side and independent analysts all produce similar output, sell-side analysts are the only ones who disclose their findings to a wider public.[1] In contrast, buy-side and independent analysts' research is not widely disseminated, but instead is essentially used internally by employers or clients. Because sell-side analyst research is the only sort that is easily available, empirical studies of analysts' production focus almost exclusively on sell-side forecasts and recommendations.

Because they provide investment research free of charge, sell-side analysts employed by investment banks, brokerage firms and integrated financial firms do not receive any direct income. Their research is primarily aimed at generating investment banking business and/or securities trading. As explained by Eccles and Crane (1988), fees generated by investment banking activities are used to fund financial analysis, inasmuch as analysts' outputs help attract new clients or market new offers. In the same way, securities trading is used to fund investment research only because this research generates trades. Thus analysts' contribution to the income of their employers is directly related to the trading volumes and investment banking activities generated by their forecasts and recommendations.

B. How Do Conflicts of Interest Arise?

As noted by Hayward and Boecker (1998), conflicts of interest arise in organizations due to the existence of interdependent groups that provide services to distinct parties and thus have conflicting goals. In investment banks, corporate finance departments compete to underwrite stock offerings and to undertake mergers and acquisitions (M&A) for both new and current clients. Optimistic forecasts and recommendations help place new issues, promote current M&A deals and win new business by sustaining demand for securities. Consequently, while they are expected to provide investors with independent and objective forecasts or recommendations, investment banks' analysts may be subject to significant pressures from corporate finance departments to portray client companies in a favourable light. In the same way, because they compete to generate trades and commissions, the goals of brokerage firms' trading desks often conflict with the duty of analysts to issue objective forecasts or recommendations. Because they collect a commission for each trade they execute on behalf of a client, these desks are the only contributors to brokerage

1. Consequently, as Dugar and Nathan (1995) point out, because buy-side analysts' employers are clients of investment banks that provide them with sell-side research, buy-side analysts can easily use this research as an input for their own investment reports.

revenues, which increase with the number of buy or sell orders they execute. For this reason, analysts may be pressured to revise forecasts frequently, purely to generate additional trades and commissions. They may also be under pressure to issue optimistic rather than pessimistic recommendations since investors are more likely to buy a stock following a positive analyst report. A negative report, in contrast, will not lead to sales of stock, except by investors who already hold the stock, or are willing to bear the additional costs of short sales – assuming that the latter are not restricted or forbidden. Accordingly, positive reports are expected to generate more commissions than negative ones. By showing that stock trading volumes are positively related to the optimism of analysts' forecasts, Francis and Willis (2000) confirm this assumption.

This situation is not, in itself, necessarily a source of conflict. Conflicts of interest in the financial analysis industry are generally exacerbated by compensation structures, since a significant portion of many analysts' remuneration depends on their contribution to their employers' revenues. Like any rational agent, analysts seek to maximize their long-term compensation. Insofar as they are rewarded for helping to market new equity offers and to promote M&A deals, and for helping to increase the trading volumes of the stocks they cover, analysts have strong incentives to produce positively biased reports aimed at facilitating stock issues, M&A deals and stock trading. However, due to the large fees involved, conflicts of interest relating to investment banking activities are potentially more serious than those relating to brokerage activities. Boni and Womack (2003) report that fees from investment banking in 1999 in the US totalled USD 24.5 billion – far more than the trading commissions generated by major integrated firms and brokerage houses, which amounted to a mere USD 9.5 billion.

C. CAN ECONOMIC INCENTIVES MITIGATE CONFLICTS OF INTEREST?

Incentives for biased research are to some extent mitigated by analysts' desire to gain reputation for integrity and expertise, since a good reputation confers numerous professional benefits. First, it helps generate investment banking business or trading commissions in the long run. Second, it increases job mobility and career advancement. Third, it provides access to higher-status clients, investors and company executives. Hong and Kubik (2003), for example, show that sell-side analysts who build a reputation for providing reliable and timely forecasts generate additional brokerage business for their firms. They are less likely to be fired and more likely to be promoted or hired by a more prestigious financial institution. Similarly, Mikhail *et al.* (1999) note that poorly performing analysts generate less trading business. They also suffer from a higher job turnover.

In a study of All-American Research Team analyst performances, Stickel (1992) explains that analysts who are on the team are among the highest earners in the US. Members of the Team are elected by more than 2,000 money managers on the basis of four criteria that underlie their reputation: stock picking, earnings forecasts, written reports and overall services. By analyzing the accuracy of their forecasts and the impact of their forecast revisions on stock prices, Stickel shows that their forecasts are more frequently updated and more accurate than those of other analysts. He also shows that their upgrades have a greater impact on stock prices than the upgrades issued by other analysts. Finally, he reports that election to the Team occurs after the issuance of more accurate forecasts and frequent revisions. If an analyst's forecasts over a particular period are less accurate than those of other team members he risks ejection from the team. This suggests that reputation is the result of a long track record of forecasts and recommendations. Consequently, the numerous advantages reputation offers to analysts over the long run might be expected to deter them from issuing over-optimistic ratings just to attract new deals in the short term. They must balance their own career concerns against the need to generate business for their employers.

II. ANALYST FORECASTS AND RECOMMENDATIONS SURROUNDING STOCK ISSUES

Investment banking includes various activities such as advising on mergers and acquisitions and marketing securities issues. These issues generally involve several investment banks. One of them is the lead manager; the other participating banks are known as co-managers. In the case of an equity issue, two types of contracts generally prevail: best effort arrangements and firm commitments. Unlike best effort arrangements, which do not guarantee the ultimate success of the issue, firm commitments do guarantee success because lead and co-managers underwrite the issue by purchasing the shares from the issuer and reselling them to investors. Because such commitments require underwriters to bear the risk of inadequate demand for the newly issued shares, the underwriters have a real interest in favourable recommendations from analysts covering the stocks in question. Considering that investment bank analysts are especially exposed to conflicts of interest when their employer underwrites a stock they cover, some researchers look closely at stock issues to see how this works out in practice. They investigate whether underwriter analysts issue more optimistic forecasts or recommendations with regard to security offerings than their non-underwriter competitors.

Many of these researchers divide investment bank analysts into 'affiliated' and 'non-affiliated'. Affiliated analysts work for lead or co-underwriters of an initial public offering (IPO) or seasoned stock offering (SEO) of a recommended stock. Unaffiliated analysts are brokerage analysts, pure research analysts or investment bank analysts others than those of lead or co-underwriters of the recommended stocks being studied. The purpose of the distinction between affiliated and unaffiliated analysts is to determine whether affiliated analysts are exposed to conflicts of interest, whether they benefit from information superiority, and how far their forecasts or recommendations are affected by the close relationships between their employers and the firms they cover. In this section we shall describe successively studies on short-term earnings estimates, investment recommendations and long-term earnings growth forecasts.

A. Studies on Short-term Earnings Forecasts

The study by Dugar and Nathan (1995) was the first to be devoted to conflicts of interest in the financial analysis industry. To test whether affiliated analysts are more optimistic than unaffiliated ones, they calculate earnings forecast errors, i.e. the difference between actual and forecast earnings per share scaled by the firm stock price. Their findings show, first, that 56 per cent of affiliated analyst estimates are higher than those of unaffiliated ones, only 33 per cent being lower. They also report a mean forecast error of −4 per cent for affiliated analysts and −2.8 per cent for unaffiliated ones. The fact that affiliated analysts exhibit a smaller negative mean forecast error than unaffiliated ones suggests that underwriter analysts are more optimistic on average than those working for non-underwriters. The fact that both affiliated and unaffiliated analysts exhibit negative mean forecast errors confirms that all analysts are systematically over-optimistic. This overall optimism bias has often been documented in the empirical literature, notably by Fried and Givoly (1982), Brown *et al.* (1985) and O'Brien (1988). Francis and Philbrick (1993) state that if analysts are naturally inclined to optimism, this is in order to curry favour with the managers who supply them with the private information they need to prepare relevant forecasts. This means that all analysts are potentially subject to conflicts of interest because they all must cultivate management relations.

Although Dugar and Nathan find that earnings forecasts and recommendations of affiliated analysts tend to be more optimistic than those of unaffiliated ones, that does not in itself prove a causal link between optimistic forecasts and conflicts of interest. Two other competing hypotheses seek to explain upward biased forecasts: the superior information hypothesis and the selection hypothesis. Suggested by Allen and Faulhaber (1989), the superior information hypothesis posits that affiliated analysts issue more accurate forecasts/recommendations than unaffiliated ones because they have preferential access to information during the due-diligence process.[2] The selection hypothesis states that firms planning a security offering prefer to select investment banks that have the most positive opinion of their future prospects. This favourable opinion suggests that the banks perceive the issue as less risky, which results in lower underwriting fees. Consequently, according to the selection hypothesis, affiliated analysts do not issue optimistic research reports because their employer is underwriting a stock they cover. The process is precisely the opposite: their employer is selected to underwrite the issue because of the optimistic opinions in their reports.

From a larger sample and a more sophisticated methodology than that employed by Dugar and Nathan, Lin and McNichols (1998) obtain conflicting results. They do not detect strong differences between affiliated and unaffiliated forecasts. Using a matching procedure to compare affiliated and unaffiliated analysts' forecasts in

2. This is why, in the US, lead managers and co-managers are strictly forbidden from issuing forecasts and recommendations during the 'quiet period' prior to IPOs. In July 2002, this period was extended from 25 days to 40 days.

similar information environments and to control for differences in the characteristics of companies analysts choose to cover, they conclude that there is no difference between affiliated and unaffiliated analyst forecasts. Current and subsequent year earnings forecasts by affiliated analysts are not significantly different from those issued by unaffiliated ones.

Lin and McNichols contend that the reluctance of affiliated analysts to issue upward biased earnings estimates is not entirely surprising since, as suggested by Francis and Soffer (1997), analysts are generally evaluated from these estimates directly. Because actual earnings are eventually disclosed publicly and earnings forecast errors are easy to measure, analysts' reputations depend primarily on the accuracy of their earnings estimates. This, according to the authors, tempers the propensity of most analysts to issue unreasonably biased estimates. Errors in investment recommendations and long-term growth estimates are much more difficult to detect. First, comparing actual long-term earnings growth rates with forecast ones is a difficult task, because how actual long-term growth rates should be measured is unclear. Second, because it is unclear over what time period recommendations should be assessed, the profitability of strategies based on investment recommendations cannot be precisely determined. Accordingly, analysts' reputations are seldom based directly on the relevance of their investment recommendations and growth forecasts. Reputation effects are therefore less likely to deter analysts from issuing over-optimistic recommendations and long-term earnings growth forecasts.

B. Studies Focusing on Investment Recommendations

By coding analysts' recommendations on a 5-point scale – 1 corresponding to a 'strong buy' recommendation and 5 to a 'strong sell' recommendation – Lin and McNichols (1998) show that the average score of affiliated analysts is 1.7 compared to 2.1 for unaffiliated ones. The statistically significant difference between these two mean scores suggest that affiliated analysts provide more optimistic recommendations relative to the stocks their employers underwrite than uninvolved competitors. Using the Zacks Investment Research database, which codes strong buy recommendations as 5 and strong sell recommendations as 1, Hayward and Boeker (1998) report more optimistic recommendations from affiliated analysts involved in debt issues, equity issues and M&A deals as compared to non-affiliated ones. Using the First Call Corporation database, Michaely and Womack (1999) corroborate this conclusion. Affiliated analysts issue 50 per cent more strong buy recommendations than unaffiliated ones during the 60 days following an IPO. Puckett and Lipson (2004) obtain similar results around both IPOs and SEOs. O'Brien, McNichols, and Lin (2005) examine analyst impartiality using a duration model. First, they compare affiliated and non-affiliated analysts covering the same firms at the same time. Secondly, they compare analysts' behaviour toward clients and non-clients. Thirdly, they repeat these comparisons for both upgrades and downgrades. Their results prove that affiliated analysts that affiliated analysts are slow to downgrade buy and hold recommendations, but are quick to upgrade hold recommendations as compared to unaffiliated analysts. They are slower than non-affiliated to upgrade from 'buy'. However, there is little evidence that affiliated analysts delay downgrades from strong buy.

The fact that affiliated-analyst recommendations tend to be more optimistic than unaffiliated ones does not mean that affiliated analysts issue biased opinions. Affiliated analysts may disclose positive recommendations simply because firms that raise capital externally are those that perform the best. An analysis of the long-term stock price performance of recommended stocks is therefore required to determine whether affiliated analysts' optimistic recommendations are upward-biased. If they appear to be associated with positive long-term abnormal stock returns, the 'conflict of interest' hypothesis must be rejected and the conclusion must be that positive recommendations are due to the superior information available to affiliated analysts. Conversely, the 'information superiority' hypothesis must be rejected, and the 'conflict of interest' hypothesis accepted, if optimistic recommendations by affiliated analysts are systematically associated with a negative stock price performance, suggesting that these favourable recommendations are unjustified, either because affiliated analysts are caught in a conflict of interest or because their lack of expertise prevents them from providing investors with relevant recommendations.

Michaely and Womack (1999) provide such an analysis. They construct two equally weighted portfolios based on 'buy' recommendations issued by unaffiliated analysts and affiliated analysts respectively. The former outperform the latter by an average 18.4 per cent after one year. Size-adjusted excess returns generated by 'buy' recommendations come to −5.3 per cent for affiliated analysts and 13.1 per cent for unaffiliated ones. Moreover, 59 per cent of the firms favourably recommended by affiliated analysts experience negative excess returns in the first year after the recommendation. Only 49 per cent of the firms positively recommended by unaffiliated analysts experience a negative stock performance over the same period. These results clearly indicate that affiliated analysts issue far more 'buy' or 'strong buy' recommendations than unaffiliated ones, and that the former's recommendations tend to be significantly upward-biased. Such results clearly tell against the 'superior information' hypothesis, but they do not help disentangle the 'selection' hypothesis (i.e. affiliated analysts are over-optimistic due to error) from the 'conflicts of interest' hypothesis (i.e. they are knowingly over-optimistic). It is therefore interesting to determine whether investors perceive differences in the quality of recommendations between affiliated and unaffiliated analysts.

Michaely and Womack (1999) determine how investors interpret 'buy' recommendations in the short term by studying excess returns of recommended stocks during the one-to-five day period following the recommendations. Mean abnormal returns related to affiliated analysts' 'buy' recommendations are lower than returns related to 'buy' recommendations from unaffiliated analysts: 4.4 per cent for the latter and 2.7 per cent for the former, showing that investors discount affiliated recommendations. This finding suggests two interesting comments. First, it supports the 'conflict of interest' hypothesis, unless we assume that investors have more information about the firm than affiliated analysts. Secondly, it shows that investors are aware of biased research emanating from affiliated analysts, which indicates that stock prices are not affected by deliberately over-optimistic recommendations.

Using the same matching approach, Lin and McNichols (1998) report slightly different but complementary results. They confirm that investors find analysts' recommendations informative, but they do not document any difference in investors' responses to affiliated and unaffiliated 'strong buy' and 'buy' recommendations. During the three days surrounding the recommendation date, both are associated with short-term positive size-adjusted returns of the same magnitude. Unaffiliated 'hold' and 'sell' recommendations are also both associated with short-term negative excess returns, but returns related to affiliated recommendations are more negative than those affected by unaffiliated ones. This implies that investors interpret hold recommendations as unfavourable rather than favourable, and unaffiliated hold recommendations as more unfavourable than affiliated ones. Using the procedure designed by Lin and McNichols, Puckett and Lipson (2004) report similar results. Mean abnormal returns surrounding affiliated strong buy recommendations do not differ from mean abnormal returns associated with their unaffiliated equivalents. In contrast, hold and sell recommendations that emanate from affiliated analysts exhibit lower negative returns (−11.7 per cent) than those generated by 'hold' and 'sell' recommendations issued by unaffiliated analysts (−6.9 per cent).

Taken together, the results of Michaely and Womack, Lin and McNichols, and Puckett and Lipson confirm that investors are aware of the conflicts of interest that bias affiliated analyst recommendations. Unaffiliated analysts' positive recommendations give a better idea of the future prospects of the firm than those emanating from affiliated analysts, who are expected to strategically avoid 'sell' recommendations. For the same reason, because they are aware that affiliated analysts have no incentive to issue negative recommendations, investors assign strong information content to affiliated analysts' negative recommendations.

To gauge the relevance of affiliated analysts' recommendations, Lin and McNichols examine stock returns associated with lead underwriter and unaffiliated analysts' recommendations over a 250-day period starting two days after the recommendation date. They show that size-adjusted returns associated with unaffiliated 'strong buy' and 'buy' recommendations are significantly positive. Excess returns associated with unaffiliated 'hold' and 'sell' recommendations are negative. Moreover, the returns related to affiliated analysts' recommendations do not differ from those related to unaffiliated ones, suggesting that affiliated recommendations are as relevant as unaffiliated ones. The fact that long-term excess returns associated with 'hold' recommendations do not differ, combined with the fact that returns associated with affiliated 'hold' recommendations are more negative than those associated with unaffiliated ones during the three-day period surrounding the recommendation date, suggests that all the implications of excessively optimistic affiliated 'hold' recommendations are reflected in prices during this three-day period. This confirms that investors are aware of affiliated analysts' propensity to issue over-optimistic recommendations.

C. Studies Focusing on Long-term Earnings Growth Forecasts

Dechow *et al.* (2000) focus on long-term earnings growth forecasts to assess the scale of optimism displayed by underwriters' analysts. They report that affiliated sell-side analysts' long-term growth forecasts are systematically over-optimistic about equity offerings. In the US between 1981 and 1990, the actual earnings growth of firms that issued stock averaged 5.7 per cent annually during the five years following the offering. The mean error in the five-year growth forecasts was −10.5 per cent; the estimated growth at the time of the offering was 16.2 per cent. Dechow *et al.* also show that affiliated analysts provide the most optimistic growth forecasts. While the mean forecast error of unaffiliated analysts is −10.3 per cent, the mean error of affiliated ones is −14.4 per cent. Interestingly, affiliated analysts' growth forecasts appear to be positively related to the fees paid by the issuing companies. A regression of growth forecasts on both realized growth and fees paid to underwriters scaled by the total amount of the offering indicates that forecasts are positively related to the fees paid to the analysts' employer. They are not related to actual growth rates. This indicates that fees might be the main determinant of underwriters' forecasts. Finally, Dechow *et al.* seek to explain the findings of Loughran and Ritter (1995) and Spiess and Affleck-Graves (1995) that firms experience abnormally low stock returns over the years following a SEO on the hypothesis that this underperformance may be caused by the over-optimism of analysts' growth forecasts. They show that the highest growth forecasts emanating from affiliated analysts are associated with the most pronounced post-offering underperformances. Moreover, abnormally low post-SEO stock returns disappear when the over-optimism in growth estimates is taken into account.

Using the same matching methodology and the same sample as they used to analyse earnings estimates and investment recommendations, Lin and McNichols (1988) confirm that growth forecasts issued by affiliated analysts are significantly higher than those of unaffiliated ones. Rajan and Servaes (1997) provide similar evidence for IPOs.

III. THE MAGNITUDE OF THE OPTIMISM BIAS IN INVESTMENT BANK FORECASTS AND RECOMMENDATIONS

The first empirical studies devoted to analysts' conflicts of interest were conducted in the 1990s. As shown in the previous section, they focused exclusively on analysts employed by investment banks that underwrite stock issues. Maintaining that all investment bank analysts are systematically subject to conflicts of interest, even if their employers are not affiliated to a company through a security issue or M&A deal, more recent empirical studies compare forecasts and recommendations emanating from investment bank analysts with those emanating from non-investment bank ones. These studies contend that every company is a potential client for any investment bank. Consequently, if the selection hypothesis holds good, since issuers are expected to select underwriters on the basis of analysts' views of their firms, investment bankers can be expected to discourage negative reports to avoid falling out of favour with potential future clients. If such is the case, the only analysts who should be sheltered from conflicts of interest should be those who work for pure research firms.

In this section we shall review these recent studies. First we shall provide data on the nature of financial firms that produce investment reports. Then we shall describe the main conclusions of the research devoted to short term earnings estimates. Finally we shall describe the results of studies on investment recommendations.[3]

A. WHO PRODUCES INVESTMENT RESEARCH?

To clearly understand why it is possible to consider investment bank analysts as a homogeneous group, without distinguishing between the affiliated and the non-affiliated, it is interesting to discuss some statistics concerning the providers of financial research. In an attempt to determine whether investment bank analysts' outputs are unjustifiably optimistic, Barber *et al.* (2004) classify US analyst firms into three groups. The first includes investment banks that led or joint-led one or more equity offerings between 1996 and 2003. The second includes investment banks that were syndicate members of one or more equity offerings during the same period, but were never a lead or a joint-lead underwriter. The third group includes independent research firms, i.e. firms engaged solely in research or brokerage. In 2002, 103 US investment banks were put in the first group, 62 in the second and only 50 in the third. From November 1993 to December 2002, Clarke *et al.* (2004) identify 10 independent firms, 9 pure brokerage firms, and 271 investment banks in the US. These data show that investment banks, all more or less involved in security offerings, employ the most analysts issuing forecasts or recommendations. In the same vein, Cowen *et al.* (2003) make a distinction between US analyst firms depending on whether they were listed by the Nelson Directory of Investment Research as underwriter banks, syndicate member banks, pure brokerage firms, or independent research firms. Between 1998 and 2001, they note that 80 per cent of earnings estimates were issued by analysts working for underwriter banks, 15 per cent by syndicate member banks, and only five per cent by pure brokerage firms or independent research firms. This confirms that the proportion of forecasts coming from analysts employed by firms not involved in stock issue activities is extremely small.

B. STUDIES FOCUSING ON SHORT-TERM EARNINGS FORECASTS

To assess the scale of analyst optimism, Cowen *et al.* (2003) devised a relative forecast optimism index. This index was used to measure the difference between

3. Studies focusing on long-term growth estimates are not reviewed here because they are almost non-existent.

the forecast error of specific analyst relative to the earnings of a particular firm over a particular quarter, and the mean forecast error of all analysts relative to the earnings of the same firm over the same quarter. This difference was scaled by the mean absolute forecast error of all analysts. Empirical results showed that relative forecast optimism indices were negative for underwriters and positive for non-underwriters, indicating that analysts employed by US underwriters were less optimistic than other analysts over the period under study. The results also indicate that it is pure brokerage analysts who issue the most optimistic forecasts, suggesting that the primary influences on analysts' forecasts relate to trading incentives rather than underwriting incentives. Jacob *et al.* (2003) confirm this conclusion. Comparing the earnings estimates of analysts employed by independent research firms with those of analysts employed by investment banks, they find that earnings estimates emanating from investment banks are less optimistic and more accurate than those emanating from independent firms' analysts. These results are robust to controlling for factors identified in prior research as affecting earning estimates, i.e. the age of the forecast, the number of analysts following the firm, the number of firms and the number of industries followed by the analyst issuing the forecast, and analyst seniority.

Clarke *et al.* (2006) analyse the optimism, timeliness and forecast accuracy of investment banks' analysts. They measure optimism using the same relative forecast optimism index as Cowen *et al.* and Jacob *et al.* and assess forecast timeliness from the probability that the first forecast will be issued in a given quarter. They estimate forecast accuracy from the absolute difference between each analyst's forecast and the realized earnings per share of the firm. Furthermore, since analysts with substantial resources are expected to issue better forecasts, they differentiate between large and small analyst firms on the basis of the number of analysts they employ. With respect to accuracy versus optimism, they show that it is small brokerage firms' analysts who issue the most optimistic accurate forecasts. They also show that small investment banks' analysts are more optimistic than those of large banks, but less optimistic than those of small brokers. Finally, analysts in large independent firms are more optimistic than those in large investment banks. With respect to accuracy, Clarke *et al.* find that large investment banks' analysts provide more accurate forecasts than those working for small banks or large independent firms.

Agrawal and Chen (2004) examine the difference between actual earnings and expected earnings scaled by stock price as the measure of forecast bias. They show that forecasts emanating from independent analysts are no more accurate than those issued by analysts facing potential conflicts of interest because their employers are investment bankers or brokers, even after controlling for the classic set of variables affecting forecast accuracy.

C. Studies Focusing on Investment Recommendations

Clarke *et al.* (2004) report that analysts employed by large investment banks issue a smaller proportion of 'buy' and 'strong buy' recommendations than analysts in small investment banks. However, it is analysts in independent research firms who issue the smallest proportion of buy and strong buy recommendations. Approximately 56 per cent of recommendations by investment bank analysts are either buy or strong buy. Only 46 per cent of independent research firms' recommendations are of this type. To determine whether investors think investment bank recommendations are potentially biased, and to assess the relevance of these recommendations, the authors examine both the short-term market reaction on and about the recommendation dates and the long-term abnormal performance of recommended stocks in the year following the recommendation. Bear in mind that if investors think that conflicts of interest affect investment banks' recommendations, investment banks' upgrades should induce smaller positive reactions than those issued by independent firms. In contrast, if investors believe that investment bank analysts provide more informative recommendations than those in independent firms, the market reaction to both downgrades and upgrades should be stronger for investment bank recommendations than for those by independent analysts. After controlling for analyst-specific factors, results show that short-term returns associated with large investment banks' upgrades/downgrades are lower/higher than those associated with independent analysts' recommendations. Consistent with the conflict-of-interest hypothesis, this indicates that investors think that recommendation changes from large investment banks are less informative than those that emanate from independent analysts. With respect to long-term stock performance in the year following investment bank recommendations, results indicate that positive upgrades led to consistently positive long-term excess returns. This suggests that investors under-react to investment banks' positive recommendation updates, probably because they expect these updates to be biased upward. In contrast, negative recommendation updates do not lead to significant long-term excess returns, suggesting that investors react appropriately to downgrades.

Barber *et al.* (2004) compare the long-term profitability of recommendations issued by independent analysts employed by pure research firms or by brokerage firms with no investment banking business, with the profitability of recommendations emanating from investment banks.[4] They compare the long-term profitability of recommendations issued by each type of analyst firms. They obtain insignificant abnormal returns for the portfolio of investment bank buy recommendations, and significant positive returns for buy recommendations from independent research firms. They obtain significant negative returns for hold and sell recommendations from investment banks and insignificant returns for hold and sell recommendations from independent research firms. As investment bank hold-sell recommendations outperform those of independent firms, the results suggest that hold-sell recommendations emanating from investment banks are more relevant than those from independent firms. In contrast, the fact that investment banks' buy recommendations do not increase investors' profits, while following independent firms' buy

4. In contrast to Barber *et al.*, several studies posit that investment banks that have never been lead or joint-lead underwriters are not subject to conflicts of interest, even if they sometimes act as syndicate members for equity offerings.

recommendations leads to significant positive profits, suggests biased research on the part of investment banking analysts.

IV. ADDITIONAL RESULTS RELATING TO ANALYST CONFLICTS OF INTEREST

This section examines additional analyses relating to the magnitude of conflicts of interest in the financial analysis industry. First, we will review studies aimed at determining whether forecasts and recommendations emanating from brokerage firm analysts are affected by pressures to generate trading commissions. Second, since the empirical research reviewed above produces conflicting results, showing that recommendations are upward biased while earnings forecasts are not, we will scrutinize studies aimed at determining whether the market for financial research is segmented with easily interpretable recommendations oriented to unsophisticated small investors and less easily interpretable earnings forecasts to more sophisticated institutional investors. In the third and final part of this section, we examine studies intended to determine whether biased research may be profitable for banks.

A. Do Analysts Issue Biased Research in Order to Generate Trades?

The two previous sections were devoted exclusively to investment bank analysts' output. However, as described earlier, brokerage firms' analysts may also be subject to conflicts of interest, since frequent and favourable forecast and recommendation updates are expected to generate trades. The very few studies devoted specifically to brokerage analysts tend to validate this intuition. This is not surprising since substantial empirical evidence, such as Dimson and Marsh (1984) in the UK and Womack (1996) in the US, suggests that analysts' recommendations can be used to implement profitable trading strategies, viz. buying a stock when a 'buy' or a 'strong buy' recommendation is issued, and selling it in the case of a 'sell' or a 'strong sell' recommendation. Thus, Irvine (2004) shows that including a stock in a coverage list causes abnormal trading volume in that stock. He uses a unique data set obtained from the Toronto Stock Exchange that identifies each broker involved in individual trades. By comparing trading volumes in covered and uncovered stocks, he documents a positive relationship between coverage and trading volume. By calculating the market share of a given broker for a given stock as the total volume in the stock traded by that broker over a given period divided by the total trading volume of the stock over the same period, Irvine shows that the market share in covered stocks averages 5.6 per cent against 1.8 per cent for uncovered stocks, the difference being statistically significant. He also finds that covering a stock results in higher volumes, and that providing coverage increases brokerage firms' market share by 3.8 per cent relative to uncovered stocks. These results confirm that analyst coverage influences investors' choice of broker. They also confirm that covering a stock generates trades and commissions. The positive impact of coverage on the number of trades may motivate firms offering brokerage services to pressure analysts to issue frequent optimistic forecasts and recommendations.

Agrawal and Chen (2004) confirm this conclusion. They show that brokerage analysts are more likely, and investment banking analysts less likely, to frequently update their earnings estimates than independent analysts. To generate trades, firms offering brokerage services also have a strong incentive to pressure analysts to issue optimistic rather than pessimistic recommendations. As suggested by Jackson (2005), optimistic recommendations, unlike pessimistic ones, drive buy orders that do not require already holding the recommended stocks or bearing potential short-selling costs. The results of Cowen *et al.* (2006) mentioned earlier corroborate this hypothesis with regard to small brokerage firms. The most optimistic forecasts among all those they study are issued by analysts in small brokerage firms, suggesting that trading incentives lead brokerage analysts to issue positively biased earnings estimates.

Hayes (1998) argues that pressures to generate trades should lead brokerage analysts not only to issue frequent forecast updates and over-optimistic recommendations, but also to preferentially cover stocks expected to perform well, for at least two reasons. First, forecasts for stocks expected to perform well are likely to be more accurate than those for stocks expected to perform poorly. As investors have a clear preference for precise information, accurate forecasts should increase trades. Secondly, as mentioned earlier, if short sales are restricted or costly, negative forecasts relative to a poorly performing stock are accessible only to investors who already hold the stock. In contrast, positive forecasts relating to a well-performing stock are open to any investor. Results by McNichols and O'Brien (1997) confirm this hypothesis. Analysts tend to cover firms on which they have optimistic views and tend to drop coverage on stocks they expect to perform poorly. Moreover, investment reports relating to stocks receiving initial coverage appear to be more precise than those relating to stocks previously covered. Finally, stocks receiving initial coverage attract more 'buy' recommendations than stocks previously covered.

B. Is the Market for Financial Research Segmented?

As shown in Sections II and III, empirical research based on forecasts and recommendations from investment bank analysts provides contradictory results. Studies of investment recommendations and long-term growth forecasts show that these are upward biased. Conversely, studies of short-term earnings forecasts conclude, with the notable exception of Dugar and Nathan (1995), that these are not systematically biased. These contradictory results suggest that the market for financial research might be segmented. On the one hand, recommendations are easy to interpret. They therefore seem well suited to helping unsophisticated small investors define their investment strategies. In contrast, the interpretation of earnings forecasts and their translation into buy or sell orders requires financial skills, which orients them mainly towards sophisticated investors.

Malmendier and Shantikhmar (2004a) aim to determine whether investors take account of the well-documented upward bias in recommendations issued by affiliated analysts. Their main results can be summarized as follows. Failing to recognize the impact of analyst affiliation, small investors follow all analyst recommendations literally. This trading strategy results in systematic negative risk-adjusted returns. In contrast, large investors interpret hold recommendations, in particular those emanating from affiliated analysts, as in fact being sell recommendations. They interpret buy recommendations as being hold recommendations. Such a trading strategy results in positive risk-adjusted returns. These findings indicate that small traders are not sophisticated enough to take the global and specific causes of biased recommendations into account. More surprisingly, the same research shows that small investors tend to trade more than usual following investment recommendation issues, which suggests that they are unaware of their inability to interpret analyst recommendations correctly.

In a related paper, Malmendier and Shantikhmar (2004b) explore the market reaction to contemporaneous issues of earnings forecasts and investment recommendations. Their findings shed light on the discrepancies between earnings forecasts and recommendations described in Sections II and III. Since recommendations are a by-product of earnings forecasts, recommendations and forecasts should systematically coincide. Surprisingly, this is not the case. Recommendations by affiliated analysts are more optimistic than those of unaffiliated ones, but their earnings forecasts are not. Earnings forecasts by affiliated analysts are on average even lower than those by unaffiliated ones. They are also less biased, in the sense that they exhibit a lower variance. Moreover, while upward biases in unaffiliated analysts' recommendations and upward biases in their forecasts tend to be positively correlated, the correlation between these two types of bias is negative for affiliated analysts. By indicating that affiliated analysts distort recommendations intentionally, this paradoxical result strongly supports the conflict of interest hypothesis.

Distinguishing between small individual investors and large institutional investors on the base of the size of their trades, the same two authors analyse the stock price reactions associated with recommendations and forecasts. They observe that large investors discount recommendations selectively to avoid being hit by analyst over-optimism. Large investors react less strongly to affiliated-analyst recommendations than to those of unaffiliated ones. This is not the case with small investors, who make no distinction between affiliated and unaffiliated recommendations. Moreover, while large investors react strongly to both affiliated and unaffiliated earnings forecasts, small investors do not. This suggests that the consequences of conflicts of interest are substantially different for unsophisticated (small) and sophisticated (large) investors. Sophisticated investors are aware of the impacts of potential conflicts of interest on analyst behaviour, whereas less sophisticated investors are not. This sheds an interesting light on the debate about optimal analyst regulation.

Along the same lines, Ljungqvist *et al.* (2005) provide interesting additional results. They hypothesize that sell-side analysts are less likely to succumb to their employer's pressures if they cover highly visible stocks held by institutional investors. This hypothesis is justified by the fact that performance ratings depend strongly on these investors, who are quite able to recognize biases in analyst recommendations. Ljungqvist *et al.* also hypothesize that analysts are less susceptible to pressures if they are employed by investment banks with large underwriting market shares, because these banks must preserve their reputation. Consistent with previous research, the authors find, on the one hand, that analysts are prone to issue upward biased recommendations if their employer has an existing investment relationship with the firm they cover, and moreover has significant brokerage business. On the other hand, they note that analysts refrain from over-optimism when institutional investor ownership is high, and when their employer is strongly involved in the underwriting business. This suggests that retail investors may benefit most from regulations imposed on brokerage houses and investment banks, the smallest of which being the most exposed to conflicts of interest.

C. Do Upward Biased Forecasts Generate Business for Investment Banks?

The main argument in favour of the 'conflict of interest' hypothesis is that upward biased forecasts and recommendations help gain market share in the underwriting business. In a recent paper, Ljungqvist *et al.* (2006) investigated whether the behaviour of analysts influences the likelihood of attracting underwriting mandates. They examine a sample of 16,625 US debt and stock offerings from 1993 to 2002, a period during which potential conflicts of interest were expected to be high. To isolate the impact of optimistic recommendations on the probability of winning underwriting mandates, they control for the number of previous offerings underwritten by each bank under study, the strength of prior lending relationships, the endogeneity of analyst behaviour and the bank's decision to provide coverage. The results are striking. First, they show that aggressive upward biased recommendations do not help banks attract underwriting mandates. The strength of the bank's involvement in the issuer's past security offerings and the strength of prior lending relationships are the main determinants of the likelihood of winning an underwriting mandate. Aggressive behaviour does not serve the bank's interests in either the short or the long run. Secondly, they show that analysts are aware of the trade-off between their career concerns and the gains (bonuses) provided by biased recommendations. Everything else being equal, they are more aggressive when more potential fees are at stake, though analysts with a high reputation ('all-star' analysts) are less so. Thirdly, it appears that the least aggressive recommendations are issued by the most prestigious banks with the highest underwriting market shares. Ljungqvist *et al.* attribute the absence of association between optimistic recommendations and the likelihood of winning an underwriting mandate to the information asymmetry that affects security issues. They argue that these information frictions are best resolved by a credible intermediary, so that issuers tend to select credible investment banks that refrain from biased research. This analysis suggests that conflicts of interest can be mitigated by standard economic mechanisms; this would make analyst regulation superfluous.

V. DOES ANALYST REGULATION HELP MITIGATE CONFLICTS OF INTEREST?

A. THE MAIN FEATURES OF THE NEW REGULATION

At the end of the 1990s, financial analysts were at the centre of the controversy over the Internet speculative bubble. In April 2003, following numerous incidents in which financial analysts employed by investment banks were suspected of compromising their integrity by issuing biased recommendations, the US Securities and Exchange Commission (SEC) made an agreement[5] with ten of the largest US investment banks. These incidents also led to a new regulation requiring investment banks to implement a series of reforms aimed at separating research departments from investment banking activities, matching analysts' compensation with their performance, and adding various specific disclosures to research reports. As shown by Dufournet (2005), most of these rules have been adopted or adapted by most European countries. The European regulation embraces four related topics:

- Organisational structures capable of insulating analysts from investment banking and brokerage departments;
- The extent and nature of compulsory disclosures;
- Restrictions on analyst proprietary trading;
- The qualifications, training and remuneration of analysts.

Most European regulations require investment banks to have a 'Chinese Wall' between their corporate finance and financial research departments. This Chinese Wall is intended to limit information transfers from the former to the latter, and prevent corporate finance departments from influencing the opinions issued by analysts. Chinese Walls are based on the simple – and to some extent naïve – idea that most potential conflicts of interest could be mitigated by adopting organisational structures isolating investment research from investment banking. Moreover, employers are forbidden to retaliate or threaten to retaliate against analysts issuing reports that may adversely affect the investment banking relationship.

Secondly, the new regulations stipulate that sources of potential conflicts of interest must be disclosed in research reports. With respect to conflicts resulting from security offerings, the underwriters and other investment banks involved in the issue must ensure that the investment reports they release prior to the issue contain appropriate disclosures on their relationships with the issuer. Moreover, the

5. This 'Global Analyst Research Settlement' imposed fines totaling USD 875 million on the banks involved, of which USD 432 million was used to fund independent securities research over the next five years.

valuation methods used must be clearly described, and the rating system must be defined explicitly. Both must be based on generally accepted rules and principles. In addition, the reasons why a research department decides to stop covering a particular firm must be explained in a specific report. This report must also contain statistics concerning the proportion of buy, hold/neutral and sell recommendations provided during the period covered by the report.

Thirdly, European regulations prohibit trading in recommended securities during the days surrounding the release of an investment report, an earnings forecast, a recommendation update or a price target.

Fourthly, in order to certify a minimal level of competence, the new regulations impose additional qualifications and ongoing training on financial analysts. Moreover, financial analysts' compensation should be matched to the performance of the stocks they cover.

B. THE EMPIRICAL EVIDENCE RELATING TO THE NEW REGULATIONS

As shown by the survey conducted by Leo Schrutt and Stefan Wieler (2006)[6] to gauge the opinions of Swiss portfolio managers and financial analysts on the impact of the Directives on the Independence of Financial Research developed by the Swiss Bankers Association, the new regulations impose stringent constraints whose costs are moderate. Overall, the directives are seen as positive by both portfolio managers and financial analysts, even though most of them disapprove of the ban on proprietary trading. Unfortunately, the adoption of these regulations is still too recent for any more comprehensive empirical appraisals of their effectiveness, with the exception of a study by Kadan *et al.* (2005).

Kadan *et al.* are the first – and, to our knowledge, the only – researchers to have examined the impact of the introduction of the NASD 2711, NYSE 472 and Global Analyst Research Settlement on investment recommendations. They look at whether the number of optimistic recommendations has been reduced, in particular for affiliated analysts, and how regulation has affected analyst practices. They also examine how the market has reacted to the introduction of the new regulation. Compared to previous research, the authors use smaller sample periods, since they compare the recommendations released between November 2000 and August 2002 to those disclosed between September 2002 and December 2004. Consequently they analyse a smaller number of recommendations, and thus their results may be sample-specific. In particular, the period they study is not a 'hot issue' period with high conflicts of interest. They nevertheless obtain extremely encouraging results. First, they notice that following the introduction of the new regulation, recommendations have become far less optimistic. The number of strong-buy and buy recommendations has decreased and the number of sell recommendations has increased, in particular for the ten brokerage houses that were part of the Global Analyst Research

6. See chapter 8 of this book.

Settlement. This suggests that, under the new regulation, investors find it easier to interpret both positive and negative recommendation updates. A direct consequence of this improvement is that the market price reaction associated with upgrades was twice as high during the post-regulation period as before, and the reaction associated with downgrades was significantly less negative after the adoption of the new regulation than before. Moreover, there is no noticeable difference between the market's reaction to recommendations by affiliated and unaffiliated analysts. Thus the new regulation appears to help unsophisticated (small) investors interpret investment recommendations correctly. However, more research is still needed in other environments and over longer time periods to confirm this conclusion.

VI. CONCLUSION

Analysts are assigned to issue objective and independent research aimed at helping investors evaluate the financial position of listed companies. However, sell-side analysts, whose employers provide both brokerage services to investors and underwriting services to companies, are frequently inclined to issue over-optimistic reports in order to satisfy their employers by attracting investment banking business. This potential source of conflicts of interest is intensified by the fact that analysts often earn large bonuses for winning such business.

The extensive research devoted to conflicts of interest in the financial analysis industry provides several results that help us understand how these conflicts may affect analysts' work. Existing research provides unequivocal evidence that earnings forecasts are not affected by conflicts of interest. Affiliated analysts do not issue more positively biased earnings forecasts than unaffiliated ones around equity offerings. Affiliated and unaffiliated investment bank analysts' earnings estimates do not significantly differ from those of independent research firms' analysts. This is probably because analysts build their reputation from their earnings forecasts and forecast errors are easy to measure. In contrast, errors in long-term earnings growth forecasts and investment recommendations are much more difficult to detect, and it is here that analysts' propensity to issue biased research may come into play. In conformity with this intuition, most empirical studies provide evidence that affiliated analysts, and more generally investment bank analysts, issue significantly upward-biased recommendations and growth forecasts. However, these are not likely to affect sophisticated investors since, being aware of these biases, they take them into consideration when they incorporate the information conveyed by analysts' reports in stock prices.

In order to limit the consequences of potential conflicts of interest, new regulations have recently been adopted in most developed countries. Because empirical research has consistently demonstrated that investment recommendations are significantly upward biased, the new directives regulating analyst activities will be effective if, and only if, they ensure that analysts abstain from strategic distortions in their recommendations. In a comprehensive analysis of the current trends in financial market laws, Jean-Baptiste Zufferey (2006)[7] questions whether such regulations will suffice to limit the consequences of potential conflicts of interest and promote capital market efficiency. To fully appreciate the opportunity of these new rules, we must bear in mind that Ljungqvist *et al.* (2006) clearly show that small investment banks, weakly involved in underwriting and security issues, are the most exposed to conflicts of interest. We also must bear in mind the findings of Malmendier and Shantikhmar (2004b): the main victims of analyst conflicts of interest are small investors, because they are not aware of the upward biases that contaminate investment recommendations. In other words, the empirical research shows that regulating analyst activities is to a large extent unnecessary for two major reasons. First, banks strongly involved in security offerings must preserve their credibility, which naturally prevents them from issuing misleading forecasts or recommendations. Secondly, sophisticated investors mainly focus on earnings forecasts that have been shown not to be biased. They are also able to take into consideration the impacts of potential conflicts of interest on investment recommendations so that, unlike retail investors, they are not inveigled into pursuing non-profitable strategies. Consequently, the real aim of regulating financial analysts is to protect small investors from the opportunism of small investment banks. It would therefore be detrimental if small financial institutions did not have to comply with this regulation, particularly because very early empirical results obtained in the US suggest that the new regulations tend to improve the interpretation of stock recommendations, notably by small investors. Further in-depth research is necessary to analyse the consequences of this new regulation, particularly in the European context.

REFERENCES

Allen, F., and G. Faulhaber, 'Signalling by underpricing in the IPO market' (1989) *Journal of Financial Economics* 23, 303–323.

Affleck-Graves, J., L.R. Davis and R.R. Mendenhall, 'Forecasts of earnings per share: possible sources of analysts superiority and bias' (1990) *Contemporary Accounting Review* 6, 501–517.

Agrawal, A., and M. Chen (2006), 'Analysts conflicts and research quality' Working Paper, available at <www.ssrn.com/abstract=556783> *Journal of Financial Economics*, forthcoming.

Barber, B.M., R. Lehavy and B. Trueman (2004) 'Comparing the stock recommendation performance of investment banks and independent research firms' Working Paper, available at <ssrn.com/abstract=572301>.

Block, S., 'A study of financial analysts: practice and theory' (1999) *Financial Analysts Journal* 55(4), 86–95.

7. See chapter 7 of this book.

Bouwman, M., and P. Frishkoff, 'The relevance of GAAP-based information: a case study exploring some uses and limitations' (1995) *Accounting Horizons* 9(4), 22–47.

Brown, P., G. Foster and E. Noreen, 'Security analysts, multi-year earnings forecasts and the capital market' (1985) *Studies in Accounting Research*, 21.

Clarke, J., A. Khorana, A. Patel and P. Raghavendra (2004) 'Analyst behavior at independent research firms, brokerage houses, and investment banks: conflicts of interest or better information?' Working Paper, available at <ssrn.com/abstract=562181>

Cliff, T. (2004) 'Do independent analysts provide superior stock recommendations?' Working Paper, available at <ssrn.com/abstract=540123>.

Cowen, A., B. Groysberg and P.M. Healy (2006) 'Which types of analyst firms make more optimistic forecasts?' Working Paper, available at <ssrn.com/abstract=436686> (2006) *Journal of Accounting and Economics* 41,1, 119–146.

Dechow, P.A., A. Hutton and R. Sloan, 'The relation between analysts' forecast of long-term earnings growth and stock price performance following equity offerings' (2000) *Contemporary Accounting Review* 17, 1–32.

Dimson, E., and P. Marsh, 'An analysis of brokers' and analysts' unpublished forecasts of UK stock returns' (1984) *Journal of Finance* 39, 1,257–1,292.

Dufournet, J.C. (2005) Qualité de l'analyse financière ou indépendance des analystes? Examen critique de la réglementation et de l'autoréglementation, Working Paper available at <web.sfaa.ch>.

Dugar, A., and S. Nathan, 'The effect of investment banking relationships on financial analysts' earnings forecasts and investment recommendations' (1995) *Contemporary Accounting Research* 12, 131–160.

Eccles, R.G., and D.B. Crane, *Doing deals: Investment banks at world* (Cambridge MA: Harvard Business School Press, 1988).

Francis, J., and D. Philbrick, 'Analysts' decisions as products of a multi-task environment' (1993) *Journal of Accounting Research* 31, 216–230.

Francis, J., and L. Soffer, 'The relative informativeness of analysts' stock recommendation' (1997) *Journal of Accounting Research* 35, 193–211.

Francis, J., and R. Willis (2000) A multivariate test of incentive, selection and judgmental explanations for analyst bias, Working Paper, available at <www.ssrn.com>.

Fried, D., and D. Givoly, 'Financial analysts' forecasts of earnings: a better surrogate for market expectations' (1982) *Journal of Accounting and Economics* 4, 85–107.

Hayes, R., (1998) 'The impact of trading commissions incentives on analysts' stock coverage decisions and earnings forecasts' (1998) *Journal of Accounting Research* 36, 299–320.

Hayward, M.L., and W. Boecker, 'Power and conflicts of interest in professional firms: evidence from investment banking' (1998) *Administrative Science Quarterly* 43, 1–22.

Hong, H., and J. Kubik 'Analyzing the analysts: Career concerns and biased earnings forecasts' (2003) *Journal of Finance* 58, 313–351.

Irvine, P.J., 'Do analysts generate trades for their firms? Evidence from the Toronto stock exchange' (2001) *Journal of Accounting and Economics* 30, 209–226.

Ivkovich, Z., and N. Jegadeesh, 'The timing and value of forecast and recommendation revisions' (2004) *Journal of Financial Economics* 73(3), 433–463.

Jacob, J., S. Rock and D.P. Weber (2003) 'Do analysts at independent research firms make better earnings forecasts?' Working Paper, available at <ssrn.com/abstract=434702>.

Jackson, A., 'Trade generation, reputation and sell-side analysts' (2005) *Journal of Finance* 60, 673–717.

Kadan, O., L. Madureira, R. Wang and T. Zach (2005) 'Conflicts of interest and stock recommendations – The effects of the global settlement and related regulations' Working Paper, available at <ssrn.com/abstract= 568884>.

Lin, H.W., and M. McNichols, 'Underwriting relationships, analysts' earnings forecast and investment recommendations' (1998) *Journal of Accounting and Economics* 25, 101–127.

Ljungqvist, A., F. Marston, L. Starks, K. Wei and Y. Hong (2005) 'Conflicts of Interest in Sell-side Research and the Moderating Role of Institutional Investors' Working Paper <ssrn.com/abstract=649684>.

Ljungqvist, A., F. Marston and W. Wilhelm 'Competing for securities underwriting mandates: banking relationships and analyst recommendations' (2006) *Journal of Finance*, vol. 61(1), forthcoming.

Loughran, T., and J.R. Ritter, 'The new issue puzzle' (1995) *Journal of Finance* 50, 23–51.

Maddaloni, A., and D. Pain (2004) 'Corporate "excesses" and financial market dynamics' *European Central Bank, Occasional Paper Series #17,* available at <www.wcb.int>.

Madureira, L., T. Zach, O. Kadan and R. Wang (2005) 'Conflicts of interest and stock recommendations – The effects of the global settlement and recent regulations' Working Paper, available at <ssrn.com/abstract=568884>.

McNichols, M., and P. O'Brien, 'Self-selection and analyst coverage' (1997) *Journal of Accounting Research* 35, 167–199.

Malmendier, U., and D. Shanthikumar (2004a) 'Are Investors Naive About Incentives?' Working Paper, available at <ssrn.com/abstract=601114>.

Malmendier, U., and D. Shanthikumar (2004b) 'Do security analysts speak in two tongues?' Working Paper, available at <faculty-gsb.stanford.edu/malmendier>.

Michaely, R., and K. Womack, 'Conflict of interest and the credibility of underwriter analysts' recommendations' (1999) *Review of Financial Studies* 12, 653–686.

Mikhail, M., B.R. Walther and R.H. Willis, 'Does forecast accuracy matter to security analysts?' (1999) *The Accounting Review* 74, 185–200.

Mola, S., 'Do IPO analysts issue unfavourable recommendations on non-IPO firms?' (2005) *European Financial Management,* forthcoming.

O'Brien, P., 'Analysts' forecasts as earnings expectations' (1988) *Journal of Accounting and Economics* 10, 53–83.

O'Brien, P., M. McNichols and H.W. Lin (2005) 'Analyst impartiality and investment banking relationships' Working Paper, available at <ssrn.com/abstract=709201> (2005) *Journal of Accounting Research*, 43, 4, 623–650.

Previts, G., and R. Bricker, 'A content analysis of sell-side financial analyst company reports' (1994) *Accounting Horizons* 8(2), 55–70.

Puckett, A., and M. Lipson (2004) 'Are lead analysts really optimistic?' Working Paper, University of Georgia – Athens (USA).

Rajan, R., and H. Servaes, 'Analyst following of initial public offerings' (1997) *Journal of Finance* 52, 507–529.

Spiess, D.K., and J. Affleck-Graves, 'The long-run performance following seasoned equity offerings' (1995) *Journal of Financial Economics* 38, 243–267.

Stickel, S., 'Reputation and performance among security analysts' (1992) *Journal of Finance* 46, 3–27.

Womack, K., 'Do brokerage analysts' recommendations have investment value?' (1996) *Journal of Finance* 51, 137–167.

Chapter 7

Regulation of Financial Analysts: An Illustration of the Current Trends in Financial Market Law

*Jean-Baptiste Zufferey**

At the 2004 annual Symposium of the Swiss Lawyers Society, devoted to the general topic 'Regulation, De-regulation and Re-regulation', it fell to me to present the report on banking and financial market law.[1] This contribution proposed a set of questions and tests designed to assess the current evolution of the law in this area. They deal with formal (Section III) and material (Section IV) elements of the regulating process. In this paper, I have decided to concentrate on these elements and set aside the implementation aspects (organization of the authority, means of supervision, enforcement and sanctions).

I shall apply the tests mentioned above to recent regulations bearing on financial analysts, their independence requirements and the potential conflicts among their interests. I shall not focus on technical aspects, since the existing literature on financial analysts and conflicts of interests in general is very rich, and scrutinizing them is the task of other contributors to this volume. The idea here is to go beyond

* Professor of administrative law, Faculty of Law, University of Fribourg, Switzerland, Vice-Chairman of the Swiss Federal Banking Commission. The paper expresses only personal opinions. I wish to thank Mrs. Clemence Grisel, research assistant at the University of Fribourg, for her help in editing this contribution.

1. See J.-B. Zufferey, (Dé-, re, sur-, auto-, co-, inter-) réglementation en matière bancaire et financière – thèses pour un état des lieux en droit suisse, RDS 2004 II, pp. 479–611.

L. Thévenoz and R. Bahar (eds.), *Conflicts of Interest: Corporate Governance and Financial Market*, pp. 211–226.

those aspects by observing the fundamentals of the regulation and by ascertaining to what extent it corresponds to (or even promotes) the present overall evolution of financial market law.

The analysis concentrates on primary sources, i.e. regulations in force in various jurisdictions. The selection is intended to offer a valuable sample of the national and international legal landscape surrounding Swiss law. Here is a list of the texts that have been taken into account:[2]

1. *Switzerland*:
   - SwissBanking (Swiss Bankers Association [ASB]), Directives on the Independence of Financial Research, dated 2 December 2002 (came into force on 1 July 2003); Implementing Circular, as of 15 May 2003; Portfolio Management Guidelines, version of 18 September 2003 (came into force on 1 November 2003).
   - Swiss Financial Analysts Association (SFAA), Handbook of Best Practice, June 2004 (first version dated June 2002).
   - Swiss Funds Association (SFA), Rules of Conduct, dated 30 August 2000.
2. *France*: Société française des analystes financiers (SFAF), Code de déontologie professionnelle, as of March 2002 (first version in 1992); Guide pour une meilleure communication entre les entreprises cotées et les analystes financiers (Guide de communication financière, dated May 2002).
3. *Germany*: Deutsche Vereinigung für Finanzanalyse und Asset Management (DVFA), Kodex für Finanzanalyse, as of 25 February 2003; DVFA-Standards für Researchberichte, dated May 2004; DVFA-Rating Standards, 2001 version.
4. *United Kingdom*:
   - Financial Services Authority (FSA), Conflicts of Interests: Investment Research and Issues of Securities, Handbook, May 2004 (came into force on 1 July 2004).
   - Security Investment Institute (SII), Code of Conduct, 2005; Grey Matters, 2005 (set of scenarios).
5. *United States*: National Association of Securities Dealers (NASD), Manual. With respect to financial analysts in particular: Membership and Registration Rules, Rule No. 1050 (Registration of Research Analysts, 2003, amended several times); Conduct Rules, Rule N° 2711 (Research Analysts and Research Reports, 2002, amended several times).
6. *European Union:* Commission Directive 2003/125/EC of 22 December 2003 implementing Directive 2003/6/EC of the European Parliament and of the Council on the fair presentation of investment recommendations and the disclosure of conflicts of interests (JO 24.12 2003, L 339/73).

2. For the associations and institutions mentioned below, only regulations are considered, and not all the rules and materials relating to the training and certification of financial analysts.

7. *Other sources*:
   - International Organization of Securities Commissions (IOSCO), Statement of Principles for Addressing Sell-Side Securities Analyst Conflicts of Interests, September 2003.
   - European Federation of Financial Analysts Societies (EFFAS), Financial Analysts, Best Practices in an Integrated European Financial Market, Recommendations from the Forum Group to the European Commission Services, as of 4 September 2003.
   - CFA Institute, Centre for Financial Market Integrity, Code of Ethics and Standards of Professional Conduct, 2005 (came into force on 1 January 2006; revised version); Best Practice Guidelines Governing Analyst and Corporate Issuer Relations, dated 12 November 2004; Research Objectivity Standards, 2003; Asset Manager Code of Professional Conduct, 2005.

The following contribution is an analysis of a lawyer with a particular interest in *Rechtslehre*. Hence it does not examine the material or economic adequacy of the regulatory solutions adopted in the various texts listed above, or their impact on the market for research services or on the financial markets themselves.

I. ABSTRACT

This contribution was originally designed to support the discussions that took place at the Gerzensee Symposium. Hence many formulations were left open or proposed questions for debate. The ensuing debates provided some elements of solutions which have now been integrated into this paper.

From a legal perspective, the numerous regulations and standards enacted in recent years to govern financial analysts appear to be an accurate illustration of current trends in financial market law. I shall first examine this proposition with regard to formal elements:

- Are these regulations part of the general increase in regulation of financial markets?
- Are the regulations a political reaction to market events?
- Are the regulations partly responsible for what many now allege to be overregulation?
- Is self-regulation still an adequate solution?

Secondly, and from a more material perspective:

- Are these regulations another ingredient of the regulatory amalgam that constitutes financial market law?
- Are the regulations in line with the 'traditional' objectives of financial market law – to protect the individual investor and the market itself?
- Has the regulation of financial analysts adopted a functional or an institutional approach?

– Does the regulation follow the common 'disclosure strategy' that characterizes present financial market law?

II. FORMAL ELEMENTS

The following four topics correspond to the most common debates over the current evolution of financial market law.

A. 'Regulatory Shower'

Since the end of the 1980s, the banking and financial sector has undergone a period of general de-regulation (global finance and corresponding decompartmentalization of activities; free access to remote markets, privatization and demutualization). Under Swiss law, this de-regulation has been less conspicuous, owing to the country's long tradition of liberalism.

With respect to material requirements, conversely, this period of de-regulation has been compensated by a continuous increase in regulation (in terms of both quality and quantity). This '*re-regulation*' can be linked to the additional risks that have been created by liberalization, or at least are thought to have been by market participants. In fact, this phenomenon of re-regulation is due not only to the state regulators; professional bodies too have shown an inclination to standardize the behaviour of their members. This pattern is not specific to the financial sector, but is affecting all industries anxious to defend their reputation and competitiveness.

In many ways, it can be argued that the regulation of financial analysts is consistent with these developments and *has been contributing* to the 'regulatory shower' that has been occurring in the financial sector:

1. Considering the implementation dates of the regulations listed in the introduction above, it is striking that they are all extremely recent; a '5-year regulatory tsunami' can even be identified (2000–2004), with several 'waves' since many of these texts had to be amended extremely rapidly. Prior to that period of concentrated intervention, the financial research sector was almost entirely unregulated. In other words, regulation in this area started from scratch and took in a whole new branch of economic activity. Other contributors to this volume come to a similar assessment, [3] which is a good indication that the regulation of financial research may have been a reaction to some particular event or series of events (see paragraph 2 below).
   This leads to the question of whether or not financial analysts have been officially elevated (perhaps unintentionally) to *a new category of financial intermediaries*. Under EU law, the answer to that question is 'probably not', since financial research is not, as such, a regulated service subject to

3. See specifically S. Abegglen, Chapter 5, Section II, pp. 175–179.

regulations on investment services in the securities field. Rules on insider dealing and other market abuses are now well established, as are general standards for fair presentation of recommendations and disclosure of interests or conflicts of interests. The situation is currently similar in national jurisdictions, including Switzerland. This functional and 'non conceptual' approach can be seen as a first step towards a full legal framework for financial research, implying the imposition of capital and organizational requirements on independent research institutes and a corresponding authorization procedure. In any case, this progressive extension of the scope of financial market law has generated *less reaction* than other borderline cases, such as independent asset management, external auditing or the role of rating agencies. Moreover, in all these cases, legislators have been compelled to admit that creating a new legal category does not in fact solve the problem of establishing the scope of application of the law, but only shifts it. As a matter of principle, it is no easy task for the regulator to define clear concepts with respect to financial advisers, due to the endless variety of services offered by all sorts of market professionals.

2. Since financial research was traditionally non-regulated, no process of deregulation or liberalization can be identified in this area. Nowadays, the financial research industry consists essentially of two leagues of players: individuals – who may at times work in teams for important investors – and large institutions (mainly banks and brokerage firms). The large institutions clearly dominate the market for these services.[4] This trend towards bi-polarization creates a certain bias with respect to the objectives of the regulation (Section IV.1), self-regulation (Section V.1) and implementation (Section V.4).
3. Most striking is the fact that *self-regulation* strongly contributes to the regulation of financial research. First, financial analysts must conform to existing self-regulation, e.g. stock exchange codes of conduct or banking rules;[5] secondly, many of the legal rules listed above (Section I) are private standards laid down by professional bodies. This twofold observation indicates that it would be unfair to blame governments alone for the alleged burden of re-regulation. In many jurisdictions, financial analysts have spontaneously taken the initiative to organize, regulate and supervise their industry. Some seminar participants even suggested that financial analysts, like other market professionals, do not actually believe in the efficiency of existing regulations and so have undertaken themselves to promote the interests of their economic sector. Similarly, self-regulation is often an attempt to forestall forthcoming government intervention or emerges from a more or less organized dialogue with government regulators searching for the most effective way of protecting certain interests of the public and the market.

4. For more evidence and data, see the contribution by M. Dubois and P. Dumontier, Chapter 6, pp. 187–210.
5. See SFAA Directive, Rule 2.

4. From the same perspective, it can also be pointed out that regulation of financial research is *an internal phenomenon* in many enterprises: banks and brokerage firms (directly or through their professional bodies) have enacted their own directives. They are not always forced into it by the relevant authority; internal rules are also a tool for risk management, particularly as regards reputation. This risk now bulks large in management eyes; if it is not under control, shareholders will ask for changes in management, auditors will terminate their mandate, the supervisory body will hardly glance at the intermediary in question, and clients will distance themselves from this difficult environment.
5. Inevitably, the introduction of a regulation on financial research also generates an increase in the structures of supervision:
   - The authority has a new category of 'clients' to monitor (to the best of my knowledge, the supervision of financial analysts has not led to the creation of specific authorities such as the one in charge of money laundering prevention nor to sub-institutions of the type 'PCOABs' (Public Companies Oversight Accounting Boards).
   - Alternatively, new SROs (self-regulatory organizations) must be ratified and then periodically checked.
   - In jurisdictions with a dual system, such as Switzerland, private auditors must be mandated to monitor state/soft regulation.
   - Finally, each important financial analyst must implement (and pay for) its own internal control system, especially with respect to
     (a) Compliance;
     (b) The segregation of functions within the enterprise (pertaining to securities origination, investment banking, sales and trading, credit and nostro holdings).[6]

B. Reactive Regulation

Financial market law is certainly not the only regulation to be event-driven. In this area, however, the reaction process seems particularly rapid and strong, perhaps because the transformation of individual risks into systemic risks is immediate, as a result of the activities of numerous intermediaries which re-allocate individual risks through sophisticated financial products.

As we saw earlier (III.1), the 5-year wave of regulation in the financial research sector is clearly reactive. Indeed, several scandals emerged in the late 1990s, just prior to the publication of the first draft regulations on financial research, and draft amendments to the regulations. Public abuses and conflicts of interests in the United States provoked strong reactions from the SEC and the New York Attorney General. Recent regulations in other jurisdictions even refer expressly to these cases as justification for their own existence.

---

6. See for example ASB Directive, Chapter II.a, II.b, II.c and II.d.

We must now ask ourselves whether the speed and intensity of this regulatory reaction can be regarded as a *criterion of legal quality*. The following elements must be taken into account:

1. The purpose of reactive legislation is to re-establish confidence among investors and other market participants, because confidence is fundamental to financial markets. From this perspective, it is more important that the markets believe in the efficiency of the regulatory reaction than that efficiency be objectively measured.
2. It is, in fact, extremely difficult to say whether or not a market has recovered because of, and from the time of, ad hoc regulations. Internal market mechanisms function at least as efficiently as external interventions. One could argue in this context that there is no such thing as a 'market for political excuses' which requires legislators to not only be active, but also to be perceived as such. This might also explain why sunset clauses are not at all popular under the laws governing financial markets in Europe, particularly Switzerland.
3. It is most likely too early to decide whether or not the regulation of financial research has had any positive impact on financial markets and their stability. From the same law and economics perspective – and we are all fans of this approach! – I have not seen a great deal of analysis of the impact of such regulations, particularly with respect to European markets. This confirms the existence of a gap between the attitudes of market professionals, who often attribute new regulations to academic interference or defence tactics, and the day-to-day experience of the regulators themselves. Legislators are very fond of invoking the cost-benefits-analysis, but find it much more difficult to implement systematically over and above selected studies of specific topics. Surveys may be of some help in estimating the direct costs of a new regulation to the enterprises, or to the authorities (in particular the costs of compliance and of internal and external audits), but any attempt to assess the costs of opportunity for the subjects of that regulation, or its benefits for the public and the market, 'encounters formidable methodological problems.'[7]
4. The speed of regulation is specific to each jurisdiction. Swiss legislation is not designed to be rapid. Self-regulation has been called upon to accelerate the regulatory process with respect to financial research (the Swiss Bankers Association enacts a new directive and the Swiss Federal Banking Commission ensures it is binding on all banks). However, other approaches are possible. The Commission can issue a specific directive based on the powers delegated to it by the banking statute, and an administrative decision can be taken in a particular case pursuant to some such general provision

7. This cautious statement was made by the British FSA, which is regarded as one of the leaders in regulatory impact analysis (D. Llewellyn, *The Economic Rationale for Financial Regulation*, FSA, Occasional Paper Series, No. 1, April 1999, pp. 52–53).

as art. 3(2)(b) of that same law (adequate internal regulation and organization) or art. (2)(c) (the conduct of all financial institutions must be above reproach at all times). Each of these approaches has its advantages and disadvantages, which have been assessed in the legal literature. Experience has shown that practical solutions based on a consensus between the authority and the professional bodies are more efficient than one-sided state intervention, even if state intervention is perfectly formulated, from a legal perspective.

C. OVER-REGULATION?

In almost all economic areas in which regulators have been active, accusations of over-regulation are frequent – 'over-regulation' meaning legal provisions that impair or complicate economic activity and generate costs without bringing about any material improvement. The debate has been particularly intense in the banking and financial industry since the 2000–2002 market crisis forced professionals to rationalize their costs. Faced with major legal projects, they (and their organizations) are beginning to speak in terms of 'regulatory fatigue', with particular reference to money laundering and terrorism prevention, changes in accounting standards and the ongoing implementation of the new capital adequacy system (Basel II).

Scholars have a duty to avoid facile solutions, and this applies as much to financial research as to anything else. Firstly, we must decide *from whose point of view* we should conduct the discussion; the assessment will differ depending on whether we consider the interests of independent analysts, firms or employees (bipolarization – see Section III.1 below) or the need to protect third parties (clients or independent investors).

Secondly, over-regulation is a matter of quality, not quantity: the mere number of legal provisions cannot be considered a serious criterion. Moreover, in this quantitative approach, the following sorts of regulations *should not be taken into account* in the regulatory calculation:

- Regulations that introduce no real constraint on financial research activities, e.g. the requirement for financial analysts to exercise their profession in an independent, integer, diligent, professional and ethical manner;[8]
- Regulations which refer to, or implement, pre-existing laws, e.g. financial analysts must know and comply with laws, regulations and self-regulatory rules as well as all internal rules of their employer that are applicable to their activities;[9]

8. IOSCO Principle 7 and list of corresponding measures; SFAA Directive, Rule 1.
9. SFAA Directive, Rule 2; DVFA Kodex, Chapter II.1.

- Regulations that simply establish the normal quality standards of the industry, e.g. financial analysts must ensure that the information they provide to clients and investors is of the best quality, clear and accurate;[10]
- Regulations which are designed directly to promote the interests of the industry in question, e.g. financial analysts must strive to add value, as appropriate, to their recommendations by the accuracy of their earnings per share estimates and the use made of their ratings by their financial institute; so far as this information is public, financial analysts must encourage its dissemination to investors;[11]
- Tax regulations, although it is commonly admitted that tax elements are highly significant incentives for investors as they make their financial decisions.

These limitations being set, the discussion must then identify *what counts as over-regulation*. It cannot be exclusively the level of costs or the competitive handicap imposed on market professionals. In order to nuance the description and avoid political slogans, the following additional factors can be suggested:

1. Is the regulation of financial research in a particular jurisdiction in line with international standards? Looking more closely at the regulations under review, the material consensus among them is striking: they very often use not only similar legal institutions, but also similar formulations; they even refer to each other in order to underline this emergence of an international standard.[12] It is possible to speak in terms of 'legal globalization'.
2. Does the regulation in question threaten to reduce the market incentives for financial analysts to manage their own organization, risks and quality of service? This moral hazard may arise when regulations introduce an extensive duty of public reporting (see Section IV.4 below).
3. Does the regulation have a disproportionate impact on the structure of the financial research industry? In particular, does it provoke a concentration process? With respect to services in or from Switzerland, it certainly cannot be alleged that the financial research market has been concentrated in the hands of the larger banks because of the regulations.
4. In the case of a government regulation, is the intervention entirely necessary or would other normative tools have sufficed to protect the targeted interests? Throughout their activities, financial analysts are subject to a nexus of laws other than banking and financial market law: private law (contract, tort, company, securities, real estate) as well as administrative law (anti-trust, unfair competition, consumer protection). This phenomenon is referred to as 'inter-regulation' (Section IV.1).

---

10. EU Directive, Preamble, No. 6; SFAA Directive, Rule 3; SFAF Code, Art. 1.5.
11. SFAA Directive, Rule 9.
12. The SFAA Directive expressly refers to various foreign approaches, in particular the US and the European Union (Chapter 5).

D. SELF-REGULATION

Self-regulation is essentially a mechanism that enables legislators to refrain from intervening, despite the fact that a need for such intervention has been identified, and to give a corresponding mandate to professional organizations. In other words, self-regulation is a kind of co-regulation and a particular form of regulatory delegation. The current trend towards industrial standardization and certification is helping to expand the scope of this regulatory technique. The pros and cons of self-regulation in the financial market sector have been debated for years; more recently, national legislators have tended to recoil from self-regulatory solutions, due to an increasing lack of credibility.

In this context, it must once more be stressed that financial analysts are primarily self-regulated (Section III.1). This is not necessarily a bad thing, even if the approach has to some extent been exploited to prevent or avoid possible government legislation – so long as this self-regulation is accompanied by certain *formal and material guarantees*:

1. The delegation to professional bodies must be expressly embedded in national legislation. Here, Swiss law has a peculiar system: the Swiss Bankers Association's directive on the independence of financial research has been recognized by the Federal Banking Commission as a compulsory standard for banks; hence, its application must be checked by every bank's auditors. In terms of legal legitimacy, this system is acceptable only if the directive fulfils the three conditions specified below. Moreover, a private rule should not be considered imperative if it goes beyond what is actually necessary in terms of individual and collective protection (see Section IV.2 below on the threefold objectives of financial market law).
2. Some state authority must ensure an initial and then permanent control of self-regulation. In practice, this is done by banking and financial authorities.[13] Anti-trust authorities could be more pro-active in this context and prevent SROs from becoming 'closed shops'.
3. .SROs should be forced to organize adequate legal protection for their members. Consider the following example: Rule 10 of the SFAA Directive states that effective regulation of financial analysts depends on effective penalties (warning, fine, revocation of certification, exclusion from the association); however, it is possible to appeal against these penalties to the SFAA arbitration tribunal.
4. SROs should then provide for a fair representation of all categories of market participants affected by the rules in question:
   - Members of the organization (all categories, not merely larger intermediaries);

13. For example, the Swiss Federal Banking Commission regularly publishes its interpretation of the self-regulatory directives issued by the Swiss Bankers Association. For the Directive on financial research, see Circular No. 7258 of the Association.

- Clients and investors. In many jurisdictions, however, they are not consulted at all, and the only way they can make their views heard is through public channels, e.g. the Internet;
- Individual financial analysts acting as employees of the members. Here, in general, national financial market laws do not protect their interests and pass the problem to labour law. This explains why the Swiss Bankers Association's Directive was ratified by the Federal Banking Commission, although it contains requirements which are more stringent than the SFAA Directive and are not particularly necessary to protect investors or the market (particularly as regards the absolute ban on personal purchase of securities, now under consideration).[14]

III. MATERIAL ELEMENTS

I have decided, somewhat arbitrarily, to focus discussion on four elements.

A. INTER-REGULATION

Now that financial market law has been officially recognized as a branch of law, it is seeking conceptual autonomy. However, after almost 30 years of rapid expansion (Section III.1) most scholars (at least in Europe) now admit that financial market law is and will remain a maze of regulations spread across various legal areas. And the internal coherence of that amalgam is largely an academic concern. There is no indication that the regulation of financial analysts is going to change this situation: it is simply another piece of the puzzle, designed to deal with specific market problems, and its enactment does not appear to have endangered the *de facto* equilibrium within the legal system, as it has been developed and established step by step.

In terms of legal policy, the regulation of financial research is an excellent example of inter-regulation, i.e. a single market situation is subjected to cross-intervention from *various legal areas and even various regulators*. As evidence, we can cite the following:

- Each individual regulation is integrated in the legal area relating to its addresses. Two examples: banking law regulates financial research by bank employees; portfolio management regulation prohibits investment in securities issued by entities that have connections with the portfolio manager in question.[15]

---

14. However, self-regulations of some other countries also forbid the employees' personal transactions (examples: SFAF Code, Art. 5; DVFA Kodex, Chapter IV.G).
15. See ASB Directive on portfolio management, Art. 25.

- Financial research regulations relate to more than one area of law: they require financial analysts to observe the internal rules of their employer[16] (contract law); they impose certain rules of conduct on the managers of relevant companies;[17] they may refer to elements of corporate governance[18] (company law); and they all invoke prohibitions specific to stock exchange law (such as insider trading or unequal treatment of investors).
- Penalties for breaching financial research regulations may stem from private law (termination of employment contract), administrative law (a government warning) or company law (expulsion from a professional organization).

In principle, there is no real conceptual problem associated with such inter-regulation, provided that the two risks detailed below can be overcome. Both of these risks affect financial research regulation as well.

- A specific legal system must avoid contamination by *concepts belonging to other legal cultures*. This is most likely to happen when a civil-law country introduces Anglo-American institutions into its financial market legislation. I do not believe this applies to financial research regulations, however, considering the already high degree of legal globalization in this field (see Section III.3 above). For example, even if all jurisdictions enjoin Chinese walls on financial intermediaries, this is an administrative/organizational matter and has no impact on private law.
- Administrative law, of which the core principle is proportionality (or subsidiary), should intervene only when it is absolutely necessary. The question here is whether governments need to regulate financial research at all. Almost all the rules under review here are self-regulatory in nature; even EU Directive 2003/125/EC seems to consider this approach sufficient when it speaks of 'appropriate regulation'. These are indications that *government intervention was and is not considered necessary*. The discussion can even go a step further: can the general provisions of contract, tort, company, securities, and criminal law be regarded as efficient enough to render specific (self-)regulation of financial research unnecessary – along with the corresponding administrative costs?

B. Threefold Objective

There is near-total international consensus among lawyers and even economists about the two main objectives of financial market law: first, the protection of (individual) investors, and second, the (collective) protection of the market itself. Nearly

16. See SFAF Code, Preamble.
17. See SFAA Directive, p. 9.
18. See SFAA Directive, Chapter 3 and DVFA Kodex.

all important national and supra-national regulations refer in some way to this twofold objective.

There is no doubt that the regulation of financial research, is *in line with this concept of double protection*. In fact:

- All the texts under review make express mention – in the preamble or in some specific provision – that their purpose is to protect investors and clients. The same material target is sometimes formulated negatively: the regulation does not apply until the investment recommendation is passed to the client.[19] Beyond that, the classical question would be: do all investors deserve the same level of protection, or should financial research regulation leave institutional investors to fend for themselves? National laws currently tend to apply the latter, incremental approach, distinguishing a separate category of 'sophisticated investors' in such areas as the new issues market or the distribution of investment funds and other financial products.
- All the regulations considered here also proclaim an intent to protect the financial market as a whole. This is either implied, by mention of collective values such as public interest, reputation, integrity and ethics,[20] or referred to indirectly using words such as transparency or equal treatment of investors.[21] This somewhat generic objective of protection is justified, since conflicts of interests among financial analysts may bias market prices (even if investors have some knowledge of these conflicts) as evidenced by Dubois and Dumontier (in this volume) and the literature they cite with reference to US markets. This is hardly surprising: analysts working for brokerage firms tend naturally to concentrate on companies which are expected to show good performance, so that they can justify profitable recommendations on the part of their employers.

It appears, however, that a third objective has joined the first two in most financial analyst regulation: the protection of *the interests of the institutes* (mostly banks) in which financial analysts are employed,[22] or, in the same area, the protection of the interests of the client commissioning the research.[23] These third party interests also relate to reputation and ethics, but they certainly cannot be considered equal to the interest of the market itself. This enmeshing of legal objectives is due to the bi-polarization of the financial research market, as described earlier (Section III.1). It embraces a duty for financial analysts to inform their employers about the regulations they are subject to as members of their professional association,[24] and to obey their employer's regulations, including the prohibition of transactions on

19. See ASB Directive, Rule I.2.
20. See EU Directive, Preamble, No. 1; SFAA Directive, par. 2; ASB Directive, Preamble.
21. See ASB Directive, Rule 24 and 25 (equal treatment amongst the analysts); SFAA Directive, Rule 3 and 4; SFAF Code, Art. 1.5.
22. Most explicit formulations: IOSCO Principle 2.1; SFAF Code, Preamble.
23. See DVFA Kodex, Chapter I.3.2.
24. See SFAA Directive, Rule 6.

their own account.[25] Recently, a number of well-publicized cases have confirmed just how strict employers can be and how fast they can sack an analyst when they consider that their reputation is endangered. The mere fact that civil courts may subsequently award such employees damages for wrongful dismissal is certainly not a good reason for regulators to implement the legal inter-connection mentioned above.

The question here is whether, as a matter of principle, it is possible and adequate to mix such different objectives. The types of problem that it creates have been illustrated, with respect to self-regulation and its ratification by the national supervisory authority (see Section III.4 above).

C. Function Versus Institution

Quite naturally, economists are always pleading for regulations with a functional approach, i.e. based on products, transactions and markets, services, behaviours, risks and incentives. By contrast, lawyers feel more at home with laws predicated on institutions such as banks, brokerage firms or investment funds (primarily legal persons).

Our review shows that financial research regulation remains essentially *institutional*:

- Self-regulation is institutional by definition: financial analysts are not subject to it unless they incorporate and become members of the body sponsoring the appropriate self-regulation. There is one minor exception to this: by compelling their employees to behave in certain ways, the internal regulations of banks and other financial research institutes do play a functional role by targeting certain types of activities and services.
- The regulation requires financial research providers to impose internal controls on their organization and the conduct of their employees (segregation of functions, compliance).[26]
- Regulations that are limited to rules of conduct – which, to some extent, is the approach of the European Directive on investment recommendations – can only be implemented through administrative procedures (authorization) and corresponding control measures. And the only way to impose these measures is through the financial institutes, whatever their size and legal status.

There is no real legal alternative to this institutional approach. The question is how to improve the functional character of the regulation so that it obeys the principle of 'same business, same risks, same rules'. Regulations should be based on legal concepts that are as abstract and generic as possible, so as not to have to enact new laws for every new financial service or product. Similar suggestions have been made in the past with respect to trading systems.

---

25. See SFAF Code, preamble, Art. 5 and 6.3.3.
26. E.g. IOSCO Principle 4 and the corresponding core measures.

D. Disclosure

Modern financial market law essentially *refrains from prohibitions*, be it on products, services or transactions. It considers that the best way to protect individuals and the market effectively is to inform them in all situations. Hence regulations require providers of financial services to make increasing numbers of disclosures and fixes labels on them that signal their capacities to their clients, as well as the kind of supervision that to which they are subject. The disclosure requirements also encompass information in regard to the internal structure of market professionals.

Today, being a 'financial analyst' means being subject to rules of conduct, with corresponding sanctions in case of violation. This regulation of financial research appears to be in line with the general trend, since it imposes a large set of *reporting duties* towards the public and the markets, in particular:

- Transparency on connected activities;[27]
- Transparency on remuneration;[28]
- Disclosure of the sources of information that have been used for the financial analysis, in particular non-public information[29]
- Transparency on interests and possible conflicts.[30] Participations in particular must be mentioned.[31]

Beyond this list, discussion at the symposium focused on the effectiveness of this disclosure strategy. The following points were made:

- The reporting duties confirm the regulators' recognition that conflicts are unavoidable: they use disclosure as a palliative tool. The very wording of the regulations often spells this out *a priori*. For example, Art. 11(1)(c) of the Swiss Stock Exchange and Securities Trading Act says that the securities trades shall ensure that any possible conflict of interest does not disadvantage its customers. In other words, the ultimate regulatory objective is not to combat conflicts of interests but to promote market efficiency. However, it is not certain that such official recognition of conflicts of interests is psychologically suitable for the purposes of prevention; besides, the legal consequences of non-disclosure have not been established.
- Scholars still find it rather difficult to explain how disclosing conflicts of interests produces effective market protection. Investors seem to want to be placed in a position where they can make informed decisions. Over the longer term, market confidence is increased by a policy of full information, and disclosure can act preventively by encouraging good behaviour. Leo

27. E.g. ASB Directive, Art. 12 (in particular services to issuers).
28. E.g. IOSCO Principle 3; ASB Directive, Arts. 7 and 15.
29. Examples: SFAA Directive, Rule 7.2; ASB Directive, Art. 26; SFAF Code, Art. 1.5.
30. Examples: IOSCO Principles, Core measures of Principle 1; EU Directive, Preamble, No. 7; ASB Directive, Preamble.
31. Examples: SFAA Directive, Rule 4 and 5.B; ASB Directive, Art. 21 and 33.

Schrutt's survey of the financial research community in this volume provides some interesting confirmation of this.

- Taking disclosure as a core principle, it is then extremely important to ask how it is to be implemented. And when? And under whose supervision? Regulators must also consider the sociology of communication.
- The disclosure policy is only one of the measures to manage the risks associated with conflicts of interests. Section III of Sandro Abegglen's paper describes other possible instruments: organizational measures such as Chinese walls and a corresponding compliance function; compensation rules; restrictions on proprietary trading; and rules about relationships with the companies being analyzed. To find the best combination of these legal tools is no easy task. Should financial research become an unattractive occupation, its overall quality would diminish and regulations would ultimately have generated no benefit for the markets.

I will end with one further remark: recent financial scandals have boosted regulation on conflicts of interests, but the latter can be attributed, at least in part, to simple incompetence. In the last analysis, regulation cannot solve this problem and markets have to rely on competition.

Chapter 8

Conflicts of Interest in Research: Independence of Financial Analysts – The Costs and Benefits of Regulation

*Leo Th. Schrutt and Stefan Wieler**

EXECUTIVE SUMMARY

Along with the bursting of the Internet bubble at the end of the 1990s, a series of financial scandals hit Wall Street and some of its most prestigious houses. Several financial analysts had published misleading research reports in order to boost equity sales. This method was not new, but this time it led to a series of lawsuits, with several banks paying hundreds of millions of dollars in private settlements. Moreover, the misconduct of some analysts also had an impact on the profession overall. In an effort to protect investors from fraudulent analysts, the financial regulator imposed new guidelines on financial analysts in order to prevent possible conflicts of interest. In Switzerland, the Swiss Bankers Association (SBA) developed the Directives on the Independence of Financial Research, which were subsequently validated by the Federal Banking Commission (EBK).

This paper will analyze the costs and benefits of these directives. To this end, we conducted a survey, asking portfolio managers as recipients of research and financial analysts as producers of research for their opinions. Our questionnaire was sent to all members of the Swiss Financial Analysts Association in two versions,

* Leo Th. Schrutt, Member of the Extended Executive Board, Julius Baer. Stefan Wieler, Investment Research and Portfolio Construction Private Banking, Julius Baer.

L. Thévenoz and R. Bahar (eds.), *Conflicts of Interest: Corporate Governance and Financial Market*, pp. 227–259.

French and German. We received over 150 responses, a very gratifying result. The analysis of the survey can be summarized as follows: portfolio managers generally see the directives as a benefit.

Some parts of the regulation are seen solely as unwarranted interference by both portfolio managers and financial analysts. In particular, the ban on proprietary trading leads to strong disagreement with the directives.

- The costs of the regulation are hard to measure. They largely lie in the reduced attractiveness of the profession.
- The directives missed some of their targets, such as to increase confidence in financial analysts.
- Demand for independent research will increase steadily in the future.
- Transparency of research is of the utmost importance. The guidelines have heightened this transparency.

We therefore regard the directives in general as a success. Nevertheless, a number of crucial points must still be reviewed. If the directives are to be accepted by both recipients of research and analysts, several changes must be made. The most crucial point is the ban on proprietary trading, which is seen as an unnecessary restriction by both portfolio managers and analysts; many even believe it is counterproductive. In our opinion, the relevant articles could be either deleted or changed without losing sight of the main objectives of the directives. This would lead to a broader acceptance in the financial industry, even though in some pieces of legislation, it would arguably be possible to maintain the attractiveness of the analyst's job by compensating him otherwise than through stock market trading.

I. INTRODUCTION

A. HISTORY

In 2001, the *Financial Times* published a headline: 'Shoot All the Analysts'.[1] In the preceding months, a series of scandals had shaken Wall Street and some of its most prestigious banks and brokers. As investors saw their fortunes crumble, those to blame where quickly spotted. Some financial analysts had made recommendations on certain stocks, well aware of the risk and huge downside potential, simply to boost sales and their personal income. Pressure on the regulator was high, and new rules and directives were quickly introduced. Although there was no major scandal in the Swiss market, the Swiss Bankers Association (SBA) drew up the Directives on the Independence of Financial Research, which were then implemented by the Swiss Federal Banking Commission (EBK). The directives regulate the rights and duties of financial analysts and are intended to ensure the independence and transparency of research.

During the tech boom in the late 1990s, financial analysts' salaries went through the roof. Bonuses often amounted to several times an analyst's annual salary. With

1. *Financial Times*, 'Shoot All the Analysts', 20 March 2001, pp. 21–22.

the end of the Internet boom came the collapse of the job market for analysts. Those who still had a job faced salary cuts of up to 75 per cent. Buy-side analysts blamed their sell-side colleagues, as, in their opinion, the sell-side analysts' unethical behaviour had had an adverse impact on the whole profession. But the SBA directives specifically refer to both buy- and sell-side analysts. For buy-side analysts, this means that they can no longer conduct proprietary trading in the stocks they cover. Moreover, the wider public makes no distinction between buy-side and sell-side, and therefore the buy-side analysts now must cope with a bad reputation as well. The Swiss directives speak of 'so-called buy-side' and 'so-called sell-side' analysts. In our opinion, ignoring this distinction is the correct course of action. The SBA stresses 'independent analysts' and wants to create an environment for this independence.

The reason for the unethical behaviour of some analysts can be described by means of the principal-agent theory.[2] Agency costs occur when agents in this case analysts do not work for the sole benefit of the principals: the investors. Financial analysts, particularly sell-side analysts, often had their bonuses tied to sales in other business areas, such as equity sales. For this reason, it was in the analysts' personal interest to drive the sale of stocks. A common dictum in the banking industry is, 'buy sells better'. Analysts pushed stocks they were not in fact optimistic about. The bank safeguards intended to prevent such behaviour either failed completely or did not even exist. The result was that financial analysts were no longer independent. To eliminate such behaviour, principals must control their agents, which creates additional costs. Within the framework of the principal-agent theory, these costs are referred to as monitoring costs. One way to monitor these costs is to implement a regulatory framework, such as the SBA Directives on the Independence of Financial Research. The directives impose monitoring costs on both the regulator and the banks. These costs will inevitably be passed on to the owners of the financial firm in the form of lower earnings. If the financial firm has sufficient pricing power, it can then pass these costs on to its clients, who are the beneficiaries of the regulation. The question that must be asked in regard to any regulation is whether the benefits outweigh the costs.

B. Why is There Still Research?

A number of studies show that research does not create any added value. According to most surveys, research can create superior returns, but the high costs of research cancel out these returns. The efficient market hypothesis (EMH),[3] one of the most analyzed theories in financial economics, predicts no superior return through research. The theory states that all relevant information is already implied in

2. M.C. Jensen and W.H. Meckling, 'Theory of the Firm: Managerial Behaviour, Agency Costs and Ownership Structure' (1976) *Journal of Financial Economics* 3, 305–360.
3. E.F. Fama, 'Efficient Capital Markets: A review of Theory and Empirical Work' (1970) *Journal of Finance* 25, 383–417.

security prices. New information is immediately absorbed by the market. The theory differentiates by type of information. The weak form of the EMH only assumes that all past information is already reflected in prices. It is therefore impossible to create superior returns by analyzing past price movements. The semi-strong form of the EMH goes one step further, implying that all publicly available information is reflected in prices. Fundamental research thus becomes needless. The strong form of the EMH even includes insider knowledge. Why then is there still research?

While most empirical surveys reject the strong form, opinions diverge on the semi-strong and even the weak form. Stiglitz and Grossmann published an article in 1980 in which they questioned the EMH.[4] They argued that if all relevant information were already reflected in the prices, there would be no incentive for market participants to acquire the information, as doing so entails costs. Prices, however, are based on this information. This reasoning is known as the Grossmann-Stiglitz paradox. Markets are therefore efficient only as long as research is available. But irrespective of whether or not the EMH is valid, there are several other, much more commercially relevant, reasons why banks continue to conduct research. Research has an extremely important marketing function. High-profile banks cannot afford not to have their own research. Wealthy clients who have their assets managed by banks expect them to have an opinion on the markets and securities they are invested in. It is highly unlikely that clients will quickly turn to the EMH and therefore believe only in passive management.

C. Effect of Increased Costs on Research

1. Analysis of Costs

In order to determine the costs of the SBA Directives on the Independence of Financial Research, we first must identify possible costs. As noted above, costs arise for the regulator and for the banks. In the present study, we concentrate on the additional costs for banks. We learned that the additional costs as regards compliance and structural measures are negligible. Other studies have analyzed these costs in greater detail.[5] The main costs are incurred at the analyst level. We therefore drafted a questionnaire for financial analysts in which we tried to determine direct and indirect costs.

2. Analysis of Potential Benefits

The beneficiaries of the directives are the recipients of research. Although the final beneficiaries of research are the clients of a bank, we addressed our questionnaire

4. S.J. Grossman and J.E. Stiglitz, 'On the Impossibility of Informationally Efficient Markets' (1980) *American Economic Review* 70, 393–408.
5. I. Hubli, 'Regulatory Burden: Die Kosten der Regulierung von Vermögensverwaltungsbanken in der Schweiz, Institut für Schweizerisches Bankwesen', Working Paper no. 37 (April 2004), pp. 28–38

to portfolio managers, who are likely to be best placed to answer these questions because they do not have a filter, such as a relationship manager or salesperson, as do the end users, namely the institutional and private clients. We decided to turn to portfolio managers because they are professional investors who are familiar with the directives and the business itself. The questions we want to analyze are:

- Does regulation lead to more outsourcing?
- Does regulation lead to more independent research?
- Do investors notice the expected benefits?
- Do the benefits of regulation outweigh the costs?

II. OUR SURVEY ON CONFLICTS OF INTEREST IN RESEARCH

The survey was addressed to financial analysts as producers of research on the one hand, and portfolio managers as users of research on the other. We therefore created different questionnaires for portfolio managers and financial analysts. The survey was sent to the members of the Swiss Financial Analysts Association (SFAA) in German (August 2005) and in French (November 2005). The survey was completed by 6 December 2005 and the data were collected. We obtained 134 answers from portfolio managers and 30 answers from financial analysts, 13 of whom described themselves as sell-side analysts and 17 as buy-side analysts.

A. The Questionnaire for Portfolio Managers

The questionnaire for portfolio managers was composed of six categories plus a general section on the employee and the employer. The questionnaire is reproduced in Tables 1 through 7 in the Appendix.

1. General Questions About the Interviewee and the Employer

The majority of respondents had worked in the financial industry for more then 10 years. Only five per cent replied that they had worked in the industry for less than three years. While half the portfolio managers had some experience as buy-side analysts (47 per cent), only a small fraction (18 per cent) had previously worked as sell-side analysts. Asked if they were familiar with the SBA directives on the independence of financial research, 103 (77 per cent) answered yes and 27 (20 per cent) no. Four portfolio managers did not answer this question. Interestingly, the percentage of portfolio managers who did know the directives was only slightly lower than that of the financial analysts (80 per cent), although the latter are required to obey the regulation. A total of 50 per cent of all portfolio managers worked in medium-sized banks (100 to 3,000 employees), 40 per cent in small banks (fewer than 100 employees) and the rest in large banks (in excess of 3,000 employees).

In order to find out whether the directives had led to outsourcing of research to other countries or companies, we asked the participants whether any outsourcing had occurred in the last three years or was being planned. It turned out that the majority of employers had not thus far outsourced research and were not planning to do so. The responses show that most companies that do outsource research to other companies have done so in the last three years and only 12 per cent are planning to do so in the future. Whether this indicates that the directives are putting pressure on banks to outsource research, or simply reflects the fact that employees do not know their companies' plans, has to be left open.

2. Disclosure Requirements

How well do Swiss analysts disclose possible conflicts of interest? And have the directives increased transparency? According to the SBA directives, banks are obliged to disclose all possible conflicts of interest in research reports. On a one per cent significance level, we can say that portfolio managers feel that Swiss banks and brokers now disclose possible conflicts of interest appropriately, and that they did not do this before the guidelines took effect. This finding clearly indicates that the directives have indeed led to better disclosure of possible conflicts of interest and therefore to greater transparency. Disclosure of possible conflicts of interest in research reports is highly important for portfolio managers, as the responses to question E show. Asked whether they believed professional investors (such as portfolio managers) can recognize and abstract possible bias from conflicts of interest as long as they are disclosed, the majority (57 per cent) agreed; only 17 per cent said they disagreed or strongly disagreed. On the other hand, portfolio managers do not believe that non-professional investors can use disclosure information as efficiently. Ultimately, we cannot say that portfolio managers think the overall quality of research has increased due to the disclosure requirements in the SBA directives on a five per cent significance level. One respondent went so far as to say that disclosure requirements protected banks and brokers rather than the recipients of research.

3. Proprietary Trading by Financial Analysts

What do portfolio managers think about proprietary trading by financial analysts? The Directives on the Independence of Financial Research contain the following regulation on proprietary trading by financial analysts in paragraph 33: 'A financial analyst may not acquire for his/her own account any securities which he/she researches (securities, uncertificated securities, incl. derivatives).'[6] The majority (85 per cent) of portfolio managers do not work as analysts (see Table 1). We therefore presume that the sole interest portfolio managers have in research is obtaining accurate and unbiased information from financial analysts. The personal interests

6. SBA Directives on the Independence of Financial Research (English version, 2003, p. 12).

of financial analysts do not concern portfolio managers and therefore do not affect their answers.

When asked whether financial analysts should be allowed to trade the stocks on which they conduct research, the vast majority (83 per cent) said yes. Only nine per cent disagreed and were happy with the current situation. The mean of 4.08 is actually the highest in the entire questionnaire, except for the questions about expectations from recommendations. One reason for this result might be the fact that portfolio managers also believe that analysts make better recommendations on securities that they themselves trade. While the mean for this question is 3.22 (39 per cent agree) for the portfolio managers, it is only 3.17 (36 per cent agree) for financial analysts, and we cannot reject the null hypothesis that financial analysts do not make better recommendations when they hold the security they cover. It seems that portfolio managers have more faith in recommendations of stocks held by analysts than the analysts themselves do. Several portfolio managers commented that they would like analysts to be *obliged* to buy into their own recommendations. One portfolio manager expressed it as follows: 'A car dealer who doesn't drive his own make of car is not very credible.' Some portfolio managers were also concerned that analysts with a fondness for trading might change their profession and only analysts with no market flair would remain.

Portfolio managers are also disinclined to believe that the regulation on proprietary trading has increased the overall quality of research.

4. Independence of Research

Do portfolio managers use independent research? Did the regulation change the market for independent research? When in 2001 the *Financial Times* ran its headline 'Shoot All the Analysts', numerous scandals had only recent shaken Wall Street and other financial centres around the world. In most cases, the financial analysts concerned did not have the necessary independence.

The majority (72 per cent) of portfolio managers think that demand for independent research is going to increase; fewer than seven per cent disagreed. At least 85 per cent of all respondents make use of independent research. 43 per cent think that it is useful for their work; only 14 per cent say it does not help them. Portfolio managers believe that the range of independent research has increased due to the directives, though quite a significant number had no opinion in this matter. Although portfolio managers do not believe that financial analysts will ever be truly independent, they admit that the directives have significantly increased their independence.

5. Value of Research

How valuable was financial research to portfolio managers before and after the introduction of the directives? The majority (84 per cent) of respondents clearly affirmed that external research is useful for their decisions, but most do not think that the value of research has increased since the directives were put in place.

The conclusion became even clearer when portfolio managers were asked if they had used analysts' recommendations more often since the introduction of the directives. 58 per cent said no, and only eight per cent said that they now did more trading based on a recommendation from a financial analyst.

Questions D and E in this section must be analyzed together. In question D, we asked the interviewees if a more balanced ratio between buy and sell recommendations would increase analysts' credibility. Question E then asked if this ratio had become more balanced due to the regulations. Considering that the interviewees said yes to the first question but no to the second, we conclude that the directives did not increase analysts' credibility with regard to the balance between buy and sell recommendations.

Overall confidence in financial analysts did not increase with the introduction of the directives. Only 18 per cent of all portfolio managers trust financial analysts more since the introduction. If this was a goal of the directives, it needs to be worked on. As one portfolio manager commented: 'It is a modest start.'

6. General Questions

Paragraph 1 of the SBA Directives on the Independence of Financial Research defines the scope of the regulation as follows:

> 'Financial analysts within the meaning of these directives means employees of banks or securities traders (hereinafter referred to as "banks") who are engaged in compiling and producing the banks' research reports (in particular investment and financial recommendations) which are destined for external publication. So-called "buy-side" analysts and "sell-side" analysts, in particular, fall within the scope of the application of these Directives. The Directives apply to both equities and fixed-income analysts. A financial analyst may not circumvent the provisions contained in these Directives by conducting transactions through third parties, such as members of his/her family or other persons close to him/her.'[7]

When we asked portfolio managers if they agreed with the directive's restriction of the term 'financial analyst' to fixed-income and equity analysts (but not to portfolio managers), we received quite a range of answers, distributed three ways: 31 per cent disagreed, 35 per cent agreed and only 16 per cent 'didn't know.' This leaves quite some room for interpretation. More than half the participants had previously worked as analysts and if they ever went back into research they would come within the purview of the SBA directives. Interestingly, the financial analysts' responses to the same question did not offer a much clearer picture, despite the mean of 2.38. Many portfolio managers and analysts commented that they believed the definition of analysts was 'arbitrary'. The portfolio managers felt that collaboration between themselves and the financial analysts has actually improved. The respondents also

7. SBA Directives on the Independence of Financial Research (English version, 2003, p. 3)

believe that the credibility and reputation of financial analysts has improved due to the higher ethical standards set by the directives. This stands in strong contrast to the statement in Section IV, where increased personal confidence in financial analysts was strongly denied. It appears that portfolio managers believe that the general perception of financial analysts in the market has improved, but they personally still don't trust them.

7. Additional Questions

Section VI on expectations from analysts' recommendations will be discussed in 1.2.7 on page 239 below, where the answers are contrasted with what analysts believe portfolio managers want.

B. The Questionnaire for Financial Analysts

The questionnaire for financial analysts was composed of seven categories and a general section on the employee and the employer. The questionnaire for buy-side analysts differs slightly from the one for sell-side analysts, but only in that the questionnaire for buy-side analysts contains three additional questions. Although the survey would enable us to make a separate analysis for two types of financial analysts, the limited number of replies makes it necessary to conflate the answers in order to avoid misrepresenting the data. Where possible, we have indicated the differences between the two groups, although these interpretations must be taken with a pinch of salt. The questionnaire is reproduced in Tables 8 through 15 in the Appendix.

1. General Questions About the Interviewee and the Employer

Similar to the portfolio managers, the majority of financial analysts who responded to the questionnaire have worked in the industry for more than 10 years. Most of the analysts have already worked as buy-side analysts (83 per cent) or sell side-analysts (77 per cent). Seventy-seven per cent of the interviewees are equity analysts; only 13 per cent work as fixed-income analysts; some do both (10 per cent). Nearly half (43 per cent) conduct primary and secondary research, 23 per cent conduct primary research only, 20 per cent secondary research and the rest did not respond to these questions. Three financial analysts (10 per cent) were not aware of the SBA directives they are required to obey. The majority of respondents work in medium-sized banks in terms of both number of employees (100 to 3,000) and assets under management (CHF 1500 billion). The rest are equally distributed among small and large banks. When asked about the number of employees working in research before and after the implementation of the directives, the outcome shows no significant changes. We therefore conclude that the directives had no influence on whether banks and brokers were forced to cut or increase the number of research positions.

Again we asked the interviewees whether their companies had already outsourced part of their research to other countries or were planning to do so. The answers show the same picture as for the portfolio managers. Only a comparatively small percentage (20 per cent) of all banks and brokers has outsourced research in the last three years and even fewer are planning to do so in the near future. However, unlike the portfolio managers, financial analysts see outsourcing to other countries such as India as more likely than outsourcing to other banks or brokers.

2. Additional Working Time and Effort Due to the Directives

It is usually a significant challenge to calculate the costs of regulation, while the benefits can more easily be determined. For once, it is the other way around. Trying to find the main cost drivers of this regulation, we soon realized that the additional costs that the regulator incurs are negligible, as are the costs to the compliance departments of the firms concerned. On top of this, some minor structural measures, such as electronic door locks, must be installed to serve as Chinese walls between research and other departments. All these costs are negligible compared to where the main expenses accrue, which is the additional working time and effort required of analysts on the one hand, and the reduced attractiveness of the profession on the other. In Section I, we asked the financial analysts to indicate how much additional working time they require as a result of the regulation.

Results showed that the directives incur an additional average working time of 9.18 per cent. This appears to be at the upper end of the scale. A minimal additional working time of 5.77 per cent sounds more reasonable. As a bold figure, the cost of employing an analyst averages CHF 400,000 a year, including social security payments and office costs. It is up to the reader to judge whether the costs of the regulation, as we have calculated them, are high or low. The two most time-consuming regulations are those regarding the dissemination of material, non-public information and the disclosure obligation. The average additional working time devoted to material, non-public information is 3.02 per cent. If we examine more closely how buy-side and sell-side analysts responded to this question, we can clearly see that material, non-public information affects sell-side analysts much more, with an average 3.42 per cent increase in working time versus only 2.68 per cent for buy-side analysts. Again we would like to emphasize that, due to the limited number of responses from analysts, no conclusions based on the difference between buy-side and sell-side analysts can have any statistical significance; these figures should be treated as indications only.

Nevertheless, the outcome seems reasonable, as sell-side analysts usually gain a deeper insight into the companies they cover and are therefore more likely to come into contact with material, non-public information. The same seems to apply to additional working time related to disclosure obligations. Sell-side analysts on average require much more additional working time for disclosing issues (4.21 per cent) than buy-side analysts (2.11 per cent). In total, analysts spend 3.08 per cent more working time on disclosures due to the directives. Proprietary trading rules, though one of the most criticized issues in the directives, do not create a large amount of additional work. One financial analyst stated that the main issue is not the additional working time as such, but the fact that analysts see the rules as a serious annoyance in their daily work.

3. Material, Non-Public Information

How do financial analysts deal with material, non-public information? Paragraph 26 of the Directives on the Independence of Financial Research contains the following regulation on relationships with analyzed companies:

> 'As a rule, a company shall not disclose to individual analysts any kind of privileged ("material, non-public") information. If an analyst nevertheless does receive privileged information in the course of his/her activity, he/she shall inform the company that this information must be disclosed. In addition, he/she shall immediately notify the Compliance Unit. The Compliance Unit shall decide on how to proceed, in particular, on whether to refrain from publishing the report or recommendation, as well as on whether to disclose that the information could have been privileged.'[8]

According to the financial analysts, the handling of material, non-public information has changed as a result of the directives. Only 13 per cent felt that the directives had no impact on how they dealt with situations in which material, non-public information was involved. On the question of whether the regulation on material, non-public information poses a major problem for analysts, the mean of all responses lies slightly above neutral, however, the null hypothesis cannot be rejected. Therefore, we conclude that the directives pose no major problems for financial analysts with regard to material, non-public information. Nevertheless, the respondents state that the regulation is difficult to implement. In addition, financial analysts do not believe that the only purpose of the regulation is to call analysts to account in a crisis.

Our personal comment is somewhat different. The directives here confuse what analysts should do with what the analyzed company should do. Because the regulation does not apply directly to the CEOs, CFOs or investor relations officers of analyzed companies, banks attempt to circumvent the obstacle. Some react with a mass mailing to hundreds of companies, while others try to comply with the regulation by requiring the analyst to submit a letter to the company's representative before each consultation. But in our view, the analyst cannot ultimately be held responsible if a conflict does develop.

4. Proprietary Trading by Financial Analysts

How does the ban on proprietary trading affect financial analysts? Paragraph 33 of the directive regulates proprietary trading by financial analysts: 'A financial analyst

8. SBA Directives on the Independence of Financial Research (English version, 2003), p. 10.

may not acquire for his/her own account any securities which he/she researches (securities, uncertificated securities, incl. derivatives).'[9]

Analysts strongly disagree that the directives have improved the quality of buy-side or sell-side research. In addition, asked whether feel that analysts should be allowed to trade the securities they cover, the majority (67 per cent) strongly agree. This translates into a mean of 4.52 and a median of 5, which is the highest score in the entire questionnaire. This response goes hand in hand with the answer to question F, to which the analysts reply that they regret no longer being able to conduct proprietary trading. Prior to the introduction of the directives, the majority of analysts (70 per cent) traded the securities on which they did research. As noted earlier in the discussion of the questionnaire for portfolio managers, analysts do not believe that they make better recommendations on securities they themselves trade.

One respondent noted that the Swiss regulator obviously went too far this time, as most other countries allow financial analysts to conduct proprietary trading. Another even questioned the legality of the ban on proprietary trading, which he believes is a breach of superordinate law.

5. Attractiveness of the Profession

For the last three years, financial analysts have found themselves in a much weaker position in regard to negotiating their salaries, but this mainly seems to be the result of the bursting of the Internet bubble and the market crash rather than the directives. These analysts do not believe that the regulation has led to job cuts in the research industry or forced analysts to change jobs. Asked whether they believe that the directives have made it more difficult for banks to find enough entry-level analysts, the respondents said they did not believe that the new regulatory framework would deter junior analysts from entering the profession. Nor did they fear that the regulation would increase pressure to outsource research jobs. We also asked the financial analysts whether they felt that their reputation had improved or deteriorated since the inception of the directives. Interestingly, and unlike the portfolio managers, financial analysts do not believe that their reputation has improved.

However, despite these responses, financial analysts agree that their profession has become less attractive as a direct result of the directives. More than 80 per cent of all interviewees thought that the attractiveness of their profession had decreased.

6. Quality of Research from the Analysts' Viewpoint

Financial analysts deny that the quality of either buy-side or sell-side research has improved, and do not believe that research in general has become more independent as a result of the directives. Interestingly, the buy-side analysts are much more convinced of the independence of sell-side analysts than the sell-side analysts

9. SBA Directives on the Independence of Financial Research (English version, 2003), p. 12.

themselves. Only three (18 per cent) buy-side analysts disagreed with the statement that, due to the directives, sell-side research has become more independent. However, seven (53 per cent) sell-analysts disagreed, one even strongly. The respondents had not yet observed any increase in the supply of independent research, but they clearly predicted a steady rise in demand in the future. Like the portfolio managers, the financial analysts stated that they did not believe that the ratio of 'buy' to 'sell' recommendations was more balanced than prior to the regulation, or that performance measurement had become more transparent; only 20 per cent of respondents noted an improvement in transparency.

The reponses show that the directives missed one of their targets: to improve, and help restore confidence in, the quality of financial research. The fact that the financial analysts' answers reflect those of the portfolio managers reveals some need for improvement on this issue.

7. General Questions

We then confronted our interviewees with the directives' definition of financial analysts. As expected, the financial analysts disliked the definition even more than the portfolio managers did. Only 23 per cent agreed with the definition, while more than 50 per cent disagreed, most of them strongly. From the comments, it can be concluded that the main point of criticism is that fund analysts, economists and certain other analysts are not forced to abide by the directives and are therefore allowed to conduct proprietary trading. Some analysts would have liked the directives to differentiate between buy- and sell-side analysts. Responses to the question of whether they expected even tighter regulation, or believed that deregulation was more likely, did not produce a clear result. On a one-per-cent-significance level, we cannot reject the null hypothesis and therefore conclude that financial analysts do not believe that there will be either more or less regulation in the future.

8. Additional Questions

We asked portfolio managers what they expected from analyst recommendations. Independently, we asked the analysts what they believed the portfolio managers wanted. Interestingly, both groups' portfolio managers and financial analysts felt that a good performance of the recommendations and easily and readily understandable explanations are the key requirements, while extensive company reports are less important. One reason for this unanimity may be that it seems quite common for financial analysts to become portfolio managers and vice versa.

C. Conclusion of the Questionnaire

- All in all, the directives are seen as a benefit and an improvement.
- Some aspects, such as the ban on proprietary trading by financial analysts, were not thought to increase the independence of financial research, and

the majority strongly disapproved of them. Interestingly, the majority of portfolio managers as clients or consumers of research shared this opinion.

- It seems that the critical path is no longer with the analysts, but with the companies. In other words, analysts' awareness is quite high and compliance processes appear to be in place. It is the analyzed companies that need to improve and be made more aware of these issues.
- The costs of regulation do not have as significant an impact on working time as we initially assumed. Instead, the costs are reflected in the reduced attractiveness of the analyst's profession. Analysts appear to have a strongly negative attitude towards a number of the regulations, particularly those on proprietary trading. It is the portfolio managers, rather than the analysts themselves, who fear a brain drain from research due to the regulations.
- Our respondents believe that demand for independent research will increase significantly in the future.
- Portfolio managers do not believe that regulation can lead to (full) independence.
- Confidence in analysts' buy and sell recommendations did not increase with the introduction of the Swiss code.
- Interestingly, however, the answers show that the credibility and reputation of analysts have actually increased.
- In general, it appears that transparency is of utmost importance. The portfolio managers also state that transparency has increased with the directives. We therefore conclude that one of the main goals of the directives has been achieved.

III. TABLES

QUESTIONNAIRE ABOUT THE SBA DIRECTIVES ON THE INDEPENDENCE OF FINANCIAL RESEARCH

Questionnaire for Portfolio Managers

General questions about the interviewee	0 Y	<3 Y	3–10 Y	>10 Y	N.a.
Industry experience	0	6	35	90	3
I have experience as a buy-side analyst	47	14	28	21	24

General questions about the interviewee	**0 Y**	**<3 Y**	**3–10 Y**	**>10 Y**	**N.a.**	
I have experience as a sell-side analyst	77	5	12	7	33	
	Yes	**No**	**N.a.**			
I am currently working as an analyst	16	93	25			
I am currently working as a portfolio manager	122	11	1			
I know the directives on the independence of financial research	103	27	4			
General question about your employer	**Mean**	**Median**	**<100**	**100–3,000**	**>3,000**	**N.a.**
Number of employees in the company	3,622	255	47	57	12	18
	Mean	**Median**	**<1 bil.**	**1 bil.–500 bil.**	**>500 bil.**	**N.a.**
Assets under management	83,626	4,000	28	70	5	31
	Yes	**No**	**N.a.**			
We conduct buy-side research	75	52	7			
We conduct sell-side research	46	79	9			
We receive independent research	106	22	6			
We have outsourced part of our research to other countries such as India in the last three years	13	110	11			

General questions about the interviewee	**Yes**	**No**	**N.a.**
We plan to outsource part of our research to other countries such as India	10	107	17
We have outsourced part of our research to other banks/brokers/research companies in the last three years	26	92	16
We plan to outsource part of our research to other banks/brokers/research companies	14	97	23

Table 1. Questionnaire for Portfolio Managers

The directives on the independence of financial research contain regulations regarding disclosure requirements. Banks are obliged to disclose all possible conflicts of interest in research reports. Please indicate the extent to which you agree or disagree with the following statements:

Category	Strongly disagree 1	Disagree 2	Neutral 3	Agree 4	Strongly agree 5	No opinion 6	Mean	Median	p value z test (mean)
A. Swiss banks/brokers disclose possible conflicts of interest appropriately in research reports	**3** 2%	**15** 11%	**31** 23%	**61** 46%	**16** 12%	**7** 5%	**3.57**	**4**	< 0.001
B. Swiss banks/brokers disclose possible conflicts of interest appropriately in research reports even before the new guidelines became effective	**8** 6%	**60** 45%	**36** 27%	**21** 16%	**3** 2%	**5** 4%	**2.62**	**2**	< 0.001
C. The disclosure of possible conflicts of interest has become so extensive that most clients do not even read it anymore	**5** 4%	**35** 26%	**31** 23%	**43** 32%	**15** 11%	**4** 3%	**3.22**	**3**	0.012
D. Non-professional investors require much more information about potential conflicts of interest and therefore need stricter regulations than professional investors	**7** 5%	**45** 34%	**27** 20%	**37** 28%	**12** 9%	**4** 3%	**3.02**	**3**	0.437
E. As a professional investor, I can recognize and abstract possible bias from conflicts of interest as long as it is fully disclosed in the reports	**4** 3%	**19** 14%	**31** 23%	**62** 47%	**14** 11%	**3** 2%	**3.48**	**4**	< 0.001
F. Non-professional investors can recognize and abstract possible bias from conflicts of interests as long as it is fully disclosed in the reports	**10** 8%	**42** 32%	**28** 21%	**39** 29%	**9** 7%	**5** 4%	**2.96**	**3**	0.345
G. The disclosure requirements clause in the guidelines has significantly increased the quality of research	**8** 6%	**20** 15%	**50** 38%	**41** 31%	**5** 4%	**9** 7%	**3.12**	**3**	0.078

Comments of respondents: 1) Many brokers still do not offer research that's independent of Trading or Corporate Finance. 2) Banks often don't recommend the best stocks but rather companies they have the best connections to. 3) In case of conflicts, analysis is often discontinued. In my opinion, this isn't the appropriate solution, either. 4) You can also take these directives too far. After all, lengthy disclaimers don't solve the problem. They only protect the research units from litigation. And this certainly doesn't help the investor. 5) For me, what's more important than potential conflicts of interest is the distinction between buy or sell-side analysis. Nobody reads disclaimers anyway. What is indeed interesting, however, are statements regarding positions an analyst holds. 6) The quality of research has deteriorated. The sell-side analyst used to learn a great deal about his companies when he was still involved in transactions. Now he doesn't have this kind of knowledge. As far as conflicts of interest are concerned: Everybody knew they existed anyway – even before the dotcom bubble burst. 7) Regarding your questions about research, note that we've developed our own (quantitative) models for the selection of stocks. The recommendations of research analysts therefore aren't relevant to us. What's important for the qualitative element is information on products / markets / the competitive environment. So the independence of an analyst only concerns us when it comes to rating a company's management. Our answers to these questions must be viewed with this in mind. 8) Some questions are asked the wrong way around. Basically, the questions should be less concerned with the distinction between professional and non-professional. The essential thing is that conflicts of interest are disclosed or can be detected. This varies from one case to the other and, in my opinion, can only very rarely be achieved. Today's disclaimers certainly don't solve the problem. 9) Your questions rather make reference to a specific situation; they can't very well be answered in a general fashion. / Hence the many neutral replies. 10) Non-professional investors always depend on professional advice. This is why I think the disclosure obligation is largely misguided.

Table 2. Disclosure Requirements

The directives on the independence of financial research contain the following regulation on proprietary trading by financial analysts: *"A financial analyst may not acquire for his/her own account any securities which he/she researches (securities, uncertificated securities, incl. derivatives)."* Please indicate the extent to which you agree or disagree with the following statements:

	Category	Strongly disagree 1	Disagree 2	Neutral 3	Agree 4	Strongly agree 5	No opinion 6	Mean	Median	p value z test (mean)
A.	Presumably, many financial analysts will try to avoid the directives (through undeclared bank accounts with other banks, through bank accounts of close relatives)	**5** 4%	**31** 23%	**43** 33%	**36** 27%	**6** 5%	**11** 8%	**3.06**	**3**	0.254
B.	Analysts should be allowed to trade securities they do research on for his/her own account - obviously in accordance with front-running rules.	**3** 2%	**10** 8%	**8** 6%	**64** 48%	**47** 35%	**1** 1%	**4.08**	**4**	< 0.001
C.	Analysts who trade securities they do research on make better recommendations	**8** 6%	**6** 17%	**21** 35%	**15** 23%	**8** 14%	**1** 5%	**3.22**	**3**	0.012
D.	The regulation on proprietary trading by financial analysts has increased the quality of research	**21** 16%	**21** 39%	**15** 27%	**3** 7%	**3** 2%	**3** 9%	**2.35**	**2**	< 0.001

Comments of respondents: 1) A distinction should be made between analysts who have a great influence on stock movements and secondary analysts, for instance, those who can't influence the market. 2) It's not about the quality of research but about the possible abuse of the analyst's recommendation, which is only indirectly tied to the quality of research. 3) Buy-side analysts should definitely be allowed to buy stocks they cover. When it comes to sell-side analysts, a company's market capitalization should be taken into consideration (e.g. holding Nestlé would be no problem). 4) A car dealer who doesn't drive his own make of car is not credible – the same goes for an analyst. But he should disclose his transactions.

Table 3. Proprietary Trading by Financial Analysts

One reason for the introduction of the directives on the independence of financial research was the lack of trust in the research industry after the international scandals in 2002. In most cases, the involved financial analysts did not have the necessary independence. Please indicate the extent to which you agree or disagree with the following statements:

	Category	Strongly disagree 1	Disagree 2	Neutral 3	Agree 4	Strongly agree 5	No opinion	Mean	Median	p value (2-tailed z test), H0: μ=3
A.	The independence of financial research in Switzerland is guaranteed	**5** 4%	**23** 17%	**52** 39%	**43** 33%	**7** 5%	**2** 2%	**3.18**	**3**	0.011
B.	The independent research I receive usually is useful for my work	**1** 1%	**17** 13%	**35** 27%	**47** 36%	**9** 7%	**20** 16%	**3.42**	**4**	< 0.001
C.	The demand for independent research will further rise	**0** 0%	**9** 7%	**23** 18%	**73** 56%	**22** 17%	**4** 3%	**3.85**	**4**	< 0.001
D.	Due to the regulation, the range of independent research has increased	**0** 0%	**14** 11%	**52** 40%	**39** 30%	**3** 2%	**23** 18%	**3.29**	**3**	< 0.001
E.	Performance measurement in research has become more transparent due to the introduction of the directives	**0** 0%	**21** 16%	**53** 40%	**46** 35%	**2** 2%	**10** 8%	**3.24**	**3**	< 0.001
F.	Financial analysts will never be truly independent due to the threat of a "freeze-out" (the management of a researched company refuses to talk to an analyst who issued an unfavorable report)	**1** 1%	**21** 16%	**26** 20%	**63** 48%	**16** 12%	**4** 3%	**3.57**	**4**	< 0.001
G.	The independence of financial research has increased significantly since the introduction of the directives	**2** 2%	**21** 16%	**55** 42%	**40** 31%	**2** 2%	**11** 8%	**3.16**	**3**	0.014

Comments of respondents: 1) Banks are too intertwined with the industry! These are the problems of large banks. Every company that's being analyzed is also a client. 2) A lack of independence is less important than the pressure to make 'hot' recommendations. If an analyst makes no contribution to the turnover that's often generated by such recommendations, he loses his job. As a result, conducting serious analysis is impossible anyway – and most clients don't demand it, either. 3) How do you define independence?? 4) With regard to independence, we must make a clear distinction between Anglo-Saxon countries and Switzerland. In Switzerland, the independence has always been relatively complete, amongst others because the IPO and M&A business was less prominent.

Table 4. Independence of Research

Please indicate the extent to which you agree or disagree with the following statements:

Category:	Strongly disagree 1	Disagree 2	Neutral 3	Agree 4	Strongly agree 5	No opinion 6	Mean	Median	p value z test (mean)
A. External research is useful for my decisions	**3** 2%	**4** 3%	**13** 10%	**85** 64%	**26** 20%	**1** 1%	**3.97**	**4**	< 0.001
B. The value of research in making my decisions has increased since the directives were put in place	**8** 6%	**41** 31%	**56** 42%	**24** 18%	**2** 2%	**1** 1%	**2.78**	**3**	0.002
C. I trade more analyst recommendations since the introduction of the directives	**14** 11%	**63** 48%	**42** 32%	**11** 8%	**0** 0%	**2** 2%	**2.38**	**2**	< 0.001
D. A more balanced ratio between buy and sell recommendations would increase analysts' credibility	**9** 7%	**25** 19%	**27** 20%	**49** 37%	**20** 15%	**2** 2%	**3.35**	**4**	< 0.001
E. The ratio between buy and sell recommendations is more balanced since the introduction of the directives	**7** 5%	**24** 18%	**56** 42%	**30** 23%	**0** 0%	**15** 11%	**2.93**	**3**	0.189
F. My trust in financial analysts has increased since the introduction of the directives	**14** 11%	**36** 28%	**54** 42%	**21** 16%	**2** 2%	**3** 2%	**2.69**	**3**	< 0.001

Comments of respondents: 1) Research renders information 'more liquid,' but it isn't the best of solutions! 2) In my opinion, the quality of research has deteriorated. 3) It's still too early for me to make a clear statement. I believe that analysts are much too influenced by short-term company results (quarterly results) and don't develop a long-term point of view. 4) The guidelines have not influenced my view of analysts in any way. As always, I focus on the quality of the text, the opinion and the arguments. 5) In isolated cases, the 'value' of research can increase – as much as it can decline. / A double-edged sword. / 'Value' can be judged after years of use and after analyzing large quantities. 6) I don't believe that research has no value, on the contrary. I believe that directives only rarely achieve what they're supposed to achieve (regardless of the business). In fact, they usually have a negative effect, as has happened in the present case. 7) The ratio of buy and sell recommendations has become more one-sided (towards buy recommendations) again. 8) It's a humble start.

Table 5. Value of Research

Please use the following information to answer the questions below. The directives on the independence of research define a financial analyst as follows: *"Financial analysts within the meaning of these directives means employees of banks or securities traders (hereinafter referred to as "banks") who are engaged in compiling and producing the banks research reports (in particular investment and financial recommendations) which are destined for external publication. So-called "buy-side" analysts and "sell-side" analysts, in particular, fall within the scope of application of these Directives.* The Directives apply to both equities and fixed-income analysts. *A financial analyst may not circumvent the provisions contained in these Directives by conducting transactions through third parties, such as members of his/her family or other persons close to him/her.*
Please indicate the extent to which you agree or disagree with the following statements:

	Category:	Strongly disagree 1	Disagree 2	Neutral 3	Agree 4	Strongly agree 5	No opinion 6	Mean	Median	p value z test (mean)
A.	The directives specify only equity and fixed-income analysts as financial analysts. Economists and fund analysts do not need to adhere to the regulation, for instance. I think this is a sound solution	**8** 6%	**42** 32%	**21** 16%	**47** 35%	**8** 6%	**7** 5%	**3.04**	**3**	0.344
B.	I believe the peak of regulation in the financial research industry is past and that deregulation will be more likely in the future	**8** 6%	**41** 31%	**46** 35%	**25** 19%	**4** 3%	**9** 7%	**2.81**	**3**	0.011
C.	The collaboration with financial analysts has improved	**0** 0%	**14** 11%	**70** 53%	**34** 26%	**0** 0%	**14** 11%	**3.17**	**3**	0.001
D.	Due to the guidelines, higher ethical standards have been established, and the credibility and reputation of analysts have therefore increased	**3** 2%	**18** 14%	**34** 26%	**63** 47%	**8** 6%	**7** 5%	**3.44**	**4**	< 0.001

Comments of respondents: 1) Analysts often have families and must do what the bank wants them to do. Otherwise, they get fired. 2) They crucial distinction would actually be between buy and sell-side. 3) As long as the investor is under the impression that analysts usually publish their opinions after company results have been released and the markets have reacted to the news, the reputation of analysts will remain tarnished. 4) The directive is hypocritical nonsense that causes more damage than good. However, it sells well and therefore helps the industry. 5) Fund managers or commodity analysts would need to be included in this category as well. Why aren't they? / Equity and fixed income tools are selected randomly! And what about real estate? 6) Buy-side analysts who cover large caps should maybe be excluded from the definition, as an individual study has a minimal impact on the share price. 7) It's a humble start.

Table 6. General Questions

Please indicate the extent to which you agree or disagree with the following statements:

Category:	Strongly disagree 1	Disagree 2	Neutral 3	Agree 4	Strongly agree 5	No opinion 6	Mean	Median	p value z test (mean)
What do you expect from analyst recommendations?									
A. Good performance of recommended securities	**2** 2%	**5** 4%	**16** 12%	**58** 44%	**49** 37%	**1** 1%	**4.13**	**4**	< 0.001
B. Numbers, models, descriptions	**0** 0%	**5** 4%	**23** 18%	**75** 57%	**28** 21%	**0** 0%	**3.96**	**4**	< 0.001
C. Quickly and easily understandable explanations	**0** 0%	**0** 0%	**1** 1%	**67** 51%	**64** 48%	**0** 0%	**4.48**	**4**	< 0.001
D. Extensive company reports	**4** 3%	**30** 23%	**47** 36%	**41** 31%	**10** 8%	**0** 0%	**3.17**	**3**	0.019
E. Good story behind the recommendation	**11** 8%	**20** 15%	**24** 18%	**54** 41%	**22** 17%	**0** 0%	**3.43**	**4**	< 0.001

Comments of respondents: 1) Looking for the keys to outperformance! 2) Experience has taught me to make my own decision and not base myself on recommendations. Nevertheless, analyses are a valuable aid when I make my decisions. 3) A 60-page study with thousands of numbers is of no interest. A well-documented story and a few key arguments to support a recommendation are the most important pieces of information. 4) Only very naive investors follow analyst recommendations, as, due to pressure from the sales department, analysts cannot afford to make recommendations that don't push stock prices up immediately. Yet since the market is on a 'random walk' in the short term, recommendations are doomed to uselessness. Every once in a while, recommendations indeed turn out to be useful, but we don't expect them to. 5) The analyst takes the time I don't have to collect, analyze and draw conclusions from statistics, archives and information in general. 6) Studies should be written on the basis that 'brevity is the soul of wit.' 7) Summary, valuation comparisons, sector comparisons and sector analyses should also include these subjects.

Table 7. Additional Question

QUESTIONNAIRE ABOUT THE SBA DIRECTIVES ON THE INDEPENDENCE OF FINANCIAL RESEARCH

Questionnaire for Financial Analysts

General questions about the interviewee	**0 Y**	**<3 Y**	**3–10 Y**	**>10 Y**	**N.a.**
Industry experience	0	1	6	23	0
I have experience as a buy-side analyst	2	8	13	4	3
I have experience as a sell-side analyst	5	8	10	5	2
	Yes	**No**	**N.a.**		
I am currently working as an Equity analyst	23	3	4		
I am currently working as a Fixed income analyst	4	20	6		
I do primary research	20	7	3		
I do secondary research	19	5	6		
I am currently working in a management position in research	20	8	2		
I am responsible for monitoring proprietary trading for research analysts	6	20	4		
I know the directives on the independence of financial research	25	3	2		

General question about your employer	**Mean**	**Median**	**<100**	**100–3,000**	**>3,000**	**N.a.**
Number of employees in the company	9,419	900	6	16	6	2
	Mean	**Median**	**<1 bil.**	**1 bil.–500 bil.**	**>500 bil.**	**N.a.**
Assets under management	55'409	41'790	5	17	0	8
	Mean	Delta				
Number of employees in research (without economists and other analysts that are not subject to the directives) **before 06/03**	11.38					
Number of employees in research (without economists and other analysts that are not subject to the directives) **after 06/03**	11.21	−1.5%				
	Yes	**No**	**N.a.**			
We conduct buy-side research	24	5	1			
We conduct sell-side research	18	11	1			
We conduct investment banking	17	12	1			
Our research is completely disassociated from other business lines	18	10	2			
We have outsourced part of our research to other countries such as India in the last three years	6	23	1			

	Yes	**No**	**N.a.**
We plan to outsource part of our research to other countries such as India	4	25	1
We have outsourced part of our research to other banks/brokers/research companies in the last three years	2	27	1
We plan to outsource part of our research to other banks/brokers/research companies	2	28	0

Table 8. Questionnaire for Financial Analysts

The SBA Directives on the Independence of Financial Research entered into force on 1 July 2003. Please indicate how much additional work you have per year relative to your overall work time as a result of the directives.

	Category	0%	1-2%	2-5%	5-10%	10-20%	>20%	No opinion	Minimum in % of working time	Maximum in % of working time	Average of min/max
		1	2	3	4	5	6	7			
A.	Material, non-public information (informing of companies, compliance reports etc.)	**8** 26.7%	**6** 20.0%	**7** 23.3%	**4** 13.3%	**1** 3.3%	**0** 0.0%	**4** 13.3%	**1.9%**	**4.1%**	**3.0%**
B.	Proprietary trading	**9** 30.0%	**8** 26.7%	**6** 20.0%	**0** 0.0%	**0** 0.0%	**0** 0.0%	**7** 23.3%	**0.9%**	**2.0%**	**1.4%**
C.	Disclosure obligation	**7** 23.3%	**5** 16.7%	**10** 33.3%	**3** 10.0%	**1** 3.3%	**0** 0.0%	**4** 13.3%	**1.9%**	**4.2%**	**3.1%**
D.	Others:	**8** 26.7%	**8** 26.7%	**2** 6.7%	**1** 3.3%	**0** 0.0%	**0** 0.0%	**11** 36.7%	**0.9%**	**1.9%**	**1.4%**
	Total:								**5.6%**	**12.2%**	**8.9%**

"No opinion" answers are not counted for calculating the average

Comments of respondents: 1) These are unknown dimensions for me. As early as 2002 did we put an independence framework in place on the Swiss level; this was expanded to the international level in 2004. 2) The additional effort, particularly for the relevant compliance department, restrictions on and prohibition of proprietary trading above all cause mental stress, as it all is very annoying. 3) We are a German universal bank which is active solely in Germany and which, as a result, is bound by German law. We therefore need not make an additional effort in Switzerland. 4) An oral comment is enough in most cases. I generally am no friend of excessive regulation, even if I've already abided by these rules in the past. In this context, one shouldn't forget the implementation of control processes, surveys on accounts, etc. Proprietary trading and compliance with the disclosure obligation are monitored by compliance officers hired for exactly this purpose. Material, non-public information: lively exchange with the compliance team.

Table 9. Additional Effort Due to the Directives

The directives on the independence of financial research contain the following regulation on relationships with companies being analysed *"As a rule, a company shall not disclose to individual analysts any kind of privileged ("material, non-public") information. If an analyst nevertheless does receive privileged information in the course of is/her activity, he/she shall inform the company that this information must be disclosed. In addition, he/she shall immediately notify the Compliance Unit. The Compliance Unit shall decide on how to proceed, in particular, on whether to refrain from publishing the report or recommendation, as well as on whether to disclose that the information could have been privileged."* Please indicate the extent to which you agree or disagree with the following statements:

Category	Strongly disagree 1	Disagree 2	Neutral 3	Agree 4	Strongly agree 5	No opinion 7	Mean	Median	p value z test (mean)
A. When I receive privileged information, it is no problem for me to convince the companies to publish this information.	**2** 7%	**1** 3%	**8** 27%	**4** 13%	**0** 0%	**15** 50%	**2.93**	**3**	0.394
B. The handling of material, non-public information has changed dramatically for analysts since the directives entered into force.	**3** 10%	**1** 3%	**5** 17%	**13** 43%	**2** 7%	**6** 20%	**3.42**	**4**	0.037
C. The regulation on material, non-public information poses a major problem for sell-side analysts, as it forces them to assume a supervisory function.	**2** 7%	**6** 20%	**6** 20%	**5** 17%	**5** 17%	**6** 20%	**3.21**	**3**	0.213
D. The regulation on material non-public information is difficult to implement.	**1** 3%	**5** 17%	**6** 20%	**6** 20%	**8** 27%	**4** 13%	**3.58**	**4**	0.009
E. In my opinion, the regulation only serves to call the analyst to account in an emergency. I don't think it will change the handling of material, non-public information.	**1** 3%	**6** 20%	**7** 23%	**5** 17%	**4** 13%	**7** 23%	**3.22**	**3**	0.186

Comments of respondents: 1) I've never experienced such a case. 2) Companies are extremely careful not to disclose any material, non-public information. 3) Today companies are very sensitive when it comes to disclosing material, non-public information. So this isn't really a problem for analysts. 4) Your questions are biased. 5) Approx. 2-5 times a year. 6) Where are the limits? What is 'material'? What is 'non-public'? If a competitor of a company tells me something, is it non-public or not? It is always a matter of interpretation. Ambiguous clauses. But if worse comes to worst, analysts are certain to get clobbered – they become the perfect scapegoats. Fundamentally speaking, too big a fuss is made about it. By definition, we only work with publicly-accessible information, and that's that. Good recommendations are not made based on privileged information but on experience and sector know-how, analytical skills and feel – and the normal kind of information one has at his disposal. 7) Since the directives entered into force, I've never been able to test them on a company, because management and Investor Relations by now are extremely alert when it comes to this issue. 8) If I answered this additional question, it would mean that, depending on the answer and the incidents reported to the compliance officer, there could be a gap that may be used against the analyst. Of course, this is not the case with my answer.

Table 10. Material, Non-public Information

The directives on the independence of financial research contain the following regulation on proprietary trading by financial analysts: *"A financial analyst may not acquire for his/her own account any securities which he/she researches (securities, uncertificated securities, incl. derivatives)."* Please indicate the extent to which you agree or disagree with the following statements:

	Category	Strongly disagree 1	Disagree 2	Neutral 3	Agree 4	Strongly agree 5	No opinion 6	Mean	Median	p value z test (mean)
A.i	This regulation has improved the quality of buy-side research. (Asked buy-side analysts only. 17 replies)	**10** 59%	**2** 12%	**1** 6%	**2** 12%	**1** 6%	**14** 47%	**1.88**	**1**	< 0.001
A.ii	This regulation has improved the quality of sell-side research.	**12** 40%	**9** 30%	**3** 10%	**2** 7%	**0** 0%	**4** 13%	**1.81**	**2**	< 0.001
B.	Analysts should be allowed to trade securities they do research on for their own account - obviously in accordance with front-running rules.	**1** 3%	**0** 0%	**2** 7%	**6** 20%	**20** 67%	**1** 3%	**4.52**	**5**	< 0.001
C.	Analysts who trade securities they do research on make better recommendations.	**3** 10%	**2** 7%	**13** 43%	**9** 30%	**2** 7%	**1** 3%	**3.17**	**3**	0.185
D.	Presumably, many analysts will try to avoid the directives (through undeclared bank accounts with other banks, through bank accounts of close relatives, ets.)	**3** 10%	**6** 20%	**7** 23%	**7** 23%	**1** 3%	**6** 20%	**2.88**	**3**	0.292
E.	Prior to the introduction of the directives, I traded securities I do research on.	**5** 17%	**2** 7%	**1** 3%	**13** 43%	**5** 17%	**4** 13%	**3.42**	**4**	0.064
F.	I deeply regret no longer being able to do proprietary trading.	**0** 0%	**2** 7%	**5** 17%	**6** 20%	**11** 37%	**6** 20%	**4.08**	**4**	< 0.001

Comments of respondents: 1) The problem with large caps or foreign shares: Recommendations do not influence the stocks. The problem with the wording of 'stocks covered by the analyst himself:' How does this phrase need to be interpreted? When does something become an analysis? 2) This paragraph must have been invented by a lawyer who has never purchased stocks himself! 3) One's own points of view do not influence the quality of research. Much rather, it is the interests of the investment bank – the employer – that do. 4) The guidelines are too broad. They concern all coverage where my name as a co-analyst is involved, even though I don't conduct any primary research per se. In order to be on the safe side, one should therefore avoid all stocks in a sector. I also see conflicts of interest when analysts hold stocks they cover themselves (which has never been the case for me). But I believe it should be up to every analyst to decide whether he wants to hold the stocks he covers. 5) I think that the behaviour of analysts was fair already before the directives entered into force and that it was monitored already as far as possible. The directives may prevent improper use in isolated cases. But those who want to use information improperly can still do so today. Perpetrators were punished even before the directives were introduced. 6) As a client, it would be in my interest for analysts to hold the stocks they recommend. 7) It has a lot to do with personal ethics.

Table 11. Proprietary Trading by Financial Analysts

Please indicate the extent to which you agree or disagree with the following statements:

	Category	Strongly disagree 1	Disagree 2	Neutral 3	Agree 4	Strongly agree 5	No opinion 6	Mean	Median	p value z test (mean)
A.	When it comes to salary and bonus, the negotiating position of analysts has deteriorated since the dot-com bubble burst.	**0** 0%	**4** 13%	**5** 17%	**14** 47%	**4** 13%	**3** 10%	**3.67**	**4**	< 0.001
B.	When it comes to salary and bonus, the negotiating position of analysts has deteriorated due to the introduction of the directives.	**2** 7%	**9** 30%	**14** 47%	**2** 7%	**0** 0%	**3** 10%	**2.59**	**3**	0.002
C.	The directives have led many financial analysts to move into other business areas and will lead many others to move as soon as the labor	**2** 7%	**5** 17%	**7** 23%	**10** 33%	**2** 7%	**4** 13%	**3.19**	**3**	0.186
D	Due to the regulations, it will be difficult for companies to find entry-level analysts in order to secure the future need of experienced analysts.	**2** 7%	**8** 27%	**6** 20%	**9** 30%	**1** 3%	**4** 13%	**2.96**	**3**	0.428
E.	The regulations have led to a loss of jobs in financial research.	**1** 3%	**11** 37%	**10** 33%	**1** 3%	**4** 13%	**3** 10%	**2.85**	**3**	0.242
F.	Due to the regulations, banks will increasingly outsource research activities (buy side and sell side). This is a change that can exclusively be attributed to the regulations.	**1** 3%	**8** 27%	**5** 17%	**9** 30%	**0** 0%	**7** 23%	**2.96**	**3**	0.415
G.	The regulations have improved ethical standards and the reputation of analysts.	**1** 3%	**8** 27%	**10** 33%	**7** 23%	**1** 3%	**3** 10%	**2.96**	**3**	0.419
H.	The profession of financial analysts has become less attractive as a result of the directives.	**1** 3%	**5** 17%	**5** 17%	**11** 37%	**1** 3%	**7** 23%	**3.26**	**4**	0.108

Comments of respondents: 1) The greater need of compliance makes research services more expensive. This puts above all small players at a disadvantage. 2) The reform process within the financial market is not driven by regulatory changes. The decisive driver is change in the basic needs of investors. 3) Some questions are difficult to answer because they require one to guess what all the others think. This point of view (what the others may think) does not necessarily correspond to one's own point of view, which is of greater relevance in some of the other questions. 4) If the Swiss regulator attaches great importance to being among the leaders in the global upward spiral of regulation, it can lead to a drain of specialized analysts to other, less regulated (banking) jobs such as compliance lawyers. Or it can reduce the recruitment potential for the analysts' profession. And a bank first needs to earn all the money needed to pay its legal experts. (Disclaimer for these statements to follow!)

Table 12. Attractiveness of the Profession

One reason for the introduction of the Directives on the Independence of Financial Research was a loss of confidence in the entire research sector following the international scandals in 2002. The directives are to heighten the quality of research and thus help regain this confidence. Please indicate to what extent you agree with the following statements.

	Category	Strongly disagree 1	Disagree 2	Neutral 3	Agree 4	Strongly agree 5	No opinion 6	Mean	Median	p value z test (mean)
A.i	The quality of buy-side research has improved due to the implementation of the directives.	**3** 18%	**6** 35%	**3** 18%	**3** 18%	**1** 6%	**1** 6%	**2.56**	**2**	0.074
A.ii	The quality of sell-side research has improved due to the implementation of the directives.	**4** 13%	**14** 47%	**6** 20%	**3** 10%	**0** 0%	**3** 10%	**2.30**	**2**	< 0.001
B.i	Buy-side research in Switzerland has generally become more independent due to the implementation of the directives.	**2** 12%	**5** 29%	**5** 29%	**2** 12%	**1** 6%	**2** 12%	**2.67**	**3**	0.123
B.ii	Sell-side research in Switzerland has generally become more independent due to the implementation of the directives.	**1** 3%	**9** 30%	**6** 20%	**6** 20%	**1** 3%	**7** 23%	**2.87**	**3**	0.269
C.	The supply of independent research has increased due to the implementation of the directives.	**1** 3%	**12** 40%	**5** 17%	**7** 23%	**0** 0%	**5** 17%	**2.72**	**2**	0.067
D.	Demand for independent research will rise further in the future.	**0** 0%	**6** 20%	**7** 23%	**12** 40%	**3** 10%	**2** 7%	**3.43**	**4**	0.009
E.	The ratio of buy to sell recommendations made by sell-side analysts has improved due to the implementation of the directives.	**1** 3%	**10** 33%	**5** 17%	**8** 27%	**1** 3%	**5** 17%	**2.92**	**3**	0.350
F.	The performance measurement of sell-side research has generally become more transparent due to the implementation of the directives.	**3** 10%	**10** 33%	**6** 20%	**5** 17%	**1** 3%	**5** 17%	**2.64**	**2**	0.047

Comments of respondents: 1) In my opinion, this is not a business case for independent research services providers. 2) Numerous other factors play into these questions. It always depends on the prevailing mood in the market as well. Suddenly, clients demand a sell-side organization that participates in IPOs, which was completely unfashionable two to three years ago. What's more, we are in the Swiss market, and the major scandals didn't primarily happen in our neck of the woods. Yet we all need to abide by the new directives. 3) The quality and measurability of analysts did not change because of the guidelines but rather because of a systematic collection and evaluation of analyst recommendations (IBES).

Table 13. Quality of Research from the Point of View of Analysts

Please use the following information to answer the questions below. The directives on the independence of research define a financial analyst as follows: *"Financial analysts within the meaning of these directives means employees of banks or securities traders (hereinafter referred to as "banks") who are engaged in compiling and producing the banks research reports (in particular investment and financial recommendations) which are destined for external publication. So-called "buy-side" analysts and "sell-side" analysts, in particular, fall within the scope of application of these Directives. The Directives apply to both equities and fixed-income analysts. A financial analyst may not circumvent the provisions contained in these Directives by conducting transactions through third parties, such as members of his/her family or other persons close to him/her.*
Please indicate the extent to which you agree or disagree with the following statements:

Category:	Strongly disagree 1	Disagree 2	Neutral 3	Agree 4	Strongly agree 5	No opinion 6	Mean	Median	p value z test (mean)
A. The definition exclusively refers to equity and fixed-income analysts as analysts. Economists and fund analysts, for instance, do not need to adhere to the regulation. I think this is a good solution.	**7** 23%	**9** 30%	**1** 3%	**6** 20%	**1** 3%	**6** 20%	**2.38**	**2**	0.008
B. I think the peak of regulation in financial research has been reached and that deregulation will be more likely in the future.	**1** 3%	**9** 30%	**6** 20%	**9** 30%	**2** 7%	**3** 10%	**3.07**	**3**	0.360
C. The cooperation with sell-side analysts has improved	**0** 0%	**7** 41%	**4** 24%	**2** 12%	**0** 0%	**4** 24%	**2.62**	**2**	0.035

Comments of respondents: 1) The guidelines should differentiate between buy-side and sell-side! 2) Fund managers should also be subject to the directives. 3) The EU will continue to exert pressure to increase regulation. 4) What hasn't been solved is the question regarding the authorization of proprietary trading of sales staff, traders, portfolio managers, investment advisors, etc. To focus solely on financial analysts is arbitrary. And what isn't solved either is the question of whether the prohibition of proprietary trading violates a superordinate law (Federal Law). 5) In addition to fund managers, equity and fixed-income analysts, one should not forget loan analysts. Banks' loan divisions also gain a very deep insight into the corporate structure, and there quite possibly is such a thing as cross-information in the decision-making committees. 6) To restrict this particular guideline to analysts only is totally arbitrary. So if you do it at all, do it properly! Equity Sales would also need to be included – or drop it completely. 7) For some time, we have been in a clear upward spiral when it comes to regulation. I'm afraid that we are placing additional obstacles in our way which – when measured against the abuse to date and the abuse the directives can eliminate – will be excessive. And once something is introduced, you can never get rid of it again; it will only be refined and made more complicated. 8) Where do you ever get fewer rules? Unfortunately. 9) By the way, in the U.S. analysts are still permitted to own the stocks they cover. But they must declare such holdings and obviously are not permitted to engage in front-running.

Table 14. General Questions

Please indicate the extent to which you agree or disagree with the following statements:

Category:	Strongly disagree 1	Disagree 2	Neutral 3	Agree 4	Strongly agree 5	No opinion 6	Mean	Median	p value z test (mean)
What do your clients expect from analyst recommendations?									
A. Good performance of recommended securities	**1** 3%	**1** 3%	**1** 3%	**10** 33%	**15** 50%	**2** 7%	**4.32**	**5**	< 0.001
B. Numbers, models, descriptions	**0** 0%	**0** 0%	**2** 7%	**19** 63%	**8** 27%	**1** 3%	**4.21**	**4**	< 0.001
C. Quickly and easily understandable explanations	**0** 0%	**0** 0%	**3** 10%	**15** 50%	**11** 37%	**1** 3%	**4.28**	**4**	< 0.001
D. Extensive company reports	**1** 3%	**7** 23%	**5** 17%	**14** 47%	**2** 7%	**1** 3%	**3.31**	**4**	0.054
E. Good story behind the recommendation	**2** 7%	**2** 7%	**6** 20%	**9** 30%	**9** 30%	**2** 7%	**3.75**	**4**	< 0.001

Comments of respondents: 1) Follow on recommendation (very important) / Risk scenario in addition to story 2) The answers very much depend on which clients we're talking about. There are major differences between retail clients and institutional clients! 3) Recommendation and target price are becoming less important, whereas the model, analysis and argumentation are becoming more important. 4) Sell-side analysts are expected to have detailed knowledge of their companies and industries. They are also expected to point out sensitivities the client can then use based on his own assumptions regarding macro economics and the company.

Table 15. Additional Questions

REFERENCES

Fama, E.F., 'Efficient Capital Markets: A Review of Theory and Empirical Work' (1970) *Journal of Finance* 25, 383–417.

'Shoot All the Analysts', *Financial Times* (20 March 2001), pp. 21–22.

Grossman, S.J., and J.E. Stiglitz, 'On the Impossibility of Informationally Efficient Markets' (1980) *American Economic Review* 70, 393–408.

Hubli, I., 'Regulatory Burden, Die Kosten der Regulierung von Vermögensverwaltungsbanken in der Schweiz', Institut für Schweizerisches Bankwesen, Working paper No. 37 (April 2004), pp. 28–38.

Jensen, M., and W. Meckling, 'Theory of the Firm: Managerial Behavior, Agency Costs and Ownership Structure' (1976) *Journal of Financial Economics* 3, 305–360.

Chapter 9

Conflicts of Interest, Especially in Asset Management

*Eddy Wymeersch**

I. CONFLICTS OF INTEREST ARE INEVITABLE IN FINANCIAL SERVICES

Until 15 or 20 years ago, asset management was largely the task of an (often large) department of a bank that dealt with securities. It was fully integrated in the overall banking business and asset managers were usually acquainted with the transactions the bank was engaged in; in the securities field, public issues, private placements, underwriting and M&A work was often done in the same department and was familiar to most of its members. Institutional and individual portfolios were managed together. The same situation existed with regard to the bank's other functions, such as its loans business or its position in the payment systems. Asset managers could obtain information about the financial standing of the firms the bank was lending to, and on that basis make their investment decisions. This raised the question of whether the bank should protect its asset management clients by selling the shares about which it had unfavourable information: did the bank not have an overriding fiduciary duty to those clients?

* Professor at the Ghent University Law School; Chairman of the Belgian Banking, Finance and Insurance Commission. The paper expresses only personal opinions.

L. Thévenoz and R. Bahar (eds.), *Conflicts of Interest: Corporate Governance and Financial Market*, pp. 261–275.

To illustrate the degree to which conflicting situations were part of the prevailing culture of that time, clients were often pleased to learn that asset managers were well informed about the bank's transactions and would take advantage of their privileged information. Even today, some asset managers continue to inform their clients that they will benefit from their (the managers') higher quality of information about the securities to be acquired for the clients' portfolios, on the basis of the bank's broad presence in the markets. Conflicts of interest abound.

A related question arises when bank directors or asset managers are appointed to the boards of listed companies; while not expressly forbidden,[1] this practice may create delicate situations, in which both the director and the asset manager are in a conflict of interest situation and will usually be bound to abstain from certain actions. For example, a bank will be expected to abstain from rendering particular services to a listed company, such as delivering a 'fairness opinion' on its shares, if one of the bank's managers is on the board of that company.

In the late 1980s, the issue of conflicts of interests became more insistent. Under US and UK influence, a new terminology was invented, including 'Chinese walls' and 'fiduciary duties;' notions not highly familiar to continental European professionals. Awareness of the impropriety of exploiting such conflicts increased, which resulted in voluntary guidelines, or more formal 'conduct of business codes', to prevent information about sensitive banking business being communicated to the asset management side. The Insider Trading Directive of 1989 and the Investment Services Directive of 1992, article 11, bear witness to these regulatory developments. New techniques for dealing with conflicts were developed in connection with the fight against 'insider trading'; 'trading windows' and 'restricted lists' are among the instruments most widely used to prevent them.

While considerable progress has been made in the prevention and combating of conflicts of interests in the provision of financial services, it has become clear that not all conflicts can be avoided, and there will always be residual cases in which the only protection is individual conscience.

II. PROVISIONS IN THE EU DIRECTIVES DEALING WITH CONFLICTS OF INTEREST

The regulation of financial services includes a good many rules that deal explicitly with conflicts of interest. A short analysis of the applicable rules follows: it is based on the EU directives, but in practice it is also necessary to look at national regulations, as they often refer in more detail to conflict cases.

The EU financial services directives contain several provisions that directly address conflicts of interest; others do so indirectly. Surprisingly enough, few

1. The Belgian Banking Act of 22 March 1992, Art. 27, relaxed the rules governing the appointment of bank directors to the boards of other companies.

comparable provisions are found in the European company law harmonization directives, except with respect to the activities of auditors.[2]

In the Market Abuse field, of the restrictions on primary insiders, nearly all are in some way related to conflicts of interest; company directors should not take advantage of insider information, first because it could be construed as stealing information from the company, and secondly because it undermines investor confidence and harms the company's reputation.[3]

More explicitly, the new rules applicable to financial analysts[4] and journalists pursue similar objectives. The preamble clearly states that possible conflicts must be disclosed, but no further measures are imposed.[5] The rules on financial analysts are obviously inspired by the fear of biased opinions that may result in legal action against the analyst and the institution to which an analyst belongs. The technique for dealing with the conflict is both general and very traditional: the analyst's report must declare any potential conflict of interest.[6] Analysts are not specifically forbidden to publish reports that reflect too closely the interests of the firm for which they work, or hold securities. But organizational measures, such as separation of functions within an investment firm, are required.[7]

The regime applicable to journalists is much the same.[8] However, in order to avoid conflicts with press freedom under the Human Rights Convention, the directive allows the regime applicable to journalists to take the form not of a national law, but of a self-regulatory instrument, provided that the law is appropriate and equivalent to the provisions of the directive. Hence journalists who are conflicted, for example, because they hold securities on which they propose to comment, would be required to disclose this ownership. The directive requires the disclosure of all 'relationships and circumstances that may reasonably be expected to impair the objectivity of the recommendation.'[9] This provision has been highly controversial on adoption and it will be interesting to see how it will be put into practice in the Member States.

A number of the provisions on market manipulation also refer to conflict situations, such as 'front running', whereby a broker takes advantage of his knowledge of

---

2. The Eighth Directive, dated 10 April 1984, refers only to the auditor's independence (Art. 24); comp. Arts. 23–25 and 40 of the revised Eighth Company Law Directive before renumbering of the articles, and Recommendation of the Commission on Auditor Independence 2002/590/EC (16 May 2002), OJ, L 191/22, 2002.
3. Directive 2003/6 (28 January 2003), OJ, L.96/16, 2003.
4. The definition is broader and includes persons who issue recommendations: see Art. 2 of Directive 2003/125 (22 December 2003), OJ L 339/73, 2003.
5. Preamble 7, *in fine*. This refers to a strict separation of the 'recommendation' activity from any other business activity performed by e.g. financial analysts or rating agencies.
6. See Art. 6 of Directive 2003/125, no. 4 above.
7. Art. 6(2) of Directive 2003/125, no. 4 above; information about such measures should be disclosed.
8. Journalists are not subject to the same rules as financial analysts, provided they are subject to appropriate and equivalent regulation, including self-regulation, and provided the effect of such regulation is equivalent to the one imposed by the directive Art. 2(4) and 5(5) of Directive 2003/125, no. 4 above.
9. Art. 5(1) of Directive 2003/125, no. 4 above.

the orders that clients have placed with him. Front running has an abusive effect on the market (it artificially increases the order flow and may mislead other investors), and also constitutes a conflict between the intermediary and the investor. Here again, it is clear that although the rule primarily protects the investor's interests, it also aims at protecting confidence in fairness of the market.

The Market in Financial Instruments Directive[10] contains a specific section that requires investment firms – including banks[11] – to take adequate measures to avoid conflicts of interest.[12] These firms must introduce organizational and administrative measures to identify and mitigate such conflicts, and, if these are insufficient, the nature and source of the conflicts must be disclosed to clients in general terms.[13]

'Best execution' rules should help protect the investor against any conflicting interest of the executing investment firm which might encourage the firm to choose a substandard execution venue in order to earn commissions or other advantages from the investor.[14] But here again the main concern is the efficiency of the market in general. The best execution rules are not principally based on disclosure: the investor should have access *ex post* to information about how the execution venue was, but the obligations imposed on the investment firms relate essentially to organizational measures and procedures to select the best venue.[15]

As the investment funds field is particularly prone to conflict of duties, the directive might be expected to contain a number of provisions on the subject.[16] The previous (1985) directive on investment funds required the functions of fund manager and depository of the fund's assets to be split.[17] Because the latter has a certain supervisory function, the split was imposed to prevent abuses and at the same time introduce a useful monitoring mechanism.[18] The Amending directives of 2001 contain a general provision urging management companies to organize and structure themselves in such a way as to minimize conflicts of interest.[19] The provision expressly refers to the case in which the management company acts for several investment companies, and for other portfolios as well (private banking, institutional asset management), when specific rules preventing conflicts of interest must be introduced.[20]

---

10. Directive 2004/39 (21 April 2004), OJ. L. 145/1, 2004.
11. According to Art. 1 of Directive 2004/39, no. 10 above.
12. Art. 18, Directive 2004/39, no. 10 above.
13. Art. 18(2), Directive 2004/39, no. 10 above.
14. See Art. 21 of Directive 2004/39; but the provision does not mention conflicts of interest.
15. See CESR technical advice 05-290b.
16. Note that a management company must have internal rules dealing with employee transactions (Art. 5f[1][a]) and rules of organization and structure to prevent conflicts between the management company and, its clients or other UCITS (Art. 5f[1][b]).
17. Art. 17(1) Directive 85/611 (20 December 1985), OJ L 375, 1985: 'no single company shall act as both investment company and depository.'
18. Art. 14 of Directive 85/611 (20 December 1985).
19. Art. 5f(1)(b); Art. 5f(1)(a), relating to the conflict between the management firm and its employees, a subject on which all asset managers today have internal rules.
20. See preamble 9, Directive 2001/107 of 21 January 2002. Art. 5(3) of the Directive.

But other conflict situations are not covered. For example, the same financial services group can take on both the management of the fund, the depository function and the sales organization. As a result, the typically European structure of the investment fund business is overwhelmingly bank-dominated. This integration of the business in the overall banking organization raises a number of conflict of interest issues that are increasingly being tackled, in part by granting extensive autonomy to the investment management business within the group, and by offering to the investors not only in-house funds, but a selection of the 'best' funds, within the 'open architecture formula.'[21] Another issue the directive fails to cover relates to the hard and soft commissions the fund manager receives from a broker as a reward for channelling orders his way; the commission may be in cash or equivalent, or may represent other advantages that are useful either to the business he runs or to the manager himself.[22]

Surprisingly, the directive contains no overarching rule that the fund should be managed in the interest of investors, although a similar provision is imposed on the depository.[23] Instead, the idea is introduced indirectly by stating that Member States should draw up rules of conduct reflecting the principle that the manager should act 'honestly and fairly and in the best interest of the UCITS and the integrity of the market' and should 'try to avoid conflicts of interest, and when they cannot be avoided, ensure that the UCITS are fairly treated.'[24] By relying on state initiatives, the directive leaves ample freedom for member states to accommodate local situations.[25]

Also relevant is the Financial Conglomerates Directive, which does not mention conflicts of interest issues as such, but addresses them indirectly under the heading 'intra-group transactions'.[26] Conflicts of interest must be subjected to supervisory overview by the coordinating supervisory body.

The Insurance Mediation Directive[27] does not specify conflicts of interest, although evidently the matter might have been raised.

This brief – and necessarily incomplete – overview of the directives shows that while they contain a number of provisions that deal directly or indirectly with conflicts of interest issues, there is no consistent overarching approach; some issues – hard or soft commissions being the most delicate – were deliberately neglected, and few if any structural measures are imposed. The ultimate aim of the conflict provisions is to protect investors, whether by intervening directly in the investor-investment firm relationship or by ensuring that confidence in the market is upheld.

21. See further Section 4.
22. These issues are dealt with in national law: hard commission are generally considered unlawful, while for soft commission disclosure is usually considered sufficient. See e.g. the Belgian law of 20 July 2004, and Royal Decree of 4 March 2005, Art. 61, which allows only 'soft' commissions.
23. Art. 17(2) UCITS Directive no. 17 above.
24. Art. 5 b, litt. a, UCITS Directive no. 17 above.
25. Art. 5 h, litt. a and d UCITS Directive no. 17 above. The latter provision states that if conflicts cannot be avoided, the management company should treat the UCITS 'fairly.'
26. Art. 8, Directive 2002/87 (16 December 2002), OJ L 35, 2003).
27. See Directive 2002/92 (9 December 2002), OJ L.9, 2003).

Both approaches – macro and micro – can be identified in a number of the directives described previously.

III. WHY WORRY ABOUT CONFLICTS OF INTEREST IN FINANCIAL SERVICES, ESPECIALLY ASSET MANAGEMENT?

Financial services regulation, particularly in the collective asset management field, shows an undeniable interest in conflicts of interest. There does not appear to be any one, single philosophy, or any overall statement about the issue. We therefore must ask what the policy objectives of these various interventions are. The objectives may be quite diverse.

The simple answer to this question why we must worry about conflicts of interest in financial services, especially asset management, is 'investor protection'. While it is undeniable that investors would often be better protected by stringent conflicts of interest rules, it is less clear to what degree that is actually the aim of the present regulations. Most conflict of interest rules impose disclosure on the conflicted party and then rely on the investor to discuss the disclosure and designate an alternative provider if he chooses. Imposing disclosure, however, does not prevent the conflict, but merely mitigates it. As is often the case, investors have no real alternatives. They can only compare the relative detrimental effects of conflict situations. By way of example, investment fund investors may be able to compare some of the charges imposed on the portfolio, but they are rarely in a position to opt out of the conflict situation altogether.

Do investors, in fact, need conflict regulations at all? As we have stated, conflicts are numerous, but also – as appears from some of the cited provisions – inevitable; hence investors will have to take them for granted. Investors do not take investment decisions on the basis of the conflict disclosures, or on the basis of the amount of fees received by the investment manager from service providers – though this might benefit investors by reducing the expenses and charges imposed on the portfolio manager and hence increasing their returns. Investors try to identify the best portfolio manager, meaning the one who will yield the highest net return. The amount that the portfolio manager receives in fees is of little, or no, importance. Entry fees vary widely throughout Europe and there does not seem to be a massive interest in the funds with lowest fees; instead, the opposite appears to be true. In addition, the considerably higher management fees charged by hedge fund managers have not prevented this sector from attracting very substantial investment.

In terms of competition, disclosure of fees is important, but is insufficient. From the investor's perspective, it would seem equally if not more important to be able to switch funds. Investors may be expected to compare returns from various funds and make their choices accordingly, although exit fees[28] may, to some extent,

28. Or, more precisely, the fees for a 'round trip', i.e. both entry and exit fees.

restrict this. Rather than impose expensive and even burdensome conflicts of interest regulations, one could argue that it would be more efficient, and more protective of investors' interests, if stronger competition enabled investors to switch funds at minimal cost.[29] The paucity of no-load funds on the European markets is relevant here.[30] Disclosure may at least contribute to making that element of the investment decision more transparent, and hence enhance competition.

The entry and exit fees charged by investment funds vary considerably in Europe. Often, even load funds are available at a zero entrance fee. It is not certain whether investors consider this factor as being of decisive importance for their investment decisions. Much of this sensitivity is due to the way in which the investment business is tied to the traditional banking groups. Unlike in the US, most European investment funds are distributed not by the fund's distribution network, but through the traditional banking channels. Internet sales do not appear to have changed that pattern. Products distributed by the banks are predominantly in-house: they are sold, not bought. Investors therefore attribute more importance to the reputation of the bank with which they are dealing than to the cost of entering or exiting the fund, because on this basis they obtain – or think they obtain – some sort of guarantee that if things go drastically wrong, the bank will stand behind them. In a number of cases, this is precisely that occurred; confronted with irregular dealings, or with a highly unfavourable investment outcome, the bank indemnified its investors. Conflicts of interest may have their advantages.

The disclosures required by most conflicts of interest not only protect investors – or ought to – but also affect the situation of the offeror of the service. By disclosing certain (usually sensitive) items, operators ought to be able to avoid exposure to public criticism so long as they desist from particular sorts of behaviour. They will, for example, need to avoid hard commissions altogether if their disclosure would create doubt about the recipient's fairness. The policing function of disclosure is a well-known phenomenon, often expressed in the slogan 'electric light is the best of policemen.' It is quite possible that some of today's regulations were intended as an invitation to market participants to offer a fairer deal to investors, e.g. by lowering their charges. The disclosure of soft and hard commissions, as discussed in some jurisdictions, is relevant here: the regulator may have been disposed to make it an outright prohibition, but this was watered down to a disclosure requirement.[31] Once again there is no evidence that this approach has been successful in all fields. With respect to fund administration, both the number of charges and the applicable tariffs have increased. Entrance and management fees have a tendency to increase, on the argument that fees charged on other markets have also gone up.

---

29. It would be worth investigating whether funds that do not charge an exit fee present a more volatile profile than those that do.
30. It would be interesting to identify the degree to which investor interest is affected by the offering of load funds with no-load conditions, which some banks do from time to time.
31. See the FSA's statement 'Bundled brokerage and soft commission arrangements,' Policy statement 05/9.

The same argument could be applied, *mutatis mutandis*, to reputation damage, because conflicts of interest are one of the abuses most damaging to public confidence. In the 1960s, a major upheaval in the US investment fund sector was a direct consequence of the discovery of hidden commissions and other fringe benefits paid to investment managers by executing brokers.[32] The crisis generated additional regulation, particularly in regard to disclosures. Substantive prohibitions, however, were generally avoided. Here again disclosure was considered an alternative to substantive regulation.

Financial services companies are becoming increasingly sensitive not only to the existence of conflicts, but also to the public perception of them, which may damage their reputation and hence undermine their clients' confidence. By stating that it avoids conflicts of interest, a firm will enhance investors' confidence. Some operators mention this argument when offering investment funds on an 'open architecture' basis.[33] They present themselves as independent advisors selecting the best funds for their clients, irrespective of whether they are promoters of the fund or mere salesmen. Even in this case, the bank is not entirely free from conflict: it remains silent on the commission it receives from the third-party fund organization.

The public authorities[34] in charge of monitoring the financial system strongly support the banks' attempts to avoid reputation damage. Although these endeavours were originally linked to money laundering, recent statements have broadened the perspective and drawn attention to the damaging effects of conflicts of interest. Large conflict cases may indeed damage a bank's reputation and even jeopardize its future. If the conflict affects not just one bank, but also a large number of market operators, this can even trigger wider concerns, such as the competitive position of a national financial system. Dealing with conflicts of interest, while primarily a micro issue, has a macro dimension in terms of the reliability of the financial system and the need to build investor confidence in the soundness of its operations and structure. The passage from the investment fund directive quoted earlier explicitly recognizes this by stating that the rules of conduct should ensure that the management company acts 'in the best interest of the UCITS it manages and the integrity of the market.'[35]

Surprisingly, in Europe, the fundamental structure of the investment management business has never been challenged on the basis of the existence of conflicts of interest. Even the directive admits that 'conflicts of interest cannot be avoided,' in which case investors must be guaranteed fair treatment.[36] Indeed, in Europe, one of the fundamental characteristics of the investment fund business is the embedding of almost all functions – portfolio management, distribution, order execution, etc. – within the banking group that acts as the promoter of the fund. In theory at least, this

---

32. See SEC, Public Policy Implications of Investment Company Growth, 1966.
33. See below p. 274.
34. The Basel Committee on Banking Supervision regularly warns of reputation risks from conflicts of interest. Among its most recent statements see: BIS, *Enhancing Corporate Governance for Banking Organisations* (BIS, February 2006).
35. Art. 5 h, no. 17 above.
36. See Art. 5 h, litt d of the UCITS Directive, no. 17 above.

is likely to give rise to numerous conflicts of interest: the bank could recommend to its clients funds for which it acts as promoter; the fund's orders could be executed in house; cash could be deposited with the bank belonging to the group. The bank may place some of the securities it has underwritten, or which it wants to get rid of, by dumping them in the portfolios of funds in the group.[37] Conflicts between funds in the group, or between collective and individual asset management, are the reason behind some of the provisions of the new UCITS Directive. And the list of potential conflict situations could be prolonged indefinitely. This structural issue is not even touched upon in the UCITS Directive, which confines itself to enunciating a general principle and dealing with a few specific items. Despite these numerous potential conflicts, and investors' awareness of them, investors still turn to their banks to invest their savings. The explanation for this passive attitude of investors has already been mentioned: they believe that placing their savings in a fund is the same as putting them in the bank, although legally the two are separate. Fund business is inherently banking business. This creates a potential risk for the bank, which can be mitigated by separating the asset management activity more clearly from the rest of the group's business. This type of structural intervention will be explored further below.

To conclude, conflicts of interest in asset management are covered by a number of financial regulations, most prominently in the field of investment funds. These rules address specific aspects of the problem, but not its inherently structural basis, which is due to the strong linkage of asset management with banking business. However, there appears to be an increasing awareness of the structural dimension, at least in some financial services groups.

IV. STRUCTURAL ASPECTS OF CONFLICTS OF INTEREST IN THE FIELD OF ASSET MANAGEMENT

In this part of the paper, I shall attempt to show that in some regulations, and more conspicuously in actual practice, banking groups are required to deal with the conflict of interest problem by taking structural measures, specifically by separating the asset management business from the rest of their banking activity. The accompanying safeguards deserve special attention.

A. Regulation

Currently there are some indications that European regulation is going down this path, though there are few very specific prescriptions.

37. E. Wymeersch. and M. Kruithof, 'Belangentegenstelingen bij het beheer van gemeenschappelijke beleggingsfondsen' [1989] *Revue de la banque (Belgium)*, 303–321.

The UCITS Directive does not contain any structural provisions on this matter, except where the depository is concerned; manager and depository should be two separate legal entities.[38]

This is a clear internal control measure, particularly because the depository has been placed in charge of certain supervisory functions. The rule aims to avoid confusing the interests of the fund with those of the fund manager. But the approach is far from comprehensive. The depository will usually be a bank in the same financial services group, acting as custodian for the securities, receiving the cash on deposit, and guaranteeing the fund obligations when required.[39] Other companies in the group will also undertake servicing activities. From the client's perspective – as stated earlier – this structure is not necessarily objectionable, because he is still investing his money with the bank, whether in the form of a fund, a deposit, a short term bond or other investment vehicle.

Although this is based on wider considerations, we could also mention the provisions in both the non-life and the life directives forbidding insurance companies to engage in any business other than insurance.[40] In view of the developments in financial services groups, particularly the creation of integrated financial conglomerates, one may wonder whether the economic justification of this prohibition is likely to be challenged.

More explicit measures are called for in the MiFID: Art. 13(3) stipulates that investment firms – including banks – should operate and maintain effective organizational and administrative arrangements with a view to taking all reasonable steps to prevent conflicts of interest from adversely affecting the interests of their clients. This rule is further elaborated in Art.18, which adds that, if the measures prove ineffective, the investment firm 'shall clearly disclose the general nature and/or sources of conflicts of interest to the client before undertaking business on its behalf.' The Commission intends to enact further detailed measures, although these have not yet been adopted. Because the provision is drafted in very broad terms, its precise purpose is unclear, nor is it clear whether or not the provision will include structural measures of the kind referred to below.

B. Factual Developments

Recently, some significant developments have taken place in numerous financial services groups, whereby the asset management activity is being located in a separate subsidiary, more precisely a sub-group that is granted a well-defined autonomy within the overall group. This development is due to various factors, with specialization, economies of scale, and specific developments in the investment fund

38. The same rule is good practice in private banking.
39. This is the case with structured funds, as far as the 'guarantee' for the capital is concerned.
40. See Art. 8(1)(b) of the Non-Life Directive 73/239 (24 July 1973), as amended, and Art. 8(1)(b) of the Life Directive 79/267 (5 March 1979), as amended, where the restriction is strictly confined to life business, excluding non-life.

business playing a dominant role. But conflict of interest considerations have undeniably contributed to this development.

In practice, European societies are growing increasingly aware of the need to deal adequately with conflicts of interest. The number of regulations addressing conflicts of interest has increased not only in the field of financial services, but in other domains as well. Some highly publicized investigations in the US have brought to light previously unsuspected forms of conflicts that can occur in financial markets. The traditional instruments – disclosure, Chinese Walls, conduct of business rules – are considered useful, but are unable to avert all suspicion of misconduct. In recent insurance cases, controversy surrounding commissions received by independent brokers raised questions about their role and caused anxiety not only in the US, but also in several European states. Stricter discipline is now considered necessary.

If the existing instruments do not provide a satisfactory solution to conflict of interest problems, what other measures can be taken to dispel suspicion? The most radical answer has been developed in the asset management field. It is based on strict separation between the asset management department of the bank and the rest of its business. Note that this development is not due solely to considerations related to conflicts of interest. It appears chiefly to be inspired by organizational and efficiency imperatives.

The spectre of the now defunct Glass-Steagall Act has been revived. A split in the business is introduced by spinning off the asset management activity – but not the entire securities business – into a separate subsidiary, with a separate board of directors (some of them independent), separate organization, business plan etc. Often there is even a physical separation. The asset manager's employees are located in a different building, or even a different country, from the main banking business. Their reporting lines are mainly financial (financial objectives, budgets), not operational. With respect to actual asset management, the company enjoys full autonomy.

Most large financial services groups now have a separate asset management entity in the group, which is not dependent on the bank, but acts as a supplier of asset management services either for the group itself or for the investment funds that are presented as group products. Usually this asset manager will be a separate company, a subsidiary not of the bank, but of the top holding company that also owns shares in the bank, the asset manager and normally also the group's insurance company. As an internal service provider, it can be seen as a factory that produces products adapted to the demands of the various markets where the groups' products are on sale. This approach therefore also aims at considerable economies of scale and other specialization imperatives.

How does this development fit into the general organizational patterns of financial services groups?

Most of the large European financial services groups offer the full range of financial services: banking in its various forms, insurance, asset management and private banking, insurance, leasing, etc., are all part of the same group. For various reasons, particularly regulatory ones, these services are located in separate legal entities, each with its own board of directors, management committees, external auditors, financial statements and so on. However, in practice, the group is largely managed as a single 'enterprise', often with centralized decision-making at the level of the top holding company's management. Often the same individuals even sit on the management committees heading the numerous legal entities, sometimes – but not always – together with a special representative of the entity itself. The management of the group's business is organized not according to legal entities, but on strict commercial lines. The 'retail' business line looks after the activities involving the public at large, e.g. banking, insurance, personal banking and so on. Wholesale banking may be another business line. Business lines, therefore, cut across legal entities, leading to new and difficult legal questions. The coherence of the managerial structure, superimposed on the legal structure, deserves further analysis from the legal point of view. The rules on groups of companies will be a primary source of inspiration in this field.[41]

Where asset management is concerned, the situation is somewhat different. Often, it is considered to be a group-internal service provider. Its products are 'sold' either directly – e.g. management of institutional portfolios for third parties – or indirectly through other parts of the group. This applies especially to investment funds, for which the asset management business line acts as a factory for setting up funds and managing portfolios that are then sold through the banking or the insurance arm, often repackaged according to applicable legal, commercial, or supervisory requirements and adapted to each of the geographical markets in which the group is active. The activity covers not only investment funds, but also asset management for institutional investors. Usually private banking is kept separate, along with management of the group's assets for its own account.

The question here focuses on the independence of the asset manager within the overall group; increasing the asset manager's independence reduces the potential conflicts of interest. By structuring the asset management as a more independent business within the group, the group is attempting to send the message that potential conflicts are addressed not so much by soft instruments – Chinese walls and the like – but by the strongest possible institutional measures. As far as the prudential approach is concerned, the structure indicates that potentially risky issues are receiving a strong institutional or structural response. In terms of protecting the investor's interest, the portfolios will be managed in an objective way, without any group interference. Conveying this message to investors indicates that the group is aware of a previously widespread negative perception of its conflicted position. At the same time, sending this message forestalls the criticism that the bank is selling its own products: even if the products are in house, they are managed in an objective way, based on arm length's contracts.

Examining the details of the structure, the first aspect worth mentioning is the strict legal separation of the management company (which is often a subgroup)

41. Among the fundamental pronouncements worth noting here is the so-called Rozenblum doctrine of the French '*Cour de Cassation*', which clarified the ground rules for group liability. See Forum Europaeum, 'Konzernrecht für Europa' ZGR [1989], 672.

from the rest of the financial services group: separate name (albeit with a reference to the main group), separate legal regime,[42] separate board and separate location, often spread across several jurisdictions. Asset management companies may usefully reinforce this image of independence by appointing one or more independent directors whose specific task is to ensure that the management takes place in an objective, arms length way, thereby looking after the interests of all stakeholders.

The relationship with the group deserves further analysis. As a rule, the group will retain full (often 100 per cent) control. But it will not intervene in actual investment decisions, and the managing directors will be adamant that the group must abstain from any intervention in actual investment decisions. Clients are informed that the assets are managed by a team that has no relationship with the overall group and takes its decisions in the interest of the portfolios managed, without any influence from the bank.

However, the group, thanks to its membership on the asset management company's board, will not stand aloof. Rather, it will ensure that its overall objectives are realized in terms of strategy, return on group investment, budgets and results, as well as in terms of group policies involving the group's reputation. Because the asset manager's products usually carry the name of the group, they may harm the group's reputation if its guidelines are not strictly adhered to. The group's reputation depends in part on respecting policies developed at group level, and on ensuring that standards of ethical conduct are respected by all the entities in the group wherever their business activity. These standards are becoming more and more important. Apart from money laundering policies, ethical or responsible investment has attracted considerable attention. Avoiding conflicts of interest will be part of these standards. Transactions with professional counterparts – e.g. cash investment, order transmission, financial analysis, etc – will take place on an arm's length basis and only after having investigated the conditions offered by different market participants; the group will not enjoy a privileged position. The 'factory' may assemble products for a third party that are then sold under that party's name. Here it is evident that any bias in the management would scare away the other partner.

Apart from the items mentioned above, the group's overall intervention will also extend to supervising the activities of the asset management team: internal controls, audit and compliance rules will all be determined and enforced on a group wide basis and be monitored by departments belonging to the overall group; the sub-group's own internal control mechanisms notwithstanding.

As far as conflicts of interest are concerned, the message is clear: these conflicts are to be avoided. But conflicts of interest are of course not the only, and probably not even the principal, reason for organising a separate asset management business line. This is also influenced by regulatory concerns, such as the requirement to organize a separate asset management company for investment funds. This requirement will

42. This could mean either an investment firm as defined in the MiFID, or a specialized UCITS management company.

be further strengthened under the recent MiFID rules, which will lead to stricter regulation of conflicts.

To what extent this structure will constitute an effective response to accusations of biased conduct is difficult to say. The relationship with the banking group will continue to exist. Ultimate policies will be decided at group level, staff will move between different departments of the overall group, procurement contracts such as insurance coverage will be contracted for the entire group. Will the presence of one independent director for all portfolios managed constitute a credible defence against accusations of unfair treatment? Even if the answer to some of these questions remains uncertain, the overall movement is towards more autonomy of the asset manager within the banking group.

Another development points in the same direction: the offering of investment funds on an 'open architecture' basis. Some banks have decided to offer not only in-house products, but also products of other selected asset managers. They tell their clients that they have selected the best products on the market, and that the clients can choose among them, often at lower entry fees. The role of the bank has changed from managing funds to selecting the best performing funds, and to advising clients according to their needs. This marketing is, according to some banks, likely to become the prevailing approach for investment funds. It eliminates the conflicting interest of the bank, and limits the financial involvement of the latter to receiving a fee, the gross amount of which may – or may not – be known to the client. In practice open architecture agreements often include a more elaborate agreement among the banks, whereby the offering bank will undertake a due diligence of the other bank's management services, evaluate the quality of its staff, procedures, organization, and of course also of the returns obtained. Agreements occasionally permit products to be sold on a reciprocal basis. Here again questions of conflict might appear, but are mitigated by the comparative analysis and adequate disclosures. Although experts might dispute that this development reflects the same fundamental drive towards less bank-embedded asset management, the banks claim that by choosing the 'open architecture' approach they make themselves more independent, free from any bias.

Some groups have envisaged other combinations. While maintaining a separate asset management entity within the group, they wonder whether the group should keep full control of an asset manager which is largely autonomous. With potential economies of scale in mind, they wonder whether joint ventures, or even mergers with other asset managers, might yield a higher return on invested capital.

Here the logic of spinning off the in-house asset management has been taken to extremes. The original banking group retains a minority stake in its former asset manager, and sells its products along with those of other suppliers. The role of the bank becomes that of a neutral marketing channel, identifying the products that offer the best returns and looking for the best fees on products sold. At the same time, the group may develop a wider range of products on offer, reduce its investment and minimize costs.

It is still too soon to be sure that the last trend is actually taking place. From the angle of the present research, it is clear that financial services groups, while attempting to eliminate conflicts of interest, are offering a credible product range to their clients.

To conclude, apart from the complex legal enactments that aim at preventing conflicts of interest or at least making them manageable the economic structure of the sector seems to be heading towards more institutional or structural concepts, which may largely eliminate conflicts arising from asset management activity within a banking group. This tendency underpins the drive of banking groups to gain the confidence of their clients and avert reputation risks. It does not mean that all conflicts are eliminated. If the trend is further confirmed, we may be moving closer to something like the US-UK scheme, whereby asset management is not necessarily located within banking groups.

Chapter 10

Conflicts of Interest in Institutional Asset Management: Is the EU Regulatory Approach Adequate?

*Marc Kruithof**

Conflicts of interest, particularly in the financial sector, have been debated for some time and regulators have introduced various rules, principles and mechanisms specifically intended to address such conflicts.[1] This article seeks to contribute to the discussion about the adequacy of these legal responses to conflicts of interest

* Lecturer in Law in the Department of Business Administration and Public Management at the University College Ghent (Belgium), Assistant at the Ghent University Law School and the Financial Law Institute (Belgium); Licentiate in Law, Ghent University (Belgium); Licentiate in Economics, Ghent University (Belgium); LL.M., Yale Law School (USA).

1. For EU regulation of the financial sector, see e.g. Art. 10 and 17 of Council Directive 85/611/EEC of 20 December 1985 on the Coordination of Laws, Regulations and Administrative Provisions Relating to Undertakings for Collective Investment in Transferable Securities (UCITS), OJ L 375/3, 1985, (hereafter referred to as the 'UCITS Directive'); Art. 10 and 11 of Council Directive 93/22/EEC of 10 May 1993 on Investment Services in the Securities Field, OJ L 141/27, 1993 (in short the 'Investment Services Directive,' usually and hereafter referred to as the 'ISD'); and more recently Art. 13(3) and 18 of Directive 2004/39/EC of the European Parliament and of the Council of 21 April 2004 on Markets in Financial Instruments amending Council Directives 85/611/EEC and 93/6/EEC and Directive 2000/12/EC of the European Parliament and of the Council and Repealing Council Directive 93/22/EEC, OJ L 145/1 2004 (in short the 'Market in Financial Instruments Directive,' usually and hereafter referred to as the 'MiFID').

L. Thévenoz and R. Bahar (eds.), *Conflicts of Interest: Corporate Governance and Financial Market*, pp. 277–335.

in institutional asset management or delegated portfolio management.[2] This issue is approached from a theoretical perspective by analyzing whether the typical legal responses to such conflicts, in particular those envisaged under the new European Market in Financial Instruments Directive (hereafter 'MiFID'),[3] address what economic analysis has shown to be the key characteristics of the problem.

Section I of the paper begins by analyzing the concept of a conflict of interest in general. After this definition of the legal concept, the insights of economic theory are called upon to pinpoint the reason why such conflicts constitute a problem that warrants special legal attention. Section II focuses on asset management, first identifying the potential conflicts of interest facing portfolio managers (SubSection II.A), and then explaining why the problems that may be caused by such conflicts call for government intervention (SubSection II.B). Section III discusses how the law has dealt with conflicts of interest in asset management. Section IV offers some concluding remarks, taking into account recent developments in the market of asset management.

I. CONFLICTS OF INTEREST IN GENERAL

A. Conflicts of Interest as a Legal Concept

In the broadest – i.e. non-legal – sense, a conflict of interests can be defined as a situation in which the protection or furtherance of different interests requires

2. Institutional asset management can take different forms. Financial institutions manage portfolios of investments, some belonging to a collectivity of investors (such as an investment company or a management company for mutual funds) – this is usually referred to as collective asset or portfolio management – and others belonging to individual clients (though these clients can themselves be institutional investors, such as pension funds or investment companies or a management companies of mutual funds that have delegated the actual management of their portfolios to a specialized investment firm, so that the managed assets economically form a collective portfolio) – this is usually referred to as individual asset or portfolio management. In this article I refer to each of these types of delegated portfolio management as 'asset management' or 'portfolio management.'
3. See no. 1 above. These rules are applicable to investment firms and banks; see Art. 1(2), MiFID. The rules on conflicts of interest in the MiFID are most likely to become, if not *de jure* then at least *de facto*, the uniform standard in the EU, as it is unlikely that any Member State will impose additional rules addressing this problem. In the implementation of the MiFID, a clear choice is made for exhaustive harmonization, leaving no room for supplementary national rules to those strictly needed for the transposition of the European rules into national law. See European Commission, *Background Note to the Draft Commission Directive Implementing Directive 2004/39/EC of the European Parliament and of the Council as regards Record-Keeping Obligations for Investment Firms, Transaction Reporting, Market Transparency, Admission of Financial Instruments to Trading, and Defined Terms for the Purposes of that Directive* (6 February 2006) (available at the Commission's website at <www.ec.europa.eu/internal_market>, hereafter the 'Commission Level 2 Background Note'); see also L. Enriques, 'Conflicts of Interest in Investment Services: The Price and Uncertain Impact of MiFID's Regulatory Framework' in G. Ferrarini and E. Wymeersch (eds), *Investor Protection in Europe: Regulatory Competition and Harmonization* (Oxford, Oxford University Press, 2006 forthcoming), references here to the working paper version available in the Social Sciences Research Network electronic library, <www.ssrn.com/abstract=782828>.

different actions; in other words, circumstances in which a choice of action necessarily implies preferring certain interests over others. Modern society applies several methods for making choices among conflicting interests, such as politics, law in general, contracts between individuals and the market mechanism. In this sense, everything the law deals with is in essence a conflict of interests, and the same can be said of economics.

But when lawyers talk about conflicts of interest, they do not mean all those situations in which the interests of different people call for different choices. In a legal context, the term 'conflict of interest' has a much more specific meaning.[4] In the legal sense, a conflict of interest arises when an individual in a certain situation has a duty to decide how to act based solely on the interests of another person, while the choice he makes also has repercussions on his own interests (*conflict of interest and duty*) or on the interests of another, third person that he is also legally bound to protect (*conflict of duties*).[5] Both types of conflicts of interest[6] raise issues, because we assume that a person usually determines how to act at least partially based on the repercussions the available alternative actions would have on his own interests.[7]

However, the fact that someone has a personal interest in the choice he is legally required to make is insufficient to create a conflict of interest in the legal sense of the term. If it were, then anytime a person was under a legal duty to act in a certain way, that person would by definition have a conflict of interest, because his personal interests would always be affected by the choice of whether or not

4. Note the distinction between the general concept 'conflict of interests' and the specific legal (or moral) problem 'conflict of interest', studied here, as suggested by M. Davis, 'Introduction' in M. Davis and A. Stark (eds), *Conflict of Interest in the Professions* (Oxford, Oxford University Press, 2001), p. 3, p. 16.
5. Cf. V. Simonart, 'Conclusions générales' in *Les conflits d'intérêts* (Brussels, Bruylant, 1997), p. 297, pp. 304–305; M. Davis (no. 4 above), 8; J.R. Boatright, 'Financial Services' in M. Davis and A. Stark (eds), *Conflict of Interest in the Professions* (Oxford, Oxford University Press, 2001), p. 217, p. 219.
6. From this perspective, a conflict of duties does not differ from a conflict of interest and duty. The latter type of conflict is considered to be a problem because there is reason to fear that the person will not fulfil his duty where doing so would damage his own interests. The same idea is the basis for considering a conflict of duties to be problematic: abiding by one duty may imply a breach of the other duty, bringing about sanctions that adversely affect the acting person's interests.
7. For this assumption to be valid, it is not necessary that a person chooses his actions based solely on his own interests; as soon as his own interests have some influence on his actions, the situation characterized as a conflict of interest becomes problematic. For an interesting psychological interpretation of the conflict of interest problem, analyzing why self-interest (perhaps subconsciously) influences our actions when such actions are thought to be geared towards other interests, see D.A. Moore and G. Loewenstein, 'Self-Interest, Automaticity, and the Psychology of Conflict of Interest' (2004/2) *Social Justice Research* 17, 189. For an analysis of how our so-called 'bounded ethicality' hinders us from recognizing situations as conflicts of interest and conflict of interest situations as problematic – further reducing the extent to which our moral sense will limit our 'automatic' tendency to consult our own interests – see D. Cugh, M.H. Bazerman and M. R. Banaji, 'Bounded Ethicality as a Psychological Barrier to Recognizing Conflicts of Interest' in D.A. Moore, D.M. Cain, G. Loewenstein and M.H. Bazerman (eds), *Conflicts of Interest: Challenges and Solutions in Business, Law, Medicine, and Public Policy* (New York, Cambridge University Press, 2005), p. 74.

to abide by this duty. The reason for this is because breaching the duty may incur sanctions, while fulfilling the duty – and thus avoiding the sanctions – represents a cost for this person as well. In this sense, a person who has a legal duty will always have interests that potentially conflict with this duty. Conversely, the fact that a legal duty requires a person to act contrary to his own interests in order to protect the interests of someone else is not enough to constitute a conflict of interest in the legal sense of the term. All duties are intended to steer the actions of a person in order to protect the interests of others and thus 'represent' their interests.[8] The fact that those interests conflict with the actor's own interests does not define a subset of all situations involving duties. Instead, it characterizes every situation in which a legal duty is present, because it is precisely the reason why the legal duty is imposed in the first place.

For this reason, we cannot say that a person is faced with a conflict of interest merely because he has a personal interest that conflicts with his legal duty, or because his freedom to further his own interests is limited by a legal duty that requires him to act in a specific way to protect the interests of others. What characterizes the situation known as a conflict of interest, in the legal sense, is the specific content of the legal duty the person is under; a duty which is commonly referred to as a duty of loyalty.[9] Two characteristics of this duty are particularly relevant here.

The first characteristic of a duty of loyalty is that the legally required action is not specifically identified: the law does not tell the person exactly what to do or how to act.

On the one hand, it is recognized that a person under a duty of loyalty has a so-called discretionary margin within which he can legally judge which action is the most appropriate.[10] Reasonable people can disagree about which of the feasible actions within this margin would be optimal, thus the fact that such disagreement

8. In a minority of cases, the legal duty is intended to steer the actions of a person so as to protect his own interests. These types of duties are mainly imposed in situations in which a person is not trusted to reliably protect his interests voluntarily, e.g. if he is judged unable to form rational judgments (e.g. minors), or when the costs and benefits of a choice tend to be incorrectly estimated by individuals (e.g. mandatory seat belts in cars).
9. Cf. A. G. Anderson, 'Conflicts of Interest: Efficiency, Fairness and Corporate Structure' (1978) *UCLA L. Rev*. 25, 738, 738 no. 2: 'The three major areas where conflicts of interest are so labeled and regulated are government, the professions and property management . . . [T]hose "conflicts of interest" recognized by lawyers are typically conflicts between self-interest and fiduciary obligations of loyalty or impartiality.' In this article, the term 'duty of loyalty' is used in its generic sense, not necessarily in the more specific fiduciary meaning as it is usually used in common law systems, with all the particular legal consequences that brings (see Section III.A below), because these special fiduciary characteristics do not constitute the *source* of conflicts of interest, but are part of the law's *solutions* for the problems stemming from the conflicts of interest imposed by any duty of loyalty, whether fiduciary or otherwise. As discussed below, civil-law systems do not recognize fiduciary law with all its equitable characteristics, but of course do impose duties of loyalty through various other mechanisms.
10. Cf. D.A. DeMott, 'Beyond Metaphor: An Analysis of Fiduciary Obligation' (1988) *Duke Law Journal*, 879, 908–910; R. Cooter and B.J. Freedman, 'The Fiduciary Relationship: Its Economic Character and Legal Consequences' (1991) *New York University Law Review* 66, 1,045, 1,046–1,047 and 1,051.

exists does not imply a particular choice was wrong. In addition, the fact that the action subsequently turns out to not have been the optimal choice does not in itself imply that the duty was breached, as long as the choice fell within the margin of discretion; that is, the range of actions within which reasonable people could disagree about what is the optimal choice. The duty of loyalty is, in that sense, open-ended, and usually worded in terms of 'best efforts' or 'prudence' or 'due care.'[11] Viewed in this way, a duty of loyalty encompasses a duty of care: it requires a reasonable effort to try to identify the optimal choice of action given the interests that must be furthered.

Conversely, a duty of loyalty is highly specific, not open-ended at all, and very different from a duty of care. Loyalty has been described as 'the willing and practical and thorough-going devotion of a person to a cause.'[12] The requirement to be loyal is thus a constraint on a party's discretion to pursue self-interest,[13] preventing him from using his powers for goals other than those for which they were intended, i.e. the furthering of the interests of the beneficiary.[14] The duty requires the person to determine his way of acting based *solely* or *exclusively* on the interests of another person. When making decisions, the person must weigh only the costs and benefits of the available alternative actions with regard to the person whose interests he is under a legal duty to protect, and choose the action that maximizes those interests. He must ignore – i.e. completely disregard – the ways in which the available alternatives may affect his own interests, including those resulting from his duties to other persons. A duty of loyalty thus applies to this decision-making process; it is not a standard by which to judge the chosen action itself.[15]

While reasonable people may disagree about which action is optimal for the interest that must be protected, and therefore several choices within the range of discretion may be legitimate from this perspective, reasonable people cannot disagree about which interest should be the yardstick to judge the actions taken under a duty of loyalty, and thus only one very specific motive is allowed to inspire these

---

11. See R. Cooter and B.J. Freedman (no. 10 above), 1,049.
12. J. Royce, *The Philosophy of Loyalty*, p. 16 (1930) quoted in A.W. Scott, 'The Fiduciary Principle' (1949) *California Law Review* 37, 539, 540.
13. D. A. DeMott (no. 10 above), 879.
14. Cf. T. Frankel, 'Fiduciary Duties' in P. Newman (ed.), *The New Palgrave Dictionary of Economics and the Law* (London, Macmillan, 1998), p. 127, p. 129.
15. Cf. C. M. Bruner, ' "Good Faith" State of Mind, and the Outer Boundaries of Director Liability in Corporate Law', Boston University School of Law, Working Paper Series, Law and Economics, Working Paper No. 05–19, p. 57, available at <www.ssrn.com/abstract=832944> (October 2005):

    '[F]iduciary duty doctrine would be rendered substantially more comprehensible and workable if the line between care and loyalty were understood functionally as an analytical distinction between minimizing agency costs through assessment of the quality of objective decisions, on the one hand, and the quality of subjective intentions, on the other. Beneath the surface of the doctrine and the terminology employed, this has always in fact been the difference between the duties of care and loyalty.'

actions. Any deviation from this principle, even the slightest, by allowing one's choice to be influenced by an interest other than the one to be protected, implies a breach of the duty of loyalty. Here, there is no margin of discretion.

The typical element that characterizes a situation as a conflict of interest, therefore, is the combined presence of personal interests that will be affected by the choice to be made, and a legal duty to *exclude* such personal interests from the decision-making process.[16] And here lies the particular risk. When the individual is given the opportunity to make choices within his discretionary margin that are not exclusively motivated by their effect on the interests of the beneficiary, he will be all the more likely to do so if his own personal interests are involved.[17]

The second characteristic of a duty of loyalty, which is in fact a consequence of the first, is that it is judged by a subjective standard, i.e. the yardstick is the required *ex ante* motive or purpose of the action, not the *ex post* effects this action may turn out to have. But while the effects of an action are very often objectively verifiable, the actor's intentions usually are not. In most instances, they cannot be deduced *ex post* from the results of the action. The effects of most actions are not completely determined by those actions alone, but are also influenced by external factors.[18] Moreover, there is an additional complication, namely the existence of a margin of discretion within which reasonable persons can disagree about which action is optimal given the stated purpose. A certain outcome may result from one particular choice of action within the acceptable range inspired exclusively by the interest to be served; however, that same outcome may equally result from the choice of another action within the same range, but which was preferable because it also served another, conflicting interest.[19] *Ex post*, it is extremely difficult, if not impossible, to distinguish between these two actions. Yet while both actions are within the margin of discretion, only one of them is a legitimate choice in the light of the duty of loyalty.[20]

---

16. Cf. M. Davis (no. 4 above), p. 4: 'Conflict of interest is a problem only in a certain domain, one in which we do not want ordinary self-interest to guide the decisions of those on whom we depend; instead we want those on whom we depend to be "independent", "impartial", "unbiased" or the like.'
17. See T. Frankel, 'Fiduciary Law' (1983) *California Law Review* 71, 795, 809–810; K.B. Davis, Jr., 'Judicial Review of Fiduciary Decisionmaking – Some Theoretical Perspectives' (1985) *Northwestern University Law Review* 80, 1, 4.
18. In economic literature this is often referred to as a 'high-noise, low-signal environment'.
19. Cf. R. Cooter and B.J. Freedman (no. 10 above), 1,049–1,051.
20. One might ask why, if the harm done to the person to whom the duty is owed is not affected by whether a particular choice of action is due to a lack of care or a lack of loyalty, the law should treat the two instances differently. Cf. A.G. Anderson (no. 9 above), 758, no. 59:

    'Disloyalty may be intuitively regarded as more "unfair" because it involves a somewhat more deliberate form of self-preference than laziness or carelessness, but both the careless and the disloyal [person] are choosing self-interest . . . over the duty to others. Negligence and self-dealing are equally costly to the person harmed, and I therefore include both in my discussion of cheating by fiduciaries.'

    However, while the harm to the principal may be the same whether the person under a duty is negligent or disloyal, the harm to society is not. The reason why the law should treat a

For this reason, enforcing a duty of loyalty is highly difficult. Because the person with the duty of loyalty can substantially gain from wrongdoing, the fact that he is unlikely to be caught out means that the incentive to breach this duty is much stronger than it is for other duties – a fact that helps explain the special legal attention paid to this phenomenon.[21]

B. CONFLICTS OF INTEREST AS AN ECONOMIC AGENCY PROBLEM

In economic parlance, a person acting in a way that affects the interests of another person or persons is referred to as an 'agent'; the person whose interests are affected by the act of the agent is referred to as the 'principal'.[22] In most instances, an agent will also have personal interests relating to his actions that affect others, and those interests may differ from the principal's. To put it more precisely, his own interests may be better served by a way of acting that does not have optimal consequences for the interests of the principal. From a utilitarian perspective, the socially optimal action is the one that maximizes the aggregate utility – furthers the interests – of both the principal and the agent.[23] Assuming no legal duties are involved, economic theory predicts that the agent will act as if he is only trying to maximize his own interests, without taking into account the consequences of his actions for the interests of the principal and thus failing to attain the social optimum.

---

breach of a duty of loyalty differently from a breach of a duty of care is, to some extent, the same as the answer to the question of why a distinction is made between mere incompetence (or lack of care) and fraud. Increasing the level of competence or care requires the investment of real resources. Here, as always, we may legitimately ask whether these resources would not be better allocated elsewhere. A reduction in fraud or an increase in loyalty, however, does not require any additional resources. An adherence to honesty would thus *always* involve a clear social gain, while an increase in competence or care will only yield a social gain if the gains are greater than the increase in resource costs. See M.R. Darby and E. Karni, 'Free Competition and the Optimal Amount of Fraud' (1973) *Journal of Law and Economics* 16, 67, 83.

21. Cf. A. G. Anderson (no. 9 above), 740: 'Special legal regulation of conflicts of interest is imposed on those occupational groups which have the greatest opportunities to cheat without detection and whose cheating imposes the most serious costs on others.'
22. Note that the terms 'agent' and 'principal' are used here without necessarily implying the legal relationship that exists between a *legal* principal and agent; legal agents and principals are also economic agents and principals, but the latter category is much broader. See in general J.W. Pratt and R.J. Zeckhauser, 'Principals and Agents: An Overview' in J.W. Pratt and R.J. Zeckhauser (eds), *Principals and Agents: The Structure of Business* (Boston, Harvard Business School Press, 1985), p. 1, p. 2; for a description of the possible principal–agent relationship present in asset management services, see Bank for International Settlements, *Incentive Structures in Institutional Asset Management and Their Implications for Financial Markets*, Committee on the Global Financial System Working Group Report No. 21 (Basel: BIS, March 2003), pp. 16–18.
23. This would be the so-called Kaldor-Hicks efficient result. This concept of efficiency is based on N. Kaldor, 'Welfare Propositions of Economics and Interpersonal Comparisons of Utility' (1939) *Economic Journal* 49, 549; and J.R. Hicks, 'The Foundations of Welfare Economics' (1939) *Economic Journal* 49, 696.

One way to overcome this problem is for the principal to bargain with the agent: in return for the agent choosing the action that is most favourable to the principal's interests, the principal will pay the agent an amount that renders it also in his interest to act that way.[24] Classic economic theory predicts that such transactions will lead to a social optimum, on the assumption that principals and agents will only – but also always – consent to such deals if they are better off as a result. The problem of the conflicting interests of individuals, therefore, automatically disappears if the market is allowed to do its job, or so classic economic theory assured us:[25] a social optimum will necessarily result.[26] In other words, classic theory did not perceive the principal–agent relation as a problem, so little attention was devoted to it.

This view has been seriously challenged by insights developed during the latter half of the twentieth century usually referred to as 'information economics'. Classic economic theory starts from the assumption that agents and principals have perfect information, not only regarding their own interests, but also about how potential alternative actions will affect those interests and about what actions are actually taking place or have taken place. Of course, in reality, this is seldom the case. For a long time economists had assumed that markets with not too imperfect information would perform very much like markets in which information was perfect, rendering the actual imperfection of information a minor 'noise', not threatening the validity of the theory or the accuracy of its predictions. Information economics, however, showed that even a minor imperfection in the information could result in outcomes *very* different from what classic theory predicts.[27] Agency theory was developed to analyze the problems caused by information asymmetry between a principal and an agent.[28]

---

24. Other methods are also used to overcome this problem. For example, the law may impose extra-contractual duties or liabilities on agents to provide incentives for them to take the interests of principals into account. However, given that the focus of this paper is on asset management, a contractual relationship, I will only discuss deals. For an entertaining introductory overview of possible applications of the economic agency model to a wide assortment of different areas of the law, see E. Posner, 'Agency Models in Law and Economics' in E. Posner (ed.), *Chicago Lectures in Law and Economics* (New York, Foundation Press, 2000), p. 225, who rightly remarks that 'once one has mastered the agency model, it is a fine game, especially on long car trips, to apply it to everything in the universe' (p. 240).
25. Cf. the formulation by Adam Smith in *An Inquiry into the Nature and Causes of the Wealth of Nations* (first published in 1776): 'by [acting] he intends only his own gain, and he is in this, as in many other cases, led by an invisible hand to promote an end [a social optimum, MK] which was no part of his intention.'
26. This is the so-called first optimality theorem, according to which if a competitive equilibrium exists and all commodities relevant to costs or utilities are actually priced in the market, then the equilibrium is necessarily optimal in that there is no other allocation of resources to services which would make all participants in the market better off. See K. J. Arrow, 'Uncertainty and the Welfare Economics of Medical Care' (1963) *The American Economic Review* 53, 941, 942.
27. See J.E. Stiglitz, 'Information and the Change in the Paradigm in Economics, Part 1' (2003) *The American Economist* 47, 6, 8.
28. See in general K.M. Eisenhardt, 'Agency Theory: An Assessment and Review' (1989) *Academy of Management Review* 14, 57–74; K.J. Arrow, 'The Economics of Agency' in J.W. Pratt and R.J. Zeckhauser (eds), *Principals and Agents: The Structure of Business* (Boston, Harvard Business

The classic theory's prediction that the market will resolve any conflict of interest problem only holds to the assumption that the person under the duty of loyalty will actually fulfil this duty completely and correctly, and if not, the law imposes a sanction or provides the principal with an effective remedy.[29] But for this to be possible, the principal has to know whether the agent has correctly performed his duty, which is difficult because the agent's duty applies to the motives for, rather than the outcome of, his actions. Such a duty is difficult to police in practice, because the agent's intentions are known only to himself.[30]

In most cases the actual motives for the agent's actions cannot be deduced from their objective outcome. First, the outcome itself may be impossible to ascertain. For example, if the task of the agent is to avoid losses to the greatest extent possible, it is very difficult to quantify *ex post* the amount of losses that were actually averted.[31] Secondly, in many cases, the objective outcome is not exclusively determined by the agent's actions, but is also influenced by external factors.[32] To complicate matters further, enforcing a duty of loyalty through the legal system requires the beneficiary to convince a court that a breach has occurred. It is not enough for the principal to 'know' what the agent's motives were: he must also be able to prove it.[33]

If for any of these reasons the assumption of classic economic theory is unrealistic, a problem develops which in modern economic literature is usually referred to as a *moral hazard*: the agent with conflicting motives has an incentive to undertake a *hidden action* with adverse consequences for the principal, and market forces alone do not suffice to avert this problem.[34]

But can we not assume that principals prefer 'moral' agents over 'rational' agents,[35] i.e. that over time principals will learn from past experience, giving dishonest agents a bad reputation that will force them to accept lower fees, allowing

---

School Press, 1985), p. 37; H.R. Varian, *Intermediate Microeconomics – A Modern Approach* (6th edn, New York, London, W. W. Norton & Company, 2003), Chapter 36, p. 667 *et seq.*

29. As E.N. White correctly points out, 'Litigation is an important part of market discipline'; see his 'Quis Custodiet Ipsos Custodes? Controlling Conflicts of Interest in the Financial Industry' in C. Borio, W.C. Hunter, G.G. Kaufman and K. Tsatsaronis (eds), *Market Discipline across Countries and Industries* (Cambridge, MA, MIT Press, 2004), p. 287, p. 296.
30. See p. 282 above. See also R. Cooter and B.J. Freedman (no. 10 above), 1,051, no. 13, referring to R. Romano, 'The Dynamics of Shareholder Litigation: An Empirical Study' (unpublished manuscript, 1990); cf. R. Posner, *Economic Analysis of Law* (3rd edn, Boston, Toronto, Little, Brown and Company, 1986), p. 418, on the paucity of litigation over trustees' investment decisions because most trust instruments give the trustee a discretionary power.
31. W. Bishop and D.D. Prentice, 'Some Legal and Economic Aspects of Fiduciary Remuneration' (1983) *Modern Law Review* 46, 289, 290 and 292.
32. See W. Bishop and D.D. Prentice (no. 31 above), 290; K.B. Davis, Jr. (no. 17 above), p. 6; R. Cooter and B.J. Freedman (no. 10 above), 1,049–1,051.
33. See J.-J. Laffont and D. Martimort, *The Theory of Incentives – The Principal-Agent Model* (Princeton and Oxford, Princeton University Press, 2002), p. 3, referring to this type of information problem as 'nonverifiability'.
34. Cf. L.S. Friedman, *The Microeconomics of Public Policy Analysis* (Princeton and Oxford: Princeton University Press, 2002), pp. 260–261 and 729–730.
35. Moral hazard had been considered only as a moral or ethical problem by most writers. It was Pauly who first explicitly pointed out that it is 'a result not of moral perfidy, but of rational economic behavior.' See M.V. Pauly, 'The Economics of Moral Hazard: Comment' (1968)

for a discount that compensates clients in advance for any potential disloyalty, so that in the end the market will deal with the problem by ensuring that only loyal behaviour is rational, even from the agent's perspective? There are situations in which this approach might work, but unfortunately there are more in which it won't if the problem is a conflict of interest in the narrow legal sense used here. In those situations, the principal does not know in advance whether his agent will be loyal and thus cannot negotiate *ex ante* compensation from a disloyal one, thereby providing effective incentives for agents to behave honestly.[36]

In many cases of moral hazard, no bad reputation can develop or stick, precisely because of the informational problems that created the moral hazard in the first place.[37] But other factors can also cause informational problems. Creating, gathering, or distributing information can be a costly exercise. Furthermore, in some cases, information in regard to the performance of an agent may not become known because nobody has an incentive to produce and/or distribute it, e.g. if all agents have the same bad characteristics to a greater or lesser degree.[38] In that case, no agent has an interest in drawing principals' attention to this 'problem'; although disclosure may increase the market share of the disclosing agent by showing him to be 'less bad' than the others, this gain could be more than compensated by the reduction in the overall size of the market as principals become aware of a risk.[39] Concerns about market effects are an important factor in the financial markets, where public confidence in the reliability of financial institutions is essential and loss of confidence in one institution can easily spill over to other institutions and the market as a whole. Moreover, a free rider problem can limit information production: it is extremely difficult to appropriate the benefits resulting from this kind of information to the one who produced it, as everybody can use the information once it is produced. As a result, nobody will be prepared to bear the cost of producing the

---

American Economic Review 58, 531, 535. In response, Arrow correctly pointed out that 'Mr. Pauly's wording suggests that "rational economic behavior" and "moral perfidy" are mutually exclusive categories. No doubt Judas Iscariot turned a tidy profit from one of his transactions, but the usual judgment of his behavior is not necessarily wrong.' See K.J. Arrow, 'The Economics of Moral Hazard: Further Comment' (1968) *American Economic Review* 58, 537, 538.

36. K.B. Davis, Jr. (no. 17 above), pp. 6–7 and 44; W. Bishop and D.D. Prentice (no. 31 above), 293; T. Frankel (no. 17 above), 812–813.
37. See p. 285 above.
38. Cf. I. Walter, 'Conflicts of Interest and Market Discipline' in C. Borio, W.C. Hunter, G.G. Kaufman and K. Tsatsaronis (eds), *Market Discipline across Countries and Industries* (Cambridge, MA, MIT Press, 2004), p. 175 and 185: 'Market discipline that helps avoid exploitation of such conflicts may be weakened if most of the competition is coming from a monoculture of similarly-structured firms which face precisely the same issues'; see also M. Knight, 'Three Observations on Market Discipline' in C. Borio, W.C. Hunter, G.G. Kaufman and K. Tsatsaronis (eds), *Market Discipline across Countries and Industries* (Cambridge, MA, MIT Press, 2004), p. 11 and 12: 'Experience indicates that markets are at their best when identifying a risky institution in an otherwise healthy financial system – the black sheep in the flock, as it were.'
39. Cf. R. Posner (no. 30 above), p. 349, citing the example of tar and nicotine content of cigarettes: 'even producers of cigarettes with low tar or nicotine content had no interest in voluntarily disclosing this to consumers not aware of the health risks of smoking.' See also no. 43, below, and accompanying text.

information. This is one of the main reasons why the market tends to produce insufficient information.[40] Finally, but no less significantly, the relationship between the principal and the agent may be what is sometimes referred to as a 'once-and-for-all' contract: a deal once reached or relationship at one time established and never subsequently changed or replaced. This factual characteristic renders the agent to some extent immune from competitive pressures.[41]

The result is that principals typically have a notion that some agents may be disloyal, but they do not know in advance whether their agent will act loyally or disloyally.[42] This in turn creates another type of asymmetric information; the principal, unlike the agent, will not generally know whether the latter is going to act loyally, and thus the agent possesses *hidden information* at the moment of transacting. In these circumstances, *ex post* knowledge about previous transactions with unreliable agents can only influence the way the principal perceives the total agent market *ex ante*. Principals will adjust by lowering their global expectations, because they cannot distinguish good agents from bad ones in advance. Through this mechanism, transactions with unreliable agents have external effects on loyal agents; even if they fully perform their duties, principals are not prepared to pay them full value because they want to cover themselves for the perceived risk that the agent may turn out to be disloyal. As a result, the market may suffer from so-called *adverse selection*: prices fall and loyal agents are priced out of the market if being honest is more costly to agents than being dishonest.[43]

If, for instance, disloyal agents confronted with conflicts of interest can charge lower fees than loyal agents with the same type of conflicts, but still make a profit because of the gains the disloyal agents realize by secretly pursuing interests other than those of the principal, the market mechanism alone is unlikely to solve this problem. Although principals may prefer agents without conflicts of interest, and would be willing to pay extra for them, and even though some loyal agents are prepared to ignore other potential conflicting interests, the market may end up offering too few, or in extreme cases no, loyal agents if principals cannot reliably recognize them.[44]

---

40. For instance, even large non-controlling shareholders may not want to invest in costly monitoring of corporate management, as the gains from this investment would perforce have to be shared with other free-riding investors. See R. Cooter and B.J. Freedman (no. 10 above), 1,049; K.B. Davis, Jr. (no. 17 above), p. 6; S. Levmore, 'Monitors and Freeriders in Commercial and Corporate Settings' (1982) *Yale Law Journal* 92, 49.
41. Cf. W. Bishop and D.D. Prentice (no. 31 above), 293; T. Frankel (no. 17 above), 815.
42. This problem is more systemic than might appear at first glance. It is not merely that principals cannot know in advance what kind of agent they are dealing with. There is also the fact that the problem is not a *bias* in the judgment of certain agents, but a *tendency towards a bias* in their judgment, which is not easy to counteract by *ex ante* measures. See M. Davis (no. 5 above), p. 12.
43. This is the modified appearance of Gresham's law ('bad' cars tend to drive out the good in the market for second-hand automobiles) discussed in the famous article by G.A. Akerlof, 'The Market for 'Lemons': Quality Uncertainty and the Market Mechanism' (1970) *The Quarterly Journal of Economics* 84, 488.
44. The circumstance that principals cannot reliably recognize disloyal agents in advance is a *conditio sine qua non* for occurrence of the so-called 'lemons' problem. The fact that reputation

In short, when agents and principals have conflicting interests and the agent has private information about his own actions during the performance of the service (*hidden action*) or about his loyalty at the time of transacting (*hidden information*), the result will not be the one predicted by classic economic theory. The first-best allocation of resources – the allocation that would be achieved in a world where all information was common knowledge and which was assumed to be efficient – will not automatically be realized by the market. This means that due to informational inadequacies, the market is not a sufficient mechanism for managing all conflicts of interest. Due to the informational difficulties the principal faces, the agency relationship involves an *agency problem* when the principal and agent have conflicting objectives. The problem is that the strategic behaviour of privately informed agents creates *agency costs*:[45] the difference between the level of aggregate utility created by the first-best allocation of resources and the suboptimal allocation resulting from the market equilibrium that is actually reached.[46]

II. CONFLICTS OF INTEREST IN ASSET MANAGEMENT

A. THE INEVITABILITY OF CONFLICTS OF INTEREST IN INSTITUTIONAL ASSET MANAGEMENT

A financial institution that offers asset management to individual clients, or manages the portfolios of collective investment schemes, essentially offers its clients its knowledge and skill in making and executing investment decisions. These decisions are supposed to be inspired exclusively by the investment interests of the client.

---

is such an important asset in certain professions is often invoked to argue against the lemons analysis as a justification for legal intervention in the market. See e.g. C. Shapiro, 'Investment, Moral Hazard, and Occupational Licensing' (1986) *Review of Economic Studies* 53, 843, 843: 'the lemons assumption that consumers have no seller-specific information seems inappropriate in the professional context, where reputations are so important.' But while this reputation-based argument may be relevant to agency problems relating to the competence and general honesty of the professional or service provider – factors on which their reputations actually depend – it is much less convincing when the agency problems stem from the requirement to completely exclude self-interest as a force directing behaviour in cases involving legal conflicts of interest (see p. 280–283 above). To my mind, this distinction is crucial. Given the extreme difficulty of monitoring such behaviour, and recognizing it afterwards, the importance of reputation may be too limited to be relevant in practice. To put it concretely: I do not think that any financial institutions have a significantly worse or better reputation than any others with regard to conflicts of interest; I do think that all multifunctional financial institutions are liable to suffer from general public distrust after certain scandals became generally known.

45. See J.-J. Laffont and D. Martimort (no. 33 above), p. 3.
46. Agency costs thus include the costs of structuring, monitoring, and bonding a set of contracts among agents with conflicting interests, plus the residual loss incurred because the cost of full enforcement of contracts exceeds the benefits. See M.J. Jensen and W.H. Meckling, 'Theory of the Firm: Managerial Behavior, Agency Costs and Ownership Structure' (1976) *J. Financial Econ.* 3, 305 and 308.

This promised, bargained for, and therefore legitimately expected loyalty creates a potential for conflicts of interest.

Such conflicts could theoretically be eliminated by changing the substance of the service rendered to the investor by the financial institution. Instead of its best efforts and full loyalty, the financial firm could promise to deliver a specified investment outcome. In the common typology of incentive contracts, this would be characterized as a pure rental contract; one in which the agent receives all the benefits resulting from his efforts and only pays the principal a fixed sum.[47] Applied to the financial investment sector, such deals of course exist, e.g. savings accounts, bond financing and some types of life insurance, where the financial institution gets the use of the principal's funds in exchange for a fixed payment.[48] This type of contract includes incentives for the agent to pursue the socially optimal result, because to do so is fully in his own interest, and therefore no conflicts of interest between the principal and the agent arise.

However, when the outcome of the agent's actions depend not just on his own efforts, but is also influenced by external factors, such a contract burdens the agent with all the risk. In situations in which the principal is less risk-averse than the agent, this type of contract would therefore not be optimal; the agent would refuse to pay the principal more than a relatively low fixed sum – because he wants to be compensated for bearing the full risk – while the principal would be prepared to bear this risk for less.[49] Thus, although such transactions do exist, they cannot replace the service of asset management, which is used precisely in those cases where the essence of the deal is that the investor is willing to bear more of the risk in return for a higher yield.

A second, theoretical way to avoid conflicts of interest would be to specify what decisions the agent should take or create strict parameters for his decision making in effect reducing his margin of discretion. Here, the risk from the effect of external factors on the outcome of the agent's actions would lie with the principal, but the actions of the agent would be constrained. In asset management, however, the investor cannot completely specify in advance what the manager has to do and when, because the services of the financial institution consist precisely in substituting the professional opinions and insights of the asset manager for the opinions of the less knowledgeable, skilled and/or experienced principal, or are called upon because the principal thinks it more efficient not to spend his own precious time on these matters or wants to take advantage of the economies of scale the agent can realize.[50] Moreover, at the time when the deal is concluded, no one can tell what circumstances

47. For a description of this common typology of incentive contracts, the pure rental contract and its economic characteristics, see H.R. Varian (no. 28 above), Section 36.7, p. 679 *et seq*.
48. See W. Bishop and D.D. Prentice (no. 31 above), 291.
49. R. Cooter and B.J. Freedman (no. 10 above), 1,046–1,049 and 1,067; K.B. Davis, Jr. (no. 17 above), pp. 6 and 17–18.
50. Cf. W. Bishop and D.D. Prentice (no. 31 above), 289; K.B. Davis, Jr. (no. 17 above), pp. 6 and 17–18; R. Cooter and B.J. Freedman (no. 10 above), 1,046–1,049; T. Frankel (no. 14 above), 128.

will prevail when the asset manager will have to act, and for investment decisions to be optimal, they must be adjusted to take those circumstances into account.[51]

In recent practice, however, there has been a clear tendency to restrict the freedom of portfolio managers by specifying what investment style the portfolio must follow and benchmarks for its performance.[52] These types of mechanisms can be seen as an attempt to alleviate the agency problems of asset management. But while it is to some extent possible to limit the freedom of the portfolio manager, it remains intrinsically inconsistent with the concept of asset management to completely specify the actions of the agent in advance. The financial service of asset management cannot effectively benefit the investor unless the portfolio manager enjoys some margin of discretion.[53]

Consequently, an asset manager will *necessarily* be confronted with conflicts of interest. However, the severity of this problem depends on what interests of the asset manager could potentially come into conflict with the customer's interests.

B. Possible Conflicts of Interest for Portfolio Managers

The following review will show that asset managers have a number of significant interests – albeit in some cases only through the interests of their other clients – that will be affected by the investment decisions they take on behalf of their clients. The following discussion provides a number of illustrative examples of possible conflicts, without attempting to be exhaustive.[54]

1. Conflicts Because the Manager has Several Clients

Conflicts can arise between the interests of the various clients of an asset manager because opportunities are limited. This type of conflict may be an unavoidable cost accompanying the economies of scale created by professionalizing asset management.

The total amount of effort the asset manager can provide is limited and may fall short of the cumulative optimal effort required to properly manage all the customers'

51. K.B. Davis, Jr. (no. 17 above), pp. 6 and 17–18; R. Cooter and B.J. Freedman (no. 10 above), 1,046–1,049.
52. See Bank for International Settlements (no. 22 above), pp. 19–20.
53. Cf. T. Frankel (no. 17 above), 809.
54. For examples of conflicts of interest, including some given here, see also G. McCormack, 'Conflicts of Interest, Chinese Walls and Investment Management' (1999) *International and Comparative Corporate Law Journal*, 1, 5 and 8–9; N.S. Poser, 'Chinese Wall or Emperor's New Clothes?' (1988) *The Company Lawyer* 9, 119–123, 159–168 and 203–209, which also appeared in *Mich. Y.B. Int'l Legal Stud.* 9 (1988), 91, and in *Rev. Sec. & Commodities Reg.* 21 (1988), 207; H. McVea, *Financial Conglomerates and the Chinese Wall. Regulating Conflicts of Interest* (Oxford, Clarendon Press, 1993), pp. 33–35. For a recent taxonomy of conflicts of interest faced by financial service providers, see I. Walter (no. 38 above), pp. 176–181.

portfolios, so that principals in effect compete for the agent's time and effort.[55] If it happens that not all individual customers are equally able to ascertain the amount of effort the manager actually devoted to their specific portfolios, or if not all customers are equally active, the asset manager has an incentive to spend proportionately more effort on the informed or critical customers than on the others,[56] thus in effect overcharging the vulnerable customers for the services they actually receive.[57] For another example: the manager may charge different fees (or other forms of compensation) to professional and to retail clients, not based on the actual costs he has incurred, but simply because retail clients are less able to exploit the competition among asset managers to their advantage.

Taking this to the extreme, even if the asset manager has limited resources to spend on all its customers, or the investment opportunity is too limited to allow all customers to participate to the extent they would prefer, and the asset manager treats all its customers equally by (for instance) allowing them all to share proportionately in the opportunity, each individual customer could theoretically complain that the duty of loyalty owed to him by the manager has not been honoured completely, because the asset manager has taken the interests of other customers into account.

Conflicts between the interests of clients can also arise because specific transactions performed for one or more clients can have repercussions for other clients.

---

55. For a discussion of such problems affecting real estate agents, compare S. Levmore, 'Commissions and Conflicts in Agency Arrangements: Lawyers, Real Estate Brokers, Underwriters, and Other Agents' Rewards' (1993) *Journal of Law and Economics* 36, 503, suggesting that uniform flat commissions, commonly used in real estate markets, serve to mitigate this problem of conflicts of interest among principals.
56. Cf. K.J. Hopt, 'Trusteeship and Conflicts of Interest in Corporate, Banking, and Agency Law: Toward Common Legal Principles for Intermediaries in the Modern Service-Oriented Society' in G. Ferrarini, K.J. Hopt, J. Winter and E. Wymeersch (eds), *Reforming Company and Takeover Law in Europe* (Oxford, Oxford University Press, 2004), p. 51–88, p. 53 ('Examples are the attribution of newly issued, oversubscribed securities to a favourite large client, a practice that unfortunately was common in the late German New Market') and p. 61; see also I. Walter (no. 38 above), p. 178 (on spinning); R.A. Schotland, 'Introduction' in *Abuse on Wall Street: Conflicts of Interest in the Securities Market* (Westport, CO, London, 20th Century Fund Report, Quorum Books, 1980), p. 3, pp. 11–12. For an actual example of a management company allocating executed orders among several collective investment schemes in response to subsequent price movements on the market, see *Conflicts of Interest of CIS Operators*, Report of the Technical Committee of the International Organization of Securities Commissions (s.l., IOSCO, 2000), p. 7, available at <www.iosco.org>; for an example of spinning, see G. Morgenson, 'Lawsuit Says Salomon Gave Special Deals to Rich Clients' *New York Times*, 18 July 2002, A1 (about a lawsuit claiming that Salomon favoured corporate clients' executives when allotting securities, in the hope of attracting or keeping their corporate business). If it is true, as has been alleged, that an experienced futures trader and personal friend of Hillary Rodham Clinton tried to tempt her into commodity trades by shifting other orders to her account after their profit became known, this would constitute another example. See 'Hillary Clinton Futures Trades Detailed' *The Washington Post*, 27 May 1994, A01.
57. This risk will only arise if individual customers cannot verify whether the asset manager has delivered the appropriate amount of effort, and/or – for whatever reason – cannot easily change their asset manager, because if they could, the market would ensure that the customers the asset manager expends less effort on are charged lower fees.

The value of the financial instruments in one client's portfolio, for example, can be influenced by transactions in those instruments entered into for other clients. Or the asset manager may organize transactions between the portfolios of two of its customers; or the knowledge that certain transactions have been decided for one portfolio may open opportunities for so-called front running on behalf of other portfolios.[58]

2. Conflicts Because the Manager Also Offers Other Services

Conflicts can also arise between the interests of clients and the interests of a financial institution that also offers other financial services to the same clients. In general, one can intuitively see that the more types of services an institution provides, the more conflicts of interest it will face.[59] The recent expansion of the range of activities by financial institutions offering asset management services has therefore increased the potential for such conflicts.[60]

---

58. I. Walter (no. 38 above), p. 177–178; see also K. Kelly and S. Craig, 'NYSE Probe Reaches 5 of 7 Specialist Firms' *The Wall Street Journal*, 18 April 2003, leading to SEC orders against these firms; see Releases Nos. 34–49498 to 34–49502 of 30 March 2004, available at <www.sec.gov/litigation/admin.shtml>. According to Art. 1(1) Directive 2003/6/EC of the European Parliament and of the Council of 28 January 2003 on Insider Dealing and Market Manipulation (Market Abuse) OJ L 96/16, 2003 (hereafter referred to as the 'MAD'), information 'conveyed by a client and related to the client's pending orders' may represent inside information for 'persons charged with the execution of orders concerning financial instruments'; front running by these persons, therefore, would violate the ban on trading using inside information envisaged in Art. 2(1) MAD. Information about a person's own pending orders, however, is not inside information as defined in the MAD (in a manner of speaking, one is allowed to front run one's own transactions). MAD does not specify how asset managers should treat the information they have about pending orders on behalf of their clients. For consistency, such information should also be considered as inside information for the asset manager concerned, but as this person is not charged with the *execution* of orders and as this information was not *conveyed by a client* and is not related to the *client's pending orders*, it most likely does not fall within the scope of the Directive.
59. See *International Conduct of Business Principles*, A Report of the Technical Committee of the International Organization of Securities Commissions (s.l. IOSCO, 1990), Part One, no. 9. See also I. Walter (no. 38 above), pp. 181–182; N.S. Poser (no. 54 above), pp. 119–120; A. Crockett, T. Harris, F.S. Mishkin and E.N. White, *Conflicts of Interest in the Financial Services Industry: What Should We Do About Them?*, Geneva Reports on the World Economy 5 (Geneva, International Center for Monetary and Banking Studies (ICMB) and London, Centre for Economic Policy Research (CEPR), (2003), p. 5: 'Conflicts of interest stand out most sharply . . . when an institution provides multiple financial services, thereby creating an opportunity for exploiting the synergies or economies of scope by inappropriately diverting some of their benefits.'
60. See Recital 29 in the preamble of the MiFID; see also the Explanatory Memorandum accompanying the Proposal for a Directive of the European Parliament and of the Council on Investment Services and Regulated Markets, and Amending Council Directives 85/611/EEC, Council Directive 93/6/EEC and European Parliament and Council Directive 2000/12/EC, COM(2002) 625 final, OJ C 71/62, 2003, p. 82; F. Buisson, 'La Directive sur les Marchés d'Instruments Financiers: Quels Enjeux pour la Protection des Investisseurs et le Maintien de l'Intégrité du Marché?' (2004/2) *Euredia – European Banking & Financial Law Journal – Revue européenne de Droit bancaire & financier*, 237, 245–246.

Typical examples include the firm that also offers order execution services and therefore has an incentive to execute all transactions on behalf of its clients itself even if alternatives may be better for the investor; or the firm that has an incentive to choose transactions it can carry out itself in preference to alternative transactions that would require other intermediaries.[61] The same can happen, of course, if the financial institution is a market maker in certain financial instruments,[62] or when the financial institution also internalizes client orders.[63] Deciding to invest, on behalf of an individually managed portfolio, in collective investment schemes sponsored or managed by the same financial group is another example. To complicate matters further, a firm may decide to invest on behalf of one collective portfolio in another collective investment scheme managed or sponsored by the same asset manager.[64] Other cases are the financial institution that also produces investment research and

---

61. Analogous problems can occur when the asset manager has an arrangement with some intermediary whereby the former receives kickback payments. For an actual example, see the IOSCO Report *Conflicts of Interest of CIS Operators* (no. 56 above), p. 6. For a discussion of conflicts of interest relating to the compensation of financial intermediaries, see J.-B. Zufferey, 'Conflicts of Interest with Respect to the Remuneration of Financial Intermediaries. Some Swiss and Comparative Aspects' in L. Thévenoz (ed.), *Aspects Juridiques de la Gestion de Fortune – Legal Aspects of Investment Management* (Brussels, Bruylant and Bern: Stämpfli, 1999), pp. 223–238.
62. For an example of collective investment schemes investing in real estate purchased from a related real estate company, see the IOSCO Report *Conflicts of Interest of CIS Operators* (no. 56 above), p. 5.
63. The European legislators had this type of conflict in mind when they broadly allowed internalization of orders in the MiFID. See COM(2002) 625 final (no. 60 above), p. 18:

    'The debate surrounding "internalisation" has thrown into sharper relief the already commonplace conflict of interest that arises when investment firms cumulate the functions of broker and dealer. Execution of client orders against the firms' proprietary positions begs the question of whether investors can be confident that their interests are paramount when the broker-dealer acts on their behalf. These concerns are exacerbated where an investment firm implements systems and procedures to maximise the number of client orders executed against proprietary positions or other client orders.'

    On internalization of orders, see e.g. D. Rolland and B. Bréhier, 'L'internalisation des ordres' *Banque & Droit* 102 (July-August 2005), 17; A. Caparrós, 'Understanding the New Regime for Internalisation of Order Flow in Europe' (2004/2) *Euredia – European Banking & Financial Law Journal – Revue européenne de Droit bancaire & financier*, 269; J.-J. Daigre, 'La libéralisation de l'exécution des ordres en interne au risqué de la fragmentation des marchés' (2004/2) *Euredia – European Banking & Financial Law Journal – Revue européenne de Droit bancaire & financier, 285.*
64. A comparable practice exists when financial institutions systematically promote so-called 'house products' to retail customers who are under the impression that they are receiving impartial investment advice. The recent trend towards so-called 'open architecture' does not eliminate this practice, as even then financial institutions usually only promote the products of suppliers with whom they have distribution agreements. See I. Walter (no. 38 above), pp. 178–179; for the example of Morgan Stanley being fined for organizing sales contests to sell in-house products, see National Association of Securities Dealers, Inc., *NASD Monthly Disciplinary Actions*, October 2003, p. D18, available at <www.nasd.com>, and A. Michaels and D. Wells, 'Morgan Stanley Fined over Mutual Funds' *Financial Times*, 17 September 2003, 32. For another example, see A. Lucchetti, 'Schwab Gives Own Funds Top Billing – Brokerage Firm's "Short List" Includes 4 of its Portfolios, Raising Concerns of Conflict' *Wall Street Journal*, 3 September

has an incentive not to use other research sources, and the financial institution that also offers asset depository services and therefore has an incentive not to use other depositories. A recent problematic example is the financial institution that provides credit or loans to investors, the proceeds of which can be used to fund investment transactions.[65]

In each of these examples, the financial institution has an incentive to use more of these other services it offers than would be optimal for the client. The best-known example is the 'churning' of the portfolio, where transaction frequency is higher than would be in the client's best interests in order to generate transaction fees for the financial institution.[66] Similarly, a financial institution could recover an undue proportion of its general investment research costs from its asset management clients by allocating to their accounts more such research than optimal.

The interests of clients using different services offered by the same financial institution can also conflict directly with each other. Such conflicts occur when the financial institution has a duty of loyalty to both clients. The most typical example in this category is the conflict between the interests of the clients whose portfolio is managed and the interests of the issuer of financial instruments which the financial institution has promised to place in the market.[67] The firm's duty to further the

---

2002; for a case in which a broker was fined because it had failed to disclose to its customers that it received huge incentives from a financial institution to promote its mutual funds through so-called neutral advice to its customers, see U.S. Securities and Exchange Commission, Administrative Proceeding Release No. 33–8520 of 22 December 2004 in the Matter of Edward D. Jones & Co., L.P., available at <www.sec.gov/litigation/admin/33–8520.htm>.

65. See I. Walter (no. 38 above), p. 178; cf. the recent disputes between Dexia Bank Nederland and various groups representing claimants and small investors which ended with a settlement agreement reached with the help of the late W.F. Duisenberg, former President of the European Central Bank. For more information about the settlement reached, see Dexia's website at <www.dexialease.nl>; for more information about the disputes and the share-leasing practice that caused them, see 'Wim Duisenberg, médiateur entre Dexia et les épargnants néerlandais' *Le Monde*, 16 February 2005, 18; 'Duisenberg to Mediate in Dexia Dispute' *Financial Times*, 11 February 2005. For a similar problem, see G. Morgenson, 'Salomon Faces Complaints Over Options at WorldCom' *New York Times*, 24 April 2001, C1; for the disciplinary decision in this matter, see New York Stock Exchange, Exchange Hearing Panel Decision 03-182, 1 October 2003, Citigroup Global Markets Inc. formerly known as Salomon Smith Barney Inc., available at <www.nyse.com/pdfs/03-182-183.pdf>.

66. See M. Mayer, 'Broker-Dealer Firms' in *Abuse on Wall Street. Conflicts of Interest in the Securities Market* (Westport, CN, London, 20th Century Fund Report, Quorum Books, 1980), p. 433, p. 436; N. S. Poser (no. 54 above), 121; I. Walter (no. 38 above), p. 179; see also U.S. Securities and Exchange Commission Investor Alert, 'Analyzing Analyst Recommendations' available at <www.sec.gov/investor/pubs_alpha.shtml>; L.S. Unger (Acting Chairman of the US Securities and Exchange Commission), 'Written Statement Concerning Conflicts of Interest faced by Brokerage Firms and their Research Analysts before the Subcommittee on Capital Markets, Insurance and Government Sponsored Enterprises of the House Committee on Financial Services', US House of Representatives, Hearing Entitled 'Analyzing the Analysts', Tuesday, 31 July 2001, p. 3, available in the 'Printed Hearings from 107th Congress' on the Committee's website, <www.financialservices.house.gov/hearings.asp>.

67. See K.J. Hopt (no. 56 above), p. 61; G. McCormack (no. 54 above), 8–9; R. Cranston, *Principles of Banking Law* (Oxford, Clarendon Press, 1997), p. 23; N.S. Poser (no. 54 above), 121; SEC

interest of the issuer in trying to successfully complete the offering creates an incentive to 'dump' the so-called '*queues d'émissions*' in portfolios it manages.[68]

Conflicts can also arise between the interests of asset management clients and those of the firm itself, because it also has clients who use other services. Even when the financial institution offers other services that do not imply a duty of loyalty towards those clients, the institution itself has an interest in keeping these customers happy so that they do not take their business elsewhere, or in attracting potential new customers for these services.[69] The asset management unit of a multifunctional financial institution, for example, may be tempted to use the voting rights attached to the portfolio's shares in a company that is a client of the investment banking arm of the conglomerate in the manner preferred by the management of that client company, which may not be in the best interests of the owner of the portfolio.[70] The opportunity to control a significant number of transactions on behalf of clients may also be a powerful argument to attract investment banking business, which would give the financial institution an incentive to use its asset management mandate to further the marketing interests of its investment banking division instead of maximizing the value of the portfolio for the client.[71]

Investor Alert, 'Analyzing Analyst Recommendations' (no. 66 above). For an example of an operator of a collective investment scheme investing managed funds in securities underwritten by an affiliated party to help the issuer reach minimum subscription standards, see the IOSCO Report *Conflicts of Interest of CIS Operators* (no. 56 above), p. 5.

68. See I. Walter (no. 38 above), p. 179; this is alleged to have happened in Belgium. See 'Rapport de la Commission des Finances' *Documents du Senat*, 1994–95, no. 1352/2, 89.
69. In general, larger companies are not pleased if their investment or commercial banker fails to show an interest in the securities they issue. See L.S. Unger (no. 66 above) pp. 3 and 13; SEC Investor Alert, 'Analyzing Analyst Recommendations' (no. 66 above).
70. See I. Walter (no. 38 above), p. 177, and in particular no. 9, pp. 22–23, offering the example of the 2001–2002 effort by Hewlett-Packard Co. to acquire Compaq Computer Corp., using its power over Deutsche Bank and Northern Trust Co., of which it was an important corporate finance client, to 'influence' voting by the asset management arm of these financial institutions. The asset management arm of Deutsche Bank was fined by the SEC for not disclosing its conflict of interest in the matter. See U.S. Securities and Exchange Commission, Administrative Proceedings Release No. IA-2160, In the matter of Deutsche Asset Management, Inc., 19 August 2003, available on the SEC website at <www.sec.gov/divisions/enforce/enforceactions.shtml>.
71. We have recently witnessed examples of such behaviour in the investment research sector. See in general 'Analyzing the Analysts', Hearings before the Subcommittee on Capital Markets, Insurance, and Government Sponsored Enterprises of the Committee on Financial Services, U.S. House of Representatives, 107th Congress, First Session, 14 June and 31 July 2001, Serial No. 107–25, available in the 'Printed Hearings from 107th Congress' on the Committee's website, <www.financialservices.house.gov/hearings.asp>; *Report on Analyst Conflicts of Interest*, Report of the Technical Committee of the International Organization of Securities Commissions (s.l., IOSCO, September 2003), available at <www.iosco.org>; for Europe, see e.g. the work of the Forum Group on Financial Analysts, appointed by the European Commission: Press Release IP/02/1763 of 28 November 2002, available at <www.europa.eu.int/rapid>, and *Financial Analysts: Best Practices in an Integrated European Financial Market*, Recommendations from the Forum Group to the European Commission Services, 4 September 2003, available at <www.europa.eu.int/comm/internal_market/securities/analysts/index_en.htm>.

3. Conflicts Because the Manager has a Stake in the Consequences of Transactions

If a financial institution also trades on its own account, or has a personal investment portfolio, it may have an interest in the consequences of transactions on behalf of clients.[72] A typical example would be transactions that can influence the market price of instruments in which the institution has a vested interest.[73] This can lead to abuses, particularly in the case of take-overs or buy-outs, where the manager exploits his control over the managed portfolios to influence the outcome of the transaction or battle by purchasing (or not purchasing, selling, or not selling, as the case may be) shares on behalf of clients.[74] Another case is the manager who channels transactions on behalf of its customers into instruments issued by related issuers, or uses transactions for the portfolios it manages to influence the market price of instruments issued by itself or by a related party.[75] In addition, a credit institution may have an interest in supporting a potentially troubled debtor by channelling investment into securities issued by that debtor, thus attempting to mitigate its own credit risk and in effect shifting it on to the managed portfolios.[76]

C. Resulting Agency Costs for Asset Management

The previous section demonstrated some of the conflicts of interest confronting asset managers. The question then becomes whether these conflicts create agency problems that cannot be solved by normal market forces based on standard legal rules and remedies; in other words, whether specific rules are required to redress the agency costs created by these conflicts of interest. Three types of reasons potentially justify intervention.

---

72. For an example involving an asset manager trading on behalf of clients and for his own account and making late allocations of these trades, see the IOSCO Report *Conflicts of Interest of CIS Operators* (no. 56 above), p. 10.
73. For a general discussion, see SEC Investor Alert, 'Analyzing Analyst Recommendations' (no. 66 above). A known practice is the so-called booster shots, where a financial institution immediately prior to the lock-up period – i.e. the period following an IPO during which the financial institution and/or its employees cannot sell the pre-IPO shares they own – supports the market price of the shares so as to liquidate its own position at a (higher) profit. See also L.S. Unger (no. 66 above), pp. 3, 6, 8 and 12.
74. For examples, see the IOSCO Report *Conflicts of Interest of CIS Operators* (no. 56 above), p. 7. See also K.J. Hopt (no. 56 above), p. 62.
75. For an example of an asset manager buying and selling a number of bonds issued by an affiliated company from and to that company, and even an example of a collective investment scheme buying and selling from and to the operator unlisted securities issued by that operator as part of its share capital, see the IOSCO Report *Conflicts of Interest of CIS Operators* (no. 56 above), p. 5.
76. L. Enriques (no. 3 above) p. 17, offers the recent examples of the behaviour of Italian banks in the Cirio and Parmalat cases. See also J.A.C. Santos, 'Commercial Banks in the Securities Business: A Review', Basle: BIS Monetary and Economic Department, Working Papers No. 56 (1998), p. 10; I. Walter (no. 38 above), p. 181. It is obviously in the interest of credit institutions to improve the creditworthiness of their borrowers. See also R. Cranston (no. 67 above), p. 23; N.S. Poser (no. 54 above), p. 121.

1. Adverse Impact on the Interests of the (Small?) Investor

The first complaint that one often hears is that conflicts of interest hurt the interests of the investor directly because some asset managers do not deliver the quality of service for which the customer has paid.[77] The increasing attention that has lately been paid to the conflicts of interest problem is partly explained by recent financial scandals breaking during a period of already relatively modest returns on investments, causing many investors to lose money contrary to their expectations.[78] Designing specific measures to regulate conflicts of interest is therefore often perceived as a necessary part of investor protection.[79]

However, this rationale assumes that the investor is not able to protect his own interests by negotiating *ex ante* compensation, e.g. by paying a lower asset management fee to compensate for the risk posed by the conflicts of interest;[80] by

---

77. For instance, Investars.com calculated *post factum* that from January 1997 to May 2001 only four of the 19 largest US brokerage firms gave investment advice that would have realized a surplus value, and the highest return that would have resulted from following the advice of any one of these firms would only have been 7.6 per cent, although during that same period the S&P 500 rose by 58 per cent and the NASDAQ more than doubled. See D.W. Tice (Portfolio Manager, Prudent Bear Fund, and publisher of the institutional research service 'Behind the Numbers'), 'Analyzing the Analysts: Are Investors Getting Unbiased Research from Wall Street', Testimony before the Subcommittee on Capital Markets, Insurance and Government Sponsored Enterprises of the House Committee on Financial Services, US House of Representatives, Hearing Entitled 'Analyzing the Analysts', Tuesday, June 14, 2001, p. 16 *et seq*., available under 'Printed Hearings from 107th Congress' on the Committee's website <www.financialservices.house.gov/hearings.asp>. For other more recent figures see <www.investars.com>.
78. See N. Moloney, 'Time to Take Stock on the Markets: The Financial Services Action Plan Concludes as the Company Law Action Plan Rolls Out' (2004) *International and Comparative Law Quarterly* 53, 999 and 1,003; A. Crockett, T. Harris, F.S. Mishkin and E.N. White (no. 59 above), p. 1–2; see also J.-B. Zufferey, Chapter 7, p. 216 above. In general, see P. Klurer, 'Mainsprings of Financial Services Regulations. Towards a Dynamic Model of Understanding Changes in Legal, Regulatory and Ethical Risks of the Financial Services Industry' in R. Waldburger, Ch. M. Baer, U. Nobel and B. Bernet (eds), *Wirtschaftsrecht zu Beginn des 21. Jahrhunderts, Festschrift für Peter Nobel zum 60. Geburtstag* (Berne, Stämpfli 2005), pp. 575, 578.
79. See e.g. Recital 29 in the preamble of the MiFID: 'It is...necessary to provide for rules to ensure that . . . conflicts [of interest] do not adversely affect the interests of . . . [the] clients [of investment firms].' See also COM(2002) 625 final (no. 60 above), p. 82, discussing the conflict of interest rules as part of the rules on investor protection in the proposed MiFID.
80. Cf. J. A. C. Santos (no. 76 above), p. 11: 'economic theory suggests that if agents are moderately rational, when they enter into a contracting relationship they will consider the other party's incentives and, as a result, they will not generally be fooled . . . .If investors perceive that a bank has been exploiting a certain conflict of interest they can take that into account by applying a 'lemons' discount to the bank's products affected by such conflict.' I would add that if investors can perceive the potential conflicts of interest risk but cannot distinguish between firms that would behave loyally and those that would not – which seems to be the case – they will apply a 'lemons' discount to the products of all these firms (see no. 43 above and accompanying text). If the investors can distinguish between the types of firms, which is what Santos appears to assume, the adverse selection problem analyzed by Akerlof (no. 43 above) simply does not arise. Therefore the term 'lemons discount' cannot properly be used for a discount that is applied to a 'bad' provider but not a 'good' one.

negotiating specific contractual duties and remedies for potential abuses of conflicts of interest by the financial institution;[81] or simply by making less use of these financial services and thus discounting the risk posed by the conflicts of interest.[82] The investor is only 'harmed' in so far as he pays for more than he actually receives. If the conflict of interest risk is fully reflected in the market price for asset management services, the interests of the investor do not need any special protection not accorded to anybody else's interests. In that sense, the potentially self-serving behaviour of asset managers is not 'bad' *per se*, as long as it is reflected in the price paid for the service by the investor.[83]

Therefore, from an investor protection perspective, conflicts of interest only warrant special attention if the market mechanism has failed to take them into account.[84] However, for this type of market failure to occur, asset managers would have to be able to effectively conceal any potential conflicts of interest, because if enough investors become aware of the problem, the market price for asset management services and/or the demand for such services will be forced down to take account of the anticipated risk. If conflicts of interest are a generally known problem, the market conditions for asset management services will protect the interests of the investor unless they systematically underestimate the risk or its consequences. Moreover, if the essence of the investor protection issue is a market failure because of missing information, the obvious legal way to overcome this problem is to impose disclosure, and disclosure alone should suffice.

From the point of view of protecting the investor, one could easily conclude that these measures should focus particularly on the small or unsophisticated investor, who is allegedly in most need of protection.[85] This would avoid the usual problem

81. Cf. J.R. Boatright, 'Conflict of Interest in Financial Services: A Contractual Risk-Management Analysis', paper presented at the Tenth Annual Meeting Promoting Business Ethics, St. John's University, 2003, The Hastings Center, Garrison, NY, 10 April 2003, available at <www.sba/luc/edu/research/wpapers/040602-B.pdf>; J.R. Macey, 'Fiduciary Duties as Residual Claims. Obligations to Nonshareholder Constituencies from a Theory of the Firm Perspective' (1999) *Cornell Law Review* 84, 1266, 1268, who both argue that fiduciary duties or more generally conflict of interest rules, in so far as they are embodied in law, are default rather than mandatory rules, since they are adopted voluntarily when the contract is made: in fact they are the outcome of the normal workings of the market mechanism. See also F.H. Easterbrook and D.R. Fischel, 'Contract and Fiduciary Duty' (1993) *Journal of Law and Economics* 36, 425.
82. Compare the way in which investors discount the forecasts and recommendations of financial analysts who are confronted with conflicts of interest, discussed in M. Dubois and P. Dumontier, Chapter 6, p. 194–195 above; see also A. Crockett, T. Harris, F.S. Mishkin and E.N. White (no. 59 above), pp. 75–76, giving several examples where they see the market mechanism discounting the bias created by conflicts of interest in several sectors.
83. Cf. K.B. Davis, Jr. (no. 17 above), p. 20.
84. See K.B. Davis, Jr. (no. 17 above) for an analysis and explanation of the differing fiduciary rules applicable to various types of fiduciaries (trustees, corporate managers, partners, etc.) based on the varying market conditions affecting the services they offer. According to his thesis, fiduciary law interferes more when the market does not adequately protect the interests of the beneficiary and less when the market seems to be functioning well.
85. The inequality between investors and financial institutions is sometimes invoked as a reason for applying stricter rules for conflicts of interest in the financial sector. See e.g. H. McVea (no. 54

with applying uniform standards to situations involving heterogeneous customers, viz. setting the bar too high for services provided to clients that need and prefer less protection.[86] However, one would expect the market to protect all investors alike, unless there is a particular reason why it should not do so. So why would the market mechanism offer less protection against conflicts of interest to retail investors than to professionals, so that one type of investor requires more protection than the other?

A first situation in which the market may fall short of protecting the unsophisticated investor is when the asset manager can effectively separate the retail and the professional investor markets, so that the prices and conditions in one are not directly influenced by those in the other. Only then will the professional investors' scepticism not lower the price unsophisticated customers must pay. In those circumstances, it may help to impose extra disclosure requirements for retail investors that are not necessary for professional clients.

Another circumstance in which the market may fail to protect the interests of the investor is when the latter is too 'loyal' to his asset manager to consider changing to another, more competitive manager. Here, a clear case can be made for special protection of retail investors. Given their limited knowledge of, insight into, and experience with financial instruments and the workings of the financial markets and in particular the specific risks involved, most retail investors are incapable of safeguarding their own investment needs. In reality, such investors have only one rational investment choice and that is to ask a financial institution to assist them in protecting those interests.[87] Professional investors are much more likely to be able to handle their own investment needs, and this provides them with an alternative to using an external professional asset manager. But even when professional investors do use the services of a professional portfolio manager, they tend to shop around much more than retail investors do. In many countries, small investors use one bank branch for all their financial needs, and it takes a big disappointment in this relationship for the client to switch banks. Thus, these financial institutions become partially shielded from competition for the individual services they render to these retail customers.

---

above), pp. 33–35; *Jirna Ltd v. Mister Donut of Canada Ltd*, 13 D.L.R. (3d) 645 (Ont. H.C., 1970) 22 D.L.R. (3d) 639 (Ont. C.A., 1972) 40 D.L.R. (3d) 303 (S.C.C., 1973), cited by E. J. Weinrib, 'The Fiduciary Obligation' (1975) *University of Toronto Law Journal* 25, 1, 6: no special protection against conflicts was imposed (e.g. fiduciary duties), *inter alia* because no such protection would be warranted in transactions between experienced business people with equal bargaining strength 'acting at arm's length'.

86. Cf. H.E. Leland, 'Quacks, Lemons, and Licensing: A Theory of Minimum Quality Standards' (1978) *Journal of Political Economy* 87, 1,328, 1,336–1,337.

87. It is interesting to see that, even though the direct accessibility of financial markets has increased of late, e.g. through the use of the internet, at the same time the share of household wealth managed by financial institutions has increased sharply. See J. Franks, C. Mayer and L. Correia da Silva, *Asset Management and Investor Protection. An International Analysis* (Oxford, Oxford University Press, 2003), p. 33 *et seq.*; see also E.P. Davis and B. Steil, *Institutional Investors* (Cambridge, MA, MIT Press, 2001).

In general, however, the agency problem created by a conflict of interest does not arise because the parties are in an unequal bargaining position at the time of transacting, which is the traditional justification for introducing measures to protect consumers. Rather this agency problem arises because investors are vulnerable to disloyal behaviour inherent in the essential characteristics of the asset management relationship *resulting from* the agreement.[88] This is because the asset manager's power over the investor's interests intrinsically is, and indeed must be, broader than is strictly necessary for him to be able to do the job: 'the purpose for which the [asset manager] is allowed to use his delegated power is narrower than the purposes for which he is capable of using that power.'[89] This means that the essential breeding ground for conflicts is in principle the same, independent of the type of investor or his level of sophistication. As a general principle, therefore, intervention should not be justified on the basis of the need to protect small investors, since, while retail investors do have special problems, the basic conflict of interest problem is essentially the same for small investors and sophisticated, informed investors capable of bargaining or negotiating for their own interests.

2. Undermining Capital Market Integrity

But there is more: the fact that asset managers may not fully deliver on their promises to investors affects not only those investors' interests, but also the wider economy. Conflicts of interest in asset management may jeopardize the integrity of the financial markets. These markets perform an important function in our economy, directing available capital to alternative productive purposes or, looking at it from the opposite perspective, offering alternative financing techniques for productive projects. To be efficient, investors' capital should be invested in the instruments that offer them the maximum utility given their needs, including their risk preferences and time horizons. If because of their personal interests financial intermediaries such as asset managers divert invested moneys to suboptimal uses, the financial markets fail in their crucial function: the optimal allocation of capital.[90] Bias in this intermediation could lead to overinvestment in certain economic sectors at the

88. E. J. Weinrib (no. 85 above), 6; T. Frankel (no. 17 above), 810.
89. T. Frankel (no. 17 above) 810.
90. See R. Glantz, 'Oral Testimony before the Subcommittee on Capital Markets, Insurance and Government Sponsored Enterprises of the House Committee on Financial Services', US House of Representatives, Hearing Entitled 'Analyzing the Analysts', Tuesday, 31 July 2001, p. 5: 'That's not only bad for the average investor, it undermines one of the primary reasons for having a stock market – the efficient allocation of investment dollars', available under 'Printed Hearings from 107th Congress' on the Committee's website, <www.financialservices.house.gov/hearings.asp>; D. W. Tice (no. 77 above) p. 15 *et seq.*; see also H. McVea (no. 54 above), p. 30.

cost of underinvestment in others,[91] overinvestment in certain regions resulting in underinvestment elsewhere, or overinvestment in certain types of instruments to the detriment of others.[92] From this perspective, designing measures to minimize these negative effects on the economy as a whole by tackling the conflicts of interest problem in the financial sector is not an issue of investor protection, but is instead in the general public interest, including the business interests of companies.[93]

But here one might ask whether the essence of this problem is not akin to the issues involved in vertical integration and restraints in competition policy.[94] Isn't a financial institution interested in steering investors towards particular investments comparable to a supermarket interested in steering customers towards a particular brand, perhaps not even offering competing brands, because it has a preferential distribution arrangement with a certain manufacturer? Wouldn't the problem be solved if there was sufficient competition on the asset management market among financial institutions with various vertical links creating conflicts of interest? In other words, wouldn't the problem be solved if investors split their assets over a number of financial institutions each with a limited market share?[95]

---

91. E.g. the difficulties faced by companies with more 'traditional' business plans when endeavouring to raise capital through new public security issues during the so-called dot-com boom of the late 1990s.
92. For instance, overinvestment in newly offered financial instruments to the detriment of underinvestment in the secondary markets, when financial institutions stand to earn more through IPOs than through brokerage on the secondary market.
93. Cf. K.J. Hopt, 'Prävention und Repression von Interessenkonflikten im Aktien-, Bank- und Berufsrecht' in S. Kalss, Chr. Nowotny and M. Schauer (eds), *Festschrift Peter Doralt zum 65. Geburtstag* (Vienna, Manzsche Verlags- und Universitätsbuchhandlung, 2004), p. 213, p. 214: specific regulation of conflicts of interest is often intended 'eine bestimmte Interessenwahrungsfunktion zu sichern oder einen ohne saubere Interessenwahrung nicht ordentlich funktionierenden Markt zu fördern.' It has been suggested that, given the importance of delegated portfolio management relationships in modern financial markets, the study of agency aspects of delegated portfolio management, and particularly of suitable incentive contracts, performance measuring systems, etc., should focus on the general equilibrium implications of these mechanisms: see L. Stracca, 'Delegated Portfolio Management. A Survey of the Theoretical Literature', ECB Working Paper No. 520, September 2005, p. 32, available at <www.ecb.int> and <www.ssrn.com/abstract=781088>, to be published in the *Journal of Economic Surveys*.
94. One could argue that this problem is in essence one of a diminishing distinction or demarcation between markets on the one hand and intermediaries or agents active on markets on the other, as more allocation decisions are taken within a financial institution instead of being the result of a traditional market transaction between financial institutions. Cf. K. Vuillemin, 'Libre propos sur la directive relative aux marchés d'instruments financiers 2004/39/CE' (September–October 2004) *Bulletin Joly Bourse* 119, 579, 580: 'La place financière européenne est devenue complexe, rendant de plus en plus invisible la frontière marchés et intermédiaires.'
95. Cf. Bank for International Settlements (no. 22 above), pp. 32–33: 'Avoidance of explicit and implicit barriers to market entry: To support market efficiency and liquidity, and to help limit volatility, care should be taken to maintain an environment that encourages market entry by pooled investment vehicles in general and by specialised investment pools seeking to exploit arbitrage opportunities in particular. . . . A similar reasoning applies to other parts of the institutional investment industry, particularly if these are characterised by a high degree of concentration and potential conflicts of interest.'

3. Suboptimal Asset Management Market Efficiency

Finally, there is a case for tackling the conflicts of interest problem in asset management, due to the effect it may have on investors' confidence in financial institutions in general.[96] In financial markets, where institutions are particularly dependent on public confidence, this issue must be taken very seriously.[97]

First, an individual financial institution under suspicion of behaving disloyally as an asset manager may suffer by losing customers, and consequently the firm's market value may diminish.[98] If this suspicion is correct, of course, the consequence is desirable and serves as a market mechanism to deter misbehaviour. However, if the suspicion is unwarranted, it may be extremely difficult – indeed nearly impossible – for the financial institution to convince the public of its honesty. Moreover, suspicions of dishonesty can easily spill over from one institution to another. Therefore, it is in the interests of every financial institution that no such suspicions should arise as a result of the behaviour of other institutions, and this may require regulatory intervention.[99]

Secondly, as already discussed,[100] the price investors are prepared to pay for asset management services may drop if they anticipate that conflicts of interest will lead to abuse by some managers. As a consequence, managers who act disloyally when faced with conflicts of interest may actually increase their market share, because they are better able to remain profitable under these market conditions. This, in turn, will encourage asset managers to abuse conflicts of interest. In other words, the market mechanism may in fact aggravate the problem rather than solving it, due to the phenomenon of adverse selection.[101] In the end, individual investors will be less prepared to use the services of asset managers than would be socially optimal, or will receive less honest services than they would desire.[102] Instead,

---

96. See also H. McVea (no. 54 above), pp. 4 and 30.
97. For a study highlighting the serious impact of limited investor trust in 'the system,' see L. Guiso, P. Sapienza and L. Zingales, 'Trusting the Stock Market', National Bureau of Economic Research (NBER) Working Paper 11648, September 2005, available at <www.nber15.nber.org/papers/w11648>.
98. See I. Walter (no. 38 above), pp. 183–184.
99. Cf. J. Clijsters, 'La déontologie bancaire et financière. Le point de vue d'un banquier' in *La déontologie bancaire et financière – The Ethical Standards in Banking & Finance*, Cahiers AEDBF/EVBFR-Belgium (Brussels: Bruylant, 1998), p. 113, p. 116.
100. See p. 287 above.
101. As Akerlof pointed out:

> 'The presence of people in the market who are willing to offer inferior goods tends to drive the market out of existence . . .. It is this possibility that represents the major costs of dishonesty – for dishonest dealings tend to drive honest dealings out of the market . . ..The cost of dishonesty, therefore, lies not only in the amount by which the purchaser is cheated; the cost also must include the loss incurred from driving legitimate business out of existence.' G. A. Akerlof (no. 43 above), 495.

102. Cf. *International Conduct of Business Principles*, A Report of the Technical Committee of the International Organization of Securities Commissions, (s.l., IOSCO, 1990), Part One, no. 7:

they may choose alternative ways of managing their savings, perhaps substituting direct investment in securities for delegated portfolio management, or they may avoid investing in securities altogether,[103] realizing a less than optimal return on their savings while at the same time increasing the cost of capital to enterprises.[104] Here, again, it would appear that tackling the problem of conflicts of interest in asset management – and financial institutions in general – is a matter of general public interest, not merely an issue of investor protection.

III. LEGAL APPROACHES TO CONFLICTS OF INTEREST IN ASSET MANAGEMENT

A. IMPOSING FIDUCIARY DUTIES

Probably the oldest legal concept specifically developed to deal with conflicts of interest is the so-called fiduciary law, originally developed in equity in common law jurisdictions. Unlike in continental European civil law countries, in which no such special system exists, not only does fiduciary law impose a duty of loyalty in circumstances where standard law does not, but – and this is the characteristic most relevant to our discussion here – this equitable or fiduciary duty of loyalty also differs from a duty of loyalty as it would be imposed by non-fiduciary or standard private law.[105] Without attempting to discuss this rather peculiar system of principles, rules and remedies fully or in depth,[106] I must draw attention to a few particularly relevant elements.

The first element deserving our attention is the applicable remedy. To appreciate this, we first must return to the 'standard' – in the sense of 'non-fiduciary' – legal relationship between a principal and an agent imposing on the agent an open-ended

---

'Smaller investors, whether they participate directly in the markets, or indirectly through mutual funds or pension funds, continue to be considered vital to the functioning of the markets. Their continued participation depends upon confidence in the integrity of the market and in the firms with which they deal.'

103. See also R.A. Schotland (no. 56 above), pp. 12–13.
104. Recent research has suggested that delegated portfolio management leads to a larger demand for risky assets than if individual investors were to invest in these assets directly, so the overall result of more widespread use of delegated portfolio management may be a lower required equity premium, consistent with market evolution in the 1990s. See S. Kapur and A.G. Timmermann, 'Relative Performance Evaluation Contracts and Asset Market Equilibrium' (2005) *Economic Journal* 115, 1,077, 1,078. It may therefore be assumed that decreasing recourse to delegated portfolio management will lead to a lower demand for risky assets and/or a higher required equity premium.
105. Thus a duty cannot be described as 'fiduciary' or equitable merely because it requires 'loyalty' as a normative content. There is a clear distinction between a 'legal' or 'standard private law' duty of loyalty and a 'fiduciary' duty of loyalty. Unfortunately, in much of the continental European literature, any duty that requires loyalty is called a fiduciary duty, rendering the term rather meaningless.
106. Fiduciary duties have been referred to as 'the law's most exotic species.' See D. A. DeMott (no. 10 above), 923.

duty of best efforts or a duty of care. In this type of relationship, the agency problem is that the agent may shirk his duties, and try to spend less effort or care than is required. The standard legal remedy against such a breach of duty, in both tort and contract, is full compensation for the damage suffered by the principal.[107] The damages that would be payable for a breach of duty, as anticipated at the time of acting, are almost always larger than the effort the agent thinks he will save by shirking his duties.[108] In this sense, damages as a remedy for a breach of a duty of care may seem punitive from the wrongdoer's viewpoint: he risks paying more than he stands to gain.[109] In general, therefore, there is no reason to think that this remedy will not provide an adequate incentive for the debtor to comply. The economic agency problem involved in a duty of care will thus generally be effectively addressed by the 'normal' or 'standard' legal technique of liability for damages caused by one's own fault which is known in both common and civil law systems.[110]

When the debtor is under a duty of loyalty, however, the situation becomes essentially different. Here the remedy of damages or compensating the victim alone will by definition not constitute a credible incentive to the debtor to comply. Such a remedy will steer the debtor away from a breach if he thinks his actions will damage the principal more than they benefit him, the agent, but not if he believes that he can gain more from breaching the duty than this breach would cost the principal. In other words, the remedy of damages encourages the agent to weigh his own interests against the interests of the principal when deciding how to act, but does not encourage him to *exclude* his own interests from the decision-making process, which is what the duty of loyalty requires. Thus, the standard legal technique of liability leading to full compensation of the victim does not adequately address the economic agency problem in what we are referring to as conflicts of interest.

---

107. For a general discussion of why damages might be a more efficient remedy against an agent failing in his duty of care than forcing him to disgorge his profits, see A.M. Polinsky and S. Shavell, 'Should Liability Be Based on the Harm to the Victim or the Gain to the Injurer?' (1994) *Journal of Law, Economics & Organization* 10, 427.
108. If the anticipated damage from the agent's behaviour does not exceed the anticipated cost of the effort required to prevent the damage, the agent will not usually be deemed to have acted negligently and therefore there will be no remedy. This, of course, assumes that the negligence standard applied approaches the so-called Learned Hand Formula, most clearly formulated by Judge Learned Hand of the US Court of Appeals for the Second Circuit in *United States v. Carroll Towing Co.*, 159 F.2d 169, 173–174 (2nd Cir. 1947), which defines negligence as a function of the probability of a harmful event occurring or the magnitude of the risk (P), the extent of the damage that may result or the gravity of the harm (L) and the cost of preventing the occurrence of the harmful event or the burden of prevention (B): according to this formula conduct is negligent if $B < PL$. See also *Restatement (Second) of Torts* § 291 (1965); see for this concept of negligence in general R.A. Posner, 'A Theory of Negligence' (1972) *Journal of Legal Studies*, 1, 29.
109. R. Cooter and B.J. Freedman (no. 10 above), 1,059–1,060.
110. It may of course occur that information problems make it prohibitively difficult for the victim to prove the debtor's fault. However, this problem could effectively be dealt with by shifting the burden of proof, rendering the debtor liable unless he shows that sufficient effort was expended.

For breach of a duty of loyalty, fiduciary law uses a remedy that is much more appropriate from an economic perspective. The agent must disgorge or transfer to the beneficiary all his profits or gains from his disloyal action.[111] This remedy – or the *no profit rule* as this principle is also called – places the disloyal agent in the position he would have been in had he not breached his duty of loyalty and thus eliminates the incentive for him to act disloyally.[112]

However, replacing the remedy of damages by disgorgement does not resolve the problem of enforcing the duty of loyalty. From the perspective of the potential wrongdoer, the anticipated cost of a breach of duty is never equal to the actual cost of the remedy if imposed; in fact, the cost of the remedy is likely to be discounted by the unlikelihood of it being imposed. For a duty of loyalty, the chance of being caught is far lower than with most other types of duties, because of the informational problems already discussed.[113] Therefore, even with a remedy such as disgorgement, the anticipated cost of being disloyal is far too often outweighed by the expected gains.[114] This brings us to the second particularity of fiduciary law as a special technique to tackle conflicts of interest: the presumption of wrongdoing.

Under standard private law, the principal would have to prove that the agent breached his duty in order to be able to invoke remedies. Applied to a duty of loyalty, this would require the principal to show that the agent actually was inspired by interests other than the principal's, and as we have said, this will not often be possible in practice.[115] Under fiduciary law, however, this burden of proof is replaced by the presumption that an agent faced with a conflicting personal interest has acted in furtherance of that interest.[116] In some cases, the fiduciary can escape by proving that his actions are objectively defensible and in the interest of the

---

111. See in general F.H. Easterbrook and D.R. Fischel (no. 81 above), 425; D.A. DeMott (no. 10 above), 882; T. Frankel (no. 17 above), 827–827: 'By classifying a relation as fiduciary, the law creates strong property rights for the entrustor as against his fiduciary' and 'By declaring that a person is a fiduciary, the law shifts the beneficial ownership (the entitlement to benefit from the power [held by the fiduciary]) to the entrustor and leaves the fiduciary with mere legal title. This shift vests in the entrustor a property right in the power. The entrustor can enforce the prohibition against abuse of power directly against the fiduciary by strong remedies available to an owner of property.'
112. K.B. Davis, Jr. (no. 17 above), p. 45–46; R. Cooter and B.J. Freedman (no. 10 above), 1,052 and 1,073, quoting *LAC Minerals Ltd. v. International Corona Resources Ltd.*, 61 D.L.R.4th 14, 47–48 (Can. 1989) ('The imposition of a remedy which restores an asset to the party who would have acquired it but for a breach of fiduciary duties or duties of confidence acts as a deterrent to the breach of duty and strengthens the social fabric those duties are imposed to protect.'); W. Bishop and D.D. Prentice (no. 31 above), 309, quoting J. Rand in *Midcon Oil & Gas Ltd. v. New British Dominion Oil Co. Ltd.*, (1958) 12 D.L.R. (2nd) 705, 716: '[Equity] by an absolute interdiction . . . puts temptation beyond the reach of the fiduciary by appropriating its fruits.'
113. See p. 285 above.
114. R.R. Cooter and B.J. Freedman (no. 10 above), 1,052.
115. See p. 285 above.
116. R. Cooter and B.J. Freedman (no. 10 above), 1,048 and 1,053–1,055: 'To overcome difficulties in proof, the law infers disloyalty from its appearance, presuming that a fiduciary will appropriate the principal's asset when it is in her self-interest to do so.'

beneficiary, but in many cases the presumption is irrebuttable and hence results in a *per se* prohibition of action when confronted with a conflict of interest, because any action in such circumstances will result in liability. In effect, these presumptions help reduce the incentive problem by increasing the chances of being caught.[117] If the agent is not allowed to act when confronted with a conflict of interest – this is often referred to as the *no conflict rule* – the only remaining risk for the principal is that the agent may be able to keep his conflicting interests a secret.[118]

In theory, both characteristics of fiduciary law – the remedy of disgorgement and the presumption of wrongdoing when a conflict of interest is present – seem particularly appropriate to address the agency problem posed by conflicts of interest. Fiduciary law offers the principal a basis for a realistic *ex post* reckoning: if there is any reason to believe the agent may have behaved disloyally, he will have to transfer all his gains to the principal. This eliminates the *ex ante* incentive for the agent to act disloyally, as he will not anticipate any gain from disloyal behaviour if he knows he will have to turn over any such profits to the principal anyway. Disloyal behaviour is no longer in the agent's interest and hence the conflict of interest effectively disappears. This makes fiduciary law in theory a good way of ensuring that principals will be prepared to 'trust' their agents to the extent required to realize efficient market outcomes.[119]

However, imposing fiduciary duties on asset managers poses many problems in modern commercial practice. As we have seen, financial institutions offering asset management services are almost necessarily confronted with conflicts of interest,[120] and thus fiduciary law would very often, if not always, require them to abstain from acting on behalf of their clients. Also, applying the no-profit rule would be impractical: even the financial institution itself is unlikely to be aware of all the indirect gains it could have realized through its actions on behalf of its clients. Fiduciary law, with all its strictness, was developed at a time when commercial and financial transactions and firms were relatively simple.[121] It does not fit well with the much more complicated financial services of today, the large-scale organization of financial services that require loyalty, or the tendency to create multifunctional financial institutions that combine almost all financial services under one roof.[122] It

117. R. Cooter and B.J. Freedman (no. 10 above), 1,054.
118. K.B. Davis, Jr. (no. 17 above), p. 45.
119. Of course, fiduciary law developed from equity precisely in cases where the Chancery wanted to protect the 'trust' or 'confidence' one party had placed in another in order to make such relationships possible. See L.S. Sealy, 'Fiduciary Relationships' (1962) *Cambridge Law Journal*, 69, 69–72; D.A. DeMott (no. 10 above), 880.
120. See Section II.A above.
121. See R. Cranston, 'Conflicts of Interest in the Multifunctional Financial Institution' (1990) *Brooklyn Journal of International Law* 16, 125, 128; P. Finn, 'Fiduciary Law and the Modern Commercial World' in E. McKendrick (ed.), *Commercial Aspects of Trusts and Fiduciary Obligations* (Oxford, Clarendon Press, 1992), p. 7, pp. 19–20; H. McVea (no. 54 above), p. 147.
122. H. McVea, 'Conflicts of Interest – Regulatory Rules and the Common Law' in R. Rider and M. Asche (eds), *The Fiduciary, the Insider and the Conflict* (Dublin, Sweet & Maxwell, 1995), p. 131, p. 142; R. Cranston (no. 67 above), p. 24; N.S. Poser (no. 54 above), p. 165.

is therefore unsurprising that, in practice, fiduciary duties are not enforced as strictly as one would expect against financial institutions.[123] If they were, the indirect effect would be to preclude financial institutions from combining asset management with other financial services. This would turn the conduct rules created by fiduciary law into an effective structural bar, requiring disaggregation of multifunctional financial institutions.[124]

B. Regulatory Conduct of Business Rules

1. A Regulatory General Standard of Loyalty

The EC's harmonized financial regulation imposes a duty of loyalty on all asset managers. For individual portfolio management, Article 19(1) of the Market in Financial Instruments Directive ('MiFID')[125] requires an investment firm to 'act honestly, fairly and professionally in accordance with the best interests of its clients,'[126] and under the Undertakings for Collective Investment in Transferable Securities Directive ('UCITS Directive'),[127] comparable requirements exist for collective portfolio management.[128]

But what does this add to the existing legal landscape? We have pointed out that a duty to act in the exclusive interests of the customer is already included in the asset management contract, at least implicitly, and therefore the investor can use contractual remedies under applicable national law if this duty is breached.[129]

123. See St. Coates, 'Conflicts of Interest in the Securities Industry' in R. Rider and M. Asche (eds), *The Fiduciary, the Insider and the Conflict* (Dublin, Sweet & Maxwell, 1995), p. 104; N.S. Poser (no. 54 above), 122; P. Finn (no. 121 above), p. 13; B. Rider, 'Conflicts of Interest: An English Problem?' in G. Ferrarini (ed.), *European Securities Markets. The Investment Services Directive and Beyond* (London: Kluwer Law International, 1998), p. 149, p. 164.

124. Cf. P.R. Wood, 'Financial Conglomerates and Conflicts of Interest' in R.M. Goode (ed.), *Conflicts of Interest in the Changing Financial World* (London, The Institute of Bankers & Centre for Commercial Law Studies, Queen Mary College, University of London, 1986), p. 59, p. 59, saying that 'If one were to take [the strict fiduciary] standard as applying to the investment banking and dealing activities of the London financial conglomerate, it would be impossible to do business.' See also N.S. Poser, 'Conflicts of Interest within Securities Firms' (1990) *Brooklyn J. Int'l L.* 16, 111, 116.

125. See no. 1 above.

126. Art. 19(1) MiFID, is declared applicable to credit institutions providing investment services by Art. 1(2) MiFID.

127. See no. 1 above.

128. See Art. 10(2) UCITS Directive (no. 1 above) ('[T]he management company . . . must act independently and solely in the interest of the unit-holders.') and Art. 5h, UCITS Directive ('[A] management company: (a) acts honestly and fairly in conducting its business activities in the best interests of the UCITS it manages . . .; (b) acts with due skill, care and diligence, in the best interests of the UCITS it manages. . . .').

129. See 'Débats', in L. Thévenoz (ed.), *Aspects Juridiques de la Gestion de Fortune – Legal Aspects of Investment Management* (Brussels, Bruylant and Bern, Stämpfli, 1999), p. 125–132; L. Enriques (no. 3 above), p. 4; P. Wéry, 'La gestion de fortune au regard du droit

EC financial regulation reinforces this duty by elevating it to a regulatory norm applicable to all financial institutions offering asset management services. Thus, as a consequence of the transposition of the MiFID and the UCITS Directive into the national laws of the Member States, not only has a duty of loyalty become a *mandatory* element of asset management contracts, but compliance with this principle can now also be supervised and breaches sanctioned by national public supervisory institutions, the securities regulators.[130] This approach is typically justified on the grounds that, as discussed previously, the loyalty of these professionals to the interests of their clients affects not only those clients, but also more general or systemic interests, such as the integrity and efficiency of the market and the financial system, investors' confidence in that system, and the function the latter can perform in our society.[131]

Due to the public interest involved, regulatory oversight seems appropriate,[132] given the justifications for specific legal intervention we identified earlier.[133] In many cases, the existence of a conflict of interest may not actually hurt the individual investor, because the market price he pays for the service offered by the asset manager reflects the risk posed by the conflicts of interest.[134] In that case, the investor will not feel any need to bring a private action against the asset manager. But as discussed earlier, even in such a situation, it is in the general interest that conflicts of interest should not be abused.[135] In cases where only general interests are damaged, public authorities seem best placed to decide whether an action against the financial institution is warranted.[136]

But the EC legislator seems to go further than this enforcement-based rationale: it seems to take the view that, in order to protect the investor, a regulatory standard requiring investment firms to act in the interest of their clients is necessary

---

commun du mandat' in B. Tilleman and B. Du Laing (eds), *Bankcontracten*, Series Recht en Onderneming No. 9 (Brugge, die Keure, 2004), pp. 319–341, para. 15 at p. 333; P. Wéry, *Le mandat*, Répertoire notarial, Vol. 9, Principaux contrats usuels, Livre 7 (Brussels, Larcier, 2000), p. 151 *et seq*.

130. Art. 8 and 51(1) MiFID.
131. Cf. also K. J. Hopt (no. 56 above), p. 63.
132. However, not everyone is convinced that the national supervisory authorities will be equipped to perform the task of reviewing the behaviour of firms under the very broad standards of fairness and honesty. See e.g. L. Enriques (no. 3 above), p. 14.
133. See Section II.C above.
134. See p. 297–298 and 302–303 above.
135. See Section II.C.3 above. One could say that the externalities of conflicts of interest justify public regulation and proactive law enforcement by regulators. Cf. L. Enriques (no. 3 above), p. 4.
136. One could also argue that the behaviour of financial institutions in such cases does not violate the rule in Art. 19(1) MiFID, as the interests of the clients are not particularly hurt, but is caught by the general rule in Art. 25(1) MiFID, requiring the investment firms to act 'honestly, fairly and professionally and in a manner which promotes the integrity of the market.' The Commission considered it desirable to split the general principle of loyalty between these two provisions because the 'Implementation of the . . . provision [in ISD 1993 containing conduct of business rules as one of the mainstays of investor protection] has been hampered by . . . overlap with market integrity issues . . ..' See COM(2002) 625 final (no. 60 above), p. 82.

because the normative content of this rule offers the investors extra protection. The Commission even goes so far as to claim that this regulatory approach will reinforce the *fiduciary duties* of investment firms.[137]

However, the Commission's view seems to be based on the assumption that each and every duty of loyalty is a *fiduciary* duty. As indicated earlier,[138] what distinguishes fiduciary duties is not the normative content of the general principle involved ('thou shalt act loyally'). That content is part of *any* duty of loyalty, whether it is imposed by fiduciary law – historically equity – or by standard private law. What differentiates a fiduciary from a non-fiduciary duty of loyalty is the remedy attached to a breach (disgorgement instead of damages, resulting in an effective no-profit rule) and the principle that a breach is deduced from the mere appearance of impropriety (presumption of disloyalty, resulting in an effective no-conflict rule).

Continental European civil law seldom, if ever, recognizes any such general rules applicable to situations involving conflicts of interest.[139] In other words, in most EU Member States there are no 'fiduciary' duties to 'reinforce' by regulation. But more importantly, nowhere in the MiFID or in any other existing European legislation, or in implementing Level 2 rules,[140] can the remedies and presumptions

---

137. Thus, for instance, the Commission commented that 'In terms of concrete policy and technical choices . . . [its] proposed approach at Level 2 consists in *reinforcing the fiduciary duties* of the investment firms towards their clients (and especially towards retail clients)' and 'Since . . . [it] proposed reinforced fiduciary duties, in formulating the information requirements as part of the conduct of business rules . . . [it] took the view that the information which firms must give to their clients should be limited to those elements that are essential for the client to understand the nature of his relationship with the firm, and the services and instruments offered by the firm. Accordingly . . . [it has] tried as far as possible to avoid overloading clients, and retail clients in particular, with information that would be of no immediate use to them.' European Commission, Internal Market and Services DG, *Explanatory Note to Working Document ESC/23/2005 and to the Addendum of the Working Document ESC/17/2005 on Investment Research*, Working Document ESC/24/2005, 11 July 2005, p. 2 (emphasis added); see also the *Commission Level 2 Background Note* (no. 3 above), p. 15:

    'Art. 19, 21 and 22 of the Level 1 Directive and the accompanying implementing measures in the implementing Directive establish a *rigourous investor protection regime that clearly stipulates* the basic information requirements and the *fiduciary obligations* of investment firms towards their clients. The implementing Directive provides for a balanced combination of information disclosure in some areas . . . and *stronger fiduciary duties* for the firm to take care of the client interests in other areas.' (emphasis added).

138. See Section III.A above, especially p. 303–306.
139. Some continental European private law systems may recognize some variation on the rule that a legal agent cannot represent both sides of a transaction. However, in many countries, neither the courts nor academic opinion seems to be willing to interpret this rule as a specific application of a wider standard prohibiting any person under a duty of loyalty from entering into a situation that creates a conflict of interest for him. See A. Meinertzhagen-Limpens, 'La représentation et les conflits d'intérêts en droit comparé' in *Les conflits d'intérêts* (Brussels: Bruylant, 1997), p. 261, pp. 273–277, paras 14–18; K.J. Hopt (no. 56 above), pp. 71–72.
140. The provisions in the MiFID have to be implemented by Level 2 measures by the European Commission under the so-called Lamfalussy method. See B. Sousi, 'La Procédure Lamfalussy

that characterize duties as fiduciary be found. Of course, the application of the European rule in national courts might effectively turn it into something like a fiduciary duty when it is backed up by equitable remedies under national law. However, that will only be possible in common-law jurisdictions with a national law that already imposes fiduciary remedies. It is not a consequence of the MiFID or any other European law.

Apart from the question of whether it would be desirable to impose fiduciary duties on financial institutions,[141] it does not help matters – nor do much to underpin public confidence – if investors are given the false impression that they are owed a more special protection than 'normal' legal duties would offer them.[142] Breaches of the general rule in Article 19(1), MiFID, will offer the investor only the remedies already available under national private law,[143] which in most continental legal systems just means damages, making this loyalty principle virtually unenforceable in practice.[144]

à l'épreuve de la directive concernant les marches d'instruments financiers' *Euredia – European Banking & Financial Law Journal – Revue européenne de Droit bancaire & financier* (2004/2), 209; for this legislative method in general, see e.g. E. Ferran, *Building an EU Securities Market* (Cambridge, Cambridge University Press, 2004), pp. 61–84; N. Moloney, *EC Securities Regulation* (Oxford, Oxford University Press, 2002) pp. 861–871. The Level 2 rules relevant for the subject of this paper can be found in Commission Directive 2006/73/EC of 10 August 2006 implementing Directive 2004/39/EC of the European Parliament and of the Council as regards Organisational Requirements and Operating Conditions for Investment Firms and Defined Terms for the Purposes of that Directive, OJ L 241/26, 2006 (hereafter referred to as MiFID Level 2 Directive).

141. Cf. p. 306–307 above.
142. In the shorter run, however, the false feeling of protection given to investors by the regulatory rules may cause them to overestimate the average value of the financial services they receive. Applying the lemons mechanism in reverse, this would lead to a market equilibrium at too high a level of services provided and price paid, a situation good for the financial industry but not optimal for society. Cf. D. McGowan, 'Some Realism About Parochialism: The Economic Analysis of Legal Ethics', University of San Diego School of Law, Legal Studies Research Paper Series, Research Paper No. 07–20, October 2005, p. 12, available at <www.ssrn.com/abstract=819984>.
143. The conduct of business rules included in the ISD turned out to offer the investor very different kinds of remedies depending on the applicable national law, and in some member countries could not even be relied upon by private parties in a dispute against an investment firm because they were interpreted as relating solely to the relationship between the financial institution and the supervisory authorities. See M. Tison, 'Conduct of Business Rules and their Implementation in the EU Member States' in G. Ferrarini, K. J. Hopt, and E. Wymeersch (eds), *Capital Markets in the Age of the Euro. Cross-Border Transactions, Listed Companies and Regulation* (London, Kluwer Law International, 2002), p. 65, pp. 77–80. Arguably, the MiFID changes this and requires the Member States to allow private parties to enforce its conduct of business rules in liability suits. See M. Tison, 'Financial Market Integration in the Post-FSAP Era. In Search of Overall Conceptual Consistency in the Regulatory Framework' in G. Ferrarini and E. Wymeersch (eds), *Investor Protection in Europe: Regulatory Competition and Harmonization*, (Oxford, Oxford University Press, 2006 forthcoming).
144. See p. 304–306 above.

As a consequence, the imposition of a regulatory duty of loyalty does not in itself help to solve conflict of interest problems. In fact, to put it cynically, the presence of such a duty is precisely what creates a legal conflict of interest, and therefore the only advantage of imposing a duty of loyalty where it is not already part of the contractual arrangement would be to transform an existing economic conflict of interests into a legal conflict of interest,[145] requiring effective remedies that would take into account the difficulties of enforcing the duty of loyalty as discussed above. For this reason, it may be worthwhile to investigate and debate the desirability not just of introducing a European regulatory rule requiring asset managers to act loyally or in the best interests of their clients, but also of providing investors all over the EU with uniform appropriate remedies and suitable rules of evidence that would address the real problems.[146]

2. Imposing Specific Rules for Asset Management Services?

If the duty of loyalty were imposed only by general private law, as a 'vague' or 'open' standard, fine-tuning the application of the principle to specific cases or financial services would, in fact, be left to the judiciary. Given the relatively limited amount of litigation between individual investors and asset managers, owing probably to the remedies problems discussed above, it is unlikely that many helpful guidelines will develop, resulting in significant uncertainty for asset managers and investors alike.

Incorporating the general duty to act in the interest of the client into public regulation of investment firms provides an opportunity to create specific, precise regulatory prescriptions or prohibitions by tailoring the general principle to different financial activities, transactions and situations. The MiFID itself, referred to as the Level 1 text, does contain some conduct of business rules that can be considered to subsume the general principle of loyalty, such as the 'know your customer' principle, as adapted to different services and different types of clients,[147] the best execution principle,[148] and the client order handling rules.[149] Moreover, the MiFID also anticipates that the general principle in Article 19(1) will be implemented in so-called Level 2 Commission directives or regulations so as to further specify and flesh out the general rule.[150] Unfortunately, the European Commission is not

145. See p. 280 above.
146. In Recital 5 of the MiFID Level 2 Directive (no. 140 above) the Commission stresses that the conduct of business rules 'should be designed to ensure a uniform level of investor protection to be applied in a uniform manner through the introduction of clear standards and requirements governing the relationship between an investment firm and its client.' This, of course, requires not only uniform conduct of business rules but also uniform remedies against breaches of such rules.
147. Art. 19(4), (5) and (6) MiFID; see p. 314 *et seq.* below.
148. See Art. 21, MiFID.
149. See p. 317 *et seq.* below.
150. According to Art. 19(10) MiFID, the Commission is to adopt implementing measures to ensure that investment firms comply with the general duty of loyalty included in Art. 19(1) MiFID,

apparently planning to issue many such Level 2 rules specifically detailing the principle of Article 19(1), MiFID.

In its Level 2 Directive, the Commission included only one implementing rule specifying how the general duty should be understood in particular circumstances; namely a rule relating to acceptance of inducements by an investment firm.[151] The current draft version of the rule starts from the assumption that an investment firm must not, in relation to the provision of an investment or ancillary service to a client, pay or receive any fee, commission or non-monetary benefit.[152] However, some exceptions are made. Such benefits are of course allowed if they are received from or paid to the client or if they are necessary for the provision of investment services that by their nature cannot give rise to conflicts.[153] Secondly, benefits paid or provided to or by a third person or a person acting on behalf of a third party are allowed on condition that (1) the existence, nature and amount or method of calculation are disclosed to the client prior to the provision of the service,[154] and (2) the benefit is designed to enhance the quality of the relevant service to the client and does not impair compliance with the firm's duty to act in his best interests.[155] Disclosure must be comprehensive, accurate and understandable to the client, but may be confined to the essential terms of the arrangements in summary form, provided that the firm undertakes to disclose further details at the client's request and honours that promise.[156] The Commission commented further that:

> [S]ome more thought should be given to this issue, it would be preferable to categorize the different kinds of inducements and provide for a differentiated treatment according to each category so as to maintain the flexible policy

---

when providing investment or ancillary services to their clients, taking into account the nature of the services offered or provided to the client, the type, object size and frequency of these transactions, the nature of the financial instruments involved, and the retail or professional nature of the client. The idea behind this system was apparently to produce something more akin to a European conduct of business rulebook than to a set of high-level principles at a European level with the detail being left to national implementation measures as was the case under the ISD. See J. Herbst, 'Revision of the Investment Services Directive' (2003) *Journal of Financial Regulation and Compliance* 11, 211, 215.

151. Actually, Art. 44 and 45 of the Draft Commission Level 2 Directive (no. 140 above) also base the Level 2 rules on best execution and the client order handling rules on Art. 19(1) MiFID, inasmuch as they are applicable to the service of portfolio management. This, however, is a consequence of a drafting error in the Level 1 text, because these rules are to be considered specifications of the norms to be found in Art. 21 and 22 of MiFID. See no. 187–190 below and accompanying text.
152. See Art. 26, MiFID Level 2 Directive (no. 140 above).
153. Art. 26(a) and (c) MiFID Level 2 Directive (no. 140 above).
154. Art. 26(b)(i) MiFID Level 2 Directive (no. 140 above). Cf. Paragraph 17 in Box 9 of *CESR's Technical Advice on Possible Implementing Measures of the Directive 2004/39/EC on Markets in Financial Instruments – 1st Set of Mandates*, CESR/05-024c, January 2005, p. 58, available at <www.cesr-eu.org>.
155. Art. 26(b)(ii) MiFID Level 2 Directive (no. 140 above). Cf. Paragraph 9 in Box 7 of CESR/05-024c (no. 154 above), p. 44.
156. Art. 26, MiFID Level 2 Directive (no. 140 above).

> where that is appropriate, while imposing more restrictive requirements where necessary to protect the interests of clients.[157]

It is remarkable that the Committee of European Securities Regulators (CESR), which advises the Commission on these matters, originally considered a Level 2 rule based on the general principle of Article 19(1), MiFID, that was slightly more specific and would have required:

> the transactions carried out by an investment firm that provides portfolio management services to retail clients . . . [to] be exclusively motivated by the interests of such clients and in accordance with the management objectives set out in the retail client agreement.[158]

This proposed rule apparently drew heavy criticism from the industry. First, some respondents in CESR's consultation process took the view that to oblige the firm to act in accordance with the retail client agreement is redundant, as the firm would be bound by that agreement anyway.[159] While this is of course true, if the regulations did not include a duty to comply with a private law contract, the public supervisory bodies would have no authority to monitor and if necessary sanction breaches of that contract that did not involve a breach of any specific rule in the actual regulations. Secondly, some respondents apparently 'objected to the concept of 'exclusive motivation' as being too absolute, saying that other legitimate reasons, such as the interest of the firm in attracting additional clients by achieving portfolio performance superior to that of its competitors, should naturally not be ruled out.'[160] This fact is disturbing. In most cases, the firm's interest in attracting additional clients by achieving superior portfolio performance does not conflict with the interests of the clients. This means that in most circumstances a rule imposing exclusive loyalty to clients' interests would not prohibit the firm from striving for superior portfolio performance, giving the industry representatives no reason to object to the proposed rule. The only instances in which the proposed rule would prohibit the firm furthering its interest in achieving superior portfolio performance would

---

157. ESC/24/2005 (no. 137 above), p. 3.
158. See Rule 2 in Box 7 of *CESR's Draft Technical Advice on Possible Implementing Measures of the Directive 2004/39/EC on Markets in Financial Instruments – 2nd Set of Mandates, Consultation Paper*, CESR/04-562, October 2004, p. 42, available at <www.cesr-eu.org>. This rule already existed as a CESR Standard for Investor Protection (see Principle 137 in The Committee of European Securities Regulators, *A European Regime of Investor Protection – The Harmonization of Conduct of Business Rules*, CESR/01-014d, April 2002, p. 25, available at <www.cesr-eu.org>), having been proposed by its predecessor FESCO in 2001 (see Standard 151 in FESCO, *Standards and Rules for Harmonizing Core Conduct of Business Rules for Investor Protection, Consultative Paper*, Fesco/00-124b, February 2001, p. 32, available at <www.cesr-eu.org>).
159. See *CESR's Technical Advice on Level 2 Implementing Measures on Mandates of the First Set where the deadline was extended and the Second Set of Mandates – Markets in Financial Instruments Directive – Feedback Statement*, CESR/05-291b, April 2005, p. 21, available at <www.cesr-eu.org>.
160. Ibid.

be when this would not be in the interests of existing clients, which only happens when the asset manager overinvests in the services it renders, i.e. when the asset manager actually expends *and charges for* more than the optimal effort from the perspective of the existing clients. Do industry representatives actually believe it is acceptable for asset managers to overinvest in their efforts and charge their clients for it?

In the end, CESR decided for whatever reason not to maintain the rule in its final advice to the Commission,[161] and thus far the Commission has given no sign of proposing such a rule.

3. Specific Requirements of Suitability of Investment Decisions

One of the specifications or applications of the general principle of loyalty for portfolio management services can be inferred from Article 19(4), MiFID. This Article adapts the 'know your customer' principle to asset management and investment advice.[162] As such, it only imposes a duty on the asset manager to gather information. The information to be collected relates to the client's knowledge and experience in the relevant investment field,[163] the client's financial situation,[164] and

---

161. See CESR/05-291b (no. 159 above), pp. 21–22.
162. Art. 19(4) MiFID reads:

 'When providing investment advice or portfolio management the investment firm shall obtain the necessary information regarding the client's or potential client's knowledge and experience in the investment field relevant to the specific type of product or service, his financial situation and his investment objectives so as to enable the firm *to recommend* to the client or potential client the investment services and financial instruments that are suitable for him' (emphasis added).

 This Level 1 text is not optimal, because there are no 'recommendations' in the case of portfolio management: the investment firm will execute the investment decisions itself, albeit on behalf of the customer. This terminological problem was noticed by CESR, and therefore the problem has been dealt with in its advice to the Commission on the Level 2 measures (see *CESR's Technical Advice on Possible Implementing Measures of the Directive 2004/39/EC on Markets in Financial Instruments – 1st Set of Mandates where the deadline was extended and 2nd Set of Mandates*, CESR/05-290b, April 2005, p. 26, available at <www.cesr-eu.org>; see also the earlier CESR/04-562 (no. 158 above), p. 42, and the Level 2 measures based on this provision (see Art. 35[1] MiFID Level 2 Directive [no. 140 above]).
163. According to the Level 2 rules, this includes information on the types of services, transactions, and financial instruments with which the client is familiar, the nature, volume, and frequency of the client's transactions in financial instruments, and the period over which they have been carried out, and the level of education and profession or relevant former profession of the client. See Art. 37(1) MiFID Level 2 Directive (no. 140 above). This is analogous to CESR's advice on the issue (see Rule 1.a) in Box 10 of CESR/05-290b (no. 162 above) p. 27, and not very different from what was already envisaged in CESR's 2002 Conduct of Business Rules (CESR/01-014d [no. 158 above], p. 46, no. 15).
164. According to the Level 2 Directive this includes information on the source and extent of his regular income, his assets, including liquid assets, investments, and real property, and his regular financial commitments (see Art. 35[3] MiFID Level 2 Directive [no. 140 above]), again very similar to CESR's advice (Rule 1.b) in Box 10 of CESR/05-290b (no. 162 above), p. 27.

the client's investment objectives,[165] and is to be used to judge what is called the 'suitability' of the investment that has been recommended or made. This contrasts with the know your customer principle as applied to other investment services, where only information relating to the client's knowledge and experience in the relevant investment field has to be collected in order to judge what is referred to as the 'appropriateness' of the envisaged investment service or product.[166]

The distinction between the rules applicable to asset management and investment advice on the one hand, and other investment services on the other, is more than a difference in the kind or quantity of information to be collected. The two regimes also reveal two different reasons for requiring the information, due to the fact that the general duty in Article 19(1), MiFID, is interpreted differently when applied to portfolio management and investment advice than in the case of other investment services.[167]

In the case of investment advice and portfolio management, the investment firm apparently has a duty to choose investments that are suitable for its client. This implies a margin of discretion for the investment firm coupled with a duty of loyalty, requiring the firm to decide based exclusively on the interests of the customer. In order to properly ascertain the interests of a particular investor, the asset manager will need the type of information specified in Article 19(4), MiFID.

In the case of other investment services, however, the investment firm does not have a duty to choose for the client. Here, in principle, the client himself decides what is in his best interest, and the investment firm merely helps him execute the decision. Hence, the only underlying duty assumed by Article 19(5), MiFID, is the duty of an investment firm to warn an investor when he is making decisions with potential consequences he does not fully comprehend.[168] The investment service provider is not required to substitute its own judgment as to whether or not the proposed investment decision is in the investor's interests. In such cases, the investment firm apparently does not have a duty of loyalty.[169]

In this light, it makes perfect sense that the information duties included in Article 19(5), MiFID, do not apply when investment services are offered to profes-

165. According to the Level 2 Directive, this includes information on the length of time for which the client wishes to hold the investment, his preferences regarding risk taking (risk profile), and the purposes of the investment (Art. 35(4) MiFID Level 2 Directive (no. 140 above), which is also what CESR advised (Rule 1.c) in Box 10 of CESR/05-290b (no. 162 above), p. 27, and what was already the rule in the CESR 2002 Conduct of Business Rules (CESR/01-014d [no. 158 above], p. 46).
166. See Art. 19(5) MiFID; Art. 36, MiFID Level 2 Directive (no. 140 above).
167. Cf. *Commission Level 2 Background Note* (no. 3 above), pp. 20–21.
168. See Art. 19(5), para. 2, MiFID: 'In case the investment firm considers . . . that the product or service is not appropriate to the client or potential client, the investment firm shall warn the client or potential client.'
169. Cf. B. Inel, 'Investment Advice and Execution-Only Services in the Single European Market: The New FIMD Regime' (2004/2) *Euredia – European Banking & Financial Law Journal – Revue européenne de Droit bancaire & financier*, 301, 311–312, describing the duty imposed by Art. 19(5) MiFID, as a 'light-touch profiling system for clients not requiring a personalized assessment. In this sense, it is meant to be distinct from investment advice.'

sional clients.[170] A professional client under the MiFID is 'a client who possesses the experience, knowledge and expertise to make its own investment decisions and properly assess the risks that it incurs,'[171] so the underlying duty assumed by Article 19(5), MiFID, will not apply. But the problem tackled by Article 19(5), MiFID, relates to the time of contracting, which is part of the law relating to pre-contractual information provision and thus has nothing to do with the issue of conflicts of interest.

However, it is more questionable whether it is consistent with the rationale of Article 19(4), MiFID, to excuse the asset manager from verifying whether investment decisions for a professional client are such that he can afford to bear the risk of any loss the investment may cause. Nonetheless, this was what the Commission appeared to be considering in its initial drafts for the Level 2 implementation of Article 19(4), MiFID.[172]

An asset manager takes investment decisions on behalf of the investor, so it is the asset manager that has to judge the desirability of the transactions from the investor's interests. According to the Level 1 text, this desirability/suitability is to be judged based on the client's 'financial situation and his investment objectives,' meaning that these elements at least are aspects of the investor's interests that have to be taken into account. The fact that the investment firm is justified in assuming that the professional client 'possesses the experience, knowledge and expertise to make its own investment decisions and properly assess the risks that it incurs' is irrelevant here, as it is not the client who is making the investment decisions. If it is the asset manager's duty to make investment decisions in the best interests of the professional client, it has to know what these interests are, even if its client is a professional. This is a conflict of interest issue, and these issues arise not at the time of contracting, but during the performance of the contract, and therefore no distinction between the types of clients is warranted.[173]

This could be why the Commission, in its actual Level 2 Directive, qualified the rule so as to limit the presumption that professional clients are able to bear the financial risk of any loss that the investment may cause to investment advice,

---

170. According to the Level 2 rules, 'an investment firm shall be entitled to assume that a professional client has the necessary experience and knowledge in order to understand the risks involved in relation to those particular investment services or transactions, or types of transaction or product, for which the client is classified as a professional client.' See Art. 36, Draft Commission Level 2 Directive (no. 140 above).
171. See Annex II to the MiFID, OJ L 145/43 of 30 April 2004.
172. See Art. 11(1) *Draft Commission Working Document on Conduct of Business Rules, Best Execution, Client Order Handling Rules, Eligible Counterparties, Clarification of the Definition of Investment Advice and Financial Instruments*, Working Document ESC/23/2005, 7 July 2005: 'An investment firm shall be entitled to assume that professional clients are . . . able financially to bear the risk of any loss that the investment may cause,' still present in the first revision of this Working Document: Art. 11(2)(b) *Draft Commission Working Document on Conduct of Business Rules, Best Execution, Client Order Handling Rules, Eligible Counterparties, Clarification of the Definition of Investment Advice and Financial Instruments*, Working Document ESC/23/2005-Rev1, 9 September 2005.
173. See p. 300 above.

thereby implicitly excluding asset management; the asset manager's duty under Article 19(4), MiFID, to collect information about its client's ability to bear risk remains fully operational even in the case of professional clients.[174]

4. Client Order Handling Rules

The MiFID requires investment firms to implement and maintain 'procedures and arrangements which provide for the prompt, fair and expeditious execution of client orders, relative to other client orders or the trading interests of the investment firm.'[175] These so-called client order handling rules do not judge how well a client order has been executed in view of conditions in the wider market place; that is the province of the best execution duty.[176] Fairness and expediency in this regard should be understood as referring to a comparison with the handling of other client orders or proprietary transactions by the investment firm.[177]

This provision is particularly aimed at tackling the conflicts that can arise among the interests of several clients using the same investment service from the investment firm.[178] It contains an important modification of the general duty of loyalty applicable to the relationship with each individual client: instead of being required to maximize the interests of each individual client, this rule makes clear that the firm is only bound to treat each investor 'fairly' as compared to other investors. While the personal interests of an investment firm under the duty of loyalty may never enter the equation, the interests of other clients apparently have to be taken into account so as to treat clients equally. Where conflicts of duties exist towards several clients, the duty of loyalty is transformed into a duty of equal treatment.

This principle must be considered to be a *moderation* or limitation of the fiduciary duty of loyalty, which in its strictest form would make it difficult for a fiduciary to have numerous competing clients.[179] In effect, the Level 2 implementing rules under this principle eliminate the conflicts of interest that can arise between competing clients of an investment firm by partially replacing the firm's duty of loyalty to its clients with a duty that specifically prescribes what the firm is to do in certain situations.[180]

---

174. See Art. 35(2), MiFID Level 2 Directive (no. 140 above); the change appeared first in the second revision of the working document preparing the draft: see Art. 10(2)(b) *Draft Commission Working Document on Conduct of Business Rules, Best Execution, Client Order Handling Rules, Eligible Counterparties, Clarification of the Definition of Investment Advice and Financial Instruments*, Working Document ESC/23/2005-Rev2, 29 September 2005.
175. Art. 22(1) MiFID.
176. The best execution duty, as included in Art. 21(1) MiFID, requires investment firms to 'take all reasonable steps to obtain, when executing orders, the best possible result for their clients taking into account price, costs, speed, likelihood of execution and settlement, size, nature or any other consideration relevant to the execution of the order.'
177. COM(2002) 625 final (no. 60 above), p. 84.
178. See Section II.B.1 above.
179. Cf. p. 306–307 above.
180. See p. 289–290 above.

For instance, the Commission compels investment firms to carry out client orders sequentially and promptly, unless the nature of the order or the prevailing market conditions make this either impracticable or not in the best interests of the client.[181] Once executed, orders must be promptly and accurately recorded and allocated.[182]

Aggregation of orders for several clients should only be permitted if (1) it is unlikely to work overall to the disadvantage of any client involved; (2) the investment firm has disclosed to each client involved that the effect of aggregation may work to his disadvantage in relation to a particular order; and (3) the investment firm has established, and effectively implements, an order allocation policy providing for the fair allocation of such orders and transactions in sufficiently precise terms.[183] The allocation of aggregated orders on behalf of clients and on the firm's own account must not be detrimental to any client.[184] If an aggregated order is only partially executed, the related trades must be allocated according to the firm's allocation policy.[185] When client orders have been aggregated with transactions on the firm's account, allocation should give the client priority. Only if the firm can demonstrate on reasonable grounds that without the aggregation it would not have been able to carry out the order on such advantageous terms is it allowed to allocate the order proportionally.[186]

Some discussion has focussed on whether the MiFID's client order handling principle is applicable to portfolio management. At first glance, the Level 1 text may argue against such application, as Article 22(1), MiFID, applies to the 'execution of client orders' and one could argue that an asset manager does not receive any 'orders' from its clients and does not 'execute' an order when it accesses execution venues indirectly.[187] Some respondents in CESR's consultation argued that this rule was drafted for sell-side firms only, particularly brokers and dealers. They pointed out that portfolio management is not a transaction service and should not be

181. Art. 47(1)(b) MiFID Level 2 Directive (no. 140 above). This is very similar to the existing CESR 2002 Conduct of Business Principles: CESR/01-014d (no. 158 above) Rules 97 and 196.
182. Art. 47(1)(a) MiFID Level 2 Directive (no. 140 above).
183. Art. 48(1) MiFID Level 2 Directive (no. 140 above). CESR had proposed much the same requirements: see paras 8 and 9 of Box 17, CESR/05-290b (no. 162 above), p. 44, already included in the 2002 CESR Conduct of Business Principles. See Rules 96, 99, 100 and 108 in CESR/01-014d (no. 158 above).
184. Art. 49(1) MiFID Level 2 Directive (no. 140 above). This rule is analogous to CESR's advice: para. 12 in Box 17 of CESR/05-290b (no. 162 above), p. 44.
185. Art. 48(2) MiFID Level 2 Directive (no. 140 above). Cf. CESR proposal, para. 14 in Box 17 of CESR/05-290b (no. 162 above), p. 44. This was also the rule in the 2002 CESR Conduct of Business Principles; see Rule 115 in CESR/01-014d (no. 158 above), p. 22.
186. Art. 49(2) MiFID Level 2 Directive (no. 140 above); cf. CESR's rather similar advice, para. 15 in Box 17 of CESR/05-290b (no. 162 above), p. 44.
187. *CESR's Draft Technical Advice on Possible Implementing Measures of the Directive 2004/39/EC on Markets in Financial Instruments – Aspects of the definition of Investment Advice and of the General Obligation to Act Fairly, Honestly and Professionally in the Best Interests of Clients – Best execution – Market Transparency, Second Consultation Paper*, CESR/05-164, March 2005, p. 15, para. 10 , available at <www.cesr-eu.org>.

regulated as such.[188] However, as CESR correctly recognized, this ignores the fact that poor or unfair execution has an adverse impact on portfolio performance and is therefore relevant to a duty relating to the resulting global yields.[189] While the Draft Commission Level 2 Directive still subjected portfolio managers to the rules for client order handling by way of spelling out to portfolio managers their general Level 1 duty to act in the best interests of the client the final MiFID Level 2 Directive is silent on the issue.[190]

Unfortunately, replacing the general duty of loyalty as applicable to order handling by a rule specifically prescribing equal treatment of or specific consent by the investors (which is precisely what the order handling rules do) is only of limited use when applied to the service of asset management. Here, the problem involves not only the timing of the execution and the allocation of executed orders among clients, but also – and more fundamentally – the timing and allocation of the investment *decisions* resulting in these orders. Once the decisions are taken, such order handling rules can ensure that execution is fairly distributed among clients. But the rules as such do not influence whether the investment decisions *themselves* are fairly 'distributed' among the clients. To give just one example, CESR stressed that if an investment firm is not allowed to benefit when its own and clients' aggregated orders are only partially executed, but not aggregating those orders would have resulted in worse execution conditions for the clients, this would remove any incentive for firms to aggregate orders in such circumstances, ultimately hurting the investors.[191] But how is one to tell whether or not the firm came up with the decision to order on behalf of its clients precisely because it could aggregate such orders with its own and so realize better conditions? While for execution purposes an equal treatment rule may be practical and sufficient, such a rule would become impossible to enforce when applied to the investment decisions themselves and hence to asset management.

C. Specific Measures to Tackle Conflicts of Interest

EC regulation requires multifunctional financial institutions offering investment services to 'maintain and operate effective organizational and administrative

---

188. CESR/05-164 (no. 187 above) p. 18, para. 25.
189. CESR/05-164 (no. 187 above) p. 18, para. 26.
190. See Art. 45, Draft Commission Directive implementing Directive 2004/39/EC, 6 February 2006, available at the commission's website at <http://ec.europa.eu/internal_market> 'Member States shall require investment firms, when providing the service of portfolio management, to comply with obligations analogous to those imposed under Art... 22(1) of Directive 2004/39/EC when carrying out transactions that result from decisions to deal, as if references in... [that] Art... to executing orders were references to carrying out transactions that result from decisions by the investment firm to deal in financial instruments on behalf of its client.' Compare CESR's advice: Paragraph 1 in Box 13 in CESR/05-290b (no. 162 above), p. 37.
191. Cf. CESR/05-291b (no. 159 above), p. 39: 'CESR believes it is important to maintain the general principle of priority to client orders in the allocation of partial fills, especially because of the risk of abuse. However, it accepts that this risk needs to be weighed against the benefits of allowing clients to benefit from the aggregation of their orders with own account transactions, which may be lost if clients are provided with priority in all cases.'

arrangements with a view to taking all reasonable steps designed to prevent conflicts of interest . . . from adversely affecting the interests of its clients.'[192] Management companies of UCITS have to be 'structured and organised in such a way as to minimise the risk of UCITS' or clients' interests being prejudiced by conflicts of interest . . .'[193]

It is interesting that neither text expects the financial firm to prevent conflicts of interest from arising, as general fiduciary law would require.[194] Instead, the rules only require organizational measures that are designed to prevent existing conflicts of interest from *adversely affecting* or prejudicing the interests of clients.[195] In other words, investment firms are required to organize their operations in such a way as to neutralize the potential adverse impact of conflicts of interest on clients.

1. Which Conflicts of Interest?

The EC rules require an investment firm to make a reasonable effort to identify the conflicts of interest with which it is confronted.[196] Conflicts are understood to arise only in cases where the interests of the firm conflict with the duty the firm owes to a client or where there is a conflict between the different interests of two or more clients to whom the firm owes in each case a duty.[197] According to the MiFID Level 2 Directive, the firm has to draw up, maintain and implement an effective conflicts of interest policy, which as a first component must identify, for the specific investment services, activities, and ancillary services the firm offers, the circumstances that constitute or may give rise to a conflict of interest entailing a material risk of damage to the interests of a client.[198]

But what does it mean for the 'interests of clients' to be 'negatively affected,' 'prejudiced' or 'damaged'? We have seen that the most fundamental economic problem of conflicts of interest in institutions functioning in a sufficiently competitive market environment is not that the individual client pays for more than he receives.[199] Due to market forces, most conflicts of interest – if not kept secret – will eventually result in an adjusted market price and demand for the service involved. In such circumstances it is hard to maintain that the interests of clients have been prejudiced or negatively affected, as they did not bargain for, nor pay for, more than

192. Art. 13(3) MiFID. This provision does not fundamentally differ from the corresponding rule in Art. 10, ISD, requiring the investment firm to be 'structured and organized in such a way as to minimize the risk of clients' interests being prejudiced by conflicts of interest between the firm and its clients or between one of its clients and another.'
193. Art. 5f, UCITS Directive.
194. See p. 305–306 above.
195. See also CESR/05-024c (no. 154 above), p. 41.
196. Art. 18(1) MiFID. L. Enriques (no. 3 above), p. 5, calls this a 'red flag' system.
197. See Recital 24, MiFID Level 2 Directive (no. 140 above); *Commission Level 2 Background Note* (no. 3 above) p. 12.
198. See Art. 22(2)(a) MiFID Level 2 Directive (no. 140 above).
199. See Sections II.C.1 and II.C.3 above.

they got, even if what they get is a riskier transaction than they would have preferred. The essence of the agency problem lies in the suboptimal market equilibrium that will result under these circumstances. Therefore, even if clients' interests are not damaged because they anticipated the risk posed by the conflicts of interest, the problem persists and should be tackled. However, the MiFID seems to leave such instances untouched. To me, this appears to indicate that the EC legislator views conflicts of interest too much as an investor protection problem and not enough as a market efficiency issue.

The Level 1 text of the MiFID mandates the Commission to adopt Level 2 measures that establish criteria for determining the types of conflict of interest intended.[200] But rather than give criteria that would help to interpret the Level 1 text in a general, systematic way, the Commission prefers giving a 'clear, although open, list of the generic situations that should be treated . . . as conflicts of interest detrimental to the client for the purposes of the MiFID',[201] because it brings legal certainty.[202] The list includes five situations:[203]

- An action is likely to create a financial gain or avoid a financial loss for the investment firm or a person in some way related to the firm, at the expense of the client;
- The firm or a person in some way related to the firm has an interest in the outcome of an action which is distinct from the client's interest in that outcome;
- The firm or a person in some way related to the firm has an incentive to favour the interests of one or more clients over the interest of another or other client(s);
- The firm or a person in some way related to the firm carries on the same business as the client;
- The firm or a person in some way related to the firm receives from a third person an inducement in relation to a service provided to the client other than the standard commission or fee for that service.

As a general, clarifying principle, the MiFID Level 2 Directive clarifies that '[i]t is not enough that the firm may gain a benefit if there is not also a disadvantage to a client, or that one client to whom the firm owes a duty may make a gain or avoid a loss without there being a concomitant possible loss to another such client.'[204] Again, this shows a rather limited view, considering conflicts of interest to be a mere investor protection issue.

---

200. Art. 18(3)(b) MiFID.
201. European Commission, Internal Market and Services DG, *Explanatory Note: Main Differences between Working Document ESC/17/2005 and the CESR Level 2 Advice*, Working Document ESC/18/2005, 13 May 2005, p. 5.
202. ESC/18/2005 (no. 201 above) Annex, p. 6.
203. Art. 21, MiFID Level 2 Directive (no. 140 above).
204. Recital 24, MiFID Level 2 Directive (no. 140 above).

2. Structural and Organizational Measures

Under the MiFID, the Commission has to implement Level 2 rules that 'specify the concrete organizational requirements to be imposed on investment firms performing different investment services and/or activities and ancillary services or combinations thereof.'[205]

According to the MiFID Level 2 Directive, the organization of the investment firm should 'ensure that relevant persons engaged in different business activities involving a conflict of interest . . . carry on those activities at a level of independence appropriate to the size and activities of the investment firm, and of the group to which it belongs, and to the materiality of the risk of damage to the interests of clients'.[206] For the sake of clarity and certainty, the Commission added a list of organizational measures that will be mandatory if they are appropriate to the type of conflicts the firm is subject to.[207] This list includes:[208]

- Measures to prevent inappropriate exchange of information;
- Measures to ensure separate supervision of personnel;
- Measures to ensure independence of remuneration;
- Structures to prevent or limit inappropriate influence; and
- Measures to prevent or control the simultaneous or sequential involvement of a person in separate investment or ancillary services or activities.

However, where these measures would not be appropriate or sufficient, firms are allowed and required to apply additional or alternative measures.[209] Such separation must be maintained in particular between the activities of portfolio management and proprietary trading and corporate finance.[210]

Internal procedures to separate activities within a financial firm are known as Chinese Walls. This type of mechanism, however, should not be confused with a firewall, such as was imposed between commercial and investment banking in the 1930s. Whereas a firewall is primarily intended to protect an institution providing one financial activity against the risks inherent in – and the potential financial problems for the firm caused by – another (i.e. keeping the 'fire' started in one department from spreading to other departments, or addressing the contagion problem within financial institutions),[211] a Chinese Wall is intended to prevent the free

205. Art. 13(10) MiFID.
206. Art. 22(3) MiFID Level 2 Directive (no. 140 above).
207. See ESC/18/2005 (no. 201 above) p. 5.
208. Art. 22(3) MiFID Level 2 Directive (no. 140 above).
209. Art. 22(3) MiFID Level 2 Directive (no. 140 above); see also ESC/18/2005 (no. 201 above) p. 5.
210. See Recital 26 in the MiFID Level 2 Directive (no. 140 above).
211. See P. Graham, 'The Statutory Regulation of Financial Services in the United Kingdom and the Development of Chinese Walls in Managing Conflicts of Interest' in E. McKendrick (ed.), *Commercial Aspects of Trusts and Fiduciary Obligations* (Oxford: Clarendon Press, 1992), p. 43, p. 49; R. Cranston (no. 67 above), pp. 104–105.

flow of information within a firm.[212] This practice was originally developed to forestall criminal liability for insider trading: not only to prevent inside information available in one division of the financial institution being used as the basis for transactions by another, but also to defend the institution against claims from clients based on an alleged use of privileged information or a failure to act on certain information that it had at its disposal.[213]

Although these types of barriers and procedures have become a standard part of the mechanisms used to manage conflicts of interest in financial institutions, their contribution to alleviating these problems is modest. One reason is that while Chinese Walls may restrict the flow of information,[214] and recent regulations intensify the effect by including measures to sever direct lines of reporting, supervision, influence and remuneration, they do not in themselves do anything to avert conflicts of interest.[215] Moreover, they do not influence the loyalties of the personnel involved.[216] Chinese Walls may be effective in preventing an institution from using one client's privileged information against the interests of that client to further the interests of another client or itself, but these cases only represent a very small fraction of the conflicts problems faced by financial institutions. The information that is most often relevant to the transactions for investment clients cannot be kept

212. Cf. H. McVea (no. 54 above), pp. 123 and 126; G. McCormack (no. 54 above), p. 30; N.S. Poser (no. 54 above), 119.
213. See H. McVea (no. 54 above), pp. 124–125; N.S. Poser (no. 54 above), 119 and 159–163; see also N.S. Poser (no. 124 above).
214. And there is even legitimate doubt whether Chinese Walls are actually leak proof. See e.g. A. Lehar and O. Randl, 'Chinese Walls in German Banks', June 2003, available at <www.ssrn.com/abstract=424010>.
215. See also the UK Department of Trade and Industry (DTI) White Paper *Financial Services in the United Kingdom: A New Framework for Investor Protection* (Cmnd. 9432, January 1985), pp. 19–20: 'The Government are not convinced that total reliance can be placed on Chinese walls because they restrict flows of information and not the conflicts of interest themselves,' quoted in P. Graham (no. 211 above), p. 50; B. Rider (no. 123 above), p. 163: 'The courts have shown no great enthusiasm for Chinese Walls and similar devices which, while they may serve to inhibit or at least control the flow of information within a multiple function fiduciary, do not address the inherent conflict of interest.'; see also N. S. Poser (no. 54 above), 166 and N. S. Poser (no. 124 above), 112.
216. See also P. Finn (no. 121 above), p. 26 (1992): 'Whatever efficacy 'walls' etc. may have as information protection devices, segregation is not a loyalty-engendering contrivance'; H. McVea (no. 54 above), p. 223: 'Chinese Walls are useful defence measures for conglomerates to protect themselves from liability in certain circumstances, but should not be relied upon as a means of discharging duties owed.' Moreover, recent research in behavioural economics has shown that self-serving behaviour is not necessarily the result of a conscious choice by the actor, so that all too often a person is under the honest conviction that he has acted without taking his own interests into account while in fact his behaviour turns out be significantly influenced by them. See e.g. D.A. Moore, P.E. Tetlock, L. Tanlu and M.H. Bazerman, 'Conflicts of Interest and the Case of Auditor Independence: Moral Seduction and Strategic Issue Cycling' (2006) *Academy of Management Review* 31, forthcoming in no. 1, Harvard Business School Working Paper No. 03115; Harvard PON Working Paper; CMU Tepper Working Paper, available at <www.ssrn.com/abstract=667363>; see also M.H. Bazerman, G. Loewenstein and D.A. Moore, 'Why Good Accountants Do Bad Audits' (2002/1) *Harvard Business Review* 80, 87.

private by Chinese Walls or other internal measures, as it is publicly available. To give but one example: how could a Chinese Wall prevent the asset management division of a firm knowing that the investment banking division is underwriting certain securities offerings, whereupon the former division may consider it is in the interest of the firm to help by placing these securities in controlled portfolios?[217] And finally, would not a truly effective Chinese Wall undo all the advantages of conglomeration?[218]

3. Disclosure Requirements

Disclosure has long been a standard item in the anti-conflicts of interest toolkit. It is apparently considered to be a more 'flexible' legal instrument.[219] Perhaps more importantly, disclosure is much less intrusive than alternative regulatory interventions such as prohibition of certain actions or mandatory segregation of specific activities.[220] As such, disclosure can be characterized as involving 'minimal disruption of the status quo.'[221] However, since disclosure in the modern financial world has become a very costly activity, it is well worth wondering whether existing disclosure requirements pertaining to conflicts of interest actually are an effective and efficient way of tackling the problem.

The first way that disclosure can help is by providing the principal, in this case the client, with *ex post* information on how the agent, in this case the portfolio manager, performed his functions. This type of information is intended to enable the principal to take effective legal action against an agent that breaches its duties.[222]

217. See also L. Enriques (no. 3 above), pp. 12–13.
218. It has been argued that the economic advantages of conglomeration are mainly realized in information-gathering activities. See L. Van den Berghe and K. Verweire, *Creating the Future with All Finance and Financial Conglomeration* (Dordrecht, Kluwer, 1998), pp. 56–57. However, it is precisely the sharing of information which a Chinese Wall should inhibit. See H. McVea (no. 54 above), pp. 128–129, 205–206 and 225–227; cf. N.S. Poser (no. 54 above), 205; N.S. Poser (no. 124 above), 115: 'Chinese walls tend to defeat the business reasons for creating multiservice firms.'
219. K.J. Hopt (no. 56 above), p. 67.
220. Cf. J. Surowiecki, 'The Financial Page: The Talking Cure' *The New Yorker Magazine*, 9 December 2002, 54:

> 'It has become a truism on Wall Street that conflicts of interest are unavoidable. In fact, most of them only seem so, because avoiding them makes it harder to get rich. That's why full disclosure is suddenly so popular; it requires no substantive change.... Transparency is well and good, but accuracy and objectivity are even better. Wall Street doesn't have to keep confessing its sins. It just has to stop committing them.'

221. D.M. Cain, G. Loewenstein and D.A. Moore, 'The Dirt on Coming Clean: Perverse Effects of Disclosing Conflicts of Interest' (2005) *Journal of Legal Studies* 34, 1, 3; see also D.M. Cain, G. Loewenstein and D.A. Moore, 'Coming Clean but Playing Dirtier: The Shortcomings of Disclosure as a Solution to Conflicts of Interest' in D.A. Moore, D.M. Cain, G. Loewenstein and M.H. Bazerman (eds), *Conflicts of Interest: Challenges and Solutions in Business,* Law, Medicine, and Public Policy (New York, Cambridge University Press, 2005), p. 104 pp. 107–108.
222. K. J. Hopt (no. 56 above), p. 68.

However, requiring an asset manager to disclose *ex post* facts that may have implied a conflict of interest does not necessarily provide the investor with a legal remedy, because the mere existence of a conflict does not imply a breach of duty in standard continental civil law in general, or European regulation of asset management in particular. In addition, the investor would be required to prove not only that the asset manager had conflicting interests but also that he based certain investment decisions on those inappropriate interests, which in practice is very difficult.[223] For this purpose, therefore, this type of *ex post* disclosure will not help without some modification to the material law applicable to asset management.

Secondly, disclosure can be relevant in relation to fiduciary duties. As a general principle of fiduciary law, a fiduciary confronted with a conflict of interest must either fully inform the beneficiary of the existing conflict and its potential consequences and obtain his informed consent, or abstain from acting on behalf of the beneficiary. The origin of this rule, often referred to as 'disclose or abstain,' can be linked to the principle that the fiduciary may not make any secret profits.[224] However, it can also be seen as a way of eliminating the conflict of interest. If the beneficiary is fully informed and himself decides whether to consent to the transaction or not, the arbitrage between the conflicting interests is not performed unilaterally by the fiduciary, but is the result of arm's-length negotiation between two parties. Disclosure effectively relieves the fiduciary of his duty of loyalty for that specific transaction, as it is the beneficiary himself who will further his own interests in the matter. As the fiduciary is no longer acting '*en fonction fiduciaire*' as it were, the law switches from 'fiduciary mode' to 'contract mode,'[225] so that no fiduciary duties are applicable.[226] Disclosure, therefore, is not only fiduciary law's answer to conflicts of interest; it also provides a way out of the realm of fiduciary law.

More generally, irrespective of whether or not a legal system contains fiduciary duties accompanied by equitable remedies, *ex ante* disclosure of conflicts of interest makes it theoretically possible for the principal to reappraise the situation and decide whether he wants to go on delegating power to the agent or not.[227] If he chooses to end or temporarily suspend the delegation of power based on a disclosed conflict, the agent is effectively relieved of his duty of loyalty, so the conflict of interest disappears.

223. See p. 305–306 above.
224. See L. S. Sealy, 'Some Principles of Fiduciary Obligation' (1963) *Cambridge L. J.*, 119, 135.
225. See T. Frankel (no. 14 above), p. 131; K.B. Davis, Jr. (no. 17 above), p. 47: 'By fully disclosing her interest in the transaction, [the fiduciary] becomes free to deal with the principal because the principal's independent judgment is presumably now triggered as a safeguard against the fiduciary's opportunism.'
226. For historical notes on the development of the disclosure duties in fiduciary law, see L.S. Sealy (no. 227 above), 125–126.
227. K.J. Hopt (no. 56 above), p. 68. See also M. Davis (no. 5 above), p. 13: 'Disclosure . . . prevents deception and gives those relying on P's judgment the opportunity to give informed consent to the conflict of interest, to replace P instead of continuing to rely on him, or to adjust reliance in some less radical way (e.g., by seeking a 'second opinion') or by redefining the relationship (e.g., by requiring recusal for a certain range of decisions).'

In the context of asset management, this can only work if separate disclosure is required for every individual investment decision of the portfolio manager that poses a conflict. If only general *ex ante* disclosure is required, that information will not enable the principal to take the relevant investment decisions himself. Nor will it enable principals to distinguish 'good' asset managers from 'bad,' as it will inevitably reveal that all asset managers that are part of a multifunctional financial institution are confronted with similar conflicts of interest, without indicating which of these institutions will abuse such conflicts and which will not.[228] Such a general disclosure requirement will not avoid Akerlof's so-called 'lemons' problem[229] but induce it. It will reduce investors' confidence in the average quality of the services offered by asset managers, and as a result they will invest less than they really want to. General *ex ante* disclosure, therefore, may protect the interests of investors in that it may enable them to negotiate across-the-board *ex ante* compensation for the general or average risk of conflict of interest abuse, but as discussed above, that is not the most compelling argument in favour of specific legislation to tackle the entire conflict of interest problem.[230]

And unfortunately there are more problems. Disclosure is most often advocated as an appropriate remedy because it supposedly reduces the information gap or asymmetry between informed financial professionals and uninformed, unsophisticated investors.[231] The effectiveness of this remedy depends on the assumption that disclosure will enable the informed principal to properly discount the value of the agent's performance, and so defend his own interests by making less use of the agent's services or paying less for them. This, in turn, will provide the proper incentives for the agent to adapt his behaviour to the preferences of informed principals.[232]

However, recent research suggests that disclosure of conflicts of interest may not only fail to produce the intended effect, it may often have unintended perverse effects, increasing rather than reducing the inefficiencies created by conflicts of interest. This is because, in most situations, principals are unable to sufficiently discount the agent's actions, while the disclosure paradoxically often leads to more self-serving behaviour by the agent, as he tries to compensate for the reduced

---

228. This kind of disclosure is scarcely going to encourage the development of reputations by which customers can distinguish 'good' service providers from 'bad'. See no. 44 above.
229. See p. 287 above
230. See p. 288 and Section II.C.3 above.
231. See e.g. P.M. Healy and K.G. Palepu, 'Information Asymmetry, Corporate Disclosure, and the Capital Markets: A Review of the Empirical Disclosure Literature' (2001) *Journal of Accounting and Economics* 31, 405, 412.
232. On the effectiveness of disclosure in general, see A. Fung, D. Weil, M. Graham and E. Fagotto, 'The Political Economy of Transparency: What Makes Disclosure Policies Effective?', Ash Institute for Democratic Governance and Innovation, John F. Kennedy School of Management, Harvard University, Working Paper OP-03-04, December 2004, available at <www.ssrn.com/abstract=766287>.

confidence of the principals, but at the same time feels less inhibited by ethical considerations.[233]

This may come as a surprise to students of security regulation, given the overall reliance of such regulation on disclosure as a mechanism of investor protection.[234] Surely nobody would dare to question the wisdom of that approach? The explanation must partially be sought in the distinction between the investor protection dimension, which in many instances does require disclosure, and the conflict of interest dimension, which does not necessarily. The root cause of the problem is the characteristics of the duty of loyalty.[235] Here, disclosure can only be a remedy in the sense that disclosing a conflict of interest will allow the principal to take his interests back into his own hands and thus relieve the agent of the duty of loyalty in respect of the specific transaction the disclosure is about, in effect dissolving the conflict of interest. But this is fundamentally different from using disclosure to enable the principal to discount the agent's actions so that the market mechanism can take care of the problem. Such discounting is simply not highly feasible in the case of conflicts of interest.[236]

The MiFID, interestingly, does not require an asset manager to disclose *all* potential conflicts of interest. Disclosure is only required in cases where 'organizational or administrative arrangements made by the investment firm . . . to manage conflicts of interest are not sufficient to ensure, with reasonable confidence, that risks of damage to client interests will be prevented.'[237] In other words, if the firm believes that a conflict is unlikely to damage the client's interests because the way

233. See D.M. Cain, G. Loewenstein and D.A. Moore, 'The Dirt on Coming Clean' (no. 224 above), 4–8; Ibid., 'Coming Clean but Playing Dirtier' (no. 221 above), pp. 108–119.

234. Cf. F. Easterbrook and D. Fischel, 'Mandatory Disclosure and the Protection of Investors' (1984) *Virginia Law Review* 70, 669, 670: 'The dominating principle of securities regulation is that anyone willing to disclose the right things can sell or buy whatever he wants at whatever price the market will sustain.' See also P. Mahoney, 'Mandatory Disclosure as a Solution to Agency Problems' (1995) *University of Chicago Law Review* 62, 1,047.

235. See p. 280–282 above.

236. Cf. D. T. Miller, 'Psychologically Naive Assumptions about the Perils of Conflicts of Interest' in D.A. Moore, D.M. Cain, G. Loewenstein and M.H. Bazerman (eds), *Conflicts of Interest. Challenges and Solutions in Business, Law, Medicine, and Public Policy* (New York, Cambridge University Press, 2005), p. 126, p. 127. Miller distinguishes between two types of discounting; one involving recalibration and the other involving diagnosing the motives that underlie the acts of the agent. While the first type of discounting is prohibitively difficult, the second would simply lead to dismissing the services of the conflicted agent out of hand. It is this second type of discounting that disclosure in the case of conflicts of interests was intended to produce – something similar to disclosure functions within fiduciary law – and not the first kind of discounting, which would be the intended result of the kind of disclosure imposed as a method of consumer or investor protection in general.

237. Art. 18(2) MiFID. In its earlier consultations while drafting revisions to the ISD, the Commission took a stricter line that would have required firms to abstain from any action when confronted with a conflict of interest if their organization was unable to prevent all risk of prejudice to their clients. Only after heavy lobbying on this point, apparently, did the ultimate rule allow investment firms to act even when confronted with a conflict of interest for which their organization did not fully protect the interests of the clients so long as they at least disclosed the existence of the conflict. See J. Herbst (no. 150 above), 215–216.

the firm manages that conflict is considered to be appropriate, specific disclosure is not mandatory.[238] In that case, the customer will have to make do with the *ex ante* general disclosure of the investment firm's conflict of interest policy,[239] namely the general measures it has taken to manage the standard conflicts of interest posed by its various activities.[240] This is linked to the so-called 'identify, manage and disclose' structure of the MiFID's conflicts of interest approach, which is designed to compel firms to act in order to prevent the risk of damage to clients in case of identifiable conflicts, rather than allowing them to rely on disclosure alone to tackle conflicts.[241] However, the text goes further, by reducing disclosure to a remedy of 'last resort,' *only* to be used when other preferred methods fail.[242]

Moreover, the Commission recently considered a proposal to limit the transaction-specific disclosure required under Article 18(2), MiFID, to retail investors.[243] However, while Article 19(10), MiFID, which gives the Commission the regulatory power to adopt implementation measures for the general information duties of Article 19(3), MiFID, requires those Level 2 measures to take into account 'the retail or professional nature of the client or potential clients,' Article 18(3), MiFID, which instructs the Commission to adopt implementation measures for the conflict of interest rules in Article 18, MiFID, does not contain any such mandate. It does not even mention the distinction between different types of clients. I therefore fail to see on what specific legal basis the Commission would have the jurisdiction to reduce the normative content of Article 18(2), MiFID, as applied to the relationship between investment firms and professional clients, to a mere duty to respond to a client's request for information.[244]

---

238. See also L. Enriques (no. 3 above), p. 6: '[T]he disclosure obligation is conditional upon the firm's judgment that the organizational and administrative arrangements in place cannot ensure the prevention of damage to clients. A bona fide judgment that those arrangements can prevent such risks, in turn, will imply no violation of the disclosure requirement, even if it turns out ex post that a client's interests actually have been damaged.'
239. Investment firms have to provide retail or potential retail clients with a description of their conflicts of interest policy. See Art. 30(1)(h) MiFID Level 2 Directive (no. 140 above).
240. See p. 320 above.
241. See *Commission Level 2 Background Note* (no. 3 above) p. 13; cf. Recital 23, MiFID Level 2 Directive (no. 140 above): 'While disclosure of specific conflicts of interest is required by Art. 18(2) of Directive 2004/39/EC, an over-reliance on disclosure without adequate consideration as to how conflicts may appropriately be managed is not permitted.'
242. See *Commission Level 2 Background Note* (no. 3 above), p. 13.
243. While the first two working versions of the Commission's Level 2 rules did not contain a distinction based on the type of client, the third draft limited the implementation provision of Art. 18(2) to disclosures to retail clients (Art. 23, European Commission, Internal Market and Services DG, *Organisational Requirements and Identification, Management and Disclosure of Conflicts of Interest by Investment Firms*, Working Document ESC/17/2005-Rev2, 9 September 2005) and the third revision specified that 'An investment firm shall provide the information [required by Art. 18(2) MiFID] to professional clients upon request' (Art. 23(2) European Commission, Internal Market and Services DG, *Organisational Requirements and Identification, Management and Disclosure of Conflicts of Interest by Investment Firms*, Working Document ESC/17/2005-Rev3, 27 September 2005).
244. Cf. the remark by CESR in answer to some respondents: 'the disclosure obligations under Art. 18(2) cover all categories of clients.' *CESR's Technical Advice on Level 2 Implementing*

More importantly, limiting the disclosure requirement of Article 18(2), MiFID, to retail clients is inappropriate to tackle the problems posed by conflicts of interest. As regulation relating to conflicts of interest is linked to information asymmetries, it may seem logical to differentiate between the wholesale or professional domain on the one hand and retail on the other.[245] But conflict of interest problems are just as prevalent in relations with professional clients, and the fact that such clients are more likely to know when conflicts are present does not mean they are no longer entitled to expect loyalty from their asset managers.[246] As I pointed out earlier,[247] the agency problems created by conflicts of interest are not the result of the parties' unequal bargaining positions at the time of transacting, which would suggest that the problems do not exist for professional clients. In fact they are the result of clients' vulnerability to disloyal behaviour, which is inherent in the characteristics of the duty of loyalty *resulting from* the asset management agreement, and these characteristics[248] are as serious in contracts with professional clients as they are in contracts with retail clients.

Therefore, it is fortunate that the MiFID Level 2 Directive does not limit the conflicts of interest disclosure duty to retail clients.[249] Indeed, as the Commission itself now explicitly recognizes, '[t]he status of the client to whom the service is provided – as either retail, professional or eligible counterparty – is irrelevant for [the] purpose [of the regulation of conflicts of interest].'[250]

Is disclosure sufficient in itself, or must the informed client also consent before the firm can provide or continue to provide the service or services or execute the transaction in relation to which the conflict arose? CESR advised requiring the client's consent, and in its first working version the Commission followed this advice.[251] However, this paragraph was dropped without explanation from the

---

Measures on the First Set of Mandates. Markets in Financial Instruments Directive. Feedback Statement, CESR/05-025, January 2005, pp. 23 and 25, available at <www.cesr-eu.org>).

245. See e.g. I. Walter (no. 38 above), p. 184; cf. also Recital 5 ('as regards investor protection, and in particular the provision of investors with information or the seeking of information from investors, the retail or professional nature of the client or potential client concerned should be taken into account') and Recital 44, MiFID Level 2 Directive (no. 140 above).
246. Given the familiar distinction between retail and professional clients when describing the specific protection offered by securities regulation, it might seem 'normal' to limit conflict disclosure obligations to retail clients. However, to show how inappropriate this assumption is, we need only imagine reactions to a proposal that in future law firms and attorneys would no longer have to inform their professional clients of the conflicts of interest they face in representing them, unless specifically asked to do so. I cannot imagine that such a rule change would be accepted on the argument that professional clients are expected to fend for themselves and ask for this information if they consider it to be relevant.
247. See p. 300 above.
248. For these characteristics, see p. 280–282 above.
249. Art. 22(4) MiFID Level 2 Directive (no. 140 above).
250. Recital 25, MiFID Level 2 Directive (no. 140 above).
251. Art. 23(2) European Commission, Internal Market and Services DG, *Organisational Requirements and Identification, Management and Disclosure of Conflicts of Interest by Investment Firms*, Working Document ESC/17/2005, 13 May 2005, p. 17: 'Where an investment firm has made a disclosure to a client in relation to a conflict of interest in accordance with Art. 18(2)

subsequent working versions of the Commission's Level 2 text.[252] Instead, the version of the Level 2 text requires the disclosure to contain sufficient detail to enable the client to take an informed decision with respect to the service in the context of which the conflict of interest arises.[253] Could it be that the Commission is only thinking of one-off transactions where disclosure of the conflict before the client even asks for the service can be assumed to imply his consent when he subsequently confirms the order? Applied to financial services such as asset management, this provision becomes problematic: shouldn't a portfolio manager be required to disclose conflicts of interest that relate to individual investment decisions he might have to take in the performance of his asset management contract? Can such disclosure suffice, even if it is not followed by any action by the client that can be understood to imply his informed consent?

As such, the disclosure requirement of Article 18(2), MiFID, is in practice more likely to lead to a general system of disclaimers issued by investment firms,[254] instead of the type of disclosure that would be required to effectively resolve conflicts of interest. While disclosure is presented as a method of preventing conflicts of interest from creating problems for agents under a duty of loyalty, what this disclosure requirement in fact threatens to do is to materially change the duty the investment firm owes the client. Indeed, there is a serious risk that the investment firm will try to use disclosure to reduce the expectations of its clients,[255] which then can be used as an argument for limiting its liabilities to a general duty of care, not a duty of loyalty.[256] Hence, unfortunately, the rules may end up throwing away

---

of the Directive, it shall not provide, or continue to provide, the service or services in relation to which that conflict arises, without the consent of the client.' CESR's advice contained the same requirement: Paragraph 11(b) CESR/05-024c (no. 154 above), pp. 44 and 42.

252. See European Commission, Internal Market and Services DG, *Organisational Requirements and Identification, Management and Disclosure of Conflicts of Interest by Investment Firms*, Working Document ESC/17/2005-Rev1, 20 June 2005, p. 19; ESC/17/2005-Rev2 (no. 243 above), p. 20; ESC/17/2005-Rev3 (no. 243 above), p. 18.

253. Art. 22(4) Draft Commission Level 2 Directive (no. 140 above); see also J. Krol (Administrateur, Commission Européenne, Direction Marché Intérieur) 'Présentation générale de la directive MIF et de sa mise en œuvre' (July-August 2005) *Banque & Droit* 102, 4, 6: 'le client doit être informé de la source et la nature des conflits pour qu'il puisse prendre une décision en toute connaissance de cause.'

254. Cf. K. Vuillemin (no. 94 above), 590.

255. How else are we to interpret the boilerplate conflicts disclosure reportedly used by Charles Schwab & Co.: 'Schwab and/or its employees or directors as well as consultants to Schwab may have had clients with positions in securities or companies referenced in Information, including Research Reports, and may, as principal or agent, buy from or sell to customers. From time to time, Schwab may perform investment banking or other services for, or solicit such services from, companies mentioned in Information.' D.M. Cain, G. Loewenstein and D.A. Moore, 'Coming Clean but Playing Dirtier' (no. 221 above), p. 111.

256. See N. S. Poser (no. 124 above), 122–123, summing up the usual disclaimers in common agreements with investment-management clients, concluding that '[t]hese kinds of clauses may have the effect of avoiding a firm's liability for failing to meet fiduciary duties owed to its clients.' See also D.M. Cain, G. Loewenstein and D.A. Moore, 'The Dirt on Coming Clean' (no. 221 above), 3, comparing this with the result of the warning labels on cigarette packets:

the baby with the bathwater. While the problem of potentially unfulfilled investor expectations may be avoided, the potential for reaching a higher level of efficiency on which the asset manager really does act in the investor's exclusive interests is lost. Were conflicts of interest a mere investor protection issue, this consequence would be acceptable; however, as the main risks from conflicts of interest are to market efficiency, this result unfortunately fails to solve this problem.

IV. SOME CONCLUDING REMARKS

Asset management traditionally involved the portfolio manager explicitly or implicitly promising to loyally serve his client's investment interests. Such a duty of loyalty inherently creates conflicts of interest when the asset manager has personal interests that are affected by the investment decisions he has to take on behalf of his clients, or has several clients whose interests may come into conflict. Multi-functional financial institutions offering asset management services are very often confronted with such circumstances.

As it stands, European regulation does not adequately address the problems created by conflicts of interest, for a number of reasons.

The rules do not contain realistic remedy provisions that take into account the essential characteristics of the conflict of interest problem, characteristics that make it insoluble by the market mechanism if governed by standard private law. This is because of the inherent difficulty of proving the true motivation of an asset manager who is necessarily mandated to act with considerable discretion, and/or the extent of his personal gains from his actions.

Application of enforcement mechanisms such as common-law fiduciary duties could solve this problem, but would require massaging to be realistically applied to institutional asset management. Thus far, however, both the Level 1 text of the MiFID and the Level 2 Directive fail to properly specify the general duty of loyalty as it should be applied to asset management services in order to avoid the enforcement problems of a general duty of loyalty.

Another problem is that the EC legislator appears to start from a mere investor protection rather than a global market efficiency rationale when designing conflict of interest rules. This approach is misguided because although the market mechanism may often provide investors with sufficient protection against abuses from financial institutions, the market as such is unlikely to reach a socially optimal equilibrium.

As a practical matter, this unfortunate focus on investor protection results in an unwarranted distinction between professional and retail clients with respect to conflict of interest rules. Both types of clients should be able to rely on the

---

a requirement that was intended to protect consumers ended up shielding tobacco producers from liability for damages suffered by smokers who had been warned. In other words: *caveat emptor*!

loyalty of their asset managers, and the agency problem that undermines this confidence and thus limits market efficiency is a consequence of inherent characteristics of an asset management contract, not of the lack of sophistication of certain investors.

Finally, the rules that have been considered rely on disclosure to solve problems it cannot solve. Disclosure is generally agreed to be an efficient measure for addressing asymmetric information problems at the time of contracting or taking investment decisions. However, in conflict of interest situations using disclosure to redress an informational asymmetry at the time of contracting is not very helpful because the asymmetry reappears every single time the asset manager takes an investment decision.

Hence, to solve the conflict of interest problem, disclosure will only work if it effectively acts to end the delegation of power to the agent and allow the principal to take the decision himself, or at least to force the agent to disclose all gains he will realize and has realized from exploiting the conflict, in order to permit both *ex ante* and *ex post* negotiation between agent and principal and so allow market forces to allocate these gains between principal and agent. This kind of disclosure would seem to undermine the very reason why investors use institutional asset managers – namely to take investment decisions on their behalf without bothering them – and hence it is not surprising that the disclosure measures contemplated in MiFID are geared to the time of contracting. The problem is that the required disclosure is unlikely to be effective against the conflicts of interest problem faced by institutional asset managers.

As long as returns on investment are satisfactory or in line with expectations, investors will not complain about conflicts of interest in the asset management sector. However, when the market takes a downturn – as it did at the beginning of this decade – financial institutions risk being burdened with complaints and lawsuits by investors trying to recover part of their losses. Abuses of conflicts of interest and the resulting damage to the investor may be difficult to prove in practice, resulting in enforcement problems, but an accusation of such abuse is almost impossible to disprove, resulting in a legal risk for financial institutions. Moreover, the potential loss of small investors' confidence as a result is undesirable for service providers and for the market as a whole.

Interestingly, the asset management sector has recently shown three developments that could be seen as partially redressing some conflicts of interest problems.

First, the industry has been moving away from the traditional single asset manager controlling a broad-based portfolio towards very specialized mandates focused on narrowly defined asset classes and clearly defined investment styles and strategies.[257] Performance is being evaluated based on general or specialized market indices; if none is available for the investment category involved, peer group

257. Apart from obviously being included in the agreement between the firm and the client, the draft Level 2 rules require the portfolio manager to provide retail clients with a summary of the types of financial instruments that may be included in the client portfolio and types of

benchmarks are employed.[258] Such contractual arrangements make it more difficult for asset managers to get away with deliberately harming the client's interests by making suboptimal investment decisions. Given competition forces, these developments allow the market mechanism to reduce the conflicts of interest problem to a level below the radar, i.e. a level at which no *ex post* verifiable bias can be measured.

Secondly, most asset management contracts include disclaimers limiting the potential liability of the financial firm.[259] Not only are such clauses designed to inform the client in advance of any potential conflict of interest, thereby shielding the firm from any future claim based on such a conflict, but they also aim to limit the duties the portfolio manager owes his client. Under the broadest of such exonerating clauses, the asset manager merely promises to make a reasonable effort to generate an investment result that conforms to industry standards, without being required to take the best decision for the investment interests of the client at every turn. In other words, asset managers are trying to substitute a traditional duty of care for the potentially problematic duty of loyalty and so avoid the conflict of interest problem altogether.

While these two developments may prove helpful in limiting the potential liability of asset managers and thus restricting their legal risk, they do not help solve the most essential problem created by conflicts of interest – reduced market efficiency. Reduced investor confidence in financial institutions, and limited client expectations of what their professional service providers have to offer, will result in a market equilibrium at a lower level than optimal. In other words: investors may very well use fewer asset management services and hence keep a smaller proportion of their savings in risk-bearing assets than would be optimal for the economy.

Remarkably, multifunctional financial institutions seem to be moving towards voluntarily segregating activities more than is required by regulation. The move from closed to open architecture in the distribution of collective investment schemes is an example, but even more typical is the fact that several larger financial firms have brought all their asset management activities – both individual portfolio management and the management of collective investment schemes such as UCITS – together as a separate subsidiary of the financial institution or separate corporation within the conglomerate, with no other activities.[260] Although clearly inspired by a

---

transactions that may be performed on such instruments, including any limits, the management objectives, the level of risk to be reflected in the manager's exercise of discretion, and any specific constraints on that discretion. See Art. 30(3)(d)-(e) MiFID Level 2 Directive (no. 140 above).

258. See Bank for International Settlements (no. 22 above), p. 19; if a benchmark is being used, the retail client will have to be informed. See Art. 30(3)(c) MiFID Level 2 Directive (no. 140 above).

259. See nos. 254–256 above and accompanying text.

260. The combination of individual and collective portfolio management within one company was permitted by the 2001 amendments to the UCITS Directive. See Art. 5(3) UCITS Directive, as amended by Directive 2001/107/EC of the European Parliament and of the Council of 21 January 2002 amending Council Directive 85/611/EEC on the Coordination of Laws, Regulations

desire for economies of scale, this structure can also be seen as a way of producing the level of separation of activities required by the regulation.

However, while separate legal personality, combined with liability limited to the assets of each corporation, is an effective mechanism for creating a firewall designed to insulate each activity centre from the financial distress existing in another centre, it does not sever lines of loyalty. As corporate careers of staff members often involve hopping from one conglomerate entity to another, loyalty can attach to the conglomerate as a whole, ignoring the specific corporate structure of the companies constituting the group. For loyalty to be restricted to the asset management activity alone, it may very well be necessary to completely sever the links between the asset management corporation and the rest of the financial group, attracting a different set of shareholders for the asset management company.

Interestingly, there appears to be some desire in the market to do precisely that.[261] It can bring marketing advantages on the buy side of the market, as the separateness and thus independence can be highlighted as a strength. In effect, this is a way for asset managers to signal to potential clients that they are truly independent of the sell side of the market and therefore not subject to the conflicts of interest arising from a combination of activities, which also enables them to avoid a so-called lemons' discount.[262]

The ultimate question is whether such separation should be legally imposed. Today, most regulators clearly do not favour mandatory separation as a way of tackling conflicts of interest problems.[263] As a justification for this position, CESR noted that there is no proof that the benefits to clients from disaggregation of

---

and Administrative Provisions relating to Undertakings for Collective Investment in Transferable Securities (UCITS) with a View to Regulating Management Companies and Simplified Prospectuses, OJ L 41/20, 2002, 20.

261. E.g. the recent efforts of the Fortis Group to find a joint venture partner for its asset management business, in particular the reported talks between Fortis and Lloyds TSB bank with a view to merging their respective asset management corporations. 'Lloyds in Talks to Merge Widows Fund Arm', *The Independent*, 11 November 2005; T. Braithwaite and L. Saigol, 'Lloyds in Talks with Fortis on Asset Management Deal' *Financial Times*, 12 November 2005, 15.

262. See no. 80 above.

263. This may be related to past experiences with the separation of commercial and investment banking. See e.g. E. N. White (no. 29 above) p. 296:

'Perhaps, the most potent example of a misplaced remedy is the separation of commercial and investment banking by the Glass-Steagall Act. The separation imposed a high cost; and only after a long struggle, was the act was [*sic*] reversed in 1999. Market discipline that forced institutional changes on banks worked fairly well before 1929. The repeal of Glass-Steagall moved back to a greater emphasis on disclosure and oversight that were originally recommended by contemporary experts.'

I think that to consider the Glass-Steagall Act a 'misplaced' remedy points to a confusion between the rationale for the separation of commercial and investment banking – mainly to avoid financial risks spreading from one activity into the other by imposing a firewall – and the rationale for the separation of asset management from other supply-side financial services – mainly to avoid conflicts of interest. See p. 322–323 above. This, however, does not stand in the way of a conclusion that the regulatory separation of commercial and investment banking long had the effect of creating structural barriers to certain conflicts of interest which became

large financial firms would outweigh the costs.[264] However, it would be worth investigating – empirically as well – what real economic benefits are gained by combining buy side portfolio management with sell side activities or services in the same firm. Is combining these functions in one firm or one group of firms actually efficient from a social point of view, or only from the point of view of the firm involved? If the only economic advantages that can be named are economies of scale or scope, do they actually outweigh the costs resulting from the inherent conflicts of interest, not least the compliance cost from the special regulations that would be unnecessary if the functions were totally separate? Above all, would segregation not ultimately allow the market to reach equilibrium at a higher level as global investor confidence in the loyalty of asset managers increased?

In 2000, the SEC, fully aware of the problems of conflicts of interest in the auditing industry, considered but rejected a mandatory separation of audit and consulting services and chose only to impose disclosure as a remedy.[265] Less than two years and one particularly publicized and therefore politicized scandal later, the US changed its mind and imposed a ban on combining auditing with non-auditing services for the same client in the Sarbanes-Oxley Act.[266] Let's hope it does not take another scandal to convince the regulators that control over the investments of savers (buy-side, asset management services) had better not be in the same hands as control over the production and distribution of objects that can be invested in (sell-side services and market organizing or transaction execution services).

In medicine, if you want patients to feel secure in the conviction that their doctors' prescriptions are issued on purely medical grounds and not because the doctors stand to gain from them, it is a good idea to have a mandatory separation between medical practices and the distribution of medication through pharmacies. Why should it be fundamentally different for asset management?

---

prevalent very soon after the passing of the Gramm-Leach-Bliley Act (Public Law No. 106–102, 12 November 1999, 113 Stat. 1341), of which Section 101(a) repealed the Glass-Steagall Act (12 U.S.C. 377). See I. Walter (no. 38 above) p. 175.

264. See CESR/05-024c (no. 154 above) p. 41; for an earlier reference see *CESR's Advice on Possible Implementing Measures of the Directive 2004/39/EC on Markets in Financial Instruments, Consultation Paper*, CESR/04-261b, June 2004, p. 40, available at <www.cesr-eu.org>. The actual CESR wording ('the costs associated with disaggregation cannot be shown to outweigh the benefits to clients.') seems to be a mistake.

265. See SEC, Final Rule: Revision of the Commission's Auditor Independence Requirements, Release No. 33–7919, 21 November 2000, codified in 17 C.F.R. Parts 210 and 240.

266. See Section 201 of the Sarbanes-Oxley Act, Pub.L. 107–204, 30 July 2002, codified as 15 U.S.C. 78j-1(g).

Chapter 11

Conflicts of Interest in the Distribution of Investment Funds

*Luc Thévenoz**

> 'Open architecture provides greater choice but introduces the possibility that customers will be sold the funds that pay the highest commission rather than those that are most suitable.'
>
> *The Financial Times*, 18 July 2005

While in the next chapter Tamar Frankel mostly discusses conflicts of interest arising from the relationship between the manager of an investment fund and the brokers executing securities transactions on behalf of the fund,[1] this paper focuses on the relationship between the manager of an investment fund and the firms distributing its shares to the public. To incentivize distributors, the manager agrees to share revenue by retroceding to distributors part of the fees obtained from its activity. I shall examine in greater detail retrocessions paid to distributors out of the management fee charged to the fund and the conflicts of interest that result from them, as well as possible approaches to preventing or managing these conflicts.

In this paper, 'investment fund' refers to any variety of collective investment scheme, whether in corporate form (SICAF, SICAV, investment trusts and so on), based on a contract (*fonds de placement, fonds communs de placement, Anlage-fonds*), or based on a trust arrangement (unit trusts). 'Fund provider' refers to a

---

* Professor, University of Geneva, Director, Centre for Banking and Financial Law, Commissioner, Swiss Federal Banking Commission. This contribution expresses the author's personal opinions.

1. See below, page 370ff.

L. Thévenoz and R. Bahar (eds.), *Conflicts of Interest: Corporate Governance and Financial Market*, pp. 337–361.

financial institution that designs, creates and promotes an investment fund. The provider does not necessarily manage the assets of the funds, a task which is often partially or totally outsourced. 'Fund distributor' refers to the firm or person controlling the relationship with the individual investor and acting as an intermediary in the investment process. Distributors vary widely in types and sizes, from a bank to an independent licensed or unlicensed[2] financial advisor, including securities brokerage firms, insurance companies, tied agents, etc.

While this paper concentrates on policy issues rather than on any specific legal system, I shall often refer to the European Union legal environment as well as to Swiss laws and regulations. Reasons for the first choice are fairly obvious. On this side of the Atlantic, investment funds are a major area of financial services where governments, regulators and the industry are seeking to achieve closer and more efficient integration while maintaining a high degree of investor protection.[3] The second choice is prompted not only by the institutional context in which this book originated, but also by the fact that revenue sharing between fund providers and distributors has recently attracted a great deal of attention in Switzerland. Over the past three years, the regulator (the Swiss Federal Banking Commission) has questioned the extent and practicalities of retrocessions out of the management fee, which in turn prompted the industry association (the Swiss Funds Association) to a adopt self-regulatory disclosure standard sanctioned by the regulator.

I. GENERAL CONTEXT

The volume of assets in EU-regulated investment funds[4] is estimated at EUR 4 trillion.[5] The figure for Switzerland is CHF 505 billion, or approximately EUR 330 billion.[6] It is no wonder that the distribution of these funds to retail and private-banking customers has become a major line of business and source of revenue for

2. Unlike in the European Union, the provision of financial advice or portfolio management services in Switzerland is not *per se* a regulated service.
3. See recently the public consultation initiated by the EU Commission on its Green Paper on the Enhancement of the EU Framework for Investment Funds of 12 July 2005, SEC(2005) 947, COM(2005) 314 final. It is supplemented by a valuable Background Paper published as a Commission Staff Working Paper. Both are available at <www.europa.eu.int/comm/internal_market/securities/ucits/index_en.htm>.
4. Such investment funds (known as UCITS) are subject to national legislation implementing the Council Directive 85/611/EEC of 20 December 1985 on the coordination of laws, regulations, and administrative provisions relating to undertakings for collective investment in transferable securities, OJ L 375/3, 1985, (hereafter: UCITS Directive). This directive has been modified by several subsequent directives. A current, consolidated text is available at<eur-lex.europa.eu/LexUriServ/LexUriServ.do?uri=CELEX:01985L0611-20050413:EN:NOT>.
5. Annex (p. 12) to the Green Paper (no. 2 above).
6. Swiss Funds Association, *SFA fund statistics – Q3 2005*, 30 October 2005, <www.sfa.ch>.

most financial services providers such as banks, securities brokers, independent financial advisors, etc. Unlike in the USA and the UK, the distribution of collective investments in continental Europe is largely dominated by universal banks. At the same time, banking groups are the most significant providers of funds. Traditionally, banks used to distribute almost exclusively their own products through their proprietary network. Over the last several years, however, 'open architecture' has gained in popularity. European banks and other funds providers are trying to distribute their funds through other, non-captive channels such as regional banks, securities brokers, insurance companies,[7] and independent financial advisers. At the same time, European banks are opening their own distribution networks to funds created and managed by other providers.

However significant, this trend toward open architecture (or cross-distribution of investment funds) is still at an early stage. A study by PriceWaterhouseCoopers published in 2002, for example, found that non-proprietary channels contributed 14 per cent of the inflow of new assets from the home market, but 82 per cent of the inflow of new assets from export markets.[8] Data published by the EU Commission confirms the progressive opening up of proprietary distribution channels to funds provided by third parties. In 1998, cross-border funds accounted for 11 per cent of all EU regulated funds. This figure was 13 per cent in 2002 and 16 per cent in 2003, indicating a significant speeding up of the process.[9]

Conversely, Europe is characterized by an extremely large number of funds of sub-optimal size: EU data indicate that the 28,830 EU (regulated) funds have on average five times fewer assets under management than the corresponding 8,046 US investment funds.[10] This makes it difficult for the industry to reap economies of scale. A number of reasons may explain this excessive fragmentation of the European fund industry. Cross-border funds (funds sold in several or many EU Member States) are increasing sharply, but remain difficult and costly to launch. Administrative barriers, differences in tax regime, obstacles to cross-border fund mergers and pooling techniques, client preferences varying from one country to another, all contribute to an offer of funds which is fragmented and biased towards national products.[11]

---

7. Life-insurance companies typically distribute investment funds through 'unit-linked policies' (premium buys life insurance plus investment in funds) or 'with-profit funds' (policyholders share in the return on the fund), see Commission staff's Background Paper (no. 2 above), p. 10 at footnote 16. Other intermediaries may also repackage investment funds, e.g. through private labelling, by incorporation into a certificate or other derivative or structured financial instrument, or by way of a fund of funds.
8. PriceWaterhouseCoopers, *Eurofunds Survey 2002: Challenging Markets: Distributing Too Many Products to Too Few Clients* (Luxembourg), <www.pwcglobal.com/lu/eng/ins-sol/publ/pwc_eurofunds_flyer.pdf> (03 January 06), p. 23.
9. [EU Commission's Directorate of General Internal Market and Services, *Financial Integration Monitor 2005* : Background document (June 2005) p. 45, Figure 11.
10. Ibid., p. 46, Table 5.
11. Commission's staff Background Paper (note 2 above), p. 9.

The still prevailing state of high fragmentation of European investment funds inevitably impacts on the costs of funds distributed cross-border in Europe. A recent study of investment fund expenses highlights the fact that the Total Expense Ratios (TERs)[12] of US and European funds diverge widely.

Table 1. TER of US, UK, and European Cross-border Funds

	Equity funds (overall)		Bond funds (overall)	
	Asset-weighted average TER	Average fund size (USD mil.)	Asset-weighted average TER	Average fund size (USD mil.)
USA	0.92%	3,238	0.86%	1,883
Europe (cross-border Ucits)	1.79%	1,221	1.35%	992
UK	1.68%	687	1.24%	233

Source: Lipper[13]

While the fund size significantly affects the TER, it does not explain the difference between US and European funds of similar size, as can be seen from a comparison between midsize funds (USD 100 million to 1 billion of assets under management).

Table 2. TER of midsize US, UK and European Cross-border Funds

	Equity funds between USD 100 mil. and USD 1 bil.		Bond funds (overall) between USD 100 mil. and USD 1 bil.	
	Asset-weighted average TER	Average fund size (USD mil.)	Asset-weighted average TER	Average fund size (USD mil.)
USA	1.25%	432	0.93%	407
Europe (cross-border Ucits)	1.86%	413	1.30%	382
UK	1.69%	426	1.25%	295

Source: Lipper[14]

This paper does not purport to explain why European investment funds, particularly those distributed in more than one country, are significantly more costly than US funds. Whatever the number of factors, my point is that costs are significant to

12. According to IOSCO's Technical Committee, 'the Total Expense Ratio of a fund is equal to the ratio of the fund's total operating costs to its average net assets,' calculated at least once a year. It includes all recurring and non-recurring costs, except transaction costs of asset purchases and sales. See Annex 2 of the Technical Committee's Final Report on Elements of International Regulatory Standards on Fees and Expenses of Investment Funds, November 2004, available at <www.iosco.org>.
13. Lipper, *A Comparison of Mutual Fund Expenses Across The Atlantic*, 26 September 2005, Tables 1 and 2.
14. Ibid., Tables 3 and 4.

investors because they directly affect the performance of their investments. This also applies to distribution costs as well as to other costs.

Obviously, distribution is not only a matter of costs, but also of quality of service. By focusing on the conflicts of interest in the distribution of investment funds, I will show that both are closely connected. The fact that, in the retail market, funds distributors are significantly, and often exclusively, remunerated by fund providers creates conflicts of interest that may increase the costs ultimately borne by investors without promoting a choice of the funds best suited to the interests and needs of the individual investor.

II. REMUNERATION OF FUND DISTRIBUTORS – AN OVERVIEW

Depending on its contract with the investor, the distributor may or may not receive a fee directly from the investor. Financial advice paid for by the retail investor is not yet very common, while discretionary management of portfolios most certainly is. Nonetheless, under its contract with the provider of the fund, the distributor will in most cases obtain some form of remuneration from the fund provider, in one or more ways:[15]

- The investment in the fund may be subject to an entry (or load) fee paid by the investor to the provider. Most of the fee is typically paid back by the provider to the distributor. A 2002 survey shows that the average retrocession for equity funds varied between 79.5 per cent of the entry fee in France to 95.6 per cent in the UK and 95.8 per cent in Switzerland.[16]
- Whether or not the investment is subject to an entry fee, the distributor receives a retrocession (a so-called trail fee) on the management fee paid to the provider in accordance with the fund regulations. The same survey shows a wider range of retrocession on the management fee of equity funds, from 45.8 per cent in the UK and 56.8 per cent in Switzerland to 106.7 per cent in Spain.[17]

I use the word 'retrocession' here to refer to revenue sharing arrangements by which some part of the remuneration paid to the provider by the investor, directly or out of the assets under management, flows back to the distributor as a remuneration for its services to the provider and/or the investor.

Both types of fees and retrocessions differ in their source and periodicity. The entry fee is paid once by the investor to the provider as a percentage of (and

15. This paper discusses only retrocessions from entry fees and management fees. Similar issues may arise in connection with retrocessions from other (redemption, switch, etc.) fees charged by the fund provider to the investor.
16. *Eurofunds Survey 2002* (no. 8 above), p. 32.
17. Ibid. A figure above 100 per cent indicates that the provider spends all of the management fee plus money from other resources to distribute the fund

in addition to) his investment. The management fee is charged by the distributor directly to the fund, paid out of the assets managed, in accordance with the fund rules;[18] its cost is borne by all investors in the fund since it is deducted from the net asset value (NAV).

It is worth noting that retrocessions are also paid by funds providers to fund distributors within the same firm or financial group.[19] There are at least two reasons for such intra-firm or intra-group retrocessions. First, whether they operate as separate legal entities in the same financial group or as separate business units within the same legal entity, assets management (typically responsible for providing funds), private banking, and retail banking are different profit centres. Each is accountable for its own revenue and profit. The distribution of investment funds must be profitable to the profit centres in charge of the distribution. Secondly, the number of products offered to private investors is steadily increasing; pushing an investment fund all the way through to the ultimate investor requires incentives comparable with those offered on substitute investments, be they investment funds provided by other firms or other financial products such as structured products. This is true not only from the perspective of the managers of the distribution units, but also from the financial perspective of the employee managing the relationship with the customer.

The above figures[20] show that retrocessions are a substantial part of the management fee. Increased competition for 'shelf-space' is driving them up rather than down. This is particularly true of cross-border distribution. Alan Ainsworth, deputy chairman of Threadneedle Investment Services, was recently quoted by the *Financial Times* as saying that cross-border funds based in Luxembourg or Dublin 'have made progress over the last few years by paying higher retrocessions.'[21] Though I do not have any chronological data on retrocessions, this affirmation matches well with the constant increase in management fees observed over more than 10 years.

While the total volume of funds has been increasing sharply, management fees are also on the increase. The most likely explanation, and the one which is offered informally by many actors, is that retrocessions to distributors drive up the management fee out of which they are paid.

The above mostly applies to funds distributed to (retail and private banking) individual investors. Institutional investors (including high net worth individuals) usually have direct access to the provider of the fund and thus need not pay the cost of a distributor. If they do not, and employ an asset manager or a financial advisor to invest in a fund, the terms of the contract will almost always require the advisor to pass on to them any remuneration received from a third party.

---

18. In this paper, the term 'fund rules' includes the instruments of incorporation of an investment company.
19. Page 32 of the *Eurofunds Survey 2002* (no. 8 above) reads: 'For manufacturers [funds providers] that have access to proprietary channels, rebates [retrocessions] offered to the latter are higher than those offered to external partners. For the vast majority of respondents, the rebates offered to the proprietary channel are the upper limit. No external [distribution] partner gets more.'
20. See no. 17 above.
21. *Financial Times*, 18 July 2005.

Table 3. TER and Management Fee

	1993	1994	1995	1996	1997	1998	1999	2000	2001	2002	2003 (prov.)
Total Expense Ratio (%NAV)	2.20	2.00	2.00	2.00	1.89	1.90	1.87	1.84	1.93	2.08	2.05
Management fee including distribution (%NAV)	1.15	1.17	1.19	1.21	1.23	1.25	1.29	1.31	1.34	1.36	1.37
Managed assets in EU (billion EUR)[22]						2,262	3,070	3,333	3,487	3,200	3,599

Source: Fitzrovia International[23]

The scope of this paper is thus limited to conflicts of interest in the distribution of funds to individual investors. These clients have neither the sophistication nor the commercial clout to make their financial advisor or manager agree to pass on to them any remuneration received from third parties in connection with their own investment.

III. CONFLICTS OF INTEREST AT TWO LEVELS

The factual settings of fund distribution and the resulting flows of remuneration give rise to two conflicts of interest: one in the person of the distributor, the other in the person of the provider. These conflicts are legally relevant only if the provider and the distributor are respectively subject to a duty of loyalty to the investor, i.e. a duty to actively protect and promote the investor's interests.[24]

A. Fund Providers

For investment funds subject to regulatory approval, the fund provider will always be a regulated entity subject to a legal, contractual or regulatory duty of loyalty to investors.

---

22. The data on assets managed by UCITS investment funds are taken from the Background Paper (no. 2 above), p. 6. Note that it refers to the overall EU market, while TER and management fee refer to equity funds domiciled in Luxembourg and Dublin. The investment fund volume is given here as a proxy for the development of the total market, from which Luxembourg and the Irish Republic profit probably more than other member states.
23. Presentation by Ed Moisson at the Fund Forum International on 8 July 2004. These figures apply to 'mainstream actively managed equity funds domiciled in Luxembourg and Dublin.'
24. See the introductory chapter of this book, pages 3–4; see also V. Simonart, 'Conclusions générales' in *Les conflits d'intérêts* (Brussels, Bruylant, 1997), pp. 303–304.

1. Duty of Loyalty

The law of the European Union imposes a clear duty of loyalty on the fund provider ('management company'). Article 5h of the UCITS Directive[25] requires the provider to try 'to avoid conflicts of interest and, when they cannot be avoided, ensure that the UCITS it manages are fairly treated,' and to ensure that it 'complies with all regulatory requirements applicable to the conduct of its business activities so as to promote the best interests of its investors.' This wording would seem to distinguish between duties of the provider to the UCITS it manages (to avoid conflicts of interest) on the one hand and its duties to investors in these UCITS (to promote their best interests) on the other. However, Article 5f (1)(b) requires Member States to adopt prudential rules aimed at 'minimiz[ing] the risk of UCITS' or client's interests being prejudiced by conflicts of interest . . . .' It is doubtful whether the interest of a UCIT and the interest of its investors can be distinguished. Losses and other detriments suffered by a UCIT are of necessity borne by all investors in it in proportion to the size of their investments.

Article 12 of the 1994 Swiss Investment Funds Act[26] requires the management company[27] and its agents to safeguard exclusively the interests of investors. As a result, the management company may only obtain and keep the remuneration spelled out in the fund rules; any other compensation or advantage must benefit the fund itself.[28] Conflicts of interest are not specifically mentioned in the 1994 Act. However, the Rules of Conduct adopted in 2000 by the Swiss Funds Association include three general rules dealing with conflicts of interest (adequate organization, employees' compensation policy, regulation and supervision of staff securities transactions).[29] The Swiss Federal Banking Commission, which is also the regulator for the fund industry, has mandated compliance with these rules for all management companies and requires their auditors to report on compliance.[30]

To summarize, both EU and Swiss law impose a duty of loyalty on fund providers and require them to avoid conflicts of interest that may affect the interests

25. See no. 4 above.
26. French, German and Italian authentic versions at <www.admin.ch/ch/f/rs/c951_31.html>; unofficial English translation by KPMG at <www.kpmg.ch/library/gesetzestexte/en/11972.htm> January 2006.
27. Investment funds contemplated by this provision are exclusively contractual arrangements – 'common funds managed by management companies' (see Art. 1(3) of the UCITS Directive) – not unit trusts or investment companies. A new Collective Capital Investment Act is currently being considered by the Swiss Parliament, which will extend this duty to investment companies and other collective investments falling within the (extended) scope of the Act, see *Feuille fédérale* 2005 5993, available at <http://www.admin.ch/ch/f/ff/2005/index0_43.html>.
28. See Arts. 14 (1) and 12 (2) of the Act.
29. Paragraphs 11 – 13 of the Code of conduct for the Swiss fund industry of 30 August 2000, <www.sfa.ch/index.php?setLN=e&site=2&page=13>.
30. See paragraph II.1 of the Annex to the Circular no. 04/2: Self-regulatory rules recognized as minimal standards by the Federal Banking Commission, 21 April 2004, <www.ebk.admin.ch>.

of investors in their funds. If such conflicts cannot be avoided, these interests must be 'treated fairly,' i.e. must not be 'prejudiced.'[31]

2. Retrocession Paid by Fund Providers on the Management Fee

Does the retrocession of some of the management fee by the fund provider to the distributor create a conflict of interest? One might be tempted to answer in the negative. The management fee paid to the fund provider out of the assets under management, in accordance with its contract with the investors, is legitimate compensation that it should be free to use as it wishes. Why should the fund provider's duty of loyalty extend to the use of such compensation? In particular, why should there be any problem in using a (significant) part of its compensation to remunerate distributors?

Though coined as 'retrocession out of the management fee,' the payments only nominally come out of the fees earned by fund providers. In reality, they are commissions negotiated between a fund provider and every distributor, calculated as some fraction (expressed in basis or percentage points) of the net funds invested in the fund by clients of that particular distributor. These commissions are paid out of the assets under management and are then accounted for as part of the so-called management fee. Indeed, the commissions are paid for by the investors collectively. In economic and accounting terms, such payments to distributors flow out of the accounts of the investment funds, not of the fund provider. When negotiating the amount of the distributors' compensation, the fund provider is therefore in a fiduciary position and owes a duty of loyalty to the investors, whose money it uses to pay for services provided by third parties, as it does for custodian banks, asset managers and other service providers.

The provider's conflict of interests comes from the fact that it has a personal interest in increasing assets under management (and its own compensation) by using such commissions to induce distributors to sell more fund shares. While the interest of investors requires compensating distributors for the services investors receive, fund providers have an interest of their own in inducing more sales by paying higher commissions out the investors' assets.

There is an additional component to the provider's conflict of interest, which lies in the potentially corrupting effect of such payments on fund distributors, which may conflict with the best interests of some investors. Compensating distributors for their efforts to bring in new investors or keep current investors in the fund is legitimate up to the point where such compensation induces them to recommend that particular fund in breach of their own duty to the investors. As we shall see below, distributors of funds (unlike distributors of cars or household appliances) are generally under a duty of loyalty to their customers, which is distinct from the fund provider's own duty of loyalty. It should not be the fund provider's responsibility to make sure that the distributor is fulfilling its duty of loyalty, e.g. by second-guessing

31. Comp. Art. 5h (d) and 5f (1)(b) of the UCITS Directive.

recommendations made by distributors to investors. However, the fund provider's own duty of loyalty prevents it from inducing the distributor to act against the investor's interests. After all, an investor induced by a distributor to invest in a given fund is the customer (and principal) of both the distributor and the fund provider.

'Retrocessions out of the management fee,' which are in fact commissions paid out of assets under management, compensate distributors for services rendered to the investors (advice) as well as to fund providers (promotion). When setting the appropriate level for such compensation, a fund provider is serving two interests, its own and its investors'. Retrocessions on management fees thus create a conflict of interest in the person of the fund provider as well as in the person of the fund distributors, as we shall see below.

This very conflict of interest is why, in the United States, SEC Regulation 12b-1 allows a mutual fund to pay distribution and marketing expenses out of the fund's assets provided that this has been approved by a majority of the outstanding voting securities of the investment company and is re-confirmed annually by a decision of the board of directors exercising reasonable business judgment and in the light of their fiduciary duties.[32]

3. Retrocession Paid by Fund Providers on Entry Fees

Entry fees are paid by investors upfront; they are distinct from the money invested in the fund. Who benefits from this entry price is not necessary relevant to the investor. Where the contract between the investor and the distributor does not provide for an explicit advisory fee or brokerage commission, the investor should expect that some or all of the entry fee will serve as remuneration to the distributor. When the investor explicitly pays for the service she gets from the distributor, she may not stop to think that its contractual partner may be getting some additional compensation from a third party, a benefit that the distributor may not be allowed to retain for itself. But this is relevant to the investor's relationship with the distributor, and not to the fund provider.

Do retrocessions out of entry fees raise the same conflict of interest as retrocessions out of management fees? We have just observed that both compensate the same service, viz. the distributor's contribution to the investor's initial decision to invest in a given fund. However, the corrupting effect of sharing the entry fee between the provider and the distributor seems much less problematic because:

- The entry fee is fixed (as opposed to the management fee, the actual amount of which will be determined year on year by the fund provider up to the cap defined by the rules of the particular fund) and easily recognizable by the investor; and

32. Rule 12b-1,'Distribution of Shares by Registered Open-End Management Investment Company,' was adopted by the Securities and Exchange Commission in 1980. The text of the Rule is available at <www.law.uc.edu/CCL/InvCoRls/rule12b-1.html>.

– The entry fee is explicitly designed as the price for being admitted into the fund, a price which reasonably entails the costs of fund distribution about which the investor may seek information from her distributor.

The investor is therefore in a much better position to guess or to find out from the distributor about the compensation the latter will obtain if the investor decides to choose that fund. This largely minimizes the problem from the viewpoint of the fund provider.

B. Fund Distributors

Investment funds can be distributed by various types of financial intermediaries – banks, securities brokers, tied agents, insurance companies and agents, independent financial advisors and portfolio managers, etc. – whose legal status and regulatory duties may differ significantly. Here again, conflicts of interest are legally relevant only if the distributor is subject to a legal, contractual, or regulatory duty of loyalty to the investor.

1. Duty of Loyalty

I shall not attempt here to determine which distributors are subject to such a duty of loyalty and will restrict ourselves to several highlights.

Under EU law, the UCITS Directive does not purport to impose duties on distributors of investment funds. However, the execution of orders or provision of advice in respect of UCITS is an investment service subject to the Markets in Financial Instruments Directive (MiFID).[33] Article 13(3) MiFID requires the investment firm 'to maintain and operate effective organizational and administrative arrangements with a view to taking all reasonable steps designed to prevent conflicts of interest as defined in Article 18 from adversely affecting the interests of its clients.' Article 18(2) provides that if the measures taken 'in accordance with Article 13(3) . . . are not sufficient to ensure, with reasonable confidence, that risks of damage to client interests will be prevented, the investment firm shall clearly disclose the general nature and/or sources of conflicts of interest to the client before undertaking business on its behalf.'

The Swiss Investment Funds Act of 1994 subjects the professional activity of distributing shares in investment funds to licensing by the Federal Banking Commission, unless the distributor is already licensed as a bank, securities house, or insurance company.[34] Apart from good repute, adequate training and experience,

33. Directive 2004/39/EC of the European Parliament and of the Council of 21 April 2004 on markets in financial instruments . . . OJ L145/1, 2004, (hereafter MiFID).

34. Art. 22 of the Act combined with Art. 23 of its implementing Ordinance, available at <www.admin.ch/ch/f/rs/c951_311.html>. The Swiss Postal Service, which provides certain financial services, is also exempted from this requirement.

liability insurance coverage, and reliable distribution methods, no specific regulatory duties attach to this status except for the requirement of a written contract with funds providers.[35] These few regulatory duties are supplemented by self-regulation adopted by the Swiss Funds Association requiring management companies to include in their distribution contracts a duty for the distributor to avoid conflicts of interest between investors and itself (and its employees) or, where this is not possible, to avoid any detriment to the interests of investors.[36] In fact, the most significant distributors of funds in Switzerland are banks that are also licensed as securities brokers, which Article 11(1)(c) of the Securities Exchange and Securities Trading Act of 1995[37] subjects to a legal duty of loyalty to their customers, including the duty to ensure that the interests of the latter are not adversely affected by potential or actual conflicts of interest. Moreover, a similar duty of loyalty will apply to all distributors of investment funds when the 2006 Collective Investment Act enters into force.[38]

2. Retrocession Received by Fund Distributors

Independent of the fund provider's conflict of interest as described earlier, negotiating for and obtaining retrocession creates a separate conflict of interest in the distributor.

Whether a distributor is required to assess the suitability of the investment for the investor, whether it owes a duty of professional advice or a mere duty of information will depend on its regulatory duties and the nature and extent of the service promised to the investor. As soon as this service includes some use of the distributor's professional judgment, the fact that the distributor receives some level of remuneration from the fund provider, whether as a one-off or periodically, may bias his judgment or appear to do so. The distributor's self-interest in maximizing its income conflicts with its duty to use its professional judgment in the best interests of the investor.

---

35. See Art. 22 (1) of the Ordinance. Whether distributors are agents (*mandataires, Beauftragte*) of the management company and therefore subject to the same duty of loyalty under Art. 12 of the Act is controversial, comp. M. den Otter, *AFG: Anlagefondsgesetz* (4th edn, Zurich, Orell Füssli, 2001), p. 58, and M. Küng & M. Büchi, *AFG: Materialien zum Bundesgesetz über die Anlagefonds . . .*, (Kriegstetten: Q Verlag, 1995), p. 148.
36. Para. III.A.3 of the Annex to the SFA Guidelines on fund distribution, 22 October 2001, <www.sfa.ch/index.php?site=2&page=12>. Pursuant to Art. 22 (3) of the Investment Funds Ordinance, the Federal Banking Commission imposes on all licensed distributors the duty to abide by the SFA Guidelines.
37. French, German and Italian authentic versions at <www.admin.ch/ch/f/rs/c954_1.html>, English translation at <www.swx.com/admission/regulation/rules_federal_en.html> (19 August. 2005)
38. See Art. 20 of the Federal Act on Collective Investments of Capital of 23 June 2006, <http://www.admin.ch/ch/f/ff/2006/5533.pdf>.

Indeed, the European legislation implementing the MiFID does recognize that receiving an inducement 'from a person other than the client . . . in relation to a service provided to the client' is a source of conflict of interest.[39]

Recognizing this conflict of interest does not mean that retrocessions should necessarily be banned and distributors be remunerated directly by the investor. This is one of several possible solutions to this conflict, and a radical one. But recognizing the conflicts that retrocessions entail for distributors of funds, as well as for their providers (see above), is a necessary preliminary to the search for possible solutions.

IV. POSSIBLE SOLUTIONS

Having established that, in most cases, retrocessions create conflicts of interest for fund providers as well as for distributors, we can start looking for solutions. As noted above, the most significant conflict arises out of sharing the management fee. For practical purposes, I shall focus largely on solutions in respect of retrocessions out of the management fee. A number of potential solutions can be envisaged, ranging from the most radical and undifferentiated to preserving the status quo. I shall go through them under three headings: prohibiting retrocessions, regulating retrocessions, and disclosing retrocessions to investors.

A. PROHIBITING RETROCESSIONS

The most radical and undifferentiated option would be to partially or entirely prohibit the payment of retrocessions by fund providers to distributors. Full prohibition would avoid all conflicts of interest arising out of such payments. This is the least liberal remedy: prohibition prevents market forces from applying. It is not *per se* unacceptable, but should only be considered if no other, lighter approach equally avoids conflicts of interest, or at least enables them to be managed so as not to disadvantage investors. A prohibition approach need not be absolute. It can differentiate between entry fees and management fees, which do not raise identical problems. It may also be subject to waiver by the investor as the party whose interests are endangered by the conflict.

Retrocessions on entry fees actually compensate the distributor for a service provided to the investor: information, transmission of order and payment, and quite often some form of advice. The provision of such services is useful and beneficial to investors. If they are not adequately remunerated, they will not be provided. At the same time, the remuneration creates an incentive to recommend (or limit the proposal of) funds based on the amount of remuneration received through retrocessions rather than on suitability to the needs of the investor. This is a problem

39. See Art. 21(e) and 26 of the Commission Directive 2006/73/EC of 10 August 2006 implementing Directive 2004/39/EC . . . as regards organizational requirements and operating conditions for investment firms and defined terms for the purposes of that Directive, OJ L241/26, 2006.

faced by buyers of complex goods and services. It is legally relevant when the distributor is subject to a duty of loyalty; a situation that does not generally apply to the sale of washer-dryers, automobiles or home cinemas. However, this conflict of interest might be effectively managed by other measures such as disclosure, as considered below.

Retrocessions on management fees can also be considered additional, deferred and periodic compensation for the same services performed at the time of investment. This does not imply that they should receive the same treatment as retrocessions on entry fees. Because retrocessions on management fees are periodic, their aggregate sum is not measured according to the extent or quality of the service provided to the investor, but according to the duration of his investment. This can also be construed as compensation for the loss on retrocessions on entry fees forfeited because the investment in the original fund is maintained. The incentives so created are not aligned with the interests of the investor.

In addition, informal discussions and queries show that individual investors are generally aware that the entry fee they are charged is used, at least partly, to compensate their distributor. The vast majority, however, are not aware that part of the yearly management fee represents regular payments to distributors. The mere words 'management fee' certainly do not suggest that a significant part of it is used to compensate and incentivize distributors.

Straightforward prohibition is nonetheless an unattractive solution. If the competitive market for distribution services ('shelf-space') calls for retrocessions, then their abolition is unlikely to achieve an efficient solution and is likely to be evaded in more obscure ways.

As an alternative, prohibition of retrocessions could be designed as a *default rule* which an *investor may agree to waive*. This in fact is the basic rule in a number of legal systems. In English and American law, fiduciaries – including financial advisors and wealth managers – are not allowed to make a secret profit out of their office.[40] Under Swiss law, the duty of loyalty includes the agent's duty to account to the principal for any benefit received from third parties in connection with his services.[41] In both systems that rule may be waived by the principal. To be valid, a waiver is generally conditional on full prior disclosure by the fiduciary. Whether or not the waiver can be implicit is a separate question; one that will be discussed later in connection with disclosure.[42]

The significance of this default rule is evidenced by the fact that experienced investors – such as institutional investors, high net worth individuals, and family officers – do not usually waive it in their relationship with their financial advisor or asset manager. They negotiate the whole remuneration structure for which they are going to be charged and therefore include in their contracts an explicit duty for

40. Rather than focusing on fiduciaries and fiduciary obligations, this paper approaches the issue through the duty of loyalty, the core equitable obligation of fiduciaries. As discussed in pages 247–248 above, most funds distributors owe a duty of loyalty to investors.
41. Art. 400 of the Swiss Code of Obligations.
42. See pages 352ff below.

the advisor or manager to account for compensation received from third parties, including brokers and fund providers.

A similar policy can take the shape of a menu approach requiring financial advisors to offer investors an explicit choice between options. This was the approach taken by the UK Financial Services Authority in its recent move towards 'depolarization'. The regulation used to oblige each financial advisor either to be 'independent' and offer products from the whole of the market, or to be 'tied' to a single provider whose products it was distributing. In 2004, FSA changed its policy and authorized advisers to offer products from a (limited) number of providers.[43] This policy is linked to a significant improvement in disclosure about the services offered and their price. It is interesting, from the perspective of this study, that 'independent financial advisors' (IFA) are now required to offer their customers a choice between a fee-based and a retrocession-based[44] approach. Customers must be free to compensate their advisor directly and exclusively if they wish, in which case they will benefit from any payments or other advantages received by the adviser from third parties.

B. Regulating the Level of Retrocessions

We have seen that the conflicts of interest that retrocessions create for fund providers and for fund distributors are not identical. Fund providers negotiate retrocessions with distributors to increase investment in their funds, which serves their own interest in maximizing revenue, but not necessarily the interests of investors, who nonetheless are charged for it. At the other end, distributors negotiate and obtain a financial incentive which may bias their professional judgment in advising investors.

The distributor's conflict of interest arises from the fact that, for any class of funds (equity, bonds, money-market, etc.), a distributor is unlikely to negotiate the same level of retrocession from different providers. This is the normal consequence of fund providers competing for 'shelf space' and privileged access to investors. One simplistic answer would be for legislation or regulation to fix a uniform level of retrocessions for each class of funds. This would suppress the incentive for distributors to advise their clients based on any other consideration than the intrinsic quality of the funds and their suitability for individual investors. By the same token, the provider's conflict of interest would be avoided because fixed retrocessions dispense providers from the need to balance their own interests with those of investors when negotiating distribution agreements.

However, it is widely accepted that regulating the price of services in a competitive industry should generally be avoided. However carefully determined, regulated

---

43. See Financial Services Authority, *Reforming Polarisation: Implementation*, November 2004, Policy Statement 04/27, <www.fsa.gov.uk>.
44. The FSA uses the terms 'commission' or 'product charge' for the compensation paid to the distributor by the provider of a financial product.

prices are likely to be less efficient than competitive prices. They do not readily adapt to market changes, and may create wrong incentives or disincentives.

In addition, price regulation is politically unacceptable. Financial markets are supposed to be the epitome of, or at least the best approximation to, a perfect market. Regulated prices, in so far as they used to exist in the guise of maximum interest rates or no-interest no-fee checking accounts, have become anathema and have been systematically dismantled.[45] Even central banks, which enjoy a legal monopoly, have moved towards implementing monetary policy mostly through open-market mechanisms.

C. Disclosing Retrocessions to Investors

It is generally agreed that where financial markets are concerned, it would be inefficient to avoid conflicts of interest absolutely. There is arguably no financial market without intermediation. Intermediaries often deal for the account of numerous clients, whose interest may conflict, and often for their own account as well. Conflicts of interest that would be perceived as unacceptable in other professions, such as the law, are not yet perceived as such in the financial industry. Because they cannot be completely avoided, conflicts of interest are tolerated provided that, when they occur, clients are 'treated fairly,' or in a manner that is 'not detrimental to their interests.' When this cannot be achieved 'with reasonable confidence,' a financial services provider 'must clearly disclose the general nature and/or source of conflicts of interest to the client before undertaking business on its behalf.'[46]

Disclosure differs from other approaches because, where conflicts of interest cannot be avoided and the interests of the client are even potentially at risk, the decision on whether that risk is acceptable is left to the client, who is empowered to take his interests into his own hands. Disclosure enables the client to either accept the risk or withdraw from the contract and, if at all possible, try to secure better terms for himself with some other intermediary.

Disclosure is the approach adopted by the Swiss Funds Association (SFA) in its Directive regarding transparency in management fees of 7 June 2005.[47,48] Partly inspired by SEC Rule 12b-1[49] this self-regulation is (to my knowledge) the first

---

45. See recently the European Court of Justice judgment of 5 October 2004 that legislation prohibiting banks from remunerating sight accounts in euros is contrary to the EU Treaty, case C-442/02, *CaixaBank France v. Ministère de l'Economie, des Finances et de l'Industrie.*
46. Article 18 (2) MiFID.
47. This directive was reviewed by the Federal Banking Commission and designated as a minimal standard applicable to all management companies. See no. 27 above.
48. After the finalization of this chapter, the SFA was authorized by the Federal Banking Commission to delay the enforcement of its Directive of 7 June 2005 while it is trying to identify an alternative approach move in line with the European Standards, especially as set out in the Market for Financial Instruments Directive.
49. See above, no. 32 and accompanying text.

of its kind in Europe, including the UK.[50] It is in the line with the IOSCO's *Final Report on Elements of International Regulatory Standards on Fees and Expenses of Investment Funds* of November 2004,[51] as well as with the *Asset Manager Code of Professional Conduct* adopted by the Center for Financial Market Integrity in 2005.[52]

The SFA regulation applies to investment funds marketed to the public, not to funds (or classes of shares) restricted to institutional investors. The regulation deals with two different issues:

– Retrocessions paid to distributors out of the management fee[53] are admissible provided that their existence and their actual or maximum level are disclosed in the fund rules and in the prospectus. When that is the case, the fund rules and the prospectus must indicate the actual or maximum levels of the following three components of the management fee: administration of the fund, management of the assets, and distribution. When (as should almost always be the case) maximum levels are disclosed, then the total sum of the three components may not exceed 150 per cent of the maximum management fee. Obviously, the sum of the actual components may not exceed the maximum management fee. This *ex ante* disclosure by way of maximums is meant to allow fund providers to negotiate retrocessions with distributors without divulging to them the actual overall level of retrocessions.

50. Schedules A (under 1.18) and C in Annex 1 to the UCITS Directive, as amended in 2001, set a rather vague standard regarding disclosure of remuneration payable to third parties. Commission Recommendation 2004/384/EC of 27 April 2004, OJ L 144/44, 2004 recommends that the simplified prospectus should give' an indication of the existence of fee-sharing agreements and soft commission' (point 2.2.1 (f)). Fee-sharing agreements are defined in pt. 2.2.2.1 as 'those agreements whereby a party remunerated, either directly or indirectly, out of the assets of a UCIT agrees to split its remuneration with another party and which result in that other party meeting expenses through this fee-sharing agreement that should normally be met, either directly or indirectly, out of the assets of the UCITS.'
51. Report adopted in November by the Technical Committee of the International Organization of Securities Commissions, <www.iosco.org>; see above footnote 12. Payments to distributors out of funds assets are only marginally discussed, see para. 12 on page 3 with footnote 3 and Annex 1 (Examples of a fee table).
52. It recommends the disclosure of conflicts of interest with brokers resulting *inter alia* from 'soft or bundled commissions, referral and placement fees, trailing commissions, sales incentives . . . 'as well as 'management fees and other investment costs charged to investors, including what costs are included in the fees and the methodologies for determining fees and costs.' See Appendix I, under F.4.a and d, at p. 17–18. Available at <www.cfainstitute.org/cfacenter/positions/pdf/asset_manager_code.pdf>.
53. Notwithstanding the need for some international convergence of terminology, the SFA directive uses the German word *Bestandespflegekommission* and the French neologism *commission d'état. Literally translated, Bestandespflegekommission* means a commission paid [to the distributor] for maintaining the assets [invested in the fund].

– *Rebates*[54] on the management fee in favour of certain classes of investors are admissible provided that they are implemented in one of two ways. For investment funds open to the public, certain classes of share may carry lower management fees provided that their eligibility requirements are transparent for all investors. Rebates are also admissible for funds restricted to certain qualifying institutional investors. In both cases, the maximum management fee for every class of shares must be disclosed in the fund rules and in the prospectus. Rebates to investors are different from retrocessions from distributors because they entail no conflict of interest but they violate the equality of treatment among investors. I shall not discuss them further here.

The SFA regulation is the result of much discussion within the industry and with the Swiss Federal Banking Commission. Since its enforcement has been postponed,[55] it is impossible to assess the impact of this solution. In the next two parts of this paper, I will discuss the pros and cons of the disclosure approach and some alternatives in its design.

The Market in Financial Instruments Directive (MiFID) is mostly based on disclosure. Article 26 of the Commission Directive 2006/73/EC implementing the MiFID deems investment firms receiving such payments not to be acting 'honestly, fairly and professionally' unless two requirements are met:[56]

> '(i) the existence, nature and amount of the fee, commission or benefit, or, where the amount cannot be ascertained, the method of calculating that amount, must be clearly disclosed to the client, in a manner that is comprehensive, accurate and understandable, prior to the provision of the relevant investment or ancillary service;
> (ii) the payment of the fee or commission, or the provision of the non-monetary benefit must be designed to enhance the quality of the relevant service to the client and not impair compliance with the firm's duty to act in the best interests of the client.'

Two differences between the Swiss and the proposed EU approaches are worth noting. The former relies on disclosure by the providers of funds while the latter, which applies to all investment firms, relies on disclosure by the distributors. In addition, the latter requires that the payments received by the distributors must enhance the quality of the service provided and not imperil its duty of loyalty.

Why has the Swiss Funds Association opted for disclosure by fund providers rather than by fund distributors? Part of the answer lies in Switzerland's regulatory

54. Unfortunately called 'retrocessions' in French and 'Rückvergütungen' in German.
55. After the finalization of this chapter, the SFA was authorized by the Federal Banking Commission to delay the enforcement of its Directive of 7 June 2005 while it is trying to identify an alternative approach move in line with the European Standards, especially as set out in the Market for Financial Instruments Directive.
56. OJ L241/16, 2006.

approach to the distribution of financial products. Unlike the European Union, where MiFID complements the UCITS Directive by mandating licensing, supervision and conduct of business rules for all distributors of investment products, the Swiss 1994 Investment Fund Act deals marginally with the distribution of funds. Distributors must be licensed, but they are subject neither to substantive prudential supervision nor to specific conduct of business rules.[57] While not entirely impossible, it would have been more difficult – and probably ineffective – to impose disclosure regarding retrocessions on fund distributors rather than on fund providers. Another reason is that disclosure at the fund provider's level (as implemented by the SFA) does not pursue the same objectives as disclosure at the distributor's level (as required by the British FSA or by the draft EU directive implementing MiFID). The former allows investors to make choices based on the distribution costs of various funds; the latter allows investors to discriminate among financial advisors based on their prices. I shall discuss this further in Section VII.

V. THE CASE FOR DISCLOSURE

Disclosure is typically used when conflicts cannot be fully avoided and are not otherwise managed. Disclosure is a necessary basis for the *client's consent* to the risk of being exposed to a conflict of interests and to its potential detrimental consequences. If not explicitly stated, consent may be implied in the client's informed decision not to terminate or renegotiate his relationship with the conflicted party. Thus, disclosure *allows the client to take his interests into his own hands*. Disclosure also *allows market forces to apply* to the management of conflicts and to the pricing of services. Clients may agree to pay more to avoid exposure to certain conflicts of interest, or may want to pay less when they take the risk of some detrimental consequences.

There are significant merits to a disclosure approach for the distribution of investment funds.

On the one hand, disclosure of retrocessions enables investors to factor this cost component, which is ultimately borne by them, into their choice of a distributor (if distributor-specific retrocessions are disclosed) and of one or more investment funds (based on fund-related disclosure). Without disclosure, the investor negotiates direct compensation (fees, commission), if any, with the distributor. Typically, an individual investor will not know of the additional compensation his distributor receives from the fund provider by way of retrocession. He cannot effectively negotiate the total compensation, including the indirect part received as retrocessions, for the service he receives from the distributor. It is true that sophisticated

57. At the time this article is finalised (May 2006), it is still unclear whether the Swiss Parliament will maintain, extend or entirely abandon the (narrow) regulation of funds distributors who are neither banks, securities firms or otherwise regulated entities.

investors who enjoy some degree of bargaining power can, and sometimes do, ask their distributors about retrocessions. In actual fact, only institutional investors and high net worth individuals can do so. When they are not dealing directly with the fund provider, thus by-passing distribution channels, they negotiate with their distributor (typically an asset manager or financial advisor) some form of direct compensation; the distributor undertakes to pass on to the investor any hard or soft compensation received from third parties. This approach does not apply to retail investors because they have neither the necessary information and expertise nor the commercial influence.

Disclosing the level of retrocessions applicable to various investment funds enables the investor to ask the distributor how he benefits from them. Transparency on retrocessions may trigger competition at two different levels:

- Providers of funds might compete on management fees by offering funds with lower retrocessions, and thus lower management fees. With the same gross performance, lower management fee means higher net performance for the investor. Distributors might not like offering funds on which they receive less retrocession, but in a market in which an excessive number of similar, under-sized funds compete for investors, investors might express their preference for such funds.[58]
- If distributors think that these low-retrocession funds do not adequately compensate their services, they may want to negotiate some (additional) remuneration to be paid directly by investors. Investors would then have to negotiate their distributor's total remuneration, something that they do not get a chance to do in the present situation.

For investors, taking their interests in their own hands means, in this context, that disclosure may provide them with more price competition at two levels, *i.e.* management fees charged to the assets of the funds and/or distributor fees and commissions charged to them directly by distributors.

Finally, better transparency on distribution costs might generate more investment in funds by improving investor confidence. A study commissioned by Bank of New York and published in July 2004 under the title *Restoring Broken Trust* strongly corroborates this argument. A survey of a sample of professionals representative of the various participants in the European fund market, it provides an insight into why the industry itself thinks investor confidence has been damaged (more strongly in the UK and in Germany than in other European countries) and what measures could help restore confidence. Among the most frequently cited factors that are important to regaining trust, three of the top four deal with 'increased integrity of promoters' (first, 87 per cent), 'putting client interests before asset gathering'

58. In its recent report (no. 13 above), Lipper notes at p. 6: 'Furthermore, it is interesting that in the U.S. 'low-cost' brands that are perceived to have proactively addressed investor concerns seem to have a competitive advantage in attracting assets. At the very least it seems worth considering whether such an arrangement is feasible for European funds.'

(third, 83 per cent), and 'payment by fees not commission' (fourth, 66 per cent). Seventy-five per cent of respondents agreed or strongly agreed with the proposition that greater transparency in the costs of funds would improve investor confidence in these products.

VI. THE CASE AGAINST DISCLOSURE

There are two main objections to disclosing retrocessions in the investment funds industry.

First, it is often suggested that retail investors do not care how, or how much, distributors are compensated; they look at the fund's performance and are only interested in the total level of costs which impact that performance, not in their components (including distribution). Regulation or self-regulation need not and should not go beyond requiring adequate (standardized) transparency on performance and the Total Expense Ratio (TER).

It is a fact that, at present, most retail investors do not seem to look actively for the best bargain. They typically decide among the funds offered by their long-term financial service provider, their bank in most cases. Since these investors do not compare the performance and costs of a wider choice of funds suitable to their needs, additional cost information is unlikely to affect their behaviour. Nonetheless, a smaller group of retail or private banking investors is indeed pro-active. Their need for information is served by specialized publications, often based on research and tables compiled by firms such as Standard & Poors (Micropal) and Fitzrovia, web sources including multi-funds platforms, fairs, and questions to their usual financial advisors.

Pro-active investors are interested in knowing what part of the management fee is compensating distribution, as opposed to asset management and administration. Research is expensive. If more of the management fee is spent on distribution, less is available for quality research.

Secondly, fund providers fear that disclosing the current level of retrocessions in any format will increase expectations from distributors and drive retrocessions up.[59] Distributors who negotiated remuneration at a lower level than the published data would want to re-negotiate their contracts.

This argument appears wrong-headed. In markets for most goods and services, the remuneration obtained by distributors vary considerably depending on the brand value of the goods or services, the distributor's market share and reputation, volume, etc. Fund providers and distributors are aware of the many factors that determine the level of retrocessions. They are also well aware of the range of retrocessions.[60] Disclosing aggregate figures for individual funds to investors will

59. This is the 'Lake Wobegon effect' referred to in R. Bahar's contribution, Chapter 3, page 118 ff. above.
60. See for example the *Eurofunds Survey* 2002 (no. 8 above), from which most figures in section II are drawn.

not bring new information to distributors. The problem lies not with the principle but with the practice, which should not compromise the capacity of providers to negotiate remuneration with distributors. This is discussed in the next section.

VII. WHO IS TO DISCLOSE WHAT, WHEN, AND HOW?

Disclosure of retrocessions for individual funds can be designed in a number of different ways. The actual design should provide information that is significant enough for investors (i) to discount the bias that retrocessions create for distributors in their selection and advice and, subject to their commercial influence, and (ii) to negotiate the total price they are willing to pay for the distribution of funds.

Who should disclose? Disclosure by distributors fulfils at least the second objective. The investor knows how much the distributor will receive from his own investment and can therefore appreciate the (total) price he is paying for this service. He can thus shop around for his preferred balance between price and extent and quality of service. However, this may not satisfy the first objective if the disclosure relates to a class of products as a whole (investment funds) and not to individual funds. For example, the 'keyfact' disclosure required by the British FSA from independent financial advisors informs investors about the average retrocession paid by investment fund providers to the disclosing advisor, but not about the specific level of retrocession paid by fund providers in relation to various investment funds.[61] It does not, and could never, provide the investor with enough information to discount the incentive effect of increased retrocessions paid by providers to promote specific funds. Indeed, the FSA policy is not meant to achieve this first objective, which is more closely related to the conflict of interest question addressed in this paper.

Fund-specific disclosure is better and more efficiently achieved by fund providers. Aggregate, non-distributor-specific figures give an indication as to the incentives offered to distributors. They allow market forces to apply to the selection of specific funds, as well as to the overall level of retrocessions paid to distributors. Both potential effects of fund-specific disclosure must be examined separately.

Comparing the level of retrocession across all investment funds, across investment funds in the same asset type or management style, or across investment funds offered by the same provider would provide the market with signals as to the aggressiveness of promotion and the incentive bias to which distributors are exposed in making their recommendations. This type of information may be used by individual, sophisticated investors. It is likely to be used by financial analysts and to be reflected in fund table-leagues, and will thus be brought to the attention of a larger audience of investors. While the TER impacts the overall performance of funds, its

61. See Tables 1 and 2 of Annex 2 to Policy Statement 04/27 (no. 45 above).

distribution component signals potential bias on the distribution side. Both pieces of information are valuable; neither quite replaces the other.

What, how and when to disclose? What can and should be disclosed obviously depends on who does the disclosing. The FSA requirements applying to independent financial advisors give an example of the degree of disclosure that can be achieved by distributors. It allows investors to make comparisons between distributors and classes of products (i.e. investment funds as opposed to life insurance policies), but not within each class.

The SFA regulation is an example of disclosure by fund providers. The exact design of disclosure will depend on the balance to be achieved between the interests of investors and of distributors. Investors may wish to obtain *ex ante* as well as *ex post* disclosure. Investment funds provide for both types of disclosure: prospectus: simplified prospectus are designed to inform investors before their investment decision; annual and other periodical reports inform investors about the performance of their investments. Since the actual level of retrocession is subject to bargaining between the fund provider and the individual distributor, *ex ante* disclosure on retrocession to distributors must almost necessarily be framed as a maximum percentage or a percentage bracket. *Ex post* disclosure may express the retrocessions actually paid or due as a percentage of the net asset value of the fund. That type of information is however quite sensitive; it affects the bargaining position of providers when setting the level of retrocession with individual distributors, creating a ratchetting effect.

The SFA has opted for *ex post* disclosure of the maximum management fee allowed (as a percentage) and a breakdown into its three components: administration,[62] asset management,[63] and distribution,[64] with a maximum percentage for each component. The total of the maximum percentage of each component must be no greater than 150 per cent of the maximum management fee. The total of each actual component, i.e. the actual management fee, must obviously not exceed the maximum management fee.

The SFA approach gives fund providers flexibility at the cost of some lack of transparency for investors. Comparing the maximums for each component *ex ante* may provide quite a different impression from the real weight of each component in the management fee as disclosed *ex post*. A hypothetical example will show how.

62. Includes administrative functions, risk management, internal control system (ICS) and compliance, monitoring and supervising authorized agents, accounting, controlling, financial statements, valuing fund assets, calculating the NAV, issuing mandatory publications, and all other functions not connected with asset management or the distribution of fund units.
63. Includes research and analysis, making investment decisions and reporting on investment policy to unit holders.
64. Includes working with sales agents/partners as well as institutional investors, marketing, road shows and sales discussions with investors.

Table 4. Hypothetical Disclosure According to SFA Regulation

	Maximum allowed	Relative weight of each component	Actual expense	Relative weight of each component
Management fee	2.0		1.59	
• Administration	0.4	13.3%	0.21	13.2%
• Asset management	1.6	53.3%	0.41	25.8%
• Distribution	1.0	33.3%	0.97	61.0%
Total of components	3.0	100%	1.59	100%

The figures disclosed to investors are highlighted in this table. *Ex ante* disclosure (column 'maximum allowed') suggests that asset management weighs more heavily than the other components, with distribution accounting for a third. *Ex post*, actual expense disclosure indicates that the total management fee remains well under control, below its maximum. But undisclosed component weighting shows that distribution really accounts for three-fifth of the total management fee, quite a different proportion from the one suggested in the disclosed maximum component. This distorting effect results from the rule that the disclosed total maximum for each component may exceed the total management fee by 50 per cent.

VIII. IS DISCLOSURE ENOUGH?

One reasonable approach for the policy-maker designing a legal rule is to look at real agreements negotiated by parties with similar sophistication and market power. Informal enquiries and inspection of a few actual contracts indicate that institutional investors negotiate fee-only remuneration with their asset managers and advisors. Payments and discounts granted by third parties are passed on to these investors. This strongly suggests that the traditional rule prohibiting fiduciaries from keeping secret benefits for themselves is optimal. It is also liberal because it allows the fiduciary and its client to depart from the legal rule and make their own deal.

For retail investors, who are less sophisticated and enjoy less commercial influence, this rule is contracted out in the guise of a general clause authorizing financial advisors, asset managers, and other retail distributors to keep for themselves benefits they might receive from third parties in connection with their clients' investment. Such clauses hide the true extent of the price paid by the investor to her direct intermediary as well as the incentives that may bias that intermediary's professional judgment. This is not acceptable unless some degree of transparency is achieved to allow the investor to take her interests into her own hands.

However smartly designed, can disclosure promote more investor awareness and more competition on distribution costs? It is too early to assess the effects either of the British FSA's depolarization policy or of the Swiss Funds Association's new self-regulation.

Additional arrangements could be devised to make use of the disclosed information on behalf of investors. This is not a new concept in the financial markets, where debenture trustees and other bondholders' representatives are appointed to monitor the issuer's solvency and behaviour and are usually empowered to make decisions on behalf of all investors (triggering acceleration clauses and the like). The FSA proposes building on the same concept when it suggests that the new requirement to disclose soft commission arrangements between fund providers and securities dealers[65] should include scrutiny by an individual or group representing the retail investors. This representative should have knowledge and experience of investment activity, authority and confidence to discuss with the fund providers, and sufficient incentive to carry out the task diligently. Based on the disclosed information, he would be required to ask questions and request explanations from the provider of the fund, and to express views in general terms or in relation to a particular arrangement.[66]

Whether or not the disclosure of certain information will prove useful to investors is often no more than an educated guess. Are investors better served by the disclosure of significant shareholdings in listed companies, or of management transactions in the same? What will be the value to investors of knowing how much distribution costs affect the performance of their investment? Beyond political arguments, lawyers will be looking for empirical research to verify the relevance of their thinking. Or will they?

65. See Policy Statement 05/9: *Bundled brokerage and soft commission arrangements – Feedback on CP05/5 and final rules, July 2005, available at* <www.fsa.gov.uk>.

66. See Consultation Paper 05/13: *Bundled brokerage and soft commission arrangements for retail investment funds*, September 2005, available at <www.fsa.gov.uk>.

Chapter 12

United States Mutual Fund Investors, Their Managers and Distributors

*Tamar Frankel**

The concept of conflicts of interest is rich, varied and complicated. Mutual funds provide a prime example of conflicts of interest issues and will be the focus of this paper. The parties are public investors in mutual funds, managers of mutual funds and distributors that sell mutual fund shares and trade in the funds' portfolios. The issues are difficult because each party can justify its claims, and public policy supports each claimant. Thus, everyone can be right, but the results of the claims of at least two parties can be completely wrong. The ultimate victims of conflicts of interest in this case are mostly the shareholders of mutual funds and the financial system as a whole. And even though the problems are not new and many solutions have been tried, none of the solutions has lasted.

This paper is divided into five sections. Section 1 deals with the nature of conflicts of interest – what they mean and when they matter. Section 2 provides an overview of mutual funds and their promoters. Section 3 discusses how mutual fund managers' relationships with distributors pose serious conflicts of interest in their relationships with investors. Section 4 examines the models and theories on which the parties base their claims. The final section, Section 5, discusses possible ways of addressing conflicts of interests between mutual funds managers and distributors and the interests of the investing shareholders. The conclusion suggests that, without an appropriate strong culture of honesty, none of the solutions will work over time.

* LL.M., S.J.D., Harvard Law School, Professor, Boston University.

L. Thévenoz and R. Bahar (eds.), *Conflicts of Interest: Corporate Governance and Financial Market*, pp. 363–394.

I. CONFLICTS OF INTEREST IN THE UNITED STATES: WHAT THEY MEAN AND WHEN THEY MATTER

Not all conflicts are wrongful. People's interests can complement each other, be identical or conflict. But only a certain kind of relationship gives rise to legal issues. The category in which wrongful conflicts of interest arise in the mutual fund area is the category of fiduciary law. It is when fiduciary law arises that conflicts of interest are wrongful.

A. When Does Fiduciary Law Arise?

Fiduciary law arises when:

- One party (the fiduciary) undertakes to provide services to another (the entrustor), and
- Public policy values the services.
- The entrustor entrusts property or power to the fiduciary. For example, an agent is entrusted with the power to bind the principal to legal obligations. A trustee is entrusted with the trust assets and the discretion (power) to manage them. Corporate management is entrusted with insider information regarding the affairs of the corporation.
- Most importantly, the entrustment is for the purpose of allowing the fiduciary to perform its services more efficiently.[1]

For example, a lawyer is entitled to his fees under a contract with the client. However, to perform his services, the lawyer must have the power to represent his client in court and in many cases to bind the client to legal obligations. A physician is entitled to a fee under a contract with the patient. However, to perform his service, the doctor is entrusted with the patient's health and well being, and at times with control over the patient's body. The purpose of the entrustment is to enable the physician to perform his services more effectively.

The fundamental point in fiduciary law is that the entrusted power or property never belongs to the fiduciary. The entrustment is not made in exchange for the services or for anything else. It is made for the purpose of benefiting the entrustor. Sometimes the benefit is exclusive, as when the money manager receives the investor's savings to manage. Sometimes entrustment may be shared, as in the case of a partnership, where each partner has an undivided interest in the partnership assets and the power to bind the partnership as a whole. Often the entrustor takes the action as a result of the fiduciary's advice, as in the case of a subscriber to an investment advisory letter. But there is always the principle that the entrusted power or property is not given as an exchange but is given for the benefit of the entrustor. Ownership remains with the entrustor.

Thus, fiduciary law recognizes a split ownership. To the rest of the world the fiduciary may be the owner of the property, as the money manager is. He can

1. T. Frankel, 'Fiduciary Law' (1983) *California Law Review* 71, 795–836.

therefore deal freely with the property, even in violation of his duties, and the public has no right to know whether he is the true owner or not (unless there is clear notice). But *vis-à-vis* the entrustor, the fiduciary has no rights to the entrusted property or power. This is why an entrustor who entrusts property to the fiduciary is called the 'beneficial owner.' The benefits from the property, though not the control of the property, belong to the beneficial owner.

For a number of reasons, the entrustor is vulnerable to abuse of the entrusted power or property. The fiduciary receives the entrusted power and property first. It is only then that he begins to perform the promised services. Thus, the entrustor gives first; the fiduciary gives (services) later. By definition, the transfer to the fiduciary is not a simultaneous exchange.

- It is highly costly to monitor, verify and ensure that the fiduciary will indeed abide by his promise and deal with entrusted power or property only for the benefit of the entrustor. Not only is the fiduciary entrusted with power or property in advance, but also he usually has expertise that the entrustor lacks. Therefore, the entrustor must take a significant risk of loss in the relationship. In fact, the cost to the entrustor may exceed the expected benefits from the relationship.
- Market monitoring and enforcing the fiduciary's obligations is ineffective, either because of the costs to entrustors or because fiduciaries do not compete on particular aspects of their services and usually because revelations about the abuse of trust by fiduciaries can be well hidden. After all, fiduciaries receive the power or property voluntarily.
- The results of the services are not always related to the honesty of the fiduciary or the quality of the services. For example, the physician may be an expert, but the patient can still die. The money manager may be honest, but the value of the portfolio may fall as the result of unrelated political events.
- The cost to the fiduciary of proving his trustworthiness is very high, and can exceed the compensation and other benefits from the arrangement.

In sum, fiduciary duties arise when the costs to the entrustor on the one hand, and the costs to the fiduciary on the other hand, are too high to induce both parties to interact.

The strictness of fiduciary duties depends on the magnitude of the conditions in which fiduciary relationships arise. The duties of the fiduciary reflect the magnitude of the entrusted power or property, the cost of monitoring the honesty of the fiduciary, and the cost to the fiduciary of guaranteeing that honesty. For example, the fiduciary duties of an agent who acts under the close supervision of the principal are lower than the duties of an agent that has broad discretion, far from the principal's reach. The duties of an adviser to the subscribers of his advisory letters are lower than the duties of an adviser that controls and manages the client's assets. The duties of a manager of a mutual fund, whose investors can sell or redeem their shares, are lower than those of a trustee that can be removed only by a court. Thus fiduciary duties are calibrated. A fiduciary's conflict of interest is dangerous because, by definition, the entrustor will not have full control over the use of the entrusted property or power. If the entrustor does not cede control, the very utility of the relationship will be undermined. However, the greater the degree of control the entrustor has over the decision regarding his power or assets, or over the fiduciary, the more the entrustor can fend for himself. Hence, the duties of the fiduciaries will depend on the degree to which the entrustor can fend for himself.

Fiduciary duties may be imposed even before the parties enter the relationship. Because in each of these cases the parties start the negotiations with an anticipation of a fiduciary relationship, fiduciary rules may apply, even before the parties reach the agreement to interact. A client or a patient who anticipates a fiduciary relationship starts the negotiation with an understanding of the nature of the relationship and the inherent entrustment that it will involve.[2] Lawyers and physicians as well as other fiduciaries are interested in creating the image of trusted persons, far more than the parties involved in sales or manufacturing. The thrust of fiduciary services is the entrustment of power and property in advance for the purpose of benefiting the entrustor.

It is important to note that the inability of entrustors to protect themselves does not arise from their lack of sophistication or other inherent weakness. Rather, the weakness stems from the very nature of the relationship. If entrustors attempt to control the fiduciaries in order to protect themselves, the very utility of the relationship will be undermined. The entrustors might not be able to monitor the investment manager for lack of expertise. Even if the investors have the expertise, the monitoring will deprive the investors of time to engage in other functions. Investors might as well manage their property themselves and save the fees. Thus, fiduciary duties are linked to a social structure that values specialization of talents and functions.

The remedies for breach of fiduciary duties include accounting. Because the fiduciary relationship results in 'beneficial ownership' that remains vested in the entrustor, the remedies for wrongful benefits reaped by the fiduciary include accounting for the ill-gotten profits. Thus, not only damages for breach of promised obligations but also accounting for the misappropriated power or property and any profits from such appropriated power or property rightly belong to the entrustor.

2. Advisers who charge fees that are significantly higher than the fees normally charged by other advisers may violate para. 206 of the Advisers Act. See, e.g., *Anthony Belmonte*, SEC No-Action Letter, 1993 SEC No-Act. LEXIS 930 (13 August 1993) ('The staff believes that an investment adviser that charges a fee for its services that is larger than that normally charged by other advisers [taking into consideration factors such as the size, location and nature of the advisory businesses to be compared] has a duty to disclose to its clients that the same or similar services may be available at a lower fee'); *Shareholder Servs. Corp.*, SEC No-Action Letter, 1989 SEC No-Act. LEXIS 159 (3 February 1989) (similar; stating staff belief that 'whether a particular fee violates section 206 depends upon whether the fee is reasonable in relation to the services provided, which necessarily involves examining the facts and circumstances surrounding a particular adviser/client relationship'); *Berkman Ruslander Pohl Lieber & Engel*, SEC No-Action Letter, 1977 SEC No-Act. LEXIS 68 (6 January 1977) ('Depending upon the specific circumstances, an annual fee of 3% of the portfolio value may require that the adviser make such disclosure').

Similarly, if the fiduciary becomes bankrupt, the entrusted property does not become part of the trustee's estate. The beneficiaries can claim the entire property, rather than become unsecured creditors of the estate in the bankruptcy proceedings.

1. The Issue of the Fiduciaries' Fees

When the entrustors establish the relationship with the fiduciaries, they can bargain at arm's length. Even then, the proposed relationship is based on an assumption that the entrustors can rely on the fiduciaries if the fiduciaries hold themselves out to provide trust services, such as lawyers' advice. In any event, even if an arm's-length bargain is reached before the entrustment of the power or property, after the entrustment the nature of the relationship changes into a fiduciary relationship. The fiduciary holds the entrustors' money or power and any further amounts that the fiduciary charges are far more within his control. At that point, even if the fiduciary renegotiates the contract terms, the bargain is not at arm's length. The fiduciary holds the entrusted power or property and the entrustors are at his mercy, and may not even have the information needed to conduct an arm's length bargain. Thus, often, in the case of millions of mutual fund shareholders, there is no negotiation. The fiduciaries hold the power to determine how much their services are worth, and how much they worked and how much compensation they deserve. The entrustors do not have the information and cannot bargain or fend for themselves.

2. The Contest of Categories

We categorize information to put our thoughts in order. The main images of categories must remain clear even if the categories are foggy at the fringes. U.S. fiduciary law is a common law-based category, which differs from the contract category. To the best of my understanding, fiduciary law is not recognized in the civil law system. And yet, both the civil law contract and fiduciary law address the same problems. Not only that, but both are guided by similar principles and policies and reach very similar results, except for the type of remedies that they provide for conflicts of interest. In fact, the different remedies they provide signal their fundamental difference.

The source theories of fiduciary law and the civil law contract are fundamentally different. Fiduciary law derives from the category of property. Civil law is contract-based. The following guidelines may help define fiduciary law.

Some academics in the United States have argued that fiduciary law is a branch of contract law. These scholars deny the necessity of a separate category of fiduciary relationship. Every consensual relationship is contractual, they argue, and these relationships form a special situation in contracts. Most scholars and courts, however, do not deny the existence of fiduciary law as a category. They do, however, water down the substance of fiduciary duties and think in terms of contracts.[3]

3. See e.g., T. Frankel, 'The Seventh Circuit Decision in Wsol v. Fiduciary Management Associates and the Amendment to Rule 12b-1' (August 2004) *Investment Lawyer* 11, 14; the court treats

Despite the arguments, a number of clear differences exist between contract and fiduciary relationships.

First, in contract, the money that the entrustor-investors hand over to their managers becomes the property of the managers, subject to the managers' contractual promises to behave according to the explicit and implied provisions of the agreement between the parties. Under such contracts, the entrustor-investors hand over their money at the outset of the relationship, and are promised payment from the gains, or offset against the losses. While the money is owned by the managers, the investment risks are borne by, and gains will be paid to, the entrustor-investors.[4]

Second, in contrast, the courts might presume that the parties have agreed upon terms and duties similar to those of fiduciary rules, unless the entrustor-investors explicitly waive these duties.[5] The duties, however, are not duties established by law, but obligations stemming from the contract.[6]

Third, contract does not recognize the remedy of accounting. It does include somewhat similar remedies, but none is based on the notion that entrusted power or assets continue to belong to the entrustor.

3. The Prohibition on Conflicts of Interest

In contract, conflict of interest is assumed, understood and accepted. The contract image is that of an exchange. Conflicts of interest exist in all exchange transactions. Each party has interests which conflict with those of the other parties. For example,

---

fiduciary law as contract law and holds that investors cannot complain if they pay 'market price' brokerage fees regardless of the actual brokerage charges.

4. It should be noted that if the investors' money is given as a loan, the debtors are not fiduciaries. The reason for this is because the contract can be designed to protect the lenders. Which is why the debtors can do with the money whatever they choose, subject to the terms of the contract among the parties. If the parties' bargaining powers are not balanced, particular provisions of the law are in place to protect them, when there is a public policy to encourage the parties' interaction. For example, public policy is designed to encourage people to use banks and insurance companies. Therefore, even though banks and insurance companies are debtors, they are required by law to conduct their business in such a way as to ensure that they will abide by their promises. Thus, even though banks and insurance companies are debtors, the law interferes to protect the creditors (depositors) and makes the conflicts of interest of the debtors acceptable. Similarly, when the investing public is the creditor and large institutions are the debtors, such as when large corporations issue bonds, the law imposes on the debtor's duties that protect the public by requiring the debtors who issue bonds to make certain disclosures. A similar distinction is made in corporate law. The corporation and the directors owe a fiduciary duty to the shareholders—holders of equity, but not to the debtors—holders of corporate bonds.
5. D.R. Fischel and F.H. Easterbrook, 'Contract and Fiduciary Duty' (1993) *Journal of Law and Economics* 36, 425–446.
6. In fact, before 1940, many investors asked wealthy people to take their money. The investors assumed that the wealthy people, who made money for themselves, would also make money for the small investors. This, however, did not happen. The wealthy people instead found ways to reap benefits from the small investors' money. For example, the small investors received non-voting types of securities. They did not receive equal profits and had no say in the division of the profits. The courts were unsympathetic. After all, the investors knew what they were buying, and the wealthy, controlling persons had no duty to meet the investors' expectations.

the buyer wants to pay less and the seller wants to be paid more. But this conflict of interest does not necessarily prevent people from interacting in an exchange. That is because their conflicts are not as strong as their mutual interest in interacting. Thus, the desires of the buyers to buy are stronger than their desire to pay less; and the sellers' wishes to sell are stronger than their desire to be paid more.[7]

The question of whether the parties should help each other in making the decision to enter the transaction involves the question of whether the 'help' is against the parties' own interests or in furtherance of their interests. Should the seller tell the buyer that the same item is sold for less in another shop across the street? Should the seller be prohibited from telling the buyer a lie, for example, that the item is of a higher quality? To what extent should each party volunteer information that is useful to the others? To what extent should each be responsible for the other's welfare? In reality, the parties may indeed help each other, for example, to establish the reputation of trustworthiness and fairness. But that is not the question. The question is whether the law requires contract parties to take care of each other's interests.

In the United States, contract law answers these questions more or less in the following manner: each party is responsible for its decision. No party is required to volunteer information unless the other party asks for it. No party is required to care for the other party's welfare. If asked, a party may refuse to answer. But if a party decides to answer, the answer should be the truth.[8] Numerous statutory laws change this basic rule. Consumer protection laws require one party to give the other certain information, often in writing.[9] The buyers of securities and corporate shareholders are entitled to full and detailed information, as specified in securities laws and corporate law.[10] But unless the statutes require, the assumption is that the parties can and should fend for themselves. The sellers may remain silent, unless their silence is misleading in the context of their relationships or the environment. They need not negotiate with the other party's interests in mind.

Thus, in exchange situations the conflicts of interest are quite clear, and each party is expected to fend for itself. In some relationships, however, within the

7. What happens in actual situations is far more complex than this bare-bones simplistic description. Often the sellers' consent to be paid less is contingent upon the promise of future benefits (e.g. receiving more work). In some cases, the consent of the buyers to pay more depends on their degree of need for the item. Each party may view the importance of the transaction differently. Each may value the collaboration and the transaction differently. As long as each party is capable of making an independent and free decision, the law will enforce the bargain. Of course, the words 'capable of making its decision' and 'free decision-making' are open to different interpretations.
8. E.A. Farnsworth, *Farnsworth on Contracts* (3rd edn, Aspen, 1990), 1:§4.9, at 465, stating that society has an interest in avoiding misleading information, notwithstanding the rule.
9. See, for example, J.C. Pendergrass: 'The Real Estate Consumer's Agency and Disclosure Act: The Case Against Dual Agency,' (1996) *Alabama Law Review* 48, 291, no. 80, which states 'Though the doctrine of caveat emptor applies to the sale of used residential real estate in Alabama, see *Hays v. Olzinger, 669* So. 2d 107, 108 (Ala. 1995), a real estate broker has a duty to disclose a home's defects to a buyer where there is a fiduciary or confidential relationship between the broker and the buyer, see *Cooper & Co. v. Bryant*, 440 So. 2d 1016, 1019 (Ala. 1983).'
10. 15 USC §77e (2000).

exchange context or outside it, one party is expected and required to deal in the interests of the other party, and the other party is entitled to rely on that requirement. Conflicts of interest in such situations acquire a different meaning and are subject to very different rules.

Fiduciary conflict of interest is not assumed, is not understood, and is certainly not accepted. The very purpose of the entrustment is to benefit parties other than the fiduciary. Some fiduciaries are paid for services but must hold the power or property entrusted to them for the benefit of the entrustors. But some fiduciaries are not paid, and yet, if they have been entrusted with valuables for the purpose of serving the entrustors they may not benefit from the entrusted valuables. For example, if I give my neighbour USD 100 to buy groceries for me and he accepts, he is my fiduciary with respect to the USD 100. If he bought groceries for less, the rest of the money is mine, not his. That is so even if he did not benefit from the relationship.

Because the relationship can involve degrees of control by the other party, the prohibited conflict of interest is calibrated accordingly. When the fiduciary has full control and the beneficiary has no actual and legal power to control the fiduciary, as is the case of private trusts, conflict of interest is fully prohibited under fiduciary law.[11] When the fiduciary has partial control, conflict of interest rules may switch to contract, to the extent that the entrustor could have monitored and prevented the conflict. Fiduciary law was never precise. Perhaps the law was never meant to be precise. The imprecision can bar fiduciaries from gaining, but it also creates a self-enforcement mechanism. It does not lend itself to a cost-benefit analysis but rather to a knee-jerk reaction to a constant question: 'Am I in a conflict of interest?'

In sum, fiduciary law requires that the interests of the entrustors be paramount. The fiduciaries must suppress their own interests and the temptations to further their interest or the interests of parties other than the entrustors. That is the understanding. In this context, conflict of interest acquires a different, pejorative meaning. There is no right to have a conflict of interest as in the case of a contract. This conflict of interest denotes abuse of trust unless it is corrected.

II. AN OVERVIEW OF MUTUAL FUNDS AND THEIR PROMOTERS

A. THE TWO PARENTAL PROMOTERS

Mutual funds are vehicles for 'mass-produced' expert investment management services. Rather than offering personalized services, mutual funds offer standardized services to numerous investors by selling them shares in a fund that is managed

11. See for example, A.W. Scott and W.F. Fratcher, *The Law of Trusts* (4th edn, Little, Brown, 1987), 1: §2.

by expert managers.[12] The added benefits from these services are reduced investment risk by diversification and savings by economies of scale from large volume of assets and transactions.[13] Thus, one kind of mutual fund promoter is an expert adviser who wishes to offer his services to numerous investors. This type of promoter originated from the prototype of a trustee that catered to wealthy persons, their families, and their heirs. These trustees had investment acumen, and some wished to expand their services to the public by creating mutual funds.[14]

The second type of mutual fund promoter is the distributor. During the 1920s, for example, when the public had an insatiable appetite for stocks, distributors established many mutual funds, including funds of funds – that is, mutual funds that held mutual fund shares – all based on one portfolio, to satisfy the public's demand.[15] Today, distributors may establish mutual funds or pool long-term investors and invest their savings for them in mutual funds. This type of group of investors is, for example, those who hold 401(k) plans.[16] The two types of promoters – the managers and the distributors – usually cooperate, each in their area of expertise.

Therefore, mutual funds have two 'parents': the descendents of the professional trustee and the distributors that sell and trade in securities. Each of these promoters has incentives to create such funds and increase their assets. The existence and collaboration of these two 'parents' explains many of the fiduciaries' conflicts of interest issues, the violations of duties to investors, as well as the growth of mutual funds and the financial success of their promoters.

B. THE STRUCTURE OF UNITED STATES MUTUAL FUNDS AND THE MANAGERS' ROLE, STATUS, AND INCENTIVES

Mutual funds can be organized in any form their promoters offer. However, superimposed on the legal form the promoters choose is a corporate form. With few exceptions, all mutual funds must have an elected board of directors,[17] some of whom must be disinterested,[18] that is, unrelated to the managers. The managers, however, operate the mutual funds much like the Chief Executive Officers of a corporation. In corporate law, it does not appear that CEOs can be outsourced.[19]

12. See T. Frankel and A.T. Schwing, *The Regulation of Money Managers* (2nd edn, New York, Aspen, 2001), 1: 1–5 (hereinafter: T. Frankel and A.T. Schwing).
13. T. Frankel and C.E. Kirsch, *Investment Management Regulation* (3rd edn, Fathom, 2005), 1 (hereinafter: T. Frankel and C.E. Kirsch).
14. T. Frankel and C.E. Kirsch, p. 11.
15. J. K. Galbraith, *The Great Crash, 1929* (New York, Houghton Mifflin, 1988), pp. 46–65.
16. 26 USC §401(k) (2000 & Supp. II 2002).
17. 15 USC §80a-16 (2000).
18. 15 USC §80a-2(a)(19) (2000 & Supp. II 2002).
19. There is one instance in which corporate directors can be deputized by an entity. That is under section 16 of the Securities Exchange Act of 1934, 15 USC §78p (2000 & Supp. II 2002). However, even in these types of cases the director is a person and not an entity, and the context is quite limited. See *Dreiling v. American Express Travel Related Services Co.*, 351 F. Supp. 2d 1077 (2004).

CEOs cannot form an entity that offers CEO services to more than one corporation. Mutual fund managers, however, face no such restrictions. To a great extent, these managers resemble a law office that offers legal advice to clients in contrast to an in-house general counsel. Therefore, the managers invest their own money and hire their own portfolio managers, accountants, and lawyers, buy their own software, and establish their own controls and other parts of the operational infrastructure of the funds that they manage.

1. Managers' Incentives Focus on the Sale of Their Mutual Funds Shares, as Compared to Trustees of Private Trusts

We refer to those who offer investment advice to individuals and groups as 'managers'. We also use the term managers to refer to those who manage mutual funds. 'Trustees of private trusts' are those who manage the assets under a trust instrument for relatively few persons, usually families. Managers are highly regulated in the United States.[20] In contrast, the contents of the financial products offered by mutual funds and by managers are rarely regulated. And if they are, the regulation is usually in the form of required disclosure.[21]

C. The Managers Manage Funds as Chief Executive Officers Manage Corporations

However, because managers serve more than one fund, they act as 'outsourced CEOs'. From their perspective, these managers manage one enterprise, much like a law firm. From the perspective of the investors in each fund, the managers manage different enterprises, much like the view of each client of the law firm.

The measures used to compensate managers vary. Some managers charge hourly fees.[22] Managers who act as financial planners may charge a one-time commission; that is, a percentage of the amount of investments that the investors make.[23] Some managers charge subscription fees for their advisory letters. But usually the compensation which is charged by managers of mutual funds who manage the investors' money is similar to the compensation paid to trustees of private trusts. These managers and trustees charge a percentage of the assets under management. There are, however, managers of mutual funds who charge a percentage of the profits that the investors receive, that is, performance fees. Such a measure is limited

20. Investment Advisers Act of 1940, 15 USC §§80b-1 to -21 (2000 & Supp. II 2002); Investment Company Act of 1940, 15 USC §§80a-1 to -64 (2000 & Supp. II 2002); a minor amendment to the Investment Company Act in 2004 is not included in the 2002 Supplement.
21. See 15 USC §80a-8(b) (2000).
22. J.J. Haas and S.R. Howard, 'The Heartland Funds' Receivership and its Implications for Independent Mutual Fund Directors' (2002) *Emory Law Journal* 51, 209.
23. S.K. Foster, 'Financial Planning: Is It Time for a Self-Regulatory Organization?' (1987) *Brooklyn Law Review* 53, 148–149. There are three types of financial planners: fee-and-commission, fee-only and commission-only planners. Fee-and-commission planners charge for their plans and sell on commission some or all of the products that they recommend.

to managers who serve sophisticated investors or investors who have a minimum amount, such as USD 1 million.[24]

Underlying the measures of compensation are certain assumptions about the incentives that managers (and trustees) are offered, linked to their relationships with the investors. The assumptions underlying compensation in the form of a percentage of the assets under management are that managers and trustees will have an incentive to increase those assets. If they do, the managers' and trustees' compensation also increase. The percentage is calculated on a higher amount of assets.

However, at this juncture, the managers and trustees part ways. Trustees can increase the trust assets under management mostly by performance. In addition, traditional trust law requires trustees to segregate trust assets from their own assets, or from the assets of others, subject to express exceptions. Thus, trustees cannot benefit from economies of scale that result from the growth of assets under management, except when the trust assets appreciate by performance.

In contrast, managers of mutual funds are not prohibited from pooling investors' money.[25] Thus, mutual fund managers can increase the amount of assets under their management not only by performance, but also by selling more shares in the portfolios that they manage. Any pool of money can be incorporated and any such pool could become the issuer of securities that offers the securities (a piece of the managed portfolio) to the public.

It should be noted that, even when trustees are permitted to pool trust assets, as bank trust departments are free to do, the comptroller of the currency's rules do not permit bank trust departments to aggressively advertise their investment acumen, but only their trust services.[26] Among other reasons, this prohibition maintained the distinction between bank trust departments and mutual funds.[27] Trustees may not mount an aggressive program to sell their services while managers of mutual funds may do just that.

This difference between mutual fund managers and traditional trustees is far more significant than it appears at first glance. While performance can raise the amount of assets by 20 per cent, or even 100 per cent, the aggressive sale of fund shares can raise the amount of assets under management by 1,000 per cent. Successful sales may depend on performance, but, as experience has shown, success depends as much if not more on the sales effort. The sale of mutual funds can be difficult under certain economic situations, and may require aggressive sales pressure. Americans are not ardent savers. The real effort in the mutual fund area

24. 15 USC §80b-5(b) (2000).
25. The managers can pool their investors' assets or can create a vehicle for the assets such as a limited partnership, a business trust, or a corporation. Superimposed on any such structure is a structure similar to that of a corporation. T. Frankel and A.T. Schwing 1: para. 1.02[B][2][j].
26. 12 C.F.R. §9.18 (2005) (the rule of the Comptroller of the Currency regarding bank trust departments).
27. Testimony of Richard C. Breeden, Chairman, U.S. Securities and Exchange Commission, Concerning Proposed Revisions to Rules Governing Bank Common Trust Funds, Before the Subcomm. on Telecommunications and Finance of the Comm. on Energy and Commerce, 101st Cong. 1990.

may be characterized by convincing investors to save; to part with their money and hand it to the managers for management. Thus, in contrast to trusts, for managers, the role of the broker dealers in increasing the assets under management cannot be emphasized enough.

D. SOLICITORS

There are managers who specialize in advising pension funds and other large institutional investors. Some of these managers use solicitors, either as employees or as independent contractors to solicit these institutional investors. Like distributors, the solicitors usually receive a commission calculated as a percentage of the money they bring to the adviser. The source of the contacts with the potential clients varies. But some of the contacts are broker dealers who have served the institutional investors, such as the pension funds. These distributors-contacts can be closely connected to the employees or independent solicitors for the managers. But what can the contacts provide for the solicitors? In some cases the contacts may demand part of the solicitors' compensation (a percentage of the percentage). In others, however, the best way for everyone to gain is to compensate the solicitors by providing them with brokerage business for the funds' portfolios.

But suppose the solicitors or distributors to whom the brokerage business is allocated cannot themselves execute the large transactions? The solicitor will receive brokerage business. The fund will be charged a 'market price,' for example, of six cents per share. The solicitor will then connect to a reputable broker dealer, who will execute the transaction for a fraction of the commission, for example, two cents per share. The solicitor will pocket the difference of four cents per share for the services of bringing to the adviser money to manage. Thus, the adviser benefits by gaining more valuable business at no cost. The solicitor benefits by four cents per share. The broker that executed the transaction earns a fair commission. The investors pay the 'market price.' This, in brief, is the arrangement of 'give-ups'.

E. THE DISTRIBUTORS' ROLE, STATUS AND INCENTIVES

Distributors perform two functions for mutual funds. One function is to sell the funds' shares. The other function is to sell and buy securities for the funds' portfolios. Generally, the business of selling mutual fund shares to individuals is not attractive to distributors, unless the buyers are pension funds and other institutional investors. Sale to institutions reduces the distributors' cost. But even selling to pension funds requires a great deal of effort. In addition, the sale of redeemable shares, which in previous decades constituted approximately 80 per cent of the fund shares,[28] is unattractive to distributors. Redeeming shareholders go directly

---

28. J.C. Stein, 'Why Are Most Funds Open-End? Competition and the Limits of Arbitrage' (2005) *Quarterly Journal of Economics* 120, 251–252; the majority of the mutual funds and hedge funds are open-end funds offering the shareholders the right to redeem their shares.

to the funds, and not to an intermediary. That is, they do not resort to distributors. Therefore, distributors serve only buyers of redeemable securities. The distributors are engaged only in servicing the buyers, but not in servicing the sellers. Therefore, the transactions available to distributors in redeemable securities are fewer. Not surprisingly, distributors demand higher compensation for these sales. The second brokerage function, of trading in mutual funds' assets, is lucrative for distributors. The portfolios are large and bring significant economies of scale. Therefore, distributors are eager to offer deep discounts on usual commissions to receive very large orders to trade.

F. DISTRIBUTORS' COMPENSATION

Distributors' compensation is measured by a percentage of the money that constitutes the transaction. This percentage measure reflects the recognition that larger transactions involve more work and responsibility. Unlike managers, who are paid periodically throughout their management period, distributors are paid only when the transaction is closed. That timing presumably offers distributors incentives to convince the parties to transact and to close the transaction as quickly as possible. Both measures of compensation are traditional, determined mainly by market practices.

G. THE ALLIANCE: WHAT MANAGERS WANT FROM DISTRIBUTORS AND WHAT DISTRIBUTORS WANT IN RETURN

Managers have a strong incentive to induce distributors to sell the shares of the mutual funds that the managers manage. The funds' increased size also reduces the costs of managing the fund assets. Size produces economies of scale, particularly when the shareholders are long-term shareholders. The number of fund managers does not increase proportionately to the amounts under management. Shareholder services cost less than the fee increases. Finally, the more investors purchase fund shares the more other investors they are likely to bring along. Investors often create cascades (both of purchases and of sales-redemptions). The reason for this is because most investors do not study their mutual funds to determine their worth. Instead, they simply follow others on the assumption that they have done their 'homework.' Once a cascade begins in earnest, people will follow others even in contradiction to their own information and convictions.[29]

In contrast, selling fund shares is not highly profitable for broker dealers. Selling and buying large blocks of securities is far more lucrative, which is precisely what the large investment banks seek. Moreover, few investment banks, such as Merrill Lynch, have a network of broker dealers who sell to retail investors. Banks that enter the mutual fund area often use their tellers as a sales force to steer

29. T. Kuran and C.R. Sunstein, 'Availability Cascades and Risk Regulation' (1999) *Stanford Law Review* 51, 711.

the depositors to their advisory services. This adviser then sells the depositors' mutual fund shares or other investment services. In sum, distributors and managers have dual ties. Managers seek buyers (large and small) and distributors seek large transactions (sales and purchases). This synergy of the two parties opens the door to problems for the investors, both those who wish to buy mutual fund shares and those who have invested in mutual fund shares.

The connection between managers and broker dealers and their exchange of benefits, including give-ups in one way or another, raises the problem of conflicts of interest. Regardless of the extent to which distributors were permitted to indirectly compensate managers for fund brokerage business, there was the proviso that the managers should first and foremost consider the quality of the distributors' execution of the transaction. They should choose the best distributors to execute the transactions for their funds, and assuming there were more than one broker with the same qualities offering the same conditions, then, and only then, could the managers choose the ones who were selling their funds' shares. This guide was presumed to solve the conflict of interest that tainted the decision to choose the distributors to execute the transactions of the fund's portfolio. But that was not enough.

Thus, managers are interested in the sale of fund shares, in which distributors are not eager to engage. But managers can allocate large portfolio trades to distributors, in which distributors are eager to engage. It therefore makes good business sense for managers to compensate distributors who sell fund shares. It also makes good sense for distributors to pay managers for allocating to distributors large portfolio transactions. It makes sense for managers to pay distributors for the sale of fund shares not with dollars from the managers' pockets, but with brokerage business for the funds' portfolios. If the assets in the funds belonged to the managers this would be a perfectly logical and legitimate exchange. The more a broker sells fund shares the more lucrative business of trading the funds' portfolio the adviser will allocate to the broker. This sensible business arrangement, however, raises difficult issues.

H. Give-Ups and Their Evolution

Generally, distributors who sell mutual fund shares are not the same distributors who execute large portfolio transactions for mutual funds. The sellers of fund shares are retail distributors who have ongoing contacts with clients, whether individuals or institutional. The distributors who trade in large fund portfolios' shares are those who have a wholesale facility, and are connected to other buyers and sellers of very large blocks of shares.

Managers sought to compensate those who were selling mutual fund shares. Large distributors were eager to offer managers discounts for executing large portfolio transactions. It is not surprising that the practice of give-ups developed in the 1960s.[30] Managers required large investment banks who sought large funds' port-

30. T. Frankel and A.T. Schwing 2: 15.02[A]; 4: §27.01[B][3].

folio transactions to give up some of their commissions and pay the discounts to broker dealers who sold fund shares. The discounts that these large wholesale distributors were willingly giving up were not paid to the managers directly. Instead, the discounts were paid to the distributors who sold fund shares in which the managers had an interest.

Other forms of hidden give-ups and payments for the sale of mutual fund shares abound. For example, if the adviser offers the investment bank back-room services at a substantial discount, the discount can be counted towards the sale of fund shares, or perhaps the 'introduction' to institutional investors, such as pension funds. The calculation can be easily adjusted: The more sales the bank makes, the more brokerage business it can receive either to execute in its own departments or to 'farm out' to other investment bankers at a discount and pocket the difference.

1. Revenue Sharing

Over the past 15 years, broker dealers who once sold fund shares have begun to demand what became known as 'revenue sharing'. They demanded not only a percentage of the price of the stock they sold, but also a percentage of the management fees that the managers received for managing the funds.[31] The salespersons argued that the managers were enjoying far greater compensation from the money that the salespersons brought to them and therefore demanded part of these compensations. For example, large share distribution broker dealers, such as Charles Schwab, demanded payment for a preferred higher placing of mutual funds that Schwab displayed to their customers. This idea was modelled on the way supermarkets displayed products. It appears that supermarkets charge the producers who want to display their wares on higher shelves, or to the right of the entry to the store, where most buyers usually turn. Similarly, investors do not scan the thousands of available funds, but usually choose among the first 20 to 30 funds on the list. Large managers, including the largest (Fidelity), paid Charles Schwab to place their funds close to the top of the list. But only at the beginning of 2005 did Fidelity disclose that it was making these payments to the distributor.[32]

III. MANAGERS AND INVESTORS' CONFLICTS OF INTEREST: THE SALE OF FUND SECURITIES AND ALLOCATION OF FUND BROKERAGE BUSINESS

We noted that managers are interested in the sale of fund shares, in which distributors are not so eager to engage, but managers can allocate large portfolio trades to

31. See 'Milberg Weiss Announces the Filing of a Class Action Suit against UBS-AG, and Certain of Its Affiliates, Officers and Directors on Behalf of Purchasers of Certain UBS Funds' *Business Wire*, 1 August 2005.
32. J. Waggoner, 'Investing: Fund Sales Practices Might Be Costing You' *USA Today*, *Money*, posted November 20 2003, <ssrn.www.usatoday.com/money/perfi/columnist/wagon/2003-11-20-mym_x.htm>, last visited August 18 2005; brokerage firms have 'preferred lists.' Fund managers pay to be on these lists.

distributors, in which distributors are eager to engage. It therefore makes good business sense for managers to compensate distributors who sell fund shares, not with dollars from the managers' pockets, but with brokerage business for the funds' portfolios.

However, an arrangement of this sort creates conflicts between the managers' interest and the interests of the shareholders of the funds.

A. Misappropriation of the Discounts

First, managers could be tempted to benefit from the discounts that distributors offer by diverting these discounts to distributors that sell fund shares (and thereby increasing the managers' fees). But if the managers do not own the invested money but the shareholders do, then the discounts that the distributors are ready to pay for the business of trading in funds' portfolios belong not to the managers, but to the shareholders. After all, it is the shareholders' assets that are being traded and it is the shareholders' money that is being charged with the costs of the trading. Unless the shareholders benefit from the larger size of the fund, or unless the shareholders agree to the charges and the payments to the managers, the shareholders suffer losses.

B. Poor Execution of Trades

Second, managers who use distributors that offer benefits in exchange for portfolio brokerage business face conflicts between their own interest and the interest of the shareholders. Managers face the temptation to engage those distributors rather than choose the best available broker for the transaction. Trading in large volumes of shares requires an understanding of the markets, and the knowledge of how to sell the vast number of shares without depressing the market or buy a large number of shares without raising market prices. Such distributors usually find ways to balance their sales and purchases in order to avoid market gyrations that would harm their clients' interests, or find the sellers or buyers of such large quantities of shares and negotiate the prices successfully. Thus, unqualified distributors that cannot trade in large blocks of shares but sell fund shares to individual investors or institutional investors could be allocated fund portfolio business to the detriment of the fund shareholders.[33] As a result, investors might be harmed by poor execution of portfolio transactions.

33. As mentioned earlier, the consequences of this disparity of abilities drove to a market solution. At the behest of the managers, the wholesale distributors who traded in fund portfolios 'gave up' some of their benefits to the retail distributors who sold fund shares. The adviser benefited from the larger sales: receipt of higher fees as a percentage of the assets under management. It also benefited by paying for the sales with the discounts to which the fund shareholders were entitled. The fund shareholders paid the distributors the 'market commissions' in full, and did not benefit from the economies of scale as their funds grew.

C. Increased Turnover (Churning)

Third, since placing portfolio transactions can benefit the managers by financing the sale of fund shares, managers may be tempted to increase the turnover of the portfolio transactions. This increases the investors' costs and reduces the returns from their investments.

D. Disadvantages of Fund Size

Fourth, very large funds are not necessarily beneficial to their shareholders. Size may restrict their managers' flexibility to trade when opportunities arise. To be sure, the shareholders could benefit from the economies of scale, but that depends on the adviser's frugality and moderation.

E. Misappropriation of Economies of Scale

Fifth, the issue of economies of scale raises further conflicts of interest. Large portfolios present savings to the managers: their size offers economies of scale. The cost of managing a fund of USD one billion is not ten times greater than the cost of managing a fund of USD 100 million.

If the managers use the economies of scale for their own benefit, or for the benefit of other funds that the managers are interested in shoring up, they rob the shareholders in the large funds of the benefits. The arguments concerning the fees and the expenses can be played over in this context, as well.

F. Even Direct Cash to Distributors Comes from the Investors' Pockets

Even if the managers pay dollars to the distributors who sell fund shares, the dollars in fact come from the shareholders' pockets. Managers may simply increase their fees. Unless the investors shop for mutual fund shares according to the fees they charge, or the shareholders are represented in their negotiations with the managers, or legal constraints are applied on the amounts that managers can charge, the shareholders will have to pay whatever the managers charge. And there is no limit to the amount of shares they wish to sell and the resultant fees that they want to collect.

G. Opening the Doors to Other Abuses: The Issue of Culture

More generally, if managers use the model of give-ups, they can move to other areas in which they charge investors with market prices rather than actual costs and use the differences for their own benefit. For example, managers may charge investors the market price for back-office bookkeeping, which is higher than the actual cost to the managers.

H. The Law's Response

In the late 1960s, after give-ups became widespread, the Securities and Exchange Commission reacted by holding hearings and denounced the practice. Parallel to the prohibition by the Commission, the National Association of Securities Dealers, the self-regulatory organization of all securities broker dealers, promulgated Rule of Conduct 2839(k), which prohibits distributors from offering managers benefits by selling fund securities. Thus, in the allocation of funds' brokerage business (1) managers were prohibited from accepting bribes or kickbacks by the sale of fund securities and (2) distributors were prohibited from offering bribes or kickbacks by the sale of fund securities. Regardless of the terms of the rules, the understanding was that both managers and distributors were prohibited from exchanging the managers' benefit from the sales of fund securities for the distributors and underwriters' benefit of gaining fund brokerage business.

In the 1980s the interpretation of the strict prohibition became softer. Managers were permitted to consider and take into account the contribution of a brokerage firm to the sale of shares when allocating portfolio business to it. Distributors were permitted to offer sale of fund securities to facilitate such managers' considerations. After the discovery of a direct quid pro quo among managers and distributors and many forms of indirect benefits that amounted to the same thing, this soft prohibition has now hardened again into an unconditional prohibition. Since 2003, managers have been prohibited from considering or rewarding distributors who sold fund shares with brokerage business of the funds. And distributors are prohibited from offering such sales in exchange for fund brokerage business.

I. Another Crack in the Wall: Permissible Soft Dollars Arrangements

Since 1975 distributors have been permitted to offer managers and managers were allowed to receive free 'research' from distributors.[34] Research was broadly defined.[35] Thus brokerage business allocation became a source of benefits to managers, and could influence their choice of distributors to whom the managers will allocate fund brokerage business. In recognition of the conflict of interest that such free research might produce, managers were required to ensure that the distributors they choose for fund portfolio transactions would provide 'best execution'.[36] However, best execution of the transactions did not imply the cheapest execution.

The prohibitions on paying for sales and research by brokerage business were relaxed on the same grounds: the complaints of small distributors and the desire to equalize their position with those of the large underwriting firms. Small distributors could not provide best execution of fund portfolio transactions. Neither did small distributors have the facilities to offer the research that large underwriting firms

34. 15 USC §78bb(e) (2000); Frankel & Schwing 2: §15.02[D].
35. Brokerage and Research Services, Exchange Act Release No. 34–23170 (23 April 1986).
36. Ibid.

prepared. In both cases, their sales of fund shares were not compensated by the lucrative brokerage business. The relaxation was aimed at equalizing their situation with that of the large firms.[37] In the large brokerage firms that offered both services – selling fund shares and trading in funds' portfolios – the conflicting interests surfaced between the departments that sold fund shares and the departments that traded in the shares. The sellers demanded benefits knowing that the traders would have received less brokerage business otherwise.

J. THE DILEMMA: THE COMMODITY CONTRACT APPROACH

The recognition of conflicts of interest in the fiduciary category, which are prohibited, can be vigorously disputed if the managers' services are viewed as the sale of a commodity under a contract.

Unlike other fiduciaries, such as lawyers and doctors, advisory services can be viewed as more similar to commodities. The results of managers' services are quantifiable and can be compared to the results of other investment managers' services. The investors either gain or lose specific amounts of US dollars. These are somewhat different from the specific results of a particular court case or particular patient. Each court case and each patient is unique.

In addition, if managers are judged by the long-term results of their services, they cannot blame events beyond their control. The assumption is that the results cannot be consistently disappointing in the long-term. In face-to-face negotiations, the parties establish a benchmark, and the results are based on a long-term period, such as three or often even ten years. This aspect of advisory services points to the sale of a commodity rather than the service of a fiduciary.

In addition, small investors do not negotiate with managers. These investors most often evaluate advisory services the way they evaluate any commodity—by the short-term results. Even if they receive information about performance after one, five and 10 years, most investors will judge the particular managers on a far shorter-term basis. Therefore, it may be argued that the managers should be treated as the sellers of a commodity. In that case, they are carrying on a business.

In addition, managers not only manage, but also invest in the infrastructure of mutual funds. The managers are the owners of the operational aspect of the management. Thus, they run a business and ought to be treated as such. Therefore, the buyers of commodities have no claim to information, or to any savings, or to the profits that the sellers or manufacturers have made. The price of the commodities is

37. Prior to 1986, managers were permitted to receive only 'research' that was produced by the firms who executed portfolio transactions. In fact, it was the practice of such large firms was to provide such research, for example, on particular corporations, as a courtesy and an advertisement. In 1986, the Securities and Exchange Commission allowed small distributors to purchase research in the market and provide it to managers in exchange for brokerage business. If the distributors did not have the facilities for executing the transactions, they then farmed out the execution to the large firms for a smaller amount and captured the discount. During the past 25 years a large market has developed in soft dollar 'research'.

all the buyers are entitled to evaluate, so long as the buyers can shop for cheaper or better commodities, the exchange of which is subject to specific consumer legislation. If a competitive market exists for the managers' services, the services (and the costs) should be treated as commodities. Thus, the difficulty in deciding who should benefit from the discounts that broker dealers offer for large portfolio transactions disappears. Similarly, the issue of just who is entitled to the economies of scale when the funds have grown disappears.

The savings that managers manage to squeeze out of performing the service belong entirely to the managers. If fund managers manage to save costs by a smart use of managerial techniques or software or attraction of the right talent, the benefits belong to the managers and not to the shareholders. The following story illustrates this approach.

1. One Case

In this case, an adviser who caters mainly to institutions employed a solicitor who was paid a commission for any business that he generated. He had previous contacts with distributors from whom he sought help. One of these distributors, the 'introducing broker' who solicited institutional business for this adviser's employee, induced the trustees of a pension fund to transfer to the adviser USD 260 million for management.[38] But even broker friends do not help get business for nothing. These distributors wanted portfolio fund brokerage business. The employee-solicitor persuaded the adviser's personnel to allocate to the 'introducing broker' a certain amount of fund brokerage business at six cents per share, known as the 'market price'. The introducing broker could not perform the services. He transferred the execution to a reputable broker for 2 cents per share and pocketed the four cents per share. That was the broker's compensation for the introduction. The employee-solicitor received a commission from the adviser.

What was wrong with this transaction, if anything? According to the Court of Appeals of the Seventh Circuit, nothing whatsoever.[39] After all, the investors paid the market price of six cents for execution. The introducing broker guaranteed the good execution (even though he was a crook). The adviser did not receive anything of value, but instead was paid for the services it provided to the pension fund. The adviser received nothing by getting USD 260 million to manage, even though it hired and paid a solicitor to generate the business. It appeared that the court did not consider getting the business of any value, and that the court did not consider the fact that the investors paid more for the execution of the transactions than two cents per share, which was the actual, not market, price paid. It did not consider the fact that a third party pocketed the difference.

---

38. This influence included bribery. *Wsol v. Fiduciary Management Associates*, 266 F.3d 654 (7th Cir. 2001), *cert. denied*, 535 U.S. 927 (2002); see also T. Frankel, 'The Seventh Circuit Decision in Wsol v. Fiduciary Management Associates and the Amendment to Rule 12b-1' (August 2004) *Investment Lawyer* 11, 11–16.
39. Ibid.

It seems that the court viewed the duties of the adviser to the investors as contractual. Investors bought services and agreed to pay the 'market price' for transactions in their portfolio. The savings that the adviser could shave off belonged to the adviser. Or at least, the savings were not the business of the investors, but instead were the profits of the adviser. The adviser, after all, was smart enough to gain new business and pay for it with the investors' transactions money (below what they presumably agreed to pay: the market price). The model of the relationship dictated the results. The conflicts of interest were fine. Investors should protect themselves if they do not like the results of the services. After all, many managers must compete ferociously for business.

This case demonstrates the difference between conflicts of interest in a contract relationship and conflicts of interest in a fiduciary relationship. Contract and fiduciary relationships share a basic feature: both are voluntary and consensual. Contract and fiduciary categories are not mutually exclusive. Some provisions of a consensual transaction may be judged under contract law, but others must be judged under fiduciary law.[40] As a result, some conflicts of interest fall into the category of contractual relationships, while others fall into the category of fiduciary relationships. In fact, there is a slippery slope in the definition and duties regarding conflicts of interest.

In the contract relationship, the adviser promises the investors a managed portfolio. He also promises to incur no more than the market costs for the product: the managed portfolio. The adviser in fact has either 'rented' or borrowed the assets of the clients. In both cases, the adviser can do what he likes with the assets for his own benefit, as long as he pays the investors what he promised. He promises the clients a return linked to the performance of the markets, repayment of the investments under certain terms, and charges in accordance with market prices. The rest of the benefits from controlling the money belong to the adviser.

A fiduciary relationship is entirely different. Theoretically, the same rules that now compose fiduciary law can also be presumed and embedded in the contract arrangement. The contract may state that investors' money never becomes the adviser's money; that the benefits from everything that the money produces belong to the investors, not to the adviser; and that if the adviser receives a deduction in price or charge, the deduction belongs to the investors. The contract can emphasize that the only amount that belongs to the adviser is the fees and charges explicitly and specifically agreed upon. And nothing else. In this case, the question would be whether the investors can waive these 'contract' provisions, and whether the court can have the flexibility to fashion other presumed rules into contracts in somewhat different situations. In that case, there is no difference between fiduciary duties and contract duties. There will be no difference between fiduciary conflicts of interest and contractual conflicts of interest.

Fiduciary duties and contractual duties will coincide, except for three additional items. First, the courts should be more inclined to broadly interpret the agreement

40. Ibid.

and the presumed basis on which the former type of duties is grounded. They should not be as constrained to follow the wording of the contract. Second, a breach of this fiduciary type of agreement should be considered abuse of trust and embezzlement, carrying with it a stigma that is extremely different from a mere contractual breach. It should carry with it the branding of dishonesty. And third, remedies for a breach of the fiduciary duty should include not only damages to the victims, but also every penny of profit that it received directly and indirectly in connection with the transaction. That should include not only the particular breach, but any other profit emanating from the relationship, even if not in breach. When all this is done, the difference between the contract and the fiduciary duties disappears.

A number of objections are voiced against this approach. First, even when managers compete among themselves, it is extremely difficult for investors to ascertain and evaluate the services that the managers offer. In addition, the quality of the services may be high, but the results may not. If the managers' 'commodity' cannot be evaluated by the results of their services, the managers should collect their fees even on disappointing results. Their fees should reflect the quality and efforts of their services, but the savings from discounted commissions should belong to the investors.

More importantly, investors expect managers to serve the investors' benefits exclusively, with the exception of the advisory fees. All fees and expenses must be clearly specified, and never hidden, so that investors can know and agree to them. The residue belongs to the investors. This is the investors' basis for trusting managers. Performance cannot gain trust if it is coupled with a high risk of embezzlement. This brings us back to fiduciary duties.

Congress, regulators and most courts have rejected the contract analysis. The Securities and Exchange Commission charged the adviser in the case described above with using investors' brokerage business and the discounts for its own benefit, by paying with what belonged to the investors (allocation of brokerage business) for new business (which was worth a great deal to the adviser). The employee-solicitor was charged as well for the pressure he put on the adviser's personnel to allocate brokerage business to his broker-contacts so that they would 'introduce' him to institutional investors and generate new business for the adviser.[41]

IV. THEORETICAL MODELS FOR MANAGERS TO ADDRESS MANAGERS' CONFLICTS OF INTEREST

A. What is Wrong with Rewarding Managers with Benefits from Their Control over Investors' Money?

If a broker charges two cents per share and gives the adviser four cents, the broker has paid a kickback that will injure the shareholders of the fund. That is because

41. See e.g., *Wsol v. Fiduciary Mgmt. Assocs.*, 266 F.3d 654 (7th Cir. 2001), *cert. denied*, 535 U.S. 927 (2002); T. Frankel, 'The Seventh Circuit Decision in Wsol v. Fiduciary Management Associates and the Amendment to Rule 12b-1' *Investment Lawyer* 11 (August 2004), 14.

the broker was prepared to offer his services for two cents per share and the fund shareholders paid six cents per share for the service. The fund shareholders paid more than the cost of the broker's services.

But what if the shareholders agreed that the adviser would charge them the market price and pocket whatever he could squeeze out of the distributors? One could question such an agreement, considering the disturbing possibility that the adviser might not choose the best broker, or the cheapest, but the broker who would pay him the most. The second assumption would be that such a broker would seek to recoup these costs by providing the least expensive service. In short, the fund will be paying for services that cost more than they are worth, and the adviser will collect the difference. This is the adviser whom the shareholders trusted to manage their money for their benefit. The shareholders would not be able to spot the broker's payment to the adviser because the shareholders do not have control over the managers' operation. If brokerage expenses are charged to investors at cost, then kickbacks of any sort (whether by increasing the price or reducing the quality) constitute a diversion of the investors' money to the managers for the managers' benefit. The answer to conflicts of interest differs depending on the choice between contract and fiduciary categories. The answer depends on how we view the managers and their relationships with the investors in the mutual funds. What model should we use to resolve the issues?

Are the managers offering personal services to the funds and indirectly to each of the fund shareholders, or are the managers managing a business of offering management services? Managers for individual wealthy investors are viewed as fiduciaries in personal relationship with their clients. What is the status of the relationship of the managers to mutual funds? In fact, a similar question is often asked in the corporate context: is the relationship between the corporation and its managers personal or is it derivative? In other words, is the relationship linked to the corporation rather than to each shareholder?

The issue in mutual funds is somewhat different from that of corporations, essentially because the services that the adviser offers the shareholders of the mutual fund are very similar to that offered to individual investors. The difference lies mainly in the fact that the services are standardized and not tailored to the needs of each investor. Unlike the corporate enterprise, the mutual fund enterprise replicates personal management services. Even though shareholders of mutual funds are limited in their ability to sue the managers directly, the nature of the services the adviser renders and the resulting duties on the funds' directors are similar to those offered to large individual investors. The funds, representing a pool, are an aggregate of such personal advisory relationships. Managers of mutual funds are similar to law firms that serve individual and corporate clients. This is the view of managers under the Investment Company Act of 1940.[42]

In fact, the prohibitions on managers' conflict of interest transactions are quite detailed. Under the Investment Company Act of 1940, they are permitted only by an

42. 15 USC §§80a-1 to 80a-64 (2000 and Supp. II 2002)

exemption of the Securities and Exchange Commission.[43] When the number, assets and transactions of mutual funds grew dramatically, the Securities and Exchange Commission allowed some conflict of interest transactions by rules, subject to the approval of the majority of the funds' disinterested directors.[44]

As far as advisory fees and advisory contract terms, however, the American policy is to avoid government involvement in business negotiations. Hence, the fees were to be determined by negotiation between the managers and the boards of directors of the funds. Early on another provision required that the majority of the disinterested directors on the board agree on the fees and other terms in the advisory contract. The contract must be approved annually.[45] In 1970 Congress added a special section in the Investment Company Act, 36(b), which imposed a fiduciary duty on managers regarding excessive fees, and established a special procedure to allow shareholders of mutual funds to challenge excessive fees in the courts.[46] Cases on this issue demonstrate the theoretical models on which the courts based their interpretation of the section.

Prior to the recent round of litigation, regulators and others considered advisory fees to cover only the value of the advisory services. Therefore, if the managers used the fees for anything other than the services that they offered, these additional amounts were considered excessive. Hence, managers who used their fees to pay distributors for selling fund shares were considered to have charged excessive fees. In sum, fees could cover only the cost of providing the advisory and other services to the funds.

During the early 1980s, including the later fees litigation,[47] the model of managers as personal fiduciaries of the investors changed. The emphasis shifted from the type of services that the managers offered to the fact that the managers were managing a business that offered fiduciary services. Therefore, if advisory fees include profits, the managers can do whatever they want. Hence, managers could use their fees to compensate distributors for selling fund shares.

B. THE DISCLOSURE AND IMPLIED CONSENT SOLUTION

Most fiduciary duties are default rules. If the fiduciary discloses the conflict and the entrustor agrees to the transaction, the fiduciary is relieved of liability.[48] In the context of mutual fund fees, the issue is more complicated. The fees are disclosed in the prospectuses that each investor receives. There are other easy-to-reach sources that offer the information. Why, then, should the managers be burdened with a fiduciary duty with respect to the fees? It should be noted that the fees are part of the

43. Ibid. §80a-10(f), 17(a),(b),(d),(e), 23.
44. See e.g., Rule 12b-1, 17 C.F.R. §270.12b-1 (2005).
45. 15 USC §80a-15(a) (2000).
46. Ibid. 15 USC §80a-35(b) (2000).
47. E.g. *Krinsk v. Fund Asset Management, Inc.*, 875 F.2d 404 (2d Cir. 1989).
48. T. Frankel, 'Fiduciary Duties as Default Rules' (1995) *Oregon Law Review* 74, 1,209–1,220.

exchange process—definitely a contract posture, even though it is established with a fiduciary. In the case of mutual funds, the directors, including the majority of the disinterested directors, are supposed to represent the investors. These disinterested directors are expected to negotiate with the adviser at arm's length.[49] However, these directors for many years rarely pressed the managers on the fees and expenses issues – even in appropriate situations; a situation which has led the Securities and Exchange Commission to tighten the rules recently. The agency required the directors to disclose their reasons for approving the advisory contract, including the reasons for approving the advisory fees.[50]

The counterargument to these demands is that the shareholders who purchase fund shares, and those who have the freedom to redeem the shares, should not be protected by the disinterested directors.

One could argue that investors evaluate advisory fees as they do any other commodity, and therefore fiduciary rules should not apply to fees. Since the investors in shares are not in personal relationship with the adviser, the adviser cannot influence them. They can and should shop for the best advisory services, including the least expensive, as they would for any other commodity available on the market. Since managers compete fiercely, the protection of investors under fiduciary law is misguided. In such cases the conflicts of interest appear loud and clear. There is no need to distinguish between what is conflicted and what is not. The argument aims at the results. If the investors can fend for themselves, then there is no need for the imposition of fiduciary duties, and the contract regime should apply. This argument is linked to the shift from personal advice to the impersonal sale of advice as a commodity. If such a shift is effected, the chances are that the shareholders will view their relationship with the adviser as less fiduciary and more contractual, and that they will better understand that managers are not the trustworthy servants they might appear to be. The long-term results may be to truly change the relationship into a contractual relationship. Whether the investors would then entrust their savings to the managers is another matter.

C. Mutual Funds as Businesses

The view of managers as businesses brought with it a permission to do what they liked with the profits, and opened the door to Rule 12b-1.[51] The Rule allows the funds to finance the distribution of their shares, the way any business finances the distribution of its products. To be sure, the rationale of the rule based its permission on the benefits to the shareholders. The larger the fund, it was expected, the

49. Division of Investment Management, Securities and Exchange Commission, 'Report on Mutual Fund Fees and Expenses' (December 2000), available at <www.sec.gov/news/studies/feestudy.htm> (last modified 10 January 2001).
50. Proposed Amendment to Rule 12b-1, 17 C.F.R. para. 270.12b-1 (2005), IC-26356, 2004; Amended NASD Conduct Rule 2830(k), approved by the Securities and Exchange Commission, Rel. No. 34–50883, Dec. 12, 2004.
51. 17 C.F.R. §270.12b-1 (2005).

more economies of scale the shareholders would receive. The reality, however, was different. Large funds did not significantly reduce their fees. Rather, managers based the lack of reduction on new and additional services that they were offering investors, and on the fact that investors continued to invest.[52] That is, they did not care about the fees. The conflict of interest on this score came full circle. The investors financed the sales of the fund shares directly (up to one per cent of the assets in the funds). The managers financed additional sales from profits that they were entitled to receive. They also borrowed to finance additional sales.

In sum, to release fiduciaries from strict prohibitions on conflicts of interest under United States law, a number of theoretical shifts are possible:

- Shift a transaction from fiduciary law category to contract law category.
- View the managers as conducting businesses for the sale of fiduciary services as commodities and not as fiduciaries who give trust services for the benefit of their clients. If the managers are businesses plying for the sale of their wares then they have the right to charge investors as much fees and expenses as the market would bear, to hire solicitors and to pay them from the profits the managers make. It is then no one's business, except the Internal Revenue's and their own shareholders, how much they earn.
- View the funds as businesses managed at the managers' discretion including the sale of funds' shares.

D. Theoretical Frames for Remedies on Conflicts of Interest

Conflicts of interest can be addressed in two ways: by liabilities or by exercise of ownership rights. In an article entitled 'Conflicts of Interest in Publicly-Traded and Closely-Held Corporations: A Comparative and Economic Analysis,'[53] Zohar Goshen classifies two responses to conflicts of interest. One response is by resorting to the court's decision that would impose liabilities on violators of fiduciary duties.

---

52. Securities and Exchange Commission, Release Nos. 33–6254, IC-11414, File No. S7–743, *45 FR 73898*, 7 November 1980:

> 'The Commission is taking these actions because it believes that directors and shareholders of open-end management investment companies should be able to make business judgments to use fund assets for distribution in appropriate cases but that, in view of the investment adviser's conflict of interest with respect to any recommendation to bear distribution expenses and because of uncertainties about whether such companies are likely to benefit from such expenditures, any such exercise of business judgment should be subject to conditions designed to ensure that it is made by persons who are free of undue management influence and have carefully considered all relevant factors.' and 'The directors must decide, in the exercise of their reasonable business judgment and in light of their fiduciary duties under state law and under the Act, that there is a reasonable likelihood that a plan will benefit the fund and its shareholders.')

53. Z. Goshen, 'Conflicts of Interest in Publicly-Traded and Closely-Held Corporations: A Comparative and Economic Analysis' (July 2005) *Theoretical Inquiries in Law* 6, 277–300.

The other response is by imposing on fiduciaries a duty to seek the owners' consent. Liabilities are imposed by the courts, and are subject to the constraints and dictates of the law. The owners' consent is not constrained. However, while liabilities are accompanied by the power to impose punishments on violators and award remedies to victims, the owners are not empowered to impose such legal punishments and remedies.[54] In addition, while the decision of the courts strives to be objective, the decision of the owners to consent or refuse consent to conflicts of interest can be subjective. Owners need not explain or justify their consent or refusal to consent.[55]

E. Mutual Funds Regulation Adopted Both Responses to Conflicts of Interest

First, the law establishes directors as the spokespersons of the owners and empowers them to approve (or not approve) the contract with the adviser.[56] The directors are also required by law to monitor the adviser's activities, codes of ethics, expenses, and operations.[57] However, because the directors are fiduciaries, they lack the freedom of the owners to determine arbitrarily the fees and expenses of the managers. Thus, in addition to their powers the directors are required to follow both process and substantive principles in their approval of the contract between their mutual funds and the managers.[58] Advisory contracts may be approved by the shareholders as well.[59] These shareholders are not constrained by standards or qualification except the ownership of the shares. The remedy against the managers is a 'market remedy' however. It is simply to not renew the contract. In light of the fact that such a non-renewal may be very damaging to the shareholders, there are very few cases in which such a non-renewal occurred. Therefore, this market solution is not very powerful or effective. It does, however, allow directors to deal with the adviser in the shadow of this strong remedy.

In addition, most mutual funds in the United States are of the open-end vintage. The market remedy for wayward managers in this structure is far stronger than the legal remedy. The shareholders of such funds have the right to redeem their shares at *pro rata* share asset value within seven days of demand, with very few extreme exceptions.[60] The shareholders' power is the owner's power. They do not have to comply with any standard of fairness or otherwise. Their decision is subjective. Their redemption is powerful because they can liquidate the funds' assets, not merely the price of the fund shares in the markets. That reduces the managers' fees and increases the costs of managing the funds.

54. Ibid. at 282–284.
55. Ibid. at 284.
56. 15 USC §80a-15(a), (c) (2000).
57. 15 USC §80a-15(c) (2000).
58. See T. Frankel and A.T.. Schwing 2: §§9.05, 12.03[D][5].
59. 15 USC §80a-15(a) (2000).
60. 17 CFR §270.22c-1 (2005).

Similarly, investment companies that issue non-redeemable shares are subject to the shareholders' ability to sell the shares on the market and thus reduce the share price if supply exceeds demand for the shares. This does not reduce the funds' assets, but makes it difficult for the funds' managers to increase money under management by issuing new securities. Finally, such funds may be subject to hostile takeovers, when the fund shares are sold at a discount and the funds show very poor performance. Redemption and sale of shares are the owners' remedies. They require not objective reasons. However, they are also not accompanied by the punishments and remedies that regulators and the courts have at their disposal. In recent activity of the Securities and Exchange Commission, the agency passed rules to increase the power of the disinterested directors and required the chairperson of the board to be a disinterested director. This move has spawned litigation.[61] In addition, there are currently a number of cases brought by investors on the fees, and attempts to reconsider the basis for the advisory fees.[62] Not surprisingly, there are academic arguments in support of both trends.

Moreover, the law imposes specified direct legal constraints on the fiduciaries, and subjects them to liabilities. The enforcement of these constraints is left to the Securities and Exchange Commission and the courts. These entities follow principles established in the law.

F. The Change in Judicial Interpretation of Statutes

Before 1975, courts tended to interpret the statutes by examining the problems that the legislators sought to address and the policies that they adopted. Since 1975 the courts' tendencies and directions have changed. The focus has been on the 'ordinary' or 'literal' meaning of the statutory language and the specificity of the prohibitions, including prohibitions on breach of fiduciary duties. Thus, the fiduciaries could read the statute narrowly, and whatever was not expressly prohibited or required was interpreted as being permissible.[63] This form of interpretation for fiduciary duties had an effect of allowing fiduciaries to gain more in gray areas. That could be deemed efficient: allowing fiduciaries to create value for themselves. However, by eliminating the gray areas the interpretation dramatically increased the cost of enforcing the prohibitions.[64] No amount of rules would prevent circumvention of the spirit and purpose of the law. The Library of Congress could not hold all the rules that would be required to specifically prohibit activities that would result in abuse of trust. Thus, the literal interpretation not only limited judicial activism

61. *Chamber of Commerce v. Securities and Exchange Commission*, 412 F.3d 133 (D.C. Cir. 2005).
62. See, e.g., *Krantz v. Prudential Invs. Fund Mgmt.*, 305 F.3d 140 (3d Cir. 2002) *cert. denied*, 537 U.S. 1113 (2003); *Green v. Nuveen Advisory Corp.*, 295 F.3d 738 (7th Cir.) *cert. denied*, 2002 U.S. LEXIS 9267 (2002); *Green v. Fund Asset Mgmt.*, 286 F.3d 682 (3d Cir.), *cert. denied*, 2002 U.S. LEXIS 6512 (2002); *Olmsted v. Pruco Life Ins. Co.*, 283 F.3d 429 (2d Cir. 2002).
63. See T. Frankel, *Trust and Honesty, America's Business Culture at a Crossroad* (New York, Oxford, Oxford University Press, 2005), Chapter 8.
64. Ibid.

but also increased the need for more rules, greater supervision of fiduciaries, and tighter punishments. It may well be that the literal interpretation and the specificity approach have contributed to increasing conflicts of interest transactions and hidden and new ways to bribe and receive kickbacks in the mutual fund area. Fiduciary duties must be interpreted with a view to furthering the purpose of the rules. Rules that are designed to avoid conflicts of interest should be designed to provide a gray area and uncertainty to help enforce the purpose of the rules.

G. THE PUZZLE AND THE DANGER

For the past 25 years the relaxation of the prohibition on conflicts of interest has progressed. Prohibitions were especially avoided or simply violated during the 1990s. This behaviour is hard to explain. It is especially puzzling because the 1990s were the bubble period during which the stock market rose significantly, until it fell in the year 2000. One may speculate that the financing of the sale of mutual funds contributed to the bubble of those years. But whatever the reason, managers gained much and sought to gain more.[65] This is not the first time that the enforcement of barriers against temptation has decreased during prosperous years and heightened during the lean years.

The new puzzle is not that rogue managers and distributors have violated the law and abused their trust. The puzzle is that so many have either accepted fraud as 'a way of life' or justified it: 'It is bad, but not so bad. Besides, everyone does it, and I must do it too to survive in a competitive market.' A yet more pernicious approach has emerged when so many actors are violating the law that enforcement becomes too expensive and embarrassing. In such a case the prohibition has been redefined to weaken or even eliminate it. The mutual fund industry and some academics are attempting the redefinition approach. Theories, such as contract relationships, market transactions, and the sale of fiduciary services as commodities have helped water down or eliminate the prohibitions on fiduciaries' conflicts of interest or the entire fiduciary category. Some arguments are based on a comparison between what the investors lose and what the managers and distributors gain. For each investor the amounts that managers misappropriate are very small, although over the years it may slowly become significant. Yet a very small daily amount taken for each investor becomes quickly enormous for the managers and distributors. It is so easy to earn so much by taking so little. It is easy to justify the taking by exaggerating the adviser and broker contribution to passive investors and berating investors' demand for more. And it is still easier to take when 'everyone takes.'

The law can help constrain temptation of fiduciaries to abuse their trust, but it cannot be fully effective. During the 5 years from 2000 to 2005, regulators conducted investigations, brought cases, and obtained either judgments or settlements against many mutual fund managers. It is not clear, however, whether these cases

---

65. Ibid. See also T. Frankel, 'Regulation and Investors' Trust in the Securities Markets' *Brooklyn Law Review* 68 (2002) 439–448.

will produce a more self-limiting cadre of managers in the future. The conflicts of interest are significant, the temptations to abuse trust are powerful, and close monitoring is rare if not impossible. Distributors and managers can communicate in very subtle ways. There are so many ways in which the quid pro quo bribery and kickbacks can be hidden. More importantly, many distributors and managers berate the laws and the government that enforces them. The greatest danger to the financial system is when the taking becomes a habit for fiduciaries and suspicion and risk of misappropriation bring about investors' demands for higher returns.[66]

H. Is the Concern About Conflicts of Interests Described in This Paper Exaggerated?

Even if we reject the theories that justify the conflict of interest transactions described in this paper, and even if we view the transactions as prohibited, is the concern in regard to the conflicts not exaggerated? Viewing the scene as a whole, it seems that:

- There are enormously strong incentives for managers and distributors to benefit from servicing millions of investors.
- The losses investors suffer as a result of the conflicts of interests are rather small as compared to the enormous benefits that managers and distributors can reap from such transactions.
- The costs of monitoring and enforcing the current rules are prohibitive.

Thus, from a cost-benefit viewpoint, a simple and more reasonable solution would be to allow the offering of mutual funds securities to state one number that investors would be charged. That would contain the fees and costs, whatever they are, and whoever receives them.

I. The Issue of Culture

The solution suggested in the previous section, however, ignores human nature and the impact of habit and culture on human behaviour. If that solution is allowed, the current arrangements are likely to expand to other areas. After all, there is no limit to how much money one can have. For example, higher performance can be coupled with higher risks, which investors may find hard to gauge. Besides, not all investors follow their investments closely, and some might not overcome their inertia. There are also cases in which investors follow charismatic managers, regardless of performance.

As always, the concern is that investors may trust market actors for a sustained period, and then, with little warning, decide to withdraw that trust. The decision may

66. This speculation is based on G.A. Akerlof's famous article 'The Market for "Lemons": Quality Uncertainty and the Market Mechanism,' (1970) *Quarterly Journal of Economics* 84, 488–500.

be reasoned. It may also depend on the persons and ideas that the investors follow. If, for whatever reason and under whatever circumstances, investors decide that they will withdraw trust, and if there might be other competitors for the investors' money, then mutual funds will be decimated and remain only with tax-deferred investments. Even those tax-deferred investors may find ways to escape the mutual funds. To be sure, this scenario is speculative, but here again, the cost and probability of such a run must be factored into the calculation described above.

Moreover, permitting managers and distributors to view investors' money as partly their own can become a habit and solidify into a culture. A culture is a social habit. Like a habit, a culture implies that members of society assume that everyone behaves in a certain way and that everyone expects others to behave in the same way. In Western culture, no competitor assumes that competitors will kill each other. In the culture of the Mafia, at least in the past, it was assumed that competitors would kill each other at the first opportunity. Like custom, culture grows with repetition. Like habit, it becomes an irrefutable assumption, as to both one's own behaviour and the behaviour of others. A culture in which distributors and managers deal with investors' money in conflict of interest will affect the investors' culture as well. Investors will expect such a conflict of interest (whether or not it exists in reality). The reaction of the investors may differ. They may continue to trade but agree to pay less for fees, or demand guarantees or cease to buy mutual funds altogether. Thus, regardless of what investors do, the costs to the managers, to distributors and to the system are bound to rise.[67]

As a result, managers might not even consider alternative options. Here, perhaps, lies the greatest danger to the financial system generally, and to the mutual funds system in particular. The 1990s sowed the seeds of the approaches that came to fruition, and that are still rooted in the managers' approach and attitudes. To be sure, there are arguments about where the line to conflicts of interest should be drawn.

If the arguments cease and the conflicts are allowed and legitimized, there is a good chance that the conflicts will spread on the same basis and rationale to other areas of services. The benefits to managers and distributors might be still greater and the cost to investors might rise. If the current conflicts do not shake investors' trust, other conflicts will, at some point, shake them into action.[68] These are of course speculations. However, so is the idea that nothing will happen if the current conflicts are permitted.

V. CONCLUSION

The fee structure of mutual fund managers is fraught with incentives leading to conflicts of interests; that is, provided the managers are viewed as fiduciaries who

67. T. Frankel, *Trust and Honesty, America's Business Culture at a Crossroad, (New York, Oxford, Oxford University Press, 2005), Chapter 4.*
68. Ibid.

manage other people's money and not as the sellers of a commodity composed of a piece of a managed portfolio. The buyer of such a commodity, however, is exposed to serious risks regardless of how the relationship is characterized. The legal response in the United States was to provide investors with (1) representatives to monitor managers and approve the terms of the contract with the adviser on the investors' behalf; (2) monitoring by the regulators; and (3) resort to the courts. These mechanisms must be based on principles and standards. Directors, regulators and the courts must all follow the principles, standards and processes prescribed by law. Investors are afforded a fourth protection by the redeemability of the investors' shares. Unlike directors, regulators and the courts, redeeming shareholders need not follow any principles and standards. They have the owners' right to withdraw from the relationship for whatever reason.

Despite these protections, conflicts of interest are very strong when the losses each investor suffers are very small as compared to the enormous benefits that the managers and the distributors can stand to gain from an arrangement. The previous section suggests that the key to maintaining investors' trust and the financial system is a culture of honesty among managers and distributors. The key is in their self-imposed self-limitation and barriers to temptation. Rules can help. But culture is the decisive factor.